GROSSMAN'S
GUIDE
to Wines,
Beers, and Spirits

SIXTH REVISED EDITION

GROSSMAN'S GUIDE TO WINES, BEERS, AND SPIRITS

SIXTH REVISED EDITION

HAROLD J. GROSSMAN

Revised by

HARRIET LEMBECK

CHARLES SCRIBNER'S SONS
New York

Frontispiece: Handsome Sangiovese grapes at Montemasso vineyard near Florence. (*Courtesy I. L. Ruffino, Pontassieve, Italy*)

Library of Congress Cataloging in Publication Data

Grossman, Harold J.
   Grossman's guide to wines, beers, and spirits.

   Previous editions published under title:
Grossman's guide to wines, spirits, and beers.
   Bibliography: p.
   Includes index.
   1. Alcoholic beverages.   I. Lembeck, Harriet,
joint author.   II. Title.   III. Title: Guide
to wines, beers, and spirits.
TP505.G76   1977   641.2   77-13950
ISBN 0-684-15033-6

1 3 5 7 9 11 13 15 17 19 Q/C 20 18 16 14 12 10 8 6 4 2

Printed in the United States of America

CONTENTS

PREFACE

In the many years since *Grossman's Guide to Wines, Spirits, and Beers* was first published in 1940, Harold J. Grossman's book has been accepted as the definitive reference and textbook for everyone interested in this field, professional and amateur alike. The continued growth of the alcoholic beverage industry has sparked a need for knowledge by a wide range of professional people who are concerned with the industry, whether in finance, advertising, legal work, or production. This knowledge is, of course, essential for all marketing levels of the industry. *Grossman's Guide* is to be found in the working library of almost every executive in the industry as well as in hotel schools, buying offices, and retail stores, including those operated by the various control states.

The *Guide* has necessarily been updated and revised periodically over the years. Reference books, unlike some wines, do not improve through aging, and Harold Grossman recognized his responsibility to keep his work as useful as possible by making the necessary changes and additions dictated by new technologies, revisions of laws and regulations, and changing taste trends in the marketplace. This dedication to keeping *Grossman's Guide* as current as possible is the primary reason for this new edition.

To assume the challenging responsibility of editing the sixth edition of *Grossman's Guide*, Scribners chose Harriet Lembeck, whose credentials are highly impressive. One of Mr. Grossman's star pupils eleven years ago, she has since been closely identified with the Beverage Program, which he started. For the past three years she has conducted four courses each year, and from this vantage point she knows the *Guide* page by page and line by line. She is aware of the reactions and needs of the students who use it as a text. In scanning reader letters to *Vintage* Magazine she has found many questions repeated again and again, and the answers to most of them have been incorporated into the revised edition of the *Guide*.

James Beard maintains that those fortunate people who have perfect pitch in music are likely to be equally sensitive to the aroma and flavor nuances of food and wine. This may explain some of the abilities of Harriet Lembeck, who was a major in music at Bryn Mawr College and is distinguished for her perception of tone and pitch as well as for her taste memory.

Harriet Lembeck is chairman of the Wine Committee and a director of the Wine and Food Society of New York, a Chevalier of the Confrérie des Chevaliers du Tastevin, on the faculty of the Sommelier Society of America, wine coordinator and columnist for *Vintage* Magazine, and a member of many other wine societies. She has devoted countless hours to the meticulous editing of this new edition, which entailed revising obsolete material and recognizing improved technology, tightened quality controls in various countries, the impact of economic factors on our imported wine profile, and the ever changing taste preferences of the American public (for example, the rapid expansion of the use of white wines as aperitifs). With all this Harriet Lembeck has done an admirable job of preserving the tone and character of Harold Grossman's original work.

We have also enjoyed and benefited from the ability and experience of Harriet's husband, William Lembeck, Professional Engineer. With a wide knowledge of wines and spirits added to his repertoire, he has been most helpful in researching the appendices and contributing specialized information on such subjects as fermentation.

The task of updating and revising the various chapters of the *Guide* was aided immeasurably by the cooperation and suggestions of many industry executives and veterans who were long-time friends of Harold Grossman. I am proud to be a member of the editorial team for this new edition of *Grossman's Guide*. It is as comprehensive, up-to-date, and accurate as many months of effort can make it.

GORDON BASS

FOREWORD

There are few books that can be read for pleasure, provide satisfactory browsing, be prized as an encyclopedia, be useful as a pronouncing dictionary and technical manual, and, withal, constitute an ideal textbook. *Grossman's Guide* is one of those rarities and is a direct reflection of the author, his profound knowledge of any and all alcoholic beverages, and his lifelong endeavor to gain more and more information and to pass it on to others, consumers and industry members alike.

Harold Grossman was born in Champaign, Illinois—prophetic, even though the spelling of his native town is not exactly vinous. As a young man he went to Cuba to work in the family-owned Hotel Plaza in Camaguey, and eventually he became its owner-manager. The wine cellar of the hotel was his particular pride and joy, and to build and replenish it young Harold made many buying trips to Europe, thus becoming a firsthand expert. These were the years of Prohibition, and while Harold became a knowledgeable enthusiast, the rest of his countrymen in the United States suffered from legal aridity. During this period he became friendly with Richard L. Blum, who then resided in Havana.

When Repeal came in December 1933, Blum, who was back in New York, persuaded Harold to leave the hotel and become education director of Julius Wile Sons & Co., Inc. His job was to teach what had been forgotten for a generation. Harold shared his knowledge with the entire industry—his employers, distributors and their sales staffs, retailers, hotel and restaurant personnel, and the press. He lectured and wrote and consulted and advised and above all answered questions. He appeared on radio and television programs and for over five years conducted the hotel training course for the International Geneva Association.

With the encouragement, aid, and collaboration of his wife, Florence, this book was written and first published in 1940, when it was eagerly purchased by a public still starved for information.

During World War II Harold went on a mission to Argentina with fluent Spanish as part of his equipment. He remained there for some years in the import-export business—dealing in wines and spirits, of course, among other things. Eventually he returned to New York, became a consultant to the trade, and resumed his writing on alcoholic beverages. In 1959 he instituted a series of tasting lectures using his own book as a text. This fifteen-week series was given twice a year. Upon Harold's death in 1967 volunteers continued the course in session, and it then came under the trusteeship of three of his close industry friends. Until Florence Grossman died it was called the Grossman Memorial Lectures. Today the course still goes on under the same trustees but is now called the Beverage Program. It is conducted by Harriet Lembeck, Harold's pupil, acolyte, assistant, and friend.

Those of us who knew and admired Harold Grossman, who believe, as he did, that the liquid products of grapes and fruits and grains exist for man's well-being, health, and pleasure, derive much satisfaction from the knowledge that his long years of education and instruction continue in this book and in the lectures based upon it.

JULIUS WILE

ACKNOWLEDGMENTS

It is a tribute to the vision of Harold J. Grossman that a thorough revision of his book has taken more than two years and has involved the help of so many people in all facets of the wine and spirits industry. That a book of this breadth, with no models or predecessors, was written in 1940 by a man who taught himself about wines and spirits is most impressive.

With this revision I have tried to update technical material and to bring older attitudes more in line with current thinking. I also have tried to maintain Harold Grossman's passion for accuracy and objectivity. For example, brand names have been deliberately omitted except where they have historical significance.

Knowing that this book was designed to be a handy tool for quick reference as well as for more detailed study, the appendices, especially, have been expanded to include material needed for today's market. I hope that *Grossman's Guide* will be the book reached for first when the need for such material arises.

My interviews with so many people in the wine and spirits industry and related hospitality fields have served to reinforce for me just how widely respected Harold Grossman was and how much cooperation he inspired. Many people have given a great deal of time and effort to all of the editions of *Grossman's Guide* since the 1940s. To all those go our continued thanks. Many industry leaders helped me now as they helped Harold Grossman in the past, and often my assistance has come from the next generation of authorities. For this totally and completely revised sixth edition go my sincere thanks to all those who are specifically involved.

Two close industry friends of Harold Grossman, Gordon Bass and Julius Wile, ensured the continuation of Harold Grossman's classes in wines and spirits after his passing. They have kept a weather eye on them as trustees and have now been closely involved with this book. They have given immeasurable time and talent, not only by checking all of the material but by drawing on their own vast experience and contacts to obtain and verify information. No point was too small to be overlooked. They are true educators and have been a source of inspiration and guidance.

Gordon Bass has been in all phases of the alcoholic beverage industry since Repeal in 1933. Having been a retailer, wholesaler, distiller, and importer, he is now wine marketing consultant to Schenley Affiliated Brands. He is chairman of the Tastevin Wine Library and Museum at the Culinary Institute of America, an outstanding wine reference library to which he has generously contributed rare wine books and antique wine bottles. He is a past president and board chairman of the Wine and Spirits Wholesalers of America, a past director of the Licensed Beverage Industries, and a past member of the National Association of Alcoholic Beverage Importers (N.A.A.B.I.).

Gordon Bass's membership on the board of the Sommelier Society of America and his guest lectures at the Culinary Institute of America are a special source of pleasure, since there is nothing he likes more than to share his knowledge of wines and spirits and their place in the good life. In 1975 he received the honorary degree of Master of Aesthetics of Gastronomy from the Institute.

Not content to be simply a member of various societies, Gordon Bass has risen to Grand Officier of the Confrérie des Chevaliers du Tastevin and Sénéchal Honoraire for the United States of the Confrérie de la Chaîne des Rôtisseurs. He is a forty-year member of the New York Wine & Food Society, and in 1977 he was awarded the Cross of the Chevalier du Mérite Agricole.

Julius Wile represents the third generation of the wine and spirits business founded in 1877 by his grandfather, Julius Wile. He served his apprenticeship in the important wine and spirits areas of Europe, and after an outstanding forty-year career with Julius Wile Sons & Co., Inc., he recently retired as senior vice-president.

Since 1952 he has been on the faculty of the Cornell University School of Hotel Administration and has lectured for the Sommelier Society of America, as well as for other courses. His rôle as an educator includes membership on the Executive Committee of the Culinary Institute of America, where he is vice-chairman of the Board of Trustees.

Julius Wile was also chairman of the Table Wine Committee of N.A.A.B.I. for seventeen years. He contributed annually to the *Encyclopaedia Britannica* on the subject of alcoholic beverages and is presently updating the authoritative Schoonmaker *Encyclopedia of Wine.*

He is a governor and founding member of the Commanderie de Bordeaux and a director of the New York Wine & Food Society. In 1962 he received from the French government the Cross of Chevalier de l'Ordre de l'Économie Nationale, and in 1972 he was awarded the Cross of the Chevalier de l'Ordre National du Mérite.

Special thanks must also go to my husband, William Lembeck. His talents as a Professional Engineer combined with his love of wines and spirits have been of immeasurable help with the technical aspects of this book. His artistic style and abilities as a draftsman are demonstrated by the custom-drawn wine maps throughout the book. With the public's increased interest in the technical aspects of wines and spirits, it has been very helpful to have an engineer-in-residence.

Another friend who has assumed overall involvement with the text is Richard L. Becker, of the import department of Julius Wile Sons & Co., Inc. His painstaking accuracy, collection of data, and careful research have been most valuable.

The complex chapter on the wines of France received the help of Jean-Pierre Gachelin of the French Commercial Consulate of New York and Jean Fourcade of the French Commercial Consulate in Washington, D.C. Mary Lyons, of Food and Wines from France, helped with the Burgundy section; Alain Blanchon and Judy Platt, of Bell & Stanton, helped with the material on Bordeaux and Alsace, as did Michael Buller of *Vintage* Magazine. Irving Smith Kogan and Marie-Claude Stockl of the Champagne News and Information Bureau assisted with the material on Champagne. Robert Tinlot, of the Service de la Repression des Fraudes in Paris, was helpful with some of the finer points of the *Appellation Contrôlée* regulations. Special thanks must go to Charles S. Mueller, executive vice-president of Kobrand Corp., who gave his time generously to review the entire chapter on French wines.

The Wines of Italy had the help of Mary Mulligan of the Italian Trade Commission and industry members John Mariani, Jr., of the House of Banfi and Donald St. John Sozzi of the Jos. Garneau Co. Earlier editions of *Grossman's Guide* mention help given to Harold Grossman by Ercole Sozzi, Donald Sozzi's father. Paul F. Hille, Jr., a friend and wine lover, made good suggestions for this chapter as well. Mario Daniele, of C. Daniele & Sons, graciously made himself available for questions and discussions on the wines of Italy.

For the Wines of Germany, special thanks go to Peter M. F. Sichel for all of the information he provided. His help in organizing the material was invaluable. John Woodford Rapp, Jr., of the offices of H. Sichel Sohne, also contributed his time. Alan Olson, able director of the German Wine Information Bureau, and his assistant, Brenda Mezrahi, were always ready to help with the information gathering. Anne P. Griffiths, a graduate of the German Wine Academy, also checked the material.

The major part of the sherry information was reviewed by Arthur Humbert of Williams & Humbert and his very good friend Julian Jeffs of London. Good source material was provided by the Sherry Institute of Spain, headed first by Luther Conant and then by his successor, Smitty Kogan. Don José Ignacio Domecq, of the famous Domecq family in Jerez, and Antonio Montes, Consejo Regulador of Jerez, both answered many technical questions.

The chapter on the wines of Portugal was strengthened by Victor Espirito Santo, of the Portuguese Government Trade Office. Kenneth L. Onish, of Château and Estate Wines Co., was particularly helpful with the material on Vintage Porto.

The material on the wines of smaller countries was also checked carefully. For Hungary, the task fell to Alexander Campbell McNally and Thomas J. Martin, both authorities from Heublein, Inc. The wines of Israel were reviewed by Yehudah Levinberg, of the Carmel Wine Co.

The names of the people who helped with the Wines of the United States chapter reads like a *Who's Who* of all phases of the American wine business. The wines of California were checked by Dr. Maynard A. Amerine, Harvey

Posert, Brian St. Pierre, and James M. Seff, all of the Wine Institute. Gerald Asher, vice-president of "21" Brands, Inc., provided his usual good sense and perspective with many creative suggestions. Darrell F. Corti, an innovative retailer in Sacramento, contributed an overview of the wines of his state. The information gleaned from Fromm & Sichel's *Data Annual,* sent by Jim Lucas, also contributed to this overview. Dr. Richard G. Peterson, president of the American Society of Enologists and Monterey Vineyard, Inc., provided technical information on the winemaking process. Joseph Concannon of Concannon Vineyards, Inc., was helpful with the regulations on sacramental wines. John W. McConnell made valuable comments on the book as a whole and especially on the grape varieties of California.

The wines of Washington State were reviewed by Joel K. Klein and Vic Allison of Ste. Michelle Vineyards. Information on the wines of Oregon came from Bill Fuller of Tualatin Vineyards and from the staff at Oregon State University.

For the section on the wines of the eastern United States Dr. John R. McGrew of the U.S. Department of Agriculture in Maryland provided well-documented technical information.

From the American Wine Society, Margaret Jackisch, executive secretary, and Philip Jackisch, consulting enologist, also carefully reviewed the material on the wines of the eastern United States, which have changed tremendously since Harold Grossman first wrote about them.

The chapter on beers was reviewed by Desmond G. Sharp-Bolster, of the Guinness-Harp Corp. Material was also obtained from Pat Jones, librarian, and Gary Maintman, head of the Legal Department, of the United States Brewers' Association, Bill Siebel of J. E. Siebel & Co., Inc., Jack Varick and James D. Ritchie of Jos. Schlitz Brewing Co.

The chapters on spirits were read by many industry members. Of great assistance on whiskies were John L. Brady, Jr., George W. Pacowski, and Merce Maleski, all of Joseph E. Seagram & Sons, along with Alice Gross, librarian; Weil Herzfeld and Marsha Lane of Schenley Affiliated Brands Corp.; and Jack McGowan, of Irish Distillers, Ltd. Rums were checked by William A. Walker of Bacardi Imports, Inc. Tequila and vodka were reviewed by Christopher W. Carriuolo and Erik J. Pierce of Heublein, Inc. French brandies were checked by the aforementioned Messrs. Jean-Pierre Gachelin and Jean Fourcade of the French Commercial Consulates, and American brandies were reviewed by James R. McManus of the California Brandy Advisory Board. Michel Garnier of the Fleischman Distilling Corp. and W. Ray Hyde of Schieffelin & Co. offered assistance on liqueurs.

For the material on cocktails and mixed drinks, menu and wine list making, beverage control, and bar operation, much help was given by members of the Hilton Corporation: Eugene R. Scanlan, manager of the Waldorf-Astoria

Hotel, Norbert Rademaker, Guenther Richter, Réné R. Varela, Michael R. Cross, and Louis Pappalardo. These sections were also reviewed by the Culinary Institute of America, directed by its president, Henry Ogden Barbour.

The photographs of how to open bottles of wine were made possible by Kevin Zraly and Barbara Kafka, of Windows on the World, and photographer Andrew B. Wile. Information on recorking old bottles of wine was provided by specialist Roger Mason.

Retailing practices were explained by Michael Aron of Sherry-Lehmann, Inc., and Arthur Amster of Manhattan Château Wine & Liquor Corp. In the section on merchandising I was ably assisted by Margaret Stern and Stephanie Shames of Schieffelin & Co., Jim Angelone and Gary Tobin of United Vintners, Alan Schwartz of *Liquor Store* Magazine, and many others.

Laws and regulations were meticulously checked by Eiko Narita of the National Association of Alcoholic Beverage Importers. Alan Graham of the Bureau of Alcohol, Tobacco, and Firearms answered questions relating to regulations. George McCrory, of the American Wine Society and a consumer advocate on this subject, was also helpful. Marvin R. Shanken, of Impact, provided reliable statistical information.

Some reference books that have been constant companions throughout this project are *The Encyclopedia of Wines and Spirits* by Alexis Lichine, the *Encyclopedia of Wine* by Frank Schoonmaker, *The World Atlas of Wine* by Hugh Johnson, and the *Great Book of Wine*.

Thanks must also go to the good people of Julius Wile Sons & Co., Inc. They provided the use of their Wine Library and many other facilities to help with this important project. They have not forgotten their long-time associate Harold J. Grossman, who was their original director of education. Special thanks must go to chairman Richard L. Blum, Jr., president Neil Bianchini, vice-president Brian Abbott, and office manager Arlene Duvin.

A book of this encyclopedic nature requires immense coordination on the part of the publisher. To Charles Scribner, Jr., goes special appreciation for undertaking the project when the need for thorough revision became apparent. His loyal staff put in many extra hours to ensure that the accuracy and care put into the manuscript were not lost to the gremlins of production. To Barbara Wood, who makes a specialty of precision, and to Doe Coover, my editor, who became a great friend in the process, go particular, heartfelt thanks.

HARRIET LEMBECK

It is with great pleasure that we find ourselves in a position to contribute a note to *Grossman's Guide to Wines, Beers, and Spirits.*

Some of our fondest memories are of the magnificent dinners at the home of our great-uncle Harold. His love of fine wine, together with his wife's supreme culinary skills, made dinner with them unforgettable.

Grossman's Guide represents a work of considerable scholarship and a marvelous reference work for amateur and professional alike. As beneficiaries of the royalty income we recognize a special responsibility to ensure that it is kept up to date. After a number of revisions by the author himself the task was continued by his wife and subsequently taken over by the publisher. In this Scribners has been strongly supported by Harold Grossman's former colleagues and friends, including Julius Wile and Gordon Bass. For the current edition we are indebted to Harriet Lembeck.

We feel convinced that these changes would have been welcomed by Harold Grossman himself and that he would have been the first to acknowledge the improvements that have been incorporated into this latest edition.

Alexandra Farrow
Pamela Chown

GROSSMAN'S
GUIDE
to Wines,
Beers, and Spirits

SIXTH REVISED EDITION

1
INTRODUCTION

The liquor "industry" is almost as old as man himself, and our knowledge of it is made up of widely scattered information in every language written or spoken. The subject is continually developing and consequently is always intriguing.

The development and improvement of the quality of alcoholic beverages have been the natural results of the advance of science and civilization. The role of science has been limited to ensuring uniformity of quality and sound products year in and year out, for nature still insists on having something to say in the matter, even when it comes to distilled spirits.

The vine, the brewing kettle, and the still have accompanied the spread of Christianity, establishing certain honorable traditions that the trade proudly upholds today. It is also interesting to note the esteem in which the wine trade is held abroad. It was the first "trade" considered sufficiently honorable and dignified for a member of the aristocracy to engage in, and many of the leading European firms are directed by members of noble families.

In England a wine merchant is consulted in matters pertaining to wines, beers, or spirits just as a lawyer is in legal matters. The confidence thus placed in him gives the merchant a keen consciousness of his responsibility. Also, as he knows that his descendants will continue the business he builds, family pride leads him to pass on an impeccable reputation. It is not unusual to find firms that have been doing business under the same name in the same place for hundreds of years—in some cases more than four hundred years. This is the European custom, and we are happy to note that it is beginning to take hold in the United States.

One of the leading Champagne shippers illustrated this point when he told us: "When I ship my wine, my name appears on the label. It is I who guarantee the quality. My reputation is more important to me than any pecuniary profit I may derive from the sale. It took my forebears two hundred years to establish this reputation for shipping wines of quality, and rest assured that I am going to pass on as good a name to my successors as I received." It is men of this type who have placed the wine and spirit trade on the high plane that has become traditional.

Based on these traditions, certain firms have established their brands so well that the public asks for their product by the name of the shipper. This has been particularly true in the case of Cognac and whiskies, but since the American public is "age conscious," many people buy dates rather than brands in whose names we have confidence. This has happened in the case of wines, as well. It is true that certain wines do improve with age—up to a point—but there are other wines that are more pleasant if drunk when young, as is the case with light white wines, whose charm lies in their freshness.

The industry as a whole today is a most important part of our business life, employing, directly or through allied enterprises, millions of men and women. It is one of the three most important sources of tax revenue for the federal and state treasuries.

Just as prohibition is bad, so is excess, and in no case is this more evident than in the use of alcoholic beverages. There is no better word of advice on this point than that which Lord Chesterfield gave to his son in a letter from London, dated March 27, 1747: "Were I to begin the world again with the experience I now have of it, I would lead a life of real, not imaginary, pleasures. I would enjoy the pleasures of the table, and of wine; but stop short of the pains inseparably annexed to an excess of either."

The leaders of the industry unanimously prefer that more people drink and enjoy beverages, rather than that individuals drink more.

It is gratifying to note the moderation exercised by the public in the use of alcoholic beverages. A per capita consumption in the United States of slightly over two gallons of spirits per year indicates an average of seven-tenths of an ounce per day. Wine consumption is a little over half an ounce, while the beer average is seven ounces. Normal bodily functions can eliminate more than ten times these average amounts. A people whose alcoholic beverage consumption is so low may, without fear of contradiction, be called temperate.

The *Guide* has been divided into five main sections: wines; beers and ales; spirits; uses, merchandising, and control; and, finally, the appendices, which contain useful, quick-reference data. All of the material has been carefully indexed to make the book easier to use for reference purposes.

Condensed information on the entire industry is given, including the description of a product, its method of production, selling, care, and uses in public and private places. The practices described are those generally used in the United States, unless otherwise specified.

It is our hope that libraries will find the *Guide* a comprehensive source of information on all phases of the subject; that producers, vintners, distillers, and brewers will find it valuable as a general reference and as a means of equipping their sales representatives with information about the other phases of the industry; and that the wholesale distributor will find it invaluable as a training manual for his staff and as a reference book. The various appendices also have been compiled with a view to practical use.

Particular care has been taken to provide information on every phase of the industry for retail establishments, whether off-premise (stores) or on-premise (hotels, restaurants, or clubs).

After reading the book, it may be useful for store owners to review certain chapters when promoting particular products. For example, during the Christmas season there is an opportunity to sell liqueurs in their fancy bottles. It is good business to be aware of these details and to refer to the *Guide* if one is asked, for example, for a liqueur whose style or character may have been forgotten.

It is also advisable for the hotel, restaurant, or club manager to keep his service personnel well informed. They are his sales staff and cannot be expected to increase the sale of beverages if they are not familiar with them. This applies equally to the wholesaler and distributor. The sales staff that is trained and can give information will become salesmen instead of order takers.

While the *Guide* has been designed primarily to be of use to the trade, it is our earnest hope that it will be read by the person who is most important to the entire industry: the consumer. It is to please and serve him that the industry constantly strives. A greater familiarity with the beverages discussed in this book, we believe, not only would aid him in purchasing with assurance, but would, perhaps, point out to him many intriguing qualities he may have overlooked and therefore increase his enjoyment.

To provide the reader with practical information, to increase his knowledge and enjoyment, and, above all, to impart something of the fascination of the subject are the purposes of this *Guide*.

2
DEFINITIONS

I t is important to explain the various terms we use, so that there may be no misconceptions or confusion. The definitions and axioms that follow are important because they are the basic elements on which the book is built.

what is alcohol?   Alcohol is a volatile, colorless liquid with an ethereal odor, obtained through the fermentation of a liquid containing sugar. There are many members of the alcohol family, but ethyl is the best-known alcohol and the one that concerns us most, as it is the principal alcohol to be found in all alcoholic beverages. The chemical formula for ethyl alcohol, or ethanol, is C_2H_5OH. Chemically, alcohols are hydroxides of organic radicals. There is nothing in ethyl alcohol that in itself is poisonous or injurious to a person's health.

what is an alcoholic beverage?   Literally, any potable liquid containing from $\frac{1}{2}$ to $75\frac{1}{2}$ percent ethyl alcohol by volume is an alcoholic beverage. However, for the purposes of taxation, the federal and state governments have set certain definite standards as to what constitutes an alcoholic beverage. Whereas beers containing as little as 2 percent alcohol by volume are taxable, certain bitters and medicinal compounds, which often contain upward of 40 percent alcohol, are not taxed because they are not considered alcoholic beverages. In 1919 Congress established by law that an alcoholic beverage containing more than $\frac{1}{2}$ percent alcohol by volume was intoxicating, yet in later years liqueurs containing 12 percent alcohol by volume were permitted to be sold as "nonalcoholic" cordials. One may draw the conclusion that by 1930, which was still during Prohibition, the government held that 12 percent alcohol in a permissible liqueur was not as intoxicating as beer, a forbidden beverage, with as little as 1 percent alcohol.

what is wine?   Wine is the naturally fermented juice of ripe grapes. Ideally these have been freshly gathered and pressed at or near the place where gathered.

4

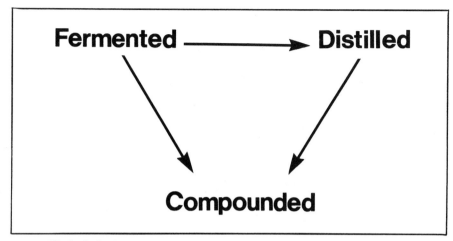

All alcoholic beverages fall into one of three basic categories: (1) fermented beverages, which are made from agricultural products such as grains and fruits and have alcoholic strengths ranging from $4\frac{1}{2}$ to 14 percent; (2) distilled or spirit beverages, which result from a pure distillation of fermented beverages; and (3) compounded beverages, which are made by combining either a fermented beverage or a spirit with flavoring substances.

Regulations under the Federal Alcohol Administration Act, however, apply the term more broadly to the fermented juice of other fruits, such as blackberry, elderberry, and peach, and of other agricultural products. Wine is more than just water and alcohol, however; it is a complex liquid in a constant state of change.

Beer is an alcoholic beverage fermented from cereals and malt and flavored with hops.

what is beer?

A spirit is a potable alcoholic beverage obtained from the distillation of a liquid containing alcohol. It makes little difference whether the original liquid contains a small or a large amount of alcohol. Once the principles of distillation are applied, nearly all of the alcohol may be separated from the liquid. In this process, however, it is inevitable that certain other matters will also be separated and it is these congeners that give the several spirits their distinct characteristics, usually after the spirits have been matured in wood and the congeners, or impurities, have fully developed.

what is a spirit?

There are only two colors in wine: red and white. Any wine containing the slightest tinge of red is a red wine. A rosé wine, therefore, is considered a red wine.

axioms

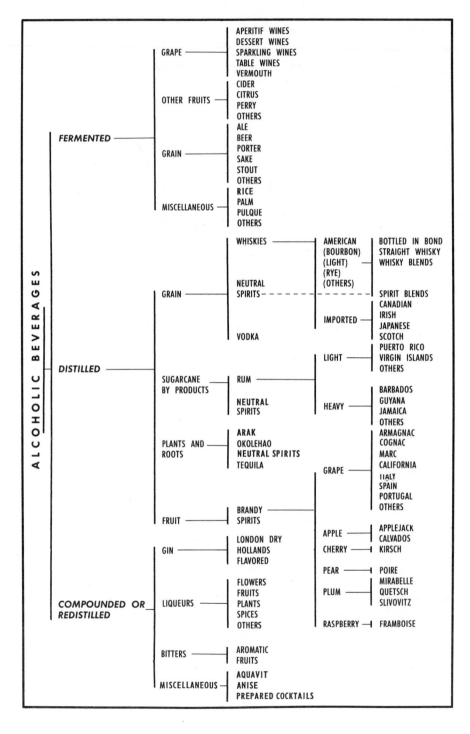

White wines range from the very palest straw color to deep, dark brown. There is no wine that is absolutely colorless.

Red wines are generally dry. (Exceptions are Porto and port-type wines, some Italian and one or two Hungarian table wines, and kosher wines.) Rosé wines can be very dry but more often are somewhat sweet.

White wines vary in sweetness, from the extreme dryness of a manzanilla to the rich, sweet lusciousness of a Tokay Eszencia.

The word *dry* is used in the wine trade to describe the opposite of *sweet*. Literally, it means "lacking in sugar."

FOUR MAIN CLASSIFICATIONS OF WINES

LIGHT BEVERAGE (natural still wines). Red and white Bordeaux, Burgundy, Alsatian, Rhine, Moselle, Italian, Spanish, Portuguese, Hungarian, American, etc. Alcohol content 14 percent or less.

SPARKLING. Champagne, sparkling Burgundy, *vin mousseux,* Asti Spumante, Sekt, etc. Alcohol content 14 percent or less.

FORTIFIED.° Sherry, Porto, Madeira, Marsala, Málaga, etc. Alcohol content over 14 percent, but not over 24 percent.

AROMATIZED. Vermouth (both Italian and French), quinined wines, etc. Alcohol content 15½ to 20 percent.

° The Bureau of Alcohol, Tobacco, and Firearms (B.A.T.F.) classifies these as dessert wines.

Standard shapes of bottles generally used in the wine trade for packaging products. LEFT TO RIGHT: Champagne and sparkling wines; Burgundy wines; Bordeaux wines; Alsatian and most German wines; *Bocksbeutel* for Franconian wines; sherries and Portos; vermouths. (*Photo by Norman Schaffer, Montclair, New Jersey*)

Wines containing less than 14 percent alcohol improve after bottling. Fortified and aromatized wines improve very little or not at all, with the exception of Vintage Portos and Madeiras.

CLASSIFICATIONS OF MALT BEVERAGES

BEERS.   Light-colored brews commonly called lager. Alcoholic strength about 4 percent by volume.

ALES.   Darker and more bitter brews. Alcoholic strength about $4\frac{1}{2}$ percent by volume.

PORTER AND STOUT.   Very full-bodied, rich malt brews. Alcoholic strength about 6 percent by volume.

SAKÉ.   A specially treated and fermented brew made from rice, produced in Japan and Hawaii. Alcoholic strength 14 to 16 percent by volume.

CLASSIFICATIONS OF SPIRITS

BRANDIES.   Cognac, Armagnac, Spanish, Greek, Italian, American, etc.

FRUIT BRANDIES.   Kirsch (cherry), Calvados (apple), Slivovitz (plum), etc.

WHISKIES.   Scotch; Irish; Canadian; American: Bourbon, blended, light, rye, etc.

RUMS.   Jamaican, Demeraran, Cuban, Puerto Rican, Martinique, Haitian, etc.

GINS.   London Dry, American, Hollands, etc.

VODKAS.   American, Russian, Polish, etc. Unflavored and flavored.

OTHER SPIRITS.   Tequila, Aquavit, bitters, etc.

LIQUEURS.   Generic types, such as menthe, cacao, anise, blackberry, curaçao, etc., are produced in many countries. In addition there are a large number of proprietary specialties that have earned international popularity, such as Bénédictine, Chartreuse, Drambuie, Galliano, Southern Comfort, Kahlúa, etc.

Spirits mature—improve—as long as they are stored in porous containers, usually wood, although sometimes, notably in Holland, they are stored in earthenware crocks, where the action of the air mellows the spirit through oxidation.

Spirits do not improve in glass. Once bottled with an airtight closure, they remain unchanged.

METRIC BOTTLE SIZES

The Bureau of Alcohol, Tobacco, and Firearms (B.A.T.F.) of the U.S. Treasury Department has declared metric standards of fill for wines and spirits sold in the United States. For wines, these standards became effective on January 1, 1975, with a mandatory compliance date of January 1, 1979. The permitted number of bottle sizes for wines is seven, reduced from the sixteen sizes previously allowed for American wines and the twenty-seven sizes for imports. Any wine bottled abroad before January 1, 1979, may be imported if the bottling date is certified by the producing country.

For spirits, the standards went into effect on October 1, 1976, and total conversion, on a state-by-state basis, must be completed by January 1, 1980. The number of bottle sizes permitted for spirits has been reduced from ten to six.

During the four-year conversion periods, both the metric contents and the U.S. fluid-ounce contents must be shown, either molded into the bottle or printed on the label.

The alcoholic beverage industry was a pioneer in adopting the metric system in the United States. The metric measures for wines and spirits are shown below.

PRE-METRIC TERMINOLOGY	METRIC TERMINOLOGY°	METRIC CAPACITY	FLUID-OUNCE CAPACITY	BOTTLES PER CASE	LITERS PER CASE
		WINES *(Still and Sparkling)*			
Miniature	Miniature	100 ml†	3.4	60	6
Split	Small	187 ml	6.3	48	9
Tenth	Medium	375 ml	12.7	24	9
Fifth	Regular	750 ml	25.4	12	9
Quart	Large	1.0 liter§	33.8	12	12
Magnum	Magnum	1.5 liters	50.7	6	9
Jeroboam	Extra Large	3.0 liters	101.4	4	12
		SPIRITS			
Miniature	Miniature	50 ml†	1.7	120	6
Half-Pint	Small	200 ml	6.8	48	9.6
Pint	Medium	500 ml	16.9	24	12
Fifth	Regular	750 ml	25.4	12	9
Quart	Large	1.0 liter§	33.8	12	12
Half-Gallon	Extra Large	1.75 liters	59.2	6	10.5

° Except for *magnum*, these terms are not legal designations and may not appear on a label.
† *ml* means milliliters, or 1/1000 liter.
§ 1 liter equals 1,000 milliliters.

3
FERMENTATION

The story of alcoholic beverages must begin with an understanding of the process whereby alcohol is obtained. Alcohol is produced from sugar or from a product that can be changed into a sugar. Once sugar is present, it can be transformed into alcohol by the natural process of fermentation.

Essentially, fermentation is the result of chemical changes in which a molecule of sugar is split into two molecules of ethyl alcohol and two molecules of carbon dioxide gas. The gas escapes into the air and the alcohol remains. The metamorphosis that takes place is similar to that which changes milk into cheese. Nature provides its own chemical agents to see that the job is accomplished efficiently in each case. The agent in fermentation is a yeast. Yeast, a living plant organism capable of self-reproduction, has many individual strains, a number of which have been identified and given scientific names. The yeast in grape juice, whose job it is to change the juice into wine, is called *Saccharomyces*.

It might be said that transforming grape juice into wine by fermentation could be left entirely to nature without any interference from man, except in the case of sparkling, fortified, or other such wines. And this is true—up to a point. Grass grows quite naturally in the fields in a wild state, but it takes constant care to make an attractive lawn. Wine allowed to ferment upon its husks will draw color from the skins, if they are those of black grapes. But if left too long it will also draw from the pips, stalks, or the small peduncles excess tannin, and more of the unsuitable acids, which would prove objectionable later. It is man's job, therefore, to control fermentation, leaving most of the work to the yeast, or *Saccharomyces*.

The *Saccharomyces* spores, dormant during the winter, settle on the outside of the grape skins as the grapes begin to ripen. When the grapes are gathered and the juice is expressed, the yeast creates enzymes that cause the grape juice to ferment and become wine. The grapes themselves are not affected by the yeast's presence, since its action does not commence until the juice is expressed. In the grape must (unfermented grape juice), with sugar and other necessary nutrients present, the yeast begins to multiply at a prodigious rate. This early yeast growth is stimulated by the presence of oxygen in the surrounding air, but *Saccharomyces* will not produce alcohol if it continues to grow in an atmosphere rich in oxygen. In other words, air is needed to get the yeast to start its rapid multiplication, but further fermentation to produce alcohol must be carried on in the absence of oxygen.

Saccharomyces works violently at first, when there is an abundance of grape sugar to work on, and then more quietly as the sugar is changed into alcohol and carbon dioxide. When all the sugar has been used up or the wine attains an alcoholic strength of approximately 14 percent, the action of the yeast is inhibited and the fermentation process complete. The violent phase is accompanied by the release of much heat, and because *Saccharomyces* works most efficiently between 65 and 80 degrees Fahrenheit, the winemaker must control the temperature level at all times during this period.

Saccharomyces performs its job of fermentation by creating catalytic agents called enzymes. The enzymes are nonliving complex chemicals that cut, chop, and change the sugar into ethyl alcohol and carbon dioxide. What was originally must has now become wine. But the importance of the yeast does not end with its function of producing alcohol. It has a definite influence on the character of the wine itself. It is a living plant organism and is influenced by

Grape must fermenting. (*Courtesy Paul Masson Vineyards, San Francisco, California*)

climate, soil, and geographical conditions existing in each wine-producing region. In some areas winemakers use specially propagated strains of yeast to eliminate undesirable characteristics without losing environmental character, instead of, or in addition to, the natural yeasts present on the grapes.

A good case in point is that of some of the white wines of Burgundy and Champagne. In both instances the Chardonnay grape is used, yet two more distinct and different white wines are hard to find. Admittedly, the difference in soils is a contributing factor, but the character of the *Saccharomyces* has much to do with explaining this phenomenon.

Still another example appears in the sherry district at Jerez, Spain, where the yeast that develops a film on the surface of the wine, known as the flower, is entirely different from that in the manzanilla warehouses of Sanlúcar de Barrameda on the seacoast.

To sum up, the process known as fermentation is one that consists mainly of the splitting up of each molecule of grape sugar present in grape juice into two molecules of carbon dioxide and two molecules of ethyl alcohol. But it must be remembered that there are other fermentable substances in grape juice besides grape sugar and that there are enzymatic catalysts that render possible secondary reactions that take place at the same time or later; these are responsible for the presence, in wine, of compounds that did not exist in the grape juice.

Grape juice, indeed, is a very complex aqueous solution. It contains, besides water and grape sugar, acids and numerous other substances, most of them in very small quantities, of both vegetable and mineral origin:

1. Substances, other than water, that are the same in must and in wine, such as grape sugar, *Saccharomyces*, acids, tannins, pigments, essential oils, proteins.

2. Substances, other than ethyl alcohol, present in wine but not in must, such as glycerine, various acids, alcohols other than ethyl, esters, aldehydes. (See Appendix H for a more technical explanation of fermentation.)

We have been discussing fermentation in wine, in which sugar is naturally present in the form of grape sugar in the grape juice. It is also present in other fruits, most particularly in sugarcane, whose juice, when properly treated, gives us the sugar we use in our coffee and, as a by-product, molasses, which when fermented produces the alcohol we distill off and call rum.

Alcoholic beverages are often obtained from basic ingredients that contain no natural sugar but that are rich in starch, such as grains, cereals, and potatoes. This is possible because, under the proper conditions, the starches can be converted into sugar (maltose and dextrin) by the action of diastase (amylase), which is the principal enzyme contained in malt (usually barley malt). Once the sugar is there, the yeast enzymes finish the job of fermentation. This will be explained in more detail in Chapter 17.

4
WINE
IN GENERAL

The winemaker's life is not a happy one, even when nature is most cooperative. Making wine is not merely a matter of gathering grapes, pressing
them, and leaving them to ferment. It is not the simplest and most
profitable of agricultural pursuits, when one considers that every vine must be
carefully watched, pruned back so that all its strength will not go into the stalk
or excess grapes or foliage but into producing grapes of rich quality, and
sprayed against the many diseases always waiting to attack. The producer must
take care that birds, which love the grapes, do not eat up the entire crop; he
must gather the grapes when they are just ripe, press them, and see that
conditions favorable to a perfect fermentation are present. He must watch
carefully over the casks of new wine to make sure that *Mycodermae aceti*
(vinegar yeasts) that are in the air do not get in and ruin his product; and after
the wine gets in the bottle, he hopes that eventually it will reach an appreciative buyer. Add to this his eternal worry over too much rain or too little
sunshine, and it is a wonder that men have the courage to carry on such an
arduous task.

Man has made wine almost as long as he has husbanded the earth. Paleon-
tologists have found evidence of masses of grape pips, skins, and stems that
apparently had been crushed by prehistoric man. No one knows when wine
was first made. It is possible that a cliff dweller who had gathered wild grapes
to use their sweet juice as a thirst quencher returned from a hunting trip,
picked up the vessel he had left, and discovered, to his amazement and delight,
that the grape juice had become a different drink, one that made him
happy—the grape juice had fermented and become wine.

The Egyptians credit Osiris, and the Greeks Dionysus, with the gift of wine,
while the Hebrews say Noah first introduced it. The numerous references in the
Bible indicate that not only wine but also stronger beverages were made, as

indicated by the following words: *yayin*, the Hebrew word most often used to describe wine; *homer*, fresh, young, unmixed wine; *tiros*, strong wine; *sekhor*, strong drink; and *meseg*, mixed wines.

Phoenician traders introduced the vine into Europe at the Mediterranean coastal trading posts they established, and later the Roman legions carried it into Gaul, Germany, and across the Channel into England. Although England is one of the best markets for wine, the English have never been able to produce wine successfully in commercial quantities.

The greatest single influence upon wine has been the Church. Indeed, the development of the vine has accompanied the spread of Christianity. Wine was needed for sacramental functions, and the priests recognized its food value. Since they made the wine for their own use and not for commercial purposes, they were more interested in quality than in quantity and their every effort was directed toward improving the vines and perfecting the wines they made. As a result, the winemakers outside the Church began to follow their example, and the general standard of winemaking was raised to a higher level.

Evidence of the priests' work still exists in France today. The vineyards of Châteauneuf-du-Pape near Avignon were started by Pope Clement V in the early fourteenth century, and they still produce wines that we enjoy. Dom Pérignon, the Bénédictine monk of the Abbey of Hautvillers, probably did more for Champagne than any other man, and as we lift the sparkling wine we still hear echoed in our ears his rapturous cry as he first sipped Champagne, "Oh, come quickly! I'm drinking stars!"

It was men of the Church, too, who first made elixirs from wine and brandy, combined with herbs and plants, that were originally used for medicinal purposes. The two most notable examples, with their secret formulas still in use today after hundreds of years, are the famed Bénédictine and Chartreuse liqueurs.

Even the vinicultural history of California begins with the efforts of Padre Junipero, a Dominican missionary, who planted vines he had brought from Spain around the missions.

But while the development of viniculture was greatly stimulated by the Church, the making of wine antedates it by thousands of years. Among the Laws of Hammurabi, the lawgiver-king of Babylonia, handed down over four thousand years ago, are regulations governing innkeepers and the manner in which their hostelries could be conducted. The penalties called for the loss of a limb—and in extreme cases death—for permitting riotous drinking on the premises. The penalties seem to have been rather trying for the unfortunate violators, but they indicate, as did our more recent "noble experiment," that man will not be made temperate by force or by stringent prohibitory laws. It is apparent that, from the beginning, the majority of people have enjoyed alcoholic beverages temperately and that there has always been a small minority who abuse the privilege to their own and their fellows' detriment.

Attempts to protect this minority have led to periodic restrictions on the rest for more than four thousand years.

The vine has played an important part in our own land, as well as throughout the world. One of the first concerns of the early European settlers on our eastern seaboard was the cultivation of the vine, both native and imported. These efforts, unfortunately, were doomed to failure for reasons discussed in Chapter 11. However, it is interesting to note that some twenty grape varieties, or more than half of the known species of the world, are indigenous to North America.

The American influence, oddly enough, has been felt in every viticultural region in Europe, not because of our taste for wine or our lack of it, but because of a certain grape pest (*Phylloxera vastatrix*) that reached Europe with a shipment of American vine plants imported for experimental purposes. In every part of viticultural Europe havoc was caused by the insatiable appetite of *Phylloxera* before an effective remedy was found. Chemicals, sprays, and turning over the land were of no avail. After twenty-odd years of suffering and experimentation, it was found that *Phylloxera* did not attack the American plants, which have much hardier roots. Thereupon, the European varieties (*Vitis vinifera*) were grafted onto American roots (*Vitis aestivalis, Vitis riparia,* or *Vitis rupestris*). There are people who say that for this reason our wines must be just as good as European wines because "their grapes grow from American vines." It is important to understand that the grape continues to have the identical character it had before being grafted onto American roots, since these particular rootstocks do not impart any of their own characteristics.

Although man had been making wine and beer since time immemorial, it was not until the early 1860s that anyone actually knew how the miracle occurred. It was the great scientist Louis Pasteur who, by his revolutionary research in the field of vinous and malt fermentation, proved that fermentation was caused by the presence of minute organisms called ferments. He further demonstrated that if grape juice or brewer's wort is exposed to air from which these minute organisms have been removed, no change takes place; but if ordinary air is present, fermentation begins. Based on Pasteur's studies the business of winemaking and brewing began a new era. Exact scientific knowledge replaced guesswork. Certain things no longer "just happened"; the winemakers understood at last how they happened and why, and they knew at last what to do.

Wine, like a human being, is born, passes through adolescence, matures, grows old, and, if not drunk in time, becomes senile and finally dies. Its life span, like that of a person, is unpredictable at the time of birth. It suffers from maladies to which some wines succumb but from which others recover. Some wines are aristocrats, some plebeians, but most wines are just sturdy, honest, good fellows. Yet all are interesting, more so as one gets to know them better, because no two vintages of the same wine, or any two wines, are ever identical.

Each has individuality. There are family resemblances and characteristics that can be recognized quite readily, but the more one studies the subject and notes these intriguing differences, the greater will be the enjoyment from wines.

*tasting—what
to look for*

Three factors govern the appreciation of wine—color, aroma, and taste. Wine offers a threefold sensory appeal. That is why those who love wine first hold the glass to the light, then smell it, and finally taste it. The pleasure of anticipation is half the fun, and in drinking wine each step in the process adds to the enjoyment.

A wine must be clear and brilliant, have a clean, pleasant bouquet, and have a clean, sound, pleasant taste on the palate. There is beauty in its brilliant color, whether it be the pale gold of a white wine, reminding us of sunshine, or the warm ruby depth of a red wine. The color also gives the first indication of the wine's body; the deeper the color, the fuller the wine will be. Naturally, this applies to wines of the same type. Two totally dissimilar wines cannot be compared.

After the appeal to the eye, the sense of smell is pleased by the subtle, pleasant perfume a wine gives off in the form of esters. As a matter of fact, more than three-fourths of our sense of taste is actually our ability to smell. The bouquet, aroma, perfume—call it what you will—of a wine tells much of what the taste will be. In subsequent chapters, in describing the taste of wines, we shall be forced to use what may seem to be strange comparisons. We shall refer to some wines as having a strawberry, violet, or flowery bouquet, trying to give a taste picture in terms of familiar experiences.

Finally, after the aroma of the wine has promised a certain taste, the palate should confirm it and add the aftertaste that is experienced after the wine has been swallowed.

If wine is being tasted critically, with a view to purchasing or judging salability, it should be compared with a similar wine of the same price to establish its quality. Is the taste more pleasing? Is the quality better than the wine with which it is being compared? Tasting is a business and should be carried out very carefully and seriously. But in drinking wine for pleasure, enjoyment should not be encumbered by any critical analysis of its delicate nuances. The important thing, in this instance, is the pleasure the wine gives. Do not be hypercritical.

CULINARY USES OF WINE

It is not necessary to be a professional chef in order to use wine in cooking. A knowing dash of wine in the pot seasons, tenderizes, and imparts rare flavor and bouquet. The alcohol quickly boils off when heat is applied, leaving the wine's flavorful bouquet.

The use of wine in cooking goes back to the first viniculturists—and that is a long, long time. They looked upon wine as food and used it as naturally in cooking as they would any other ingredient.

Why do you use herbs? For flavoring, of course. Jars of dried herbs of every description are found in every kitchen. If you use them with a heavy hand, all you taste is the herb and every dish seems to taste the same. If you look upon wine as the most delicate of all flavorings you will realize its potential in cooking. Knowing how to use it is easier than you think.

The French are recognized as the world's best cooks. They make the most of the ingredients they use to create superb dishes from soups to desserts. Their use of wine in cooking gives the simplest dish an elusive, subtle flavor. They know from long experience that wine will produce the best results if handled delicately. Too much will spoil the effect. It is not the wine you taste in the finished dish but rather the goodness of the food itself that the wine enhances.

Carême, who was chef to George IV of England and later to the Roth-schilds, wrote in his memoirs that his thoughts were first turned to the art of cuisine by the delightful aroma that tantalized him as he stood one day, all but starving, outside a Paris restaurant. That aroma was produced by the wine in which the dishes were being cooked. From that moment on his course was set. Carême became the greatest of all chefs. He was able to produce a thousand different tastes with his seasonings, just as a painter with a few colors can create an infinite variety of nuances and tones. Wine was one of the principal ingredients he used.

In the United States one can find every type of food. Many dishes have been adapted and simplified, but we also have our own heritage. In colonial days sherry, port, and Madeira were the favorite wines of hospitality, and soups, shellfish, and desserts were prepared with these wines. (See Appendix T for a list of recommended modern cookbooks that feature cooking with wine.)

THE THERAPEUTIC VALUE OF WINE

"Wine," said Pasteur, "is the most healthful and hygienic of beverages." From the earliest days it has been looked upon as a natural remedy for man's ills. In ancient times it must have been invaluable to physicians whose medical knowledge was limited, and European doctors today use it extensively in their practice. In Europe, indeed, where enotherapy has long been practiced with success, doctors regularly prescribe various wines in cases of anemia, arterio-sclerosis, constipation, diarrhea, malaria, pneumonia, illnesses of the liver, kidneys, gall bladder, and so forth.

However, it is as an aid to recovery during the convalescent period that wine can give its best service. Many of the tonics prescribed by physicians, to say nothing of the many patent medicines, could not be made without such wines as sherry, Madeira, Porto, or Tokay. All of these wines, rich in minerals and easily assimilated by the system, are used daily to help those who are run down, anemic, or fatigued. Champagne is the first food permitted after an abdominal operation. It is almost the only nourishment the stomach can receive and hold after the operative shock. The medicinal value of Champagne and other sparkling wines in cases of seasickness is well known. Sherry, rich in iron, is mentioned in the pharmacopoeias of many nations.

More important, however, than wine's medicinal properties is the fact that throughout the ages man has looked upon it as a food. The Bible refers to it in this sense time and again, for example, in Isaiah: "Until I come and take you away to a land like your own land, a land of corn and wine, a land of bread and vineyards." And later, "Thus saith the Lord, As the new wine is found in the cluster, and one saith Destroy it not; for a blessing is in it."

There is a blessing in it. Wine is a food and an aid to health. A quart of wine containing 10 percent alcohol furnishes 850 calories, or the alimentary equivalent of a pound of meat, or twenty ounces of milk, or a pound of bread. In France wine is called the milk of the aged.

In "Tables of Food Values—Revised and Enlarged" by Alice V. Bradley, published by Chas. A. Bennett Co., Inc., Peoria, Illinois, caloric values of several wines are listed as follows:

TYPE OF WINE	CALORIES PER OUNCE	TYPE OF WINE	CALORIES PER OUNCE
Red table wine	18	Port (U.S.)	43
Dry white table wine	20	Porto (imported)	39
Champagne (brut)	21	Sherry (U.S.)	36
Champagne (extra dry)	29	Sherry (dry, imported)	32
Catawba (sweet)	30	Vermouth (dry, French)	27
Madeira	32	Vermouth (sweet, Italian)	44

All light wines contain vitamins, particularly B and C, which are important to the digestive tract, as they help to activate the secretions of the ductless glands whose proper functioning is necessary to our general well-being. As can be seen from the chemical composition of wine, it contains valuable alcohols, acids, and minerals in minute quantities.

In wine-drinking nations wine is considered a food and is consumed at mealtimes.

In the United States as recently as 1960 less than one-third of the wine consumed was light wine, while wines containing more than 14 percent alcohol constituted over two-thirds. In recent years wine has become more and more a part of our regular diet; by 1976 wines under 14 percent constituted over 70 percent of our consumption, while wines of higher alcohol content have fallen to just under 30 percent. Our per capita annual consumption of all wines is only 1¾ gallons, but it is a healthy improvement over the ⁹⁄₁₀ gallon that was the average in 1960.

THE WINE LABEL IN GENERAL

Every label that appears on the bottle of an alcoholic beverage sold in the United States must be approved by the B.A.T.F. of the U.S. Treasury Department. It is mandatory that the public be furnished with clear, correct information as to the product: brand name, type of wine, country of origin, name and address of the bottler of a domestic wine or the importer of a foreign wine, and the net contents. A generic wine (see page 199) must state any qualifying place of origin, for example, New York State Chablis.

If the wine is over 14 percent alcohol, the percentage must be stated. If under, the words *table wine* or *light wine* may be substituted.

Among the items that may be mentioned or included on a label are the following:

1. Vintage date, the year in which the grapes used to make the wine were gathered, pressed, and the juices fermented into wine

2. Village, parish, district, or state in which the grapes were grown

3. Vineyard in which the grapes were grown

4. Wine made from special-quality grapes

5. Wine made from a specific grape

6. Special reserve quality, according to the producer

7. Vineyard owner's name and address

8. Bottling: estate, domaine, or shipper

9. Shipper's name and address

10. Official government guarantee of the wine's authenticity and proper labeling

11. Local trade association seal of authenticity of origin

IMPORTANCE OF WINE IN THE ECONOMY OF THE NATION

One of the world's greatest wine-producing and wine-consuming nations is France. Annual per capita consumption is now almost twenty-eight gallons. To satisfy this demand, 7 percent of the arable land, or some four million acres, is planted in vineyards. These vineyards are owned by $1\frac{1}{2}$ million individuals who give employment to many more. Figures of the other important wine-producing and wine-consuming nations of Europe—Italy, Spain, Portugal, and Germany—are comparable.

In contrast, the American consumption figures are absurd. People with a far different standard of living, recognizing the food value of wine, use about eighteen times as much as our $1\frac{3}{4}$ gallons per capita. If we could increase our consumption of light wines in this country to one-quarter of the French rate, or a little more than 7 gallons per capita (about four glasses of wine per week), we would require, on the basis of the French figures, $3\frac{1}{2}$ million acres of land, involving 2 million farmers, and the employment of perhaps two or three times as many persons. And this would be only the beginning. Distribution and sale, and the allied industries, such as bottle makers, label printers, and so on, would add to the number of employables because of this increase in wine consumption. As a means of encouraging this, state governments and the federal administration should recognize that for actual revenue through taxation, wine is a poor contributor.

The present tax rates are:

	FEDERAL	STATE
Light wines under 14 percent	$0.17 per gal.	$0.10 per gal.
Fortified wines up to 21 percent	0.67 per gal.	0.10 per gal.
Natural sparkling wines under 14 percent	3.40 per gal.	$0.53\frac{1}{3}$ per gal.

The state tax rates shown are those levied in New York. Each state levies its own taxes, and there is some variation; in most of the so-called controlled or monopoly states there is no specific tax as such, since the state sells to its citizens at a profit. See Appendix R for a list of federal taxes and import duties on all alcoholic beverages.

In 1939, when the federal excise taxes were $0.05 and $0.10 per gallon on light wines and fortified wines respectively, the federal and state governments

OPPOSITE PAGE. There are six basic types of wine labels.

TOP LEFT: Estate- or château-bottled wines are those for which the grapes are grown, processed, and bottled on the same property.

TOP RIGHT: Domaine labeling refers to wines for which the grapes are grown, processed, and bottled by the owner but not necessarily on one property.

CENTER LEFT: Regional labeling refers to wines made from grapes grown in one parish or region. If wine or grapes from out of the area are used, local custom or law controls the percentage.

CENTER RIGHT: Varietal labeling indicates the wine by the grape from which it is made. The proportion of wine from that grape may vary from 51 to 100 percent, depending on local law.

BOTTOM LEFT: Generic labeling refers to wines that use the name of a famous wine or wine area that has now come into general use. These names have no legal meaning but identify the general type of the wine. Terms such as Burgundy, Sauterne, or claret indicate the general type of wine and are always preceded by the name of the place of origin.

BOTTOM RIGHT: Monopole or brand labeling is used where the actual name of the wine has no real significance but gains consumer identification and acceptance through advertising or other consumer marketing techniques.

1970

COS D'ESTOURNEL

APPELLATION SAINT-ESTEPHE CONTROLÉE

MIS EN BOUTEILLE AU CHATEAU

SOCIÉTÉ DES DOMAINES PRATS PROPRIÉTAIRE A SAINT-ESTÉPHE
PRODUCE OF FRANCE

VIN DE BORDEAUX
PRODUCED AND BOTTLED IN FRANCE

CONTENTS
1 PT. 8 1/2 FL. OZS   **PRATS**   ALCOHOL 11¾ BY VOL.

PRATS FRÈRES NÉGOCIANTS-ÉLEVEURS, BORDEAUX (GIRONDE) FRANCE

Joseph Drouhin

RED BURGUNDY TABLE WINE   CONTENTS : 1 PINT 8 FLUID OZS.
                               ALCOHOL BY VOLUME 13°

Beaune
APPELLATION BEAUNE CONTROLÉE

Clos des Mouches

RÉCOLTE DU DOMAINE
MIS EN BOUTEILLE PAR

JOSEPH DROUHIN

A BEAUNE, COTE-D'OR, AUX CELLIERS DES
ROIS DE FRANCE ET DES DUCS DE BOURGOGNE

Dreyfus, Ashby & Co

PRODUCE OF FRANCE

NET CONTENTS   ALCOHOL 12%
1 PINT 8 FL. OZS   BY VOLUME

SOAVE
CLASSICO
DENOMINAZIONE DI ORIGINE CONTROLLATA

BOLLA

ITALIAN DRY WHITE WINE
PRODUCED AND BOTTLED IN THE CLASSIC ZONE OF
SOAVE - ITALY
BY

FRATELLI BOLLA · PRODUTTORI
VERONA - ITALY

SOLE DISTRIBUTORS FOR THE U.S.A. THE JOS. GARNEAU CO. · NEW YORK, N. Y.

Vineyards Established 1852

ALMADÉN
California Mountain

CABERNET SAUVIGNON

An extraordinary wine, full of the characteristic bouquet
and flavor of the great Cabernet grape of Bordeaux,
grown in mountain vineyards at Paicines, California

PRODUCED AND BOTTLED BY
Almadén Vineyards, Los Gatos, California
Alcohol 12½% by volume

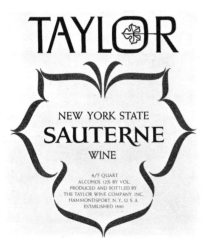

TAYLOR

NEW YORK STATE

SAUTERNE

WINE

4/5 QUART
ALCOHOL 12% BY VOL.
PRODUCED AND BOTTLED BY
THE TAYLOR WINE COMPANY, INC.
HAMMONDSPORT, N. Y., U.S.A.
ESTABLISHED 1880

MATEUS

PRODUCE
OF
PORTUGAL

ROSÉ
STILL WINE

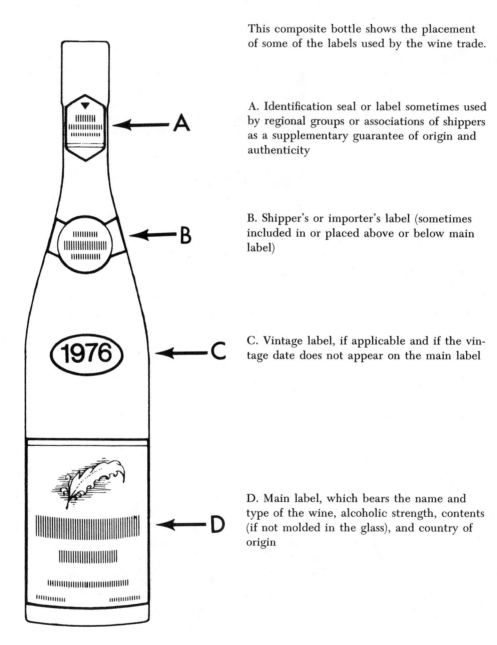

This composite bottle shows the placement of some of the labels used by the wine trade.

A. Identification seal or label sometimes used by regional groups or associations of shippers as a supplementary guarantee of origin and authenticity

B. Shipper's or importer's label (sometimes included in or placed above or below main label)

C. Vintage label, if applicable and if the vintage date does not appear on the main label

D. Main label, which bears the name and type of the wine, alcoholic strength, contents (if not molded in the glass), and country of origin collected $15 million through wine excise and fortifying taxes. In 1952, when total volume had almost doubled and the federal taxes had been increased by more than three times over those of 1939, tax collections increased to a little over $100 million. In the first five years of the 1970s, federal wine tax collections averaged $180 million a year. The prospect now is that, at current rates, because of increased plantings and consumption, federal and state revenues from wine sales will double in less than a decade.

The only increase in federal taxes on wine since 1952 was a jump from $2.72 to $3.40 per gallon for natural sparkling wines, exactly twenty times the 17-cent rate for light wines. This is the most illogical excise tax rate. But all in all, the tax from wine is rarely as much as 4 percent of the total tax revenue from alcoholic beverages. Generally speaking, these taxes are low and quite reasonable when compared with those levied on spirits. However, it is the high license fees, for both production and sale, that are the greatest hindrances to a more rapid expansion of winemaking and that tend to increase the cost of wine to the consuming public.

As long as wine is looked upon as an alcoholic beverage and not as a food, its wide use will be curtailed. When the day arrives that wine can be made and sold freely with a minimum of special tax and license burdens, when it can be distributed through outlets that sell other foods, much as coffee and tea are sold today, then and only then is our country likely to become a wine-drinking nation. Then the federal and state treasuries will derive an increased revenue from wine through the larger income tax payments of the farmers, who will turn to winemaking when they find it profitable.

The picture is not entirely discouraging, however. Annual wine consumption has reached about 350 million gallons—over four times as much as in 1939—according to Wine Institute figures. This means many more acres planted to vineyards and greater employment in the vineyards, at the wineries, and in every phase of the industry. It is to be hoped that the wine industry will continue to prosper.

In the following chapters we will discuss the wines produced throughout the world, devoting a chapter to each of the major wine producers and consumers of Europe and North America. Most of the wines these countries produce are enjoyed in the United States and are readily available on the larger markets. There are many wines of the world, however, that, regardless of the quantity made, are not among the major imports to the United States. Some, such as those from Chile, used to be more important years ago. Others, such as U.S.S.R. wines, may become a factor on the market in a few years because of recent reciprocal distribution agreements. The situation varies with changing tastes, international marketing, value, and production ability to fulfill the demand for quality and consistency.

These smaller wine-producing countries have been separated into four chapters: Other Wines of Europe, Other Wines of the Americas, Wines of the Middle East and Africa, and Wines of Australia, New Zealand, and the Far East. Within each chapter the countries will be discussed in alphabetical order. Appendix Q lists the quantity of wine produced in each country. Appendix R tells which of these nations enjoy most-favored-nation status, which affects import taxes and duties.

WINE-PRODUCING COUNTRIES OF THE WORLD

OTHER EUROPEAN COUNTRIES
- ENGLAND
- LUXEMBOURG
- SWITZERLAND
- AUSTRIA

- CZECHOSLOVAKIA
- HUNGARY
- YUGOSLAVIA
- ROMANIA
- BULGARIA
- GREECE
- U.S.S.R.

GERMANY
FRANCE
ITALY
SPAIN
PORTUGAL

UNITED STATES

OTHER AMERICAS
- MEXICO
- CANADA
- PERU
- BRAZIL
- ARGENTINA
- CHILE
- URUGUAY

AFRICA
- EGYPT
- TUNISIA
- ALGERIA
- MOROCCO

SOUTH AFRICA

MIDDLE EAST
- TURKEY
- ISRAEL
- CYPRUS

FAR EAST
- JAPAN
- CHINA

AUSTRALIA AND NEW ZEALAND

The temperate climates of the world produce the grapes and other fruits that make wine. The areas in boldface are discussed in separate chapters in this book.

WILLIAM LEMBECK

5
THE WINES OF FRANCE

I n any discussion of wines it is natural that France should be uppermost in our minds. Although vying with Italy as one of the largest wine-producing nations in the world, France continues to be a major importer as well as a major exporter of wine.

It is her fine wine that France exports, and it is this policy of exporting only such goods as will enhance the nation's reputation, whether wine or chefs or fashion, that has made the French among the most astute merchandisers in the world and given France a position from which she sets the fashion in the art of good living. Poor wine, badly made clothes, and downright bad cooking may be found in France, but they stay there.

It is not, however, because of the quantity of wine she produces or drinks, but because of the quality and variety of wines she offers to the world, that France comes at the head of our list.

France is politically subdivided into ninety-five departments (states), which are further subdivided into communes or parishes (counties). The three most important departments, in which are produced the most famous wines, are the Gironde (red and white Bordeaux), the Côte d'Or (red and white Burgundy), and the Marne (Champagne). After these leaders come the departments of Yonne (Chablis), Bas-Rhin and Haut-Rhin (Alsace), Saône-et-Loire (Pouilly-Fuissé and Mâcon), Rhône (Beaujolais), and various departments along the Rhône River, which produce Côte Rôtie, Hermitage, and Châteauneuf-du-Pape, as well as those along the Loire River, which produce, going from east to west, Pouilly-Fumé, Vouvray, Saumur, Anjou, and Muscadet. In every department but two the vine is cultivated.

MAKING THE WINE

The harvest in France usually begins sometime during the last two weeks of September. The *vendangeurs* ("vintagers")—men, women, and children—are

25

organized in groups under a foreman, who supervises the work to see that only ripe, sound grapes are picked and that the work is done thoroughly and conscientiously. The bunches of grapes are cut off the vine with special pruning shears and are placed in small baskets, which, when full, are emptied into large, wooden, hodlike receptacles known as *hottes*. The *porte-hotte* ("hod carrier") takes his full *hotte* to a wagon or a truck that has two tubs, called *douils*, into which he dumps the grapes. The driver of the truck pushes the grapes down firmly until the *douil* is filled. (A solidly packed *douil* will produce a *barrique* ["cask"] of 225 liters of wine.) When both *douils* are filled, the wagon or truck proceeds to the *pressoir* or *cuvier* ("pressing house"), where the grapes are unloaded and weighed.

Here the grapes are passed through a mechanical destemming and crushing device. The purpose of crushing is simply to break the skins so that the juice will run out freely. The yeast can then begin the fermentation. Some winemakers still destem by hand, grasping bunches of grapes and rubbing them back and forth over wooden slats. The grapes, crushed and loosened from the stems, fall through the slats into the vat below. Otherwise the mechanically crushed grapes, along with their juice, which is now called must, are pumped into the fermenting vat.

At this point the winemaking processes differ for making red, white, and rosé wines. Red wine is made by fermenting the juice with the grape skins and pips still in it, to give the wine color, body, and tannin. Tannins are complex compounds that give stability and longevity to the wine.

The juice of the usual wine grapes is colorless, and the color in red wine is obtained from the inside of the grape skin. Grape juice will not dissolve the pigments, but the alcohol and heat formed during fermentation extract the color from the skins. When fermentation first begins, not much color is yet dissolved by the small amount of alcohol produced. After about a day a red wine is just pink in color. If the must is separated from the skins at this point, with the balance of the fermentation continuing away from the skins, a rosé wine will result. Because rosé wines begin as red wines do and have some red color in them, they are considered red wines.

A white wine is made by separating the juice from the skins before fermentation begins. After the destemming, or *égrappage*, the grapes are pressed and the expressed juice is pumped into closed vats (to avoid oxidation), where it begins to ferment. In making white wines, white grapes are used almost exclusively. Black-skinned grapes can be used, however, if the must is separated from the skins before any color is extracted. The most notable example of this is the process of making Champagne.

Saccharomyces, or wine yeast, whether naturally present on the skins or provided by the winemaker from specially propagated strains, begins to multiply with amazing rapidity in the favorable elements of grape juice and plenty of air, and fermentation begins almost at once. At first it is violent and quite boisterous. In fact, the verb *to ferment* comes from the Latin *fervere*, "to boil," and a vat of fermenting must looks like boiling liquid. The escaping gas causes the surface to boil, bubble, and hiss. During the period of violent fermentation in making red wine, the skins, pips, and all the other residue in the must float to the top, forming a cap three or four feet thick. The cap is broken up with wooden appliances to allow carbon dioxide to escape, to let out excess heat, and to recirculate the skins with the must. Fermentation gradually simmers down and stops when the alcohol content is about 14 percent or when the yeast dies. Sometimes there is still some sugar left, as with the sweet wines of Sauternes. This is called residual sugar.

Fermentation of red wines usually takes from seven to ten days, while fermentation of white wines, accomplished at a lower temperature, takes longer. As soon as the fermentation is completed, the new wine is "racked" (drawn off) into clean, sulfured *barriques* of 225-liter capacity, which are placed in the *chai* ("warehouse"), or cellar, if the vineyard boasts such a luxury.

During the first few months, because of evaporation, there will be a certain loss of wine, which will leave an air space (*ullage*), into which the bad ferments are prone to penetrate, ready to undo all the work of the yeast, making the wine sick or even turning it to vinegar. The preventive is to keep the cask filled up to the top with sound wine. The casks are topped off twice a week during the first two months and every two weeks thereafter until the wine falls "bright" (clear) five or six months later.

During this period of continued activity, the wine throws off certain impurities and superfluous solid matter, which are deposited at the bottom of the cask and are known as the lees, consisting principally of cream of tartar, yeast cells, coloring, precipitative material, and other proteins.

At this point, while the wines are still in the cask, some red wines undergo a malolactic fermentation, in which the harsh malic acid is converted into the softer lactic acid. Since carbon dioxide is also formed, a loose glass bung is used to permit the gas to escape without allowing any air to enter.

It is not good for the new wine to remain in contact with the lees too long, so the new wine is racked into fresh casks three times during the first year: in the early spring, March or April; in June, when the vine flowers; and in October.

After the third racking a wooden bung is driven home and the cask stored so that the bung is on the side, entirely covered with wine. This ensures complete closure and prevents the entrance of any air. Of course, while the wine is in the cask, it is in contact with the air it breathes through the porous wood, and its development continues.

Changes in vinification methods have made it possible to bottle red wines earlier than had been customary. The lighter-bodied red wines are ready for bottling after two years in wood. The fuller-bodied red Bordeaux and red Burgundies, in big years, may require two and a half years' development in cask, but the traditional three or more years are no longer generally practiced.

The heavier solids precipitate of their own weight to form the lees, but a few lighter particles may remain in suspension, floating in the wine. To ensure only perfectly clear, bright wine, it must be fined. This clarifying process is done as follows: a small amount of albuminous material, which may be isinglass, gelatin, or white of egg, is mixed with a little wine and poured into the cask. This albuminous matter coagulates the solids in the wine, forming a heavy film, which slowly precipitates, acting as a filter and carrying with it all extraneous matter, leaving the wine in a brilliant condition for bottling. The fining process takes one or two weeks and is usually done twice. Just before bottling the wine may be filtered to ensure clarity.

On the day selected for bottling the cask is broached, the entire contents bottled, and the bottles corked. Much as a human being accustomed to an active outdoor occupation dislikes the confinement of an office job, so the wine resents the change from the cask to the confinement of the bottle. It usually takes several months for it to accustom itself to the change. During this period the wine is not in prime condition since it is suffering from a malady known in the wine trade as bottle-sickness. After the bottle-sickness period the wine resumes its slow development in the bottle, which will continue as it develops toward its prime. The wine will reach a plateau that can last for several years under good storage conditions.

It is difficult to say how long a red Bordeaux, for example, will live. No two vintages are alike. While the less successful vintages reach their peak in five to ten years, better vintages will continue to improve for twenty, thirty, or forty years. If the wine is not drunk, it will gradually become senile and die. Red wines that have suffered man's ingratitude in this manner can easily be recognized. They have lost color, bouquet, body, and flavor; they have become dead and lifeless.

Normally, the older the wine, the greater the amount of deposit there will be in the bottle, and the more delicate it will be. Sediment is a natural phenomenon and can be expected of most wines, particularly red wines. In the course of time the wine throws off some of its bitartrates, and in the case of red wines a certain amount of tannin also; these make up the deposit that settles on the side or bottom of the bottle, depending on how it is stored. The sediment, however, in no way affects the quality of the wine; it is simply one proof of age.

An extremely old red Bordeaux or Burgundy, recently arrived and fit to drink, would be a rarity in the United States today because of the rigors of an ocean voyage. However, there is no reason why a wine sent here when young and laid down in this country should not mature just as well as in France and be just as enjoyable. Experience shows that the ocean trip accelerates the maturing of the wine by at least a year.

WINE REGIONS OF FRANCE

BELGIUM

ENGLISH CHANNEL

LUXEMBOURG

Seine R.

Marne R.

Moselle R.

GERMANY

Paris

CHAMPAGNE

ALSACE

Loire R.

Rhine R.

CHABLIS

LOIRE

JURA

ATLANTIC
OCEAN

SWITZER-
LAND

BURGUNDY

BORDEAUX

Dordogne R.

ITALY

BERGERAC

Garonne R.

CAHORS

**CÔTES
DU
RHÔNE**

BEARN

Rhône R.

MIDI

SPAIN

CÔTES DE PROVENCE

MEDITERRANEAN
SEA

WILLIAM LEMBECK

APPELLATION CONTRÔLÉE

Although the vine has been cultivated commercially in France since the Roman occupation, and with greater care and intelligence than in other countries, it is only since the 1930s that regulatory laws have been passed, guaranteeing the authenticity of origin and place names commonly found on wine labels.

The first delimitative laws were passed after the 1911 "Champagne Wars," in which the *vignerons* who were making their wine exclusively from grapes grown within the province of Champagne rose up in arms against certain merchants who imported grapes at low prices from outside the traditional Champagne region and sold their Champagne at cut prices. The riots resulted in laws that fixed the boundaries within which the grapes must be grown to produce wine legally entitled to the name Champagne.

Since then further laws have fixed the geographic limits of all the major wine- and brandy-producing districts. More recently these laws have been refined to fix the physical limits of the world-famous vineyards and have set the maximum quantity of quality wine each may produce of a given vintage. Setting the legal maximum of quantity assures the maintenance of quality. Under this law, called *Appellation d'Origine Contrôlée* (A.O.C.), the production of each vineyard is controlled. The vineyard owner is obliged to report to his local board, which in turn reports to the central or national board of *Appellation Contrôlée* wines, located in Paris. Wines produced under this system of control of origin and quality will bear on their labels the phrase *Appellation Contrôlée*, which has become a French government guarantee of origin and, to a certain degree, of quality as well.

The basic conditions for a wine to be entitled to an *Appellation Contrôlée* are set up by the *Institut National des Appellations d'Origine des Vins et Eaux-de-Vie* (I.N.A.O.), an official body whose members belong either to the French civil service or to the wine industry.

Some of these conditions pertain to district boundaries according to the nature of the soil, grape varieties, maximum quantity of wine per acre allowed to be produced, minimum alcohol content of the wine, and viticultural and vinicultural methods. Growers and shippers must follow these regulations if they wish to label their wines with the name of the vineyard, the commune, or the district. There are exceptions: very old bottles of wine do not carry the *Appellation Contrôlée* statement because most of the laws date only from 1935.

Technicians exercise controls to enforce these regulations. The quality regulations, of course, increase in stringency in relation to the fame of the place of origin of the wine. For example, a wine entitled to be labeled Appellation Pommard Contrôlée must come from any vineyard of the Pommard zone and have a minimum of $10\frac{1}{2}$ percent alcohol. But for the wine to have the legal right to be labeled Appellation Pommard Les Épenots Contrôlée, it must be made entirely from grapes grown in the Les Épenots vineyard of the Pommard zone. It must also have a minimum alcohol content of 11 percent. In both cases the maximum quantity of wine that may legally be produced each year is 35 hectoliters per hectare (equivalent to 374 gallons per acre).

Some wines bear on their labels the letters *V.D.Q.S.* (*Vins Délimités de Qualité Supérieure*), which indicate that they are a second classification of high-quality wines of specified origin. They are subject to regulations similar to those of *Appellation Contrôlée* wines; that is, these wines have been harvested from strictly defined vineyards and vines, by traditional methods. The label shows that the wine conforms to standards set jointly by the I.N.A.O. and the Ministry of Agriculture. V.D.Q.S. wines, about sixty of them, are grouped into seven general places, where reds, whites, and rosés are produced. Someday the V.D.Q.S. wines may be absorbed into the *Appellation Contrôlée* classification.

The wines from each section are so markedly different and have such individual characteristics that they have been accepted as basic types. Their names are often misused and the wines imitated in almost all wine-producing countries, so in order to study the wines of the country properly, we must take each geographical division separately. Each will be considered in the order of its importance to the wine trade in general.

1 . B O R D E A U X

If France is the most famous wine-producing country, then the Bordeaux district (Gironde) is the most famous in the production of great red wines. The district produces three distinct varieties of wine, equally distinguished: magisterial clarets of great breeding; clean, dry, white Graves; and luscious, golden Sauternes.

history

Fifty years before the birth of Christ, Burdigala (Bordeaux) was the chief town and commercial center of Biturigis Vivisi. Later, in the fourth century, it was made the capital of Aquitanica Secunda. Its fame, then as now, was irrevocably linked with the excellence of its wines, which were praised by Columella, renowned Roman writer of the first century.

Through his marriage to Eleanor of Aquitaine in 1152, Henry of Anjou acquired the Sénéchaussée of Bordeaux (Gascony) and the vast Duchy of Guyenne. Two years later he became King Henry II of England, and for three hundred years Gascony belonged to the English crown. Its wines enjoyed wide popularity in the British Isles, a taste that exists to this day.

The history of the famous wines of Bordeaux began more than two thousand years ago. We do not know who first produced a wine of the claret type, but the poet Ausonius sang of its charms and virtues during the Roman occupation. The famous Château Ausone is supposed to have been his vineyard.

What is claret? The term was originally used by the English when they referred to the red wines of Bordeaux. The English made up a large part of the market for Bordeaux wines, and many English words have gained common usage in the wine world, not only in Bordeaux. The word *claret* has definite geographic origins in Bordeaux, but it is not a legal term in France. Many other countries use the term to describe a red wine they feel is similar to the type made in Bordeaux. This usage, unfortunately, has detracted from the elegant connotation of a château-bottled red wine.

geography   The Bordelais (Bordeaux country) viticultural region is divided into five main (left) and four lesser (right) districts:

Médoc	Premières Côtes de Bordeaux
Graves	Bourg
Saint-Émilion	Blaye
Pomerol	Entre-deux-Mers
Sauternes	

There is a further subdivision, the commune, or parish. The parish is a geographical, political, and, formerly, religious subdivision, as a parish priest and church were required to administer to the spiritual needs of a community. The Church worked out such a perfect geographical subdivision that the state saw no reason to change it and took it over.

Médoc   The most important district is the Médoc, a triangular peninsula stretching north some fifty miles from Bordeaux to Soulac and varying in width from six to ten miles. It lies between the Gironde River on the east and the Atlantic Ocean on the west and is divided into Médoc and Haut-Médoc. Of the appellation wines produced in the area, Médoc accounts for 25 percent and Haut-Médoc produces 75 percent. With few exceptions (for example, the dry white wines of Pavillon Blanc du Château Margaux, Château Loudenne, and Château La Dame Blanche), only red wines are produced in the fifty-three communes that make up the entire Médoc. The four most important—Pauillac, Saint-Julien, Margaux, and Saint-Estèphe—are all located in the Haut-Médoc, which extends thirty miles from Bordeaux to just north of Saint-Estèphe.

Graves   The Graves takes its name from the gravelly or pebbly quality of the soil. The district stretches for twenty-five miles to the southwest of Bordeaux and is for the most part level plain that becomes hillier to the south. Here are produced both red and white wines. The most important communes of the Graves are Pessac, Léognan, and Martillac.

WINE REGIONS OF BORDEAUX

SCALE

0   25 km

Borders
of Bordeaux
Appellation

Gironde R.

MÉDOC

BLAYE

ATLANTIC OCEAN

SAINT-
ESTÈPHE

PAUILLAC

SAINT-
JULIEN

BOURG

MARGAUX AND
CANTENAC

**HAUT-
MÉDOC**

POMEROL

SAINT-ÉMILION

Dordogne R.

**PREMIÈRES CÔTES
DE BORDEAUX**

Bordeaux

Garonne R.

ENTRE-DEUX-MERS

GRAVES

BARSAC
PREIGNAC
SAUTERNES { BOMMES
SAUTERNES
FARGUES

WILLIAM LEMBECK

Saint-Émilion and Pomerol

In Saint-Émilion there are five communes, all situated on somewhat hilly ground north of the Dordogne River, in the vicinity of the town of Libourne. The single commune of Pomerol is important enough to be considered a separate district. The wines from these vineyards, because of the high proportion of Merlot grapes, have depth of color and fullness of body and are considered the Burgundy wines of the Bordeaux district.

Sauternes

In the southern portion of the Graves we come to a district smaller than the island of Manhattan but viticulturally favored as are few regions in the world. The rich, luscious, highly perfumed wines of the Sauternes are entirely distinct from all the other wines of Bordeaux and have an excellence all their own. The Sauternais (Sauternes country) lies in the southeast of Graves and on the left bank of the Garonne River. Five communes compose Sauternes country: Sauternes, Barsac, Bommes, Fargues, and Preignac. The wines from any of these communes are known by the regional name of Sauternes. Barsac, however, even though it is a Sauternes, has its own appellation, and many of its châteaux prefer to use it rather than the larger Sauternes appellation.

Premières Côtes de Bordeaux, Bourg, Blaye, and Entre-deux-Mers

In these districts are produced the smaller but useful wines, both red and white, that are generally shipped simply as Bordeaux Blanc or Bordeaux Rouge or under the shipper's brand name.

soil

One would think that rich soil would be required to produce fine wine. Nothing could be further from the truth. In fact, the soil of the Bordeaux wine region is mainly gravel, limestone, or sand with a clay subsoil. More unfriendly soil for agriculture would be difficult to find, and yet the vine flourishes best in just these types of soil. Where no other crop can be grown successfully, the vine gives the best quality of wine grape. This is equally true in the other famous viticultural regions of the world.

grape varieties

The principal vine used in the production of the great clarets of the Médoc and Graves is the Cabernet Sauvignon. Growing in small, close-set bunches, its violet-scented grapes are small and sweet and give the wine its vinosity. Other vines, such as Malbec, Petit Verdot, and Carmenère, are planted to give special qualities to the wines. In Saint-Émilion and Pomerol, however, the principal grape is the early-ripening Merlot, the balance being mostly Cabernet Franc (also called Bouschet). The best white wines are made from the Sémillon and Sauvignon Blanc grapes, which will be discussed later.

The vine in Bordeaux is not allowed to grow wild; in fact, it is cut back close to the ground after the vintage, so that the winter appearance of a vineyard is that of a bare field dotted with an orderly series of stumps. The vines are not allowed to grow more than $2\frac{1}{2}$ to $3\frac{1}{2}$ feet high so that what strength they derive from the soil will go into producing grapes of quality rather than trailing vine.

There are more than thirty thousand vineyards in the Bordeaux wine region, most of which are called *château*, meaning "castle." In many cases the property boasts a medieval castle, but when the term is used as generally as it is in Bordeaux, the majority of these "castles" are simply farmhouses used only for pressing grapes and storing wine. *Bordeaux wine trade*

Obviously, if each of the vineyard owners were to attempt to sell his wines directly to buyers from all over the world, there would be no end to the confusion. Hence there evolved many generations ago clearinghouses in the form of Bordeaux wine merchants, brokers who buy the wine from the different vineyard owners, sometimes bottled, but more often in larger quantities in the wood. The broker ships the wine as he receives it, or he blends it with wine from other vineyards and bottles it, not under the château or vineyard name, but under his own proprietary brand name. With few exceptions the vineyard owner never markets his own wines but depends on the wine merchant to do it for him.

The Bordeaux wine trade has developed five types of labels: *labeling*

1. Château bottled
2. Château wine bottled by a cooperative or by a wine merchant
3. *Monopole* or trademark
4. Commune or regional
5. Varietal

There are two distinct types of labels used on château wines. The first, château bottled, indicates that the wine has been produced, cared for, and bottled at the vineyard property where the grapes were grown. It has on the label, or sometimes on the capsule, the phrase *mis en bouteille au château*, which means "bottled at the château." The vineyard owner delivers this wine, bottled, labeled, and cased, to the wine merchant or shipper. The cork is always branded with the château name and the vintage year. Examples are Château Lafite-Rothschild, Château Latour, and Château d'Yquem.

The second type of label, château wine bottled by the wine merchant, indicates that the wine has been produced at the château named on the label but has been purchased in the cask and bottled by the shipper in his Bordeaux cellars. The shipper's name appears on the label.

There are some châteaux that do not practice château bottling at all; they have found it more profitable to sell their wines in wood to the different wine merchants who bottle them. On these and other A.O.C. wines the following phrases may be found: *mis en bouteille à la propriété, mise d'origine,* and *mis en bouteille dans la région de . . .* , followed by the name of the specific region.

Whereas château bottling guarantees authenticity of origin, it does not have to guarantee quality. Because of changing vintage conditions, château-bottled wines vary in quality from year to year. This has a direct influence on the price governing each vintage and explains why a younger vintage will sometimes fetch a higher price than an older one of the same wine. A good example is the 1970 Château Lafite-Rothschild, which costs more than three times as much as the less desirable 1968.

In order to take care of his customer's needs in every part of the world, the Bordeaux shipper must always have a wide assortment of château wines. Although there is no wine "stock market" in Bordeaux, château bottlings are traded in somewhat the same manner as stocks and bonds. Through the centuries the trade has evolved a system that is eminently fair and satisfactory, both to the vineyard owner and to the shipper.

Suppose, for instance, that the 1971 vintage of Château Latour totaled 300,000 bottles, all château bottled. Eight wine merchants agree to buy up the entire vintage and split it among themselves. Each of them would then have the same wine to offer to the trade, identical in every respect as to labeling, capsules, cases, and so forth, and their prices would be more or less the same. Along comes a ninth merchant who needs this wine for one of his customers. As the eight merchants have cornered the market on this wine, he must buy from one of the original purchasers and pay him a profit, and he must also make a profit for himself on the sale. Therefore, when buying château-bottled Bordeaux wines, shop for the lowest price, since it is all the same wine, assuming it has been properly stored.

The third type of label is the *monopole,* or private brand. Each shipper has his own private brand label on which he stakes his reputation for honesty and his knowledge and ability as a wine merchant. A *monopole* wine is almost invariably a blend of various wines from different parts of the Bordeaux region that the shipper maintains year in and year out at the same standard of quality; examples are Grande Marque, Prince Blanc, Mouton-Cadet, and La Cour Pavillon.

The fourth label is the commune, district, or regional label. A bottle so labeled contains wine produced in the commune, district, or region named, for example, Médoc (wine in this bottle was produced in the Médoc district). This wine does not necessarily come from one vineyard but may be from several in the commune, district, or region named. It probably is a blended wine, bottled by the shipper at his Bordeaux cellars. For this reason it is possible to obtain wines of widely varying quality and price bearing identical place names and vintages from different shippers. One shipper may use better-quality wine in his blend, while another feels that price is more important than quality. The Bordeaux shipper, like any other businessman, tries to satisfy his customers'

TOP LEFT: Château-bottled wine. Note the phrase *mis en bouteille au château.*

TOP RIGHT: Monopole or trademark brand. Note the word *déposée*, meaning "registered brand."

BOTTOM LEFT: Varietal wine, bottled by the shipper.

BOTTOM RIGHT: Regional wine, bottled by the shipper.

needs. Beware of bargains, compare prices, and taste a bottle before you buy a case.

The varietal label is the fifth type. This term has been used in the United States to indicate that the grape variety named on the label predominates in the wine itself. The purpose was to break away from generic names that were not definitive and to identify more precisely the nature of a wine. This practice was formerly used only in Alsace, Switzerland, Italy, and a few other regions in Europe. In recent years the shippers of Bordeaux, Burgundy, and the Loire have also started to use varietal labels. The French authorities require the use of 100 percent of the grapes named; the German minimum is 85 percent, while the U.S. minimum is 51 percent. This is a departure from the traditional style of winemaking in France, which involves using more than one grape variety in wine.

vintage   There seems to be some confusion as to the exact meaning of the word *vintage* in reference to wines, whether they are imported or produced in the United States. The word has two meanings:

1. *Vintage* means gathering the grapes, pressing them, and making wine. There is a vintage (harvest) every year.

2. The date on a bottle of wine signifies the year in which the wine was produced, the vintage year. Some vineyards bottle and date every year's production. Certain regions, such as Champagne, date only the wines of exceptional years. Since this is not done every year, the dated wines are known as vintage wines.

A vintage chart, judiciously used, can be helpful, but it is important to remember table wines change constantly. No two wines, even from the same district, develop at a constant rate. Furthermore, not all wines made in a great year are great, and not all wines made in a relatively poor year are poor. Sweeping generalities of this kind cannot be applied when one considers the thousands of vineyards involved. However, the chances are better for good wines when conditions are generally favorable, and with these reservations in mind, a vintage chart can be useful (see Appendix B).

CLASSIFIED GROWTHS

In 1855 a number of Bordeaux wines were to be exhibited at the Exposition in Paris. There was some question about the order in which the wines should be shown as, inevitably, there was rivalry among the best-known vineyard owners as to who produced the finest wine. In order to settle the matter once and for all, a jury of wine brokers was selected to classify the outstanding clarets and Sauternes in order of merit. Although this was done nearly a century ago, for the most part these classifications still hold and are accepted the world over.

Fifty-seven red wines of Médoc and one from Graves were chosen and classified in five classes or groups, while twenty Sauternes were grouped in two main classes, and one Sauternes was placed in a special class. After 1855 some vineyards were sold and subsequently divided. This accounts for the different number of classified châteaux found in different source books, depending on when the vineyards were counted, but at present the generally accepted number is sixty-one (see Appendix C). Below the fifth growth in the Médoc and the second growth in the Sauternes are further classifications: *crus exceptionnels, crus bourgeois supérieurs, crus bourgeois, crus artisans* (obsolete), and *crus paysans* (obsolete).

In 1953 the leading wines of Graves were officially classified. In 1959 the list was revised, and this time thirteen red and eight white wines were selected. In 1955 an official classification was made of the top clarets of Saint-Émilion. Twelve were chosen as first classified great growths and seventy-two as great classified growths. Both of these classifications have been adopted by the *Institut National des Appellations d'Origine des Vins et Eaux-de-Vie* (see Appendix C).° Because of the demand and the high prices of the great classified growths, more and more wines with regional labels and proprietary brands are being sold.

the classified claret growths

To differentiate between a classified claret and a *cru bourgeois* is easy. To tell the difference between a second and a third growth is very difficult. Most of the sixty-one vineyards produce excellent wines whose main differences lie in nuances of nose (bouquet), body, and delicacy easily apparent to the connoisseur, but not to the layman. However, certain basic, distinguishing marks are apparent in wines from different parishes or sections. For example, the wines of Pauillac (Château Lafite-Rothschild, Château Latour, Château Mouton-Rothschild, and so on) have more body than those of Margaux (Château Margaux), which have finesse and delicacy, while the red wines of the Graves (Château Haut-Brion, Château La Mission Haut Brion, and so on) are fuller than the Médoc wines mentioned. Even fuller and sturdier are the Pomerol (Château Pétrus) and Saint-Émilion (Château Ausone, Château Cheval Blanc, and so on).

CHÂTEAU LAFITE-ROTHSCHILD.   Lafite is spelled with one *f* and one *t* and should not be confused with similar names such as Laffite or Laffitte. According to a document dated 1355, Château Lafite belonged to a certain Jean de Lafite. In 1868 Baron James de Rothschild acquired it at private auction for the reputed sum of 165,000 pounds, and it is still held by his heirs. In a good year

---

° In 1787, sixty-eight years before the Bordeaux classification of 1855, Thomas Jefferson wrote, "The cantons in which the most celebrated wines of Bourdeaux are made are Medoc down the river, Grave adjoining the city, and the parishes next above; all on the same side of the river. . . . Of red wines, there are four vineyards of the first quality, *viz.*, 1. Château Margau, . . . 2. La Tour de Segur, . . . 3. Hautbrion, . . . 4. Château de la Fite. . . ."

Château Lafite-Rothschild has a magnificent deep color, a softness and delicacy of flavor, and a violet bouquet.

CHÂTEAU LATOUR, also a first growth, takes its name from an ancient tower. This, according to legend, is the only remaining vestige of the original castle of Saint-Lambert, supposedly destroyed by Du Guesclin when the English were driven out of Gascony. The retiring English, say the ancient tales, left a vast fortune buried in or near the tower. But the fortune, as we well know, was buried not below but above the ground, for the great wines of Château Latour have more body and a more pronounced flavor than those of either Lafite or Margaux.

CHÂTEAU MARGAUX, in true medieval splendor, once boasted a stout fortress surrounded by moats a hundred feet wide, which were connected to the Gironde by canals so boats could sail up to its gates. In 1447 it was the property of Baron François de Montferrand. After him it passed through many hands until, in 1879, it came to Count Pillet-Will. Today it is owned by a corporation. The wines of Château Margaux are generous without being too full bodied, are elegant, and have a delightfully fragrant bouquet. In one of the best parts of its vineyard a limited quantity of fine white wine is produced from the Sémillon and Sauvignon Blanc grape varieties. It is labeled Pavillon Blanc du Château Margaux.

CHÂTEAU HAUT-BRION, in the parish of Pessac in the Graves, is the last of the original 1855 listing of first growths and the only wine of the sixty-one to be chosen from outside the Médoc. It is, in fact, in the suburbs of Bordeaux. Haut-Brion, pronounced *o-bree-ohn,* is, according to some chroniclers, the French spelling of O'Brien; this is possible, as there must have been some Irishmen in Gascony during the English period. As far back as the fourteenth century, at the court of Pope Clement V, these wines were highly regarded. Lacking the softness and lightness of their fellow first growths, these wines are renowned for their full, generous body and beautiful, deep color. This superb vineyard has been the property of Clarence Dillon, the American financier, for a number of years.

CHÂTEAU MOUTON-ROTHSCHILD, whose owners were outspoken against the 1855 classification, did not accept tamely having their wine rated below the first four growths and as a result adopted this challenging motto:

Premier ne puis	First I cannot be
Second ne daigne	Second I do not deign to be
Mouton suis.	Mouton I am.

In 1973, after much work by Baron Philippe de Rothschild, the vineyard was classified in Bordeaux as a first growth. (The 1855 classification remains unchanged.) The Baron then wrote a new motto:

First, I am
Second, I was
But Mouton does not change.

Judging by the prices Mouton usually fetches, this move was more than justified. Over the years Mouton has consistently brought more money than the average of the four first growths. Although the 1855 classification is still amazingly accurate, many inequities have developed. On the basis of market prices, Château Pétrus of Pomerol and Château Cheval Blanc of Saint-Émilion deserve top classification among the clarets of Bordeaux.

Well-known second growths in the American market are the wines of Châteaux Léoville-Lascases, Léoville-Barton, Léoville-Poyferré, Gruaud-Larose, Ducru-Beaucaillou, Lascombes, Rausan-Ségla, Brane-Cantenac, Pichon-Longueville (Baron), Pichon-Longueville-Comtesse de Lalande, Cos d'Estournel, and Montrose.

Aerial view of the beautiful Château La Mission Haut Brion at Pessac, Graves. (*Courtesy Henri Woltner, Bordeaux*)

Among the third growths Châteaux Giscours, Palmer, Kirwan, and Calon-Ségur are fairly well known in America, while among the fourth growths the wines of Châteaux Prieuré-Lichine, Talbot, and Beychevelle are often seen here.

Finally, there are the fifth growths, of which the better known in the United States are Châteaux Pontet-Canet, Grand-Puy-Lacoste, Grand-Puy-Ducasse, Lynch-Bages, Mouton-Baron-Philippe, and Batailley. There are too many people who turn up their noses at fifth growths, considering them poor or even inferior. What they forget or overlook is that fifth growths are still part of that special group of sixty-one wines that were selected from among thousands of the better red wines of Bordeaux. The fact is that they are still great wines, though not peers of the first growths.

Graves clarets The fine clarets of the Graves region were not classified officially in 1855. It was not until 1953, and again in 1959, that official quality classifications were at last made and published (see Appendix C). From the Graves come such outstanding wines as Châteaux La Mission Haut Brion, Pape-Clément, Haut-Bailly, Smith-Haut-Lafitte, Bouscaut, and Domaine de Chevalier. They are fuller bodied and not quite as delicate as the wines of the Médoc, but Graves clarets make up in richness what they lack in finesse.

Saint-Émilion and Pomerol Politics or jealousy must have had something to do with the 1855 classification, as the wines of Châteaux Ausone and Cheval-Blanc in Saint-Émilion, and Pétrus, L'Évangile, and Vieux Château Certan in Pomerol, were not included. These wines, because of their high percentage of Merlot grapes, have a deep color, rich bouquet, and fullness of body. They also mature earlier than wines made with more Cabernet Sauvignon grapes. Because of all these factors, the wines of Saint-Émilion and Pomerol are often called the Burgundies of Bordeaux. Ausone, whose average yield is quite small, Cheval Blanc, and Pétrus all produce magnificent wines that almost invariably command prices equal to the great Médoc clarets. Saint-Émilion clarets were finally classified in 1955 (see Appendix C). Still other wines of great repute are Châteaux Figeac, La Gaffelière, Canon, Magdelaine, Pavie, and Clos Fourtet in Saint-Émilion. In Pomerol famous wines include Petit-Village, La Fleur-Pétrus, Nenin, and Trotanoy.

WHITE WINES OF BORDEAUX

Graves More white wine than red is made in the Graves (pronounced *grahv*). The white wines are clean, dry, and fresh and have a pleasant, fruity bouquet of their own.

Most of the Graves wines are shipped by the Bordeaux houses under private brand labels as standard blends, each house having several brands varying in quality and dryness in order to please the tastes of their several world markets.

There are several outstanding château-bottled white Graves: Châteaux Olivier, Carbonnieux, and Laville Haut Brion. Of these the best known in this country is Château Olivier, from an estate whose castle and vineyards were renowned in the twelfth century. Here the Prince of Wales, known as Edward the Black Prince, had a hunting lodge during the time when Aquitaine was an English domain and he was governor general of Gascony.

The ancient legends of these old châteaux have the perfume and enchantment of the wines themselves. It is related of Château Carbonnieux that, in order to convince a certain sultan of Turkey of the merits of French wine (wine being prohibited to the Faithful by the Koran), Château Carbonnieux was shipped to him labeled "Mineral Water of Carbonnieux." So impressed was the Commander of the Faithful upon drinking the wine that he exclaimed, "When they have water that is so pure and so agreeable, how can the French drink wine?"

Other well-known white wines of the Graves are Châteaux Bouscaut, Domaine de Chevalier, and Haut-Brion Blanc.

The grape varieties in the Graves are the Sémillon and the Sauvignon Blanc. The Sémillon gives wine finesse, velvetiness, color, and aroma. The Sauvignon Blanc produces a wine that is full in body and rich in bouquet. Sauvignon Blanc has the acidity to stand on its own as a varietal wine. Although the same grape varieties are used in the Graves as in the Sauternes, the Graves produces a dry wine because the grapes are gathered when they are ripe and are not left to hang on the vine until overripe, as is done in Sauternes, where climatic conditions are different.

Sauternes

There are five communes in the Sauternes area: Sauternes (which gives the regional name to the entire section), Barsac, Bommes, Fargues, and Preignac. Wine produced from grapes grown in any of these five communes is legally permitted to be called Sauternes.

There is a pronounced difference in the way Sauternes are made as compared with the Graves. In fact, the wine originally resembled the Graves. But many years ago, it seems, the owner of a château in this district, reputedly Yquem, was away on a hunting trip. He was delayed and therefore did not return in time to order the gathering of the grapes when they were ripe. As his men had no authority to start this work, they waited for the master to appear some four weeks later. The grapes were overripe, shriveled, and covered with mold, but the owner decided to gather them nonetheless and see what could be done. To his own surprise as well as that of everyone else, the wine that developed from these overripe grapes was unlike anything they had tasted before. It was delicious—very rich, luscious, and highly perfumed.

Today we understand what happened. When the grapes reach a certain stage of maturity beyond the full stage of ripeness, a special mold settles upon them, known technically as *Botrytis cinerea*.

When gathering grapes in Sauternes the workers do not begin until the sun is high, about half past eight in the morning, and they stop before the sun goes down because the dew washes off some *Botrytis cinerea*. The French call this condition of overripeness *pourriture noble,* meaning "noble rottenness." The grapes are not, of course, rotten, as rotten grapes are removed lest they spoil the wine; they are merely overripe. Only bunches in a perfect condition of overripeness are picked, and therefore a vineyard may be gone over as many as eight times before all the grapes are gathered, a procedure that naturally adds to the cost of production.

Leaving the grapes on the vine until they attain *pourriture noble* makes their skins become porous and the water in the grapes evaporate, thus concentrating the sugar, increasing glycerine, and reducing acidity. This gives a smaller yield of juice, or must, per acre, but it ensures richness. Sauternes, consequently, are always rich, sweet wines. There is no such thing as a dry Sauternes.

Because these wines are rich in sugar, it is difficult to keep them from refermenting during unseasonably warm weather. The only preventive is to sulfur the casks well before they are filled. The sulfur fumes sterilize the cask, destroying any bacteria that might be present, and, when the wine is poured in, the sulfur acts as a deterrent to the yeasts remaining in the wine, as they are ready to continue their fermentation job at the least provocation.

The wines of the five Sauternes communes are all very similar in character, and they are all sweet. Sweetness and dryness, of course, are relative qualities. Some Sauternes are sweeter and richer than others, but compared with white wines from the Graves or any other section of the Bordeaux wine region, they are much softer, sweeter, and fuller bodied.

This does not mean that a rather dry white wine cannot be produced. The Appellation of Origin law and its *Appellation Contrôlée* regulations do not prevent production of such a wine in Sauternes, but they forbid its being labeled Sauternes or Barsac. It can only be labeled Bordeaux Blanc. This happens in years when conditions do not permit *Botrytis cinerea* to develop properly.

the question of Barsac   Of the five communes entitled to use the regional term Sauternes, Barsac is the most enterprising. While the vintners in the communes of Bommes, Fargues, and Preignac are content to market their wines simply as Sauternes, those of Barsac prefer that their wines be known by the name of their commune. To say that the wines of Barsac are identical to those of the other communes of Sauternes is as wrong as to say that Barsac wines are dry—as many people believe. As far as sweetness is concerned, there is little difference between Barsac and the rest of Sauternes, at least when château-bottled wines are compared.

Château Olivier, with its moat, at Léognan, Graves. (*Courtesy Louis Eschenauer, Bordeaux*)

Famed Château d'Yquem, whose crenellated walls and towers enclose the residence, offices, winery, and cellars, in the heart of Sauternes. (*Courtesy Marquis Bertrand de Lur-Saluces, Bordeaux*)

However, comparing Sauternes and Barsac shipped under the label of a Bordeaux wine merchant is another story. These are blended wines, and when the shipper blends he can control the result. He can blend for sweetness, relative dryness, perfume, or body. He knows perfectly well that if his Sauternes and Barsac are identical, there is no reason to buy both wines. So he blends one wine for more sweetness than the other, thereby establishing two different wines. There is no consistency among shippers as to which of the two wines will be sweeter.

Haut Sauternes and Haut Barsac

Haut in French means "high," but it has no official significance for Sauternes and Barsac wines of the region. The word is sometimes used on labels for the American market to denote the producer's level of quality. As a rule, these wines cost more than the simple Sauternes or Barsac of the same vintage and the same shipper and are generally sweeter. *Haut* has no geographical significance, as there is no portion of Barsac or the Sauternes region known or designated as Haut Barsac or Haut Sauternes.

the classified Sauternes growths

In the classification of 1855 the wines of the great Sauternes vineyards were classed in order of merit in the same manner as the clarets. This classification embraced twenty-one growths, but because of the split-up of several vineyards, the number today is twenty-seven (see Appendix C).

CHÂTEAU D'YQUEM. In the fourteenth century when Edward II was king of England, his wine merchant and buyer in Bordeaux was Pierre Ayquem (also spelled *Eyquem*). It was he or one of his descendants who gave the family patronym to the vineyard whose storied wines have evoked more and greater hyperbole than almost any other wine since the celebrated Falernians of Roman times. A few of these are: "the extravagance of perfection," "a ray of sunshine concentrated in a glass," and "a ray more brilliant than the sun's."

In 1859 Grand Duke Constantine of Russia paid the fabulous sum of 20,000 gold francs for a tun (twelve hundred bottles) of the 1847 vintage. This was about $3.50 per bottle, an unheard-of price in those days.

There is no question about d'Yquem's wines being in a class by themselves, as demonstrated by their 1855 classification as Premier Cru Supérieur, and meriting the apparent exaggerations of poets intoxicated by such perfection. The finer vintages of Château d'Yquem combine richness of perfume, depth of vinosity, and fullness of body in perfect balance. There are differences among vintages and some are sweeter than others. D'Yquems will vary in their luscious richness, depending on their age and the vintage.

CHÂTEAU LA TOUR-BLANCHE. According to ancient documents, this fine vineyard was at one time the property of Jean Saint-Marc de La Tour-Blanche, treasurer general to the king. Sometime after the French Revolution its ownership passed to M. Osiris, who bequeathed the entire property to the state for a viticultural school. Its wines are elegant, full, and rich.

Note the spelling of *La Tour* as two words. Many people confuse Château La Tour-Blanche, the Sauternes, with Château Latour, the claret.

CHÂTEAU DE RAYNE-VIGNEAU.   Property for generations of the Vicomtes de Pontac, Rayne-Vigneau has had a glorious history. Its most notable exploit was defeating the best German wine in a blind tasting at the World's Fair of 1867 and being selected as the finest white wine of that age. The two wines in question were a Château Vigneau 1861 and a Rhine wine of the same vintage.

CHÂTEAU SUDUIRAUT, bordering Château d'Yquem, was formerly controlled by the crown. Today its wine labels bear the legend *ancien cru du Roy* ("former property of the king"). The wine is vigorous, with a rich aroma, and commands very high prices.

CHÂTEAU GUIRAUD (formerly Bayle) is a beautiful property that includes a fine vineyard—about 150 acres in extent—a park of 350 acres, and a lovely old château. The wine of Château Guiraud is famed for its delicacy, perfume, and body.

CHÂTEAUX COUTET AND CLIMENS.   The wines of these vineyards, situated in the commune of Barsac, are first growths and possess the typical firmness and elegant bouquet of Sauternes. They are rich Sauternes like the other growths of Bommes, Fargues, Preignac, and Sauternes.

CHÂTEAUX LAFAURIE-PEYRAGUEY, CLOS HAUT-PEYRAGUEY, RIEUSSEC, RABAUD-PROMIS, AND SIGALAS-RABAUD.   These other first growths are all excellent wines that are sometimes available in the United States.

Among the second growths the best known on our market are Château Filhot, in the commune of Sauternes, and Château Myrat, in the commune of Barsac. Château Caillou, also from Barsac, ages gracefully. Although classed as second growths, they are nonetheless excellent wines possessing a fine, rich bouquet and body.

other white wines of Bordeaux

There are districts other than the major ones discussed previously that produce distinguished, useful, and usually less expensive wines. For example, Entre-deux-Mers, "between two seas," a large section lying between the Garonne and Dordogne rivers before they meet, produces a vast quantity of white wine, some dry and some sweet. Bourg and Blaye, across the Gironde from the Médoc, produce clean, dry white wines as well as robust, fruity red wines, some of exceptional quality.

2. BURGUNDY

"None other will I have," said Duke Philip the Good of Burgundy when he set his heart on marrying the beautiful Princess Isabella. This thoroughly typical phrase was adopted as the ducal motto of the House of Burgundy. It represents the attitude of Burgundians then and now, proud of their race, their lineage, and their wines. It was their wont to style themselves "Dukes of Burgundy and Lords of the finest wines in Christendom."

history   The history of wine in Burgundy dates back to Caesar's conquest of Gaul and is almost as turbulent as the political story of the region. The Roman legions planted vines from Italy, and when the wine began competing with that of the mother country, Emperor Domitian ordered the vines uprooted and the fields planted in corn. This was in A.D. 96. Fortunately the edict was enforced only halfheartedly and was finally rescinded entirely by Emperor Probus in A.D. 278.

Long before the wine of the region was known by the regional term Burgundy, the Church—which here, as elsewhere, had a strong influence in the development of quality wines—had made famous among medieval gourmets the names of such vineyards as Clos de Bèze, Corton-Charlemagne, Romanée, Clos de Vougeot, Meursault, and Montrachet.

Wine from these vineyards—first known as wine of Auxerre, since the wine went to Paris and the outside world by boat down the Yonne River from the "port" of Auxerre, and later as wine of Beaune—did not acquire the name Burgundy until the sixteenth century. When Petrarch advised Pope Urban V to remove from Avignon to Rome, according to legend His Holiness demurred because his entourage complained, "There is no Beaune wine in Italy, and without Beaune wine how unhappy we would be." This difficulty seemingly was overcome during the pontificate of Gregory XII.

geography   Wine has always been Burgundy's chief source of fame, but, unlike wine from other regions, Burgundy wines do not all come from a small, densely cultivated geographical locale. Because of the acquisitiveness of Burgundy's dukes, who reached out on all sides for more and more land, the area known as Burgundy was created by gradually adding small parcels of land. Wine produced in every part of the duchy became known simply as Burgundy. This wine-producing region includes vineyards in four different departments: Yonne, Côte d'Or, Saône-et-Loire, and Rhône.

First is the "true Burgundy," the Côte d'Or or "golden slope," divided into the Côte de Nuits and the Côte de Beaune. The Côte d'Or is a string of low-lying hills extending thirty-eight miles from Dijon in the north to Santenay in the south; the width of the vineyards is from 550 to 600 yards. Second, farther south lie the Côte Chalonnaise and the Mâconnais, in the Department of Saône-et-Loire. Beaujolais begins in the Saône-et-Loire but lies mainly in the Department of the Rhône. (This department should not be confused with the large, general wine-producing area called Côtes du Rhône, farther south.) Last, about halfway between Dijon and Paris, north of the Côte d'Or, in the Department of the Yonne, there are fifteen hundred acres of vineyards around the town of Chablis that produce the famous white wine of the same name.

The wine regions of Burgundy. (*From Pierre Poupon and Pierre Forgeot,* The Wines of Burgundy, *courtesy Presses Universitaires de France*)

The soil of the Côte d'Or, rich in iron, is chalky, argillaceous, and rocky. The slopes take their name from the burnished gold appearance they present in the late fall when the leaves have turned golden.

grape varieties

The fine red wines come from the Pinot Noir grape, while the white wines of repute are produced from the Chardonnay. The Pinot Noir and Chardonnay are noble plants that produce quality but not quantity, and here as nowhere else is the *vigneron* tempted to increase his output at the sacrifice of quality.

The other red grape variety in Burgundy that predominates in the south is the Gamay, a more productive variety that gives a poor wine in the Côte d'Or but produces an extremely enjoyable red wine in the clay and granite soil of Mâcon and Beaujolais. Other white grapes of Burgundy are the Aligoté, which is highly productive and makes a simple and short-lived white wine, and the Pinot Blanc, which is used in regional blends. The Chardonnay is not part of the Pinot family, although Mâcon white wines made from Pinot Blanc or Chardonnay grapes may use the appellation Pinot-Chardonnay-Mâcon.

vineyards

The most famous vineyards are found on slopes with a southern exposure. They neither extend to the summit of the hills nor reach the lower plains. The fine vineyards form something like a wide, continuous ribbon laid along the gentle slopes, rarely dropping below the eight-hundred-foot elevation or rising above the thousand-foot level. The plain is seven hundred feet above sea level, and the higher hills are fifteen hundred feet.

It is on these slopes that the Pinot Noir seems to do best and the Gamay is rarely found. On the plains and summits, however, the Gamay is most in evidence. Wines resulting from a mixture of the two varieties are known as Bourgogne Passe Tout Grains and contain at least one-third Pinot Noir grapes.

In Burgundy, as in other viticultural regions, *Phylloxera* did its devastating work, and today the vineyards have been replanted with American *Phylloxera*-resistant roots on which the native Chardonnay, Pinot Noir, Gamay, and other varieties have been grafted. The last native stocks were removed in the early 1950s.

The laws controlling the origin and labeling of wines limit the production of the vineyards that are capable of producing fine wines in order to ensure the highest quality possible, thus forcing the *vigneron* to prune his vines properly. As the quantity is strictly limited, he does everything in his power to aid the vine in giving quality.

The system of vineyard ownership in Burgundy is different from that in any other viticultural region of France and is duplicated to any extent only in Germany. To begin with, the vineyards are all very small. The largest, Clos de Vougeot, is only 126 acres, and Romanée is just about 2 acres, the average being under 25 acres. Not only are the vineyards extremely small, but with rare exceptions they are held by anywhere from three to sixty or more owners, each proprietor having title to a small parcel of the vineyard. This is in direct contrast to the Bordeaux system, where some of the well-known vineyards are owned by one person or corporation and the entire product is controlled by one management.

At Clos de Vougeot, for example, there are sixty-six owners who cultivate their individual parcels of the vineyard, gather the grapes from their own vines, press them, and vinify the resulting must. As the human element enters into production, it is understandable that, although the same Pinot variety is planted in the entire vineyard, and all the operations of making the wine take place at the same time, there may be sixty-six different wines produced, all legally entitled to the appellation Clos de Vougeot.

Under this system there can be no château bottling, as is practiced in Bordeaux. However, "estate bottling" received great impetus after Repeal in the United States. American connoisseurs began to demand château-bottled Burgundies, and there simply was no such thing. Estate-bottled Burgundies have been grown, vinified, and bottled by a specific producer, whose name appears on the label, and are the equivalent of château-bottled Bordeaux. Estate-bottled wines are labeled *mis en bouteille au domaine*.

While this is good merchandising and benefits the consumer, since in theory the Burgundians would strive to offer only the very best quality, estate bottling guarantees only the authenticity of vineyard origin and that the wine comes from the grapes of a single producer and has not been blended with wines from any other producer or from any other vineyard. The practice of estate bottling has proliferated so since World War II that it is not uncommon today to see estate bottlings of wines labeled Gevrey-Chambertin, Chambolle-Musigny, Vosne-Romanée, and so forth, which contradicts the entire meaning and objective of the system. For example, a wine labeled Gevrey-Chambertin is a blend of wines produced in any part of the Gevrey-Chambertin commune. When the label also states it is estate bottled, the blend is made entirely of wines from the producer's vineyard holdings in Gevrey-Chambertin. These can be, although they are not necessarily, parcels in the great Le Chambertin and also from the most poorly rated vineyards in the commune. We believe that estate bottling should be reserved and practiced for only the unblended wine of the great vineyards that is bottled by the actual producer who is a proprietor, no matter how small his holding.

Not all of the growers ship their own wines, and if the shippers were to keep each grower's wines separate their lists would not only be interminable but also very confusing. For this reason it has been only natural for shippers to buy, say, Clos de Vougeot from several growers, blend these wines together, and offer them as their own (the shippers') quality of Clos de Vougeot. This also tends to equalize the price.

Wines that are not estate bottled may be labeled *mis en bouteille à la propriété* or *mise d'origine*.

labeling   A Burgundy wine bears the best-known or most famous name to which it is legally entitled. If the name of the vineyard whence it originates is world famous, rest assured that is the name under which the wine will travel. If, however, the commune is more renowned than the vineyard, then the wine will travel under the commune name. If neither is well known, the wine will go forth as Côte de Nuits, or Côte de Beaune, or simply as red or white Burgundy.

For example, wine from the Chambertin vineyard, in the commune of Gevrey-Chambertin, will invariably be shipped as Chambertin, which, having its own appellation, will be labeled Appellation Chambertin Contrôlée. Wine from a different vineyard whose name is not as well known as its commune name of Gevrey-Chambertin will simply be labeled Appellation Gevrey-Chambertin Contrôlée.

Wine from any vineyard in the communes of Comblanchien or Corgoloin will be labeled Côte de Nuits-Villages or simply Bourgogne Rouge, because neither the vineyards nor the communes are well known outside the district. Most of the red wines of the communes of Meursault, Puligny-Montrachet, and Chassagne-Montrachet suffer the same fate and are shipped as Côte de Beaune, as these communes, while world famous for their white wines, are not too well known for their reds.

The famous vineyards of the Côte d'Or have been classified by the *Appellation Contrôlée* authorities. Those who have drunk these wines and matched one against another have established a hierarchy of quality of Burgundy wines that is generally accepted. At least the prices these great wines fetch indicate that present-day Burgundy devotees are in agreement with the order of classification (see Appendix D).

The most expensive red wine of Burgundy is that of Romanée-Conti, a rather small vineyard in the commune of Vosne-Romanée. Like all things, its price is governed by supply and demand. The area planted in vines is a little less than $4\frac{1}{2}$ acres. Its two big rivals, Chambertin and Clos de Vougeot, both much larger vineyards, produce great wines, honorably challenging Romanée-Conti's place in the Burgundy sun. Unquestionably the most famous vineyard among the white wines is Le Montrachet.

CÔTE DE NUITS

The red wines of the Côte de Nuits are generous and full bodied and have a deep, fruity, unique bouquet that is the result of the combination of the Pinot Noir grape and the Burgundian soil. They develop less rapidly than the wines of the Côte de Beaune and should be kept longer, so that their early roughness will develop that full roundness that is characteristic of the great Burgundies.

CHAMBERTIN. Napoleon, so the story goes, would drink no other wine and planned all his great military and civil victories when warmed by the generous fire of Chambertin. But when he was before Moscow his supply ran out,

Ancient Château du Clos de Vougeot, set in the very center of the vineyard, property of the Confrérie des Chevaliers du Tastevin, at Vougeot, Côte d'Or. *(Courtesy Confrérie des Chevaliers du Tastevin)*

resulting in his disastrous retreat from Russia. Knowing his penchant for Chambertin, the allies generously permitted that he be supplied with it at Saint Helena.

No one knows the date of origin for the vineyard of Chambertin, but like all ancient vineyards it is rich in legends. One story connected with it throws some light on the entire history of viticulture in Burgundy. In the year 630, according to the records, the Duc d'Amalgaire gave a parcel of vineyard, with an area of thirty-five acres, to the Abbey of Bèze. Henceforth the vineyard was known as Clos de Bèze, and in time its wines acquired much renown. Sometime later, but before 1219, when we have our next parchment record, a peasant named Bertin, who owned the field bordering Clos de Bèze, reasoned that if he planted the same grape varieties as grew in the famous Clos de Bèze vineyards, his wines would be good, too. The French word for field is *champ*, and the vineyard then must have been known as Champ de Bertin. This was finally contracted to the present Chambertin, and since 1219 the wines from the two vineyards have been confused and looked upon as one and the same. Today the total area of Chambertin and Chambertin-Clos de Bèze is sixty-seven acres. Chambertin-Clos de Bèze may be labeled either Chambertin-Clos de Bèze or simply Chambertin. Chambertin may not be labeled Chambertin-Clos de Bèze. Both wines are big, heady wines that acquire a firm roundness with age. They have the qualities that make great wines—color, bouquet, body, and finesse.

LES MUSIGNY AND LES BONNES MARES.   These two great rival vineyards lie in the commune of Chambolle-Musigny, but Les Bonnes Mares, which has 34 acres in Chambolle-Musigny, also has 4½ acres in the commune of Morey-Saint-Denis. Both wines are known for their finesse, suppleness, and elegance, but, although they are similar in character, Les Musigny, with only 14 acres, is the more famous of the two. In 1882 the leaders of the commune decided that the sale of all its wines would be increased if the commune were to adopt the name of its most famous vineyard, and therefore Chambolle became Chambolle-*Musigny*. This system has been adopted by the communes of Gevrey-*Chambertin*, Flagey-*Echézeaux*, Vosne-*Romanée*, Nuits-*Saint-Georges*, Aloxe-*Corton*, Puligny-*Montrachet*, Chassagne-*Montrachet*, and others.

CLOS DE VOUGEOT.   These are fruity wines, having flavor, color, body, bouquet, and infinite grace and character. The elegance of its wines has merited Clos de Vougeot an honor that is today traditional. During the Napoleonic wars one Colonel Bisson, marching past the gates of the Clos de Vougeot at the head of his column, ordered that a drum roll be beat and that his men present arms before a vineyard whose wines were so magnificent.

It is said that the Little Corporal, conqueror on the fields of Austerlitz and Marengo, and now all-powerful emperor, heard of the excellent wines made at Vougeot. He sent word to Dom Gobelet, the last clerical cellar-master at Clos de Vougeot, saying that it would please him to taste these superlative wines. "If he is that curious," replied the venerable Cistercian haughtily, "let him come to my house."

The beautiful, imposing Château du Clos de Vougeot is situated on the upper slopes in the very center of the vineyard. For many centuries it belonged to the Cistercian Abbey of Cîteaux. The earliest available records of the abbey vineyard ownership date back to 1110. The present château was begun in the thirteenth century and completed sometime in the sixteenth. Its primary function was to serve as the pressing house and cellars for the wine-production activities of the Cistercian Order, who owned it until the French Revolution, when it was secularized. Today the château is the property of the Confrérie des Chevaliers du Tastevin, the "brotherhood of gentlemen of the tasting cup." The great ceremonies, functions, and dinners of the Confrérie are held there.

ROMANÉE-CONTI is the accepted king of Burgundy, always having all the qualities of great wine: body, vinosity, bouquet, and character. These wines are rich and long lived.

ROMANÉE, ROMANÉE-SAINT-VIVANT, LE RICHEBOURG, AND LA TÂCHE.   The commune richest in great vineyards is Vosne-Romanée. These vineyards vary in size from the bare two acres of Romanée, fifteen acres of La Tâche, and twenty acres of Le Richebourg, to the almost twenty-four acres of Romanée-Saint-Vivant. The wines of these great growths differ, but it would take one long accustomed to drinking them to identify these differences. Suffice it to say that they all have beautiful color, a deep bouquet and flavor, body, elegance, and, above all, breed.

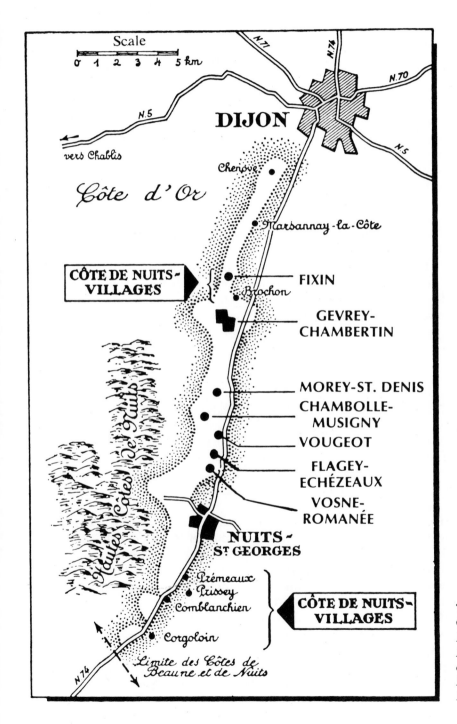

The communes of the Côte de Nuits. (*From Pierre Poupon and Pierre Forgeot,* The Wines of Burgundy, *courtesy Presses Universitaires de France*)

LES GRANDS ECHÉZEAUX AND ECHÉZEAUX.   The former's twenty-three acres and the latter's seventy-four acres are neighbors to the west of Clos de Vougeot, and there is a close resemblance among all of these wines. While in the commune of Flagey-Echézeaux, these wines are thought of in the same breath as the wines of Vosne-Romanée because the vineyard of Les Grands Echézeaux once belonged to the Abbey of Saint-Vivant. The wines are big and colorful, with breed.

CLOS DE TART, CLOS DE LA ROCHE, AND LES SAINT-GEORGES.   The first two vineyards, with acreages of $17\frac{3}{4}$ and 38 respectively, lie in the commune of Morey-Saint-Denis. The $18\frac{1}{2}$ acres of Saint-Georges are in the commune of Nuits-Saint-Georges. These three fine vineyards of the Côte de Nuits have rich wines, with color, body, and character, and in good years they are comparable to any of the great Côte de Nuits.

The most northerly commune of Côte de Nuits before Dijon is Fixin. Here the wines are similar to those of Gevrey-Chambertin and are sometimes their equal. La Perrière (not to be confused with Les Perrières of Meursault) and Clos-du-Chapitre produce good, strong Burgundy wines.

The appellation Côte de Nuits-Villages is restricted to the wines of the five communes of Fixin, Brochon, Prissey, Comblanchien, and Corgoloin. In the near future the communes of Marsannay-la-Côte, Couchey, and Premeaux-Prissey will also share this appellation.

CÔTE DE BEAUNE

The medieval city of Beaune is the headquarters of the Burgundy wine trade. Most of the great shipping houses have their cellars in the city itself and it is in Beaune that we find the world-famous Hospices de Beaune.

The red wines of the Côte de Beaune develop more rapidly and are ready for drinking sooner than those of the Côte de Nuits. They show a pleasant, fruity bouquet, softness, and finesse and are tenderly supple, which makes them most agreeable wines at all times.

HOSPICES DE BEAUNE.   There are many well-preserved examples of Beaune's long history—churches, parts of the old city wall, and battlements —all still in use in one way or another; but her proudest monument is Les Hospices de Beaune, a charitable hospital built in 1443. It has rendered continuous and devoted service to the poor of the region for over five hundred years, wars and revolution notwithstanding.

The Hôtel-Dieu, or hospital, is an exquisite example of Flemish architectural style. It is a four-story-high, block-square building, surmounted by a slanting roof whose green, yellow, and black slates are arranged in a classic pattern. The cobblestone open central courtyard—the Court of Honor—was the original locale for the Hospices' annual wine auctions.

Central courtyard of fifteenth-century Hospices de Beaune, where the annual Hospices' wine auctions were formerly held. (*Courtesy Julius Wile Sons & Co., Inc., New York*)

Over the centuries modern improvements have been adopted in the care of the sick, but some of the original wards, kitchens, chapels, and the museum have been preserved in their original fifteenth-century state. The museum contains many works of art, including paintings of Nicolas Rolin and his wife, Guigone de Salins, and the magnificent altarpiece of the Last Judgment, all on wood, which she commissioned the Flemish painter Roger van der Weyden (1440–1464) to paint expressly for the Hospices de Beaune.

In 1441 Pope Eugene IV authorized the creation of the Hospices de Beaune as a hospital to care for the poor and indigent people of Beaune. Nicolas Rolin, tax collector during the reign of Louis XI, and his wife donated the property and erected the building. They also gave the Hospices several parcels of vineyards so that the Hospices might be supported by the sale of its wines.

The legend of the period has it that Nicolas Rolin could well afford to provide such a charity for the poor, as he had created so many of them. Whether or not that is true, the Hospices de Beaune has proved to be a remarkable institution. Its principal support has always come from the sale of wines produced from vineyards that devout Burgundians have willed to the Hospices. Today these comprise some thirty parcels that are known by the names of the donors (see Appendix D).

For over four centuries the Hospices' wines were sold privately, but since 1859 they have been sold at a festive public auction on the third Sunday of every November. All of the Hospices de Beaune vineyards are located in the Côte de Beaune, from Aloxe-Corton to Meursault, but because they represent the first real opportunity for buyers to taste the wines of each vintage, the prices fetched at the auction determine to a great extent the rating of the vintage for all Burgundy wines. For example, in 1972 they produced F (French francs) 7,609,604 ($1,700,000), an all-time high, with prices up 36 percent over 1971. After that, prices dropped 25 percent, but in 1976 they were just about back up to the 1972 levels. Often these figures are more than the individual wines are really worth, but the factors of charity and publicity unquestionably influence the bidding.

LE CORTON, LE CLOS DU ROI, LES BRESSANDES, AND LES POUGETS. In the commune of Aloxe-Corton lie the famous vineyards of Le Corton with an area of 28 acres, Le Clos du Roi with 26 acres, Les Bressandes with 42 acres, and Les Pougets with 24½ acres. Le Corton is considered by many to be the best red wine of the Côte de Beaune. It is usually solid and robust. With bottle ripeness it expands and possesses a wealth of bouquet, roundness, body, and breed and can be compared with the great Côte de Nuits wines. Le Clos du Roi and Les Bressandes are also big wines, but they are more like Beaune wines in character. They have a lovely color, aroma, and finesse. The wines from Les Pougets vineyard are always very fine, with excellent color, flavor, and body.

ÎLE-DES-VERGELESSES AND LES BASSES-VERGELESSES. These vineyards have areas of twenty-three and forty-four acres, respectively, in the commune of Pernand, and their wines are renowned for their finesse and distinction.

LES FÈVES AND LES GRÈVES. These are the two outstanding examples from Beaune itself. Les Fèves, with 10½ acres, and Les Grèves, with 78½ acres, produce wines noted for their fine, rich softness and elegance.

LES RUGIENS AND LES ÉPENOTS. The commune name, Pommard, is probably the most famous Burgundy wine name. It is certainly far better known than that of its finest vineyard, Les Rugiens (33½ acres). For that reason most of its wine comes to our table labeled simply Pommard, and because of the demand its price is usually somewhat high. Should you come upon authentic and properly matured examples of Pommard-Rugiens or Les Épenots (27 acres), you will find them generally delicate, fruity, and well-rounded wines of character.

The red wines of the communes of Volnay and Monthélie are light red in color, elegant, and delightful. Those of the commune of Auxey-Duresses are

The communes of the Côte de Beaune. (*From Pierre Poupon and Pierre Forgeot,* The Wines of Burgundy, *courtesy Presses Universitaires de France*)

somewhat like those of Pommard and Volnay, and the red wines of the commune of Chassagne-Montrachet have a richness and fullness that remind one of those of the Côte de Nuits.

The appellation Côte de Beaune-Villages applies to only red wine and is restricted to sixteen communes: Auxey-Duresses, Blagny, Chassagne-Montrachet, Cheilly-les-Maranges, Chorey-les-Beaune, Dezize-les-Maranges, Ladoix, Meursault, Monthélie, Pernand-Vergelesses, Puligny-Montrachet, Saint-Aubin, Saint-Romain, Sampigny-les-Maranges, Santenay, and Savigny-les-Beaune.

WHITE WINES OF BURGUNDY

All of the main subdivisions of the Burgundy wine region produce white wines, each of which is of an individual character and has its following. The Department of the Yonne gives us the very popular Chablis. The Côte de Nuits sends us three unique white wines, although the majority of the great white wines of Burgundy come from the Côte de Beaune. Still farther south is Mâcon, which produces considerable quantities of crisp white wines, including Pouilly-Fuissé and Mâcon-Villages, which are great favorites in the United States. In neighboring Beaujolais a small amount of Beaujolais Blanc is produced.

grape varieties

For making white wines the *plante noble* is the Chardonnay. Other varieties of grapes are used, but to a very minor degree, with the exception of the copious Aligoté, which produces large quantities of an agreeable but short-lived wine that is mostly consumed locally. This wine may be labeled varietally, as Bourgogne Aligoté, and it may have some Chardonnay in it.

Chablis

The wine the world knows as Chablis comes from the northernmost part of Burgundy. Its distinguishing characteristic, not to be found in every vintage, is an austere, flinty quality, much prized by those who have had the good fortune to encounter it. Chablis is, perhaps, the driest and palest of table wines. Its color should be a pale straw yellow.

The flinty quality is known as *pierre-à-fusil* ("gun flint"), and the taste is like a sharp, metallic tang. Added to this effect is the wine's delicate, fruity bouquet, and herein lies its cooling, refreshing quality. Although in good years Chablis is a long-lived wine, we prefer it young and fresh. There is no wine that can match Chablis with oysters. They were made for each other, as you will discover if you try this combination.

Chablis is classified, in descending order of quality, as follows: Chablis Grand Cru, Chablis Premier Cru, Chablis, and Petit Chablis. The best vineyards are crescent-shaped hillsides just north of the village of Chablis and make up the Grand Cru classification. They are Blanchots, Bougros, Les Clos, Grenouilles, Les Preuses, Valmur, and Vaudésir.

Chablis Premier Cru comes from twenty-nine vineyards, situated in ten communes, which are considered superior. Chablis is a blend of wine from several vineyards. Petit Chablis comes from the outskirts of the area. As with other wines of Burgundy, the reputation of the shipper is the best guarantee of quality.

The Chablis region and its Grand Cru vineyards.
(*From Pierre Poupon and Pierre Forgeot,* The Wines of
Burgundy, *courtesy Presses Universitaires de France*)

Baskets of grapes in a Côte de Beaune vineyard. (*Courtesy Joseph E. Seagram & Sons, Inc., New York*)

Côte de Nuits   In the Côte de Nuits, at the famous Musigny vineyard in Chambolle-Musigny, about 100 cases of Musigny Blanc are produced by Comte Georges de Vogüé. To the south, next to the Château du Clos de Vougeot, famous for its red wines, are five acres planted with Chardonnay grapes from which 450 cases of Clos Blanc de Vougeot are made. In the commune of Nuits-Saint-Georges some 250 cases of Nuits-Saint-Georges Blanc are produced. These are distinguished wines, possessing full flavor and body.

Moving south to the Côte de Beaune we find the greatest white wines of Burgundy in the communes of Aloxe-Corton, Meursault, Puligny-Montrachet, and Chassagne-Montrachet.

CORTON-CHARLEMAGNE.   This renowned white wine is made in the commune of Aloxe-Corton, at the forty-two-acre Charlemagne vineyard, so named in honor of the great emperor. It is an excellent wine and must be included in any list of white Burgundies, even though the commune is still more famed for its red wines.

LES PERRIÈRES, LES GENEVRIÈRES, AND LES CHARMES.   These famous vineyards, with 42, 42, and $38\frac{1}{4}$ acres respectively, lie in the commune of Meursault. The wines are not as big as those of Le Montrachet, but they are full bodied and dry and have finesse and elegance.

At the southern end of the Côte de Beaune lie the communes of Puligny-Montrachet and Chassagne-Montrachet. Shippers' blends of wines from these two communes can be very good and offer excellent value. Like their counterparts in the Côte de Nuits, they have affixed the name of their most famous vineyard, Le Montrachet, to their own names.

LE MONTRACHET.   There is no question that this is one of the world's great white wines. It is full bodied and robust yet possesses elegance, perfume, and dignity that are hard to match. Coming from a rather small vineyard, only $18\frac{1}{2}$ acres, half of which lies in the commune of Puligny and half in that of Chassagne, the wines are in such demand that they usually fetch prices equal to those of the great red growths of the Côte de Nuits. H. Warner Allen has called Le Montrachet the Château d'Yquem of Burgundy.

CHEVALIER-MONTRACHET AND LE BÂTARD-MONTRACHET.   Chevalier-Montrachet has $15\frac{1}{2}$ acres in the commune of Puligny-Montrachet, and Le Bâtard-Montrachet, totaling $29\frac{1}{4}$ acres, is in both Puligny- and Chassagne-Montrachet. The wines of these two growths are very much like those of Le Montrachet, although, while very fine, they do not quite reach its heights of quality. They have a wealth of bouquet and finesse and are never inexpensive.

CÔTE CHALONNAISE

The Côte Chalonnaise lies just south of the Côte de Beaune. The soil, grapes, and wines of the Chalonnaise are quite similar to those of the Côte de Beaune, but they do not often attain the same quality. The four communes having appellations are Rully and Montagny, producing mostly white wines, and Mercurey and Givry, producing mostly reds. A considerable amount of sparkling wine is produced in the Chalonnaise, especially in Rully.

The wine regions of Mâcon and Beaujolais. (*From Pierre Poupon and Pierre Forgeot,
The Wines of Burgundy, courtesy Presses Universitaires de France*)

MÂCONNAIS AND BEAUJOLAIS

On the rolling low hills south of the Côte d'Or lie the districts of Mâcon and Beaujolais. Although each makes both red and white wines, Mâcon is more famous for its white wines and Beaujolais is better known for its reds.

In Mâcon the Chardonnay is still the most important grape. Pinot Blanc is also grown, and the two may be mixed under the appellation Pinot-Char-donnay-Mâcon. The most famous white wine, made only from the Chardonnay, is Pouilly-Fuissé, named for the twin towns where the vineyards lie. Saint-Véran, a lower-priced crisp white wine, is also made only from the Char-donnay. Both are appealing when young and fresh. The red wines of Mâcon are made mainly from the Gamay grape and are regionally named.

In Beaujolais the granitic soil brings out the best in the Gamay grape, which is not successful in the Côte d'Or. The best growths, or *crus*, in the north are limited to nine: Brouilly, Chénas, Chiroubles, Côte de Brouilly, Fleurie, Juliénas, Morgon, Moulin-à-Vent, and Saint-Amour. These may use the name Burgundy on their labels. The second classification is Beaujolais-Villages, which is limited to the wines of thirty-nine communes. Third comes Beaujolais-Supérieur, whose alcohol content is the same as Beaujolais-Villages, but which comes from a larger area; and, finally, enormous quantities of plain Beaujolais.

The wines of the region have a clear, brilliant red color and a fairly light body when compared with those of the Côte d'Or. Their primary characteristic is fresh fruitiness. They are most pleasant while in the fresh vigor of youth and for this reason should not be kept for many years. In France most of these wines are drunk before they are two or three years old.

For details on the Burgundy vintages, see Appendix B.

SPARKLING BURGUNDY

The discovery of sparkling wine in Champagne set off the spark that became a conflagration in all the wine-producing regions of Europe, and even to this day sparkling wine continues to be made fairly successfully wherever wine grapes grow. Burgundy's sparkling wines have enjoyed public acceptance throughout the world.

Sparkling wines may be made in Burgundy from white, rosé, or red wines. Red sparkling Burgundy, and for that matter all red sparkling wines wherever they are produced, are much fuller bodied than Champagne because the red wines from which they are produced are fuller bodied by nature. At least 30 percent of the blend of sparkling Burgundy must be from Pinot Noir, Pinot Gris, Pinot Blanc, or Chardonnay grapes. The balance may be Aligoté, Melon, Sacy, and/or Gamay à Jus Blanc. As a general rule, sparkling Burgundies are sweeter than Champagne.

Sparkling Burgundies are made by the approved *méthode champenoise,* which will be explained in the following section on Champagne. After 1980 all sparkling wines from Burgundy, whether red or white, must qualify under the appellation Crémant de Bourgogne (see page 76). They may never be called Champagne.

3. CHAMPAGNE

The word *Champagne* is synonymous with happiness, gaiety, and laughter, for it is the joyous wine of festive occasions. "Champagne," said André L. Simon, "has always been, still is, and will ever be an extravagant wine and the most charming and fascinating of wines."

There is a difference between La Champagne and Le Champagne. The former is the name of the ancient French province, part of which is today the Department of the Marne; the latter is the sparkling wine produced in the delimited Champagne region, about the size of Washington, D.C., located ninety miles east of Paris.

Wine has been made in Champagne since early Roman times, when Caesar conquered Gaul. That early wine was a still wine, however, and even today a nonsparkling wine is made in the region under the appellation Côteaux Champenois. But the name Champagne is reserved for the sparkling wine of France whose qualities and unique characteristics are the results of a second fermentation within a tightly corked bottle and which originates from the strictly delimited area of Champagne.

history   The histories of the province and its wine are intertwined. The most important city, Reims, was named for Saint-Remi, one of its first archbishops, who in A.D. 496 converted the first Frankish king, Clovis, to Christianity and at the baptism presented Clovis with a cask of Champagne from his own vineyard.

It was not until the seventeenth century that the sparkling wine we associate with the name of Champagne came into use. Some say that Dom Pérignon (1639–1715), a blind Bénédictine monk who was treasurer and cellarer of the Abbey of Hautvillers near Épernay, is the man who put the bubbles in Champagne.

Actually, the bubbles occurred naturally. Champagne is the most northerly wine-producing region of France, and the early arrival of winter often slowed down or halted fermentation before it was complete. After the wine was bottled, the arrival of warm spring weather would start a second fermentation inside the bottle. Carbon dioxide was released inside the closed bottle, which made the wine sparkle.

It was Dom Pérignon who was the first to use the bark of the cork tree as a stopper for Champagne bottles. Although cork bark had been used in other wine regions, Dom Pérignon introduced it in the Champagne region to replace the bits of tow soaked in oil that were used as stoppers, making it possible to retain the sparkle within the wine for long periods of time. Being an excellent taster, he soon observed that the wines of one vineyard were consistently dry, those of another richer and fuller bodied, while those of a third possessed more finesse. He decided to try blending these wines to produce a more balanced wine with a completeness that the component wines could not show individually. The result was that he made better wines than had been produced before, and to this day the system is followed to obtain a wine of uniformly high quality and distinctive house style.

With all this development in the bottle, there was the problem of removing sediment that had collected so the wine would be clear. Removing the sediment was time consuming, and effervescence was lost in the process. It wasn't until the nineteenth century that the system of *remuage,* which is still used today, was developed.

From 1927 to 1937 the *Appellation Contrôlée* laws were being developed in France. A separate clause dealing with Champagne processes defined the *méthode champenoise,* making Champagne one of the most rigorously controlled and most carefully made wines in the world.

geography

The Champagne growing area consists of forty-four thousand acres of vineyards in 250 different villages, most of which are clustered around the

REIMS

PETITE MONTAGNE DE REIMS

Sillery

Rilly-La-Montagne

Verzenay

Verzy

MONTAGNE DE REIMS

Trepail

VALLÉE DE LA MARNE

CHÂTEAU THIERRY

Marne R.

Venteuil

Dizy

Hautvillers

Bouzy

Ambonnay

Marne R.

Boursault

EPERNAY

Ay

CÔTE DES BLANCS

REGION OF CHAMPAGNE

Cramant

Avize

Oger

Le Mesnil

Vertus

Vineyard areas

L.M.

cities of Reims and Épernay. The Marne River, which flows from east to west, forms an important line of division. North of the Marne mainly black grapes are grown, around the towns of Ay and Hautvillers and in the Montagne ("mountain") de Reims section at Mailly, Verzy, Verzenay, Bouzy, and Ambonnay. South of the river lies the Côte des Blancs, where white grapes are grown around the towns of Cramant, Avize, Oger, Le Mesnil, and Vertus.

soil   Chalk is important to the Champagne region, both for growing the vines and for aging the wine in the deep chalk cellars. A thin top layer of earth covers a chalky, porous subsoil that extends down for hundreds of feet. The porosity allows excess water to drain, while maintaining the proper amount of moisture necessary for growth of the vines.

grape varieties   The three grape varieties from which Champagne may be made are the red Pinot Noir and Pinot Meunier and the white Chardonnay. The Montagne de Reims vineyards are planted mainly in Pinot Noir, the grape that gives full flavor and body to the wine. Pinot Noir and Pinot Meunier are grown in the valley of the Marne. The Côte des Blancs, or "white slope," is so named because it is planted with Chardonnay. This grape contributes freshness, lightness, and elegance to the final blend.

All the Champagne vineyards are rated for quality. Most achieve from 80 to 100 percent, with some going down to 50 percent, depending on soil, exposure, and microclimate. When the grapes are harvested, the price for that vintage is agreed on, and the vineyards rated 100 percent get paid 100 percent of the price, and the other vineyards are compensated proportionately. The well-known Champagne houses usually buy the grapes from vineyards rated between 90 and 100 percent.

THE CHAMPAGNE METHOD (*MÉTHODE CHAMPENOISE*)

The art of making Champagne really begins with the selection of grapes. Most of the important Champagne houses own vineyards, but to meet their needs all of them must also buy additional grapes from eighteen thousand small growers in Champagne's main vineyard areas. The vineyards are primarily family holdings averaging $2\frac{1}{2}$ acres. Since Champagne is a blend of twenty to thirty still wines made from grapes grown in a number of different vineyards, no vineyard name appears on the label; consequently the name of the blender or shipper, which is always there, takes on importance.

the harvest   Harvesting the grapes begins at the end of September or in early October, one hundred days after the vines flower. The exact time is determined by the *Comité Interprofessionnel du Vin de Champagne* (C.I.V.C.) after the laboratory tests of grape sugar content and acidity have been made and the grapes are

The *épluchage*. Highly skilled workers select only perfect bunches (culling out any imperfect grapes) before the *caques* are trucked to the wine press. (*Courtesy C.I.V.C., Épernay*)

Typical Champagne hydraulic press. (*Courtesy C.I.V.C., Épernay*)

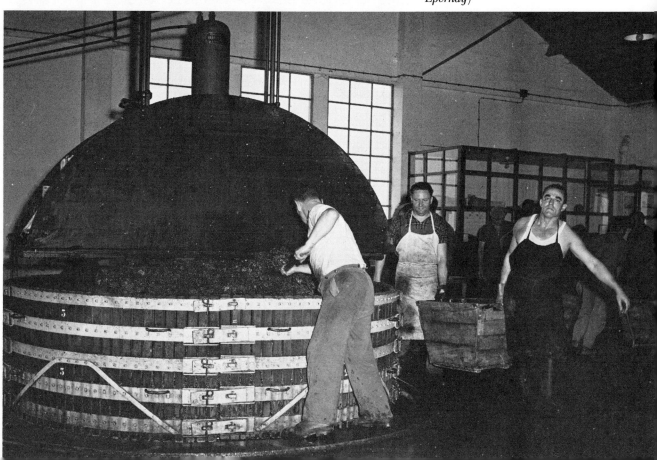

fully ripe. Within ten days an army of seventy thousand workers does the harvesting.

The ripe grapes are gathered in baskets, called *paniers*. When a *panier* is full it is taken to the side of the road, where experienced sorters cull out any green, overripe, or defective grapes to ensure that only perfect, sound fruit goes to the press. This selection process is called *épluchage* and is practiced by the leading producers. After the *épluchage* the grapes are placed in *caques* or *clayettes* ("large baskets") and carried to nearby pressing houses.

pressing   The press may belong to a Champagne firm, to the local village, to a cooperative of vineyard owners, or to brokers or middlemen. To avoid coloration of the juice, wide but shallow hydraulic presses that hold eighty-eight hundred pounds are used. Each basket is weighed and marked to ensure the exact quantity being placed in the press. The amount of grapes that makes one loading of a press is called a *marc*. From each *marc* four pressings of juice are obtained, known as *cuvée, première taille, deuxième taille,* and *rebèche.*

Pressure is applied twice for the *cuvée,* and after each pressure the grapes are worked toward the center of the press with wooden shovels. For the *première* and *deuxième tailles* pressure is applied only once. For the *rebèche* the *marc* is removed to a smaller press. The finest houses, or *Grandes Marques,* which pride themselves on the quality of their wines, use only the *cuvée* and *première taille* pressings and sell the wine resulting from the *deuxième taille* in cask. *Rebèche* wine cannot be used for Champagne; it is used for distillation.

As the juice is pressed from the grapes, it gushes out from the bottom of the press through a channel and is gathered in a cistern below the presses, whence it is transferred at once into vats or casks and carefully labeled with the name of the vineyard where the grapes were grown.

first   The first fermentation, as with all other white wines, starts out vigorously
fermentation and gradually slows down during the second week. Fermentation may take place in traditional oak barrels, glass-lined tanks, or stainless steel tanks. With modern equipment, the temperature is maintained around 70 degrees Fahrenheit for the three weeks necessary to complete fermentation.

The new wine is racked to remove large particles that have settled to the bottom, and it is now chilled. This used to be accomplished by opening the winery doors to the cold winter air. Now modern refrigeration methods are used. This chilling causes the soluble tartrates to form insoluble bitartrates, which precipitate out, leaving the wine clear and stable.

By spring the *chef de cave,* or "cellar-master," will know whether he is making vintage or nonvintage Champagne. If nonvintage, he must decide which wines, from which vineyards and in what proportions, should be married to older reserve wines to produce the characteristic house style of Champagne with the desired quality, aroma, elegance, and durability.

Highly skilled workman deftly performing the *remuage* operation of shaking the sediment down onto the inner surface of the cork. (*Courtesy Champagne News and Information Bureau, New York*)

The new wines are then pumped, in the proper proportions, into large blending vats where they are thoroughly combined.

A small amount of sugar dissolved in old wine, together with special yeasts, is added to the blend to ensure uniform secondary fermentation. This is called the *liqueur de tirage* or *dosage de tirage* ("bottling dosage"). The quantity of sugar varies from year to year, depending on the natural sugar the new wine contains. The wine is then bottled and corked. The corks are secured by either metal clips known as *agrafes* or crown caps such as those used on soft drink bottles. *second fermentation*

The bottles are stacked on their sides in the cellars that are hewn out of the solid chalk subsoil of the region. The yeasts discover the sugar and go to work, creating additional alcohol and carbon dioxide gas. Since the gas cannot escape it becomes a component of the wine.

During the first couple of years in the chalk cellars the stacks of bottles are examined for breakage—which is inevitable, as there are bound to be a few imperfect bottles that cannot stand the strain of the 90 to 110 pounds per square inch pressure developed by the newly created gas. In the early days the percentage of breakage was very high (sometimes as much as every other bottle), but today, with improved methods of bottle manufacture and the scientific use of the saccharometer to measure the exact sugar content of the wine, breakage has been reduced to less than 1 percent.

remuage

The action of fermentation is like a fire, and where there is fire, there are ashes. As a result of the secondary fermentation that has taken place in the bottle, "ashes," or dead yeast cells, have been left in the form of a sediment that must be removed to achieve a clear and brilliant wine. Removing the sediment is not easy, however. In this long, hard, tedious job the bottles are placed in specially built racks, called *pupitres*. At first the bottles are set at a forty-five-degree angle, and the angle is gradually increased until the bottles are standing perpendicularly, head down. A workman grasps each bottle, gives it a shake, a slight turn, and an increased tilt (*remuage,* or "riddling"), and lets it fall back into its slot on the rack with a small jolt. This is repeated every three days for each bottle. The object of this *remuage* is to move the sediment down onto the cork in a spiral movement. This operation takes about six to eight weeks. A skilled *remueur* can handle from thirty thousand to fifty thousand bottles a day.

When the wine is perfectly clear, the bottles are restacked, this time head down. They remain in this position until they are to be prepared for shipment. The time varies; some wine is shipped when it has been in the bottle three to four years, but vintage wine is shipped five or more years after the vintage.

Only those bottles that are going to be shipped at once have the sediment removed at this time. The bottles that are to be held for later shipment are kept in the cellars, still head down, so that the sediment will always remain on the cork.

dégorgement

Dégorgement is the process of removing the collected sediment from the corked bottle. The neck of the bottle is dipped into a very cold brine or glycol solution that freezes a little wine on the cork into a sludge with the sediment. Traditionally, a skilled workman, wearing a leather apron and often a wire-covered mask to protect his face in case of a bursting bottle, grasps the bottle. Standing opposite a barrel and protected by a shield, he releases the *agrafe* with a pair of pliers or removes the crown cap and at the same time turns the bottle right side up. The cork flies out, taking the frozen bit of sediment with it. He gives the neck of the bottle two sharp raps to loosen any bit of sediment that may have adhered to it. A small amount of the wine foams out. He examines this foam to be sure the wine has a perfectly clean bouquet, and then he hands the bottle to another workman sitting nearby, who adds the *liqueur d'expédition,* or *dosage d'expédition* ("shipping dosage").

Today the disgorging process is automated in many houses.

The wine that has been lost during the *dégorgement* must be replaced. This is done by adding wine from previously disgorged bottles. Simultaneously some sweetening liqueur is added, the amount varying with the desired sweetness of the final product. This *liqueur d'expédition,* or *dosage d'expédition,* is a concentrated solution of the finest sugar, dissolved in mature wine. *liqueur d'expédition*

The shipping cork, which must say *Champagne,* is now driven in by machine and tightly wired down. During disgorgement some of the gas is lost, and the final pressure after recorking is reduced to sixty to ninety pounds per square inch. The bottle goes back to the cellars for several months of further rest before the labels and the plastic or lead-foil capsules are put on. When this is accomplished, the Champagne is ready to start its journey to our tables, to help us celebrate our most joyous and triumphant moments.

Because tastes vary, and some people prefer a dry and others a sweet Champagne, shippers have adopted a simple system of labeling to indicate how sweet the wine in the bottle is. The following list should serve as a general guide to denote the varying degrees of sweetness. All shippers use these descriptive terms. There is, however, some variation. Thus, while a Brut is always drier than an Extra Sec, one shipper's Brut may be slightly drier than another's. *labeling*

TYPE	DESCRIPTION	SUGAR CONTENT/LITER
Brut	very, very dry	less than 15 grams
Extra Sec or Extra Dry	somewhat sweeter but fairly dry	from 12 to 20 grams
Sec or Dry	medium sweet	from 17 to 35 grams
Demi Sec	quite sweet	from 33 to 50 grams
Doux	very sweet	more than 50 grams

As in other wine-producing regions, the quality of Champagne grapes and the resultant wine varies greatly according to summer weather conditions. Two qualities of vintage are possible: fairly good wines, which can be enhanced by blending with wines of a previous vintage; and fine, well-balanced wines that need no assistance and can stand on their own merit. The latter happens two, three, or possibly four times in a decade, and bottles of wine in this category are dated with the year in which the grapes that produced them were grown. These are known as vintage wines. Vintage wines are usually Brut. Wines in the first category, blends of several vintages, are not dated and are known as nonvintage wines.

The minimum standards specified under the existing *Appellation Contrôlée* regulations establish that nonvintage Champagne must be matured in bottle one year and vintage wines three years. However, the leading producers usually age their wines, nonvintage and vintage, at least four years and often longer before they ship them to market.

vintage
Champagne

A Champagne label carries a vintage year only when the *chef de cave* feels it is warranted. This decision is made by the individual house, based on the merits of the harvest. Fine old vintage Champagne is one of the most delicate of all wines, and keeping vintage Champagne longer than ten years is risky. A fine vintage develops and matures nobly with the years if it is properly stored and undisturbed, but it becomes oxidized with age. On the other hand, young wines have a light, fruity freshness that is their most charming characteristic. Late-disgorged Champagnes are the only exception to these general comments. Many of the fine French Champagne producers store small quantities of various vintages undisgorged in their cellars for their personal use on great occasions. The House of Bollinger, however, has marketed late-disgorged Champagne labeled *R.D., Récemment Dégorgé* ("recently disgorged"). The label shows both the vintage date and the date of disgorgement. Limited quantities of the best vintages are put aside and left undisturbed for years, then disgorged and shipped. Late-disgorged Champagnes not only retain all their qualities but also benefit considerably from greater maturity.

nonvintage
Champagne

Champagne is produced every year. In the years when the harvest is not up to vintage standards, it is helped by blending with wines kept in reserve from successful previous crops and shipped as a wine without a vintage date on the label. These are the Champagne houses' standard wines. Nonvintage Champagne is always less expensive than vintage, but this does not mean that the quality is necessarily less. Most houses will readily agree to be judged on the basis of their nonvintage bottlings. Krug, for example, considers its nonvintage Private Cuvée as its top label, and it sells for a higher price than other nonvintage Brut Champagnes.

English market

The first Champagne salesman was the Marquis de Sillery, of the seventeenth century. He was one of the richest vineyard owners of the region and in great favor at court. He introduced sparkling Champagne there and was the first to ship it to England.

What the Marquis de Sillery did for sparkling Champagne in France, Saint Evremond did in London. Soldier, writer, philosopher, and courtier, he was last but not least a gourmet and a connoisseur. Having incurred the displeasure of his king, he left France and settled in London, where he became one of the brightest lights of London society. He made it the fashion to drink Champagne, and the English ever since have been recognized as the most discriminating connoisseurs of fine Champagne and are the region's best customers outside France.

In those early days Champagnes were generally sweet to appeal to the tastes of the period. In the nineteenth century, however, Veuve Pommery reasoned that the sweetness masked the lively, delicate taste of Champagne and that Champagne might prove more enjoyable if the *dosage* was reduced.

Her experiments led her to dry and extra dry Champagnes, which she introduced commercially. These became especially popular in London, and the term *English Market* has since come to mean very dry Champagnes.

A unique development in Champagne production was established by Pierre Taittinger, who felt that many people would prefer a lighter and more delicate Champagne. Knowing that Chardonnay grapes could impart these qualities to the *cuvée*, he departed from the usual proportions of two-thirds red grapes and one-third white, which is the traditional *cuvée*. Pierre Taittinger made a wine of 100 percent Chardonnay grapes from extensive holdings in vineyards south of Épernay in the Côte des Blancs. This Champagne is marketed as Blanc de Blancs and is dry, elegant, and expensive. Many houses produce this style of Champagne today.

Blanc de Blancs

Once a bottle of Champagne is uncorked, it should be consumed in its entirety. Recorking is impractical. For this reason shippers bottle the wine in various sizes of containers:

bottle sizes

NAME	SIZE	
	U.S. measure (fluid ounces)	Metric standard (liters)
Split	6.5	0.187
Half-bottle	13	0.375
Bottle	26	0.75
Magnum (2 bottles)	52	1.5
Jeroboam (4 bottles)	104	3.0

The bottles listed below are hand blown into individual private molds and they vary in size. Because of this they will not be permitted in the United States under the metric bottling regulations.

NAME	SIZE (ounces)
Rehoboam (6 bottles)	156
Methuselah (7 to 8 bottles)	179–208
Salmanazar (10 to 12 bottles)	270–312
Balthazar (16 bottles)	416
Nebuchadnezzar (20 bottles)	520

Champagne, as is the case with most wines, develops better in a large container than in a small one, but it is important to know that the shippers rarely develop their Champagnes in sizes other than the half-bottles, bottles, magnums, and sometimes jeroboams. All other sizes are filled by decanting from bottles. Therefore, the best size to use is the magnum if there are enough people in the party, and the next best is the bottle.

Rosé Champagne—
Pink Champagne

Some shippers offer Rosé or Pink Champagne. In nearly all cases it is produced by adding the desired proportion of still red table wine of the Champagne district—generally from Bouzy or Ambonnay—just before second fermentation in the bottle. Rosé Champagne is usually a vintage wine, always Brut quality, and therefore extremely dry and very elegant in character.

uses of
Champagne

Champagne is one of the most delicate and delightful of all wines, but because it takes so long and is so costly to produce, it can never be cheap. This puts it in a class by itself as the "glamor" wine. It is indispensable at weddings, receptions, and formal banquets, but it is not limited to special occasions. Champagne is just as much at home with oysters as it is with ham or dessert, if a Champagne of the proper sweetness is chosen. Most people would not enjoy an extremely dry Brut with strawberry mousse, but a Demi Sec would be very pleasant. A chilled glass of Champagne makes a delightful aperitif to a wine-accompanied meal. Champagne also has its uses in the kitchen. Indeed, there is no hour of the day or night when Champagne cannot properly be served.

Côteaux
Champenois

Before 1975 no still wine was permitted to be exported from the Champagne district, as, according to the *Appellation Contrôlée* laws, Champagne could only be a sparkling wine. To avoid confusing the public, a new appellation was created, called Côteaux Champenois. This wine is made from the same grapes as are used in making Champagne and is otherwise controlled by the same laws. Bollinger and Moët et Chandon, among others, have exported these fresh, dry white wines.

vin mousseux

Vin mousseux refers to all sparkling wines, although the name Champagne may be used only for sparkling wine made in the delimited district of Champagne. Almost every wine region of France produces a *vin mousseux*. In addition to Champagne, there are only sixteen other French *vins mousseux* that are entitled to carry an *Appellation Contrôlée*.

The finer producers of *vin mousseux* use the *méthode champenoise*, although other methods of production may be used. When the *méthode champenoise* is used in certain areas that have an appellation of origin, the sparkling wine is called *crémant*. During the last century *crémant* designated a Champagne with a light foam. Now the term is used to separate *mousseux* of specific regions made by the Champagne method from *mousseux* of other areas made by less expensive techniques. Examples are Crémant de Bourgogne, Crémant de Loire, and Crémant d'Alsace.

Vin Mousseux-Produit en Cuve Close is the designation for sparkling wines made by the Charmat or bulk process (see Chapter 11).

Finally, there are wines that are made sparkling by artificial carbonation. These wines must be labeled Vin Mousseux Gazéifié.

For the past several years France has exported as much or more *mousseux* as Champagne itself.

4. ALSACE

Alsace, the bone over which the Frank and Teuton dogs of war have been scrapping for hundreds of years, is the buffer province on the left bank of the Rhine that extends from Strasbourg south to Switzerland and lies between the Rhine and the Vosges Mountains.

Alsace has been an important wine-producing region since the Roman conquerors occupied the valley of the Rhine. Undoubtedly they planted the vine in Alsace before they did in Germany. The vines they brought from Italy were not the same as those that flourish there today, but the records do not show when the change occurred.

history

During the half-century of German suzerainty, the Alsatian identity of these fine wines was submerged, and while much wine was made, it was all consumed in Germany or used for blending purposes. Quantity rather than quality was the order.

The Alsatian winemaker's life has never been an easy one. There is a record that in 1473 the vintage was so abundant that thirty-five gallons of wine were exchanged for only a basket of turnips.

". . . a fertile country," wrote Julius Wile, "fields and valleys waving with grain, hillsides covered with symmetric rows of vines marching up and up until they merge with the orchards, bearers of the fruits from which are distilled the famous *eaux-de-vie d'Alsace,* Quetsch and Mirabelle [plum brandies] and Kirsch [cherry brandy]; and the orchards finally give way to the mighty forests which top the hills and cover the Vosges Mountains—forests filled with game—deer, wild boar, fox, hare, and all varieties of birds.

"There is an atmosphere in Alsace—one of close alliance between man and soil, an aura of maturity combined with a freshness of spirit, of physical youngness that one finds even in the aged, of a people that has known the past, lives in the present, and does not fear the future; of a life that includes the good things of old and yet leaves space for the changes of today.

"It is something of all this that one finds in their wines. Wines that are firm and winy, and at the same time fresh, flowery and delicate—white wines of distinctive characteristics, not the finest wines of France, but worthy of their own separate place in the sun."

geography   From the north southward the towns whose surrounding vineyards are famous are:

BARR.   This is the home of the famous Clos Gaensbroennel ("little goose fountain") vineyard.

RIBEAUVILLÉ AND RIQUEWIHR.   Located in the center of the region, they have long enjoyed a reputation for producing excellent Alsatian wines.

AMMERSCHWIHR.   The important vineyard here is Kaefferkopf.

GUEBWILLER AND THANN.   Almost in the shadows of Switzerland, these are the southernmost towns of the region. There is a hill at Guebwiller called Kitterle, or "leg cutter." These leg-cutter wines are said to have been among Napoleon's favorites.

grape varieties   Only wines produced from a limited number of grapes are entitled to the *Appellation Contrôlée* Vin d'Alsace. Allowed for the production are Riesling, Gewürztraminer, Sylvaner, Muscat d'Alsace, Tokay d'Alsace (Pinot Gris), Klevner (Pinot Blanc), and Pinot Noir. There are other permitted varieties, but they are gradually being phased out. The Riesling is considered the king of Alsatian grapes. It has a subtle bouquet and fruity quality and is full bodied. The Gewürztraminer has a unique, spicy bouquet, with full flavor and flowery qualities. In some years the Riesling and Gewürztraminer are affected by "noble rot," and the wine made is rich and luscious. The Pinot Noir makes a rosé wine here, not a deep red wine.

labeling   In Alsace the name of the wine is generally determined by the grape variety from which it is made. Exceptions can be the name of a vineyard, such as Clos Gaensbroennel; the name of the grape in conjunction with a village, such as Gewürztraminer of Ribeauvillé; a shipper's trademark name, such as Cuvée Les Amours; and local blends, such as Edelzwicker or the more common Zwicker, depending on which grapes are used.

Labels on Alsatian wines include the following:

1. The words *Vin d'Alsace* or some variant, such as *Vin Fin d'Alsace*

2. The grape variety or trademark name

3. The shipper-grower's postal address

4. If a wine has 11 percent or more alcohol, it may be called either Grand Cru, Grand Vin, Grande Réserve, or Réserve Exceptionnelle. These wines not only meet the standards mentioned but are the vintner's best.

All Alsatian wines must be bottled in the green Alsace flute, which is a tall, slim bottle. The wines must be bottled in the region and cannot be shipped in casks.

What is of utmost importance is the name of the shipper, which may or may not be coupled with the grape name or otherwise displayed, but which in

WINE REGIONS OF ALSACE

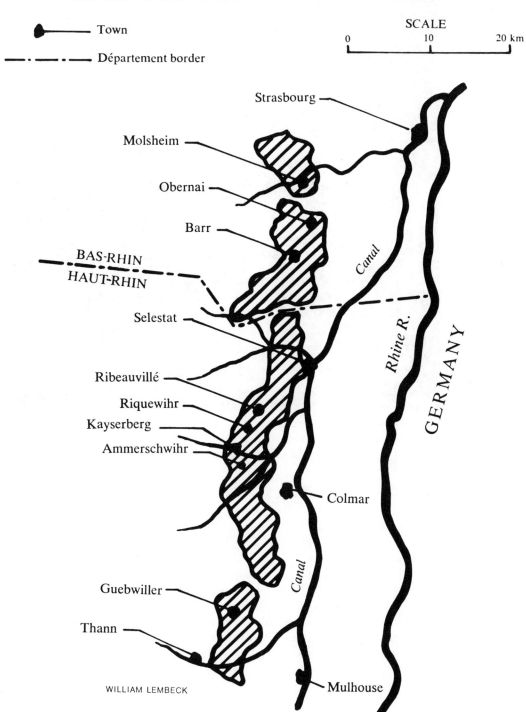

Town

Département border

SCALE

0   10   20 km

Strasbourg

Molsheim

Obernai

Barr

BAS-RHIN

HAUT-RHIN

Selestat

Ribeauvillé

Riquewihr

Kayserberg

Ammerschwihr

Colmar

Canal

Rhine R.

GERMANY

Canal

Guebwiller

Thann

WILLIAM LEMBECK

Mulhouse

Typical wine village in Alsace. High above this carefully preserved town lie the sloping hills and the vineyards. (*Courtesy Alsace Wine Information Bureau, New York*)

any case will appear as part of the address. The Alsatian shipper is usually a wine grower and a winemaker as well. As in Champagne, he buys grapes to supplement those from his own vineyards and then vinifies the wine. Because vineyard designation is often not important here, it is the name of the shipper that is paramount.

Growing the vine and the vintage in Alsace do not differ radically from other white-wine regions in France except that, because of Alsace's more northerly location and cooler climate, the vines are trained high and allowed to reach for the sun. The grape varieties do not ripen at the same time, and since many vineyards are planted with three, four, or more varieties they must be picked over several times during the vintage.

5. RHÔNE WINES

The Rhône River stretches 140 miles, from the gastronomic center of Lyon to the ancient and historic city of Avignon. It flows through the northern and southern vineyards, which produce two different styles of wines.

The Rhône River has been a means of transportation and communication, and the area has had historical and religious importance. South of Lyon, near the ancient Roman city of Vienne and across the river from Condrieu, lie the vineyards of the Côte Rôtie ("roasted slope"). The wines from this district were highly praised by Pliny the Younger, Plutarch, and Columella. *history*

Thirty miles south of Lyon, on the left bank of the Rhône near Tain, the renowned hill of Hermitage rises up majestically. Sir Gaspard de Sterimberg, a Crusader returning from the Albigensian Crusade, in southern France, decided to settle on these heights in 1209 and live the contemplative life of a hermit at the Chapel of Saint-Christophe at Hermitage. From the south he had brought a vine cutting, which he planted on the hill. According to legend it was the first Syrah brought to the Rhône. He tended his vine patiently and eventually it bore fruit, from which he made a fine wine that, ironically, brought him fame.

For seventy-two years, 1305–1377, the papacy was occupied by French-men, who, fearful of the perils of Rome, maintained the Holy See at Avignon. This period is sometimes called the Babylonian Captivity of the popes. The first of the Avignon popes was Clement V, who, as a native of Bordeaux and archbishop of Bordeaux, was familiar with viticulture and left us the legacy of that grand Graves claret—Château Pape-Clément, the vineyard which he is said to have owned.

When Clement V decided to settle the Holy See at Avignon, he built a fortress-palace just outside the town. This edifice was dubbed the new château of the pope, Châteauneuf-du-Pape. Since wine is important to a man from Bordeaux, Clement had vines planted, and they still produce the wine that is known as Châteauneuf-du-Pape.

Flowing southward, the turbulent Rhône River cuts its swath to the Mediterranean. Along its route there are two widely separated sections that produce red, rosé, and white wines of repute. *geography*

The northern part has terraced cliffs, giving the vines good exposure to the sun. The soil contains granite and shale. The southern part is covered with large stones that hold the heat, and the climate is more typically Mediterra-nean. Throughout the Rhône Valley the growing season is long and hot, creating robust, alcoholic wines that take time to develop.

grape varieties   The principal grape varieties of the Côtes du Rhône are the Syrrah (sometimes called Sirrac, Sirah, Serrine, or Petite Sirah), which is unrelated to the Petite Sirah grown in California. The Syrrah is the red grape of Côte Rôtie and Hermitage. Of twenty authorized grapes, other important red grapes are the Grenache, Clairette, Bourboulenc, Mourvèdre, and Cinsault. White grapes include the Viognier, Roussanne, Marsanne, and Picpoul. These are used both for making white wines and for softening some of the red wines (a famous example of which is Châteauneuf-du-Pape).

At Châteauneuf-du-Pape the wine is the result of judicious blending of as many as thirteen grape varieties. Baron P. Le Roy Boiseaumarié, president of the Syndicate of Vineyard Owners of Châteauneuf-du-Pape and proprietor of Château Fortia, stated in 1932 that the choice of grapes to produce a perfect Châteauneuf-du-Pape is as follows:

1st group	For warmth, richness, and roundness	Grenache and Cinsault	20 percent
2nd group	For solidity, keeping power, color, and the right flavor	Mourvèdre and Syrrah	40 percent
3rd group	For vinosity, agreeableness, freshness, and bouquet	Counoise and Picpoul	30 percent
4th group	For finesse, fire, and brilliance	Clairette and Bourboulenc	10 percent

vineyards   The red wines of Châteauneuf-du-Pape traditionally have been big and slow to develop, but today with more modern methods of vinification they are ready for drinking somewhat sooner. Another development is the production of small quantities of white wine at Châteauneuf-du-Pape. It is a pleasant wine of body, flavor, and character, although not as fine as the red.

The wines of Côte Rôtie are very deep in color and have a rich headiness and a roughness that takes some years to throw off. The wines spend three years in wood before bottling. As they grow older they lose some of their color, throw a rather heavy deposit, and rid themselves of their youthful harshness. Twelve to fifteen years is the youngest at which Côte Rôtie should be drunk.

Some white wine is produced at Condrieu and at Château Grillet from the Viognier grape. Production from both is very small and it is rare to find these wines in commerce. If you are fortunate enough to come across any Château

CÔTE-RÔTIE

CHÂTEAU GRILLET — CONDRIEU

CROZES-HERMITAGE

SAINT-JOSEPH — HERMITAGE

CORNAS
SAINT-PÉRAY

Valence

WINES OF THE
CÔTES DU RHÔNE

SCALE

0   10   20 km

KEY

SPECIFIC
APPELLATION

CÔTES DU RHÔNE
APPELLATION

CITY

Rhône R.

RASTEAU

GIGONDAS

BEAUMES
DE VENISE

CHÂTEAUNEUF-DU-PAPE

LIRAC
TAVEL

Avignon

WILLIAM LEMBECK

Grillet, you will find it to be pale in color and medium bodied, but with a wealth of character and a magnificent bouquet. It will be expensive. Château Grillet is France's smallest *Appellation Contrôlée* area.

The vineyards of Hermitage are fewer than four hundred acres and produce both red and white wines. The red wines, which Professor Saintsbury called the "manliest of wines," are big, full bodied, strong, and deep colored and have marvelous keeping qualities. The white wines are full and medium dry and have a deep bouquet. When mature they have an amber gold color and a lovely mellowness.

The appellation Crozes-Hermitage has been in effect since 1952; it applies to wines produced in eleven townships around the famous hillside of Hermitage. They are similar to Hermitage wines but have somewhat less character. Cornas and Saint-Joseph are not as well known but are enjoyable and well priced.

While the entire Rhône area may be called Côtes-du-Rhône, the only wines that are actually so named are regional blends from the area. They come mostly from the area between Côte Rôtie and Hermitage in the north and from around Tavel and Gigondas in the south. Most are red wines.

Tavel Rosé   Across the river from Avignon is the town of Tavel, which gives its name to one of the most delightful of all the rosé wines. Tavel combines the dryness of a red wine with the fresh lightness of a white. Several grapes are used, including not more than 60 percent Grenache and at least 15 percent Cinsault. It has a delightful coral color; is clean, fresh, and dry; and usually has a lovely, fruity bouquet and flavor. Tavel is best when young, no more than five years old. It should be served chilled, like a white wine. Rosé wines are often shipped in tall flute bottles.

Rhône wines, both red and white, are bottled in the same type of bottle used in Burgundy. They are more like Burgundy in character than any other wines. For these reasons many people have been confused, and on many a wine card Châteauneuf-du-Pape is erroneously listed as a Burgundy.

HOW AND WHEN TO SERVE
BORDEAUX, BURGUNDY, RHÔNE, AND ALSATIAN WINES

The place on the menu of any wine is a matter of personal taste and opinion. Fortunately, most wines lend themselves to many foods, and personal preference is the deciding factor.

Bordeaux   In general, red wines go well with almost all foods except those from the sea. Experience has shown that a perfectly dry wine, one completely lacking in sugar, will taste better with foods that are not sweet. Of course you can drink a claret with fish and it will do you no physical harm, but you will enjoy the wine much more if it accompanies a meat dish. This is especially true if the claret is a fine old château bottling.

The white, crisp, dry Graves, on the other hand, is more versatile and may be served with all foods. It shines its brightest in the company of fish and does nobly with fowl and white meats.

Sauternes is a wine that people enjoy at the end of a meal. Since the wine is sweet and has a rich perfume, it does not seem appealing with dry-tasting foods. It is lovely with a dessert such as honeydew melon. Sauternes also go well with blue-veined cheese and with pâté de foie gras.

Red Burgundies, being perfectly dry like clarets, are also somewhat unsat-isfactory with fish. They are good with high-protein foods. Game, red meat, or ripe cheese shows them off to the best advantage. Being rounder and softer than classical clarets, they often follow them at a formal dinner. *Burgundy*

White wines are at home with all foods, but a good, crisp Chablis or a fresh Pouilly-Fuissé with just-opened oysters is food for the gods. When ordering wine, it is a good rule to match the dish that will show it off best, and it is our experience that fish brings out the best qualities of white Burgundies.

The red wines of the Rhône, being full bodied and related to red Bur-gundies in character, may be served with the same type of food: roasts, game, or cheese. Hermitage and venison are classic companions. *Rhône*

The white wines are at home with most foods but are best with fish, white meats, or fowl.

A chilled bottle of dry Tavel is a delightful luncheon wine with most dishes and is a good choice on a summer evening when the weather calls for a wine that is refreshing.

Since they are delicate, light, and flowery, Alsatian wines may be served with almost all foods and are particularly attractive as luncheon wines. The wines should be served well chilled. They are, of course, ideal summer wines and are quite delightful in punches or for spritzers. *Alsace*

Alsatian wines are generally bottled when very young, in the spring or summer, following the vintage. They are at their best when relatively young since freshness is one of their most pleasant characteristics. Occasionally, however, some of the better wines are capable of attaining great age (ten to twenty years) and retaining their fruit and vigor.

6 . OTHER WINES OF FRANCE

THE LOIRE VALLEY

The château country of the tourist folder—issued by the *Commissariat National du Tourisme*—is not, as you might suppose, the Bordeaux wine region, but the part of France that inspired enchanting and exciting novels. Because of the proximity of the Loire Valley to Paris, the people of fashion in the time of the several Louises had to have châteaux there. The wines of the region were pleasant, and the courtiers at the royal court vied with one another showing off the wines from their Loire properties, thus making them popular in court circles.

Almost the entire length of the valley of the Loire River, about six hundred miles, is a series of wine-producing areas from which come a variety of pleasant wines. Muscadet from the west and Pouilly-Fumé and Sancerre from the east are dry white wines, while from the middle, around Anjou and Vouvray, the wines have a touch of sweetness, may be still or sparkling, and can be red, rosé, or white. Aside from Muscadet, whose name is the same as the grape variety from which it is made, the wines of the Loire are named for the districts in which they are grown. From east to west, as the river flows, they are:

POUILLY-SUR-LOIRE AND POUILLY-FUMÉ. South of Paris the town of Pouilly-sur-Loire lies on the right bank of the Loire. The vineyards about Pouilly are planted with Sauvignon Blanc, known locally as the Blanc Fumé, and the Chasselas. When the wines are made from Sauvignon Blanc, they are called Pouilly-Fumé. When the wines are made from Chasselas, they are named for the district and are called Pouilly-sur-Loire. Pouilly-Fumé is a delicate, soft, dry white wine, and the best examples have a slightly smoky quality to the bouquet. Pouilly-sur-Loire is less delicate than Pouilly-Fumé but is attractive when drunk young. Do not confuse Pouilly-Fumé of the Loire with the Pouilly-Fuissé of Burgundy; they are completely dissimilar.

SANCERRE, QUINCY, AND REUILLY. On the left bank of the river, almost opposite Pouilly, we find Sancerre, while a little farther west on the Cher River are the towns of Quincy and Reuilly. The vineyards of these regions produce white wines similar in character to Pouilly-Fumé, although somewhat lighter and not quite as elegant.

VOUVRAY AND SAUMUR. These are wine districts around the city of Tours that produce most of the pleasant medium-dry sparkling wines of the Loire. As of 1975 these wines are allowed the appellation Crémant de Loire. The leading producers make their wines by the *méthode champenoise* but do not, and

WINE REGIONS OF THE LOIRE

ANJOU

MUSCADET DE
SÈVRE-ET-MAINE

Angers

Nantes

MUSCADET

CÔTEAUX
DU LAYON

Layon R.

Loire R.

SAUMUR

BOURGUEIL

Tours

CHINON

VOUVRAY

Orléans

Loire R.

Cher R.

QUINCY

REUILLY

SANCERRE

POUILLY-SUR-LOIRE
AND
POUILLY-FUMÉ

WILLIAM LEMBECK

SCALE

0   50   100 km

cannot, call their wines Champagne. The grape varieties used are distinguished by their ability to produce effervescence and by the quality of the musts they produce. The main grape is Chenin Blanc or Pineau de la Loire, but Cabernet Franc, Cabernet Sauvignon, Gamay, Pinot d'Aunis, Pinot Noir, and Chardonnay are permitted.

CHINON AND BOURGUEIL.   These districts produce two similar red wines made from Cabernet Franc grapes. Chinon was the home of Rabelais, lover of the good life, who consumed Chinon in vast amounts and praised it lavishly. It may be that his judgment was befuddled by local patriotism, but still the wine is pleasing and satisfying. Both wines should be drunk young, and do not be afraid to cool them.

ANJOU. This region, near the city of Angers, produces large quantities of white and rosé wines. Some of the most popular rosé wines in the United States are the Anjou rosés, unquestionably because of their touch of sweetness and attractive pink color. Rosés produced from the Gamay and Pinot d'Aunis grapes are labeled Rosé d'Anjou. Rosés made from the Cabernet grape are varietally labeled. Sparkling wines are entitled to the appellation Crémant de Loire.

CÔTEAUX DU LAYON. The vineyards along the banks of the Layon River, a tributary to the Loire, produce delightful medium sweet or very sweet white wines from the Chenin Blanc grape. These wines are not too well known outside France, but eventually they will be.

MUSCADET. On both banks of the Loire, as it flows into the Atlantic near Nantes, the vineyards are planted with Muscadet grapes, locally known as Melon. The light, soft, bone-dry wine is called Muscadet. The best is from Sèvre-et-Maine, the heartland of the region, and is called Muscadet de Sèvre-et-Maine. When labeled *sur lie*, the wine has been bottled shortly after it was made, without having been racked. Muscadet is the most popular white wine of the Loire.

CÔTES DE PROVENCE

Although red and white wines are made in this region, some of the smoothest, freshest rosés come from the Côtes de Provence. This region runs from Nice to Marseille, although the vinicultural heart lies between Saint-Raphaël and Aix-en-Provence. When the wines are young they have a delightful bouquet; older, they lose some bouquet but gain in softness. Other areas of the Côtes de Provence include Cassis, famous for its whites; Bandol, famous for reds, as is Palette; and Bellet, near Nice, which produces reds, whites, and rosés. Regional wines are bottled as Côtes de Provence. Many of these wines appear in distinctively shaped bottles.

MIDI

West of the Côtes de Provence, along the Mediterranean, lies a huge plain that extends down to the Spanish border. This area, called the Midi, produces immense quantities of ordinary table wines. The better wines of the area are the reds from Corbières, Minervois, and Roussillon. Sweet dessert wines are also made in this area. The most famous are Muscat de Frontignan and Banyuls.

JURA

This region near Switzerland was famous in the past for its wines, but today only the Rosé d'Arbois and the wines of Château d'Arlay and Château-Châlon retain some fame. The latter two are interesting in a special way.

At Château-Châlon the Savagnin grapes (considered the same as the Gewürztraminer grown elsewhere) are picked as late as possible, sometimes in December, and fermentation takes place in vats that have been cut out of the rock. Because of the late vintage, fermentation is rather slow. Some wines are then racked into very old casks that have held many previous vintages, and they remain in partially filled, sealed casks for a minimum of six years before they are ready for bottling. This wine will be a *vin jaune*, or yellow wine.

During this period a yeast film forms on the surface of the wine in the cask and performs its miraculous work. This is one of few wines in which this phenomenon occurs. An exception is sherry from Jerez, in which the *flor* is commonplace. As a result, Château-Châlon develops an alcohol content, usually about 15 percent, that gives extraordinary keeping qualities. It is said to live for decades and to have an austere dryness coupled with a delicate, nutty flavor, such as one encounters in a very old, dry sherry.

A few miles west of Château-Châlon lies one of the oldest vineyards known, Château d'Arlay, which produces wine similar to Château-Châlon, as well as red and white table wines. But it is the white, or rather straw-colored, *vin de paille*° that is most distinguished. Only wines of better-than-average-quality vintages are bottled. The twenty acres that compose the vineyard can produce upward of thirty thousand bottles, but the quantity is usually less.

BÉARN

In the Pyrénées and a former part of the Royaume de Navarre are the vineyards of Jurançon, which produce a rich, sweet wine of breed and character. Around Pau, the capital, Rosé de Béarn, a fine pink wine, is produced.

OTHER WINES OF THE SOUTHWEST

Near Bordeaux, from the Dordogne River to the Pyrénées, are some less famous areas that produce attractive wines. Cahors is a dark red wine, made mainly from the Malbec grape, which is highly tannic. This wine requires a great deal of bottle age to smooth out.

Bergerac, another region of the southwest, produces both red and white wines. Its most famous wine is Monbazillac, a rich dessert wine that reminds one of Sauternes.

° The term comes from the fact that the grapes are spread upon straw (*paille*) to dry for a period of time before pressing.

Castello della Sala in the heart of the Orvieto wine region. (*Courtesy Julius Wile Sons & Co., Inc., New York*)

6
THE WINES OF ITALY

history

The length of the Via Latina was once dotted with statues of Bacchus that were destroyed as pagan idols with the march of Christianity. The cult of Dionysus, during the Golden Age of Greece, taught man the contemplation of his own divinity, and wine was an important part of the cult's ritual. All Hellas honored the vine and spread the cult to Rome and Asia Minor. Plato records that Socrates drank unbelievable quantities of wine but was never intoxicated.

It is unquestionable that we owe to the Romans the spread of the vinification of the grape; however, we are inclined to wonder at Martial, who speaks of *"immortale Falernum"* with a reverence that borders on idolatry, when we consider that this wine was generally diluted. It is also difficult to believe the ancient historians when they speak of the merits of two-hundred-year-old wine or to understand how wine could have been preserved so long and still be good.

The Romans were good agriculturists and good winemakers, but they must have been limited to naturally fermented wines. These, however, were of great strength, concentrated to the consistency of jelly, and served only after dilution with water; they were spiced and flavored with such substances as aloes, myrrh, resin, pitch, seawater, marble dust, perfumes, spices, and herbs.

The Romans had capable winemakers who were familiar with the use of cork and glass. From the Greeks they took the method of lining their *amphorae* and *dolia* with pitch or resin, for these earthenware containers were porous. Apparently they also used oak barrels, but these were never in such general use as the earthenware vessels.

After the fall of the Roman Empire, the Church took up the work of cultivating the vine, and the barons, under the sway of the Church, cooperated, for "mighty was the thirst of the Templar."

In the fourteenth and fifteenth centuries it became fashionable to live well,

91

even if one had to live dangerously. The literature of the Renaissance is full of references to wines and vines. The banquets of the Medicis and the Barberinis were supreme exhibitions of aesthetic magnificence, with wines served in golden goblets and toasts sung in immortal rhymes.

The vine grows everywhere in Italy, profusely, almost wantonly, as though flaunting the bounty of nature through the fertility of her soil. In fact, Italy is one vast vineyard, from the snow-covered Alpine borders in the north to the volcanic southern tip of the boot.

From birth the Italian absorbs the love of the vine with no conscious effort. Wine is the common drink—inexpensive, natural, and sound. Because no germs harmful to man can live in wine, it is a safer drink than water, which in years past was often polluted with typhoid bacteria. As a result the annual per capita consumption of wine in Italy is high, $28\frac{1}{2}$ gallons, as compared with about $1\frac{3}{4}$ gallons in the United States.

Italy has often been called the vineyard of the world. Where nature is so bountiful, man is prone to leave things in the lap of the gods. Vines were permitted to luxuriate over fertile plains, to climb at will over fence and tree, and to grow in festoons. Viticulture was often careless in some regions of Italy, and many grape varieties were grown without selection as to suitability of soil and climate. In recent years, however, economic realities, particularly Common Market trade policies, have necessitated the disciplining of those Italian vineyards that had not previously maintained such strict standards.

Because the vine grows so luxuriantly and bears so abundantly throughout Italy, it is often said that the Italian winemaker is more concerned with quantity than with quality. While this is not entirely true, most of the wine made year after year is plain, honest wine.

THE WINE LAW OF 1963

Much of the stimulus behind the modernization of the Italian wine industry in recent years has come from a new government and industry policy of tighter control of all aspects of wine production. The Wine Law of 1963, passed after thirty years of preliminary thought and effort, consolidated and defined all legal aspects with which the wine industry must comply. Its basic aims are to protect the name of origin and the sources of musts and wines and to provide measures for the prevention of fraud and unfair competition. For example, chaptalization (a process sometimes used in northern countries with short, cool growing seasons whereby sugar is added to the must to increase the alcohol content of the wine) is forbidden by law in Italy. This can be enforced because the government distributes sugar.

The 1963 law delimits zones of production so that the same type of natural environment is provided for the production of grapes for a specific type of wine. There are three different denominations, graded as follows:

1. *Denominazione Semplice* ("Simple Denomination") is a simple statement of the region of production; for example, Rosso Toscano is a red wine from anywhere inside the region of Tuscany. Such wines do not carry any official guarantee of quality.

2. *Denominazione di Origine Controllata* ("Controlled Denomination of Origin") is an appellation reserved for wines that have met stipulated standards of quality. The label must state the area of origin. Natural conditions of the locality, such as soil type and geography, determine the traditional varieties of grapes permitted to be grown. Production practices must conform to approved methods of planting, cultivating, fertilizing, and other viticultural practices, and the maximum yield is controlled. Bottling specifications and minimum alcohol content and aging requirements are also controlled. Documents on these wines and on their sales are subject to inspection. All vineyards producing such wines are listed in an official register, and their wines carry the D.O.C. label.

3. *Denominazione di Origine Controllata e Garantita* ("Controlled and Guaranteed Denomination of Origin") encompasses all of the requirements of D.O.C. wines but is even more stringent. The wine must be bottled and sealed with a government seal by the producer. A government inspector can test and analyze the wine at any time. The label of such a wine must state that its origin, as well as the net contents of the bottle, the name of the grower and bottler, the place of bottling, and the alcoholic strength, is controlled and guaranteed.

The law is quite comprehensive, covering every phase of grape cultivation and wine production, with strict controls all along the line.

Any wine that is exported must comply with the 1963 law. In addition, the wine is tested by the *Instituto Commercio Estero* (formerly called the *Instituto Nazionale Esportazione*), which grants the red I.N.E. seal, mandatory on all bottles shipped to the United States, Canada, and Mexico. This seal indicates that the wine has met the standards of the export laws applicable to these countries and ensures the wine's authenticity.

labeling

If an Italian wine qualifies under the D.O.C. laws, the words *Denominazione di Origine Controllata* appear on the label, either above or below the name of the wine. The producer and bottler are indicated, as well as the zone of origin. Whether any further descriptive words can be used on a given label depends on the individual D.O.C. rules for each type of wine.

Some of the more common words that appear on Italian wine labels, whether D.O.C. wines or not, are the following:

Classico	Classic—may be used by any producer to describe his wine. In certain regions, such as Chianti, it means that the wine has come from a specific central area
Imbottigliato all'origine	Estate bottled

Modern, scientifically planted vineyard. (*Courtesy Fratelli Folonari, Brescia*)

Vineyards planted in the more traditional style of Italy, with trellised vines. (*Courtesy Fratelli Folonari, Brescia*)

Riserva	Reserve—indicates extra aging in cask or bottle, the number of years varying with the D.O.C. requirements for different areas
Riserva Speciale	Special Reserve—wine is aged longer than Riserva
Superiore	Superior—wine has slightly higher alcohol content and sometimes greater age than a wine that does not have this designation
Vecchio	Old—a term found in Italy, but not permitted on U.S. labels. Vecchio wines are aged longer than Superiore but not as long as Riserva.

Vintages may be given on either the main label or the neck label. *Annata* means "year," and *vendemmia* means "vintage." Other descriptive terms are:

Amaro	tart, dry	*Rosato*	rosé
Secco	dry	*Chiaretto*	light red
Abboccato	semidry	*Rosso*	red
Amabile	semisweet	*Nero*	deep red
Dolce	sweet	*Frizzante*	crackling
Bianco	white	*Spumante*	sparkling

Extra and *Fine* may not be used

A growers' regional organization may add another seal guaranteeing authenticity, and the seal may provide additional information. The *Consorzio Vino Chianti Classico*, for example, surrounds its black rooster symbol with different-colored concentric rings, which indicate a Chianti Classico or a Chianti Classico Riserva. As the D.O.C. regulations become more generally effective, however, the use of the seals is diminishing, and some of the best-known shippers are discontinuing their memberships and use of the local seals.

The same grape variety is often grown in several districts. Wine made from grapes grown in the mountainous northern region where the soil is watered by glacier-fed rivers, however, is distinctively different from that produced from the same grape grown in volcanic soil containing a great many minerals. That is why a varietal wine labeled with the name of the grape always lists the area where it was grown on the label as well. Sometimes the grape gives its local name to the wine; in other cases the wine may take its name from the town or village around which the grapes were grown.

geography

A map of the world shows that Italy lies in the same latitude as Canada and New England; Naples is in the same latitude as New York. The entire Italian peninsula is covered with mountains. In the west and north lie the majestic, snow-capped Alps; toward the east are the Venetian Alps—the picturesque needles of the Dolomites. Despite the handicaps of weather, snow, ice, erosion, and avalanche, the vine thrives because the valleys are fertile and the people are hard-working. Some of the finest vines are grown on forbidding ledges, which must be carefully terraced and tended.

The peninsula is split by the Apennine Mountains, which run from the Po River in the north to the very tip of Calabria in the south. While the Apennines are not as forbidding as the Alps, they are rocky and bleak and submit only to the constant struggle of industrious peasants whose forebears have fought the elements for over two thousand years.

The northern part of Italy is often foggy and rainy; the eternal snows on the Alpine peaks cool the warm sirocco from the south. Southern Italy is semi-tropical with a climate much like that of Florida. Sicily is the island of perpetual sunshine. The vine grows profusely in all of Italy, yet so varied are the climatic conditions, the soil, the methods of cultivation, and the varieties of vines used that Italian wine probably can satisfy the most discriminating requirements of any connoisseur.

grape varieties

From the Po River down to the Vesuvius region, with its hot, sandy, volcanic soil, Italy runs the entire gamut of varieties of grapes. There are so many types of vines that it is next to impossible to make an accurate estimate of their numbers, but counts run as high as three hundred varieties. The fifty most important of these are listed in Appendix E with the areas in which they are grown and the wines in which they are used.

red grapes

The noble grape of Italy is the Nebbiolo, a red-wine grape producing the rich, full wines of Piedmont and Lombardy. Barbera and Grignolino are also grown in those regions but produce softer, lighter wines. The Sangiovese grape is grown in several regions, but it is best known as the principal grape of Chianti. The Brunello grape is grown near the Chianti area. The Lambrusco grape makes the popular wine of the same name in Emilia-Romagna. In the Veneto the Corvina Veronese grape produces both Bardolino and Valpolicella. Grapes discussed previously in Chapter 5, the Cabernet Sauvignon, Merlot, and Pinot Nero (Pinot Noir), are grown successfully in the northern regions that border on Switzerland and Austria: Lombardy, Trentino–Alto Adige, and Friuli-Venezia-Giulia.

white grapes

One of the most widely planted white grapes, the Trebbiano, grows in the north and central parts of Italy. Trebbiano is in such famous wines as Soave, Lugana, Orvieto, Frascati, and Est! Est!! Est!!!, and a small amount is even used in Chianti to soften the blend of red grapes. The Verdicchio grape produces, in the Marches, the varietally named Verdicchio wine. Pinot Bianco, Pinot Grigio,

WINE REGIONS
OF
ITALY

WILLIAM LEMBECK

Riesling, Traminer, and Tocai grapes are seen elsewhere in Europe and make charming white wines in the northern region of Friuli-Venezia-Giulia. Many varieties of Malvasia grapes are planted throughout Italy, and they appear in various table wines. Assorted varieties of Moscatos produce sweet dessert wines from Piedmont in the north to Sicily in the south, as well as on the island of Sardinia.

PIEDMONT

Piedmont produces the majority of Italy's most regal red wines, yet it is the most austere region in the country. The red wines are hardy and masculine, travel well, and improve with age. From the glaciers of the Alpine banks the land descends in a series of charming valleys and fertile plains to the Po River, from which it again rises gradually to the hills of Monferrato, where the vine is cultivated with religious fervor. Piedmont is entirely surrounded by mountains, forming a cup around the Alpine foothills. This is where the famous wines Barolo, Barbaresco, Gattinara, and Asti Spumante are produced.

The region is ruled by Turin (Torino), the home of vermouth and the center of industry. It is the richest market for wines in the region. The Piedmontese are tenacious, industrious, and faithful to their land. Their vineyards are neat and symmetrical.

Barolo is the name of a town as well as the name of the surrounding area encompassing over two thousand acres under vine. The area is situated on a hill of porous rock, which undoubtedly is an extinct volcano. On this hill Nebbiolo grapes grow best, and they give one of the finest and most justly celebrated red wines Italy has. In good years Barolo is a big, full-bodied wine, with a ruby-red color that takes on a brownish shade as it ages; it can be classed as one of the kings of wine. The Barolo Riserva Speciale is aged five years. It is generous yet austere, rich in alcohol, but, with age, always soft and velvety, with an unmistakable violet bouquet.

Northeast of Barolo is the district of Barbaresco, which produces Barbaresco wines. The city of Alba lies between Barolo and Barbaresco. The hillside vineyards surround the old red-towered remnant of Barbaresco Castle on the crest of the hill, overlooking the stone houses below. The hills are also planted with Nebbiolo vines, but because of the differences in the soil, the wines are less austere than those of Barolo and mature more quickly.

It is interesting to note that in Julius Caesar's *Commentaries* there is a reference to these wines, which he greatly appreciated and wanted to introduce to Rome. The particular wine to which he referred came from the little village of Morra (Murra). "From Murra," he wrote, "we brought the best wine to our city of Rome."

After Barolo, probably the second most important red wine from Piedmont is Gattinara, principally made from the Nebbiolo grape, locally called Spanna.

An aging cellar in the Nizza Monferrato in Piedmont. (*Courtesy Joseph E. Seagram & Sons, Inc., New York*)

Gattinara is a small area, with about eighty acres under vine, in the northeast part of Piedmont, which borders on Lombardy. The Sesia River flows through Piedmont. The wine is aged at least four years, after which it begins to get a velvet quality. It is a wine of great complexity.

Barbera is the half brother of Barolo, produced from the plentiful Barbera grape. This grape generally produces a dry, full-bodied wine that puckers your lips. Barbera wines are marketed with a place name affixed to the grape name, such as Barbera d'Alba and Barbera d'Asti.

SASSELLA — VALGELLA
— GRUMELLA
— INFERNO

FARA AND
SIZZANO —

GHEMME —

BOCA —

GATTINARA —

VALTELLINA

CALUSO
PASSITO —

BARBERA
D'ASTI —

RIVIERA DEL GARDA

FREISA —

Sesia R.

LOMBARDY

Brescia

*LAKE
GARDA*

Adda R.

Po R.

TURIN

LUGANA

Tanaro R.

Po R.

PIEDMONT

FRECCIAROSSA

BOTTICINO

OLTREPÒ PAVESE

CELLATICA

BARBERA D'ALBA

FRANCIACORTA

CORTESE

ASTI SPUMANTE

WINE REGIONS
OF
PIEDMONT AND LOMBARDY

GRIGNOLINO

BARBARESCO

WILLIAM LEMBECK

BAROLO

DOLCETTO —

SCALE

0   100 km

Grignolino, made from the grape of the same name, is a light, rather dry wine that sometimes has a slight natural effervescence. Dolcetto is another light red wine that is faintly bitter, but which makes an excellent carafe wine, without the character of the Grignolino. Another grape variety, Freisa, is so named for its raspberry bouquet. It makes both a dry red wine and a sweet, slightly sparkling, or "crackling," wine. Dolcetto, Grignolino, and Freisa have a place name after the grape variety.

Boca, Fara, Ghemme, and Sizzano are four other red wines made from the Nebbiolo, Vespolina, and Bonarda grapes. These are good red wines but with limited production.

From the Cortese Bianco is produced Cortese, a light-bodied, straw-colored wine with a greenish cast. It has a delicate, pleasant, and fresh aroma.

Asti, the sparkling wine center of Italy and the home of the famous white Asti Spumante, is a town with a great historical background. The hills of Asti are now honeycombed with cellars excavated for the purpose of storing the fermented juice of the Moscato grape which, when vinified into sparkling wine, is sold throughout the world as Asti Spumante ("sparkling wine of Asti"). Bismarck showed such predilection for it that he exclaimed: "I want one good bottle for each of my officers. It will serve to keep their heavy heads awake."

The actual production zone of Asti Spumante lies south of the town. The vineyards along the rugged banks of the Belbo around Canelli produce the most highly prized Moscatos of all.

Asti Spumante is the most popular Italian sparkling wine. It is a delicious wine with a pleasant, decidedly sweet Muscat flavor that gives it a lovely, fresh fruitiness. Most of the shippers have changed over from bottle fermentation to bulk (Charmat) fermentation (see Chapter 11). Aside from the time and expense savings, they claim that the fragrance of the Muscat grape is captured much better by this method. Many of the Italian sparkling wine producers do use the *méthode champenoise* in years of exceptional heat and sugar content. Drier sparkling wines are made from transplanted French grapes, including the Pinot Nero and Pinot Bianco. A sparkling wine that used to be made in Piedmont was Lacrima Christi, but this is no longer allowed. The wine is now made in Campania, the best coming from the zone of Mount Vesuvius.

A sweet dessert wine, Caluso Passito, is produced north of Turin from the white Erbaluce grape. These grapes undergo a drying process that raisins them and leaves them rich in sugar.

LOMBARDY

The Swiss Alps frame the lake region of Lombardy with breathtaking beauty, and the surrounding hills have a corrugated appearance as row upon row of carefully tended vineyards extend as far as the eye can see. The Adda River splits the valley of Valtellina, and Milan lies to the south, wearing the filigree crown of the Duomo, its famous cathedral.

The best wines of Lombardy come from an area known as the Valtellina, the northernmost region of Sondrio, which was formerly Swiss. The vineyards are carved out of the mountains and are tended by hardy individuals. Both red and white wines are made, but the Sassella, Grumello, Inferno, and Valgella reds are the most famous and are made from at least 95 percent Nebbiolo grapes, known locally as Chiavennasca. Differences in soil and altitude give these wines a different character from the Barolos and Gattinaras, even though they are made from the same grape. Riservas are produced from wines with four or more years of age. One year of aging makes a wine labeled Valtellina, while two years of aging will make a Valtellina Superiore. A unique, high-alcohol, rich red wine, made with semidried grapes, is called Sforsato (Sfursat), which means "forced" in Italian.

South of Lombardy is the Oltrepò Pavese area, where many good, inexpensive wines are made for local consumption, primarily from the Barbera grape. One proprietary brand, Frecciarossa, is produced by the Odero family, whose château bottling dates back to the last century. Frecciarossa is made from different grape varieties, many brought from France, and appears as red, white, and rosé wine.

Near charming Lake Garda is produced a pleasant, light white wine called Lugana, made from the Trebbiano grape. It is most enjoyable when young, especially so with a freshly caught broiled trout . . . yes, fresh from Lake Garda. The most famous wine from this area is the Riviera del Garda Rosé. Called Chiaretto, which means "light red," it is a ruby-hued rosé with a gentle flavor, soft texture, and a hint of bitterness. It is made from a mixture of grape varieties. Franciacorta, Cellatica, and Botticino are light, flavorful reds from Brescia, to the west of Lake Garda. These wines are not as popular as Chiaretto.

VENETO

The morning sun rising above the Adriatic gilds the *guglie* of the Dolomites in the north long before it touches the golden cupolas of San Marco. The land drops precipitously from rugged mountain to dismal swamp. In the intervening space rushes the Adige River. Here, at romantic Verona, where you can visit the houses of the Montagues and Capulets, where you can stand in the courtyard and gaze up at Juliet's balcony and visualize the poetic trysts of the fated lovers, there also stands majestically the Palazzo Scaglieri, where Cangrande toasted his guests with Vernaccia and where Dante Alighieri found refuge and protection.

Here, too, is Lake Garda, along whose eastern shores are produced bright red Bardolino and again dry white Lugana. The long, narrow valley running north from Verona is where the Corvina, Rondinella, and other grape varieties join to produce one of Italy's loveliest red table wines—Valpolicella. Valpolicella is a fine wine, ruby in color, of delicate bouquet and softness, and with a pleasantly bitter tang.

An even finer Valpolicella produced in limited quantities is called Recioto della Valpolicella-Amarone. It is made entirely with grapes taken from the upper part of the bunch, that is, the grapes that have benefited most from the sun and will be the best, the ripest. To the imaginative person these grapes represent the "ears" of the bunch, ergo *Recioto*, which means "ears." The grapes are dried on reed trays in a shed for three months and then are vinified. The high sugar concentration ferments down to a rich, dry wine with a high

WINE REGIONS OF NORTHEAST ITALY

LAGREIN

SANTA MADDALENA

CALDARO

TRENTINO–

LAGREIN

ALTO ADIGE

AMBELLARA

SOAVE

ALPOLICELLA
ND RECIOTO
ALPOLICELLA

ARDOLINO

LUGANA

Adige R.

Verona

VENETO

Adige R.

Po R.

LAMBRUSCO

EMILIA-
ROMAGNA

FRIULI-

VENEZIA-

GIULIA

COLLI ORIENTALE
DEL FRIULI

COLLI GRAVE
DEL FRIULI

COLLI
GORIZIANO

Trieste

CONEGLIANO-
VALDOBBIADENE

RABOSO

Venice

BREGANZE

SCALE

0   100 km

WILLIAM LEMBECK

alcohol content. Amarone actually refers to this process or style of wine-making. *Amaro* is the Venetian equivalent of "slightly bitter," which has a pleasant connotation to it and is a characteristic that is not at all unattractive.

From the vineyards around the ancient walled city of Soave, the Garganega and ubiquitous Trebbiano grapes produce the very appropriately named Soave. It is a really suave white wine, light, fairly dry, with a pleasant, subtle bouquet, soft, velvety texture, and a bit of piquant bitter undertone.

Soave, Bardolino, and Valpolicella are available as Classico wines, with a more defined zone of production, and the best are Classico Superiore.

A wine similar to the Soave, the Garganega di Gambellara, is produced in the bordering province of Vicenza. Other excellent white wines, such as the Pinot (white) or the Vespaiolo, are found in the same area. Recently, especially in the Breganze area, the production of good red wines has become much better; they are being obtained from imported vines such as Merlot, Pinot Nero, and Cabernet.

The white wines produced in the province of Treviso are of excellent quality. The best known is the Conegliano-Valdobbiadene, which comes mainly from the Prosecco grape. Raboso is the local red.

TRENTINO–ALTO ADIGE AND FRIULI-VENEZIA-GIULIA

Italy's northernmost region, bordering on Austria, is Trentino–Alto Adige. It produces many red and white wines using the traditional grapes grown in France and Germany. Some varietal red wines are Trentino-Cabernet, Trentino-Merlot, and Trentino-Pinot Nero, which use 100 percent of the grapes named. Among the whites are Trentino-Riesling, Trentino-Pinot, and Trentino-Traminer Aromatico. These wines are similar to those made in the grapes' homelands and offer good values.

The province of Bolzano (Upper Adige) produces a wide variety of quality wines, but the best known are Santa Maddalena and Caldaro—dry, red wines—and Lagrein—a dry, fresh rosé made from the Lagrein grape.

Nestled between Veneto and Yugoslavia is the individualistic region of Friuli-Venezia-Giulia. Some areas, such as Trieste, have been part of both Yugoslavia and Italy at different times and have developed cultures encompassing those of both countries. The wines come from three main areas: Colli Orientale del Friuli (Eastern Friuli Hills), Colli Grave del Friuli (Western Friuli Hills), and Colli Goriziano (Gorizia Hills). Some grapes used, as in Trentino–Alto Adige, are the Pinot Nero, Cabernet, and Merlot, which produce full, rich reds. Pinot Bianco, Pinot Grigio, Tocai, and Riesling Renano produce characteristic white wines. The Verduzzo grape, grown in the eastern and western hills, makes a full-bodied and slightly tannic white wine called Verduzzo.

EMILIA-ROMAGNA

We now come to the richest and most fertile region of the Po Valley. On the hills around Bologna, home of sausage and Parmesan cheese, the subsoil is chalky like that of the Champagne region of France. Along the valley of the Trebbia River is grown the fine Trebbiano grape, which is greatly in demand for making sparkling wine. Much of the unfermented must obtained from these grapes is exported to other countries for this purpose.

Vineyards grow right up to the remains of the medieval fortress and battlements that protected the ancient city of Soave, near Verona. (*Courtesy Fratelli Folonari, Brescia*)

A delightful and popular wine is Lambrusco, made from Lambrusco grape varieties. A lively, *frizzante*, semidry red wine with a fruity taste, it is served chilled.

In the southeast corner of this region, near the tiny Republic of San Marino, the full red Sangiovese di Romagna and the dry white Trebbiano di Romagna are produced.

TUSCANY

To the poets this region is Arcady—the home of Dante, Boccaccio, the Borgias, Saint Francis of Assisi, Saint Catherine of Siena. It bears the marks of the orgies and extravaganzas of its sinners and the pious virtues of its saints.

To most people it is the home of Italian wines, for the mention of Chianti immediately calls forth the picture of the typical straw-covered flask (*fiasco*) with the red, white, and green stripes. Of all containers for wine, it is the most picturesque and the most unsatisfactory: delicate and difficult to fill, to cork, and to stack.

After many years of squabbling, it appears that agreement has finally been reached on the geographical boundaries of the region legally entitled to call its wine true Chianti. This area is subdivided into seven districts, all of which lie on the beautiful rolling hillsides around and between Florence (Firenze) and Siena (see map on page 107). Wines produced from the heartland may be called Chianti Classico.

Here the vines grow profusely and produce enormous quantities of fruit. Farther south the appearance of the vineyards is very different from that of the orderly, well-tended ones of the north. Where nature is lavish, the vines are left more and more to their own devices. They are allowed to grow wild, their only support from weeping willows and poplars that are set up as props, the vines festooned from one tree to another.

There are exceptions to this manner of doing things, of course, the principal one being the vast vineyard of Barone Ricasoli, whose Brolio Chianti is distributed worldwide. To Barone Bettino Ricasoli must go the credit for having brought Piedmontese viticultural methods into Tuscany by the nineteenth century. The Brolio vineyards are today an example of scientific cultivation, the cellars are perfection, and the work of improvement in vinification has set an example that other vineyard owners have followed.

Chianti is made from several different grape varieties. The informing grape is the Sangiovese, which makes up about 70 percent of the must; the other 30 percent are Canaiolo Nero, Trebbiano, and Malvasia. Up to 15 percent other grapes are permitted. The proportions of these grapes vary with the style of Chianti to be made.

Three qualities of Chianti are generally produced: the wine for early local consumption, a better quality for bottling in the traditional *fiasco*, and the best quality for long aging. It is not uncommon for these Chiantis to be kept in vats up to six years before bottling. Chianti contains a substantial amount of tannin, which makes for rough, full-bodied wine while young that softens with proper bottle aging. Great improvements have been made in the vinification and subsequent care of the wine during the present century.

For Chiantis meant to be drunk young, a process called *governo* is used in Tuscany. It consists of setting aside a small percentage of the harvest on mats to become raisins. These are pressed late in the year and their fermenting juice is added to the new Chianti. A slow second fermentation takes place that makes the wine drinkable six months after the fermentation; it is lively, with a slight sparkle. Increased glycerine develops the wine's bouquet. Some large producers use refrigeration and judicious filtration to make the wine softer and rounder without detracting from its native character.

All red wines must acquire bottle ripeness, during which time they throw

WINE REGIONS OF CENTRAL ITALY

SAN MARINO

RUFINA
(Chianti)

COLLI FIORENTINI
(Chianti)

Florence

COLLI PESARESI

MARCHES

VERDICCHIO DEI CASTELLI DI JESI

ROSSO CONERO

ONTALBANO
(Chianti)

VERDICCHIO DI MATELICA

LLINE PISANE
(Chianti)

ROSSO PICENO

IANTI CLASSICO

Siena

COLLI SENESI
(Chianti)

Perugia

COLLI ARETINI
(Chianti)

TUSCANY

UMBRIA

ELBA

BRUNELLO DI MONTALCINO

VINO NOBILE DI MONTEPULCIANO

ORVIETO

ALEATICO DI GRADOLI

LATIUM

Tiber R.

EST! EST!! EST!!!

Rome

FRASCATI
CASTELLI ROMANI

WILLIAM LEMBECK

SCALE

0   100 km

off their youthful roughness. Chianti is not given this opportunity when the raffia-covered *fiasco* is used because the shipper must pack and ship promptly. If he does not, he runs the risk of the raffia's deteriorating, with consequent loss through bottle breakage. The straw Chianti flask was originally made for home consumption and was never intended for export. It was not corked, and the wine was protected from the air by a film of olive oil. Since the *fiaschi* are becoming expensive, as well as being impractical, some producers are using the

View from Brolio Castle of the vineyard, winery, and offices in the heart of the Tuscan Chianti hills. (*Courtesy Ricasoli, Florence*)

Chiantiogiona bottle or other exclusively designed bottles. The best-quality Chianti is always found in the regular claret-style bottle, since the wine must rest and develop in the bottle for years. Such Chianti will be a splendid, soft, rounded, and mellow wine of great character. After three years of age it may be labeled Riserva; Riserva Chianti must also have a higher minimum alcohol content than non-Riserva Chianti.

For all its roughness, young Chianti is an ideal wine to drink with rich, well-seasoned, oily foods because its tartness is just the thing to help digest this rich food. Older Chiantis with bottle age have more elegance.

From Montepulciano, near Siena, comes another wine on the style of Chianti, called Vino Nobile, as well as the Vernaccia di San Gimignano, a light, dry, pleasant white wine with a slightly bitter aftertaste.

Southwest of Siena the hill town of Montalcino produces a noble red varietal wine called Brunello di Montalcino, made from a variety of the Sangiovese grape, the Brunello di Montalcino. It must spend at least four years in wood and is called a Riserva after five years. It is very long lived.

White wine has always been made in Tuscany, since white grapes such as the Trebbiano and Malvasia are grown in abundance. It used to be shipped as White Chianti, but the D.O.C. laws defined Chianti as a red wine. Even though the white wine is produced in the Chianti district, it is now shipped as Vino Bianco Toscano ("White Tuscan Wine").

The traditional white wine for which Tuscany justifiably does claim some fame is her Vin (Vino) Santo, a rich, generous, sweet dessert wine with a Muscat flavor and high alcohol content. Practically all winemakers in the region produce some. The white Trebbiano and Malvasia grapes are gathered when fully ripened and the bunches are strung on poles that are suspended under the attic-roof of the house. There they remain to dry until late December, when they will be pressed; the rich juice ferments very slowly during the cold winter months.

The historic island of Elba provides clean, pleasant, dry white, red, and rosé wines. The Trebbiano is the most important vine but there is some Sangiovese as well. Some iron ore in the soil gives these wines distinction.

MARCHES AND UMBRIA

The region of Marches on the Adriatic side of the peninsula is very hilly and exposed to the north wind. Several good wines are grown in this region. One in particular demands attention: the fine, light white wine Verdicchio dei Castelli di Jesi. It is one of Italy's distinguished white wines and the most crisply dry. It has a pale greenish cast and a delicate bouquet and flavor, with a slightly tart aftertaste. It is customarily shipped in a graceful green amphoralike bottle.

Another very similar wine, not as well known, is the Verdicchio di

Matelica. The same grapes are used as for the first Verdicchio, but in different blending proportions. In general, the reds of Marches are good, ordinary wines. The best known are Rosso Piceno, Rosso Conero, and Sangiovese dei Colli Pesaresi.

Farther southwest is Umbria, where the beautiful cities of Assisi, Perugia, and Orvieto are located. It is a land of pastoral beauty, temperate climate, and rolling hills through which flows the Tiber (Tevere) River. The well-drained soil is especially suited to growing grapes for fine white wines.

Traditionally, Orvieto wines have been bottled in a long-necked *fiasco* called *pulcinella*—without question a most impractical bottle. Fortunately, the D.O.C. laws permit a more practically shaped bottle, which does not have the expensive straw wrappings.

The white wines of Orvieto are both *secco* ("dry") and *abboccato* ("semi-dry"). The *abboccato* is sometimes affected by "noble rot," called *muffa nobile* in Italy. Both are light straw-colored and have a fruity freshness, with a bitter undertone. The premium Orvieto wines are labeled Classico.

LATIUM

Latium was the home of Horace, and his poetry tells of Tusculum (now called Frascati), of the vines that he grew, and of the trees that he loved so well.

The proud Romans left the shores of the Tiber for the pleasures of the countryside, and on the hills adjacent to Rome they built their villas. Hence the wines produced on the estates of these nobles are called Vini dei Castelli Romani.

Chiefly white wines are made, as the conditions of soil and climate are more favorable for them, but some good reds are made also.

In Rome every restaurant offers the light white Frascati; the red, white, and rosé Marino; and other Castelli Romani wines from the hills around Rome. These wines are most enjoyable when young and fresh.

A little farther north around the ancient town of Montefiascone on Lake Bolsena is produced a brilliant, straw-yellow dry wine with a fruity and fresh bouquet, poetically named Est! Est!! Est!!! While the wine is very good per se, the manner in which it got its name is most interesting.

As the story goes, a long time ago—perhaps four or five centuries—a German bishop named Johannes de Fuger was on his way to the Vatican to pay his respects to the Holy Father. Being a man of taste and discrimination, he sent his secretary-valet ahead to find suitable accommodations. Where the food, and especially the wine, was good, the valet was to write with chalk the word *Est* on the wall of the inn. When this good man tasted the wines at Montefiascone he could not describe them truthfully with just one "It is," so he chalked on the wall of the inn *Est! Est!! Est!!!* ("It is! It is!! It is!!!"). When

The traditional method of transporting wine in the Chianti region of Tuscany. (*Courtesy Julius Wile Sons & Co., Inc., New York*)

Trebbiano grapes hanging from the attic rafters to dry out before being pressed for making Vin Santo. (*Courtesy Ricasoli, Florence*)

A bottle label of Est! Est!! Est!!! shows the Bishop de Fuger's arrival at the Montefiascone Inn.

the bishop arrived he agreed with his valet's judgment. In fact, he tarried so long and drank so freely that he finally died at Montefiascone, without ever reaching Rome.

We wished to verify this story, and on our last visit to Italy we made a special trip to Montefiascone to find the bishop's tomb. It is there, just within the entrance to the Basilica of Saint Flaviano. The inscription is almost illegible from the thousands of feet that have trod the marble slab through the centuries, but one can still make out the words: *Est, Est, Est et propter nimium est, Johannes de Fuger, dominus meus, mortuus est,* which means, "It is, it is, it is, and through too much it is, my master, Johannes de Fuger, dead is."

The sequel to the story is that the grateful winemakers of Montefiascone who produce Est! Est!! Est!!! commemorate the anniversary of Bishop de Fuger's demise by spilling a barrel of Est! Est!! Est!!! wine over his tomb. So we may presume that his bones have continued throughout the centuries to enjoy uninterruptedly the wine he loved so well.

In the same area the sweet Aleatico di Gradoli is produced from the Aleatico (Moscato Nero) grape; it achieves a high alcohol content.

CAMPANIA

This region, dominated by Mount Vesuvius, is one of the most beautiful spots on earth. The dust of the volcano spreads imperceptibly over the land and fertilizes it. Hot springs and fissures evidence the volcanic nature of the soil.

The climate is ideal and vegetation is luxuriant—three crops a year are rotated on farms. The vine is cultivated intensely, for the area is limited and the demand worldwide. Falernum, prized by the Romans, has fallen from popularity, and in its stead rules Lacrima Christi.

The still Lacrima Christi, made in the shadow of Vesuvius, is a golden wine, not too dry, with a softness, delicacy, and somewhat aromatic bouquet that it gets from the hot volcanic soil. Some red Lacrima Christi is also made.

Today you can get both red and white Falerno, but this modern wine does not evoke the poetic rhapsodies of its ancient namesake, Falernum, of which Juvenal IX tells that Sufeja was able to drink thirty-five gallons at a sitting, without getting drunk, simply by tickling his throat with a peacock's feather. Gragnano, a dark red, rich, fruity wine, comes closer to the storied ancient wine. Red Taurasi, made from the Aglianico grape, and white Greco di Tufo, made principally from the Greco grape, are also popular wines in the region.

In this magical setting, surrounded by blue waters, lies Capri. Little original Capri wine is available, and most of it is used by the islanders themselves. More often than not, what we get is wine from the neighboring island of Ischia, where Ischia Rosso and Ischia Bianco are produced.

APULIA

One of the most prolific wine-growing regions is Apulia, or Puglia in Italian. It produces generous, alcoholic wines because of the great amount of sunshine that bathes the land. This region is known as the wine cellar of Italy, for the wines are commonly shipped to northern Europe for blending with wines with lower alcohol content. As much wine is produced in Apulia as in Piedmont and Lombardy combined.

Typical of the region are the sweet, liquorous, nectarlike Moscato di Salento, Moscato di Trani, and Aleatica di Puglia. The majority of the red wines are very dark in color and high in alcohol content, but they often lack acid. A few areas do produce better-balanced wines, such as Castel del Monte and San Severo, which are available in red, white, and rosé; and Santo Stefano and Torre Quarto, both of which are red. Castel del Monte wines are made with varying amounts of Bombino Nero, Bombino Bianco, and Uva di Troia grapes. The San Severo wines in the north are made with Bombino Bianco and Montepulciano. Santo Stefano and Torre Quarto, made in the northern province of Foggia from a variety of grapes, are very big red wines that can take up to ten years of aging.

CALABRIA

Here, in a wild country of bare, high mountains and fertile valleys, a country of contrasts, of chilly winds and tropical shores, the vine is cultivated extensively. It produces only good local wines of rather light alcohol content. Much *vin ordinaire* comes from this section.

The best wine of the region is the Cirò. The white is made from the Greco grape, and the red and rosé from the Gaglioppo grape. The red can be aged. A superb dessert wine, Greco di Gerace, is produced from the Greco Bianco grape. The wine is round, velvety, and rich in glycerine and has a bouquet reminiscent of orange blossoms.

SICILY

Homer speaks of Sicily as the land where "spontaneous wine from weighty clusters flows." "The Sicilians," said Plato, "build as if they were always to live, and sup as if they never were to sup again."

The soil of Sicily is incomparable for growing the grape and is so varied that every variety of vine finds suitable space.

The first to appreciate the enchanting beauty of the island were the English, who practically monopolized the output of Marsala, which produced Lord Nelson's favorite wine.

The volcanic regions of the occasionally active Mount Etna produce a wine of great strength and aggressive bouquet that is much in demand for blending with weaker wines in northern countries.

One of the great wines of Italy is Corvo, from an area near Palermo in western Sicily. The vineyards are kept with the same care and severity as the French employ in pruning and in growing for quality instead of quantity. This wine is a development of Duke Salaparuta, whose desire to improve viticulture in Sicily has been fulfilled. Corvo is a fine, dry wine, both red and white, with much character and the fieriness of Sicily racing through it.

Segesta is a mellow wine from the ancient Greek city of that name. It is available in both red and white.

Many sweet dessert wines are made in the western part of the island from the Zibibbo, which is a variety of the Moscato di Allessandria grape, and from several Malvasia varieties. Sicily is famous for Marsala, although recent figures show that Marsala accounts for only 40 percent of Sicily's wine production.

Marsala is a fortified wine obtained from the Catarratto, Grillo, and Inzolia grapes. It is sweet, is dark walnut brown in color, and has a rather acid undertone because of the volcanic nature of the soil in which the grapes grow. In this respect it comes close to Madeira but it does not resemble it. Marsala is an individual wine with its own character. It is a blended wine, and each producer maintains a *solera* system on the order of the Jerez houses (see Chapter 8).

Marsala also finds many uses in the kitchen, where it is indispensable for the making of zabaglione, scaloppine alla Marsala, and numerous sauces and desserts. In Italy there is a prepared egg and Marsala drink that is imported to the United States.

SARDINIA

The cork, the olive, and the vine grow well on the island of Sardinia. The wines are mostly heady, liquorous, and strong. "Drink this wine," said an unknown poet, "thou needest no garlands." Like nearby Sicily, Sardinia is better known for dessert wines than for table wines, but her well-known Vernaccia di Oristano is an exception. It is an amber-colored wine, dry and tonic, with a delicate almond-blossom bouquet and a pleasingly bitter tang. Nuragus is another good dry white wine, but Sardinia's two best-known red wines—Cannonau and Oliena—are too tannic and heavy for most visitors.

Moscato di Cagliari and Malvasia di Bosa are two white dessert wines with the characteristic flavor of the grape varieties from which they are made, while the Girò di Cagliari is a red dessert wine on the order of port.

HOW AND WHEN TO SERVE ITALIAN WINES

The wines of Italy run the gamut of the wines of the world. There are some with a rough, downright earthiness, and others with finesse and elegance. Some are meant to be drunk young, and others can be laid away. The lighter beverages may be drunk with simple foods or by themselves. The sturdier wines give the greatest enjoyment when served with rich, well-seasoned foods. The finest wines match the most complex dishes.

In the past decade Italian wines have improved considerably and are ranked among the finest in the world. They offer many advantages to the consumer: there is seldom a poor vintage year, there is seldom a scarcity of supply, and the prices are moderate. With the D.O.C. laws consumers are assured of consistent wines.

7

THE WINES OF GERMANY

As one sails down the Rhine between its vine-clad hills, the orderly beauty makes a profound impression. But one rarely recalls that this is the result of centuries of unremitting toil. Considering the perfect weather conditions that are required to produce a good wine even in such temperate regions as Bordeaux and Burgundy, one must marvel at the courage and tenacity of the vineyard owners of the Rhine and Moselle valleys, the northernmost wine regions in Europe.

No grape grower has ever had a more discouraging or difficult task than have these Rhenish farmers, but they have triumphed magnificently over the tremendous obstacles nature has placed before them—lack of heat, a variable climate from year to year, precipitous hillsides to which the vines cling precariously, and natural diseases of the vine. Fortunately the growing season is long, with more frost-free days in Germany than in other vine-growing areas. This enables Germany to rank tenth among wine-producing countries, contributing some of the world's great wines.

The greatness of German wines is indicated by the fabulous prices they occasionally fetch. While it is still in cask, a great Trockenbeerenauslese may bring as much as $75 a bottle at auction. This sort of wine is available only on rare occasions, of course, and then only at the large estates, where never more than one-quarter cask, or four hundred bottles, of this quality can be made. Little of this wine reaches the channels of commerce; it is generally purchased by private connoisseurs.

history   In Germany, as in France, the traditions of wine are intertwined with the roots of the country's history. As far back as the time of Charlemagne (A.D. 800) the vineyards of the Rhine, probably planted by the Romans of Caesar's time, enjoyed great fame.

During the eighteenth century most of the Rhine wine shipped to England was labeled Hochheimer. The English found this word difficult to pronounce and promptly shortened it to Hock. Today in all English-speaking countries the

116

term *Hock*, or *Hocks*, means Rhine wine. This, of course, does not include the wines of the Moselle or those from Franconia.

The monastic orders of the Church in Germany did much to develop viticulture. Johannisberg takes its name from the Chapel of Saint John, erected in A.D. 853 by the Bénédictine monks of Saint Alban's of Mainz. On this hill is the castle (*Schloss*) whose vineyard produces very fine Rhine wines.

GERMAN WINE LAW

The German government published a new wine law on July 19, 1969, which became effective on July 19, 1971. It aligned the old German law with the laws prevailing or being promulgated in other wine-producing countries of the European Economic Community. It also defined and controlled more strictly the different types of wine being made in Germany through the selective picking method. All German wines being sold as of the 1971 vintage and later vintages are subject to this law.

Under this new wine law there are three broad categories of German wines: Deutscher Tafelwein, Qualitätswein, and Qualitätswein mit Prädikat. Tafelwein is an ordinary wine that need not attain any particular alcoholic strength or come from any particular grape or place. However, it must be produced from approved grape varieties grown in Germany in one of the five major Tafelwein regions: Mosel, Rhein, Main, Neckar, and Oberrhein. The region must be designated on the label with the German spelling. The label may carry the name of a smaller community within the region, but it cannot specify the name of a vineyard. The name of the bottler (*Abfüller*) must appear on the label, and brand names may appear for further identification.

Qualitätswein and Qualitätswein mit Prädikat are wines made from permitted grape varieties and fermented in their areas of production. They have to contain a minimum must weight and be approved by an official tasting panel that assigns a control number to be printed on their labels. They must come from one of eleven regions, each of which is called a *Gebiet*, and their taste has to be characteristic of wines produced in that region. The next smaller geographic area from which the wines may come is a subregion known as a *Bereich*, or district. The subdistrict is called a *Grosslage* and is made up of several vineyard properties where the grapes are similar in taste. The smallest division is the *Lage*, or individual vineyard. The name of the region is always on the label of a Qualitätswein or a Qualitätswein mit Prädikat. The name of the *Bereich*, *Grosslage*, or *Lage* precedes or follows the local village name.

If the labels on these wines specify a grape variety, there must be at least 85 percent of that grape used, and the taste of the wine must be characteristic of the grape. If the labels carry a vintage year, the year specified must constitute 85 percent of the wines in the blend, and the taste must be characteristic of that year.

The inspection control number as it appears on the label of a bottle of German wine. (*Courtesy German Wine Information Bureau, New York*)

Tafelwein and Qualitätswein may be sugared before fermentation to bring up the alcohol content of the wine (this is also permitted when required in Burgundy and Bordeaux), but Qualitätswein mit Prädikat cannot have any sugar added to the must. The minimum must weight of wines in the last category is 75 *Öchsle,* a measure of the amount of sugar in the must; 75 *Öchsle* can yield a wine of 10 percent alcohol (see Appendix I). Qualitätswein mit Prädikat wines include Kabinett, Spätlese, Auslese, Beerenauslese, Trockenbeerenauslese, and Eiswein.

Kabinett wines must be made from ripe grapes that will ferment without the aid of additional sugar; the minimum must weight is 75 *Öchsle* (or 70 *Öchsle* in certain cold areas like the Moselle).

Spätlese wines must be made from fully ripened grapes gathered after the general harvest; the minimum must weight is about 80 *Öchsle,* depending on the region.

Auslese wines are made from fully ripened bunches of grapes gathered selectively for their ripeness at any time during the harvest; minimum must weight is about 90 *Öchsle,* depending on the region.

Beerenauslese wines must be made from individually selected ripe grapes; minimum must weight is about 120 *Öchsle,* depending on the region.

Trockenbeerenauslese wines must be made from individually selected, overripe, shrunken grapes that are attacked by the *Edelfäule* mold; minimum must weight is 150 *Öchsle* in every region.

Eiswein wines must be at least Kabinett wines but are made from grapes that were caught in a deep frost during harvest and pressed before thawing. Eiswein will appear on the label after the quality designation, for example, Auslese Eiswein.

Qualitätswein and Qualitätswein mit Prädikat, which include all of the above wines, must be made solely from permitted grape varieties. When sold, they must specify whether they are Qualitätswein or Qualitätswein mit Prädikat and carry a control number. As a further guarantee of quality, the German wine law has special provisions for listing the name of the producer, the person responsible for the wine. Every quality wine has to list the bottler (*Abfüller*) on the label. If the wine is bottled by the producer, the person who owns the vineyard, then the label states *Erzeugerabfüllung* ("bottled by the producer") or *aus eigenem Lesegut* ("from his own grapes"), both of which are similar to estate bottling in France. If a shipper bottles a wine coming from an estate, he can indicate this on the label by stating *aus dem Lesegut von* and the name of the estate. This means literally "out of the harvest of. . . ."

Trocken describes a wine that is extemely dry. These bone-dry wines are not typical of German wines in general and are more suitable to being served with food than they are to being served by themselves. Trocken has been permitted on labels since 1976.

Germany's wine quality control occurs in three stages:

1. During the grape harvest a wine grower must officially register the category of wines he intends to produce, such as Spätlese or Auslese, with the mayor of his town. Thus the government controls the quality of both the grapes and the must.

2. When bottling begins, the wine is analyzed by government officials. Only officially designated wine laboratories can make the chemical analysis.

The German wine-tasting panel at work. (*Courtesy German Wine Information Bureau, New York*)

3. Finally, the wine is tasted by a panel of experts. Clarity, bouquet, color, and flavor are checked on a standard point system. An official certification number is awarded only when the necessary points are recorded. The tasting commission retains sealed samples of the wine in case of consumer complaints.

The eleven designated regions of Qualitätswein and Qualitätswein mit Prädikat are different from the five regions of Tafelwein (see page 117). The eleven are Ahr, Mittelrhein, Mosel-Saar-Ruwer, Nahe, Rheingau, Rheinhessen, Rheinpfalz, Hessische Bergstrasse, Franken, Baden, and Württemberg.

labeling   The following designations are found on German wine labels:

Qualitätswein bestimmter Anbaugebiete—Q.b.A.—("quality wine of designated regions"). A quality wine bears the control number assigned by the tasting panel. It can be labeled by region (*Gebiet*), district (*Bereich*), subdistrict (*Grosslage*), or vineyard (*Lage*). The label usually bears the name of the village where the vineyards are located.

Qualitätswein mit Prädikat ("quality wine with distinction"). Wines in this category are divided, in ascending order, into Kabinett, Spätlese, Auslese, Beerenauslese, Trockenbeerenauslese, and Eiswein, as described previously.

It is customary for each fine wine to bear the branded cork of its producer; the cork must also have the official number of the bottler.

The new German wine law has consolidated vineyards. Germany had fifty thousand individual vineyards that the government consolidated in the two years before the 1971 law went into effect. No vineyard can now be less than $12\frac{1}{2}$ acres. As in Burgundy, these vineyards have many owners tending their own rows of vines and making their own wines.

geography   German viticulture is found in the Rhine Valley and the valleys of its tributaries, the Nahe and the Main, and in the Moselle Valley, with the valleys of its tributaries, the Saar and the Ruwer. The other important areas are Baden and Württemberg. (The Baden-Bodensee area is along the Rhine from Lake Constance to above Baden-Baden opposite Alsace; the Württemberg area includes vineyards on both sides of the Neckar River.)

The Rhine Valley, like all Gaul, is divided into three parts: the Rheingau, which embraces the right bank of the river from above Lorch to and including Hochheim on the Main; the Rheinhessen, which includes the land on the left bank of the river from Worms to Bingen and that lying between the Nahe and the Rhine; and the Rheinpfalz, or Palatinate, a triangle formed by the Rhine, the Harz Mountains, and the French border.

Rising in the Vosges Mountains, the Moselle River wanders through Lorraine, becomes part of the Franco-German border, continues northward to form the border between Luxembourg and Germany, and enters Germany

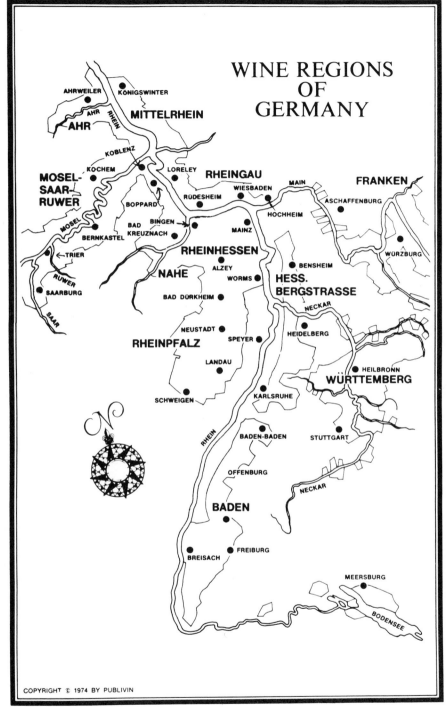

(*From Fritz [S. F.] Hallgarten,* A Guide to Vineyards, Estates, and Wines of Germany, *edited by Michel Roux, courtesy Publivin Publishing Company, Dallas, Texas*)

proper, where it is joined by the Saar and a little farther along by the Ruwer, from which point it winds and twists through its picturesque course until it reaches the Rhine at Koblenz.

Viticulturally, the Moselle Valley is divided into three parts: the Upper Moselle, from Wasserbillig (in Luxembourg) to Trier, with its famous cathedral; the Middle Moselle, from Trier to Traben-Trarbach, twin cities on opposite sides of the river; and the Lower Moselle, from the twin cities to Koblenz.

The Middle Moselle section is the most important from the standpoint of the number of famous vineyards; the valleys of the Saar and Ruwer, the Upper Moselle, have a few excellent wines; while the Lower Moselle produces none of importance.

Along the Main River are such famous cities as Würzburg and Karlstadt. The wines of this region are sold as Frankenwein and bottled in the distinctive *Bocksbeutel.*

Up to the turn of the century the regions of Baden, Bodensee, and Württemberg, with 100,000 acres of vines, made Bavaria the largest wine-producing area of Germany; but the destructions of pests, diseases, and wars reduced the vineyards by over 60 percent. It is only since World War II that serious efforts have been made to reestablish production of better-quality wines there.

soil

As in other wine regions of the world, the soil is most forbidding, suited to no other crop. The land is extremely rocky. The vineyards are planted along the steep, terraced slopes of the hills. The terraces are very narrow and must be maintained constantly, a task that must be carried on by hand. The slopes are so steep that carts cannot be used. In the Moselle Valley there is a predominance of slate in the soil, to which is attributed the "slatey" dryness of the wines.

grape varieties

The *plante noble* of the Rhine and Moselle vineyards is the Riesling. It is a small grape that produces abundantly and ripens very late. When nature smiles, the grape gives a glorious wine full of character, perfume, and body.

The Müller-Thurgau grape, a cross between the Riesling and the Sylvaner, is the biggest producer. Today 26 percent of all the grapes grown in Germany are Müller-Thurgau. It is found in nearly all districts, although the top Rheingau and Moselle vineyards are still planted entirely with Riesling. The main attraction of the Müller-Thurgau is that it ripens earlier than other varieties. It produces very pleasant, highly aromatic, and light-bodied wines.

The Sylvaner is grown in the Rheingau, the Rheinhessen, the Rheinpfalz, Baden, Württemberg, Nahe, and Franconia.

The Traminer, also called Gewürztraminer, is grown mainly in Baden-Württemberg, the Palatinate, and Rheinhessen. It is used both for blending with other varieties and for making spicy wine by itself.

The Ruländer, or Pinot Gris of Burgundy, is one of the most widely grown varieties in Baden. It can and does produce some charming wines with full aroma and flavor.

A complete list of all the grape varieties and the regions in which they are planted appears in Appendix F. New strains are being developed which produce greater yields with higher sugar content. These new grapes will mean more Qualitätswein mit Prädikat wines in the future at reasonable prices, but the wines will not have the longevity of wines made from the classical varieties.

The Blauer Spätburgunder is the Pinot Noir of Burgundy and Champagne fame and, along with the Portugieser grape, is used to produce the few red wines of the Rheinpfalz, Ahr Valley, Baden, and Rheinhessen. It is not her red wines, however, which on the whole are rather thin and commonplace, on which Germany's vinicultural fame rests, but the magnificence of her white wines.

vintage

When the summer has been sunny, with at least 100 days of sun between May and October, there will be a good wine; if there are 120 days of sun there will be a great wine. The date of the general harvest is set by each village and is subject to strict regulations. If the sun holds, the grower picks only part of his crop right away and leaves the rest to be picked later, allowing the remaining grapes to become even riper. This means a sacrifice of quantity. The grapes that are picked later are made into wines designated as Spätlese, Auslese, Beerenauslese, and Trockenbeerenauslese.

Three weeks after the general harvest, Spätlese (*Spät*—"late," *lese*—"picking") takes place. Only fully ripened bunches of grapes are gathered. Auslese (*Aus*—"selected," *lese*—"picking") means that each bunch of grapes is gathered selectively as it ripens, any time during the harvest. Auslese wines are sweeter, richer, and fuller than Spätlese wines; these designations are strictly controlled by the specific density of the must.

Often *Edelfäule* can be discerned in great Spätlese and Auslese wines. *Edelfäule*, a mold that forms on the skin of the grape, reducing its moisture and concentrating its richness, occurs in great years, producing a full and luscious wine. The mold, *Botrytis cinerea*, is also known as "noble rot" in English and *pourriture noble* in French. It is usually present in Beerenauslese (*Beeren*—"berry," *auslese*—"selected picking"), a top-designated wine made from individually selected berries. If all the individual grapes are dried and shriveled as a result of *Edelfäule*, then Trockenbeerenauslese (*Trocken*—"dry," *beeren-auslese*—"selected berry picking"), the highest-designated wine, is made. It is very rich, luscious, elegant, and costly.

The wines are bottled very young—from six to eighteen months. Even the great wines are bottled young, as they live longer in bottle when they spend less time in wood. Most are equalized by blending the wine of many casks before bottling, although some casks are bottled separately, and the price is determined by the quality of each cask.

Harvesting grapes near the ruins of Castle Ehrenfels at Rüdesheim on the Rhine. (*Courtesy German Wine Information Bureau, New York*)

WINES OF THE RHEINGAU

On the right bank of the Rhine, from above Lorch to Hochheim, is the celebrated Rheingau, one of the most famous viticultural regions in the world. Compared with other wine-growing regions of Germany, this is one of the smallest—but its wines are famous, many of them unsurpassed anywhere. Among the better-known villages in the Rheingau that have become famous over the years on wine labels are:

Eltville	Johannisberg
Erbach	Kiedrich
Geisenheim	Oestrich
Hallgarten	Rauenthal
Hattenheim	Rüdesheim
Hochheim	Winkel

In this area are the well-known estates of Schloss Johannisberg, Schloss Vollrads, Schloss Eltz, Schloss Schönborn, and Schloss Reinhartshausen, the last belonging to the Prinz zu Preusen. The most famous vineyards of this area are Steinberger, the largest single vineyard under one ownership in this region, belonging to the state government and bearing a German eagle on its label; Schloss Johannisberg; and Marcobrunn. Marcobrunn is traditionally translated as "spring of Saint Marcus," as *Brunn* means "spring," and many German locations are named after saints. But the inscription on the arch over the spring is *Gemarkung,* which means "boundary" or "marking." As the spring is on the boundary between the towns of Hattenheim and Erbach, Marcobrunn is also taken to mean "boundary or marking spring."

Charlemagne is supposed to have selected the site for Schloss Johannisberg, although it is more than likely that wines from the Johannisberg hill vineyards already existed in his time. During the French Revolution the vineyard and castle on the crest of the hill came into the possession of William, Prince of Orange, from whom it was confiscated by Napoleon after the Battle of Jena. Napoleon presented the prize to Marshall Kellermann, Duke of Valmy, whose name, appropriately enough, means "cellarman."

After the Battle of Waterloo the vineyard again changed hands, passing to the Austrian emperor Franz I, who, in gratitude for services rendered, presented the castle and vineyards in perpetuity to his great chancellor, Prince von Metternich-Winneburg, whose descendants still own it.

The wines of all these vineyards combine every attribute of greatness in a good year. They have bouquet, body, flavor, character, and breed. The Rheingau wines generally have an austere fruitiness and a certain hardness, in which lies their character. They are the longest lived of all German wines.

WINES OF THE RHEINHESSEN

Rheinhessen is Germany's second-largest wine-producing region. Wines from here are softer and fuller than those of the Rheingau. The main villages producing fine wines are:

Bingen	Nackenheim
Bodenheim	Nierstein
Dienheim	Oppenheim
Laubenheim	Worms
Mettenheim	

At the southern border of the Rheinhessen is the rather dull, smoky, gray town of Worms. Neither dull nor gray are the legends about Worms, however, for it is the locale of the ancient story of the Nibelungs, of Siegfried's marriage to Brünnhilde and his death by treachery.

Within the city limits of Worms stands the *Liebfrauenkirche* ("Church of Our Beloved Lady"). Surrounding it is a vineyard that has produced wines of some renown for many centuries—first under monastic or ecclesiastic control, but since secularization at the beginning of the nineteenth century as the private property of a number of people. The vineyard is called Liebfrauen-stift-Kirchenstück and is now owned by two shippers, Langenbach and Valckenberg.

The wines from this site (*Lage*) or vineyard are nearly always estate bottled and the labels normally read Wormser Liebfrauenstift-Kirchenstück. The word or name *Liebfraumilch* does not appear on the label. The wines are pleasant and good but somewhat lighter in body and character than those from the better Hessian vineyards of Nierstein and Oppenheim.

Liebfraumilch   Liebfraumilch is without question the best-known German wine name. Liebfraumilch is not a vineyard or a district, but rather a collective name for Rhine wine, just as Moselblümchen is for Moselle wine.

Tradition has it that the name derives from the *Liebfrauenkirche* of Worms. Who invented and first used the name is not clear, but it has been in use since 1744. Originally Liebfraumilch applied only to Rheinhessen wines, but today, and since a court decision of 1910, "the name of Liebfraumilch applies exclusively to Rhine wines of good quality and delightful character." This is recognized by present-day German wine-labeling regulations, which have defined the area from which the wines come and the quality they must attain. They must all be wines of Qualitätswein bestimmter Anbaugebiete quality.

In most cases Liebfraumilch is a blended wine. The better, more responsible shippers employ mostly the finer Hessian wines for their Liebfraumilch blends. To distinguish their individual blends, they identify their Liebfraumilch with an added registered trademark. Examples are Blue Nun, Hanns Christof Wein, Crown of Crowns, Madonna, Seagull, Sonne des Rheins, Glockenspiel, and Wedding Veil.

Liebfraumilch is an all-purpose German wine, usually of consistent quality from vintage to vintage.

WINES OF THE NAHE

One of the less well-known areas of Germany is that surrounding the Nahe, a stream that lies between the Moselle and the Rhine, into which it flows at historic Bingen. The wines harmoniously blend the hearty, masculine quality of good Rhines with the light tingle of Moselles. They are not as sturdy as the one, not as light as the other. Growing and shipping are both centered in Bad Kreuznach, where the wizard Professor Dr. Faustus once taught. The best-known villages producing fine wines are:

Kreuznach	Rüdesheim (not to be confused
Langenlonsheim	with the Rüdesheim in the Rheingau)
Niederhausen an der Nahe	Schloss Böckelheim
Norheim	

WINES OF THE RHEINPFALZ

The Palatinate (Rheinpfalz region) is the largest wine-growing area in Germany. The Upper Palatinate (südlicher Weinstrasse) produces the largest amount of table wine in Germany, the wine that is the daily diet in the German *weinstube*. In addition to several good white wines, this area produces 25 percent of all German red wines, most of which are drunk locally and seldom exported. Palatinate wines are known for their earthiness and full body.

The area best known for wines of great quality is the Mittelhaardt in the Palatinate. Unlike other German wines, those produced here are heavy, earthy, and long lived. The finest communities producing wine in the Rheinpfalz region are:

Bad Dürkheim	Königsbach
Deidesheim	Mussbach
Edenkoben	Neustadt
Forst	Ruppertsberg
Hambach	Wachenheim
Kallstadt	

Workers in the vineyards of the Rheinhessen district. (*Courtesy German Wine Information Bureau, New York*)

WINES OF THE MOSELLE

Moselle wines have a charming lightness, delicacy, fruity bouquet, elegance, and dryness that is most pleasing. But their most appealing quality is their spritz, or tingling sharpness, as though they were trying to be sparkling wines—and almost succeeding. The quality disappears after a few years, so Moselles are best when young because they are livelier and racier.

The soil of the Moselle Valley is, if such is possible, more forbidding than that in any other region, and harvesting is proportionately more difficult. The vineyard owners carry up the steep slopes pieces of slate that have been washed down the hillsides by the spring freshets, and as they go through the vineyards they laboriously arrange and rearrange the bits of slate so that they will preserve the warmth of the sun during the cool nights and help the development of the roots. It is to this backbreaking toil and infinite patience that we owe an exquisite glass of wine.

Moselle wines are the lightest fine wines made. They are very low in alcohol content, between 8 and 10 percent by volume, which is part of their charm.

There are two ways of recognizing the difference between Rhine and Moselle wines without opening the tall, flute-shaped bottle or tasting the wine. One is the color of the bottle, as Rhine wines always come in brown bottles, and the Moselle bottles are always dark green. The other is by the township name. The towns along the Rhine as a rule end in *heim*, while those of the Moselle do not. (There are, however, exceptions to this rule.)

It is simple to detect the differences in character in the wines of the Rheingau, Rheinhessen, and Rheinpfalz, but we have never found anyone who can make a similar claim about the wines of the Moselle, Saar, and Ruwer. They are all equally pleasant and intriguing, so it is not a matter of great importance.

One of the most famous vineyards of the Moselle is the Doctor at Bernkastel. In the year 1360, according to legend, Boemund II, Archbishop of Trier, fell ill with a fever while on a visit to Bernkastel. The doctors of the region did not know what to do for him. But Ritter von Holstein, whom the bishop had helped, recalled that he had cured himself of a similar ailment. He brought his finest Bernkastel wine to the bishop and told him, "Drink this and it will cure you." The bishop did so and fell into a sound sleep. The next day he awoke to find the fever gone. "This wine!" he cried. "This splendid doctor has cured me!" Since that day, over six hundred years ago, the vineyard has been known as the Doctor vineyard.

According to the records, the Bernkasteler Doctor *Lage* was the property of the Grafs von Hunolstein until the middle of the seventeenth century, when it passed to the Grafs von der Leyen, who held possession until 1804, when it was acquired by Anton Cetto, the mayor of Bernkastel, from whom it was eventually inherited by his nephew, Nikolaus Lauerburg. In 1882 the Lauerburgs sold a part of the vineyard to the Thanisch family and in 1900 they sold another portion to the Deinhards of Koblenz. The portion of the vineyard that Karl and Walter Lauerburg own today is planted with the original, ungrafted Riesling vines.

Because of the fame of the vineyard, the demand always exceeds the supply and, like Château d'Yquem, the wine fetches considerably higher prices than its neighbors.

Another famous vineyard in the Middle Moselle is Wehlener Sonnenuhr ("the sundial of Wehlen"), and its wine commands almost as high a price in the marketplace as Bernkasteler Doctor.

The sundial at Wehlen on the Moselle. (*Courtesy Joh. Jos. Prüm, Wehlen*)

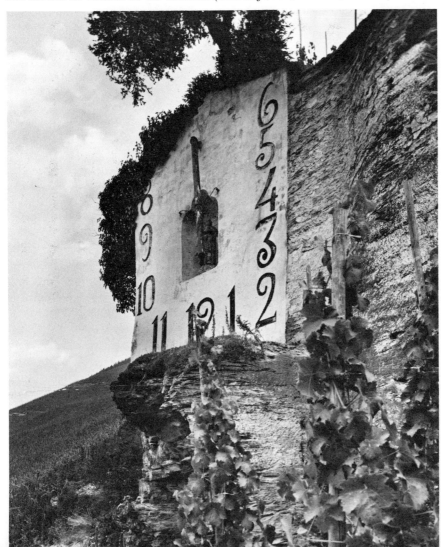

The villages that produce excellent wines are:

MOSELLE	SAAR
Bernkastel	Ayl
Brauneberg	Oberemmel
Dhron	Ockfen
Erden	Wiltingen
Graach	
Kröv	RUWER
Piesport	
Traben-Trarbach	Eitelsbach
Trittenheim	Maximin Grünhaus
Ürzig	Waldrach
Wehlen	
Zell	
Zeltingen	

Other well-known vineyards that produce superb wines in the Middle Moselle are Trittenheimer Apotheke, Dhroner Hofberg, Piesporter Goldtröpfchen, Graacher Himmelreich, Josephshöfer (the property of the Kesselstatt family), Zeltinger Himmelreich, Zeltinger Sonnenuhr, Erdener Treppchen, and Brauneberger Juffer.

Two fine vineyards on the Saar are Scharzhofberger and Ockfener Bockstein.

Moselblümchen ("little flower of the Moselle") is a name used for a blended Moselle made of wines coming from anywhere in the region. It is not a vineyard but a pleasant little wine, sold invariably as Tafelwein.

WINES OF BADEN-WÜRTTEMBERG

While the states of Baden and Württemberg have been officially merged, their wine regions remain distinctively separate, each having wines of its own special taste. The Black Forest separates most of Baden from Württemberg, but in the northern section there is little difference in wines grown along stretches of the Neckar River.

Along the shores of Lake Constance in southern Baden, the so-called lake wine, or Seewein, is the traditionally pink-tinted Weissherbst, a white wine pressed from red Spätburgunder grapes. Actually, the better-quality red wines of the Baden-Württemberg region are made from the Spätburgunder grape. The Gutedel (the Swiss Chasselas) and Ruländer (the French Pinot Gris) produce the popular white wines, which are both very rich and fruity and in the big years quite full bodied.

Württemberg produces more red wine than white, and most of the wines are consumed locally. The best white wine is Riesling, followed by Sylvaner. The important red-wine grape variety in Württemberg from the standpoint of quantity is the Trollinger, which produces a rather light wine. Better red wines are obtained from the Spätburgunder vine, originally the Pinot Noir of Burgundy.

FRANKEN WINES IN BOCKSBEUTEL

Finally we come to Würzburg and its squat, flasklike *Bocksbeutel.* Würzburg's robust wines, made largely from Müller-Thurgau and Sylvaner grapes, possess more body, hardness, and keeping qualities than the Rhine and Moselle wines. They also take longer to develop. The outstanding communities are Würzburg, Escherndorf, Iphofen, Randersacker, and Veitshochheim. The outstanding vineyards are the Würzburger Stein and Würzburger Leiste, which are parceled out among a number of proprietors, including two public institutions—the Juliusspital and Burgerspital—and the Bavarian Staatliche Kellerei (the organization controlling the Bavarian state-owned vineyards).

All Franken wines are sold in the traditional flat, squat *Bocksbeutel* (see page 7).

German vintages

The wide variation in vintage conditions causes considerable difference in delicate wines. An evaluation of recent German vintages and a vintage chart are given in Appendix B.

to sum up

It is not true that a wine must bear a famous name to be good. Much excellent, clean, pleasant wine comes to us labeled simply with the township name, such as Bernkastel, Piesport, Brauneberg, Rüdesheim, Hochheim, and Nierstein, or with a generic name, such as Moselblümchen or Liebfraumilch. Inevitably, in describing the wines of a region, one talks more about the great names than about the smaller. But what we have said about the fine wines of a locality applies generally, to a lesser degree, to the other wines of the same place.

Most German wines, particularly the smaller ones, are at their best when the fresh bloom of youth is on them. In fact, we recommend that they be drunk when they are under ten years old, except for the very fine Auslese, Beerenauslese, and Trockenbeerenauslese wines. Almost any recent vintage from 1971 through 1976 will be enjoyable. These are not wines to keep for years, although the top wines from great vintages, such as 1971, 1975, and 1976, will live a long time.

SEKT

West Germany is the world's largest producer and consumer of sparkling wine. Almost 220 million bottles are consumed annually there. (Worldwide consumption of Champagne from France averages over 150 million bottles yearly.) Most of this wine is marketed in West Germany as Sparkling Hock (Rhine wine only), Sparkling Liebfraumilch, or Sparkling Moselle. When sparkling wine is exported, the term *Sekt,* or *Schaumwein,* is used since the use of the word *Champagne* is forbidden in Germany by treaty with France for anything but true French Champagne.

Sekt is made by all the known sparkling wine production methods. The more reputable houses employ the traditional *méthode champenoise.* Sekt is a pleasantly fruity wine that comes in varying degrees of sweetness, as does Champagne. Most are somewhat sweet, but those marked Trocken are dry.

HOW AND WHEN TO SERVE GERMAN WINES

White wines, light wines, fresh wines go well with almost all foods, particularly those that come from the sea. They are dry and sharp, without being acid, and when they are sweet they are not cloying. A well-chilled bottle of Moselle wine is the summer luncheon or dinner wine par excellence.

Another pleasant way to drink German wines is with soda water, mixed half and half. This produces a spritzer. Having a pleasing, flowery perfume, German wines also lend themselves admirably to punches.

German wines are often drunk by themselves after a meal instead of with the meal. In Germany they are commonly served at eleven A.M.—the equivalent of a U.S. coffee break.

8
THE WINES OF SPAIN

The first records of Iberia tell of intrepid Phoenician sailors and merchants establishing trading posts. Before long the vine was planted, for nothing else would grow in the hard clay soil.

During the period of Rome's greatness the Iberian Peninsula did a thriving *history* business with the Romans, as is indicated by the wine jars of Spanish make found among the ruins of Pompeii.

Even during the suzerainty of the Moors, the vine flourished and prospered under the patronage of the Alhambra caliphs.

1. SHERRY

It is Jerez de la Frontera and its renowned sherry wine that concern us most when we think of Spanish viniculture. Jerez has been a formally constituted trading post, town, and city for at least three thousand years. It was first a Phoenician outpost and town called Xera. During the Roman era it was called Seritium; later the Moorish kings and caliphs spelled it Scherris. Its present name, Jerez de la Frontera, was granted officially by King Don Juan I in his royal decree of April 21, 1380.

A first impression a visitor has of Jerez is that of a very clean, peaceful city with endless whitewashed walls. One feels at once that this is the way it has been always and the way it will continue to be.

Throughout the centuries the region has produced wines that have always won high praise, beginning with the Roman Martial, to Chaucer, Shakespeare, and Samuel Pepys. But the history of sherry wine, as we know it today, began four centuries ago, when an enterprising wine merchant decided to take some wine to England, his vessel laden with casks branded:

VINO DE JEREZ
SACA

Arriving on the Thames, he discovered not only that the English could neither read nor speak Spanish but that they refused to try. If they had to use foreign words, and they did not take kindly to the idea, at least they would see that the words sounded as English as possible. The word *Jerez* (*heh-rehz*) they promply Anglicized to *jerries, sherries,* and finally to its present form, *sherry.*° *Saca,* after passing through several transmutations, became *sack.†* *Sherry* is, therefore, simply the English spelling of the Spanish *Jerez.*

Jerez de la Frontera is the city around which the sherry vineyards lie and the sherry trade revolves. The principal shippers have their *bodegas* ("warehouses") there, and the vast reserves of wine that make possible sherry as we know it are kept in Jerez, Puerto de Santa María, and Sanlúcar de Barrameda.

Jerez de la Frontera is in the province of Andalucia, the southernmost part of Spain, and to understand the wine of the region one must know something about the Spaniard, particularly the Andaluz.

Spain is a confederation of the thirteen ancient kingdoms and peoples who have always inhabited the Iberian Peninsula. It has never been and perhaps never will be one people. Even today the Catalan from Barcelona speaks a different language from the Castilian of Madrid; he has different customs and, although he carries a Spanish passport, he will always, and with pride, call himself a Catalan—not a Spaniard. Most Spaniards, then, are regionally rather than nationally minded.

In Andalucia there is brilliant sunshine and the people are gay; they dress in flaming colors and worship objects of beauty, whether they be gardens, Arabian stallions, or the magnificent sherry wine. The Andaluz is the Spaniard of romantic song and story.

"Para los gustos, Dios hizo los colores" ("To please our tastes, God created colors"), say the Andalucians, and this proverb applies most aptly to the wines of Jerez. For in sherry, as in a rainbow, almost any shade of color and taste may be found.

Pasquil's *Palinodia* (1619) contains one of the countless encomiums to sherry:

> Give me Sacke, old Sacke, Boys!
>   To make the muses merry
> The life of mirth and the joy of the earth
>   Is a cup of good old Sherry.

° Manuel Ma. González Gordon in his definitive *Jerez-Xerez-Scheris* attributes the present-day English spelling of *sherry* as "obviously a corruption of *Scherrisch,* the old Moorish name of the town."

† The word *sack* as a term meaning sherry is archaic. Its rightful use today is limited to the registered trademark of the sherry shippers Williams & Humbert.

WINE
REGIONS
OF
SPAIN

WILLIAM LEMBECK

The greatest and best salesman sherry ever had was not, strictly speaking, in the trade, but he liked sherry so much that he wrote about it constantly. His name was William Shakespeare. Sherry and sack crop up often in his plays, but most of all in *Henry IV*, in the words of Falstaff. "A good Sherris-sack," said the immortal rogue, "hath a two-fold operation in it. It ascends me into the brain; dries me there all the foolish and dull and crudy vapours which environ it; makes it apprehensive, quick, forgetive, full of nimble, fiery, and delectable shapes; which delivered o'er to the voice—the tongue—which is the birth, becomes excellent wit."

And Samuel Pepys, most famous of all diarists, refers often to sack, indicating that he must have been very partial to it.

geography   Andalucia, the most southern province of Spain, extends from the Portuguese frontier on the west to the Mediterranean on the east.

The sherry district lies between the Guadalquivir and the Guadalete rivers, with the Atlantic seaboard on the west and a line paralleling the coast a few miles north of Jerez on the east. Nature has endowed this little piece of land with qualities that are unique, although a "sherry" is made wherever grapes are grown. In this region all types of sherries are produced, from the very driest to the sweetest.

soil   Three predominating types of soil divide the region into three sections. Around and a little to the north of Jerez itself is found the *albariza*—a soil composed primarily of chalk, magnesium, clay, and lime—from which the finest sherries are produced. Each producer must use grapes from the *albariza* zone for at least 40 percent of his production.

South of Jerez is the *barros* (clay). This reddish clay contains a great deal of iron. Both *barros* and *albariza* produce from $2\frac{1}{2}$ to 3 butts (132-gallon casks) of wine per acre.

The *arenas* (sandy soil) is found toward the seashore and near the rivers. The *arenas* produces as much as six butts to the acre, but as quantity increases, quality decreases.

grape varieties   The Palomino is the classic and finest grape variety grown for making sherry wine. Ninety percent of the vines planted in the Jerez region are Palomino. The *albariza* vineyards are planted almost exclusively with it. The Mantúo Castellano, Mantúo de Pila, and Cañocazo are of secondary importance. Finally there is the Pedro Ximenez, which is used for making very sweet wines and for blending sherries, which are important to U.S. distillers in making their blended whiskies.

All the Jerez vineyards were destroyed by *Phylloxera*, which invaded the region toward the end of the nineteenth century. Since then the traditional varieties have had to be grafted onto American *Phylloxera*-resistant rootstocks. This grafting resulted in a 20 percent increase in production.

vintage   The actual gathering of the grapes begins when they are fully ripened. This varies from year to year, from the last week of August to the second week of September, depending on the climatic conditions of the preceding summer months. However, the feast of the Nativity of the Virgin, which falls anywhere from September 8 to September 12, is the usual official commencement of the vintage.

Under the auspices of San Ginés de la Jara, patron of winemakers, the gay, very colorful *Fiesta de la Vendimia* ("Vintage Festival") is celebrated for four days. There is pageantry, fireworks, a horse show, a solemn *Te Deum*, the

WILLIAM LEMBECK

Guada lquivir R.

Sanlúcar
de Barrameda

Macharnudo
(amontillados)

Carrascal
(olorosos)

Miraflores
(manzanillas)

Añina
(finos)

Balbaina
(finos)

Los Tercios
(finos)

Guadalete R.

Jerez de
la Frontera

Puerto de
Santa María

Cadiz

SCALE

0   5   10 km

Albariza
(chalky soil)

Barros and arenas
(clay and sand)

DELIMITED SHERRY ZONE

treading of a "first" butt of wine, and much happy singing and flamenco dancing. Hundreds of white pigeons, each bearing an original verse in praise of sherry, are released into the bright, sunlit sky from the steps of the *Real é Insigne Iglesia Colegial* to announce to all Spain the beginning of the new sherry vintage.

After the *Te Deum* within the church, a colorful ceremony takes place on the steps before the image of San Ginés de la Jara. Baskets of Palomino grapes, borne by the vintage queen and her maids of honor, who are dressed in traditional local costumes, are blessed by the monsignor and then emptied into a specially erected *lagar,* or "pressing trough." Four treaders, who have won the honor, tread and press out this "first" butt of the new vintage.

Meanwhile, in the vineyards the work of the vintage goes on in all its intensity. The heavily laden rows of Palomino vines growing on the grayish white *albariza* soil of the best districts of Macharnudo, Balbaina, Carrascal, Añina, and Los Tercios are invaded by men with sharp knives. They cut the large bunches of grapes, placing them in baskets, which are then carried by cart or in panniers on muleback to the whitewashed pressing house in the center of each vineyard. Here the baskets are emptied onto round woven *esparto* grass mats in the yard. The grapes are allowed to dry in the sun for twelve to fourteen hours. If they remain overnight they are covered with similar mats to protect them from the dew.

In the cool of early morning, beginning at three o'clock and continuing until noon, the grapes are brought into the pressing hall. This is a long, narrow room lined along one side with a battery of wooden pressing troughs, the *lagares.* They are sixteen to eighteen feet square and about two feet deep, and they are tilted forward from the wall to permit the juice to run freely through a doorlike opening. The *lagar* is raised three feet above the floor. Sixty baskets, or fifteen hundred pounds, of golden Palomino grapes are the precise *marc* for each *lagar;* when treaded and pressed, the *marc* fills one butt.

Four men work each *lagar.* Wearing special treading shoes, with properly spaced hobnails, they work the mass with a mincing sort of backward and forward dance step until the grapes are broken into a pulp. The mass is then sprinkled with several handfuls of gypsum (calcium sulfate) to ensure an increased tartaric acid content in the wine. Then comes the actual pressing. From the center of the *lagar* a screw post rises about seven feet. Using wooden spades, the men pile the grape mass evenly around the screw post and simultaneously wrap an eighty-two-foot-long woven grass ribbon around the grape mass to hold it in place. A wooden block is slipped over the screw post and above it is placed a threaded sleeve with two three-foot handles, which the men grasp and begin to turn. The juice gushes forth, filtered through the grass ribbon, out of the *lagar* and into the waiting butt.

Although this treading and pressing method is the traditional one that has been employed for many generations, rising labor costs have forced the sherry producers to develop new, automated methods. Today grapes are carried by truck to mechanized pressing stations where they are destemmed and crushed in modern presses.

The butts of freshly expressed must (juice) are trucked at once to the shippers' *bodegas* in Jerez, Puerto de Santa María, or Sanlúcar de Barrameda. They are placed in the fermenting warehouse and allowed to become wine. For the first week or so the fermentation process is violent. The must hisses, bubbles, and boils until most of the grape sugar has been converted. Fermen-

LEFT: Palomino grapes arriving at pressing house yard in panniers and spread on *esparto* grass mats to dry in the sun.

BELOW: Typical Jerez vineyard pressing house, showing treaders working ten *lagares*.

ABOVE: Grape mass being built up about the central post in the *lagar* ("pressing trough"). Note that the mass is held in place by a ribbon of woven *esparto* grass wrapped around it.

RIGHT: Hobnail Jerez treading shoes. (*Photos courtesy Julius Wile Sons & Co., Inc., New York*) tation then continues at a quieter, more leisurely pace through December, when the wine falls bright, which means that the insolubles have precipitated to form the lees and the wine has clarified itself. It will be racked off into fresh butts, which are filled only to seven-eighths of their capacity to allow the *flor* to develop.

In the ordinary sense of winemaking the grape juice has by this time become wine; however, it is still called *mosto,* since it has not yet become sherry. For this to occur, the unique phenomenon of the *flor* ("flowering") must take place.

flowering   *Flowering* is the term used to describe the development and growth, sometimes to a thickness of over a quarter of an inch, of the yeast film on the surface of the wine. It is a natural yeast associated with that which produced the original fermentation. The *flor* appears most strongly each spring and autumn. Together with matters of soil and climate, the *flor* contributes to sherry's distinctive characteristics, especially its delicacy, aroma, and nuttiness.

Flowering is peculiar to sherry. The only other wine-growing regions we know of where flowering has occurred naturally are South Africa, Russia, and in the Jura Mountains of France.

classifying   The new wine is carefully examined and classified. Sherry is the most
the new wines   unpredictable of all wines, and when the winemaker presses his grapes, he has not the slightest idea of the type of sherry wine that will result. No two butts of must ferment into identical wines, even though the must has come from grapes of the same vineyard, was pressed at the same time, and has been treated identically. No one knows what causes this variation.

Some butts show signs of developing into the pale-colored, light, delicate fino type and have a thick *flor* layer; others have a deeper color and fuller body and a very thin layer of *flor,* indicating that they will become the oloroso type; while other butts develop coarsely and will be separated for distilling or will become vinegar.

A simple system of chalk marks has evolved through the centuries to identify these various qualities. The butts of the palest and finest wines are marked with one stroke / (*raya*); these are destined to be finos. The heavier wines receive two strokes // (*dos rayas*); these are destined to be olorosos. Lower-quality wines are marked with three strokes /// (*tres rayas*); ordinary wines to be used for seasoning and cleaning casks receive four strokes //// (*cuatro rayas*); and a grid ⧢ (*parilla*) marks the wines to be distilled or to be removed from the winery and turned into vinegar. These and the additional marks used in further classification vary somewhat from one sherry shipper to another.

At the time of the first classification the new wines are lightly fortified with brandy. The *rayas* have their alcohol content raised to 15 or $15\frac{1}{2}$ percent, and

FLOWLINE CHART OF A SOLERA SYSTEM

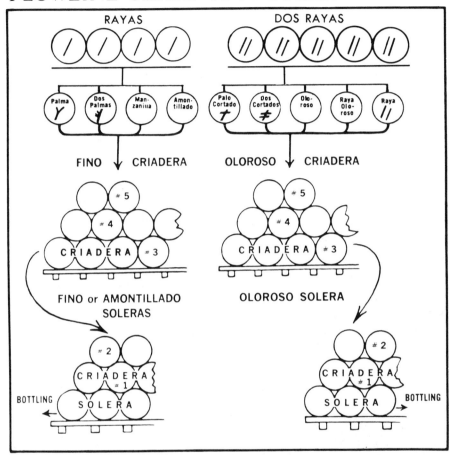

the *dos rayas* are fortified more strongly, to 17 percent. Since *flor* disappears at 16 percent, only the *rayas* continue to be affected by it during further development.

During the next year or two the *bodega* master, or *capataz*, continues the tasting and classification so that he can decide on the final type of wine that will develop and which *solera* it will eventually refresh.

He uses an instrument called the *venencia*, employed only in Jerez—a tall, narrow silver cup attached to the end of a long, springy whalebone handle. It is a tricky gadget, the use of which requires considerable skill. The cup is dipped deep into the butt through the bung in order to get a sample of clear wine. Then it is withdrawn and the wine is poured into a glass from a height, all in one motion. This looks simple until the uninitiated tries it, when he will discover that he is more likely to pour the wine down his sleeve than into the glass.

The original *rayas* are divided into *palmas*, one ⟋ , two ⟍⟋ , three ⟍⟍⟋ , and four ⟍⟍⟍⟋ , according to quality and age; these are true finos.

Manzanilla describes a fino made or matured in Sanlúcar de Barrameda, where the sea air imparts an echo of saltiness to the wine.

Amontillado is a *raya* that has become nuttier, fuller bodied, and darker than the finos.

Some original *dos rayas* develop fino characteristics and are divided into *palo cortado*, one ⟋̵ , two ≠ , three ≢ , and four ⫤ (cut sticks) according to quality. These are rather rare, however, and most of the *dos rayas* wines become olorosos.

An oloroso, in accordance with its name, has a characteristic aroma and also possesses more body than the finos. Cream sherry is a full oloroso.

The wines that develop body but not the proper finesse retain the original *raya* markings and are called either *raya* or *raya oloroso*.

The sherries are now ready to enter the *solera* system.

the solera
system

The heart of the entire sherry trade is the *solera* system by which a uniform style, character, and quality are maintained year in and year out. Every sherry shipped from the Jerez region has gone through its *solera*.

Solera comes from the word *suelo* ("ground") and refers to the butts nearest the ground. It is created by laying down a number of butts of particularly

Deft use of the *venencia*. Williams & Humbert's *capataz* ("*bodega* master") pouring a sample that he has just drawn from the Dry Sack *solera*. (*Courtesy Julius Wile Sons & Co., Inc., New York*)

fine-quality wine of a given style. The next year an equal number of butts of wine of the same style and character are placed above it to form a second tier, and the next year a third tier is placed above the second. Depending upon the needs and the desired quality of age, further lots of similar wine are set aside in succeeding years as additional tiers or scales to back up the original three.

All the tiers (scales) above the first one are called *criaderas* ("nursery reserves"). The number varies from one *solera* to another and one house to another. Each *criadera* tier is numbered. We have seen *soleras* that were backed up with six *criaderas* and others with as many as twelve. There is always a year's difference between each *criadera* number.

It is only when the shipper has established his full line of *criadera* tiers that he is ready to begin selling wine from the *solera*. He then draws wine from the original tier of butts and replaces the wine he withdraws with wine from the next youngest *criadera* tier and so on. When the wine from the youngest *criadera* is used up, it is replaced with vintage wine that has been set aside for the particular *solera*. Never more than half the wine in the oldest tier is withdrawn at one time. Once a *solera* is started, it can go on forever. The wine that will be vintaged this year will take from seven to ten years or longer to travel through the *solera* system before it reaches the bottle. In this way a constant process of blending goes on year after year, and thus a definite standard of quality can be maintained indefinitely.

Consequently, there is no such thing, commercially, as a vintage sherry. *Sherry is always a blended wine.* Occasionally a *solera* is dated, such as Solera 1870. This indicates the year when the *solera* was started, but it does not mean that the wine in the bottle is of the 1870 vintage. When you see a bottle labeled Vintage of 1900, you are being misled.

The sherry shipper, indeed, can supply the finest shades of difference in color and taste by judicious and intelligent blending. Basically, all sherries are dry. The various degrees of sweetness are the result of the careful use of a special sweetening wine made from raisined Pedro Ximenez grapes, and the depth of color is obtained by blending in a small amount of color wine (*vino de color*).

Vino de color is made by boiling the must before fermentation begins. The result is a very dark, heavy, syrupy concentration of grape sugar. If, in this process, the must is reduced to one-third of its original content, it is called *sancocho;* if down to one-fifth, *arrope.* To this are added eight or ten parts regular sherry wine of the same vintage, and the whole is known as *vino de color.* The color and sweetening wines are of great importance to the shipper, who maintains *soleras* of them, blends them, and ages them for many years. As he uses small amounts in each blend of sherry, the quality must be on a par with the wine it is to color or sweeten. The final blending of the wine to be bottled includes the proper proportion of color wine.

It is interesting to note that, because of evaporation, the strength of the wine increases slightly, so that wine that started out with 16 percent alcohol will have 18 percent or even more after a few years. This varies with the type of wine and with the shipper. Some shippers send their pale dry wines out with an alcohol content of 17 to 19 percent, while others fortify all of their wines up to 20½ percent.

The final step before bottling or shipping the wine is to fine it, in order to ensure clarity and brilliance. The best fining material for sherry is egg whites mixed with a small amount of wine (see page 28). In addition, some sherries are refrigerated for a period of time and then filtered. This procedure removes excess tartrates and stabilizes the wine.

SHERRY TYPES

All shippers produce the same general types of sherry. Each shipper, however, offers various qualities of each type, and in order to differentiate not only the various qualities but also his own brand from that of his competitors, the shipper has developed the custom of giving his *solera* a trade name.

The sherry shipper further subdivides the fino and oloroso styles as follows:

Transferring wines in a *solera* system. (*Courtesy Julius Wile Sons & Co., Inc., New York*)

TYPE	DESCRIPTION
	FINOS
Manzanilla	Very dry, very pale, light body
Fino	Very dry, very pale, medium body
Amontillado	Dry, pale to light gold, full body, nutty
	OLOROSOS
Oloroso	Usually sweet, deep golden, full body, nutty
Cream	Sweet, deep golden, full body, nutty
Brown	Very sweet, dark brown, full body, nutty

MANZANILLA. This is a very pale, very dry fino that has developed in the *bodegas* located at Sanlúcar de Barrameda, where the salt air of the Atlantic Ocean has a very definite influence and contributes to the wine's fragrance, lightness, and even slightly bitter tonic undertone. Must from the same vintage and vineyard developed in Jerez will become a fino without manzanilla characteristics. As a matter of fact, if a butt of manzanilla is moved to Jerez it loses its manzanilla character and turns into a typical Jerez fino.

FINO is the basic very pale, very dry, elegant wine of Jerez. It is a wine with a slight pungency.

AMONTILLADO is a deeper-colored fino that has developed considerable nuttiness and body. Usually it is a fairly dry wine, but some shippers blend their amontillados to be less dry.

OLOROSO is a deeper golden wine, which can be quite dry but generally is fairly sweet. It has a full body and is nutty. The term *amoroso* was formerly used for a somewhat sweet and velvety oloroso.

CREAM is a rich, golden, sweet, soft wine of full body. Cream wines are from old, extensive oloroso and color wine *soleras*.

BROWN is always a very dark walnut brown sweet wine of full-bodied nuttiness. This type is very popular in England and Scotland, but it has lost much of its appeal in the United States, where it has been replaced by the cream type.

Note: These sherry styles are the basic types shipped today. Each shipper varies his final blends according to what he believes will have the widest appeal. Some ship younger wines, while others use older wines.

PEDRO XIMENEZ

According to legend, the Pedro Ximenez grape was brought to Jerez from Germany by a man named Peter Siemens, whose name was Hispanicized to Pedro Ximenez.

Wine made from this grape is usually called P.X. and is treated differently from regular sherry. The grapes are lusciously sweet and very low in acid. Before pressing they are spread on straw mats and left in the sun to dry for ten days to two weeks. After the sunning the grapes become almost raisinlike. The must that is obtained is not allowed to ferment because it is so syrupy that fermentation would be slow and arduous. Instead the must is run into butts containing a small amount of brandy so that all the natural sugar remains in the wine. P.X. wines go through their own *soleras*.

Obviously, this is an expensive wine to produce. In Spain and Latin America Pedro Ximenez wine is popular, but its main use is to lend richness and softness to the blends of rich oloroso and brown sherries. In the United States and Scotland this is the blending sherry used to soften blended whiskies.

SHIPPERS

Sherry shipping firms do not spring up overnight. It takes years to form the *soleras*, and unless a firm can purchase a complete *bodega*, it takes many years to become established. That is why most of the well-known firms have been in existence for over a hundred years. As a firm does not stay in business unless it gives quality and deals fairly with its customers, the people managing these old firms handle fine wines and have solid reputations. In many cases the directors of these firms are direct descendants of the founders and are well aware of their responsibility to maintain the reputation of the firm on the same high plane as that of their forebears.

For this reason, and because sherry is always a blended wine, the shipper's name is of paramount importance in selecting a sherry. Every bottle bearing his label carries the shipper's assurance of honesty, ability, skill, and reputation for shipping wines of consistently high quality.

Every shipper, of course, handles both fine wines and inexpensive wines. Do not compare one shipper's fine wine with another's less expensive wine in trying to establish their relative merits as shippers.

HOW AND WHEN TO SERVE SHERRIES

Pale dry sherries, such as manzanilla, fino, and amontillado, are ideal aperitifs. They lose nothing by chilling and we recommend that they be served chilled or on the rocks. Serve them before meals with hors d'oeuvres, with soup, or at any time, afternoon or evening. Sherry is an ideal wine of hospitality.

The dry and medium olorosos may be served, like the drier wines, at room temperature, slightly chilled, or on the rocks. It is a matter of personal taste.

The richer oloroso or brown wines are too full bodied to be chilled and should be served at room temperature. They make delightful afternoon drinks to serve at the bridge table, with dessert, or after dinner.

Sherry has many virtues. It can be used in mixed drinks, such as coolers, cobblers, and flips, and it is indispensable in the kitchen.

Because sherry is fortified and has a higher percentage of alcohol than table wines, it is a wine whose flavor is not impaired by smoking. It is sturdy, does not suffer from travel, and therefore is an ideal wine to take traveling or on a picnic. Furthermore, it is an economical wine, as once a bottle is opened, especially an oloroso, it does not deteriorate and will keep almost indefinitely either in the bottle or in a decanter. A fino is more delicate and may oxidize if held too long.

Naturally there are exceptions. Manzanillas and finos do deteriorate in the bottle. Their color deepens perceptibly and they lose their freshness. Our advice is always to try to buy fresh manzanilla or fino sherry, and not to keep them overlong—a few months to a year at most.

On rare occasions olorosos may deposit some sediment. This is cream of tartar, which is natural to the wine. Stand the bottle up for an hour and the deposit will fall to the bottom so that clear wine may be poured. This deposit varies from one shipment to another of the same wine, the result of temperature fluctuations.

OTHER FORTIFIED WINES OF SPAIN

Montilla-Moriles

Another wine was shipped for generations from Jerez, although it was produced near Cordoba, over a hundred miles away from the sherry region. This wine is named Montilla because it is made in the Montilla Mountains. It is made much the same as the wine in Jerez, except it is fermented in enormous earthenware jars, called *tinajas*, instead of in oak butts. The wine is later transferred to oak butts for maturation in the *solera*. Montilla wines average 15½ to 16 percent alcohol and are made primarily from Pedro Ximenez grapes.

Montilla wines develop a dry, nutty character and are primarily aperitifs. It is from this basic wine that the word and type of sherry wine called amontillado is obtained. *Amontillado* means "in the style of Montilla."

Because the Jerez houses shipped the wines of Montilla for many, many years, we came to accept them as sherry wines. Today Spanish wine laws delimit the Montilla-Moriles region, and its wines can no longer be classified as sherries.

Málaga

Many of Spain's better-known wines of former times have gone out of fashion in a world that, temporarily at least, has turned against very sweet wine. An important sweet wine region for many centuries has been the province of Málaga on the southern Mediterranean coast.

A dozen types of Málaga wine are made, ranging from medium sweet to very sweet and from 14 to 23 percent alcohol. Several varieties of grapes are used, but the two dominant ones are Pedro Ximenez and Muscat. To the juice is added brandy and *vino de color* to make a strong, dark wine. The grapes are often sun dried before crushing and have high sugar and low acid content.

Before Prohibition Málaga wines were extremely popular in the United States, but after Repeal they never regained their popularity. Their market is primarily Spain and Latin America.

Tarragona   The highly individualistic region of Catalonia (Cataluña), with its beautiful capital, Barcelona, produces interesting fortified wines of Tarragona and Sitges. Tarragona port is a red wine made in a manner similar to that employed in Portugal. The wine, however, is not as fine. In Spain it is called Priorato, named for the mountainous district near Tarragona.

Tarragona also produces white fortified wines from the Malvasia, Muscat, and Macabeo grapes for use as altar or sacramental wines. The famous old firm of Augusto de Muller was the accredited purveyor of altar wines to the Vatican and the various cardinals of Spain.

Farther north, but still south of Barcelona, around the seaport of Sitges in the Panadés region, are produced the most famous Moscatel wines of Spain. These are prepared in the same manner as the Pedro Ximenez wines. They are light golden in color, have a pronounced Muscat flavor, and are very rich and soft. As a rule, they have an alcoholic strength of 16 to 18 percent. These wines are popular in Spain and in Latin America, although they are unknown to the North American market.

2. TABLE WINES OF SPAIN

Spain's annual production of wine exceeds one billion gallons and gives work to about 15 percent of the population. The bulk of this production is not sherry but light, fresh table wine, most of which is consumed locally during the year of the vintage, as in France and Italy. However, certain other regions of Spain export quality wines.

Besides Jerez, there are twenty-seven other controlled regions of Spain regulated by the *Instituto Nacional de Denominaciones de Origen* (I.N.D.O.). These regions produce mainly table wines and enhance Spain's position in the world market. The most important of these are Rioja, Valdepeñas, and Catalonia.

Rioja   The name with the most prestige among dry table wines of Spain is unquestionably Rioja. In the northern province of Logrono, in Navarre, lies the triangular basin of the Río Oja, whence rises the Ebro River and where lie most of the Rioja vineyards. Vineyards are also planted in the provinces of Alava and Navarre. The production and exportation of the wines from this strictly defined Rioja zone is controlled by an official authority (about twenty-eight producers are entitled to the Rioja certificate of origin), and only those produced in this area may be labeled Rioja wines.

The grapes of Rioja are native Spanish varieties—for white wines, Malvasia and Viura; for red wines, Graciano, Mazuela, Tempranillo, and the internationally known Garnacha, or Grenache.

Rioja wines are best left to mature in oak casks for not less than two years to allow them to get over their "teething" troubles; after that they begin to improve immensely, for, like all good wines, they improve in bottle for many years, attaining a mellowness and character that delight lovers of wine.

Wines from the Rioja zone are entitled to have a small square symbol of origin in the corner of the label. The finer wines are classified as Reserva or Reserva Especial, which means they have spent even more time in wood. *Consecha* ("harvest") followed by a year indicates the vintage. Other words that might be found on a label are *tinto* ("red"), *blanco* ("white"), *seco* ("dry"), and *dulce* ("sweet").

Younger or lesser wines of the Rioja can be somewhat rough but are still well suited to an outdoor meal or to accompany highly seasoned food. They, and other Spanish table wines, are also pleasant for wine cups—sangria —whether you make your own or buy the conveniently prepared product from Spain, which is a red wine flavored with citrus fruit juice and usually sweetened. It goes well with almost any food or is pleasant simply by itself as an occasional drink. See page 408 for instructions on how to mix your own sangria.

Valdepeñas

The favorite table wine of the Madrileños is Valdepeñas, produced on the plains of La Mancha around the town of Valdepeñas from the red Cencibel and white Airen grapes. Both red and white are available everywhere in Madrid. The white Valdepeñas is a dry, rather full-bodied golden wine with plenty of character and flavor. The red is almost as light in color as a dark rosé, is well balanced and fairly high in alcohol content, with a considerably fruity taste. The wines of La Mancha and Valdepeñas are most enjoyable when very young and are exported at about ten to twelve months old, when they are still fresh and vigorous.

Catalonia

The Catalonians produce several table wines of good quality, particularly dry white and rosé wines suitable to drink with their excellent fish. From the Alella vineyards north of Barcelona comes a pleasant, light, dry beverage wine named Alella, which is shipped in the typical long, flute-shaped Rhine-wine bottle. The granite in the soil gives the wines good acidity.

Panadés, south of Barcelona, has both mountain and coastal vineyards producing red and white table wines. The soil is chalky. The central area, Villafranca de Panadés, makes the best sparkling wines in Spain. The *méthode champenoise* has been used for more than a century. These wines are known as Espumosos and are gaining in popularity as reasonably priced sparkling wines.

9

THE WINES OF PORTUGAL

1. PORTO

"Claret is for boys, Port for men," declared Dr. Samuel Johnson, affirming not only his own but also England's preference for the sweet, warming wine of Portugal. Indeed, to many port was considered an English wine, for it was the English who changed it from a natural wine to the rich, fortified wine it is today, the English who created the markets for it, and the English who controlled the trade of this wine in Portugal. The Portuguese themselves, in fact, prefer the light table wines of their country; port is a bit too rich to drink in their climate.

history   In Roman times Portus Cale, the harbor at the mouth of the Douro River, was the most important center of life and trade of ancient Lusitania. It eventually gave its name to the country, modernized to Portugal, and retained for itself the simple title of Oporto, "the port." In ancient days it was customary to close the port each night to prevent pirates from coming in. This was done by swinging heavy chains from one bank to the other because the harbor, called a *bar,* had a narrow mouth.

The history of the port wine trade, like that of Burgundy, is wrapped up in politics and wars. Although port has been sold in England since the fourteenth century, it was not until the Methuen Treaty, signed in 1703, that the wine trade began to develop. English merchants had first settled in Lisbon and Oporto in the sixteenth century, after the discovery of Brazil led to increased trading possibilities. When the crews of English boats began stopping there, as the years went on, England gradually became acquainted with the Portuguese wines.

In 1703 Queen Anne's forces were at war with France. As a blow against the French wine trade Queen Anne had the English ambassador, John Methuen, draw up a commercial treaty with Don Pedro II whereby, in exchange for free entry of English woolens, port wine was given an advantageous preferential duty over all other wines coming into England.

At first the wine, despite its low price, was not popular, being both harsh and sharp. After long experimentation, however, the enterprising English wine merchants in Oporto discovered that by adding brandy to the wine before all the sugar had been fermented out, they had a wine suited to the English taste and climate. It won ready acceptance at home, and the port trade was established on a firm foundation.

Like so many of our great wines, port takes its name from the place whence it was first shipped. It is defined by the Anglo-Portuguese Treaty of 1916 as a "fortified wine produced in the delimited Douro region and exported through the Bar of Oporto." Any wine that does not fit this description cannot be sold in England as port, even if it bears a qualifying name, such as Tarragona Port. Until 1968 the same held true in the United States, except that port-type wines with prefixed American names, such as California Port or New York State Port, were allowed. But in 1968 it was established legally, with the concurrence of Portuguese and U.S. authorities, that the fortified wine of Portugal is a geographical product made only from grapes grown in a small, delimited area in the Douro region. To protect the genuineness of this unique and esteemed wine, and to distinguish it from any American-made product, the Portuguese wine must be called Porto or Vinho do Porto in the United States. Wines bottled after 1968 and shipped to the United States must conform to the ruling. Actually all port bottled in Portugal bears a government seal and is called Porto. The rest of the world may continue to call fortified Portuguese wines port or port wine.

grape varieties

The Douro region, one of the most beautiful wine countries in the world, is a rough, mountainous district, with a river winding, twisting, and turning between steep slopes of striated rock. The vineyards, known as *quintas* ("farms"), are planted in terraces so that the vines cannot be washed down into the river.

There are many varieties of grapes grown in the Douro Valley, but only two types are essential to making Porto. The first, including such *plantes nobles* as the Touriga, Mourisco, and Bastardo, produces a juice lacking in color, fairly light bodied, but giving the wine character and finesse. The second type of vines includes the Tinta Cão, Tinta Francisca, and Souzão, which contribute some balance and color to the must.

It is usual for a *quinta* to be planted with anywhere from ten to fifteen grape varieties, which are all gathered and pressed together, each contributing its individual character to produce a balanced wine.

The principal grape varieties employed in making white Porto are the Rabigato, Moscatel Branco, Malvasia Fina, and Verdelho.

vintage

The vintage begins at the end of September or the beginning of October, depending on the weather. Men and women gather the grapes, carrying them in single file down the mountain in huge baskets on their backs, supported by a head harness, balancing themselves with a crooked stick. The grapes may also be piled in squeaking, two-wheeled, oxen-drawn carts, and it is amazing to watch these lumbering beasts cart the grapes down the steep, narrow roads to the pressing house without accident.

As in Spain, vintage time in Portugal has a festival spirit, and the lively music of the *machete* ("mandolin") accompanies the work. The grapes, with their skins and pips, are placed in an oblong stone *lagar* ("pressing trough") until it is half full, and men and women tread them until almost all the juice is expressed. In recent years, however, the purple "stockings" of the treaders have begun to disappear, and modern crushing methods are used. Newer fermenters of the percolation type have entered the scene.

fermentation   Fermentation begins almost at once and is allowed to continue for from two to three days. The difference between Porto and other wines occurs at this stage, and therefore the fermentation is carefully watched. The sugar content of the must is measured periodically with a mustimeter, and when just the requisite amount of sugar remains unfermented, the must is run off into pipes (138-gallon casks), which contain sufficient brandy, distilled from wines of the district, to raise the alcohol content to approximately 20 percent. This stops fermentation, and the unfermented grape sugar remains in the wine as sweetening. Because of this, Porto is always a sweet wine. The amount of sweetness varies with the choice of each vineyard owner; but if a lot of sugar is left in, more brandy must be added.

After the free-run juice has been run into pipes, the balance of the must is pressed to express the last drops of juice. The wine made from this pressing sometimes becomes Porto, but usually brandy is distilled from it to be used in fortifying the Porto wines.

The new wines are kept at the *quintas* until the following spring, when they are racked off into fresh pipes and sent down the Douro to the shippers' wine lodges in Oporto or Vila Nova de Gaia, twin cities on opposite banks at the mouth of the river. The wines used to be shipped down the Douro aboard picturesque sailboats, called *rabelos*, but are now shipped by truck or railroad. Today one *rabelo* remains at anchor in Oporto as a symbol of the past. At the wine lodges the wine is carefully stored until it is decided whether it will be shipped as Vintage, Crusted, Ruby, or Tawny Porto.

PORTO TYPES

Vintage Porto   Table wines of Portugal ripen, mature, and are at their best in two to ten years, as in other wine-producing countries, but the richly fortified Vintage Portos require upward of twenty years to reach their prime.

Vintage Porto is wine of any exceptional year, when weather, rain, sun, and soil cooperate to produce a big wine with character, bouquet, and balanced flavor. It is bottled within two years of the vintage. On the average, the shippers are able to ship about three such vintages in every decade.

Vintage Porto sometimes bears two dates on the label, the vintage date and the bottling date.

Vintage Porto must be bottled in Portugal. The wine must rest for a considerable period of time, varying with different vintages; but at least eight to ten years are required for it to mature, and it will continue to develop for many more years.

A generous, full wine such as Vintage Porto throws a heavy deposit as it matures, consisting of argol, cream of tartar, and coloring matter, which settles as a fairly solid crust on the side of the bottle. Once this begins, shipping the wine becomes difficult, for unless it is handled most carefully, the crust may break up, clouding the wine. The wine will then need a lot of time, standing upright, for the deposit to collect at the bottom, so that it may then be decanted.

In his *Romance of Wine* H. Warner Allen tells a story about his great-grandfather's uncle, who was greatly addicted to Porto: ". . . and when gout and old age at last drove him to bed, his old servant explained to his nephew

Gathering the grapes at a typical Upper Douro *quinta* during the vintage. (*Courtesy Casa de Portugal, New York*)

how he was nursing his master: 'I keeps a-turning of his Worship 'cause you see, Sir, he's got that much Port in his inside, he'd be bound to get crusted, if I let 'un stop too long on one side.'"

Vintage Porto has the deepest ruby color, the fruitiest bouquet, and the most body of all styles of Porto. Until fully matured it is quite rough. Thus it has been customary for the English to lay down a considerable quantity of an approved Vintage Port, which they buy cheaply, permitting it to mature and triple in value in twenty-odd years. It is not an uncommon practice to purchase Vintage Porto when a child is born so that the wine may be enjoyed when both reach maturity.

Ruby and Tawny Portos   These are blended wines that are matured in wood rather than in the bottle as with Vintage Portos (they are also called wooded Portos). The blending, or vatting, is employed in the Porto lodges to ensure that a definite standard of style and quality is maintained for each brand a shipper offers. The object in blending is to balance the qualities that are lacking in one wine but are present in the other—the wine that has finesse and delicacy but is light bodied is blended with wine that has a great deal of body but less finesse; the two complement each other, giving a more balanced wine. The shipper sometimes uses as many as thirty or more wines in his blend, including those from different years.

While the wine is maturing in the pipe, it throws a deposit (crust) just as it does in the bottle. Some of the deposit is not heavy enough to precipitate and remains in suspension, causing the wine to have a dull, or "blind," appearance. This is overcome by fining. Experience has proved that wines develop best if kept in a good, brilliant condition. They are therefore fined on an average of twice a year. The material used may be a commercial fining material, but for better wines the shippers generally use whites of eggs.

As the film formed by the fining process settles, it carries down with it not only the sediment of fliers that were floating in the wine, but also a certain amount of the coloring matter. As a result, the longer a wine is kept in wood, the greater the number of times it is fined, and the less color it retains. An old wooded Porto, consequently, is paler in color than a young wine.

The quality of paleness is called tawniness because as the wine loses redness, both from repeated finings and from oxidation during wood storage, a tawny amber glint appears. As it increases in tawniness, a Porto becomes drier, so that an old Tawny will be drier than a young Tawny. The word *dry* is used, in this case, in a relative sense.

A Tawny Porto is a blend of well-matured wooded Portos; it is softer than Vintage or Ruby Portos. It does not possess the fruitiness of the others, but an old Tawny is a soft, delicate, and elegant wine. Tawny Porto may not have an age statement on the label.

Ruby Porto is a bright, ruby-colored blend of young wooded Portos. It is

Historical Douro *rabelo* laden with pipes of new wine destined for the shippers' lodges at Oporto or Vila Nova de Gaia. (*Courtesy Casa de Portugal, New York*)

generally fruitier and rougher than Tawny. The wines generally shipped are the Tawny and Ruby Portos.

White Porto

White Porto is another type of wine produced in the Douro region. Except for the fact that white grapes are used exclusively, it is made in the same manner as red Porto. It is matured in wood and is generally quite soft, pleasant, and a shade drier than other Portos. It is very popular in France, where it is consumed as an aperitif. White Porto is only 10 percent of the Porto market in the United States.

Porto of the Vintage

Sometimes a wine is not intended to be a Vintage Porto but later shows promise. After a few years in cask, where it is topped off with other Portos, this wine is bottled as a wine "of the Vintage." It is actually an unblended Tawny Porto. This will sometimes have the year of bottling on the label as well as the year of the vintage. It is always less expensive than a true Vintage Porto, and care should be taken not to confuse the two.

Crusted Porto

Crusted Porto has virtually disappeared, but it used to be a close relative of Vintage Porto in that it was usually wine of a single year. Sometimes, however,

DELIMITED PORTO
VINEYARDS OF THE DOURO

WILLIAM LEMBECK

WINE REGIONS
OF
PORTUGAL

it was a blend of vintage wines from several vintages. It was bottled early or late but, because it did not quite come up to vintage standard in quality, it was sold without any date. It resembled Vintage Porto in character and deposited a crust in the same manner as a vintage wine.

HOW AND WHEN TO SERVE PORTO

Porto wine may be served at the end of a meal with dessert or coffee or with the cheese course. Several cheeses (Stilton and cheddar, for example) can be prepared with Porto. Porto makes excellent cobblers and flips. It also has many uses in the kitchen: in sauces, in Porto wine jellies, as an addition to fruit cups, and to plump up dried fruits.

OTHER FORTIFIED WINES OF PORTUGAL

Carcavelos and Moscatel de Setúbal

As previously stated, it is illegal to call a wine Porto unless it has been produced in the delimited Upper Douro region, yet sweet, fortified wines such as Carcavelos and Moscatel de Setúbal are made in other parts of Portugal, primarily on the Tagus River and in the Estremadura region.

Carcavelos, located at the mouth of the Tagus River, just west of Lisbon, is most famous for its white fortified wine known since the thirteenth century. The climate favors the production of must of higher quality because the breezes blow away the humidity that would otherwise adversely affect the grapes producing the must. A first-class Carcavelos wine has an alcohol content of 19 percent and is good as an aperitif or dessert wine, depending on the sweetness. It has a pleasant bouquet, is smooth to the taste, and ages well.

Moscatel de Setúbal, a wine with several royal charters, is produced in Setúbal, a beautiful area south of Lisbon. It owes its perfumed scent and flavor to the distinguishing characteristics of its Muscat grapes. It is golden in color, very sweet, and, like Carcavelos, improves with age.

2. TABLE WINES OF PORTUGAL

The Setúbal district is also well known for its good-quality table wines, the majority of which are red and are made from the Periquita grape.

Bucelas and Colares

Of Lisbon's local wines, the two best are Bucelas, a pleasant, fresh, dry white, and Colares, a dry red wine.

Bucelas is a town just north of Lisbon where the wine is made primarily from the Arinto grape. Dry, with a recognizable aroma and characteristic straw-yellow color, it has a fine bouquet that increases with age.

Colares is a small town on the Atlantic, west of Lisbon. The vineyards of the region are planted with the Ramisco grape, which produces a clean, full-bodied, ruby-red beverage wine. Grown in sandy soil, this grape is not attacked by *Phylloxera*, which ravaged European vineyards in the last century, as *Phylloxera* cannot exist in sand. The very deep roots of the vines may go down nine or ten feet through the sand to a clay layer below. Colares and Periquita are wines drunk today made from the same vines as those that produced wine thousands of years ago. Although the very early history of Colares wine is unknown, it is known that in 1385 it enjoyed a flourishing trade. Very little of the local Lisbon wine is exported to this country.

Dão

The Dão region is named for the Dão River, a tributary of the Mondego River, which flows midway between Oporto and Lisbon. Only a small amount of the land is under vine because of the rocky, granitic soil. Dão wines have a full-bodied strength and richness. The red wines are characterized by a ruby-red color, rich bouquet, and smooth taste and can take up to eight years of aging very well. They are known as *vinho maduro*. The Dão red is considered the best of the Portuguese red table wines. The Tourigo, Alvarelhão, Bastardo, and Tinta Pinheira grapes impart the principal characteristics to red Dão wines. They are aged at least three years in casks and spend even more time in the bottle. The white wines are dry, full, and aromatic and are produced mostly from the Arinto grape. Genuine Dão wines are guaranteed by the Federation of Dão Viniculturists, which issues certificates of origin to all wines that are entitled to them.

Vinho Verde

One of the most pleasant and simple wines of Portugal is the Vinho Verde, produced in the northern province of Entre-Douro-e-Minho. The literal translation of *vinho verde* is "green wine," but the term really means "young wine," as opposed to *vinho madura*. It is not green, but white, red, or rosé. It is always a light, somewhat acid, refreshing, slightly *pétillant,* and fragrant wine with an alcohol content of 8 to 11 percent. Being light, pleasant, and thirst quenching, it is a wine that is generally drunk in large drafts, not sipped. Vinho Verde should be drunk young, while it is fresh; it may oxidize after two years. We recall a particularly delightful luncheon at a waterfront bistro in Rio de Janeiro, the main dish of which was huge platters of roasted, crunchy shrimp, washed down with goblets of white Vinho Verde. When the host ordered a bottle per person, we thought it was too much, but we found it was insufficient and more wine had to be served.

other table wines

Other districts yielding Portuguese table wines include Pinhel, which gives a pleasant, light wine; Bairrada, producing mostly red table wines that have body with good flavor and some white wines held in high esteem; Alcobaça, whose fame dates from the twelfth century and whose fine wines are tantalizingly aromatic; Torres Vedras, producing mostly red wines with body and a high percentage of tannin, as well as some good white wines that are alcoholic, aromatic, and flavorful; and Ribatejo, a region supplying the most important urban centers in the south of the country, where alcoholic white wines with little acidity are produced, as well as red wines, dark in color and full bodied, with a high percentage of alcohol.

rosé wines

By far the greatest volume of wine exported from Portugal is in rosé wines. For a while many rosés were carbonated, and in 1969 almost 400,000 cases of these were exported. Because of increased costs and changing tastes, in 1975 fewer than 5,000 cases were exported. The still, noncarbonated rosé wines have remained a major export and for the last three years have averaged over 3 million cases a year. These wines are clean, sound, and pleasantly sweet and are served chilled with almost any food. They are mostly shipped in the flattened, round *Bocksbeutel.*

sparkling wines

There are some bottle-fermented sparkling wines made in Bairrada and Lamego, but they have not been shipped to the United States.

3. MADEIRA

When Venice dominated the commerce of the Mediterranean, it had a great trade with England in the wines of Candia, which were known as Candy or Malvasia Candiae. The Candia of the thirteenth century is today known as Crete, and its wines have given way to those of Madeira. As so often happens, the reasons were political. As long as the wine could be obtained only in Candia, the English submitted to the tyranny of Venice, but as soon as they could obtain similar wines of equal quality from Madeira, they lost no time giving their trade to the Portuguese island in the Atlantic, which is 535 miles south by southwest of Lisbon and 360 miles off the North African coast.

history

There is some question as to whether it was Prince Henry or one of his captains, João Gonçalves, surnamed Zarco, who discovered Madeira, in 1418 or 1420. Whoever it was, Zarco was named Captain of Madeira, and he founded a settlement there on the Bay of Funchal. The name of the island, which was covered with dense forest from mountaintop to seashore, meant "wooded island." When Zarco arrived with his family and a group of colonists, he found Madeira uninhabited and untillable because of the heavy forest. Being a man of action and having little manpower, he did not attempt to cut the timber but fired it instead. It is said to have burned for seven years, but when, at length, the fire went out, there was added to the volcanic quality of the soil, and the accumulation of centuries of leaf mold, the potash of the burned forest, which made Madeira one of the most fertile of all islands.

Before long sugarcane and grapevines were planted, and Portugal had a rich colony. The grapevines were brought primarily from Candia and were of the Malvasia variety that is still grown on the island.

By the end of the fifteenth century Madeira was exporting wines to Europe; these wines found favor both in France and in England. Shakespeare mentions Madeira in several of his plays, notably in *Henry IV* where Poins greets Falstaff: "Jack! how agrees the devil and thee about thy soul, that thou soldest him on Good Friday last for a cup of Madeira and a cold capon's leg?"

There is also the unforgettable story of the early Duke of Clarence, who so loved his Madeira that he drowned in a pipe of it.

The sailing vessels of the American colonies and English ships sailing to America made it a practice to stop at Madeira for water and provisions. Here they invariably loaded a few pipes of Madeira wine, and it became the fashionable wine of the American colonies, a fashion that remained until the turn of the twentieth century.

During the early decades of the nineteenth century Madeira wines were often known by the names of the great shipping families of the Atlantic seaboard whose ship captains brought pipes of wine to their owners. There were famous Madeiras shipped to Boston, New York, Philadelphia, New Orleans, Charleston, and Savannah, but Baltimore was considered the Madeira capital of the United States.

Some of the ship owners gave the wines the name of the ship that brought them to America. Some wine historians credit the name of Rainwater to a Madeira enthusiast, Mr. Habisham of Savannah, who employed a secret fining process that made the wine paler in color without impairing its bouquet or character. Today Rainwater is a light, pale blend.

Unfortunately Madeira, after being in vogue for many years, receives little attention in the United States today.

grape varieties   The principal grape varieties grown on the island are the Verdelho, which makes up two-thirds of the planted vines; the Sercial; the Bual or Boal; and the Malvasia, from which is made the famous Malmsey Madeira. The original Malmsey was produced in Greece in Monemvasia, and in the Middle Ages red and white Malmseys were shipped all over the world. Later this type of wine was produced not only in Madeira but in Italy, Spain, and the Canary Islands as well. The name Monemvasia becomes Malvasia in Italy, Malvoisie in France, and Malmsey in England. The Malvasia grape requires a very dry soil and intense heat and is not gathered until it is shriveled and raisinlike.

Minor grape varieties grown in Madeira are the Tinta or black grape, the Bastardo, the Terrantez, the Listrão, and the Maroto.

Madeira vineyards are generally small and are planted with several varieties of vines. The cultivator does not bother to separate the different species before pressing them in the *lagar.* As a result, there is a rich and somewhat deep-colored wine from the admixture of black grapes, some of which are found in every vineyard.

In the larger vineyards the various kinds of grapes, especially the Verdelho, Sercial, Bual, and Malvasia varieties, are pressed separately and the must from each is kept separate.

vintage   The system of viticulture in Madeira differs in some ways from that of other wine regions. Most of the land is cultivated under the old feudal system of small tenant farmers, known as *caseiros.* The *caseiro* pays half of his grape crop as rent.

Every inch of ground on the island of Madeira is utilized. The hillsides are so steep that one can hardly find foothold, yet they are made up into tiny terraces, each complete with water channels for irrigation.

Madeira has not sufficient rainfall for its needs, and the land depends on irrigation for its moisture. The water is brought down from the hills in shallow channels that usually run by the roadside. The network of these channels covers the entire island, and the water is managed by committees appointed by the *caseiros.* A farmer may be entitled to so many hours of water every fifteen days and at a given hour—whether it be three o'clock in the morning or three o'clock in the afternoon—he is advised, "It is your turn to get water." The stream is turned into his farm, and at the end of his time it is shunted to the next farm. This organization is extraordinarily efficient.

The Madeira farmer knows little of modern implements or scientific methods and does all his cultivating with the primitive *enchada*, a cross between a pick and a hoe. The hillsides are so steep that not even wheelbarrows can be used, and everything is carted in baskets carried on the head or shoulders.

The vines are not carefully pruned as on the Continent, as it has been found more practical, because of the luxuriant growth, to grow them on trellises four to six feet high, with vines fifteen to twenty feet long.

It is the custom on the island for merchants and shippers to buy the produce of the vineyard while the grapes are still on the vine. Their agents watch to see that grape picking is not begun until the proper time, and they supervise the work up to the time that the must is delivered to the shippers' cellars.

As only the ripest grapes are picked, it is often necessary to go over the vineyard as many as four times. The grapes are emptied into a large wooden *lagar*, where they are trodden out by six men who stand, three on each side of a large central beam, jumping up and down to the tune of a *machete* ("mandolin").

After the grapes have been thoroughly trodden out, they are piled up in the center and a large stone, weighing well over a ton, is forced down on them by means of a wooden screw, until there is practically no juice left in the grapes. This system is ancient, but its results are better than those of the modern press. The contact of the naked feet on the grapes brings out the soft jellylike layer found on the inside of the skin, in which lies the principal flavor.

VINEYARDS OF MADEIRA

Model of an old wooden Madeira wine press. (*Courtesy Casa de Portugal, New York*)

The must is then placed in goatskins and carried down from the hills by men called *borracheiros* and is emptied from the goatskins, which hold about twelve gallons and weigh 110 pounds, into casks in the shippers' lodges. Here the must remains during fermentation, usually from two to four weeks. About 3 percent brandy is added to stop the fermentation when making the sweeter varieties. The brandy is made from Madeira wine. (When a wine is fortified with brandy, the brandy is usually distilled from the wine of the region.) Drier wines are fermented to completion. The wine is now known as Vinho Claro.

Madeiras are treated in a manner peculiar to the island. They are matured in *estufas,* or "hothouses." These vary in temperature from 110 to 140 degrees Fahrenheit according to the length of time the wine is to be baked. If it is to be kept for six months in the *estufa,* the temperature is 110 degrees, but if it is going to be kept only three months, then a higher temperature is used. During this treatment wines that enter a deep purple color undergo a change and emerge amber colored.

This method of maturing the wine is costly, as there is a loss through evaporation, but a well-matured wine is safe against after-fermentation. All of the work is carried out under government supervision. When the wine comes from the *estufa* it is known as Vinho Estufado. It is allowed to rest for a period of time and is then racked into fresh casks, becoming Vinho Trasfugado.

The heating process originated many years ago, when it was discovered that Madeira wine was greatly improved by a long voyage in the hold of a ship. At one time, indeed, it was a regular practice to send wine in the hold of sailing vessels bound for India and thence back to Europe or America, where it was known as East India Madeira. Whether it was the intense heat of the tropical seas through which the wine sailed or the motion of the ship that matured the wine, no one knew. In any case, Madeira merchants have learned that the *estufas* produce the same result.

It used to be customary in America for famous shipping families to keep a cask of Madeira slung in a rocking cradle that was placed in the entrance hall of the shipping office. It was the duty of every person who passed through the hall to give the cradle a shove. In this way the wine was kept in motion from morning until night. Of all wines Madeira is the only one that enjoys motion, and there is none that is a better sailor.

The Vinho Trasfugado is additionally fortified to bring it up to an alcoholic strength of around 20 percent, and it then becomes known as Vinho Generoso. After this it is blended with other wines of similar character and matured for a number of years.

Wines made from a mixture of grapes are shipped under trade names, while those made entirely from one grape variety are shipped under the grape name. As previously mentioned, there are four, corresponding approximately to degrees of sweetness.

SERCIAL, the driest wine of Madeira, can be pale or golden, delicate, with a refreshing acid undertone. It is a perfect aperitif but is suitable for any occasion. One Sercial that was extraordinarily dry was described by the late André L. Simon as "so soft and refined that it has no body, no sugar, no color left, and yet it has bouquet and power; the sort of wine that Rabelais, had he known it, would have called 'A Soul with a Nose.'"

VERDELHO is a medium-rich, golden wine with a dry finish. It is a good all-purpose wine and can be enjoyed before or after meals.

BUAL OR BOAL is a golden wine, fragrant and slightly less sweet than Malmsey. It is distinctly a dessert wine.

MALMSEY is a full-bodied, soft-textured, very fragrant, dark brown wine. It is the sweetest of all Madeira wines. In fact, it is of an almost liqueurlike sweetness.

The Rainwater Madeira mentioned previously is a blend of Sercial, Verdelho, and/or Bual. It is a pale, moderately sweet wine suitable for almost every occasion.

Madeira is one of the most long-lived of all wines, and even one-hundred-year-old wines are magnificent and continue to improve as do no other choice wines. In the past it was customary to keep the vintages separate, and the wines were sold as vintage wines. Since *Phylloxera* devastated the vineyards nearly a century ago, however, the old vintage wines have been used to improve the new. As a result, true vintage Madeiras are very difficult to obtain today, although a few wine merchants have offered such prize bottles as 1862 and 1898 Verdelho; 1864 and 1898 Sercial; 1869, 1870, 1882, and 1891 Bual; and 1880 and 1885 Malmsey.

In 1960 we were presented with an unusual bottle by the late Horace Zino of the Madeira Wine Association. It was one of the last seventeen bottles remaining of an 1835 Sherman Sercial, the wine reserved for shipment to General William Tecumseh Sherman. This wine was still superb, full of aroma and great vigor. It had such wealth of bouquet and depth of vinosity that the taste remained in the mouth several hours after drinking it.

One basic characteristic that all Madeiras have in common is a subtle acid undertone or tang that is found in all wines produced from grapes grown in soils of volcanic origin.

HOW AND WHEN TO SERVE MADEIRA

Madeira may be drunk as an aperitif, served with the soup course in formal dinners, or sipped as a dessert wine. It finds its greatest usefulness, however, as a wine to serve in the afternoon or evening, accompanied by cakes or cookies that are not too sweet. Madeira is rich in phosphates, iron, and minerals and thus is also useful as a tonic.

Madeira is one of the most useful of all wines in the kitchen. It may be used in soups, sauces (such as Sauce Madère), or desserts and can be used in place of sherry or Porto in most recipes. The largest export market for Madeira is France, where it is used almost exclusively in Sauce Madère and other culinary preparations.

10
OTHER WINES
OF EUROPE

1. AUSTRIA

history

Although Austria's history of winemaking goes back to Roman times, the golden age of viniculture took place shortly after the Turks occupied neighboring Hungary in the 1500s, as Hungary ceased to produce wine during that period. Vine plantings increased greatly in Austria, and it is estimated that the total vineyard acreage was five to ten times what it is now.

One law, passed during Maria Theresa's (d. 1780) reign, led to a tradition that still prevails today. The winemaker was allowed to sell his own wine without having to pay any taxes on it. A hanging branch above his doorway signified to passersby that the owner had new wine to sell. This started the tradition of the *Heurige*, which occurs every year in the countryside around Vienna. Both local residents and tourists rush to purchase the new wine.

wine regions

Northwest of Vienna the vast Wachau region has extensive vineyards along the Danube River. This region is cooler than the rest of Austria, lying just south of the massive Alpine ranges. The white wines of this area are quite fine, and the best resemble the Rieslings of Germany. The grapes, which mature slowly under these cool conditions, are fairly high in acid and give the wines from the towns of Krems, Dürnstein, Stein, Loiben, and Klosterneuburg a freshness and elegance. A local quaffing wine sometimes seen abroad is called Schluck.

The wine regions around Vienna produce mainly white wine. Grinzing, Siebering, and Nussdorf are the most famous of the Vienna suburbs that vinify wines made from the native varieties, Grüner Veltliner and Neuberger.

South of Vienna is the Südbahn region, where the famous Gumpolds-kirchner vineyards lie. Baden and Vöslau are two other towns in this region, the latter producing a red table wine called Vöslau Rotwein.

Farther to the south and to the east extensive plantings surround a large lake, the Neusiedler See. Some of the wines, made from the Furmint grape, are reminiscent of Hungarian wines made from the same grape variety. Red and white wines from the towns of Rust and Oggau are grown in sandy soil that is not hospitable to *Phylloxera;* thus these wines, which are rarely seen outside Austria, are made from ungrafted vines.

Finally, in the southern region of Styria, bordering on Yugoslavia, mostly white wines are produced and consumed locally.

grape varieties and wines   Austrian grapes are a combination of native *vinifera* vines, the Furmint of Hungary, the Kadarka of the Balkan countries, and other, more famous, varieties that have taken Austrian names. Of the native varieties the Grüner Veltliner and Neuberger produce white wines, while the Rotgipfler is used for both white and red wines. Of the more familiar varieties, the Weissburgunder (Pinot Blanc), Rheinriesling (Riesling), Traminer, Sylvaner, Müller-Thurgau, Wälschriesling, Ruländer (Pinot Gris), and Muskat-Ottonel are used to make the majority of white wines, which amount to 90 percent of the total production.

The Blauburgunder, or Spätburgunder (Pinot Noir), Blaufränkisch (Gamay), Blauer Portugieser, and Muskat Saint Laurent are the principal grapes used to make red wines.

Although Austria is a large producer of wine, averaging 60 million gallons annually, the per capita consumption is also very large, 9¼ gallons, and Austria does not produce enough wine for its needs and must import large quantities, mostly red wines. Some of the more famous whites, however, are exported in small quantities. These include Gumpoldskirchner, Kremser, and Klosterneuburger.

WINE REGIONS OF AUSTRIA

DÜRNSTEIN
LOIBEN
STEIN
KREMS
KLOSTERNEUBURG
GRINZING
SIEBERING
NUSSDORF
GUMPOLDSKIRCHEN
BADEN
VÖSLAU

CZECHOSLOVAKIA

WACHAU

Danube R.

Vienna

SÜDBAHN

GERMANY

OGGAU
RUST

NEUSIEDLER SEE

STYRIA

BURGENLAND

HUNGARY

ITALY

YUGOSLAVIA

WILLIAM LEMBECK

WINE REGIONS OF BULGARIA

WILLIAM LEMBECK

2. BULGARIA

Bulgaria, like the other Balkan countries, is a large wine producer, ranking sixteenth in world production. In some years over 100 million gallons of red and white wines are produced in this small country.

history

The earliest references to Bulgarian viticulture appear with those of northern Greece. As in Austria, winemaking in Bulgarian territory came to a halt when it was under Turkish rule. Because of suitable climate and soil, grape growing gradually returned to this Balkan country after World War I. Except for a brief pause during and immediately after World War II, Bulgaria's wine industry has continued to grow. Today the collective farms of this Communist country have become mechanized, and the advanced technology is responsible for their large production. Most of the wine is exported, primarily to the U.S.S.R.

wine regions

There are three main viticultural areas in Bulgaria, and the wines produced in all three are similar. The Danube River separates Bulgaria from Romania, and the 250-mile-long valley has vineyards along its entire length. The Maritsa Valley, the second region, is farther south and is protected by the Balkan mountain range. The third region, actually contiguous to the other two, lies to the east, along the shores of the Black Sea.

grape varieties and wines   Bulgaria's wine grapes are a mixture of local and foreign varieties. White wines produced range from dry, light, acidic wines to the sweet types typical of the Maritsa Valley. The reds range from light, fruity types to full, dark wines that need aging.

The ubiquitous Dimiat, Bulgaria's native white-wine grape, is usually vinified dry and has a crisp, fruity taste. Grapes from the Muscat family are also common and appear in some wines, as the semidry Misket Karlova, for example, whose label indicates both grape and region; or the sweet Hemus, which is a brand name. Hungary's Furmint grape makes a dry white wine named Bulgarian Sun, and Russia's Rkatsiteli grape makes a fruity white wine named Sunshine Coast. Riesling, Sylvaner, and Chardonnay are also grown in fair quantities and produce good examples of their famous counterparts.

Traditional red-wine grape varieties, such as the Melnik and Mavrud, produce full-bodied, dark red wines. Other traditional varieties, such as Pamid and Gamza (Kadarka), make fresh, light wines that are best when drunk young. Blending is an accomplished art in Bulgaria, and both locally consumed and exported wines are blends of several grape varieties. Planting noble red varieties has led the Bulgarians to vinify Cabernet Sauvignon, for example, in the Bordeaux style.

3. CZECHOSLOVAKIA

Czechoslovakia, unlike its other central European neighbors, is not a large wine producer, nor is it as avid a wine consumer, although some wine must be imported to meet its needs. This may be because Czechoslovakia's more northerly geographic position, corresponding approximately to the latitude of the wine regions of Germany, limits the grape varieties that can be grown successfully. Since production totals twenty-three million gallons, and consumption is over forty-five million gallons, it is little wonder that Czech wines are rarely seen in the export market.

wine regions   Czechoslovakia's wine production centers around three major regions: Bohemia, Moravia, and Slovakia. Bohemia, the most westerly region, borders Germany and Austria. Most of its vineyard area lies just north of the capital city of Prague. Moravia, in central Czechoslovakia, touches Poland in the north and Austria in the south. The major vineyards are along the southern border, just south of Brno. Slovakia, to the east, produces the bulk of the wine of this country. The most famous area of Slovakia is just north of Hungary's Tokaj region, around the town of Malá Trňa, but the biggest vineyard concentration is just north of Bratislava.

grape varieties and wines

Bohemian wines, because they are produced so close to Germany, are similar to those of the Rhine. The Riesling, Sylvaner, and Traminer grapes produce good white table wines with fruitiness and a touch of sweetness. Some red wines are also produced in this area from grape varieties seen also in Austria: the Blauburgunder, Blauer Portugieser, and Muskat Saint Laurent.

Moravian vineyards account for one-third of the wine of Czechoslovakia. The countryside surrounding the towns of Znojmo, Hustopeče, and Mikulov, at the Austrian border, grows the Austrian Grüner Veltliner, as well as the Rhine Riesling and Italian Riesling varieties. Only white wines are produced in this section, and these are light, dry, and crisp, with perhaps a touch too much acidity.

Slovakia, producing almost two-thirds of the country's wine, makes the majority of its wines, which are consumed locally, in the Modra and Pezinok countryside, north of the border where Austria and Hungary meet Czechoslovakia. The most famous wine made by the Slavs is their version of Tokay, produced near Hungary's famous Tokaj wine region; it is sometimes exported. Like Hungary's Tokay, the Czech Tokay is made mainly from the Furmint grape, with a little of a Muscat variety for added fragrance.

WINE REGIONS OF CZECHOSLOVAKIA

POLAND

Prague

BOHEMIA

MORAVIA

Brno

GERMANY

SLOVAKIA

U.S.S.R.

Znojmo

Mikulov

Malá Trňa

Hustopeče

AUSTRIA

Bratislava

HUNGARY

Modra

Pezinok

WILLIAM LEMBECK

4. ENGLAND

England has always been considered more of a wine consumer than a producer. The country's tradition of world commerce has aided the development of wine areas in other countries that became the most famous names in viniculture, such as Bordeaux, Jerez de la Frontera, Oporto, and Madeira. Since wines made from English vines have not measured up to imported wines, winemaking in England has had limited commercial success. In his poem "Wines of England" the late Eric Chilman, an English food journalist, said:

> The wine of England could but strive in vain
> To rival Bordeaux, and the vineyard died.
> Now is the ancient craft revived anew;
> And vineyards burgeon in the English land.°

England has long desired to make its own wine, and new techniques have made it possible to produce quality wines commercially, although on a limited scale, mostly in the southeastern part of the country.

The most successful vines in this very northerly latitude are the Riesling, the Müller-Thurgau, the Chardonnay, and other hardy white grapes in small amounts. A little red wine is being made on an experimental basis from Pinot Noir grapes. Mead (honey wine) and perry (pear wine) are also produced.

5. GREECE

The Greeks have long cultivated the vine, and their efforts have been praised in prose and poetry by all the ancient poets. Today the Greeks still produce wine in large enough quantities to place Greece twelfth in world production, with an annual production rate of 150 million gallons. The Greeks love to drink wine, and their consumption is a hearty 10 gallons per capita.

Apparently the natural flavor of the grape itself was too bland for the sophisticated Greek palate, so they stored their wines in *amphorae* ("large jars") pitched with tar. This imparted a resinous flavor to the wine, and, as if this were not enough, bags containing spices and aromatic gums were suspended in the wine to ensure its "preservation" and improved flavor. Present-day Greeks still prefer a resinated wine to a natural wine, a taste that must be acquired, as the harsh, pungent turpentine bouquet and flavor shock the unaccustomed palate. The resinated white wines are labeled Retsina while the resinated red wine is called Kokineli.

° From *The Journal of the International Wine and Food Society*, vol. 3, no. 1 (August 1976). Reprinted with permission.

The peninsula of Peloponnesus, which is virtually a huge island, since it is connected to the mainland only by a thin strip of land at Corinth, is the most important wine-producing area of Greece. *wine regions*

On the mainland a native grape variety that grows in the vineyards around Corinth, the Savatiano, is used to make all types of white wines, including the local favorite, Retsina.

The Greek islands of Chios, Coo, Corfu, Crete, Cyclades, Lesbos, Limín, Rhodes, Samos, and Santorini all produce wine today, although their products do not enjoy the majestic reputation they had when the Hellenes were masters of the known world.

Everyone in Greece drinks wine, and most of the cultivated area is devoted to vineyards, although the climate is not suitable for the best grapes for making table wine. The ancient Greeks—like those of today—preferred rich, sweet wines. *grape varieties and wines*

The grape varieties cultivated are those that have grown there for ages.

WINE REGIONS OF GREECE

WILLIAM LEMBECK

The most famous of these is the Malvasia, which originated in the region of Monemvasia, a small town in the Peloponnesian peninsula, and which is grown today in almost every wine region of the world, but most notably in Crete and Madeira (where it produces Malmsey).

The Mavrodaphne, grown in vineyards around the town of Patras along the Gulf of Corinth, is also the name of one of the most popular wines in Greece. This grape was discovered about a century ago by a viticulturist named Gustave Clauss. Because the berry reminded him of the laurel berry, he named it Mavrodaphne ("black laurel"). The wine is sweet, red, and portlike in character. It has an alcohol content varying from 15½ to 20 percent, depending on the quality of the must and the amount of brandy used for fortifying.

The Muscat is grown all over Greece, but most successfully on the island of Samos, close to Turkey. Muscat of Samos, a favorite of Lord Byron, is a pleasant, sweet, fortified white wine.

Not all Greek wine is resinated or sweet and fortified. There are many dry, light red wines, such as Demestica, Pendeli, and the dry rosé Rhoditys, made from the grape of the same name.

The dry whites are more prevalent, and these include Hymettus, named after the famous mountain near Athens, Mantinia, Kantza, Santa Helena, and the white wine of Demestica.

A big red wine from the region of Náousa is made in the northern Macedonian section of Greece from native varieties. Plantings of Cabernet Sauvignon, under the direction of French viticulturists, have also been successful in the northern region along the coastline of the Aegean Sea.

6. HUNGARY

TOKAY

When we think of Hungary and wine, we think first of Tokay.° For generations only royalty could obtain the few bottles of Tokay produced each year, so it came to be known as a royal wine. The finest vineyards in the heart of the district belonged to the royal household, and Emperor Franz Joseph made the princely gesture of sending Queen Victoria a gift of Tokay every year on her birthday, a dozen bottles for each year of her age. Year by year, as the queen grew older, the present augmented in size, until on her eighty-first birthday, in 1900, the emperor sent 972 bottles of that rare wine, Tokaji Aszú,

---

° Tokay is the name of an American dessert wine. However, it has come to be the Americanized name of the wines from the Tokaj area in Hungary. Because the use of Tokay with regard to Hungarian wines has become so widespread, we bow to that common usage, and henceforth in this section the wines of Tokaj will be called Tokay.

The letter *i* affixed to the name of a town means "from." For example, an Aszú wine from Tokaj would be labeled Tokaji Aszú.

which Professor Saintsbury called "no more a wine but a prince of liqueurs."

The wines commonly called Tokay derive their name from the small village of Tokaj in the Hegyalja country (northeastern Hungary) at the foot of the Carpathian Mountains. The delimited Tokaj district is a small plateau, less than half the size of New York City, around which rise the Carpathians. Although this district is fifteen hundred feet above sea level, the protecting mountains produce a special condition that makes possible extremes of weather highly beneficial to growing the grape. These climates vary from bitterly cold winters, accompanied by howling winds, to cool, dry weather in the spring, to very hot summer weather. The rains of early fall give way to a fine, dry Indian summer, important for the grapes, which are left hanging on the vine for extra maturing. The soil is rich in iron and contains some lime. It is of volcanic origin, and the dominant rock of the region is the volcanic trachyte.

The most important grape in Tokay is the Furmint. Young Furmint grapes are quite thick skinned, but as they ripen the skin becomes thinner and more transparent. The sun penetrates it, evaporating most of the water in the juice, with a consequent concentration of the natural sugar. Sometimes the grapes that ripen earliest are so full of juice that the skin bursts and some of the juice runs out. Oddly enough, a new skin forms over the crack and the grapes do not rot, as would normally happen. The grapes are allowed to hang on the vine until they develop *pourriture noble*. They are called Trockenbeeren.

The combination of the grapes, the minerals in the soil, the climatic conditions, and the special manner in which the grapes are treated is unique to the Hungarian Tokaj-Hegyalja. For this reason no other wine-producing region has been able to imitate Tokay. (Tokay grapes, said to have originated in Algeria, are no relation to the Furmint but are table grapes that are sometimes used to make a rather characterless wine that has no relation to the Tokay of Hungary.)

To make Tokay, the grapes are gathered in wooden vessels known as *puttonos,* which hold about 30 quarts. The universal measure in the Hegyalja is the *gönci hordó,* or "cask from Gönc," which holds 120 to 140 liters (about 30 to 35 gallons). It is the number of *puttonos* of overripe Furmint grapes per *gönc* cask that determines the quality and richness of the Tokay.

There are three main types of Tokay: Szamorodni, Aszú, and Eszencia.   *making the wine*

SZAMORODNI.   This wine is made in much the same way as any other white wine, in the lower sections of the plateau where the grapes do not shrivel and in those years when weather conditions have not been favorable for the Trockenbeeren. Szamorodni is an excellent dry wine, with a "fresh-breadcrust" flavor. It is a full-blown wine, with an alcoholic strength of 14 percent. In years when there are not enough Trockenbeeren to make a commercial quantity of Aszú, they are pressed with the other grapes and a sweet Szamorodni results. It does not, of course, begin to approach the richness of the Aszú.

Aszú. When one considers that the average yield of all the vines in the Tokaj-Hegyalja is only 2,650,000 gallons and that Aszú wine represents less than 1 percent, it is apparent that this wine is extremely rare.

In making Aszú (very rich Tokay), the Trockenbeeren are first kneaded into a pulp in a trough. Then the proper proportion of must, pressed from ordinarily ripened grapes, is poured over the pulp, and the mixture is stirred at intervals. The wine is racked after twelve to forty-eight hours of fermentation. In the *gönc* cask, where the bung hole is not tightly closed, a slow fermentation-oxidation proceeds for several years in cool surroundings.

It is the number of *puttonos* of Trockenbeeren (overripe Furmint) that determines the quality of the wine. The wines are labeled three, four, or five *puttonos* in accordance with the number of *puttonos* of overripe Furmint grapes added to the must. Three Puttonos contains about 30 percent Trockenbeeren; Four Puttonos contains about 40 percent; and Five Puttonos, the richest and finest quality that we see in this country, contains about 50 percent Trockenbeeren. Aszú wines are not made every year, only when the vintage is moderately successful.

P. Morton Shand relates Robert Druitt as saying that "Tokay has a flavor of green tea, but an amalgam of the scents of meadow-sweet, acacia-blossom, and the lime-tree in flower, rendered perceptible to the palate . . . is possibly somewhere nearer the mark. No wine possesses such a tremendous force and volume of flavor."

It is the natural sweetness and natural high alcohol content, often exceeding 14 percent, that raise Tokaji Aszú wine so high in the estimation of wine lovers.

ESZENCIA, ESSENZ, OR ESSENCE. In exceptionally successful and plentiful years only Trockenbeeren are put in a cask. The juice that collects without any pressure other than the weight of the Trockenbeeren is allowed to ferment apart and is called Eszencia. This is a fabulous wine that takes years to develop and will live for centuries. There were Eszencias, notably in Poland, over 200 years old. A newspaper account of the marriage of the president of Poland in 1933 reported that toasts were made with 250-year-old wine: "The wine, if good, could only have been Essence of Tokay, and the centuries-old friendship between Poland and Hungary would seem to support this conclusion."

Very little Eszencia is ever made. It is rare and almost unprocurable, as what little is produced is used mostly for enriching the Aszús of poorer years.

HOW AND WHEN TO SERVE TOKAY

Dry Szamorodni should be served well chilled. With its full-bodied dryness it makes an excellent aperitif or all-around table wine.

Sweet Szamorodni may be served at room temperature or cooled. It can be used as any sweet white wine is, but it is more properly a dessert wine.

Aszús have a ripe, luscious quality and should be slightly cooled. They are dessert wines of the first order, but they are more often enjoyed by themselves. A small glass is often one of the most tonic and wholesome restoratives one can take.

Tokay wines, as they come to us, are generally blends of various vintages, but the wines are kept in cask three or four years before bottling. Tokay wines take a long time to ripen and are rarely shipped much before ten years. There are some vintage wines available. The one-half-liter (seventeen-ounce) long-necked bottle has been and still is the standard size and shape.

OTHER HUNGARIAN TABLE WINES

Winemaking is an important part of Hungarian agriculture, as wine is produced in fifty of her sixty-three *Megye* ("counties"). Most of this wine is drunk locally, but Hungary also produces some very fine red and white table wines whose quality is known and appreciated wherever Magyars have lived.

The wine-producing regions are scattered. Near Tokaj-Hegyalja is Eger, whence comes the famous Egri Bikavér. In the central western part of the country is the region of Somló. Below that lies the largest lake in Europe, Lake Balaton. On the northern shore, where the water moderates the climate, is

wine regions

WINE REGIONS
OF
HUNGARY

WILLIAM LEMBECK

Badacsony, center of the vineyards producing the best-quality white table wines. Finally, on the southwestern border is Villány-Pècs, where both red and white table wines are produced.

Hungary contains rough, hilly, and mountainous country as well as plains. The quality wines are not produced in the plains, but in the hilly country where the topsoil appears to be, in many cases, of volcanic origin. Perhaps this explains the fiery character most of the white wines display. The combination of basalt and sand contributes to this special character of the wines.

grape varieties

Grape varieties grown today can be considered native species. Chief among these for white wines are Furmint, Hárslevelü, Kéknyelü, Leányka, and Muskotaly (Muscat). The Kadarka is an important native red-wine grape. In addition to native varieties a number of traditional European varieties are grown. Some of these are the white Rizling (Riesling), Szilvany (Sylvaner), and Sémillon and the red Cabernet, Pinot Noir, and Médoc Noir (Merlot).

white wines

Typical Hungarian wines and descriptions of their taste are:

SZEKSZÁRDI RIZLING.   A light, dry wine with Riesling character from the region of Szekszárd.

TOKAJI FURMINT.   A full-bodied dry wine made in the same district as the Tokaji wines mentioned previously. It resembles the other wines because of the common geographic origin and use of the Furmint grape. The Tokaji Furmint differs because the wines commonly known as Tokays use the Hárslevelü grape in the blend, but Tokaji Furmint does not. Unlike the Tokays, the Tokaji Furmint comes in a standard table-wine bottle.

SOMLÓI FURMINT.   A fragrant dry wine that resembles the Tokaji Furmint but is from the region of Lake Balaton.

BADACSONYI KÉKNYELÜ.   From the Badacsony district on the north shore along Lake Balaton comes this gold-green, medium-dry wine, with a bouquet reminiscent of new-mown hay. Kéknyelü is the name of the vine and it means "blue-stalked."

BADACSONYI SZÜRKEBARÁT.   A medium-dry, golden table wine from Badacsony. The vine is named Szürkebarát, which translates as "gray friar"; it is the Pinot Gris of France. The wine derives its distinctive flavor from the volcanic soil of Mount Badacsony.

DEBRÖI HÁRSLEVELÜ.   A medium-sweet wine with a pleasing perfume from the small wine district of Debrö in northern Hungary, near the town of Eger. It is produced from the Hárslevelü grape, whose name means "linden-leaf."

LEÁNYKA.   A light table wine from the traditional vine-growing mountain villages around the city of Eger. The name, meaning "young girl," refers to the softness and delicacy of the wine.

MUSKOTALY.   One of the lightest and most highly perfumed wines of Hungary, with a pronounced Muscat flavor. Made in various districts, it is always a pleasant wine, although not one of the finest.

red wines

EGRI BIKAVÉR.   Because of its deep, very dark red color, it is called Bikavér, or "bull's blood." It is a big, full-bodied dry wine with character and is probably the best-known Hungarian red wine. It is supposed to have fortified the inhabitants of Eger, enabling them to withstand the siege by the Turks in the sixteenth century.

SZEKSZÁRDI VÖRÖS.   A dry red wine from the town of Szekszárd, south of Lake Balaton. This is one of the oldest wine regions of Hungary, dating from Roman times. The wine is made from the Kadarka grape and is dry and well balanced. It was a favorite wine of Franz Liszt. Szekszárdi Vörös means "red wine of Szekszárd."

NEMES KADAR.   The name means "noble Kadar," and the wine is made from the Kadarka grape. It has a very bright red color and is light bodied with some sweetness.

From Villány-Pècs in the county of Pècs come some good red and white wines. The best-known red from this area is Villányi Burgundi. The white wines are generally shipped in long, fluted Rhine-wine bottles, while the reds travel in standard claret bottles of Bordeaux.

From the greater Lake Balaton area come three simpler, charming wines. They are a pale, spicy Riesling, a young, attractive Cabernet, and a fresh rosé made from the Kadarka grape.

Typical Hungarian vintage scene. Gathering grapes to produce the red Egri Bikavér at Eger, Hungary.

7. LUXEMBOURG

history   Vines have been grown in Luxembourg since Roman times. Until World War II, however, the wines were mostly consumed within the duchy, and many of them were blended with German wines. After World War II a brief effort was made to promote Luxembourg wines outside the country, but the combination of French and German competition and a large internal demand for wine made this effort fail.

Luxembourg is a small producer of wine, ranking thirty-sixth in world production, with an average annual yield of five million gallons. The local residents of Luxembourg rank seventh in consumption, however, with eleven gallons per capita; imports from France and Italy make up the difference.

wine regions   This inland duchy, which is 999 square miles in area, is surrounded by Belgium on the west and north, France on the south, and Germany on the east. Luxembourg is separated from Germany by the Moselle River, and it is along the Moselle that Luxembourg's vineyards lie.

The Moselle River actually begins in France, but before it reaches the famous Moselle wine region in Germany it cuts through Luxembourg, with vineyards along its western bank. This gives the vineyards an eastern slope and exposure to the morning sun.

The best wine-producing villages are Wormeldange, Remich, Wintringen, Ehnen, Grevenmacher, and Wasserbillig. Each main town has cooperatives made up of many small vineyards.

grape varieties   As in Germany, the finest grape grown is the Riesling. Pinot varieties
and wines   include Pinot Blanc, Ruländer (Pinot Gris), and Auxerrois. The Sylvaner, Müller-Thurgau, Traminer, Elbling, and Muscat Ottonel round out the list.

Luxembourg wines are light and not as flowery as their German counterparts, although they do have a touch of sweetness. They appear in Moselle-style green fluted bottles. Wines bottled under government supervision have the words *Marque Nationale* on a neck label.

8. ROMANIA

Catching up with the country's demand, Romanian wine production has reached the point where a large quantity is finding its way into the export market, with some entering the United States. Romania has always been a large producer and a big consumer as well. On an international scale this relatively small country ranks eighth in production, with an average 220 million gallons produced annually, and twelfth in consumption, averaging almost 9 gallons per capita.

Romania has always been the most important wine producer of the Balkan *history*
nations, which also include Albania, Bulgaria, and Yugoslavia. Romania's
war-torn history has alternately enlarged and diminished its land area, depending on its alliance with a conqueror nation or a conquered nation. Before
World War I the country consisted of a narrow, curved strip of land encompassing Moldavia and Wallachia. These lands were in the prime viticultural
belt that passed through France's Bordeaux and Burgundy vineyards, as well as
Italy's Piedmont region. Between 1919 and 1945 Romania's borders expanded
to include Transylvania, acquired from Hungary, and Bessarabia, from the
Russian Empire. This meant that large areas of vineyards came under Romanian rule. After World War II the loss of Bessarabia and some of Moldavia to the
U.S.S.R. cut Romania's production by about 40 percent. Continued plantings,
both private and cooperative, have now increased its output to a prodigious
amount.

Although the Carpathian mountain range covers a major portion of this *wine regions*
country, the foothills provide sunny slopes over large areas. Wine-growing
areas stretch southward from the northeast to the Black Sea and then curve
westward to the western part of the country.

The wine regions are the Cotnari vineyards in the northeast, in the province of Iaşi; the Focşani vineyards, south of Cotnari, in the Galaţi province; the Murfatlar vineyards, on the Murfatlar Hills along the Black Sea; the Dealul-Mare vineyards, just inland from the Black Sea, near the city of Ploeşti, nestled in the southeastern Carpathian foothills; the Tîrnave vineyards, the most important in Romania, spreading along the Tîrnave River in the center of Romania and in the heart of Transylvania; and the Banat vineyards, concentrated in the most westerly region of the country.

The best way to describe the wines of Romania is to show the range of grapes grown, along with the types of wines made from these grapes.

white grapes   RIESLING. Grown extensively throughout Romania, Riesling is often used as the major grape in a blend to produce such wines as Perla de Tîrnave. In addition to these aromatic and often slightly sweet wines, Riesling produces varietal wines with regional designations, such as Riesling de Tîrnave or Riesling de Dealul-Mare.

FETEASCĂ. This is a native variety that is suitable to many regions of the country. It is used in blends from such regions as Cotnari, Tîrnave, and Focşani. Its wine also appears under a varietal label, such as Fetească de Tîrnave.

CHARDONNAY. This noble grape takes on a different character when grown in the Murfatlar vineyards. It makes a dessert wine, rich and honeylike, and not the usual wine that comes from Chardonnay in the rest of the world.

GRASĂ. Grown in Cotnari, this grape often gets some "noble rot," making wine with a honeyed aroma and a full, rich taste.

ITALIAN RIESLING, FURMINT, MUSCAT OTTONEL, AND TRAMINER are other white grapes used throughout Romania.

red grapes   CABERNET SAUVIGNON. This noble grape is found in many of the quality red wines of Romania, notably those from the Murfatlar, Dealul-Mare, and Focşani regions.

PINOT NOIR. This grape is planted in the same regions as the Cabernet Sauvignon. The wines from this grape are full bodied and improve with age.

KADARKA. This Balkan grape is used to make the popular Kadarka de Banat, a big red wine with a rich aroma.

BĂBEASCĂ. This native variety is notable for a wine it produces in the Focşani region called Băbească de Nicoreşti.

9. SWITZERLAND

Surrounded by major wine-producing countries, Switzerland is intensely wine conscious. It is both a producer (about thirty million gallons in good years) and a consumer (seventy-one million gallons, or about twelve gallons per capita) and imports a great deal of wine from Italy, France, and Spain, among

Vines growing on terraced ground above Visperterminen, Valais. (*Courtesy Swiss Tourist Bureau, New York*)

other countries. Most of this is red wine, since two-thirds of the wine produced in nineteen of Switzerland's twenty-two cantons is white.

history

Swiss vineyards date back to Roman times, when vines were first cultivated around Lakes Neuchâtel, Morat, and Bienne. In the Swiss mountains, passes, such as the Simplon and Saint Gotthard, led to France, Austria, Germany, and Italy and thus became the highroads of the Middle Ages.

geography

The Alps are an important influence on Swiss viticulture. They shield the Valais area from winds and storms, for example, resulting in a temperate climate in summer, even though winters are cold.

Many vineyards are at high altitudes, carefully terraced. Visperterminen, which is at an altitude of four thousand feet, is the highest vineyard in Europe. Because of the cold climate and high altitude, most vineyards face south over lakes and rivers to benefit from both direct and reflected sunlight.

Much of the thirty thousand acres under vine is irrigated with water from melting glaciers through a system of canals.

grape varieties

While some ancient Roman vines are still grown, such as the Arvine, Amigne, Humagne, and Rèze, the invading dukes of Burgundy brought European varieties with them, and it is these grapes that are grown in Switzerland today. The early indigenous grapes have been replaced, for the most part, by Chasselas, Pinot Noir, and Gamay.

white grapes

The Chasselas is the most important white-wine grape, and it appears under several names in different parts of Switzerland. In Valais it is called the Fendant, in Vaud it is the Dorin, near Geneva it is the Perlan, and in the German cantons it is the Gutedel. In Neuchâtel it is the Chasselas, as it is in Pouilly-sur-Loire in France.

The Sylvaner grape appears in Valais, Vaud, and Geneva, while a cross between Riesling and Sylvaner is grown in the German cantons. The Traminer grape in Valais is sometimes called the Savagnin.

WINE REGIONS OF SWITZERLAND

Red-wine grapes of French origin are the Pinot Noir and Gamay of Burgundy and the Merlot of Bordeaux. In the German cantons the Pinot Noir is known as the Blauburgunder and the Clevner. The Gamay, in Valais, is called the Goron. The Merlot, a newer vine to Switzerland, grows in Ticino, an Italian region, along with the Italian varieties Nebbiolo and Bondolo. *red grapes*

The Italian and French cantons of Ticino, Valais, Vaud, Geneva, Neuchâtel, and Fribourg produce 90 percent of the wine in Switzerland. *wine regions and wines*

On the southwestern frontiers of Switzerland is the Lake Geneva region, which is subdivided into smaller regions. Chablais, southeast of Lake Geneva, produces good reds and pleasant whites. East of Lausanne is Lavaux, where one of the finest white wines, Dézaley, is produced from the Chasselas grape. West of Lausanne is La Côte, producing a fresh white wine called Dorin. On the tip of the lake is Geneva itself, the third largest producer in Switzerland. Here the white wines are called Perlan. Vaud, on Lake Geneva and the Rhône River, is the southern boundary of Switzerland. Red wines are produced in Vaud from the Gamay and Pinot Noir grapes and are labeled Salvagnin.

The Valais, a long valley along the Rhône River, is third largest in area and first in wine production. This canton is favored with good soil and climate, as well as dedicated growers. The best white wine is Fendant, from the Chasselas grape, and some wine called Johannisberger is produced from the Sylvaner. Dôle, considered the best red wine of Switzerland, is made from 60 percent Pinot Noir, the balance being Gamay.

The Seeland area, which includes Lakes Neuchâtel, Morat, and Bienne, has a chalky soil rich in limestone and makes especially good white wines. North of Lausanne, on the north shore of Lake Neuchâtel, is the home of the clean, fresh white wine called Neuchâtel. It is made from the Chasselas grape and undergoes a second fermentation in the bottle. The wine has a slight *pétillance* ("tingle") because of this and is most refreshing. A light red and a "partridge-eye" rosé are produced from the Pinot Noir in the Seeland area. The best red wine is called Cortaillod, named for the village where it is made.

Ticino (Tessin), an Italian region on the other side of the Saint Gotthard Pass from Valais, is on the southern slopes of the Alps. There are ten thousand growers around Lakes Locarno, Lugano, and Maggiore. The climate is temperate, and the Merlot has been expanded from two thousand to thirty thousand acres in the past twenty-five years. Merlot produces eight million gallons annually, and the best is labeled *Viti*, for the appellation Vino Ticinese, if it passes government inspection.

Along the Rhine River, from Chur to Basel, are the German cantons, which produce about 10 percent of Swiss wines. Here red wine, which is 80 percent of the local production, is made from the Pinot Noir, known as the Clevner or Blauburgunder. Some white wine is produced from the Riesling-Sylvaner. The climate is less conducive to viticulture than in other parts of Switzerland.

10. U.S.S.R.

The U.S.S.R. is the fourth largest wine-producing country in the world, ranking after Italy, France, and Spain with an estimated production of 730 million gallons. One would not expect such large production from a country whose severe winters are legendary, but in the southeastern region, where grapes are planted, the winters are actually mild and can be tolerated by the vine. It is the Black Sea that has this moderating effect on the climate. Viticultural techniques, such as insulating the vines for the winter under blankets of dirt, also account for successful wine production.

Wine consumption in Russia is $4\frac{1}{4}$ gallons per capita, and most of this is in sweet wines. There is a decided preference for wines on the sweet side; dry still and sparkling wines are in the minority.

WINE REGIONS OF THE U.S.S.R.

POLAND

FETYASKA
CABERNET
ALIGOTÉ
RIESLING
TRAMINER

Don R.

MOLDAVIA

Rostov

ROMANIA

Kerch

Danube R.

CRIMEA

Krasnodar

MUSCAT

SAPERAVI
MZVANE
RKATSITELI

BULGARIA

BLACK SEA

GEORGIA

TURKEY

ARMENIA   AZERBAIJAN

WILLIAM LEMBECK

IRAN

There are three main regions of wine production and a few other, less *wine regions* important, ones. The three major regions are Moldavia, Crimea, and the republics of Georgia, Armenia, and Azerbaijan (Azerbaidzhan). Table and sparkling wines are also produced around Krasnodar and around the Don River, below Rostov.

Moldavia, north of the Black Sea, is one of the smallest Soviet republics, yet it produces the greatest quantity of wine. Production from this region accounts for one-fourth of the total amount of wine produced in the U.S.S.R. The wines are similar in style to the wines of neighboring Romania and Bulgaria. In fact, Moldavia was part of Romania until 1940 and was known as Bessarabia. Both red and white table and fortified wines are produced here.

Crimea produces the highest-quality wines of the U.S.S.R. The area is a peninsula that extends far into the Black Sea and eastward across the Straits of Kerch into the Kuban Valley below the western Caucasus. Table, dessert, and sparkling wines, as well as some brandy, are produced here. Massandra is the location of the largest combine of Crimean wine collectives.

Farther east, along the southern slopes of the Caucasus Mountains, are the republics of Georgia, Armenia, and Azerbaijan, bordering Turkey. Georgia produces fine table wines, but it is fortified and dessert wines for which the republics are most famous.

In Russia there are *vinifera* varieties, local grapes, and hybrids. In the *grape varieties* Moldavian region there is Cabernet Sauvignon, Aligoté, Riesling, and Traminer. One of the local grapes, which makes a dry white wine, is Fetyaska. East of Moldavia, in the Ukraine, many hybrids had been planted, but these vineyards are being converted to *vinifera* varieties.

The Crimean region has the same grapes as Moldavia, but there is also a great deal of Muscat planted, which is used in dessert wines.

Georgia, Armenia, and Azerbaijan grow local grapes that include Saperavi and Mzvane, which produce red wines, and Rkatsiteli, a white-wine grape. Rkatsiteli has been grown successfully in the Livermore Valley in California, where it was planted experimentally in 1969 by the Concannons as part of an exchange of vines.

11. YUGOSLAVIA

The vine has always flourished wherever the ancient Greeks and Romans *history* had their influence. Yugoslavia was doubly blessed in this matter, with its southern vineyards neighboring Greece and its northern vineyards under the Roman influence.

This state of affairs continued until the Turks took over and decreed that the vines be uprooted. From then viticulture ceased until the 1800s. It was only in the north, in the lands that belonged to Austria, that vines continued to grow, and these wines continue to show the Austrian influence.

Yugoslavia as we know it today was formed after World War I from Slovenia, Croatia, Serbia, Bosnia-Herzegovina, Montenegro, and northern Macedonia. Wine production in Yugoslavia is about 150 million gallons annually, much of which is exported to Germany, Czechoslovakia, Poland, Italy, Great Britain, and the United States. Local consumption amounts to 7½ gallons per capita.

wine regions   The wine regions of Yugoslavia have maintained the identities they had when they were separate states under the Austro-Hungarian Empire: Slovenia, Croatia, Serbia, and Macedonia.

Vintage in vineyards near Belgrade. (*Courtesy Yugoslav Information Center, New York*)

Slovenia, in the northeast, has two wine districts. One is in the valleys of the Sava and Drava rivers, near Hungary; and the other is along a short stretch of the Adriatic Sea, near Trieste at the Italian border.

Croatia produces varied styles of wines in three main sections. In the north, near Slovenia, the vineyards also come under the influence of the Sava and Drava rivers, near Hungary. Light white wines are produced here, similar to those of Slovenia.

The Istrian Peninsula, in the north near Trieste, projects into the Adriatic Sea. The vines are protected by the tempering influence of this large body of water.

Dalmatia is a coastal region, stretching for almost 150 miles along the Adriatic Sea. It produces mostly red wines.

The Serbian region is the largest wine-producing area, contributing 50 percent of Yugoslavia's total wine output. It adjoins Romania and Bulgaria.

This inland area makes mostly white wines, with a few reds and rosés, all primarily from the Prokupac grape.

Macedonia is the southernmost region of Yugoslavia, with Albania to the west, Bulgaria to the east, and Greece, which has been the major influence on Macedonian viticulture, to the south.

grape varieties

All types of vines are grown in Yugoslavia. There are European *vinifera*, some native varieties, and hybrids that were planted at the time of *Phylloxera* intrusion.

White-wine grapes include Traminer, Pinot Blanc, Sauvignon Blanc, Sémillon, Malvasia, and several varieties of Rieslings, as well as the native Sipon, Zilavka, and Smedervka.

Red *vinifera* are represented by the Burgundac (Pinot Noir), Bogonja (Gamay), Cabernet, and Merlot. Native grapes are Teran, Plavac, Skadarka, Začinak, and the ubiquitous Prokupac.

wines

Yugoslavia produces table, sparkling, and dessert wines. They are either varietal wines labeled with a regional suffix or blended wines labeled with a regional name. Most vintages of different years are blended, and vintage labeling is not so important.

Slovenia, which once belonged to Austria, produces wines in an Austrian and German style. These wines are, however, higher in alcohol, and some subtlety is exchanged for more fullness. The most famous wine is Ljutomer, which is named after the town of that name.

Croatia's inland white wines are similar to those of Slovenia, with some of the same character and perfume. Istria and Dalmatia, on the Adriatic coast, produce red wines in a robust Italian style. These wines are big and full, with high alcohol and tannin content. Opol is a famous rosé wine of Dalmatia.

Serbian wines are mostly of the carafe, or jug, type and are named for the district of origin.

Macedonia, less influenced by other European countries, produces wines of a more native style. This region, with new plantings, is becoming more important.

11
THE WINES OF THE UNITED STATES

history

America is one of the richest countries in the world in viticultural natural resources. More than half of the known species of grapevines (*Vitis*) are indigenous to our continent. According to popular legend a band of Norse Vikings reached the eastern shores of America and found a profusion of wild grapes growing in the forests. They were so impressed by the abundant grapevines that they named the new land Vineland the Good, and so it was known in Icelandic sagas for centuries. The truth is that the Norsemen never came as far south as the grape country, and we know now that they mistook mountain cranberries for grapes. But had they traveled far enough south they would have found a land rich in vines after all.

The Indians used grapes as a staple fruit, and in early settlers' narrations the grape is found in the list of resources and treasures of the newfound continent that indeed proved to be a natural vineyard.

The winemaker's life is never an easy one, and in the United States it was more discouraging than in other lands. Our earliest settlers on the eastern seaboard made wine from the native grapes, but the wines were unlike those of Europe; the settlers wanted wines similar to the European types with which they were familiar.

Phylloxera

Since the native vines grew so luxuriantly, the settlers reasoned that their problem could be solved easily by planting European (*Vitis vinifera*) varieties. However, their efforts were doomed to failure in the East. In Mexico the missionary priests did much the same thing, but there they had greater success.

The reasons for the miserable failure of the eastern attempt to grow *Vitis vinifera* grapes were many, but the most immediate cause was the presence of native fungus diseases, such as powdery mildew (*oïdium*), downy mildew, black rot, and Pierce's Disease. Of secondary importance was the scourge of the grapevine, *Phylloxera vastatrix*.

189

Phylloxera vastatrix is, to the best of our knowledge, native to America. It is a plant pest of the louse family that lives on the sweet, soft roots of the grapevine. *Phylloxera* attacks the roots very slowly, over a period of years, and although the results are always ruinous, this dreaded plant louse probably did not do very much damage to the early American plantings of *vinifera* varieties. Those were destroyed by diseases before they would have been killed by *Phylloxera.*

Sometime between 1858 and 1863 Europe imported many American vines for experimental purposes. It is practically certain that the deadly *Phylloxera* was brought in on these American rootstocks, which also carried native American fungus diseases. The proximity of the European vineyards to one another facilitated the spread of *Phylloxera*. Within a few years it had become a true scourge, and from 1865 to 1890 *Phylloxera* devastated the vineyards of Europe eastward from France to Russia and northward from Spain to Germany; eventually the pest even appeared in Australia. In the United States it seriously damaged most of the vineyards of California in 1880, when, ironically, it was brought in on contaminated European vinestocks.

It is impossible today to estimate the actual pecuniary loss, but in 1888 M. Lalande, president of the Chamber of Commerce of Bordeaux, calculated that the loss to France alone amounted to $2 billion, or twice the indemnity paid to Germany in 1871 after the Franco-Prussian War.

Phylloxera subsists on the sap of the vine, which it obtains by piercing the bark of the root with its sharp proboscis. One solitary louse can do very little damage, but each lays many eggs that hatch in six to ten days. When only a few days old, the young attach themselves to the root and within three weeks they become adults that lay more eggs. It has been estimated that a single female that lays a batch of eggs in March and then dies would have twenty-five million descendants by October.

Every known method of combating diseases of the vine was employed but with little success. It was not until the European viticulturists discovered that the American rootstocks were hardier—and immune to *Phylloxera*—that they found that the solution to their problem was to graft the European vines onto resistant American rootstocks. Even then it took many years of viticultural investigation to find the best rootstocks that were suitably resistant yet compatible with European vines.

During the frantic search for a solution to the problem, many nurseries and grape specialists started an intensive program of hybridization between *Vitis vinifera* varieties and native American varieties to produce new selections with the *Phylloxera* resistance of the American parents and the wine characteristics of the *vinifera* parents.

The United States has radically and vitally influenced European and world viticulture and wine. Yet even though American rootstocks are in fairly general use in Europe, there has been no significant change in the basic character of the various grape varieties that have been grafted onto them and form the vines themselves. The wines made from these grapes are essentially the same as before grafting.

To the best of our knowledge Chilean vineyards have hardly been infested by *Phylloxera*. But every other non-American vineyard region of the world has been invaded and devastated by this louse, and all have had to graft their *Vitis vinifera* vines onto American *Phylloxera*-resistant rootstocks. There are certain scattered vineyard areas with sandy soil, such as Colares in Portugal, that are *Phylloxera*-free.

Even in California, where European varieties of grapes are grown almost exclusively, it is usually necessary to use certain resistant American rootstocks as a defense against the ever present *Phylloxera*, so truly surnamed *vastatrix* ("devastating"). Some recent plantings, notably in Monterey County where grapes had never been planted before, have been made with European varieties on their own roots. The growers have taken this calculated risk because they feel that since *Phylloxera* requires heavy soil, it may not appear in the granitic, very light, and sandy soil of Monterey County.

Near the end of the nineteenth century the U.S. wine industry was producing wines fine enough to win some medals and gain recognition in expositions in France. In fact, there are many strong indications that American wines were well on their way to becoming firmly established when another and more fatal blight was visited upon the vineyards—national Prohibition.

Prohibition

There was consternation among the winemakers in 1919. What were they going to do with the grapes, which were good only for making wine? Smaller and less sweet than table or raisin grapes, they were poor travelers because of their thin, easily bruised skins. The inevitable happened—many vineyards were uprooted and replanted with more salable types of grapes, and in some cases with other fruits.

Amateur winemaking—perfectly legal during Prohibition—flourished during this period. The true wine grapes from California, in addition to not shipping well, did not look as plump as some of the raisin and table varieties, and many of the new, inexperienced winemakers did not know enough to buy the better grapes. As a result, wine grapes were replaced by the less useful table varieties that the amateurs demanded. By the end of Prohibition amateur winemakers were producing ninety million gallons of wine per year, half of California's current table wine production, and the grape acreage was close to 35 percent greater than that in 1919. Only in 1975 did California acreage return to Prohibition levels.

The legacy of Prohibition, however, was a country almost bereft of fine wine grapes and a few scattered wineries that could still produce quality wine. The country had to rebuild its reputation for quality while it suffered from the added disadvantage of supplying quantity for a thirsty public.

MAKING THE WINE

At the time of Repeal American winemakers faced many problems. During Prohibition nearly all their vineyards had been replanted with other crops or with table and raisin grapes. Repeal came suddenly. Ipso facto, on December 5, 1933, the day of Repeal, the winemaker was expected to have wine ready even though until then it was illegal to make wine commercially. Regardless of what cold-storage grapes were used, it still took time to crush the grapes, ferment the must, and allow the wine to develop.

The first few post-Repeal years were very difficult for American wine producers, but they diligently set about resolving their production bottlenecks. New methods were tried. Some were discarded, but many were adopted and have become standard practice not only in the United States but in most wine regions of the world today.

The method of making wine in the United States varies, of course, from vineyard to vineyard and region to region. It also depends to some extent on the size of the vineyard. Even the smaller vineyards in the coastal parts of California in the counties surrounding San Francisco Bay tend to follow modern methods, from gathering the grapes to bottling the wine. In the small vineyards of Europe usually one type of wine is produced, not only in a single vineyard, but in an entire region. Very often the grower is a small farmer who makes, in some instances, only a few hogsheads of wine.

In the United States, however, where individual vineyards may run to thousands of acres and, in nearly all cases, produce several types and classes of wines, large-scale production is inevitable. Where the vineyards are extensive, and enormous quantities of grapes ripen at the same time, it becomes impossible to follow the small-scale European methods, and new, modern ones must be employed.

table wines   The grapes are trucked to the winery as soon as they are picked. After being examined and weighed, they are dumped onto conveyors that carry them to a power-driven destemmer and crusher. This breaks the grape skins without breaking the seeds, allows the juice to run freely, and, finally, separates and throws out the stems.

As in Europe, in making red wines the grapes and juice are conveyed directly to the fermenting vats, while in making white wines the juice is separated from the skins before fermentation.

To ensure normal fermentation, wild yeasts are inhibited by the addition of sulfur dioxide (SO_2), and smooth fermentation is carried out by SO_2-acclimated culture yeasts—*Saccharomyces ellipsoideus*. Since fermenting wine generates heat, the wine must be carefully watched. Temperatures are controlled and the fermenting must is never permitted to go above 90 degrees Fahrenheit for red wines and 70 degrees Fahrenheit for whites (sometimes not above 55 degrees).

A modern method for planting a vineyard. Five rows of new vines are planted simultaneously at Pinnacles vineyard. (*Courtesy Paul Masson Vineyards, San Francisco, California*)

Mechanical harvester picking grapes in a New York State vineyard. (*Courtesy the Taylor Wine Company, Hammondsport, New York*)

Outdoor fermenting tanks at Paul Masson Vineyards, northern California. (*Courtesy Paul Masson Vineyards, San Francisco, California*)

Higher temperatures tend to arrest fermentation and contribute to loss of bouquet. White wines especially benefit from a long, cool fermentation that retains the fruity character of the grape. Winemakers are increasingly using double-jacketed stainless steel fermenting tanks that have a cooling liquid pumped between the inner and outer walls. This enables them to maintain more precise control over the wine's development during fermentation.

The first, or violent, fermentation phase takes about a week, after which the still-fermenting must is run off into closed oak or California redwood vats or stainless steel tanks to complete fermentation. In some other wineries concrete fermenting tanks are employed. The total fermentation period takes about two weeks for red and three weeks for white wines in the cooler areas, but often less than one week for red in the warmer areas, since fermentation may be run at a higher temperature. After fermentation the new wine is placed in storage cooperage of various sizes to begin clarification, racking, and aging. Some wineries maintain air conditioning, which ensures dry, clean, mold-free cellars and precise and continuous temperature and humidity control.

Generally speaking, at the majority of wineries the most modern and improved methods of treating wines are in use, such as refrigeration, to ensure a perfectly bright, stable wine, a healthy wine free of heavy sediment.

Wine, table wine in particular, is constantly developing, with minute changes taking place. This occurs because of the action of the yeasts that may remain in the wine and because of the acids, the solids, and the other components of the wine that act and react, some with, and others against, one another. The result is a state of continual change. One of the natural phenomena of the development of a wine is the formation of cream of tartar, which settles in the form of crystalline sediment. This can be hastened if the wine is held at a low temperature for a short period of time. It is accomplished through cold stabilization and ensures a wine that after filtering will be less likely to throw any further sediment or deposit.

These winery workers are racking a tank of wine into smaller wooden casks where the wine will age and develop smoothness before it is bottled. Racking, or transferring by pump from a larger to a smaller container, also helps clear the wine of any sediment acquired during fermentation to ensure that the wine is brilliantly clear when it reaches the consumer. (*Courtesy Wine Institute, San Francisco, California*)

Since the consuming public has become accustomed to seeing so much brilliant, sediment-free wine, it has come to believe that a wine that has a natural sediment or deposit is not in good condition for serving. By the same token too many retail merchants, rather than explain the facts to their customers, take the easier path and request from the supplier a refund for or replacement of the "unsalable" wine.

dessert wines

In the production of dessert wines such as sherry, port, Muscatel, and Angelica, fermentation is arrested before all of the natural sugar of the must has been converted. The alcohol content is brought up to about 20 percent by the addition of fortification brandy, which in many cases is distilled by the brandy distillery associated with the winery itself. The wines are stored in large vats or casks and are treated in the same manner as are similar wines all over the world. They are racked periodically, so the wine will not remain on its lees, and then fined and filtered as necessary.

sherry*

Sherry in the United States is obtained by special methods. When fermentation is arrested in the new wine, the wine is not cellared in the same manner as other dessert wines. In California, in order to impart the characteristic sherry flavor, the wine is stored at a high temperature, that is, it is "baked." This is done by racking the wine into large tanks or vats located in cellars where the temperature is carefully maintained. The wine is kept in these baking cellars anywhere from two to six months at temperatures that vary from 100 degrees to 140 degrees Fahrenheit, depending on the length of time the wine is baked. Wine kept for only two months is held at a higher temperature and wine kept for a longer time is held at a lower temperature, similar to the baking process in Madeira. Each producer has his own formula for the method that gives the best results. The vats are heated, in some cases by hot water coils in the vat itself, while in other cases the entire cellar room is heated to the desired controlled temperature.

The baking process causes the color to deepen somewhat, gives the wine the desired tang, and develops the typical nutty flavor of California sherries.

Upon completion of the baking process, the wine is allowed to cool slowly to cellar temperature. It is then stored for aging and treated as other dessert wines to acquire mellowness, to be blended with older wines, and eventually to be bottled and marketed.

Some of New York State winemakers have developed their own methods of producing sherry. One method is the Tressler process. Niagara, Concord, Dutchess, and other eastern grapes are used to produce a wine that is then fortified. These wines are stored in special vats at a temperature of 140 degrees Fahrenheit for four to six weeks. During this time oxygen is bubbled through

---

* The B.A.T.F. considers all sherries to be dessert wines.

Traditional oak and redwood storage vats, together with stainless steel tanks, in California. (*Courtesy Paul Masson Vineyards, San Francisco, California*)

the wine. This oxidation develops the sherry character, and when the desired flavor is obtained, the wine is fined, filtered, and aged in other barrels for months or years.

In other wineries a weathering process is used in which fortified wines of sherry character, in uncharred fifty-gallon barrels, are stored on the roof of the winery and left exposed to the sun and elements for four years. After the wines have developed the desired nuttiness and mellowness, they are blended, filtered, and bottled.

The essential difference in the method of producing this type of wine between the United States and the Jerez region of Spain lies in the secondary "flowering" fermentation, described on page 140, that occurs in Jerez. Some California producers have had considerable success with film yeast, using the "submerged-*flor*" process, which has given them some unusually fine *rancio-* or nutty-flavored sherries. However, it is apparent that the American public still prefers the traditional baked type, although with time it may well learn to like film yeast sherries.

A few wineries in the United States, both in the East and in the West, have *solera* systems, begun several years ago. The sherries are aged in a way similar to the aging that is done in Spain. Some wineries even use sherry barrels imported from Spain. In this method older wines are systematically blended with younger wines.

Vermouth and the other aromatized appetizer wines are produced according to the traditional methods to be described in Chapter 15.

sparkling wines   The American Champagnes that enjoy the greatest repute are all produced in the same manner as the wines of Champagne, France, by means of the secondary fermentation in the bottle. These wines are clean, have a fine, definite flavor, and are most satisfactory examples of quality viniculture.

Practically all of the New York State Champagnes, produced mostly in the Finger Lakes region, are bottle fermented. The wines reach maturity rather quickly and are ready for marketing after a year of development in the bottle. Wines produced in this way are often labeled "naturally fermented in *this* bottle."

Because of the problems of removing the sediment from the bottles, the German transfer system has been introduced into this country. This is an attempt to retain the advantages of the Champagne method, with the second fermentation in bottles, while eliminating the disadvantages of costly riddling to remove sediment. The bottles are chilled, but not frozen, standing up, rather than tilting downward. The corks are withdrawn and the wine is emptied, under pressure, into a large tank. The sparkling wine is then filtered into another pressured tank under refrigeration. Finally, it is filtered, still under pressure, into clean bottles. Wines produced in this way are often labeled "naturally fermented in *the* bottle."

Sparkling wines made by both the Champagne method and the transfer process have the advantage of a second fermentation in the bottle. This gives the small volume of liquid intimate contact with the yeast.

Sparkling wines are also made by fermenting the wine in large tanks and bottling it under pressure. This method is known as the Charmat process, or bulk fermentation method. Wines made in this manner must be labeled bulk process or Charmat process.

Bulk-process fermentation saves several years in making the wine available for the market, and consequently it is much less costly to produce, but by the same token certain quality factors are sacrificed. The gas does not really become a component of the wine and tends to escape more rapidly once the bottle is opened. Furthermore, while the basic quality of the Champagne derives from the quality of the still wine employed, its character is influenced and enhanced by the maturation time during which the Champagne remains in contact with the yeast. Obviously, this is minimal in the case of bulk-process production.

There is still another type of sparkling wine that is artificially carbonated by adding carbon dioxide gas in much the same way in which soft drinks are made. It cannot be called or labeled Champagne; it must be labeled carbonated wine.

Special riddling racks employed to shake down the sediment in New York State Champagne. (*Courtesy the Taylor Wine Company, Hammondsport, New York*)

Pyrex glass pipes—measuring more than a mile in length—employed to transfer wines from one processing point to another at the Taylor Wine Company winery, Hammondsport, New York. (*Courtesy the Tayor Wine Company, Hammondsport, New York*)

WINE TYPES

U.S. wines fall into three types: generic,° varietal, and proprietary. Generics are merely generalized wine types with borrowed names, whose geographic origins have lost their significance, such as Chablis, claret, and Burgundy from France, Rhine from Germany, and Chianti from Italy. These names must be used with the name of the place of production as well, such as California Chablis.

A varietally labeled wine is one bearing the name of the grape variety from which the wine was made. To be so labeled, at least 51 percent of the grapes employed must be of the variety named on the label. Examples are Cabernet Sauvignon, Catawba, Chardonnay, Delaware, Johannisberg Riesling, Baco

° The correct term in the U.S. regulations is *semigeneric* because of the regional designation on the label, but *generic* is popularly used.

Noir, and Chelois. Some wineries now employ both a varietal and a generic name when that is the best way to describe a wine.

Proprietary labeling is another way that wineries can point to the uniqueness of their wines. A proprietary name is one created by the winery that no other winery may use. Often these names reflect the location of the winery or describe the wine itself. Many wineries are developing proprietary or trademarked brand names for their house wines.

labeling Both federal and California laws require specific labeling for wines, and these requirements are strictly enforced. Quite often it has been the California winemaker who has been responsible for the high standards. In addition, state wine laws° can be more stringent than those decreed by the federal government. The percentages of specific grapes used to make the wine may vary, and different terminology signifies different situations. The consumer should study these phrases:

Specific smaller region—75 percent of the grapes must come from the region

Vintage wine—95 percent of the grapes must come from that year

Vintage wine from a specific region—95 percent of the grapes must come from the year and the area

Estate bottled—100 percent of the grapes must come from the winery's vineyards or from those that are controlled by the winery and are in the vicinity

Produced and bottled by—75 percent of the grapes must be crushed and fermented at the winery

Made and bottled by—10 to 74 percent of the grapes must be crushed and fermented at the winery

Bottled by—wines purchased and then bottled at the winery

Cellared and bottled by—wines purchased, blended, and then bottled at the winery

Varietal wine—at least 51 percent of that grape in the wine

Generic wine—specific region of origin must appear on the label

Alcohol content—Table wines by law must contain not less than 7 percent alcohol and not more than 14 percent alcohol. Federal regulations allow up to $1\frac{1}{2}$ percent variation in either direction for table wines. Thus a wine labeled $11\frac{1}{2}$ percent means that the wine could have anywhere from 10 to 13 percent alcohol by volume. Dessert wines have alcohol in excess of 14 percent but not more than 21 percent. The allowable leeway on the label is 1 percent in either direction.

Sugar content—for wines labeled Late Harvest or Late Picked the sugar content of the grapes and juice used to make the wine, as well as the residual sugar of the finished wine, must be stated on the label.

°Such as Title 17, California Administrative Code.

Four common types of American labels.
TOP LEFT: Generic label with a state designation.
TOP RIGHT: Varietal label.
BOTTOM LEFT: Generic/varietal label.
BOTTOM RIGHT: Varietal label with a regional designation.

As the consuming public becomes more astute, labeling regulations may become more specific and the required percentages of grapes and areas mentioned previously may become higher. As a result of B.A.T.F. inquiries and California Wine Institute recommendations, changes in many of the rules are imminent, and the consumer should be aware of them.

The wines of the United States have fallen into two categories: California (and other western states) and New York (and the states east of the Rocky Mountains).

A wine designated as the product of a state must contain a minimum percentage of grapes grown in that state. The percentage varies; New York, for example, requires 75 percent, while California requires 100 percent.

The term *American* is also seen on labels when the producer has blended wines from two or more states, California and New York, for example, and chooses this labeling over a regional designation, which would require specific minimum percentages of grapes used.

Many American winemakers vintage-date their wines; other winemakers prefer to blend their wines to the highest possible—and unvarying—standard each year.

California wines produced from *Vitis vinifera* grapes have much in common with European wines while still exhibiting their own distinct regional personalities. Eastern wines are made from several types of vines: the indigenous varieties of American grapes that are mainly American hybrids, developed in the early stages of the eastern wine industry, and some *Vitis rotundifolia;* the French hybrids, which were developed to combat the devastation from *Phylloxera;* and, with increased viticultural knowledge, *Vitis vinifera* grapes. (All of these vine types will be discussed later in this chapter.)

No specific United States wineries are mentioned in this chapter except when they are of historical significance. A list of U.S. wineries appears in Appendix G.

1. CALIFORNIA AND WESTERN WINES

history   The records show that in 1518 Cortés, the Spanish conqueror and overlord of Mexico, ordered the establishment of a wine industry in the New World, obliging holders of land grants to plant one thousand vines per year for five years, for every hundred Indians living on the land. This agricultural program proved so successful that Spain, fearing harm to her own wine industry, ordered winemaking stopped and decreed that wine not imported from Spain should be considered contraband. The decree failed in its purpose; the vines, once planted, continued to bear fruit and wine was made surreptitiously.

Beautiful mountain setting for a northern California vineyard. (*Courtesy Wine Institute, San Francisco, California*)

Eventually the Spanish colonizers pushed west and then north, into what is today California. This movement was led by the missionaries, whose primary object was the propagation of the Faith.

It was only natural when the Church established its missions with their surrounding settlements that vines should be planted. The Franciscan padres, led by Padre Junipero Serra, planted grapes in California as early as 1769 at the San Diego Mission and for the first time found soil in North America in which the European vine would prosper and produce good wine. The arid lands of northern Mexico and Baja California did not lend themselves graciously to viticulture.

The Franciscan missionaries built twenty-one missions, reaching as far north as Sonoma, the northern terminus of the *Camino Real* ("King's Highway"). Descendants of the vines planted at these missions are still growing. The missionaries' largest winery was at the Mission of San Gabriel, near present-day Los Angeles, and the original adobe winery building, where the Indians trod the grapes, still exists with its three wine presses. There, too, the famous Trinity vine, planted by the Franciscans, flourished and bore grapes for over 170 years.

Until 1824 the Franciscans were the only wine producers in California. They did not attempt commercial production but confined their efforts to their own sacramental and table needs. At that time Joseph Chapman, an American, settled near Los Angeles and planted four thousand vines. He was followed in 1831 by a Bordeaux Frenchman, Jean Louis Vignes, who soon began producing very excellent wine and brandy. In 1832, a substantial vineyard was established in Sonoma by an Indian who grew grapes for sacramental wine for the northernmost of the missions—San Francisco de Solano. Vignes, in the meantime, was so successful that by 1840 he was chartering vessels to ship his wine and brandy to the ports of Santa Barbara, Monterey, and San Francisco. The trade, however, was still small. Then came the Gold Rush of 1849 and with it a boom in all activities. The widening of the market made it financially possible for still another and most important change in California wines.

The vines the missionaries planted came from those varieties originally brought to Mexico from Spain during the preceding three centuries. While they were true *vinifera* vines, their value for winemaking was limited. As a matter of fact, through the years one of these vines has lost its original European varietal identity, and it is today known and classified as the Mission grape.

Because the soil and climate of California were so hospitable to the European *Vitis vinifera* family of vines, no serious attempt has been made to cultivate native American varieties in California, and all grapes grown there commercially, whether for wine, table, or raisin use, are from *vinifera* vines.

Vignes brought over choice *vinifera* cuttings from France that prospered in his vineyard, and others did likewise, but it was not until after the arrival of that amazing gentleman, Count Agoston Haraszthy, in 1849—a sort of Johnny Appleseed to the California grapevine—that a real wine industry was developed.

The tireless and farsighted Haraszthy convinced John G. Downey, the governor of California, of the important part the wine industry could play in the development of the economy of the new state. As a result, he was sent to Europe in 1861 to select and bring back the widest possible selection of European (*vinifera*) grape varieties. He returned with over 100,000 cuttings of some 300 varieties, and in the space of a few short years he had a vineyard in the Sonoma Valley with 85,000 vines developed from imported stocks and a nursery of 460,000 vines. With this effort he set the course for commercial winemaking from which those who have followed him have not deviated.

Haraszthy experimented at his Sonoma Valley vineyard and nursery, selecting those vines that showed greatest promise. These were then sold or distributed in all sections of the state. Although at first the wines obtained were rather indifferent, it was not long before the winemakers learned to improve their product and were obtaining good, sound, drinkable wine that improved in quality each year. By 1875 California was producing four million gallons of wine a year.

Around the same time some vineyards whose names we know today were also being established: Paul Masson, Almadén, Mirassou, Charles Krug, Schramsberg, Beringer Brothers, and Inglenook.

California wines began to acquire characteristics of their own, and the custom of estate bottling was practiced at some of the best vineyards. In 1895 fifteen million gallons of wine were made, and most of it was shipped to other parts of the United States, Mexico, Central America, and Asia.

Gaining confidence in their early success, the winemakers began to compete with the European producers, and by 1900 they had won gold, silver, and bronze medals, a few blue ribbons, and even grand prizes at international expositions. Many of the great names associated with the development of California and the Pacific Coast were actively engaged in the wine industry as vineyard owners: Leland Stanford, George Hearst, James G. Fair, Elias "Lucky" Baldwin, John Sutter, and Lawrence Marshall, to mention only a few.

setbacks

The vineyards of California were and are no more immune to the ravages of the elements, disease, and countless other enemies than those of other wine regions of the world. One day in 1874 a vineyard in Sonoma County was found to be withering from an unknown ailment. Soon other vineyards became similarly affected, and in less than five years the vineyards of Sonoma, Napa, Yolo, El Dorado, and Placer counties were being ravaged by the same blight. The villain turned out to be the American *Phylloxera* (grape louse). We had quite innocently exported it to Europe on American rootstocks and then reimported it into California on the European cuttings.

Another plague showed up at Anaheim, southeast of Los Angeles, where a group of winemakers of German background had founded a vineyard colony. In 1884, when the mysterious disease struck, the colony had extensive vineyards and eight wineries that were producing over a million gallons of fine-quality wine annually. This ailment, which has since become known as Pierce's Disease, destroyed every vine in the short space of three years, and the vineyards of Anaheim have never been replanted.

In order to learn the cause of and find the remedy for these blights, the California State Board of Viticultural Commissioners was set up in 1880. This agency not only helped to conquer the plant diseases but also did much to improve wine quality and production practices. It also sponsored an experimental station for grape growing and wine production under the auspices of the College of Agriculture of the University of California. This station, located today at Davis, California, seventy-five miles northeast of San Francisco, has continued its research work and the teaching of viticulture and enology. It is one of the leading research establishments in its field and is visited by students and scientists from all wine regions in the world.

One of the university's important contributions to the American wine industry was recommending the use of various types of disease-resistant rootstocks, such as *rupestris* Saint George, Richter 99, and Ganzin 1. Developed abroad but tested extensively in California by the University of California at Davis, these resistant rootstocks have become the basic rootstocks of all the world's great vineyards.

The plagues visited upon the vineyards by nature were nothing compared with the man-made blight that befell the vines as a result of the Eighteenth or Prohibition Amendment to the U.S. Constitution, which went into effect on January 1, 1919.

Thousands upon thousands of acres of vineyards that had been laboriously planted to fine wine-producing varieties that were unsuited for any other use had to be uprooted and replanted with table grape varieties or other crops. In 1934, after Repeal, the whole process began a slow reversal and the vineyards were replanted with wine-producing varieties.

Since it takes time for new vines to come into production, and the immediate post-Repeal demand far exceeded supply, many of the first wines produced and shipped from California were of indifferent quality. However, all this has long since changed. In ever increasing numbers fine wines of outstanding quality are being produced, and it is generally accepted that present-day wines are, on the whole, far superior to those California produced before 1919. This is the result in great part of the efforts made by the wine producers themselves and of the severe regulations° governing standards of quality that have been adopted.

°Title 17, California Administrative Code.

WINE REGIONS
OF
CALIFORNIA

MENDOCINO

LAKE   YUBA

PLACER

SONOMA   YOLO

NAPA   SACRA-
MENTO   AMADOR

SOLANO

MARIN   SAN
JOAQUIN

GREAT
CENTRAL
VALLEY

ALAMEDA   STANISLAUS

SANTA
CLARA   MERCED

SANTA
CRUZ   MADERA

COASTAL
COUNTIES   SAN
BENITO   FRESNO

MONTEREY   KINGS   TULARE

SAN
LUIS
OBISPO   KERN

SCALE
50   100   150   200 mi

SANTA
BARBARA

SAN BERNARDINO

RIVERSIDE

SOUTHERN
CALIFORNIA   SAN DIEGO

WILLIAM LEMBECK

geography

In California the climate and soil can approximate almost every viticultural region in the world, for the seven hundred miles of vineyard extend over mountain slopes, irrigated deserts, lush inland valley floors, and the moist plains of the coast. The winemaker has little difficulty obtaining a fine red wine from the Cabernet Sauvignon grape when it is grown in one of the cool coastal counties, or a jug wine from a warmer inland region. The entire spectrum of wines is covered in California.

Viticulturally, California has two great regions: the cool Coastal Counties, extending from Mendocino, north of San Francisco, all the way south to San Diego, which produce 15 percent of California's wines; and the Great Central Valley, starting at Sacramento and ending above Bakersfield in Kern County, which produces 85 percent of the wines. These two regions encompass many smaller subregions.

It is a common misconception that north means cool and south means hot. California's temperatures do not depend on latitude but on an area's proximity to the coast. There are parts of southern California, around San Diego, that are cooler than the Sacramento Valley in northern California.

The Great Central Valley produces 130 million gallons of table wines and 120 million gallons of all other wines, which are of consistent quality year after year because of the even climate. The Coastal Counties produce 41 million gallons of the best table wines. Here the climate is not as predictable, and vintage differences can be significant, as in quality areas of Europe.

Coastal Counties

From north to south the most important coastal subregions are Sonoma County, Napa County, Alameda County, Santa Clara and San Benito counties, and Monterey County.

SONOMA COUNTY, forty to one hundred miles north of San Francisco, can be further divided into two smaller areas. The most northerly vineyards, around the border between Mendocino and Sonoma counties, are located along or near the Russian River, especially in Alexander Valley. In the southern part of Sonoma County lies the Sonoma Valley. This "Valley of the Moon" is separated from the Napa Valley by the Mayacamas Range. It is one of the most beautiful valleys in California and was a favorite of Jack London. Many of his stories took place here. Local microclimates provide good conditions for fine varietal grapes, and many excellent wines have been produced. Chardonnay, Zinfandel, Petite Sirah, Cabernet Sauvignon, and Pinot Noir have been particularly successful.

NAPA VALLEY, about ninety miles northeast of San Francisco, boasts many wineries dating back to the beginning of California viticulture. The valley has always had the natural conditions for making fine wines in the European tradition. The contour of the land and the maximum area that could be cultivated led to relatively small vineyard sizes. The entire Napa Valley has only twenty-two thousand acres of wine grapes under cultivation, approxi-

Ukiah

MENDOCINO

101

Cloverdale
Geyserville

Healdsburg

ALEXANDER VALLEY

Russian R.

Santa Rosa

SONOMA

101

SONOMA VALLEY

Sonoma

MARIN

PACIFIC OCEAN

San Francisco

SAN FRANCISCO BAY

NAPA VALLEY

29

NAPA

Calistoga
Saint Helena
Rutherford
Oakville
Yountville

Napa

CARNEROS VALLEY

SCALE

0   10   20   30   40 mi

CONTRA COSTA

ALAMEDA

LIVERMORE VALLEY

SANTA CLARA

101

SAN MATEO

Saratoga

Los Gatos

SANTA CRUZ MOUNTAINS

SANTA CLARA VALLEY

San Martin

SANTA CRUZ

**WINE
REGIONS
OF THE
COASTAL
COUNTIES
(CALIFORNIA)**

Paicines

SAN BENITO

101

Salinas

MONTEREY

MONTEREY VALLEY

Soledad

WILLIAM LEMBECK

mately 7 percent of California's total, divided among many vineyard owners, with grapes vinified by about fifty wineries. For fifteen miles or so along Highway 29 are some of the best-known names in California winemaking.

The Napa Valley produces a full range of still and sparkling wines. The area is particularly suited to growing noble varieties such as Cabernet Sauvignon, Pinot Noir, Chardonnay, and Johannisberg Riesling, as well as the ubiquitous Zinfandel, all vinified in a variety of styles.

The desire for increased production and the lack of available valley land for new plantings since 1967 has caused some of the major wineries to establish vineyards in undeveloped land along the northern rim of San Francisco Bay, at the Napa-Sonoma county line. One important example of this is the Carneros region. Smaller winemakers have established vineyards and wineries in the steep hills surrounding the Napa Valley.

LIVERMORE VALLEY, in Alameda County, is just east of San Francisco. The valley, surrounded by arid hills, has a gravelly soil like that of the Graves district in France. Its red wines are soft and mature early, while the whites are very fine and quite superior. Because of Livermore Valley's proximity to the bay area, urban encroachment has reduced vineyard holdings.

A mechanical grape harvester used to pick grapes of perfect ripeness to be made into wine. The grapes, which are crushed in the harvester, are pumped into a tanker that moves alongside the harvester as it travels down the vineyard rows. This immediate crushing ensures that the fresh grape juice will arrive at the winery in the best possible condition. (*Courtesy Wine Institute, San Francisco, California*)

Skilled hands of a vineyard worker gather a ripe cluster of Cabernet Sauvignon grapes during harvest season. (*Courtesy Wine Institute, San Francisco, California*)

SANTA CLARA AND SAN BENITO COUNTIES.   Santa Clara County includes the Santa Clara Valley as well as the foothills and lower slopes of the Santa Cruz Mountains. It stretches from thirty to seventy miles southeast of San Francisco. In San Benito, which is south of Santa Clara, forty-six hundred acres are under cultivation, mostly with noble varieties.

MONTEREY COUNTY is one of the newer vineyard areas of California. A small percentage of this land had been in row crop production, but most, being arid, was used only as cattle range. The temperature of the area had been classified as suitable for quality grape growing by viticulturists at the University of California in the 1930s, and this information was again significant in the 1970s with the increased demand for production. It was necessary only to irrigate before planting. The fact that no grapes had been planted in the area before meant that there was no *Phylloxera,* and ungrafted vines have been planted. About thirty-three thousand acres have been planted, ranking Monterey County third in wine grape production. Many of the larger wineries have added new Monterey acreage to existing holdings elsewhere.

All the way south along the coast to the special microclimates in the San Diego area are found the same wine types as in the coastal regions of Napa, Sonoma, and Monterey. New wineries and vineyards are springing up in the counties of San Luis Obispo and Santa Barbara.

Great Central Valley

The winemaking regions of the Great Central Valley, which follow along the San Joaquin River, are hot and must be irrigated. They are naturally suited for the production of dessert wines, but with increased consumption of table wines the emphasis is shifting toward production of table wines. Many new inexpensive, good-quality varietal wines have appeared on the wine scene and are becoming known as "valley varietals."

The main districts of the Great Central Valley are:

LODI-SACRAMENTO.   This is the northernmost region, centered around the cities of Lodi and Sacramento, the coolest sector of the otherwise hot Central Valley. Both table and dessert wines are produced here, supplying about 8 percent of the wine made in California.

A very old viticultural area, noted for its Zinfandel grapes, is situated in the Shenandoah Valley, a microclimate in Amador County.

ESCALON-MODESTO.   To the south, around the city of Modesto, encompassing southern San Joaquin, Stanislaus, and Merced counties, we find the largest wineries in the United States, producing about 30 percent of all California wine.

CENTRAL SAN JOAQUIN VALLEY.   The counties of Fresno, Madera, and Kings are hotter than other regions and are better suited for dessert wines. This area also provides about 30 percent of California wine production, with more dessert wines than any other area.

SOUTHERN SAN JOAQUIN VALLEY.   Kern, Tulare, and San Luis Obispo counties make up this region and produce about 11 percent of California's wines. Production is divided between table and dessert wines.

SOUTHERN CALIFORNIA embraces the Cucamonga Valley, which is falling victim to urban encroachment. Of California's total of over 325,000 acres of wine grape–producing land, fewer than 10,000 acres are left in this area.

heat summation   Different wines are produced in the coastal and central regions because of the differences in climate. The amount of accumulated heat affects the ripening of the grapes. This total heat has been measured by a system called heat summation, developed by researchers at the University of California at Davis. Climate zones, corresponding to five categories of total heat summation, were established throughout California, enabling growers to determine which regions would be best for which grapes. Monterey County, for example, had not been a grape-growing area until the 1970s, when this research was applied. There are now thirty-three thousand acres under vine there.

Total heat summation for each region is found in the following way: between April 1 and October 31 (the growing season) each day's average temperature is determined. If the average temperature is above 50 degrees Fahrenheit, the difference between 50 degrees and the average temperature is the number of degree-days for that day. For example, if the average temperature for a given day is 70 degrees Fahrenheit, then the 20 degrees above 50 degrees would be the number of degree-days for that day. The next day's average temperature above 50 degrees would be added to the total thus far, and so on. The total number of degree-days for the growing season determines the climate zone as follows:

REGION I.   2,500 or fewer degree-days (very cool). Examples are Sonoma (Sonoma County), Oakville (Napa), and Salinas (Monterey). Fine varietals do well. Similar climates occur in Germany and in Beaune, France.

REGION II.   2,501 to 3,000 degree-days (cool). Examples are Saint Helena (Napa), Healdsburg (Sonoma), and Ukiah (Mendocino). Table wine grapes do best here. Similar climates are found in Bordeaux and Piedmont.

REGION III.   3,001 to 3,500 degree-days (moderate). Examples are Livermore (Alameda), Asti (Sonoma), and Calistoga (Napa). Table wine grapes and dessert wine grapes are grown here. Climate is similar to that of the Rhône.

REGION IV.   3,501 to 4,000 degree-days (warm). Examples are Lodi (San Joaquin) and Modesto (Stanislaus). The University of California has developed grapes so that table wines with sufficient acidity can be made despite the heat. Similar climates occur in Florence and Tuscany in Italy.

REGION V.   4,000 or more degree-days (very warm). An example is most of the central and southern San Joaquin Valley. Dessert wine and brandy grapes as well as table and raisin varieties are grown here. Climate is similar to that of North Africa.

The picturesque courtyard of the Souverain Winery in the Alexander Valley. (*Courtesy Julius Wile Sons & Co., Inc.*)

Since the development of this system more variables are being studied and tabulated. Climatic factors under present investigation include amounts of sunlight (as opposed to amounts of heat) and rainfall.

GRAPE VARIETIES

Grapes are classed as wine, table, or raisin grapes. The wine grapes whose acreage is recorded by California's Department of Agriculture are the following:

TO PRODUCE RED WINES

Aleatico
Alicante Bouschet
Alicante Ganzin
Almission
Aramon
Barbera
Beclan
Black Malvoisie
Cabernet Franc
Cabernet Sauvignon
Calzin°
Carignane
Carnelian°
Centurion°
Charbono
  (Corbeau)
Early Burgundy
  (Portuguese Blue)

Gamay Beaujolais
  (strain of Pinot Noir)
Gamay Noir
  (Napa Gamay)
Grand Noir
Grenache
Grignolino
Malbec
Mataro (Mourvèdre)
Merlot
Meunier
  (strain of Pinot Noir)
Mission
Muscat Hamburg
Nebbiolo
Perelli 101°
Petite Bouschet
Petite Sirah (Durif)

Pinot Noir
Pinot Saint George
  (not a Pinot variety)
Refosco
  (Mondeuse)
Royalty°
Rubired°
Ruby Cabernet°
  (not a Cabernet
  Sauvignon variety)
Saint-Macaire
Salvador
Sangioveto
Souzão
Tinta Madeira
Touriga
Valdepeñas
Zinfandel

Of the above varieties, the ones with the greatest acreage as of 1975 were:[†]

GRAPE	COASTAL COUNTIES	GREAT CENTRAL VALLEY
Carignane	5,036 acres	25,208 acres
Zinfandel	12,262 acres	17,627 acres
Cabernet Sauvignon	23,186 acres	3,602 acres
Barbera	391 acres	20,044 acres
Grenache	1,129 acres	18,940 acres
Ruby Cabernet	752 acres	17,781 acres
Petite Sirah	5,424 acres	7,478 acres
Rubired	0 acres	12,123 acres
Pinot Noir	10,676 acres	330 acres

° These grapes originated in the California breeding program under the supervision of Dr. H. P. Olmo of the University of California at Davis.

[†] *California Grape Acreage 1975*, California Crop and Livestock Reporting Service.

TO PRODUCE WHITE WINES

Burger

Chardonnay
  (not a Pinot variety)

Chasselas Doré

Chenin Blanc
  (Pineau de la Loire,
  White Pinot, but
  not a Pinot variety)

Emerald Riesling°
  (not a true Riesling)

Feher Szagos

Flora°

Folle Blanche

French Colombard

Gewürztraminer

Grey Riesling
  (not a true Riesling)

Green Hungarian

Malvasia Bianca

Muscadelle

Muscadelle du Bordelais

Muscat Blanc
  (Muscat de Frontignan,
  Muscat Canelli)

Palomino
  (Golden Chasselas,
  but not a Chasselas)

Pedro Ximenez

Peverella

Pinot Blanc
  (Pinot Blanc Vrai)

Red Veltliner
  (called Traminer,
  but not Traminer)

Rkatsiteli

Saint-Émilion
  (Ugni Blanc,
  Trebbiano)

Sauvignon Blanc

Sauvignon Vert

Sémillon

Sylvaner
  (Franken Riesling,
  but not Riesling)

Wälschriesling

White Riesling
  (Johannisberg Ries-
  ling, the only
  true Riesling)

Of the above varieties, the ones with the greatest acreage as of 1975 were:†

GRAPE	COASTAL COUNTIES	GREAT CENTRAL VALLEY
French Colombard	3,544 acres	22,641 acres
Chenin Blanc	4,322 acres	15,461 acres
Chardonnay	10,763 acres	737 acres
White Riesling	6,895 acres	1,413 acres
Palomino	776 acres	4,817 acres

Thompson Seedless and Muscat of Alexandria are large wine producers. Because they are classed as raisin grapes, they are not on the list. These grapes are used for table and dessert wines, and half of the production is used for raisins. Thompson Seedless is planted in an astounding 232,330 acres; Muscat of Alexandria, in 13,477 acres.

Tokay, Emperor and White Malaga are also large wine producers, but they are classed as table grapes and therefore do not appear on the list.

TO PRODUCE DESSERT WINES

GRAPE	WINE PRODUCED
Alicante Bouschet	port
Carignane	port
Grenache	sherry, port
Mission	cream sherry, Angelica

° These grapes originated in the California breeding program under the supervision of Dr. H. P. Olmo of the University of California at Davis.

† *California Grape Acreage 1975*, California Crop and Livestock Reporting Service.

GRAPE	WINE PRODUCED
Palomino	sherry
Royalty	port
Rubired	port
Salvador	port, color wine
Souzão	port
Tinta Madeira	port
Touriga	port
Zinfandel	port

Dessert wines are blends of any and all grape varieties that are available. Any of the previously listed varieties can and have been used for fortified dessert wines; table and raisin grapes are also used. The grape's contribution is not so much varietal character as it is yield per acre. Exceptions are a small amount of sherry and port production and some special Muscat wines. Most of the above grapes for dessert wines are grown in the Central Valley.

Vineyards have benefited from careful research. Scientists at both the University of California at Davis and California State University at Fresno have developed disease-free rootstocks and virus-free vines. Specialists in grape cultivation and breeding have developed new grape varieties, such as Ruby Cabernet, Carnelian, Centurion, and Emerald Riesling, that yield good table wines in the warm interior valley. They have also determined that some of the traditional wine grapes, such as Barbera, Zinfandel, and Chenin Blanc, make good wine in the warmer growing areas as well.

types   There are three types of California wines: generic, varietal, and proprietary; these terms have been discussed on pages 199–202. In the past generic wines were the most salable because their names, being those of other famous wine districts, were familiar to the public. But as both winemakers and consumers have become more sophisticated, the finer producers have turned from generic labeling toward varietal and proprietary labeling.

Varietal labeling, especially, is an effort to show the unique nature of California wines, rather than presenting them as European copies. Varietal wines are named for the grape varieties from which they are made, such as Cabernet Sauvignon, Zinfandel, and Gewürztraminer. Under California regulations a wine bearing a varietal name on the label must be produced from at least 51 percent of the named variety. In many cases it comes closer to 100 percent of the designated grape variety, allowing for some judicious blending with other grapes to enhance the varietal character. All wines are under close federal and state inspection to guarantee that the wine is labeled accurately.

Proprietary labeling is an extension of the concept that puts emphasis on a producer's style, rather than on creating a European copy.

California is rich in a variety of natural soils and climates. Many important *classes* species of European grapes (*Vitis vinifera*) may be found, and consequently every wine type is made. The classes and types of California wines have been established by the Wine Institute of California. Wines are divided into five main classes: red table wines, white table wines, appetizer wines, sweet dessert wines, and sparkling wines.

RED TABLE WINES

Red table wines are those whose alcohol content range from $10\frac{1}{2}$ to 14 percent but generally ranges between 11 and $13\frac{1}{2}$ percent.

CABERNET SAUVIGNON.   A fine red wine made in the cool regions of *varietal wines* California from the principal claret grape of Bordeaux. The wine is astringent when young but develops complexity and depth as it matures.

PINOT NOIR.   A wine made from the noble grape of Burgundy, which is difficult to cultivate and vinify in California and which needs a very special microclimate. When properly grown and vinified, the wine can be excellent.

ZINFANDEL.   A claret-type wine, with a spicy, berrylike aroma and taste. The grape's origins are unknown, but it is most widely cultivated in California. The latest research, however, suggests that this grape was introduced into California from New England, where it was grown as a hothouse grape. It may be vinified in varying styles, from a *vin ordinaire*, which should be drunk cool, to a rich, full wine that should be aged.

GAMAY.   A fresh, sprightly wine made from the grape of the Beaujolais area that in California is called Gamay Noir or Napa Gamay.

GAMAY BEAUJOLAIS.   A medium- to full-bodied wine with a fruity aroma, but not resembling the French Beaujolais. Its grape has been identified as a strain of the Pinot Noir and should not be confused with the Gamay.

PETITE SIRAH.   This wine has a deep red color and is exceptionally full and tannic, with a spicy nose.

BARBERA.   A dark, robust, full-bodied wine that has a pleasant tartness. The grape, which originated in Piedmont, Italy, has enough acidity to do well in the warmer central regions.

RUBY CABERNET.   A fruity wine with a deep ruby color. The grape is a cross between Cabernet Sauvignon and Carignane and should not be confused with its Cabernet Sauvignon parent. It was developed to have enough acidity to be successful in the warmer interior area.

MERLOT.   A soft wine that tastes like Cabernet Sauvignon but with less tannin and astringency. It is often used to soften Cabernet Sauvignon in California, as it does in Bordeaux.

Other varietal wines are made, but in limited quantities. Examples are Carignane, Charbono, and Grignolino.

generic wines   CALIFORNIA BURGUNDY.   A full-bodied wine that is soft and smooth on the palate, with medium to deep red color. It is bottled in the traditional Burgundy-shaped bottle (see page 7).

CALIFORNIA CLARET.   A dry, tart wine with medium body and medium color. This wine is not as prevalent as California Burgundy.

CALIFORNIA CHIANTI.   A full, dry wine without any of the rough character associated with some of the *fiaschi* types.

These generic types vary from one winery to another. Burgundies from two different wineries may be entirely different.

ROSÉ WINES

It is important to remember that wine that contains *any* red coloring (which is obtained from the grape skins that are allowed to remain in contact with the must during fermentation) is classified as a red wine. There are only two colors in wine—white and red—and red wines vary in color from the very pale pink-hued rosés to the very deep, inky reds of some Barberas.

In a rosé wine varietal character is less significant than in a red wine. In a generic rosé, emphasis is on pigmentation. In a varietal rosé specific character is reduced because the must is removed from the skins after only twelve to sixteen hours. Because some rosé wines are made from fine varietals, innovative winemakers have begun drawing off the pigmented must and adding the skins, which are still rich in pigment and tannin, to working red wine fermenting tanks of the same grape. This creates a bonus of very rich, concentrated red wines, while making some elegant and fruity rosés. The alcohol content in rosé wines ranges from 10 to 14 percent.

varietal wines   CABERNET ROSÉ.   Has a more distinctive flavor and is best made in the cooler regions.

GAMAY BEAUJOLAIS ROSÉ.   Full wine with a deep rose color and good fruitiness.

GAMAY ROSÉ.   A fine, delicate rosé with a good fruity character.

GRENACHE ROSÉ.   A slightly sweet popular wine with orange tones. The grape is used extensively in California because of its high yield and strong color.

PINOT NOIR ROSÉ.   Has a pale, partridge-eye (tea rose) color and delicate flavor.

ZINFANDEL ROSÉ.   Has some of the bramble character of the grape, with a deep color.

generic wine   CALIFORNIA ROSÉ.   Usually a commercial wine with some sweetness and light body; refreshing as a summer wine.

WHITE TABLE WINES

White table wines, as the class name implies, are the light white beverage wines whose alcohol content can be as low as 10 percent, does not exceed 14 percent, and averages about $12\frac{1}{2}$ percent. Although these wines are described as white, no wine is colorless. White wines vary from a very pale straw yellow to a very dark brown. In taste they vary from bone dry to very sweet.

CHARDONNAY. A dry and full wine, with complexity, that can take some bottle aging. Sometimes erroneously called Pinot Chardonnay, this wine is made from the grape of Burgundy and Champagne, which produces the finest wines of the coastal regions.

WHITE RIESLING OR JOHANNISBERG RIESLING. A fruity wine, with a distinctive perfume and often a touch of sweetness, from the fine grape of Germany and Alsace. In some areas and only in some years, cool, humid weather causes the grapes to get *Botrytis cinerea,* "noble rot." Rich, exquisite, and expensive sweet wines are made.

SAUVIGNON BLANC. When made from only this grape, it is a wine of considerable character, sometimes labeled Fumé Blanc. When the grapes are attacked by "noble rot," a sweet Sauternes-type dessert wine is made.

CHENIN BLANC. Also called Pineau de la Loire, this fragrant wine can range from dry to semisweet, as it does when produced along the Loire River. In humid microclimates grapes with "noble rot" make a very sweet wine.

GEWÜRZTRAMINER. Often slightly sweet, with spiciness, this wine, which is from the grape of Alsace, has a highly aromatic bouquet and a distinctive character.

OTHER RIESLINGS. The grape that makes Grey Riesling produces a wine in California that is soft and mildly spicy, lacking in finesse. Wine made from the Franken Riesling, or Sylvaner, grape, which has German origins, is delicate and pleasant. The Emerald Riesling grape is a cross between White Riesling and Muscadelle, developed at the University of California. This variety has not proved too successful, and its wine appears darker than other white wines.

There are other white varietal wines produced, but in smaller quantities. The Pinot Blanc is probably the finest of these, second to the Chardonnay in quality. Other attractive varietal wines are French Colombard, Green Hungarian, and Sémillon.

varietal wines

CALIFORNIA CHABLIS. This is the most common of the California white generic table wines and comes closest to being an all-purpose dry white wine. It is straw colored and crisp, with medium body, and is generally made from the Chenin Blanc, French Colombard, Burger, Palomino, Green Hungarian, and other varieties growing anywhere in California.

generic wines

CALIFORNIA SAUTERNE (note spelling without final *s*).   This is usually a light, golden, pleasant wine. It is soft without noticeable acidity. When dry, it is sometimes labeled Dry Sauterne, clearly a contradiction in terms.

CALIFORNIA RHINE AND MOSELLE.   These wines have a pale color and medium body and acidity. They should have the fruity character of the Riesling varieties and usually have a slight sweetness—between Chablis and Sauterne. When the wine is made from grapes such as the Grey Riesling and the Franken Riesling, which are not true Rieslings, it can be labeled Riesling, but this designation is being replaced with the name Rhine or, less commonly, Moselle.

White wines often have a slight sweetness and are served chilled—two factors that account for their popularity.

APPETIZER WINES*

Appetizer wines are those that, as the class name implies, are popularly used before meals as appetite sharpeners. They include sherry (more often the drier types), vermouth, and aperitif wines.

CALIFORNIA DRY VERMOUTH (French type).   A straw-colored, herb-flavored wine with a minimum of 15 percent alcohol and some vermouth character. Light Dry Vermouth is lighter in color, aroma, and flavor, with less character, and was developed for cocktail use.

CALIFORNIA SWEET VERMOUTH (Italian type).   This is used as an appetizer wine despite its high sugar content. It is dark amber, with a pronounced herb character, and may have a Muscat aroma.

California vermouth is not marketed just as vermouth, but rather under the distinctive brand of the producer. This is because the aromatizing formula used by the producer is his very distinctive secret.

CALIFORNIA DRY, OR COCKTAIL, SHERRY.   This is the type produced by baking (see page 196). It is pale amber, with a nutty character, and is light bodied and smooth. It is sometimes sold as Pale Sherry.

CALIFORNIA MEDIUM SHERRY.   This is also sold as simply California Sherry. It is medium amber in color, full bodied, rich, developed, nutty, and well balanced.

CALIFORNIA DRY FLOR SHERRY.   This is the type produced with an alde-hyde-producing yeast, and there is no baked character. Hence it has a less pronounced nuttiness. The color is light amber, and the wine is light bodied. It is sometimes sold as Flor Fino Sherry.

CALIFORNIA MEDIUM FLOR SHERRY.   This wine is light amber in color and medium bodied and has some *flor* character.

California Sherry and Flor Sherry have 17 percent minimum alcohol.

° The B.A.T.F. classifies appetizer wines as dessert wines.

A terraced California vineyard nestled high in the foothills. California is blessed with ideal growing conditions for many of the world's finest wine grapes. (*Courtesy Wine Institute, San Francisco, California*)

Information recorded on each carved cask of wine aging in this California winery cellar is carefully checked by a worker. (*Courtesy Wine Institute, San Francisco, California*)

*DESSERT WINES**

California dessert wines include all the rich, sweet, full-bodied wines that were formerly known in the trade as sweet wines. Their alcohol content is usually under 20 percent, the minimum being 17 percent for sherries and 18 percent for port, Madeira, Muscatel, and Angelica, the upper limit being 21 percent. They range in taste from medium to very sweet and include both white and red wines. If the wine name is preceded by the word *light*, the alcohol content can be as low as 14 percent.

CALIFORNIA PORT.   This is rightfully one of the more popular dessert wines. The color can range from medium to deep ruby red, and the wine is made from grape varieties known for their high pigmentation, such as Carignane, Salvador, Rubired, Zinfandel, and Alicante Bouschet. Tinta Madeira, Touriga, and Souzão have enough quality and aroma to make varietally labeled ports. The wine is always fruity, with a youthful character.

CALIFORNIA TAWNY PORT.   This wine has a reddish brown or tawny color that comes from aging or baking. Tawny Ports are produced either from grapes that are not so rich in color or by blending white port with ruby port to reduce the pigmentation.

CALIFORNIA WHITE PORT.   This wine ranges from light straw yellow to pale gold and has a mellow taste. It is generally produced from the Thompson Seedless grape.

All California port is very sweet in taste, having as much as 10 to 15 percent unfermented natural grape sugar.

CALIFORNIA SWEET SHERRY.   This is the baked-type sherry and is also known as Cream or Mellow. It is dark amber colored, with full body and a rich, nutty flavor. When it is baked in the absence of air, the color is lighter.

CALIFORNIA ANGELICA.   Originating in California and produced mostly from Mission grapes, this wine is always very sweet, having 10 to 15 percent unfermented sugar and low acidity. It is full bodied, fruity, and smooth.

CALIFORNIA TOKAY.   Do not confuse this wine with the Tokay of Hungary; the only connection is the name. Nor does the wine get its name from the Flame Tokay grape, which may or may not be used in the production of California Tokay. This wine is always a blend, with port, sherry, and Angelica

---

* Dessert wines are generally considered fortified wines, and the term *fortified* has long been and is still used to describe wines that have brandy added to them for the purpose of arresting fermentation, or simply to increase the alcohol content above the level at which wines will normally ferment out. *Fortified* cannot, however, legally be used in the United States, a rule in effect since 1939, when Regulations No. 4 relating to Labeling and Advertising of Wine (Bureau of Alcohol, Tobacco, and Firearms of the U.S. Treasury Department) were adopted. The regulations include the statement that no advertisement for wine, label, wrapper, container, and so on, can contain: "any statement, design, device, or representation which relates to alcoholic content, or which tends to create the impression that the wine has been 'fortified.'"

used in the production. A slightly nutty flavor comes from the sherry in this amber-colored blend.

CALIFORNIA MALAGA, MADEIRA, AND MARSALA.   These wines are rarely produced in this country anymore. Malaga is a blend, similar to Angelica. Madeira and Marsala are produced like the sweeter sherries.

CALIFORNIA MUSCAT WINE.   Muscat is sometimes called Muscatel when produced from the white Muscat of Alexandria. Wines labeled Muscat Canelli or Muscat de Frontignan are made from the White Muscat grape, which originated in Frontignan, France, and Canelli, Italy. Red Muscat and Black Muscat are obtained from the Aleatico and Muscat Hamburg grapes. All Muscat wines have a distinctive Muscat fragrance.

SPARKLING WINES

California sparkling wines include Champagne, Sparkling Burgundy, Pink Champagne or Sparkling Rosé, Sparkling Moscato, and Sparkling Malvasia Bianca. They are produced by the traditional French bottle-fermented method, the Charmat process, and the transfer process, as described on page 198.

CALIFORNIA CHAMPAGNE.   This can be pale straw yellow to light gold color. The wines are marketed in varying degrees of sweetness, following French Champagne labeling practices: Natural, Brut, Extra Dry, and Sec. California Champagne is made from a number of grape varieties, such as Chenin Blanc, French Colombard, Folle Blanche, Sémillon, some Riesling varieties, and Burger. Pinot Blanc, Pinot Noir, and Chardonnay are used in the finer Champagnes, which have limited production. Chardonnay is sometimes specifically named on the label. Additional information has begun to appear on some labels, such as Blanc de Blancs for a wine made of only white grapes, Blanc de Noir for a wine made of only black grapes, and Oeil de Perdrix for a pale Rosé Champagne.

CALIFORNIA SPARKLING BURGUNDY.   This sparkling wine is produced in the same way as California Champagne, which is either bottle fermented or bulk fermented. It is made with red wine instead of white and usually has some sweetness.

CALIFORNIA PINK CHAMPAGNE.   Also called Sparkling Rosé, it is light pink in color and is produced in the same manner as California Champagne, except that it is made with pink or rosé wine.

COLD DUCK.°   A combination of Champagne and Sparkling Burgundy, it is usually semisweet or sweet. These wines have a distinct Concord taste that

°Cold Duck is a combination of white sparkling wine and sparkling Burgundy and has a sweet taste. It is supposed to have originated in Bavaria among the hunting set, where it was customary to drink Champagne before starting off. Much of it was left in the open bottles, and when the hunters returned, rather than waste it, they mixed it with cold sparkling Burgundy and called it *Kalte Ende*—"cold end." Before long the *Ende* became *Ente*, and the Americans translated it literally into "Cold Duck."

comes from concentrate of Concord grapes shipped in from nearby Washington State.

CALIFORNIA SPARKLING MUSCAT. A sparkling wine usually made from the Muscat of Alexandria grape, with strong Muscat bouquet. It is generally sold as Moscato Champagne or Spumante.

CALIFORNIA SPARKLING MALVASIA BIANCA. A sparkling wine made from the fragrant Malvasia Bianca grape.

CARBONATED WINES. Sparkling wines that are made effervescent by artificial carbonation, somewhat less expensive than naturally sparkling wines. Both red and white and dry and sweet wines are produced.

EXPANSION IN
THE CALIFORNIA WINE INDUSTRY

Over the years, the studies and research of men such as Dr. Maynard A. Amerine, Harold H. Berg, Dr. William V. Cruess, Dr. M. A. Joslyn, Dr. Harold P. Olmo, Dr. Albert J. Winkler, and other great enologists of the University of California at Davis have caused a revolution in viti-viniculture. The effect of their work on commercial wine production has been tremendous for both the winemaker and the consumer. The general quality of wine has been very much improved, within the limitations that soil and climatic conditions present. Today enologists and viticulturists come from all over the world to study at Davis, California, with its experimental vineyards, winery, and distillery.

The increased demand for wine in America began in the mid-1960s and led to an expansion of vineyards and wineries. At the end of 1975 there were 647,200 acres planted with grapevines, half of which produced wine grapes. This was in contrast to the 477,400 acres of vines under cultivation a decade before, when only 30 percent of this smaller amount was devoted to wine grapes.

During the past decade new important wine-growing areas have opened in California. The east and west sides of the San Joaquin Valley in Kern, Tulare, and Fresno counties is the largest area. The upper Salinas Valley in Monterey County and the Paicines Valley in San Benito County south of Hollister are also significant. Some vineyard land has been planted in the southern coastal region, notably in the Paso Robles area in San Luis Obispo County and a few areas in Santa Barbara County, where suitable microclimates have been found, making possible the planting of premium varieties. Older wine-growing areas such as Napa, Mendocino, Sonoma, Stanislaus, and Alameda counties have had new plantings wherever vineyard land could be found.

Sales have kept pace with production. From 1966 to 1975 sales of California wine have increased from just over 140 million gallons to over 270 million gallons. These are made up of the popular and inexpensive jug wines and the highly individual premium varietal wines. No longer wishing to produce wines in the shadow of Europe, winemakers have been developing their own styles of wines, and the public has responded with a new awareness and appreciation of these wines. California has been recognized as one of the world's premier wine-growing regions, and many connoisseurs feel that California's finer wines rank with the best in the world.

WASHINGTON AND OREGON

Although the wine regions of Washington and Oregon are not nearly as developed as those of California, regional variations are emerging and wine production is becoming significant. In 1976 Washington produced 1,200,000 gallons and Oregon produced 200,000 gallons of table and dessert wines. Many vineyards and wineries are in their infancy, and this northwestern area is nowhere near realizing its potential.

In the 1870s, almost one hundred years after the Franciscan missionaries *history* planted grapes in California, the beginnings of viticulture in Washington and Oregon were tied to the early settlers' western migrations over the Oregon Trail. The first known wineries in Oregon were established by Ernest Reater in 1880 and Adolph Doerner in 1890. In Washington, Lambert B. Evans planted the first vines in 1872, in the southern part of the Puget Sound area—a location

WINE REGIONS
OF
WASHINGTON AND OREGON

SCALE

0   50   100 mi

WILLIAM LEMBECK

that is now reduced to about one hundred acres because of sudden, damaging rains. Plantings continued sporadically until 1906, when irrigation from the Cascade watershed, which separated the cool, rainy western part of Washington from the dry eastern section, opened up the arid Yakima Valley in the east. During Prohibition only sacramental wines were produced. Repeal brought new winery development along the Columbia River, between Washington and Oregon, with the biggest areas around Seattle and the Yakima Valley. Many fruit wines were produced, as were table and dessert wines.

While it was reasoned that the climate might be conducive to growing *vinifera* vines, the biggest advance in fine winemaking in Washington did not come until 1967, when André Tchelistcheff instructed the American Wine Growers on growing and vinifying procedures. The results were the successful varietal wines produced in the Yakima Valley.

At the same time in Oregon, the Willamette and Tualatin valleys were also being planted with *vinifera* vines, with the cooler locations proving good sites for the White Riesling.

grape varieties and wines   The choice of grapes first planted in Washington and Oregon was governed by the harsh winter temperatures and consisted of hardy eastern grape varieties, such as Concord, Delaware, Diamond, and Campbell Early. An interesting development of these early plantings was the discovery of Island Belle, a grape very similar to Campbell Early that was suited to areas of high rainfall, while its counterpart thrived in dry areas. Both Campbell Early and Island Belle are grown to make sweet table wine as well as grape juice, jams, and jellies. The wines are marketed under the more familiar name of Concord.

Despite a recent surge in *vinifera* plantings, 85 percent of the acreage is still in non-*vinifera* grapes. The market for these grapes is Cold Duck and sacramental wines, with the balance being used for juice, jams, and jellies.

Learning from experimental plantings of *vinifera* varieties in the early 1930s, Washington grape growers discovered several ways to protect tender vines from winter kill. Carefully selected, virus-free *vinifera* rootstocks were planted, ungrafted, in the *Phylloxera*-free sandy loam soil. To this day the soil remains free of *Phylloxera*.

The area around Grandview-Sunnyside, in the lower Yakima Valley, is the equivalent of Regions I and II in California, 2,300 to 2,800 degree-days. Long daylight hours in this high-latitude region, combined with slopes that face south or southwest, aid in warming the vines during the day to develop sugar. The coolness of the night helps retain the acidity necessary for the proper sugar-acid balance. The slopes also provide good air flow to reduce fall frost damage.

The *vinifera* vines currently planted in Washington and Oregon include Cabernet Sauvignon, Carignane, Grenache, Merlot, Pinot Noir, Zinfandel, Muscat of Alexandria, Muscat di Canelli, Chardonnay, Chenin Blanc, Gewürztraminer,

Palomino, Sauvignon Blanc, Sémillon, and White Riesling. So far, white wines have been more successful than red wines.

The Washington and Oregon winemakers, unencumbered by precedent, have explored new techniques dictated by their unique climate and location. Extremely large grape yields per acre, which would be considered overcropping in conventional vineyards, are normal for this region. Pinot Noir, not suitable for making a big red wine in this region, is being vinified as white table and experimental sparkling wines. Other experiments include inoculating grapes with *Botrytis cinerea* to produce sweet *Botrytised* wines.

Washington has 23,000 acres planted in wine grapes, of which 3,000 acres are *vinifera* vines. Oregon has about 1,000 acres under cultivation. The two states have a combined potential of planting 200,000 to 300,000 acres in premium varietals, but it is unlikely that this potential will ever be required. The available space is conducive to higher efficiency in planting, as mechanical harvesters can be used between the rows.

Traditional fruit wines are still made in large quantities. The most popular types are made from loganberries, blackberries, and currants. Fruits are often frozen and made into fruit wines later on in the year, after grape-wine operations have been completed. Thus equipment is used all year long and is not idle most of the time.

2. EASTERN WINES

history

Early travelers and colonists left records of the wealth of wild grapes found in many sections along the eastern seaboard. In 1565 Captain John Hawkins spoke of the grapes he found in the Spanish settlements in Florida and mentioned that the Spaniards had made twenty hogsheads of wine from the wild grapes—probably *Vitis rotundifolia* (Muscadines), best represented by the Scuppernong, found along the Atlantic seaboard from Maryland to Florida.

Still later, Thomas Hariot, writing of the advisability of establishing colonies in America, mentioned grapes that were of two kinds; one was small and sour, the size of the European grape, while the other was larger, sweeter, and more luscious.

In the early 1600s colonizer Captain John Smith wrote in greater detail. "Of vines," he said, "great abundance in many parts, that climbe the toppes of highest trees in some places, but these beare but few grapes except by the rivers and savage habitations, where they are overshadowed from the sunne; they are covered with fruit though never prunned nor manured. Of these hedge grapes we made neere twentie gallons of wine, which was like our British wine, but certainly they would prove good were they well manured. There is another sort of grape neere as great as cherry, this they [Indians] call messamins; they be fatte and juyce thicks, neither doth the taste so well please when these be made in wine."

It is understandable that the newly arrived colonists should find the wines made from native grapes with their strange, wild taste a shock to their palates. Instead of recognizing the merits of the new wine, however, they insisted that it be like the old, with which they were familiar. If these early settlers had attempted to adapt to native wines, it is possible that succeeding generations would have accepted them.

It was Lord Delaware, governor of Virginia, who first suggested that a wine industry be established in America, when he wrote to the London Company in 1616. The idea was enthusiastically approved, and expert French vine dressers and a wide assortment of the finest European vine cuttings were sent to this country. But because of the easy culture and high price of tobacco, the settlers failed to grow European vines.

Even so, over the years many attempts were made, vine dressers changed, vines varied, but all to no avail. For two centuries after Lord Delaware's first efforts, a few winemakers stubbornly continued their efforts to grow the foreign vine, and it was not until the nineteenth century, when they understood the devastation wrought by the endemic pests on foreign vines, that they were able to succeed. Then and only then was a serious effort made to permit the native grapes east of the Rockies to stand on their own.

The vine can and does prosper in almost every state in the Union, but not every grape variety makes good wine, and there are certain regions in the eastern United States where wine grapes grow more successfully than in other regions.

REGIONS

When discussing eastern wine-producing areas, we feel that it is better to discuss geographic areas of similar climate and geology than to group areas by states. Many wine-producing areas cross political boundaries. The Chautauqua area of western New York, for example, lies in New York State, but the wines realistically should be grouped with those around neighboring Lake Erie.°

Finger Lakes   The most important wine-producing section of the East is the Finger Lakes region of New York, about fifty miles from Rochester, where the soil, drainage, and climate bear a striking resemblance to those of the French Champagne region. It is a beautiful countryside of rolling hills, dotted with lovely lakes. The region is devoted almost entirely to viticulture. All types of wine are made, but sparkling wine predominates.

°See Appendix G for a list of commercially important eastern wineries.

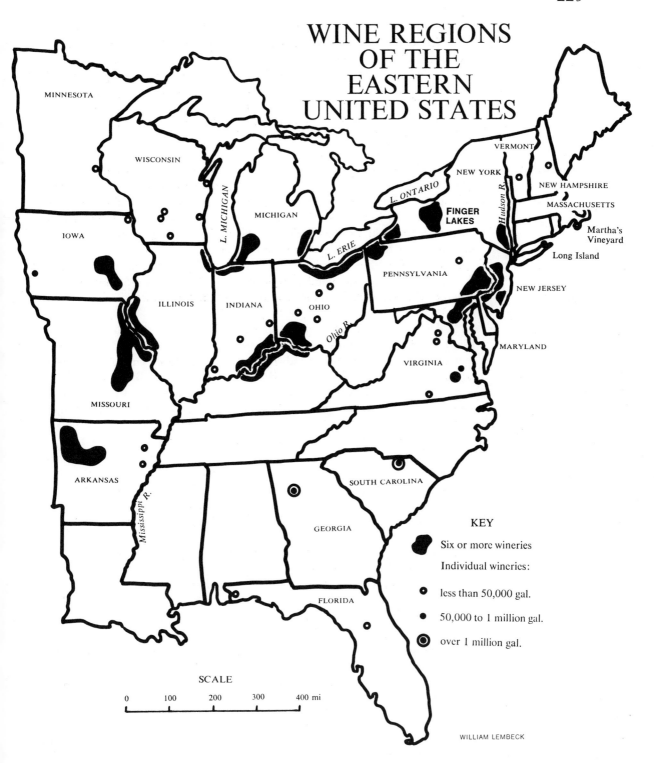

WINE REGIONS
OF THE
EASTERN
UNITED STATES

MINNESOTA

WISCONSIN

L. MICHIGAN

MICHIGAN

IOWA

ILLINOIS

INDIANA

OHIO

Ohio R.

L. ERIE

L. ONTARIO

VERMONT

NEW YORK

FINGER
LAKES

Hudson R.

NEW HAMPSHIRE

MASSACHUSETTS

Martha's
Vineyard

Long Island

PENNSYLVANIA

NEW JERSEY

MARYLAND

VIRGINIA

MISSOURI

ARKANSAS

Mississippi R.

SOUTH CAROLINA

GEORGIA

FLORIDA

KEY

Six or more wineries

Individual wineries:

less than 50,000 gal.

50,000 to 1 million gal.

over 1 million gal.

SCALE

0   100   200   300   400 mi

WILLIAM LEMBECK

The center of the region is Lake Keuka, with Hammondsport at one end, Penn Yan at the other, and Naples and its vineyards nearby to the northwest. A section of the west side of Lake Seneca is also becoming quite important.

By 1867 the Pleasant Valley Wine Company at Hammondsport, which made both sparkling and still wine, produced American Champagne of such excellent quality that it won a gold medal at the Paris Exposition. Gold Seal Vineyards also produced both wine types and received awards in Vienna in 1873 and in Paris in 1878.

Hudson Valley

The Hudson River Valley is one of the nation's oldest wine-producing districts. There are steep slopes that descend to the Hudson River, whose ameliorating effect on the climate has made grape growing possible. This area is very close to New York City, and several large wineries are popular with tourists. Some small producers who are devoted to making quality wine in this area feel that this region has great potential.

Farther east, grapes are being grown successfully on the northeastern tip of Long Island, where the combination of a bay, Long Island Sound, and the Atlantic Ocean produces a moderating effect on the climate.

Lake Erie

Lake Erie is bordered on its eastern and southern shores by many vineyards that actually lie in Pennsylvania, Ohio, and western New York. The Pennsylvania wineries are mostly around the city of North East. The Ohio wineries stretch from the eastern border of Ohio and Pennsylvania all the way west to Sandusky. In New York the Chautauqua area extends westward from Buffalo to Pennsylvania. Grapes are often sold among these states, and winemakers enjoy a cooperative spirit.

Lake Michigan

As is Lake Erie, Lake Michigan is bordered by several states. These are Michigan, Indiana, Illinois, and Wisconsin. Michigan's wineries have the most favorable sites, including the eastern shore of the lake. This location offers the most protection from the prevailing westerly winds. Local winemakers acknowledge that the climate is similar to that of Germany, and they often vinify white wines in a German style.

If the number of wines produced around Lake Erie and Lake Michigan were totaled, the Great Lakes wineries would be the third largest group of producers in the United States, after California and New York.

Ohio Valley

Most of the wineries of southwestern Ohio, along the Ohio River, are small, but Meiers is a giant, the thirteenth largest winery in the United States. The history of this area goes back more than 150 years to Nicholas Longworth, who founded the Ohio wine industry around Cincinnati. It was he who helped make Ohio the premier wine state in the country at that time. Eventually plant disease and Longworth's death led to the downfall of the Ohio River wine industry. It was not until after Repeal that the wine industry was reborn, and the region is once again flourishing.

On the eastern coast of the United States there is a cluster of small vineyards and wineries in New Jersey, eastern Pennsylvania, Maryland, and Virginia. The wine industry in New Jersey centers around Egg Harbor. In eastern Pennsylvania grapes are grown around the Main Line area. Maryland's viticultural history has been distinguished by Lord Baltimore's directive to plant vines in 1662 and by Philip and Jocelyn Wagner, who established a winery in the 1940s. The Wagners have been responsible for distributing hybrid vines from their nursery and for educating the public through many books and articles. Grape growing in Virginia predates that in Maryland, as Lord Delaware planted grapes in Virginia in 1619. Today there are wineries along the Roanoke River, in Petersburg, and in the foothills of the Bull Run Mountains, west of Washington, D.C.

Middle Atlantic states

New England has a few modest wineries located in Laconia, New Hampshire, along the Rhode Island Sound, and in Martha's Vineyard, an island off Cape Cod in Massachusetts. In the Midwest a narrow belt of established wineries stretches from Iowa, through Missouri, into Arkansas and Oklahoma. Kentucky, the Carolinas, Mississippi, Texas, and a number of other states have vineyards and wineries, and interest in wine production is high in West Virginia, Tennessee, New Mexico, and Colorado.

other states

INDIGENOUS VARIETIES

Of the many grapevines native to our country, only a few are important to wine production. The most important species of grapevine found in America is *Vitis labrusca,* the ancestor of all the present native American grapes. Strictly speaking, no *labrusca* grapes are used for winemaking. As far as enologists know, all of the varieties currently used for wine are natural or deliberate crossbreedings with other native varieties or with *vinifera* varieties. To make this distinction explicit, the proper term for the eastern grape varieties is *Vitis labruscana* (*labrusca* type).

The wines made from our native American grapes have a distinctive flavor unlike those of any other part of the world. As the grapes grew wild the early settlers attributed the strong, strange taste to the fact that the grapes were not cultivated or domesticated, and so called the taste wild or "foxy." (At night the scent of these aromatic grapes attracted foxes.) The term *foxy* has been greatly misunderstood. Its original and only meaning is "strangeness, wildness," different from the familiar (European) wines. It refers to the general character of the wines and has nothing to do with their quality. It derives from the very difinite "grapey" aroma and character. In recent years enologists have traced this

View of a vineyard near the shore of Lake Keuka in the New York Finger Lakes wine region. (*Courtesy the Taylor Wine Company, Hammondsport, New York*)

distinctive aroma to the highly odorous ester methyl anthranilate. The average person can detect as little as one part ester mixed with ten million parts wine. The *labruscana* grapes also tend to be high in acid and low in sugar, characteristics that pose a challenge to eastern winemakers.

There are at least eleven important varieties of Muscadines, but the two most important in winemaking are the famous Scuppernong and the lesser-known Creek. The Scuppernong, a bronze-colored grape, grows profusely and naturally south of the Mason-Dixon line, particularly in Virginia, the Carolinas, Tennessee, Georgia, and Florida. It gives a rather sweet, rich white wine with an individual taste. The Creek is a reddish black grape that produces a wine rather high in acidity.

The *labruscana* grapes used by winemakers are:

white grapes   DUTCHESS.   Originated by A. J. Caywood, according to Valear, "from a white Concord seedling fertilized by Delaware." It is a light green, thick-skinned grape, best suited for late picking. It is a quality grape, but it is easily destroyed by cold and disease.

NIAGARA.   Originated by Hoagland Clarke of New York in 1872, it is the most abundant American white grape, presumed to have been obtained from a Concord crossed with another *labruscana*.

ELVIRA. Originated by Jacob Rommel of Missouri in 1863, it is used for making sparkling wines and baked sherries.

NOAH, ONTARIO, AND PORTLAND. These have ceased to be used in any meaningful quantities.

CONCORD. The most important of all *Vitis labruscana* grapes, the Concord was introduced in 1854 by Ephraim Wales Bull. It has since served as a base for crossbreeding and is the most widely used grape we have. From the Concord is produced all the commercial grape juice that is consumed in the United States. Practically all the grape jelly and preserves are made from Concords too, as is most of the kosher wine made both commercially and privately.

black grapes

The only other black grapes of some importance are Ives and Isabella. The Fredonia, grown in some parts of the Lake Erie district, is blended with the Concord for juice or wine. The Clinton, Lenoir, and Norton have practically disappeared in winemaking.

DELAWARE. Popularized by Abram Thompson of Delaware, Ohio, about 1848, this is a small, light red, very sweet grape and one of the best fine-wine grapes produced in the East. The Delaware is used for white beverage wines and is indispensable for making sparkling wine.

red grapes

CATAWBA. Popularized in the wine trade by John Adlum, it was known since 1823 when it was originally found growing along the banks of the Catawba River in North Carolina. The Catawba is a fairly large red grape on a par with the Delaware, with which it is often used. From the Catawba, which when thoroughly ripe has a fairly high sugar content, are produced some of the best sweet white beverage and sparkling wines in America.

DIANA, IONA, AND VERGENNES. These varieties are available now only in small quantities and are used in making limited amounts of varietal wines.

The Catawba attained its greatest fame because of the energy of Nicholas Longworth. As a hobby Mr. Longworth made a sparkling Catawba that was so good and so popular that it won gold medals in foreign competitions. He used to sell upward of 100,000 bottles a year, produced at his vineyards near Cincinnati, Ohio.

Catawba history

Among his papers is a letter Mr. Longworth wrote to the members of the Cincinnati Horticultural Society, dated September 10, 1845, which is particularly interesting because it indicated the progress wines had made and their bright future. It read in part:

The day is not distant when the Ohio River will rival the Rhine in the quantity and quality of this wine. I give the Catawba the preference over all other grapes for a general crop for wine. Sugar was formerly added. The Germans have taught us better. Where the fruit is well-ripened, sugar will injure it where intended for long keeping;

where the grapes do not ripen well, I should still add from 6 to 10 oz. of sugar to the gallon of must. It rivals the best Hock and makes a superior Champagne. . . .

If we intend cultivating the grape for wine, we must rely on our native grapes and new varieties raised from their seed.

If I could get my lease of life renewed for 20 or 30 years, I would devote my attention to the subject, and I would cross our best native varieties with the best table and wine grapes of Europe. We live in a great age. Discoveries are daily made that confound us, and we know not where we shall stop.

Still widely used in making both sparkling and still wines, the Catawba is used in conjuction with other varieties, primarily the Delaware, which today has replaced it as the best fine-wine grape. The wine has a pleasant though slightly wild aroma and flavor distinctly different from any European wine.

HYBRIDS AND NEW VARIETIES

Considerable work has been done to develop new wine-grape varieties by crossbreeding *vinifera* varieties with native American ones. Curiously enough the outstanding hybrids have been developed in France because of the search for fungus- and *Phylloxera*-resistant vines. These French hybrids were introduced to New York State winemakers by Philip Wagner, who first proved their worth by growing them in his own Boordy Vineyard at Riderwood, Maryland.

The first leading French hybridizer was Louis Seibel. Out of the more than thirty thousand hybrids he grew, only a few—less than one in a thousand—have proved satisfactory. Other well-known French hybridizers have been Seyve-Villard, Ravat, Landot, Baco, Bertille-Seyve, Joannès-Seyve, Burdin, Couderc, Galibert, and Kuhlmann. Certain of their hybrids are particularly suited to the eastern American wine districts.

Some of the grapes used with considerable success are:

TO PRODUCE RED WINES

Seibel 5898 (Rougeon)	Seibel 10878 (Chelois)
Seibel 7053 (Chancellor)	Baco No. 1 (Baco Noir)
Seibel 8357 (Colobel)	Kuhlmann 188-2 (Maréchal Foch)
Seibel 13053 (Cascade)	Kuhlmann 192-2 (Léon Millot)
Seibel 9549 (De Chaunac)	Joannès-Seyve 26-205 (Chambourcin)

TO PRODUCE WHITE WINES

Seibel 5279 (Aurore or Aurora)	Seyve-Villard 12-375 (Villard Blanc)
Seibel 9110 (Verdelet)	Ravat 51 (Vignoles)
Seyve-Villard 5-276 (Seyval Blanc or Seyval)	Vidal 256 (Vidal Blanc)

Vineyards need year-round care. Here workers prune vines in winter. (*Courtesy the Taylor Wine Company, Hammondsport, New York*)

For the past few years the New York State Experiment Station in Geneva, New York, has been seriously engaged in hybridization and in testing new varieties. Introduced in 1972, Cayuga White was the most successful vine. It was hybridized from the French hybrid Seyval, the California *vinifera* Zinfandel, and the American hybrid Ontario. The station is also engaged in a new program of scientific work for the improvement of winemaking.

The planting of French-American hybrids in the eastern United States is of immense importance if the total number of vineyards, rather than the total acreage, is considered. More and more amateur winemakers are planting their own grapevines to ensure a continuous supply of raw material for their hobby, and these vines are mostly French hybrids. Out of the ranks of these amateur winemakers have sprung the small wineries in the East. Because the hybrids are hardy and relatively disease resistant, the vineyards and wineries are not limited to any perfect viticultural region. Every state is capable of producing quality wine.

VINIFERA VARIETIES

Possibly one of the most important developments in the New York State wine industry occurred in the early 1950s when Charles Fournier of Gold Seal Vineyards, who always dreamed of growing *vinifera* vines in New York State, met Dr. Konstantin Frank at the Geneva Experiment Station. Dr. Frank had great experience in growing *vinifera* grapes in the Ukraine and persuaded Charles Fournier that it could be done here, too. Fournier set aside a piece of land for Dr. Frank to work and the experiments began.

Dr. Frank's success and enthusiasm have since stirred many people to start vineyards of their own using *vinifera* varieties. At first these followers searched out microclimates in areas near the Finger Lakes region of New York, but eventually the distances increased to include vineyards around Lake Erie in Pennsylvania and Ohio and around Lake Michigan in Michigan, Indiana, and Illinois. Today *vinifera* vines are grown in such diverse areas as New England and Long Island, Maryland and Virginia, Arkansas and Texas, and, most recently, Colorado, Utah, Arizona, and New Mexico.

The White Riesling, Chardonnay, Gewürztraminer, and other white-wine grapes can now be grown successfully and commercially with expert handling. Aside from the northern areas around the Great Lakes, where the red grapes have not fared so well, premium varieties such as Cabernet Sauvignon, Pinot Noir, Gamay Beaujolais, and, in some places, Zinfandel have been grown successfully.

The White Riesling has done so well in specific locations in New York, Ohio, and Michigan that in certain years humidity conditions are often just right to promote the growth of *Botrytis cinerea*, or "noble rot." Dr. Frank, at his Vinifera Wine Cellars, has produced some wine that he labeled Trocken-beerenauslese.

EASTERN WINE TYPES*

The eastern wineries produce all classes and types of wines. Some are marketed under varietal labels. William Widmer was a pioneer in vintaging varietal wines and others have followed his leadership.

The eastern producers have been better known for their white wines. However, because red-black French hybrid grapes have been planted, red wines produced from them are beginning to appear on the American market.

The care exercised in the vineyards while the grapes are maturing and at vintage time is very much the same as in European wine regions. Winery operations include the best of the old-fashioned methods to which the most modern advances have been adapted.

Champagne   It is in making sparkling wines that eastern winemakers excel and have made a name for themselves. The two main grape varieties employed are Catawba and Delaware. Because of the color in the skins of these grapes it is necessary to remove the juice from the grape pulp as soon as it is pressed in

---

*For a review of the descriptions of wine types, see pages 199–202.

Original entrance to Great Western's Champagne cellar, the oldest cellar in continuous use in the United States. (*Courtesy Pleasant Valley Wine Company, Hammondsport, New York*)

order to produce a white wine. Wines from hybrid grapes are now used more and more in the blends of Finger Lakes Champagnes. The major Champagne districts east of the Rockies are located in the Finger Lakes region of New York and in the small area around Sandusky, Ohio, on Lake Erie. Cold Duck is also made in the East, which has a plentiful supply of *labruscana* grapes, which are necessary for making Cold Duck (see page 223).

kosher wines

The increased market developed for commercially produced kosher wines is primarily the result of the intensive advertising and merchandising effort made by the two or three principal firms specializing in the production of these wines. At the same time the product has a wide appeal to the consuming public.

Kosher wines are of high quality. They are not inexpensive but in our opinion their ready acceptance and wide sales come from the fact that they are sweet to the taste. The average consumer who has never tasted wine finds their sweetness more appealing to his palate than the very dry red or white table wines of America and Europe. Sampling these wines, he finds a beverage with a pleasant, fruity bouquet and flavor and at the same time a rich sweetness in taste. The sale of these wines is reputed to be four million cases a year.

Although producers of kosher wines offer a wide assortment including varied sparkling wines, table wines, and fruit wines, far and away their largest seller is the wine they make from the Concord grape. The wines are made under rabbinical supervision and meet all Talmudic stipulations for making pure, unmixed wine. For example, employees who handle the wine must be orthodox Jews, and nonkosher food may not be brought into the plant.

Kosher wine for ritual use, especially the Concord grape wine, is often made from grape juice concentrates. This enables the wines to be made at wineries far from the vineyards. It also allows production throughout the year, not just at harvest time. Monarch Wine Company, for example, has vineyards in upstate New York, from the Finger Lakes to Lake Erie. At harvest time the grapes are pressed into juice and frozen in bulk at plants in Dunkirk and Fredonia. The winery itself is in Brooklyn, New York.

Other states producing kosher wines besides New York are Illinois, New Jersey, Michigan, Washington, and California.

When the trade speaks of kosher wine, it is really referring less to a religious wine than to sweet Concord grape wine. It is generally sweetened with the addition of cane sugar.

Certainly the consumption of kosher wines is no longer confined to people of one religious faith. Many kosher wines sell more at Christmas than they do at Jewish holidays. One of the biggest markets for kosher wines is Puerto Rico. They are also shipped to other major cities in the world, including Bangkok, Tokyo, and Hong Kong. The United States' production used to be sufficient to supply these markets, but wines from Israel are also being shipped now to satisfy the demand.

THE DEVELOPMENT OF
THE WINE INDUSTRY IN THE UNITED STATES

Before 1919 the American wine industry was making slow but steady progress. Whereas in 1900, 30.1 million gallons of wine were consumed in the United States, by 1919 consumption reached 55 million gallons (12 percent of which was imported wine), according to Report No. 134, Second Series, of the United States Tariff Commission. Based on a population of slightly over 100 million, this was a per capita consumption of 0.54 gallons.

Since Repeal in 1933 wine consumption has made steady, healthy progress and today per capita consumption is over $1\frac{3}{4}$ gallons. This is not very impressive when compared with per capita consumption figures of 20 to 30 gallons for wine-consuming countries such as Italy, France, Portugal, Argentina, and Spain. However, the most encouraging wine-consumption trend that began in the United States during the sixties is the steady increase in consumption of light table wines containing 14 percent or less alcohol.

All of this is the result of several factors. One is that the public is taking a greater interest in wine, possibly in answer to the wealth of advertising that has appeared in the press and on radio and television. Another factor is the great increase in travel abroad, where American tourists sample local wines and observe how Europeans use wine as a regular part of their diet. Following the example of the French, Italian, and other wine-drinking peoples, they begin to enjoy a glass of wine with their meals and continue this custom after they return home. The administrator of one of the monopoly state operations told us that he could tell when summer tourists had returned by the number of special orders that flooded his office for some particular wine or spirit that people tasted and liked while on a trip.

The Wine Institute, founded in California after Repeal, has developed into a very efficient instrument of the industry. Practically all California producers are united as Wine Institute members and, as a result, subscribe to the self-regulation that has produced such excellent results. The Wine Institute has also succeeded in obtaining much of the wine legislation that has been passed in several states. In addition it has prepared for free distribution to the trade and the public a series of handbooks on the uses of wine.

All of this type of work, with time, will produce beneficial results for the entire wine trade. There are still many obstacles to overcome, not the least of which are the high taxes levied at almost every step wine takes from the vineyard to the consumer's table.

It is possible to buy wine in food stores in several states, but not in two of the most populous, New York and Pennsylvania. As it is now, wine must be retailed either by specially franchised outlets, which by law cannot engage in any other business, or, as in Pennsylvania, by the state itself. The most important way that naturally fermented wines should be used is with food, and we shall not think of light wine as a food until we can buy it in a food store.

If and when wine is classified as a food and relieved of its present tax burden, so that it can be sold at much lower prices than is possible today, we predict that we shall become a more important wine-consuming nation. Of the ten leading wine-consuming states, California and New York now account for one-third of the total U.S. consumption. With Illinois, New Jersey, Florida, Pennsylvania, Michigan, Texas, Massachusetts, and Ohio, these states consume twice as much wine as the entire rest of the country. The per capita consumption of wine has increased in the last decade from 0.9 gallons in 1964 to 1.72 gallons in 1975. In 1964 the amount of all wine entering distribution channels in the United States was 185.6 million gallons, and by 1975 the total amount almost doubled to 367.6 million gallons.

12
OTHER WINES OF THE AMERICAS

1. CANADA

The vineyards of Canada can be considered extensions of the vineyards of the northern United States because the areas where grapes can be grown successfully in Canada are contiguous to American regions.

Canada is a very small producer, making about as much wine as the island of Cyprus, or about fifteen million gallons annually.

history Canada's first vineyard and winery were established in 1811 by John Schiller in Ontario province. Generally, Canada's winemaking history parallels that of the United States, with a period of Prohibition for each country at about the same time. Both countries also planted experimental grapevines at about the same time.

geography In the eastern regions of Canada grapes are planted on the southwest shore of Lake Ontario and the northern shore of Lake Erie, in the Niagara Peninsula, which is in the province of Ontario. The mitigating effects of Lakes Erie and Ontario on the climate temper the winters and cool the summers. *Labruscana* grape varieties such as Concord, Niagara, Elvira, Agawam, Fredonia, and Catawba are planted, as are French hybrids such as De Chaunac, Maréchal Foch, and Baco Noir. Some *vinifera* grapes have been successful in small amounts; these include Chardonnay, Riesling, Gewürztraminer, Gamay Beaujolais, and Pinot Noir. Seventy-five percent of all Canadian wine is made in this area of the Great Lakes.

In the western part of the country the Okanagan Valley, in the province of British Columbia, produces the balance of Canada's wines. The seventy-five-mile-long Okanagan Lake lessens the effects of the low winter temperatures. Even so, it is Concord and Thompson Seedless grapes that are planted in large quantities. Hardy Rieslings and other *vinifera* varieties are little more than experimental plantings. Much wine made in this region is blended with wine made from grapes that are harvested in California and trucked north for vinification.

240

WINE REGIONS OF CANADA

WEST

EAST

Both eastern and western Canadian wineries produce table wines, baked *wines* and *flor* sherries, ports, and Tokays. Some wines are not vintage dated because of the need to blend for uniformity and quality.

Wine practices are controlled by individual provinces. The only way wines may be purchased anywhere in Canada is in a government-owned liquor store or in a restaurant. A small amount of wine is exported; most is consumed locally.

2. LATIN AMERICA

South of the Río Grande wines are produced in a number of Latin American countries, but of these only wines from Argentina and Chile find their way into the United States. Brazil, Peru, and Uruguay produce wines for home consumption. Two-thirds of South America lies in the tropics and is not as hospitable to the vine as North America.

ARGENTINA

Argentina is the largest producer of wine in the Western Hemisphere, ranking fifth among world producers. Only Italy, France, Spain, and the U.S.S.R.° outrank it. The country's vineyard acreage is over 750,000, about 15 percent more than that of California, but because the average yield per acre is almost double that of California, Argentina ranks much higher in total production, which is over 700 million gallons per year.

history   The earliest known vineyards in Argentina were planted in 1556 by the Jesuit Father Cedron in the Mendoza region. The variety planted was the Mission grape, called the *Criollo de vino* in Argentina. The later missionaries who brought the grape to South America belonged to the same religious order as those who brought the grape to California.

It was the Italian immigrants, arriving in Argentina during the latter part of the nineteenth century, who established the present wine-producing areas, methods, and grape varieties. Like their relatives who went to California, they worked hard, irrigated the land, and converted arid areas into magnificent grape- and fruit-producing regions. Finding that the grape had been cultivated with success since the establishment of the missions by the Spanish explorers, these settlers naturally paid attention to the expansion of vineyards and the production of wine. This activity, coupled with the Buenos Aires–Mendoza railway link, completed in 1884, turned winemaking into a viable industry.

geography   The three principal wine regions of Argentina, all lying in the South Temperate Zone, are in the provinces of Mendoza, San Juan, and Río Negro. Here spring is from October to December, summer is from January to March, fall is from April to June, and winter is from July to September.

Mendoza lies in the west, on the Chilean border, and is the "California Great Central Valley" of Argentina. It is only in the last hundred years that the province has been developed. Mendoza was a vast, arid, sandy desert, showing green patches only along the banks of the several rivers that cut through in draining off the melting Andean snows. Today Mendoza accounts for 70 percent of Argentina's total annual wine production and 90 percent of its table wine production.

The province of San Juan lies immediately north of Mendoza and has similar soil conditions, irrigation being always necessary. Because climatic conditions are on the whole somewhat hotter, the San Juan vineyards are the source of dessert wines, wines for vermouth production, and almost all the table or eating grapes, as well as the magnificent raisins that are available in

---

° Since production varies from year to year, there are some years when Argentina produces more wine than the U.S.S.R., and it then moves to fourth place in world production.

PERU

Lima

Ica

Cuzco

Arequipa

Moquegua

BRAZIL

MINAS
GERAIS

SÃO
PAULO

Rio de Janeiro

CHILE

ATACAMA

COQUIMBO

ACONCAGUA

Santiago

TALCA

MAULE

BÍO-BÍO

ARGENTINA

SAN
JUAN

MENDOZA

CÓRDOBA

Villa Dolores

RÍO
NEGRO

SANTA CATARINA

RIO GRANDE
DO SUL

URUGUAY

Paysandú
Florida
Maldonado
Canelones
Montevideo
San José

WINE REGIONS
OF
SOUTH AMERICA

WILLIAM LEMBECK

such profusion in Argentina's public markets. San Juan also produces some very pleasant table wines that enjoy wide popularity. This province produces about 20 percent of Argentina's wine.

In the province of Río Negro, south of Mendoza, the climate is comparable to the Champagne and German wine regions of Europe. Here are produced some of Argentina's best white table and sparkling wines. The quantities produced are small, from 3 to 5 percent of the country's total production. Very little, if any, irrigation is required in Río Negro, and the soil is less sandy, being more argillaceous and containing sections that are quite chalky in character.

While some wine is produced in practically every province of Argentina, all that is produced outside the three principal provinces does not amount to more than 5 percent of the country's total annual production. In the mountainous Córdoba province there is a small region around Villa Dolores where interesting wine is produced. The quantity is small but both the red and the white are uniformly good—fruity, full bodied, and well balanced. They are wines of character.

Argentina's vineyards, like those of other wine regions, have suffered from and been subjected to attack from various diseases, such as downy mildew, *oïdium* ("powdery mildew"), and *Phylloxera*, which have ravaged vineyards, particularly in Mendoza and San Juan.

In Mendoza and San Juan the wines generally are made on a mass-production basis similar to the methods used in the large wineries of California. A dozen or so giants of the wine industry control about a quarter of the annual production. Some of the largest wineries and wine cellars in the world are found in Mendoza.

The viticultural and vinicultural experiment station that forms part of the University of Cuyo at Mendoza has made significant contributions to the advances and modernization of winemaking in Argentina.

grape varieties

The *vinifera* varieties are cultivated exclusively for commercial wine production and are controlled by government regulation. Varieties permitted for red table wines are the Criolla, Malbec, Cabernet Sauvignon, Barbera, Petite Sirah, Pinot Noir, Tempranilla, Merlot, Sangiovese, and Lambrusco. For white table wines permitted grapes are the Criolla, Sauvignon Blanc, Sémillon, Chardonnay, Pinot Blanc, Riesling, and Trebbiano. Fortified and dessert wines are made from the Pedro Ximenez, Muscat of Alexandria, and Malvasia varieties.

The Criolla grape is the most widely planted grape in Argentina, and it is used for both red and white wines.

wines

All classes and types of wines are produced in Argentina, and almost all of them are consumed there. The largest portion of the market is wines made from a blend of the wines of the Criolla, Malbec, and Barbera grapes.

Premium wines are emerging both for local consumption and for export. Labels indicating varietal wines, such as Cabernet Sauvignon, and labels indicating age, such as Gran Reserve or Viejo ("old"), are appearing on the market, with the definition of some of these terms being up to the producer. Aging often takes place in French oak casks.

A number of the leading wine houses also produce sparkling wines by all the methods known in the wine trade. Argentine Champagne may be made by the traditional bottle-fermented method; by the transfer process; by the Charmat, or bulk-fermentation, process; or by artificial carbonation. Sparkling rosé is also produced, generally by the Charmat method. Champagnes are labeled Brut, Extra Brut, Sec, Demi Sec, and Dulce, in ascending order of sweetness. The Argentines prefer the sweeter types. Pinot Noir, Chardonnay, Chenin Blanc, and Ugni Blanc are the most common varieties used to make the *cuvée.*

Sherry and port wines of very satisfactory quality are offered, but the Muscatels of San Juan are of superior quality—comparable, in fact, to the Muscatel wines of the Mediterranean islands. These wines do not contain more than 16 percent alcohol.

Argentina is one of the largest consumers of vermouth, where one brand alone markets over 2 million cases a year of the 3½ million sold. Vermouth is consumed almost entirely as an aperitif, served on the rocks or with a dash of soda and a dash or two of Italian-style bitters.

Argentine table wines are well made, and most compare favorably with everyday drinking wines produced elsewhere. In Argentina wine is part of the diet. In every restaurant, whether it be the finest luxury establishment or a simple workers' eating place, there is wine on every table, while in the home it is always found on the host's table as well as the servants'. It is served as a matter of course, as coffee or soft drinks are served in the United States. The people of Argentina drink over twenty gallons of wine per capita each year.

There has been little Argentine wine for export, but a few importers have begun to bring in the finer premium wines from Mendoza. The local preference has always been for soft, well-matured, nonacid wines; but the Argentine drive for greater acceptance in the world market has caused producers to modify their winemaking techniques and produce a bouquet and taste more similar to the fresher, drier wines preferred in Europe and America.

BRAZIL

Viticulture is relatively new to the Brazilians, as grapes were not planted there until after World War I, by Italians. Even though the Portuguese originally colonized Brazil, the wines reflect this Italian influence, as well as a strong German influence. The French have also established modern wineries in Brazil and have brought over their own technologists.

history

geography   While Brazil is the largest South American country, most of it is too tropical for grape growing, and there are only 170,000 acres under vine in the most southern area. Winemaking activity is centered from about 15 degrees to 30 degrees latitude, in the South Temperate Zone, where the seasons are reversed. The biggest and southernmost area is Rio Grande do Sul, on the Atlantic. Rio de Janeiro and Minas Gerais are more northerly states where grapes are also grown. São Paulo has some vines, and it vinifies its own wines as well as makes wine from grapes of the adjoining Santa Catarina region.

grape varieties   Because of the tropical humidity, the most successful grapes are hybrids
and wines   and non-*vinifera* types. Most prominent are the Isabella and the Herbemont. Others include Dutchess, Majara, Concord, Cintiana, Gothe, Muscat, and Malvasia. Barbera, Shiraz, and Trebbiano are examples of European grapes that can succeed in the warmer temperatures.

Some noble grape varieties, such as Cabernet, Merlot, Pinot Noir, Sémillon, and Riesling, have been successful in small quantities.

Both generic and varietal wines are made in Brazil, and the types include table, fortified, and sparkling wines. The Italian influence is apparent with the production of vermouths and bitter aperitifs. The fifty to sixty million gallons produced annually are consumed locally, and some wine is imported from neighboring South American countries to augment local production.

CHILE

By comparison with Argentina across the Andes, Chile is a small country both in area and in population. From the standpoint of fine wines, however, Chile is very important, as the finest wines of South America are produced there.

history   Chile is endowed with a delightfully sunny climate, ideal soil conditions, and, above all, practically disease-free vineyards. The Chilean vines have never had a serious plague such as mildew or *Phylloxera* because of the country's fortunate terrain, climate, and location, as well as the relentless precautions taken by agricultural inspectors at the borders. Such diseases as the vines suffer are not serious; probably the worst worry the vineyard owner has is that of late spring or early summer hailstorms, which are, on occasion, quite devastating.

The vine has been cultivated in Chile since the beginning of Spanish colonization in the sixteenth century, when the early missionaries, as they did elsewhere, planted the vine for the production of wine for the Sacrament. Because of the propitious volcanic soil, it was not long before these vineyards were producing wines for more mundane purposes. It is presumed that the first vines planted in Chile were cuttings brought down from Cuzco, the ancient capital of the Incas. This must have been before 1551, because in letters of that date Don Pedro de Valdivia, one of Chile's early leaders, mentions eating locally grown grapes, and several years later he comments on the wine produced near the city of Santiago.

Cultivation of the vine and production of wine were rather haphazardly pursued in Chile for three centuries. Then in 1851 Don Silvestre Ochagavia contracted the services of M. Bertrand, a French viticulturer who brought with him the first cuttings of Cabernets, Pinots, and other grapes, and with his arrival began the modernization and vast expansion of wine production, consumption, and appreciation in Chile. During the century that has followed, M. Bertrand has been succeeded by a long series of eminent French viticulturists and enologists, such as Gaston Canu, Georges Guyot de Granmaison, Leopold Gamerre, O. Brard, and Paul Pacottet. As is evident, Chilean viniculture has developed primarily along French lines.

geography

Chile is a rather long and narrow strip of land that begins at the southern border of Peru and extends twenty-eight hundred miles south to icy Tierra del Fuego and the Straits of Magellan. At its back lies the ever present and imposing massif of the snow-covered Andes range, including the twenty-three-thousand-foot-high Mount Aconcagua, the tallest peak in the Western Hemisphere. Washing Chile's long shoreline is the equally impressive Pacific Ocean and its cold Humboldt Current. The fresh breezes striking the high wall of the mountain backdrop produce the ideal climatic conditions that have such a marked effect on all the fruits of Chile's soil. Whether they are grapes, peaches, raspberries, pears, melons, lentils, onions, or garlic, they are rich in perfume, flavor, and character. The country's wines are no exception.

From Coquimbo, about 30 degrees south latitude, south to Temuco, 40 degrees south latitude—some six hundred miles of land, including about 275,000 acres of vineyards—wine is made.

wine regions

There are three principal wine-producing regions in Chile. In the provinces of Atacama and Coquimbo in the north the wines are high in alcohol content and are mainly sweet, fortified types. The central provinces, from Aconcagua to Talca, produce the best table wines of Chile. The southern provinces, from Maule to Bío-Bío, produce the bulk wines of the country.

grape varieties and wines

The principal *vinifera* varieties are cultivated for wine production, as are table grapes and raisins. Most of the original cuttings were brought from the various European wine regions, but in recent years cuttings have also been imported from California. For white wines the varieties most used are the Sauvignon Blanc, Sémillon, Pinot Blanc, Chardonnay, Trebbiano, Riesling, Traminer, and the Chilean native variety known as the Loca Blanca. For red wines producers use primarily the Cabernet Sauvignon, Cabernet Franc, Malbec, Petit Verdot, Merlot, and Pinot Noir. The table and raisin varieties tend to be the Muscat of Alexandria, Malvasia, Malaga, and seedless varieties such as the Corinth and Thompson, of which thousands of boxes are exported annually to the American market.

Wine production in Chile follows European methods in all respects. Fermentation takes place in vats and the new wine is racked into small or medium-size cooperage for its development. The wines are generally bottled after one to one and a half years for white wines, and two and a half years for red wines.

All classes and types of wines can be and are produced in Chile, but consumption of wines other than red and white table wines is negligible by comparison. Good but rather sweetish sparkling wine is produced, mostly by bulk process. Some sherry and port types are also made, as well as vermouth.

The largest volume of wine sold in Chile is labeled simply Tinto or Blanco ("red" or "white"); it is sold generally in grocery stores, in a typically Chilean wicker-covered demijohn of five to ten liters, called a *chuico*. The customer leaves a deposit for the container that is refunded when he returns it.

In clubs, restaurants, hotels, and fine groceries, premium wines, which are abundant, are offered in the traditional European bottles. These wines, sometimes bearing vintage dates and resembling quite closely their namesakes, are labeled Cabernet, Borgoña (Burgundy), Pommard, Pinot, Riesling, Rhine, Chablis, Sauvignon, Sémillon, Sauternes, and so on. In addition, the labels bear the name of the vineyard and one of the following phrases, in order of quality (the first being the best): Gran Vino para Banquetes ("great wine for banquets"), Gran Vino, or Reservado.

With few exceptions Riesling and Rhine wines are bottled, for sale in Chile, in the *Bocksbeutel* of Steinwein of Franconia fame.

Grape growing in Chile is a very important agricultural endeavor and one that is of great concern to the people as a whole and to the government—particularly the Internal Revenue Department, which is charged with controlling every step of the wine's progress, from planting the grape until its final service on the consumer's table. Strict supervision of labeling, quality standards, and so forth, is maintained.

As a temperance measure the Chilean legislature passed a law limiting the amount of wine that can be sold within the country to 60 liters (15.85 gallons) per capita. The average consumption is actually less than this, amounting to 10.6 gallons per capita. In supervising strict compliance with this law, the Internal Revenue Department establishes quotas governing new plantings, wine production, and marketing. This does not mean that production is limited to the 60-liter-per-capita consumption figure. Any wine produced in excess of the statutory limit must be either exported, distilled into brandy or alcohol for fuel purposes, or dumped. Since under the law only 85 to 90 million gallons can be marketed internally, and Chile's production approaches 150 million gallons annually, the industry has to find a continually expanding export market if it wishes to progress and prosper. Some wine leaders have developed excellent markets for premium wines, exported in bottles to this country and the other American countries, and for standard quality wines shipped in bulk to a number of European markets, notably Belgium, Holland, the Scandinavian countries, Switzerland, Germany, and France. A much greater volume of exports is made to European countries than to the American nations.

Chilean wines have justifiably found a very ready acceptance wherever they have been offered. In the United States, where they are very moderately priced, they represent some of the best wine values available.

MEXICO

The history of wine in Mexico has been an interesting paradox. This area *history* was the portal of Spain's introduction to viticulture and viniculture to the Americas—to California, Peru, Chile, Argentina, and the rest of South America. Yet despite determined and intermittent efforts, Mexico's total production of table wine is only 4 million gallons a year; the per capita consumption is about $7\frac{1}{2}$ ounces.

Wines have been made in Mexico ever since Hernando Cortés had cuttings from Spain planted between 1521 and 1527. After that vines were planted by traveling missionaries. In 1593 and 1626 the first two commercial wineries were established four hundred miles north of Mexico City.

During three centuries of Spanish rule, vines were uprooted and could not be replanted, in order to protect the Spanish wine monopoly. After Mexico achieved independence in the early 1800s vines again were planted, but the wines produced were of low quality. The very large Bodegas de Santo Tomás was established in 1888 in Baja California, the long peninsula stretching south from California.

The history of Mexican wines is filled with names well known to California. From 1889 to 1904 John Concannon sent cuttings of the better French grape varieties from his property in Livermore. This was the first effort to replace the ubiquitous Mission, or Criolla, grape, which gave a high yield of low-grade wine.

Antonio Perelli-Minetti later planted nine hundred acres between 1910 and 1916 with Zinfandel, Petite Sirah, Malaga, and Flame Tokay grapes, managing to protect his vineyards during the Mexican Revolution.

Fifty years later Dmitri Tchelistcheff became the technical director of Santo Tomás. During a ten-year period he replanted vineyards with noble varieties and other varieties suitable to the climate and introduced sound winemaking techniques, such as cold fermentation of white wines, barrel and bottle aging for red wines, making *flor*-process sherries, making bulk-process and bottle-fermented Champagnes, and even producing a pot-still brandy.

Nazario Ortiz Garza, who became Mexico's secretary of agriculture, built

WINE REGIONS
OF
MEXICO

Valle Redondo
Tañama
Guadalupe
Ensenada
Rancho Viejo
Santo Tomás
BAJA
CALIFORNIA
SONORA
Hermosillo
CHIHUAHUA
Delicias
COAHUILA
Torreón
Parras
Saltillo
DURANGO
AGUASCALIENTES
QUERÉTARO
Guadalajara
San Juan
del Río
Mexico City

SCALE
0   200   400   600 km

WILLIAM LEMBECK

four wineries between 1929 and 1966. The first was at Saltillo and is now about two hundred acres; the second in Mexico City, supplied with grapes from farther north; the third at Aguascalientes, comprising eight thousand acres; and the last at Torreón. Also at Torreón the Mexican government established a vineyard supplied with rootstocks from the University of California at Davis to propagate and supply virus-free vines.

The Mexican Winegrowers' Association has launched a strong effort to increase the use of table wines by the Mexican people. Some highly rated European producers have built modern facilities to make table wine, vermouth, and brandy in Mexico. With all this activity, vineyard acreage has increased from 4,000 in 1939 to over 100,000 in 1977. Wine production has also increased to about forty million gallons a year, but most of it is distilled into brandy. Most of this increase has taken place in the last ten years.

wine regions   Most of the vineyards are in northern Mexico, where mile-high elevations provide cooler temperatures. One problem is a lack of water, and many areas must be irrigated.

The most important wine region is that of northern Baja California, which is within one hundred miles of the California border and is cooled by the moist ocean breezes of the Pacific. The most important valleys are Santo Tomás, Rancho Viejo, Guadalupe, Valle Redondo, and Tañama.

In northwest Mexico, south of Arizona, is the semitropical Hermosillo district in the state of Sonora. In north-central Mexico, south of Texas, is the Delicias district in the state of Chihuahua. Parras and Saltillo, in the state of Coahuila, also south of Texas, is five thousand feet above sea level. Parras was the site of the first winery, built in 1593, and is said to be the cradle of viniculture of the Americas. Another viticultural region is Torreón, at the border of the states of Coahuila and Durango. Aguascalientes, northeast of Guadalajara, and San Juan del Río, in Querétaro, complete the main grape-growing areas in Mexico. San Juan del Río is the most southern, only one hundred miles north of Mexico City, but its high altitude of sixty-one hundred feet means cool growing conditions, despite its being so far south.

grape varieties and wines

The best table wines are from the Ensenada area of Baja California. These wines are made from Cabernet Sauvignon, Pinot Noir, Barbera, Zinfandel, Riesling, Chardonnay, Sémillon, Chenin Blanc, and Aligoté grapes. The San Juan del Río area also has been successful with noble grape varieties.

Wines are named for the grape varieties used, and many wineries are establishing proprietary names as well. Vermouths and fortified wines, such as baked sherry, are popular. The Chenin Blanc is being used to make a good sparkling wine.

PERU

history

The vine has been growing in Peru for almost five hundred years, having been planted there in the 1500s. Production is small—about two million gallons a year—and all the wine is consumed locally.

wine regions

The vineyards of Peru stretch from Lima, the capital, south to Moquegua, along the Pacific Coast. There are twenty thousand acres around Ica, which is south of Lima. Cuzco, somewhat inland, and Arequipa, a cathedral town near the Pacific, are also vineyard sites.

grape varieties and wines

European Mission grape varieties are grown in Peru, producing red and white table wines resembling the Mediterranean style. Some fortified wines, similar to sherry, port, and Madeira, are also produced. The Muscat grape produces the famous Pisco brandy.

URUGUAY

history

Uruguay's vineyards were not established until the 1890s, so the viticultural attitudes are very modern. Since it was discovered that the mild climate was hospitable to the vine, the University of Uruguay has been working to develop the winemaking industry, even sending students to Italy and France for further study.

wine regions   Uruguay is the smallest wine-producing South American country, but it has fifty thousand acres under vine and produces 24 million gallons a year. Since it has a relatively high annual per capita consumption of 6.6 gallons, the wines produced remain in Uruguay.

The earliest cultivated area was around Montevideo, the southernmost city. Vineyards extend to neighboring Canelones, San José, and Maldonado, along the Río de la Plata. Paysandú to the north, next to Argentina, and Florida in south-central Uruguay are other grape-growing districts. The climate is mild, tempered by ocean breezes, with a high of 70 degrees Fahrenheit in summer (January and February) and a low of 50 degrees Fahrenheit in winter (July and August). Rainfall is generally adequate, but in some years there are droughts.

grape varieties   Most of the grapes have European origins: the Cabernet and Sémillon of
and wines   Bordeaux, the Pinot Blanc of Burgundy, and the Barbera and Nebbiolo from Italy. The most widely planted grape is the Harriague, originally from the Pyrénées. Some hybrids and *labruscana* types are also grown. Table, fortified, aromatized, and sparkling wines are all produced, mostly under local names.

13
THE WINES OF THE MIDDLE EAST AND AFRICA

The lands of the Middle East and North Africa share many common traditions. The most pervasive of these, the Islamic religion, forbids the use of alcoholic beverages. This religious prohibition is the major reason for the very slow development of winemaking in this potentially lush viticultural region. It is ironic that this huge area should rank so low in world production and consumption, since it is generally acknowledged to be the fountainhead of the stream of wine.

According to the Persians, their country (present-day Iran) was the birthplace of winemaking. Persia has given us many riches in philosophy, art, and poetry, but it has also bequeathed us a vine that has since prospered in many regions of the world—the Shiraz and the Syrrah of the Rhône (the descendants of which are the Petite Sirah of California). Shiraz and its wine must have been in the mind of Omar Khayyam when he wrote:

> I sometimes wonder what the vintner buys
> One half so precious as the stuff he sells?

In *A Book of Other Wines* P. Morton Shand recounts the Persian version of the discovery of wine. The Shah Jamshid always had a dish of grapes by his bedside, and one day, observing that some of the overripe berries were fermented, he ordered them to be thrown away, thinking them poisonous. A discarded favorite from his harem seized the grapes and drank the juice to put an end to her sorrow. This she achieved, but not in the way she had expected. When the surprised shah found her, mildly intoxicated but far from melancholy, she revealed the delightful secret of the grapes, and through her discovery of wine she recaptured the devotion of the shah.

This chapter follows the development of wines throughout the Middle East and North Africa and ends with a leap to South Africa. Although South Africa

253

is the newest of the countries to enter into winemaking, it is the second largest producer on the African continent, ranking behind Algeria.

1. THE MIDDLE EAST

CYPRUS

history   Cyprus today is an independent nation. Even though it was long held by England, it has maintained its viticultural ties to Greece, which had controlled it previously. Mythology calls this island the home of the goddess Aphrodite, and a dry white wine with a high alcohol content bears her name. The English Crusaders took over the island from Greece in the twelfth century and ruled until 1571, when the Ottoman Empire annexed Cyprus to its vast domain. During the English reign the Knights Templar glorified the rich and sweet Commandaria wine and established its use at English banquets.

Under Turkish rule the vine continued to flourish in quantity, but it declined in quality. At the end of the nineteenth century England again took control of the island and rebuilt the wine industry to its present status.

geography   Cyprus lies off the southern coast of Turkey and the western shores of Syria, no more than seventy-five miles from either mainland country. A hilly terrain, which provides many southern exposures, combined with the moderating effect on temperature of the surrounding Mediterranean Sea, converts this island into a veritable single vineyard.

WINE REGIONS OF CYPRUS AND TURKEY

All types of table, sparkling, and fortified wines are produced. A great deal *grape varieties* is exported, mostly to the United Kingdom. Of the table wines red, white, and *and wines* rosé are produced. The native Mavron grape is used to produce red wines as well as the nonresinated Cypriot version of the resinated Greek Kokineli wine. On Cyprus the Kokineli wine is a deep rosé, rather than a red. The most famous dry red wines are the highly pigmented Othello and Afames.

The indigenous Xynisteri grape is responsible for all of the white wines, which account for only a small percentage of the total production.

Of all Cypriot wines Commandaria is the most distinguished. It is made from a blend of Mavron and Xynisteri grapes that have been raisined and that yield a high residual sugar content after fermentation. The wines mature for a long time in a modified *solera* system. Commandaria is a rich, luscious, dark amber dessert wine, with a flavor like that of a cream sherry.

Cyprus also boasts many other styles of sherry-type dessert wines. These traditionally have been exported to Great Britain.

ISRAEL

According to Genesis, as soon as Noah emerged from his ark he planted a *history* vineyard. Wine production flourished until the Muslim occupation, when vines were uprooted because the Koran, or Holy Book, forbade wine drinking. Except for a small amount made for religious ceremonies, no wine was made commercially.

The modern wine industry began in 1870, when the first agricultural school was established in Mikve near Jaffa. Baron Edmond de Rothschild, an owner of Château Mouton-Rothschild, later sent a team of specialists who helped with the planting of *vinifera* vines. They also helped with the construction of two large wineries at Richon Le Zion and Zichron Jacob, with wine produced under the supervision of the baron's winemaker. The *Société Coopérative Vigneronne des Grandes Caves* was formed in 1906 by the farmers, who have continually updated viticultural practices. Israeli winemakers have glass-lined storage tanks with a combined capacity for several million gallons, and they use mechanized bottling facilities.

Vineyards are spread over a large area in Galilee, Shomron, the slopes of *wine regions* Mount Carmel, and the Judean Hills toward Jerusalem. *and grape*

Red wines are produced from the Cabernet Sauvignon, Alicante Grenache, *varieties* Carignane, and, in the last twenty years, the Israeli Concord grapes. These are all used for varietal wines. Other red grapes are Bouschet and Ruby Royal.

White varietal wines are made from the Sémillon, Sauvignon Blanc, Chenin Blanc, and French Colombard. Other white grapes include the Clairette, Muscat of Alexandria, Muscat de Frontignan, and Dabouki, a local grape.

LEFT: Carignane grapes from the slopes of Mount Carmel in the crusher at Richon le Zion, in Israel. (*Courtesy Carmel Wine Company, Inc., New York*) RIGHT: Fully automated bottling plant at Richon le Zion. (*Photo by Photo-Emka Ltd., courtesy Carmel Wine Company, Inc., New York*)

WINE
REGIONS
OF
ISRAEL

SCALE

0   10   20   30   40   50 km

SHOMRON VINEYARDS

LEBANON

SYRIA

MOUNT CARMEL VINEYARDS

GALILEE VINEYARDS

ZICHRON JACOB WINERY AND VINEYARDS

JORDAN

MEDITERRANEAN SEA

Tel Aviv

RICHON LE ZION— WINERY AND VINEYARDS

Rehovat Wine Institute

Jordan R.

Jerusalem

JUDEAN VINEYARDS

DEAD SEA

WILLIAM LEMBECK

EGYPT

Red, white, and rosé table and sparkling wines in all degrees of sweetness are produced. Dessert wines and sweet and dry vermouth are also made. All wines are kosher and are acceptable for religious ceremonies as well as for table use throughout the world.

Until 1961 many wines were generically named. When Israel signed the Madrid Pact, however, agreeing not to use territorial names outside its borders, new Hebrew names were adopted, identifying their Israeli origins:

NAME	DESCRIPTION
Adom Atic	dry, red, Burgundy type
Avdat Red	dry, red
Avdat White	dry, light white
Château Richon	semidry, golden, Sauternes type
Kadmon	sweet, amber, Madeira type
Partom	sweet, red, port type
Sharir	semidry, golden, sherry type
Topaz	sweet, golden, Tokay type

TURKEY

history

Although wine has been produced in Turkey on both sides of the Dardanelles for many centuries, it has never been an important enterprise, for, while Turkey possesses great vineyard acreage, the Islamic influence has limited winemaking to a small percentage of the total grape harvest.

Modern cultural changes, combined with a relaxation of traditional religious strictures, have greatly increased the vinicultural pursuits of this country. The government produces virtually all wines and spirits through state-owned wineries and distilleries. A few private concerns still make wine, but only for local consumption.

wine regions and wines

The best viticultural areas lie in the western part of Turkey's vast Anatolian peninsula, but there are a number of highly productive vineyards on the hilly slopes of Thrace in the European part of Turkey.

The wines of Turkey are produced from native grapes. Although very few wines are exported, some do appear on the wine lists of Turkish restaurants around the world. The red wines Adabag, Kalebag, and Buzbag, from Anatolia, and the white or red Trakya from Thrace are the most famous table wines. There are several good Turkish dessert wines, but few are exported.

Table wines are served mainly at dinnertime in Turkey, and consumption amounts to only one bottle per capita. The main alcoholic beverage is the anise-flavored spirit Raki, which is consumed, mainly by men, at all times of the day. Raki has a licoricelike flavor and a milky, pearlescent color when mixed with water.

2. NORTH AFRICA

ALGERIA

history   The Koran forbids the Faithful to drink alcoholic beverages, but the followers of Muhammad have always tended the vine wherever it would grow because they liked to eat the fruit. It was not until the early nineteenth century, when France colonized Algeria, that winemaking was begun in earnest. The devastation by *Phylloxera* in France during this period drove many French viticulturists to Algeria. Along with their knowledge of wine-making, the French brought their native vines—some, unfortunately, infested with the grape louse that later consumed the Algerian vineyards. Despite the scourge, the French succeeded in developing enormous vineyards on the slopes of sun-bathed hills, in the plains several miles inland, and along the coasts.

Before Algeria won its independence in 1962, this African country produced 400 million gallons annually. Most of these wines, as in other countries with hot climates, were quite full, deep red, and rich in alcohol. They were perfect blending wines for the thin bulk wines of France's Midi and were good base wines for some of the French proprietary wines, red table wines, and aperitifs. The colonial trade relationship allowed France to concentrate on producing quality wines for export and to supply its people with low-priced

WINE REGIONS
OF
NORTH AFRICA

WILLIAM LEMBECK

Algerian quaffing wines, while establishing a strong economic base for the people of Algeria. After 1962, when the French winemakers were forced to leave Algeria, the demand for Algerian wines diminished because French growers insisted that the importation of cheap Algerian wine be stopped. Algeria today, with a newly stabilized wine market, is still a large producer in the world market, ranking ninth, and produces 200 million gallons annually.

The vineyards of Algeria are located along the entire northern portion of the country, but the two departments of Algiers and Oran produce the majority of the wine. The Atlas mountain range separates the arable vineyard land from the vast nonarable interior. On the plains are produced light wines that mature quickly, while the hilly slopes and mountains are the source of fuller, more fragrant, and longer-lasting wines.   *wine regions and grape varieties*

The vines cultivated are mostly those of the Midi: Carignane, Mourvèdre, and Cinsault for the reds and Clairette, Ugni Blanc, and Muscat for the whites. In better soils and more favorable exposures along the slopes the better varieties of Cabernet, Pinot Noir, Gamay, Chasselas, and Grenache are grown.

EGYPT

Although Egypt is in North Africa, it is closely allied with the Arab countries of the Middle East. Because of its Muslim heritage, Egypt is neither a large producer nor a large consumer of wine.

Historical references indicate that wines were made as far south as the city of Merowe, near the Fourth Cataract in the Upper Nile. This region is now part of Sudan. Presently, vineyards extend all the way down the Nile to the point where it empties into the Mediterranean Sea.   *history*

Although the vineyards lie along the northern coast, they are as close to the Equator as they could be without suffering from the absence of the cooler altitudes provided by a mountain chain. Through a fortunate combination of soil, grape variety, and microclimate, Egypt has built up a wine industry since the start of this century that produces about two million gallons per year. Although more than one-third of it is exported, none has yet commercially reached the United States.   *wine regions*

MOROCCO

The history of Morocco's wine industry is very similar to that of Algeria's, except for the period after Morocco's independence from France in 1956. The Moroccan people gained their independence in an orderly transition without   *history* the uprisings and war that racked Algeria. Regulations and controls were laid down by the Moroccan ministry along lines already established by the French, and a channel of commerce was established with the Common Market countries to absorb Morocco's surplus production.

wine regions and grape varieties

Morocco's vineyards stretch from Marrakech in the west to Oujda in the east, bordering on the Algerian vineyards around Oran. These vineyards all lie between the coast and the northern slopes of the Middle Atlas mountain chain.

As in Algeria, the grape varieties are the popular ones found along the Mediterranean basin, producing red and white wines. Carignane, Cinsault, Grenache, and Clairette are the major varieties. The red wines they produce are generally alcoholic and fiery, with a tendency toward heaviness. They are sound, drinkable wines with no claim to greatness. They are often blended with thin, light wines, to which they give body and life. Their white wines are pleasant when young and fresh and are consumed locally.

TUNISIA

history

The wine industry in Tunisia is confined to a small area around the Gulf of Tunis, where vineyards once flourished around the ancient city of Carthage. This winemaking area has remained confined because of centuries of Muslim influence. After France took control of the country, as in Morocco and Algeria, Tunisia's production soared until *Phylloxera* attacked the vineyards in the 1930s. A twenty-year program of uprooting and replanting on grafted stocks has completely restored the Tunisian wine trade. Tunisia now produces thirty-three million gallons a year. The establishment of specific appellations in the 1940s helped this country maintain the high quality of its wines at a time when large quantities of bulk wine were needed in Europe. Tunisia's independence in 1956 did not affect its export market, which consisted mainly of France. After supplying domestic needs, Tunisia has no trouble selling its large surplus of wines on the international market.

grape varieties and wines

The familiar Mediterranean grapes are grown in Tunisian vineyards. Carignane, Cinsault, Alicante Bouschet, Mourvèdre, Clairette, and Ugni Blanc are some of the traditional varieties, but other *vinifera* grapes such as Pedro Ximenez, Sémillon, and Sauvignon Blanc have been planted to improve the white wines, which oxidize quickly in this hot climate. Muscat wines, produced from several varieties, are an important category and enjoy a special appellation, indicative of Tunisia's pride in these sweet wines.

Tunisians consume more wine, about one gallon per capita, than their North African neighbors.

3. SOUTH AFRICA

history

Although South Africa's wine industry goes back more than three hundred years, it is only since the early 1900s that wines were vinified and marketed to the rest of the world. Today South Africa ranks thirteenth in production with 132 million gallons, but approximately half of this is distilled into brandy. Consumption of wine is about 3 gallons per capita.

The first vines arrived on a ship from the Dutch East India Company in 1655. They were planted by Johan van Riebeeck, and the first Cape wine was produced four years later. The second Dutch governor, Simon van der Stel, established an important vineyard at Constantia. With the arrival of French Huguenots in 1688, vineyards were extended and wines were improved. By 1826 exports to Britain were increasing, and this continued until 1861, when shipments were reduced because the tariff advantage to the Commonwealth was eliminated. By 1885, when *Phylloxera* destroyed the vineyards of the Cape, the wine industry was almost in ruins. By grafting their vines onto American rootstocks, which were resistant to *Phylloxera*, winemaking resumed, and it reached a point where there was a troublesome surplus.

To solve this problem, the *Ko-operative Wijnbouwers Vereniging* (K.W.V.) or Cooperative Winegrowers Association was established. They set prices for wines, standardized wines for export, encouraged aging of sherries and ports, and had excess wine distilled. In this last activity the association improved brandy production by advocating wood aging and double distillation in pot stills.

This national cooperative has five large wineries at Paarl, Stellenbosch, Robertson, Montagu, and Worcester, which use temperature- and pressure-controlled fermentation and whose techniques and equipment have been purchased from the major wine areas of Europe and California. South Africa's heat makes cold fermentation a necessity.

areas of origin laws

A system of guaranteeing the area of origin and the grape was put into effect in 1973. A simple Wines of Origin (W.O.) seal appears on the capsule if the wine has a vintage date and contains at least 80 percent of wine from the area on the label and is made from specified grape varieties.

Approved areas are the following:

Constantia	Piketberg
Durbanville	Robertson
Little Karoo	Stellenbosch
Malmesbury	Swellendam
Olifants River	Tulbagh
Paarl	Worcester

WINE REGIONS
OF
SOUTH AFRICA

There are some estates that produce and sell their own wines, and fourteen of these are entitled to the designation Estate Wines of Origin. Most of these estates are from Stellenbosch: Alto, Middelvlei, Muratie, Neethlingshof, Overgaauw, Simonsig, Uiterwyk, and Verdun. Groot Constantia and Meerendal are estates in the Cape area, which is considered part of the Stellenbosch district as well. The Tulbagh region has three estates: Montpellier, Theuniskraal, and Twee Jongegezellen. Lastly, there is an estate from Paarl called Backsberg.

To achieve a seal of Wines of Origin, at least 75 percent of the wine must be from a specific grape variety (*cultivar*). If the grape is a noble variety, which might be in short supply, a special provision allows the wine to contain only 50 percent of that grape until 1983. After that the wine will have to contain 75 percent of the grape named on the label. If the grape used is in good supply, then the wine currently must contain 75 percent of the grape.

The highest seal is Wines of Origin Superior (W.O.S.). To qualify for this seal, all of the wine must be made from a single grape variety if one is stated on the label.

There are two main wine regions of South Africa: the Coastal Belt in the *wine regions* southwest and Little Karoo to the east. The best wines come from the Coastal Belt, which is under the influence of the Atlantic Ocean and which gets twenty-five inches of rain per year, most of it in the winter when the vines are dormant. Little Karoo, between the Drakenstein and Swartberg mountains, produces more ordinary wines. This region is much drier than the Coastal Belt, only ten inches of rain per year, and irrigation is a necessity.

The wine regions of the Coastal Belt include Stellenbosch, which was named for Governor de Stel and which is thirty miles from Cape Town. Paarl, another important region, is on about the same latitude south as is Jerez, Spain, in the north, and sherries have been made there since the 1930s. Paarl also produces table wines. South of Cape Town, the Constantia vineyards produce good red and white table wines, although a sweet Muscat wine brought them fame in the last century. Tulbagh, thirty-two miles north of Paarl, is especially known for its white wines, some of which are late harvested. Other areas of the Coastal Belt include Malmesbury, Wellington, Durbanville, and Franschhoek.

Little Karoo, which is at a higher altitude, contains Worcester, Robertson, Montagu, Oudtshoorn, and Ladismith.

South Africa has many different vines growing, some that are familiar *grape varieties* European varieties and others that are native grapes. One important red-wine grape, the Pinotage, is a cross between Hermitage and Pinot Noir.

Since the grapes are growing in the Southern Hemisphere, not only are the seasons reversed from the Northern Hemisphere, but so are the grapes' growing requirements. The whites do best on the cooler southern slopes, and the reds prefer the warmer northern slopes that face the sun.

Red grapes that grow in the Coastal Belt include Hermitage, Gamay, Pinotage, Cabernet Sauvignon, Cabernet Franc, Petite Sirah, and Cinsaut (Cinsault).

White grapes of the Coastal Belt are Riesling, Clairette Blanche, Steen (Stein), Chenin Blanc, Traminer, Palomino, Green, and Colombar (Colombard). Both Steen and Riesling are vinified in the German style, and sometimes sweeter wines are made from a late harvest of those grapes.

In the warmer Little Karoo area, the native grapes that can tolerate the heat are grown more successfully than the European grapes, which require cooler climates. Hermitage and Cinsaut are the important red grapes, and dessert wine grapes, such as Palomino, Muscat of Alexandria, Muscadel, Thompson Seedless, Hanepoot, Steen, and Sultana, complete the list of white grapes.

All types of wines are produced in South Africa. The Coastal Belt is known *wines* for its table wines and some sherries and ports. The white wines are fresh with a touch of acidity, thanks to cool fermentation. The best whites come from

Tulbagh, Paarl, and Stellenbosch. On rare occasions, *Botrytis cinerea* makes an *Edelkeur*. The red table wines are vinified to be aged in both wood and bottle. The most famous ones are produced in Paarl, Stellenbosch, Durbanville, and the Constantia Valley.

Dessert wines, especially sherries, are made at Paarl and Stellenbosch. Traditional *flor* yeasts occur naturally here (see Chapter 8) and both *flor* and *solera* sherries are produced. With proper aging they are considered to be quite good. As in Jerez, the Palomino is the grape used. Other dessert wines are produced in Constantia and in the Worcester, Montagu, and Robertson regions of Little Karoo.

Both bottle- and tank-fermented sparkling wines are made from the Riesling and Clairette Blanche grapes. They range in sweetness from extra dry to sweet. A carbonated *Perlwine* is also popular.

14
WINES OF AUSTRALIA, NEW ZEALAND, AND THE FAR EAST

1. AUSTRALIA

G rape cultivation in Australia began with Captain Arthur Phillip, who brought vine cuttings with his first fleet of eleven ships, when he arrived to found the penal colony of New South Wales in 1788. His cuttings came from Rio de Janeiro and the Cape of Good Hope, which had been stops along the way. Unfortunately his three acres of vineyards were attacked by fungus.

history

Three other pioneers made their mark on Australian winemaking during the nineteenth century. They were Gregory Blaxland, John MacArthur, and James Busby.

In 1816 Blaxland planted red-wine grapes, which he had obtained from the Cape of Good Hope, on his farm in Parramatta Valley.

John MacArthur and his two sons planted a commercially successful vineyard near Penrith in New South Wales and were producing twenty thousand gallons of wine annually by 1827.

James Busby, often called the father of Australian viticulture, arrived in Australia in 1824 from his native Scotland. He was given a grant to teach viticulture and to organize an agricultural institute. His main contributions were writing two treatises on planting vines and on making wine and collecting and planting 678 varieties of vines from France, Luxembourg, England, and Spain.

Many other *vignerons* started plantings in the 1800s, with their growing areas widespread throughout southern Australia. From these early times into the twentieth century, grapes were planted from the Swan Valley in Western Australia to the Hunter Valley, north of Sydney, in New South Wales—twenty-five hundred miles east across the continent.

The stable climatic conditions of Australia's southern half are well suited to the growth and ripening of wine-bearing grapes. Generally, Australia's wine-producing areas are warmer and drier than those of Europe. During the

265

summer the dry conditions help to ensure clean ripening and disease-free crops. The warmth and dryness also produce high natural sugar in the grapes, with low natural acidity (sugar is not added to Australian wines). There are also many vineyards in the higher and cooler areas, where delicate table wines are produced.

AUSTRALIAN STATES

There are many regions of wine production in Australia, and the easiest way to group them is by states.

New South Wales   New South Wales was the first state to produce grapes and in it is the most legendary region, the Hunter Valley. Actually, less than 1 percent of Australia's wines now come from this area. More recent plantings in the Murrumbidgee Irrigation Area (M.I.A.), with the help of advanced technology, have made this new area one of the most important regions. It now supplies about 20 percent of Australia's total vintage. Rooty Hill, Corowa, and Mudgee are other regions in this state.

Victoria   The most important vineyards in Victoria are in the Great Western region, where much sparkling wine is produced. In the Goulburn Valley, in Tabilk township, is one of the most picturesque wineries and cellars in Australia.

Rutherglen in the northeast and Mildura in the northwest are the centers of other important wine regions in the state of Victoria.

South Australia   South Australia is the premier wine-producing state, providing 65 percent of all wines in the country. The Barossa Valley is the best known of the winemaking areas of Australia. It supplies 10 percent of the country's wine production in this seven-mile-wide and twenty-mile-long valley. Its climate is comparable to that of Portugal, and table wines, as well as fortified wines, are produced. The Barossa Valley has escaped *Phylloxera,* and the vines are ungrafted.

The vineyards around Adelaide, the Southern Vales, and Clare-Watervale are all historic wine producers that make up a good part of South Australia's output of wine. A new area, Coonawarra, in the southeast part of the state, has been attracting attention for its quality wines in the style of German white wines and French clarets.

The Murray Valley, which is very large, produces great amounts of fortified wines and brandies, as well as everyday quaffing wines.

Western Australia   The Swan Valley, around the city of Perth, has a long history of wine-making. This small enclave on the west coast of Australia gets a great deal of

SOUTH
AUSTRALIA

NEW SOUTH WALES

HUNTER
VALLEY ●

CLARE-
WATERVALE

MUDGEE ●

BAROSSA
VALLEY

Murray R.

Murrumbidgee R.

ROOTY HILL ● Sydney

MURRAY
VALLEY MILDURA

M.I.A. ●

ADELAIDE

COROWA ●

SOUTHERN
VALES

VICTORIA

RUTHERGLEN ●

COONAWARRA

GOULBURN
VALLEY ●

GREAT WESTERN ●

● TABILK

Melbourne

● DRUMBORG

SOUTH PACIFIC OCEAN

SCALE

0   50   100   150 mi

WINE REGIONS OF AUSTRALIA

WILLIAM LEMBECK

sunshine, which helps produce grapes that are rich in sugar and low in acid. The wines are reminiscent of those found around the Mediterranean.

In Australia, instead of separate regions devoted to making one kind of wine, the principal growers make all types. By buying judiciously from independent grape growers and planting several grape varieties in their own vineyards, the big winemaking companies can produce and market sherries, table wines, sparkling wines, dessert wines, and brandy under their own labels.

There are about two hundred wineries in Australia, and they produce almost eighty million gallons of wine annually.

GRAPE VARIETIES

There are many different grape varieties in Australia, but all are from *vinifera* stock. The most prominent ones are:

SHIRAZ. This grape is the most widely planted grape for the production of red table wines and fortified wines. In Australia there are eighteen thousand acres of Shiraz grown in virtually all districts. It is often blended with other varieties, notably Cabernet Sauvignon.

red wine varieties

GRENACHE. This is second in acreage to the Shiraz, extending over sixteen thousand acres. It produces an early-maturing wine and is used for more commercial grades of red table wines and ports.

CABERNET SAUVIGNON. As in Bordeaux and California, this is Australia's premium red-wine grape. Its acreage is increasing every year, with about five thousand acres under cultivation at present. The Cabernets from Coonawarra are the most highly regarded. Because of Cabernet Sauvignon's relative scarcity, it is often blended with Shiraz.

MATARO, MALBEC, CARIGNANE, PINOT NOIR, AND FRONTIGNAN. These grapes are not of great winemaking significance because they either are grown in very small amounts or do not produce very good wines.

white wine varieties

SULTANA. Known in California as the Thompson Seedless (also a table grape), this grape is used more for commercial table wines, fortified wines, and wines for distillation than is any other variety. There are over fifty thousand acres planted with this vine, mainly in the Murray Valley irrigation districts.

MUSCAT GORDO BLANCO. Often traveling under the name Muscat of Alexandria, this grape is very versatile. It is the principal component of Australia's cream sherry, but it is also fermented dry for use as a table wine. It is delicious as both a table grape and a raisin grape. It is grown in over ten thousand acres.

DORADILLO. A very prolific grape, often producing fifteen tons or more per acre, it is used to produce spirits for fortifying wines. It is planted in over six thousand acres in the irrigation districts.

PALOMINO AND PEDRO XIMENEZ. These two grapes, which are often confused with each other in Australia, are planted in over eight thousand acres. They are used to produce dry sherry wines.

the question of Riesling

RHINE RIESLING. The Rhine Riesling is the true Riesling of Germany or California. It makes a fruity, acidic wine in the cooler regions and a smoother wine with more glycerine in the warmer areas.

CLARE RIESLING AND SÉMILLON. Over the years many growers have thought these two grapes to be the same. When the Sémillon was first planted in the Hunter Valley, it was erroneously known as the Hunter Riesling. Wines made from this grape, although labeled Riesling, were actually dry and austere and did not have true Riesling characteristics. The Clare Riesling, now believed to be an Austrian variant of the Rhine Riesling, produces a wine that is between the dryness of the Sémillon and the fruitiness of the Rhine Riesling. These two varieties are most important for dry white table wines.

TREBBIANO, TOKAY, ALBILLO, CHASSELAS, TRAMINER, CLAIRETTE, SAUVIGNON BLANC, AND CHARDONNAY. These grapes round out the balance of the grapes used throughout Australia for white-wine production.

WINES

All classes and types of wines are produced in Australia. In addition to a wide selection of table wines, dessert wines are available labeled as sherry, port, or Muscat types. Most of the better sparkling wines are made by the authentic *méthode champenoise*, although a few are fermented in bulk or are artificially carbonated. Both sweet and dry sparkling wines are produced.

Today most of the wineries in Australia use generic names for their wines—claret, Burgundy, Chablis, sherry, Sauternes, port, Moselle, and so on. However, many Australian wines are marketed under district names—such as Barossa, Hunter Valley, Coonawarra—and grape varietal names—such as Cabernet, Shiraz, Pinot Noir, Riesling—and sometimes a combination of both. Australian place names are unfamiliar to most wine drinkers, but generic labels may be particularly confusing here. For example, both a Burgundy and a claret may be made from the Shiraz grape. An Australian Moselle Riesling might taste surprisingly dry if it is made from the Sémillon or Clare Riesling grape. To purchase a wine with true Riesling character, one must buy a Rhine Riesling in Australia.

labeling

Strict government and industry regulations ensure the highest possible quality of exported Australian wines. The provisions of the Pure Food and Drug Regulations are rigidly enforced. Before export is permitted, wines and brandies are inspected by experienced officers of the federal government's Department of Customs and Excise, as well as by inspectors appointed by the Australian Wine Board.

2. NEW ZEALAND

Wines have been produced in New Zealand since the early 1800s. The history of the country includes some of the same people who fostered the development of winemaking in Australia, such as James Busby.

history

Viticulture in the early twentieth century was greatly influenced by Romeo Bragato, New Zealand's first official head of the viticultural division of the Department of Agriculture. Around the same time winemakers came to the shores of New Zealand from Dalmatia, now part of Yugoslavia. It was during this time that the vineyards, which had been planted totally with *vinifera* varieties, were replanted with French hybrids and *labruscana* varieties. This was done in an effort to produce a greater yield from growing conditions that were not always favorable. The new plantings were also more resistant to disease. Unfortunately, the wines made from these new plantings were of a lesser quality, and this, combined with increasing activity on the part of prohibi-

WINE REGIONS
OF
NEW ZEALAND

NORTHLAND

AUCKLAND

WAIKATO

NORTH
ISLAND

GISBORNE

HAWKES BAY

SCALE

0   50   100   150 mi

MANAWATU-
WELLINGTON

NELSON-BLENHEIM

SOUTH
ISLAND

WILLIAM LEMBECK

tionists, caused New Zealand's wine industry to dwindle to a few small wineries and home winemakers.

After World War II grape acreage and wine production began to increase significantly. From six hundred acres in 1940, grapes are now planted in over six thousand acres. New Zealand today produces over nine million gallons of wine annually, with 60 percent of that being table wines.

wine regions   New Zealand is made up of two large islands, all but one of the wine-producing areas being on the northern island. From north to south the areas are: Northland, Auckland, Waikato, Gisborne, Hawkes Bay, and Manawatu-Wellington. Nelson-Blenheim is on the southern island. Of all of the wine-producing areas, Auckland is by far the largest.

One of the main problems with grape growing in New Zealand is its humid climate, which encourages fungus that attacks the vines and produces heavy rains that thin the wines. This explains the temptation to plant varieties that would resist these conditions.

grape varieties   For years the largest plantings were in Palomino and Baco 22A grapes. The
and wines   Palomino grape does not ripen well in this climate, but with chaptalization it produces the sweet, fortified wines and brandies New Zealanders like. As the

trend turns toward table wines, however, it has been discovered that the Riesling Sylvaner (Müller-Thurgau in Germany) could produce an acceptable white wine. This has now become the most widely planted grape. Although Palomino and Baco 22A are still planted in quantity, Cabernet Sauvignon and Pinotage (a cross between Pinot Noir and Hermitage) are being planted in greater quantities. These are producing better red table wines.

Sparkling wines are produced either by bottle or bulk fermentation. Some wines are carbonated.

The main winemaking efforts in New Zealand are concentrated on making better-quality table wines with the use of virus-free *vinifera* vines.

3. CHINA

The first vines in China came from the Arabs in Turkestan in the late second century B.C. By the seventh century A.D. vines were widespread. One major setback came in 1322, when vines were uprooted by order of the emperor so that cereals and grains could be planted. Even though some vines were replanted, to this day more beer and rice wine is produced and consumed than grape wine. Recently, however, some agricultural experimental stations have been studying the vine, and cooperative vineyards are becoming more important.   *history*

MONGOLIA

TURFAN

HOPEH

Peking

SHANSI

SHANTUNG   YELLOW SEA

Yellow R.

HONAN

KIANGSU

TIBET

EAST CHINA SEA

WINE REGIONS OF CHINA

SOUTH CHINA SEA   WILLIAM LEMBECK

wine regions   Grapes are grown in the region around old Turkestan, called Turfan. They are also grown north of the Yangtze River and south of the Great Wall. Five provinces along the Yellow River—Shantung, Honan, Kiangsu, Hopeh, and Shansi—are growing grapes successfully. Some vines are also planted around Peking.

grape varieties and wines   The grapes growing in China include some native Asian stock, some *labruscana* varieties, and a few *vinifera* varieties, mostly Riesling and Pinot. The grapes are used for making wine, as table grapes, and as raisins.

Red, white, and rosé grape wines (*p'u t'ao chiu*) that go up to 16 percent alcohol are produced. A sweet wine called Chefoo, available in red and white, is also produced. Sparkling wines (*ta-hsiang-pih-chiu*) are also made. Dry white and red wines called Tsingtao are produced in Shantung province in northern China, which projects into the Yellow Sea. These wines are similar to dry sherry, with more noticeable acidity.

4. JAPAN

history   The wine industry is small in Japan, with production averaging six million gallons a year. Native varieties of grapes, the Koshu and Jaraku, have been planted since the twelfth century. They are believed to have European origins

WINE REGIONS
OF
JAPAN

HOKKAIDO

SEA OF JAPAN

PACIFIC
OCEAN

KŌFU VALLEY

OSAKA VALLEY

HONSHU

Tokyo

YAMANASHI
VINEYARDS

MOUNT FUJI

WILLIAM LEMBECK

that go very far back. In the nineteenth century Americans and Europeans brought in *labruscana* grapes, such as Concord, Delaware, Campbell Early, and Baily A, a Muscat hybrid. Some *vinifera* grapes were also introduced, including Sémillon, Chardonnay, Riesling, Cabernet Sauvignon, and Merlot.

The main island of Honshu contains the two most important wine-growing regions, although grapes are grown to the north and to the south. The main regions are the Kōfu Valley and the Osaka Valley, and the acreage equals more than half of Japan's total acreage under vine. Japan is generally quite humid, but on Honshu Island the humidity is lower and the grapes have a better chance against fungus, *oïdium,* and mildew.

wine regions

Other wines are produced on the island of Hokkaido in the north and at Katsunuma in Yamanashi province west of Tokyo.

As in China, wines are made from native, *labruscana,* and *vinifera* grapes. Problems with humidity and with acid soil, however, produce wines that are astringent and unbalanced. Torrential rains around harvest time point up the need for early-ripening varieties. Sugaring wines is quite common, and many more sweet and fortified wines are produced than table wines.

wines

Since making table wines in Japan is a young industry, producers sometimes appropriate, as has been done in other countries, names and label appearances of famous wines produced elsewhere.

Two women pick grapes for the production of wine in the Yamanashi Vineyard, the largest vineyard in the Orient, located near the foot of Mount Fuji. (*Courtesy Suntory International*)

15
AROMATIZED WINES

Man first learned to make his wine aromatic," said the late André L. Simon, "when he discovered that by adding honey or sage or some herb to his sour wine, it became more palatable." Since that day great strides have been made in the science of producing aromatized wines.

The ancient Greeks preferred pitched or resinated to natural wine, as do many Greeks of the present day. The Romans liked to flavor their wines with such interesting materials as pepper, spikenard, cypress, wormwood, myrrh, poppy, tar, pitch, bitumen, aloe, chalk, mastic gum, boiled seawater, and asafetida. Is it strange that one ancient Roman writer said of wine, "It biteth like a serpent"?

Aromatized wine is the fourth classification of wines, the others being still, sparkling, and fortified. It is a fortified wine in which herbs, roots, flowers, barks, and other flavoring ingredients have been steeped in order to change the natural flavor of the wine.

Aromatized wines include both dry (French origin) and sweet (Italian origin) vermouths and the quinined or other aperitif wines of the various countries such as Dubonnet, Byrrh, Lillet, Punt é Mes, St. Raphaël, Cin, and Cynar. All, including vermouths, are aperitifs, from the Latin *aperio*, meaning "to open." That is exactly what they are supposed to do. They open—whet the appetite pleasantly.

VERMOUTH

The term *vermouth* comes from the German *wermut* ("wormwood") but was first used commercially in 1786 by Antonio Benedetto Carpano of Torino, Italy, who may be called the founder of the vermouth industry. He used the white Piedmont wines nearest at hand, especially the fine Canelli Muscats, and produced a bittersweet vermouth.

About a generation later, and quite independently, about 1800, Louis Noilly of Lyon, France, developed a somewhat drier vermouth by employing the thin Hérault wines of the French Midi. Thus the sweet type has come to be referred to as Italian and the dry type as French. Today, however, the Italian producers also make vast quantities of the dry and the French make the sweet type as well. In fact, great quantities of both types are produced outside Italy and France, since locally made sweet and dry types are consumed in all wine-producing countries. For example, the United States produces more than 50 percent of its annual consumption of more than ten million gallons, and Argentina, whose per capita consumption of vermouth is probably the highest in the world, does not import any vermouth, producing more than fifteen million gallons each year. Much more sweet vermouth is drunk throughout the world than dry, except in the United States, where consumption of each type is about equal. The greater use of dry vermouth in the United States is the result of the popularity of the Dry Martini cocktail.

dry or French vermouth

The French type is the dry vermouth. According to French law, a vermouth must consist of at least 80 percent wine, which must have an alcoholic strength of at least 10 percent. Alcohol may be added later in order to raise the strength of the wine to up to 19 percent. Sugar, too, may be added in order to soften the bitterness.

The wines used for making French vermouth are produced in the Midi in the Department of the Hérault, which produces more wine than any other province of France. They are light, thin, and rather characterless wines, made from the Picpoul and Clairette grapes.

The process of maturing the wines plays a very important part in making French vermouth. The dryness of the vermouth is a perfectly natural development, since Clairette and Picpoul wines become very dry as they mature. In fact, to prevent too much dryness they are mixed with the less dry Grenache in a proportion of three to one. They are stored two to three years in thick oak casks called *demi-muids*. Part of the storage by some producers takes place in the courtyard of the establishment, where the wines can receive the benefits of the sun's rays during the day and of the coolness at night. This daily variation in temperature ages the wines more rapidly.

To give the vermouth its softness the better houses use *mistelle* or *vin de liqueur* in place of sugar. The *mistelle* is made by adding to unfermented must the amount of alcohol the must would have produced had it been allowed to ferment out. Thus *mistelle* contains both natural grape sugar and alcohol (in the form of brandy) at the same time. In making vermouth, *mistelles* of Grenache and Muscat are used. They are aged separately and for the same length of time as the other wines.

After the wines are matured, they are blended in a proportion of 80 percent Hérault wine and 20 percent *mistelle*. This is known as basic wine. The basic

Casks of maturing wine stored in an open courtyard, exposed to the elements, before being made into dry vermouth. (*Courtesy Noilly Prat & Cie., Marseille*)

wine is then flavored by an infusion obtained by steeping the special flavoring agents in the wine, according to a duly tested formula, which is the prized secret of each producing house. This brings out the characteristic vermouth bouquet, in which a complex aroma is blended in the most attractive manner.

Anywhere from thirty to fifty different types of herbs, plants, roots, leaves, peels, seeds, and flowers may go into a single formula for making French vermouth. Some of these are nutmeg, coriander seeds, cloves, cinnamon, rose leaves from Bengal, Peruvian quinine bark, hyssop, marjoram, angelica root, wormwood, bitter orange peel, camomile, linden tea, centaury, gentian, and flowers of elder.

All the plants are put in a large tank. The basic wine is poured in and left in contact with the plants for one month; then this wine, which has taken on flavor from the plants, is drawn off and new basic wine is added in its place. This is repeated several times before the flavor of the plants is exhausted. The flavored basic wines are then blended, and the resulting mixture is known as the infusion.

The infusion is mixed in a proportion of one to five with other basic wine, and brandy is added to raise the alcoholic strength of the wine to up to 19 percent.

This mixture is put into glass-lined vats where the wines are brought down to a temperature of nearly freezing and are stirred constantly by giant paddles to ensure perfect blending. The refrigeration has a purpose. Vermouth, like all wine, contains some tartaric acid, which is a natural element in the composition of wine. It is invisible, but in time it crystallizes and forms a deposit known as cream of tartar. The formation of this deposit can be forced by abruptly lowering the temperature of the wine.

Vermouth becomes darker in color as it ages, but variations in color have nothing to do with the quality of the vermouth. The trade, however, insists that it be the same color year in and year out. To ensure this, caramel is added if the color is too light; if the vermouth is too dark, it is mixed with a lighter vermouth.

It takes three and a half to four years to mature, age, and prepare a true French vermouth. This means that enormous reserve supplies must always be kept on hand and that large sums of money are invested in these stocks for a great many years. For this reason only well-established, financially sound houses can afford to finance the aging process that ensures the wines will acquire the properties of perfect maturity. In addition, the French vermouth business must be conducted on a mass-production scale; otherwise it would not be economically feasible.

sweet or Italian vermouth

The Italian vermouth is the sweet type, made from white wines. This sweetness results from the fact that the basic wine used for making Italian vermouth is sweeter and fuller than the thin white Hérault wine of the Midi and because sweetening is added later on in the production. The law in Italy specifies that vermouth be made from wines that are at least one year old. Between infusion and final filtering another year passes, so it takes approximately two years to produce an Italian vermouth.

Most of the wines used in making Italian vermouth are those from Apulia, although some Moscato di Canelli is always blended in for flavor and sweetness. These rather bland wines are infused with various herbs, roots, seeds, and a little quinine. They are allowed to mature, and as soon as they have absorbed a sufficient amount of flavor they are drawn off, fortified, and filtered, and some sugar and coloring matter are added. The brown color is obtained by adding caramel.

There is a reason for the use of quinine. When the European countries started colonizing the tropics they encountered malaria, and the best medicine for this was quinine, which has an extremely bitter taste. To get the soldiers to take their medicine, an ingenious physician gave them quinine in sweetened wine. Thus was born the taste for *quinquina* ("quinined wine"), the aperitif wines for which the French and Italians have never lost their taste.

other vermouths Vermouths are made in other parts of the world besides France and Italy. There are Spanish, Portuguese, American, Australian, Argentine, and South African vermouths. In fact, wherever wine is produced some vermouth is made. For the most part, however, these vermouths are consumed locally.

OTHER AROMATIZED WINES

The aperitif wines are made in almost all European wine-producing countries in the same manner as French vermouth, except that the proportion of *mistelle* is generally greater, making the wines sweeter.

Aperitif wines are usually quinined wines. When the aperitif is white, the basic wine used is white; when red, the basic wine is red. The variation in taste—the sweetness, bitterness, or aromatic flavor—results from the use of different formulas, which are trade secrets of each producing house.

The principal aperitif wines sold in this market are Dubonnet (red and white), St. Raphaël (red and white, but only the red is sold in the United States), Byrrh (red), and Lillet (red and white). St. Raphaël is slightly sweeter than Dubonnet. Byrrh and Lillet are slightly drier.

A recent arrival on the scene in the United States is Cynar. Cynar's name and principal flavor are derived from the artichoke. Among the ancient Romans *cynara* ("artichoke") was reputed to help "keep the liver young," but no one ever bothered to make use of the knowledge until the inquisitive Angelo dalle Molle recognized its virtues when he was doing research among ancient Latin tomes and manuscripts. As a result, he developed Cynar—a wine aperitif that is now almost as popular as vermouth in Italy.

HOW AND WHEN TO SERVE VERMOUTHS AND APERITIF WINES

In America we think of vermouths as wines to be used in preparing our favorite cocktails—Martini (dry vermouth) and Manhattan (sweet vermouth)—and that is the principal use made of them and some of the aperitif wines as well.

In Buenos Aires and other centers of South America the invariable gesture of hospitality, no matter what the occasion or the hour, is an invitation to have a *copetín*, which usually means a vermouth. In fact it is a must between five and six P.M. This time of day is known as the vermouth hour, and even the movie exhibited at that time is called the vermouth feature.

In other parts of the world, however, vermouths are widely used as aperitif wines by themselves. They are always served well chilled. The classic ways to drink them are neat, on the rocks, or with a splash of soda and a twist of lemon peel added. Lillet, however, is enhanced by a strip of orange peel. Both sweet and dry vermouths are often mixed together, half and half. (See Chapter 26 for recipes using vermouths and aperitif wines.)

Other uses for these wines are over fruit and in cooking. Because it combines wines and savory herbs, vermouth provides an easy-to-use blend of some of the world's most prized seasonings. French vermouth, for instance, can often be substituted for dry white wine in recipes calling for wines and herbs, and the amount of herbs can then be reduced.

Aperitif wines are increasing in popularity in the United States. Since spirits before dinner tend to dull the palate, many people have found that a wine aperitif is the best prelude to a wine-accompanied dinner. With increased travel abroad, where aperitif wines and vermouths are frequently consumed, Americans are bringing this sensible custom home with them.

Making vermouth at Cinzano. The still, called *alambicco* in Italian, is used to transform spices into extract. (*Courtesy Cinzano*)

16
SPECIALTY
WINES

1. WINES FROM FRUITS OTHER THAN THE GRAPE

Thus far we have discussed wines that have been made from grapes, but wine can be made from the juice of other fruits as well. Apples, pears, cherries, berries, and plums are some of the fruits that yield very attractive wines.

CIDER AND PERRY

Cider, or *sidra* in Spanish, comes from the Hebrew word *shekhar,* meaning "strong drink." Cider and perry are obtained by fermenting the freshly expressed juice of apples and pears. Their alcohol content varies from 2 to 8 percent and is sometimes slightly higher. This, of course, is the cider that in the United States is called hard cider, as opposed to the nonalcoholic sweet cider.

Both cider and perry are rather sweet beverages that are wholesome and have the pronounced flavor of the fruit. Just as good eating grapes are poor wine varieties, so apples and pears that are good to eat are poor for making cider or perry.

Normandy, in northwest France, is the apple- and pear-growing region of that nation. There cider, and not wine, is the table beverage.

In Spain and England, a secondary fermentation may be induced in the bottle or in bulk, producing a wine called Champagne Cider. All Spanish cider is treated in this manner. The fermentation is produced by adding a small amount of sugar syrup, the carbon dioxide thus created being retained. In Latin America vast quantities of it are sold as the poor man's Champagne, because it is about half as expensive as Champagne. It is somewhat sweet and has a pleasant apple flavor. It is also useful in making punch.

BERRY WINES

Berry wines include wines made from blackberries, raspberries, strawberries, elderberries, loganberries, boysenberries, and currants. All are very sweet and fruity, and each has its individual flavor appeal.

In Europe these wines are made from freshly expressed fruit juices. In the United States they are often made from fresh frozen fruit or concentrated fruit juice, although some dried fruit may also be added.

In all cases it is necessary to add water and sugar. The fruit musts have to be ameliorated with sugar to balance their high acid content. For example, the acid content of blackberry must is about 1 percent, principally isocitric acid, which gives the wine its distinctive character. In order to maintain color and fresh flavor, berry wines are not aged very long.

Most of the commercial fruit wines are marketed at 12 to $12\frac{1}{2}$ percent alcohol, but some are fortified to up to 20 percent. Berry wines are imported to the United States from Czechoslovakia, Israel, Holland, Japan, Poland, and Yugoslavia.

CHERRY WINES

Cherry wines are made in Europe from sour cherries. Denmark, which is an important producer of these wines, uses the small black native Langeskov cherries.

When the wines are being made some of the cherry pits are crushed and left in to give a subtle accent. If more than 10 percent of the stones are used, however, the flavor of the stones dominates the flavor of the cherries. Like berry wines, cherry wines cannot be aged too long.

The wines are fortified, being shipped with an alcohol content of $17\frac{1}{2}$ percent to $19\frac{1}{2}$ percent. They are rich in fruitiness and quite sweet—a good reason for their popularity. They are most pleasant if served well chilled, or in mixed drinks, and the cherry wine is finding wide use in the kitchen to give a delightful dash of cherry flavor to fruits and desserts.

PLUM WINES

Wines are made from different varieties of plums in Europe, the Far East, and California. Japan, especially, has a humid climate where the plum thrives. In California the plums are grown in the Santa Clara area.

These wines are seen in two styles, either with the natural plum flavor or with a slight almond flavor resulting from the presence of the stones during fermentation. It is not as easy to make a wine from a pulpy fruit as it is to make wine from a berry, but the plum wines on the market are all quite successful. In California an apricot wine is also made, and an unusual litchi wine comes from China. They are made similarly to plum wines.

PINEAPPLE WINE

A very fruity pineapple wine is made in Puerto Rico from the red Spanish pineapple. It is fortified with pineapple brandy and has a beautiful golden color and tart character.

CITRUS WINES

Some citrus wines, usually fortified and tasting like sherry, are made in Florida.

WINES MADE FROM DRIED FRUITS

Wines can be made from dried fruits, such as figs, dates, and raisins. The fruit is shredded and then steeped in hot water. This liquid becomes the fermenting must. Dried apricots and dried peaches become too gummy to be used successfully.

HONEY WINE / MEAD

Mead dates back to biblical times. Mead, or honey wine, is not really a fruit product but a fruit-related product, since much honey comes from the flowers of fruit trees.

Mild-flavored honey is better than strong honey for making honey wine. After the honey has fermented it may be sweetened with either sugar or more honey. It is fortified to 18 to 20 percent. Brandy may be added to the partially fermented must.

Honey wine is made in California and is also imported from England and Poland; a kosher mead is made in New York State.

HOW AND WHEN TO SERVE FRUIT WINES

Fruit wines can be drunk chilled, either neat or on the rocks. With soda they make a fine spritzer. They are delicious poured over fresh fruits or ice cream for dessert. In the kitchen they can be used in glazes for ham and as sauce ingredients for game birds.

2. SPECIAL NATURAL WINES

In 1954 a law was passed permitting a new wine type, special natural wines. By 1975 almost fifty-seven million gallons were being made every year by fifty-seven producers.

Special natural wines are flavored wines that resemble vermouths, but they are not vermouths. They are natural wines, lightly flavored with herbs, spices, fruit juices, essences, aromatics, and other natural flavorings, such as citrus or exotic tropical fruits. All flavorings must be approved by the B.A.T.F. While these wines cannot resemble natural fruit wines, lemon flavor may be used, for example, since there is no lemon wine on the market.

Special natural wines may be sweetened with sugar. If they are made in California, they must be designated as American, since California state law does not permit sugaring of its wines.

When these wines first appeared around 1960 they were fortified to 18 to 19 percent. With the trend toward lightness, however, they are now below 14 percent, and many have a slight amount of carbonation for even more freshness.

All of these "pop" wines appear under proprietary labels with creative names, such as Thunderbird, Ripple, Bali Hai, Annie Green Springs, and Wild Irish Rose. Some "pop" wines have had lasting popularity, while others appear and disappear within a short time. Since the special natural wines are different from traditional wines, they appeal to new and unsophisticated drinkers.

3. SACRAMENTAL WINES

From the beginning, as we have already pointed out, there has been a close alliance between wine and religion. Even during Prohibition in the United States wine for religious purposes was permitted. Almost all Western religions use wine in their rituals, the two most important and frequent users being Roman Catholics and Jews.

USE OF WINE IN THE MASS

Originally the wine used in the Eucharistic Sacrifice had to be pure grape juice that had been completely fermented. The Congregation of Sacraments, on July 31, 1890, said, "Provided that the alcohol has been extracted from the fruit of the grape, and the quantity added, together with that which the wine to be treated naturally possesses, does not exceed the proportion of 12 percent, there is no obstacle in the way of using such wine in the Holy Sacrifice of the Mass." This means that the alcohol contained in the juice from the grape itself, plus that added from an outside source, could not exceed 12 percent.

Since extra-sweet wines were subject to refermentation, the Holy Office amended the ruling on August 5, 1896, to allow the addition of alcohol so that the wine was not to exceed 18 percent alcohol, provided that such addition be made before fermentation was completed.

Sour wine is invalid for use in the Mass, and no chemical process, such as the use of tartrate or potassium, may be used to correct the natural tartness of the wine. In addition, the Sacred Congregation of the Holy Office declared that sugar could not be added to the wine. The wine may be either red or white.°

Wine is also used for the Communion service by many Protestant denominations.

USE OF WINE IN THE SYNAGOGUE

Rabbi A. Hyman kindly furnished the information on the use of wine in the synagogue and in the homes of pious Jews.

In order to be used for ritual purposes the wine must be made according to the rabbinical law and must be a pure, natural wine, unmixed and sound. It may be either red or white. If it becomes sour, or has impurities from the lees, it cannot be used. There is no such thing as a sanctified wine in the sense that a special wine is used in the synagogue. The same wine may be used in the temple as is used in the home.

Wine is used both at the incoming prayer of the Sabbath, Friday evening, and at the outgoing prayer at the end of the Sabbath, Saturday evening. It is also part of the services on the eve of festivals and on holy days. At wedding ceremonies the bride and bridegroom must share a glass of wine. The most widespread use of wine is on the two Seder nights of Passover, when it is obligatory for each person to drink four glasses of wine.

In the synagogue and at home the amount of wine served at services, according to ancient ritual, should equal "an egg and a half full"—about two and a half ounces—and more than half of it must be drunk.

Most sacramental wine is made primarily from the Concord grape, grown in the central and eastern states, which seems to fit in with the need for a mellow, rich wine.

The Concord wine is rich, sweet, and deep purple in color. After the wine has fermented out naturally, sugar is added to counteract the natural acidity of the grape and to balance the pronounced flavor.

For a full discussion of kosher wines, see pages 237–38.

° References: Tanguerey, *De Sacramentis in Geneve*, p. 80; Wuest Mullaney, *Matters Liturgical*, p. 56; McHugh and Collan, *Catechism of the Council of Trent*, pp. 221–223.

17
BEERS AND
ALES

Until now we have discussed wines, which are produced from grapes or other fruits rich in sugar. Living yeast cells, by the process known as fermentation, convert this sugar into alcohol. No matter what variations there are—white wines or red wines, indoors or outdoors, Europe or the United States—the basic chemistry is the conversion of sugar into alcohol and carbon dioxide.

But what if fruits are not readily available as a source of sugar? Can sugar be obtained from something else? In this chapter we shall look at alcoholic beverages made from grains rich in starch, instead of from fruits rich in sugar. Starch cannot be converted directly into alcohol. But with the help of nature, man can convert starch into sugar. Once this step has occurred the sugar can then be converted into alcohol by the familiar process of fermentation.

In order for starch to be converted into sugar, the grain that contains the starch must be germinated—dampened with warm water so it can sprout. A by-product of this sprouting is the formation of a vegetable enzyme called amylase. In the 1830s, when this phenomenon was beginning to be understood, this substance was called diastase, from the Greek word meaning "separation." Separation is significant because starch exists in long chains, each fragment of which is $C_6H_{10}O_5$. The enzyme amylase, in a water solution, acts to separate this long chain into double fragments and, at the same time, adds a water molecule (H_2O) to each, forming a maltose sugar molecule, $C_{12}H_{22}O_{11}$.

enzymatic action

To this day, in the alcoholic beverage industry the words *amylase* and *diastase* are used interchangeably. Other enzymes play a part later in the brewing and fermenting processes. Among those that may be either formed or added by the brewer are the proteases and zymase. The proteases act on insoluble protein matter, helping to make the finished beverage clear and free of haze. Zymase, a yeast by-product, converts sugar into alcohol.

history　　　In Germany in the early part of the present century, excavators discovered a jug whose contents proved to be beer mash that had been made sixteen centuries ago—probably the oldest bottle of beer in existence. And yet that mash had been made when the beer industry was already thousands of years old, for the history of brewing is as old as recorded history—over seven thousand years.

Archaeologists have found hieroglyphics that represent brewing. They have found jugs that were used for beer, and chemical analysis has proved that barley was used. They have even found some of the yeast cells by which beer was fermented. In ancient days the brewmaster and the baker were the same man. The nobility and the priesthood were interested in brewing, and there was a close association between religious ceremonies and beer.

According to Pliny, the Egyptians made beer from corn. The Greeks learned the art of preparing beer from the Egyptians. Through the ages, in every country from Egypt to the New World, the existence of beer has been recorded in all languages. Medieval history is replete with references to brewing and its importance to the development of civilization. The Kaffir peoples of Africa made, and still make, a kind of beer from millet, while the natives of Nubia, Abyssinia, and other parts of Africa prepared a fermented beverage that they called *bousa*.

The Russian *quass* or *kvass* from black bread (rye), the Chinese *samshu*, and the Japanese *saké* from rice are all beers of ancient origin.

Had it not been for the lack of beer and food, the Pilgrims on the *Mayflower* would have continued their journey to Virginia, where they had intended to make their home. Instead they landed at Plymouth Rock because, as recorded in their journal, "we could not now take time for further search or considerations, our victuals being spent, especially our beer."

Although the Pilgrims called their brew beer, what they drank was really ale, as the Germans did not introduce lager beer to America until 1840. Although most colonial households brewed their own beer, records show that a brewery was in operation by 1637. William Penn, founder of Pennsylvania, was probably the first to operate a large commercial brewery, at Pennsbury in Bucks County. Another early brewery belonged to the Dutch brewer Jacobus, whose first brewery and beer garden was located at what is now the corner of Pearl Street and Old Slip in New York City.

Among the early Americans who were brewers or who had financial interests in breweries were George Washington, James Oglethorpe, Israel Putnam, Samuel Adams, and Thomas Chittenden, the first governor of Vermont. They were all men of integrity and standing, so the industry started in America under excellent auspices.

definitions　　　BEER is a brewed and fermented beverage made from malted barley and other starchy cereals, flavored with hops. During fermentation the yeast sinks to the bottom; hence beer is a *bottom-fermentation* brew. *Beer* is also the generic term for all malt beverages.

LAGER is a bright, clear, light-bodied beer that is sparkling and effervescent, brewed from malt—and in some cases from prepared cereals such as corn grits or cracked rice—hops, and water. The resultant wort is fermented and lagered (stored) for aging and sedimentation. After this period it is kräusened, or carbonated. All American beers are the lager type.

PILSNER is a term employed universally on labels of light beers. The original and most famous is the Pilsner Urquell from Pilsen, Czechoslovakia. By labeling their beers Pilsner other brewers wish to convey the impression that their beer is similar to that of Pilsen. All Pilsners are bright, light, lagered beers, but none comes close to duplicating the original. Pilsner is not a separate type of beer, as bock beer is.

BOCK BEER, OR BOCKBIER, is a special brew of heavy beer, usually somewhat darker and sweeter than regular beer. It was originally brewed in the spring, but it no longer has any seasonal significance. Some people think the name is a corruption of *Einbecker Bier*, from the town of Einbeck in Germany. There is no legal definition for bock beer, and it varies with the brand.

MALT LIQUOR is a malt beverage, brewed like beer, that usually has a higher alcohol content than beers, the percentages of alcohol being regulated by each state. In Ohio, for example, the range may be from 3.2 to 7 percent by weight, and in Oregon it may vary from 4 to 8 percent by weight. The color is usually light and pale.

ALE is an aromatic brew made of malt or malt and cereal and is usually fuller bodied and more bitter than beer. Ale is fermented at a higher temperature than beer, and most of the yeast rises to the top of the brew; hence ale is a *top-fermentation* brew.

PORTER is the predecessor of stout and is lower in alcohol, with a dark color and bittersweet taste. As its producers increased its alcohol content it was referred to as an "extra stout" porter, and stout soon became a separate product.

STOUT is a very dark ale that is malty and slightly bitter, flavored and colored by the addition of roasted barley to the brew.

SAKÉ is a refermented brew of high alcohol content produced in Japan from rice.

BREWING PROCESS

In brewing beer, as in preparing a fine dish in the kitchen, the result is as good as its ingredients. These are much the same whether you wish to produce a light lager beer or a full-bodied creamy ale; the only difference is the way the ingredients are treated—how long the malt is dried and roasted, the quantities used, and the temperature at which fermentation takes place.

raw materials   WATER.   Although the quality of each ingredient is important, none is more so than the quality of the water, not only because it forms 85 to 90 percent of the finished beer, but because it is used in every step of the brewing operation and has a great deal to do with the character of the beer. The first consideration, therefore, is the quality and type of water. It must be biologically pure and its mineral content must be known. If the water contains certain mineral salts that may cause trouble, these salts must be eliminated. Most waters used for brewing are treated to render them suitable.

A water that is well suited for making lager-type beer does not make a good ale, and vice versa. That is why certain regions were noted for their light beers and others for their ales. For instance, the New York brewers concentrated on beer, while across the Hudson River, in Newark, New Jersey, the brewers became famous for their fine ales.

YEAST.   The fermenting agent, the pedigreed brewer's yeast, converts the wort into beer. This unicellular, microscopic plant is protected more carefully in a brewery than any other ingredient, for once the particular strain has been selected it must not be changed or the character of the beer changes with it. It is not merely that the yeast causes the sugars to become alcohol—another yeast would do that—but it performs other functions that probably influence the character of the beer more than the alcohol does. It is these secondary products of fermentation that vary according to the types of yeast. Therefore, once a quality or type of beer has satisfied a brewery's customers, you may be sure that the brewmaster will guard the purity of his yeast more closely than the Treasury guards its gold in Fort Knox.

MALT.   Brewers use only the finest barley malt. As a general rule the breweries do not do their own malting but buy malt from specialists, although the manner in which the malt is treated is specified by the brewmaster when ordering. The exact amount of kilning and the degree to which the barley is roasted are important in obtaining the amount of dryness or sweetness of the final beer or ale and in whether it will be a light beer or a dark beer.

OTHER CEREALS.   These can be either raw, such as corn and rice, or in varying stages of preparation, such as corn grits (cracked corn) and hominy, or they may even be like the breakfast cereal corn flakes. Certain types of sugars or corn syrups may be used. These are called malt adjuncts, and their use lowers costs.

HOPS.   Hops did not come into general use until the fourteenth century, and for a while there were laws in Europe forbidding their use in brewing. Up to that time other substances had been used to give the brews bitterness and character, but it did not take long for people to realize that hops were the best. The finest hops come from Czechoslovakia, although fine hops are grown in the United States in California, Oregon, Washington, and Idaho. Only the flower of the female hop vine is used in brewing. The flower is like a small pine cone and has very soft petals. It must be picked at just the right time, as under- or overripeness is detrimental to the brew. The hop is picked free of leaves and stems and is dried carefully to conserve the delicate, fine aroma essential to choice brewing. At the breweries the hops are stored in clean, air-conditioned cold-storage chambers at a temperature of 35 to 40 degrees Fahrenheit.

It used to be that the brewing value of the hops was judged solely by appearance or physical examination. Today, however, the hops are subjected to careful chemical analysis to determine the exact amount of humulone and lupulin (alpha and beta resins, respectively) they contain because of the flavor that these resins impart and the antiseptic action that they exercise, preventing the development of wild bacteria that might possibly get into the wort.

With the ingredients and the proper plant equipment the brewer is ready to make beer. The first step is malting the barley, which, as mentioned previously, is done by specialists to the brewmaster's specifications if it is not done by the brewmaster himself. *steps in making beer*

In general, the malting procedure is as follows. The barley goes to the barley-receiving room, where it is dressed, that is, sieved, or passed over screens so that small and inferior grain will be eliminated. The best grain is then steeped or soaked in water for two days until it is thoroughly softened. It then goes into germinating compartments, where the temperature and moisture levels are controlled, for about three weeks, during which time the grain begins to germinate, or sprout.

When the sprouts are about three-quarters of an inch long, the water is turned off and the grain is known as green malt. It is already malt, for malt is germinated grain. During this germination process a chemical change occurs in the grain that is important to its future function in the brewing process. The enzyme amylase has been produced, and it has the property of converting the balance of the starch into sugars—maltose and dextrin—which are fermentable, whereas the starch in its original state is not.

To stop further growth of the sprouts, the green malt is placed in a kiln and dried. The temperature and length of time the malt is roasted determine the color and sweetness of the final product. Roasting proceeds until either light, dark, or black malt is produced.

The kilned malt is now screened to remove the culm, or dried sprouts, after which it goes to the mill room, where it is ground into meal, or grist.

The next step is mashing. The ground malt first goes through a hopper into a mash tun, also referred to as a mash tub. This is a horizontal or vertical cylindrical copper or stainless steel vessel with a turbine or ribbon mixer unit. It contains a heating device and a set of temperature controls.

When a raw cereal is used, it is cooked in a cooker, a vessel similar to a mash tun, to gelatinize or liquefy the starch. Prepared or precooked cereals do not require heating. The malt, the cereals, and the proper amount of hot water are thoroughly mixed and are left to stand or are cooked as long as is necessary to obtain the maximum extraction of soluble materials. It is during this mashing operation that the brewmaster can determine the composition of the finished beer, for it is the temperature and the length of time at which the mash is maintained at a given temperature that determine the amount of fermentable and nonfermentable substances the wort will contain. It is the nonfermentable substances that give body to the brew. With modern equipment all of these operations are scientifically controlled, and the beer from a given brewery is uniform. After the cooker mash is added to the main mash in the mash tun, the starch is converted into fermentable sugars. Then the total mash is pumped into a lauter tun. This is a circular copper or stainless steel vessel containing a false slotted bottom and a series of movable rakes.

When the stirring is stopped the solids are allowed to settle. What has been going on is predigestion. Compounds have been broken down and made digestible; insoluble substances have been made soluble. The solids, which settle on the bottom, form the filter bed. The liquid, which is now wort, flows through this natural filter and passes into the brewing kettle. In order to ensure that every bit of goodness has been obtained from the grain, the solids are sparged (rinsed) with water. This rinse from the sparging is added to the wort. In the kettle, hops are added to the wort, which is then boiled for two to two and a half hours. This accomplishes the following:

1. The wort is sterilized.

2. Some excess water evaporates.

3. Certain volatile materials from the hops and malt that are not needed are lost through evaporation.

4. Some of the insoluble substances in the wort are made soluble by the high heat. The brewer calls this the hot break.

5. Because of a small amount of caramelization, a certain amount of darkening of color occurs.

After the hot break and the completed work of the hops, the wort runs from the kettle through a hop strainer, or hop-jack. There the hops are passed over a screen and the wort, which is now called hot wort, runs through, leaving the spent hops behind. The hot wort is cooled down and goes into the fermenting vat.

The temperature to which the wort is cooled depends on whether the brewer is making beer or ale. In the case of beer, fermentation takes place at a very low temperature—between 37 and 49 degrees Fahrenheit. Ale, on the other hand, is fermented at a higher temperature, between 50 and 70 degrees Fahrenheit. This is one difference. Another is that the yeast used in fermenting ale is different from that used for beer.

To start the fermentation, yeast is added at this point. There is as much

A universal six-roller malt mill, which grinds the barley malt in the brew house. (*Courtesy the F. & M. Schaefer Brewing Company, New York*)

Beer in fermentation in open fermenting vats. (*Courtesy United States Brewers Association Washington, D.C.*)

difference between brewer's yeast and ordinary yeast as there is between a Derby winner and a truck horse. The secret of the flavor in many world-famous beers is the result, unquestionably, of the strain of yeast used. The difference between lager beer yeast and ale yeast is that lager beer yeast settles to the bottom and does its work there during fermentation and after. Beer is the result of bottom fermentation.

In the case of ale, the yeasts, in multiplying, have a tendency to stick together, creating more of a surface, and do their work after rising to the top of the liquid. Ale is the result of top fermentation. This is partly because of the higher temperature at which ale is fermented and partly because of the different type of yeast used. Beer fermentation takes longer than ale fermentation—eight to eleven days being the fermenting time for beer, while five to six days are usually sufficient for ale.

Beer usually has a lower alcohol content than ale, while ale has a stronger hop flavor than beer.

During fermentation the carbon dioxide gas (CO_2) that is given off is gathered and stored to be added back later, in part, to the beer. After fermentation is over and most of the yeast has settled down, the young beer is

1. Barley grain is cleaned, graded, and stored before start of malting process.
2. Barley is soaked (steeped) in warm water to soften the grain.
3. Softened barley remains in scientifically humidity- and temperature-controlled compartments where it germinates.
4. The germinated barley, now green malt, is placed in kilns where it is dried out with heated air.
5. After kilning, the malt is cleaned and stored for aging.
6. Matured malt is ground into a meal.
7. Ground malt and corn grits, in proper proportion.
8. and 9. Separately, the malt and the corn grits are mixed with hot water and cooked briefly.
10. The mashing or starch liquefaction and conversion to maltose and dextrin. The liquid is now wort.
11. The wort is filtered through the lauter tun, which separates the wort from the grain solids, which in turn are processed for cattle feed.

12. The filtered wort is flavored with hops in the brew kettle, where it is boiled for several hours.
13. Spent hops are separated from the wort when the brew kettle is emptied.
14. Wort cools in wort-collecting tank.
15. Refrigerated wort cooler.
16. Pure yeast culture is added to the wort.
17. The wort remains in the starting tank only long enough for fermentation to begin.
18. Now beer, it is filled into the fermenters, where the process takes seven days. The CO_2 produced is gathered, compressed, and stored, to be added back to the beer later.
19. The new beer is put into storage tanks. Some young, unfermented (kräusen) beer is added to ferment slowly at a low temperature, under pressure, to give the beer its zest.
20. After several months at low-temperature storage, the mellowed beer is filtered, has a small amount of CO_2 added back, and is finally kegged, bottled, or canned.

MALTING PROCESS

1 BARLEY STORAGE

2 STEEPING TANK

3 GERMINATING COMPARTMENTS

4 KILN

5 FINISHED MALT STORAGE

17 STARTING TANK

KRAUSEN

CO_2

18 FERMENTER

19 STORAGE TANK

19 STORAGE TANK

BREWING PROCESS

6 MALT MILL

7 GROUND-MALT SCALE HOPPER

7 GRITS SCALE HOPPER

8 FORE MASHER

9 COOKER

10 MASH TUN

11 LAUTER TUN

12 BREW KETTLE

HOPS

13 HOP STRAINER

14 HOT-WORT COLLECTING TANK

15 WORT COOLER

16 YEAST CULTURE

16 YEAST STORAGE

20 BEER FILTERS

COMPRESSOR

CO_2 STORAGE TANKS

WORT/FLOW

run off into glass-lined or otherwise protected storage vats, where it is kept at a very low temperature, close to the freezing point, so that the yeast and other solids that would give it a cloudy appearance may precipitate by the natural process of sedimentation. Sometimes beechwood chips are added to attract the impurities and promote clarification. During this resting period certain chemical changes take place that develop the immature beer. The beer throws off its roughness and, as it matures, it becomes mellower and more pleasing. This is the lagering, and it usually takes from one to two months.

Finally the beer is carbonated to make it effervescent and refreshing. The carbon dioxide gas that was released by the wort during fermentation is added. Another popular method used for the carbonation of beer, known as kräusening, is accomplished by adding about 15 percent of the fermenting wort, or kräusen, to the beer in storage; this short second fermentation carbonates the total product, making it lively. Regardless of the method used, once the beer is carbonated it is refrigerated, passed through a pressure filter, and packaged.

the finished product Beers and ales are complex food products. They contain:

Water	85 to 90 percent by weight
Alcohol	3.2 to 8 percent by weight
Carbohydrates (sugars)	3 to 6 percent by weight
Protein	0.3 to 0.5 percent by weight
Calories	10 to 17 per ounce

As can be seen, the largest part of beer is water. This explains why, historically, areas with good water supplies were so important.

The alcohol content of U.S. beers varies from 3.2 percent to 4 percent by weight, while the specialized beer marketed as malt liquor varies from 3.2 to 8 percent by weight. Ales average 4.5 percent by weight, and fuller ales, such as stout, average 6 percent by weight. In Scandinavian countries there is a "motorist" beer that contains only 2.8 percent alcohol by weight. A Swiss import has the alcohol removed at the end of the brewing process, so that it has no alcohol at all yet retains the character of a malt beverage. The alcohol content of U.S. malt beverages is regulated by individual states and varies from state to state; states have held this right since Repeal. This explains why the same brand of beer may taste different in different parts of the country. The consumer does not know the alcohol content because it is not on the label.

The calories in beers and ales vary, naturally, with the alcohol and carbohydrate contents of the individual brands. The average U.S. beer has 12½ calories per ounce. Bock beer, malt liquor, special ales, stout, and porter have a higher caloric value. Low-carbohydrate beers, which have one-half to two-thirds the calories of regular beers, are available.

PACKAGING

The three forms of packaging beer are kegs or barrels, bottles, and cans. The beer, under pressure, passes through closed pipelines into the containers.

Beer cannot be kept or stored in direct contact with wood, as it will take on an unpleasant woody flavor. Previously, barrels made from wood were lined with pitch, which was tasteless, did not dissolve in the beer, and kept it from touching the wood. Metal kegs of aluminum or stainless steel are used today almost exclusively. These kegs are built to withstand a much greater pressure than is usually found in beer. Wooden cooperage can stand a pressure of forty-five pounds per square inch, while metal kegs can stand about three hundred pounds.

As these containers are safe against additional pressure that might be created by additional fermentation, beer so packaged is not pasteurized but is kept under refrigeration. Beer packaged in bottles or cans is likely to remain in the package longer and to be shipped farther away from the brewery than that in kegs, so in order to protect the package this beer is pasteurized, making it sterile and killing any yeast that might still be active. If this were not done, additional carbon dioxide gas could form and perhaps burst the bottle or can. This is the principal object in pasteurizing bottled or canned beer. Pasteurization takes place at 140 to 145 degrees Fahrenheit, at which temperature the beer is kept for about twenty minutes. It is then cooled rapidly. Flash pasteurization is sometimes used. This is a faster process whereby the beer is kept at 180 to 185 degrees Fahrenheit for one minute only.

As with milk, the pasteurization of beer in the bottle slows down but does not halt the ravages of time. The peak quality of pasteurized packaged beer is not indefinite. In cans it is four months, while in bottles it is six months.

As also with milk, the pasteurization of beer does, in some small measure, alter the taste. The principal difference between draft beer and bottled beer is that pasteurization diminishes the fresh flavor, although it does contribute to the beer's stability.

All bottled and canned beers were once pasteurized. Today, with the advent of microporous materials that filter out yeast cells, unpasteurized beer can be packaged in bottles and cans with assurance of a safe shelf life for this sterile-filtered beer, permitting it to retain its "draft" taste.

According to U.S. government regulations, the words *draft beer* on the labels and advertising of both keg beer and bottled or canned beer may be used as follows:

1. Beer in containers of one gallon or more, the contents of which are drawn off through a tap or spigot, may be described as draft beer whether the beer has been pasteurized or sterile filtered or is unpasteurized.

2. Bottled or canned beer may be described as draft beer if it is unpasteurized or has been sterile filtered.

SUGGESTIONS for KEEPING and SERVING "BEER AT ITS BEST"

SITUATION	CAUSE	EFFECT and REMEDY
If Your Beer Is WILD — SECTION 1	**Temperature too high**	Keep temperature in storage box 45° F. or lower. Also refer to Section 4. Coil boxes should be properly iced in both upper and lower box and ice kept broken up, preferably by a small stick used with a stirring motion, to prevent the arching of the ice. Do not beat ice down with a club as this is apt to flatten out pipes or kink them.
	Keg has been agitated	This disturbs the carbonic gas. Allow kegs to rest several hours after delivery. Don't move them about roughly.
	Pressure too high	Causes turbulent beer and excessive foaming. Decrease pressure as described in Section 3.
	Pitch or sediment in tap rod holes	Prevents free flow and gives turbulent beer. Clean holes before tapping. Don't ram the rod into the bottom—it might damage both rod and barrel lining.
	Uninsulated beer pipe line	Heats up the beer in warm weather.—See also Section 4.
	Kinks or dents in coils or beer pipe line	Have such kinks or dents removed; results in turbulent beer. Repairs must be effected.
	Holding glass too far from faucet	Results in excessive foaming. Try holding glass closer to faucet.
	"Cracking faucet" (Faucet partly open)	Causes artificial foam and destroys part of the quality. Open faucet wide as fast as possible when drawing beer.
If Your Beer Is CLOUDY — SECTION 2	**Old, defective beer hose**	Beer hose has a limited life. Old hose is likely to be the cause of contamination no matter how often it is cleaned.
	Sagging beer pipe line	The resulting pockets harbor slime and bacteria which are difficult to remove. Check lines for straightness.
	Beer chilled in coils	Beer, left in lines over night, usually becomes chilled, losing flavor and color, appearing cloudy. It should be discarded before serving in the morning.
	Coils not properly cleaned	Merely going through a cleaning procedure is not enough unless it is performed in an approved manner, preferably by a reliable and experienced expert on this type of work. It is poor economy to do the cleaning cheaply but poorly and thereby spoil beer and lose trade, worth many times the saving on cleaners.
	"Cracking faucet" (Faucet partly open)	This practice is harmful to the beer, having the effect of de-gassing, which sometimes leaves a cloudy appearance.
If You Have PRESSURE PROBLEMS — SECTION 3	**Too long beer pipe line**	A long pipe line causes a lot of friction, which is harmful to the beer and makes it almost impossible to draw a good glass. The keg should be as close as possible to the bar.
	Gauge and regulator away from bar	These devices should be installed at the bar so that they are readily accessible and under continuous control of the operator.
	Defective gauge or regulator	Should be checked occasionally to make sure that they function correctly.
	Air-bound coils	Results in unsteady flow. Put on extra pressure for a moment while faucet is wide open to clear the line.
	Pressure off during night	Apply pressure immediately upon tapping keg and never shut off until empty.—See also Section 5.
	Pressure leaks	Whether gas or compressed air is used, the loss due to leaks is considerable. All lines should be checked regularly.
	Air compressor system	Extreme care must be taken to prevent oil from entering beer line.—See also Section 6.
	Correct pressure	Depends entirely on: 1. distance between keg and bar;—2. condition and temperature of beer in keg.—3. whether vertical or horizontal beer line;—4. length of coil;—5. whether beer is drawn fast or slowly;—6. number of barrels tapped at one time.—Each installation has its own characteristics and it is therefore up to the operator to establish the most effective pressure. If using more than one beer be sure pressure is correctly adjusted for each beer on tap inasmuch as different pressures may be necessary.

SITUATION	CAUSE	EFFECT and REMEDY
If Your Beer Is TOO WARM or TOO COLD — SECTION 4	**Pre-cooling too great or insufficient**	Kegs on tap as well as in reserve should be kept cool. However, the temperature of the cooling compartment should be so controlled that it permits serving the beer at between 40° and 45° F. Unless this temperature is regulated to suit the rate of drawing beer, it is apt to run too cold or too warm at times.
	Cooling in coil box too great or insufficient	If considerable time elapses between servings, the beer in the line may be cooled too far, even to the point of being chilled, thus losing its fine flavor. Similarly, if the beer is drawn very fast, it may not have time to get cool enough. Control the refrigeration in the coil box accordingly.
	Uninsulated pipe lines	All exposed lines must be well insulated otherwise variations in the atmospheric temperature may have a considerable influence over the temperature of the beer drawn.
	Too much or too little equipment	Dispensing equipment cannot be overtaxed. In case of too little equipment the beer is drawn too fast and may run warm, while excessive equipment, standing idle much of the time, may result in chilled beer.
If Your Beer Is FLAT — SECTION 5	**Temperature too low**	Chilled beer appears flat and loses its flavor. Maintain 40°-45° F.—See also Section 4.
	Insufficient pressure	Will not allow beer to flow freely. Note little or no foam. Increase pressure.
	Leaky pressure line	Leaks allow the gas to escape and must be located to remedy.
	Pressure shut off during night	This allows the carbonic gas to separate from the beer. Once a keg is tapped, the pressure must be left on continuously until emptied.
	Loose bung or tap connections	May be caused by rough handling and result in loss of the gas same as through any other leak. Check carefully and tighten.
	Kegs stored in non-refrigerated compartment	Storage in a warm, dry place causes wooden kegs to dry out and spring leaks.
	Greasy glasses	Any fatty substance makes beer go flat instantly. Wash glasses in hot water without soap. Rinse in pure cold water. Do not dry glass before using.
If Your Beer Is UNpalatable — SECTION 6	**Unsanitary conditions at bar or in cellar**	Remove empty kegs from refrigerating compartment as soon as possible. Clear lines every morning of beer that has been standing in them over night. Observe strict sanitation everywhere.
	Sagging beer pipe line	Forms pocket for accumulation of bacteria and slime, which is difficult to remove.
	Uninsulated beer pipe line	Guard against the ill effects of possible high temperature by insulating all exposed lines.
	Old, defective beer hose	Replace defective hose at regular intervals—its life is limited and can be the cause of unpalatable beer.—See also Section 2.
	Coils not cleaned properly	This is a common cause of trouble. Should be cleaned by specialists at least once every week. Use compound made for purpose, never strong chemical solutions.—Also note Section 2.
	Rods and bungs	These must be cleaned regularly, and when not in use, hang on wall of box.
	Coil box	Any mud deposit which may collect in the bottom of the coil box should be removed, as this mud forms an insulation which prevents the full refrigerating effect of ice for which you pay.
	Air compressor location	If compressor is used, see that intake is extending to outside the draw front air. Should be equipped with an effective filtering device.—See also Section 3.
	Foul air line or air tank	Check tank and line for possible accumulation of oil, dust or water. Clean out occasionally. Drain tank regularly of condensed water.
	Unclean faucet	Take apart occasionally, thoroughly remove all deposits and then sterilize.

NOTE:

1—Place beer in storage box immediately when delivered.
2—A rubber emergency bung and extra wooden bungs should be kept on hand in case a bung is accidentally split.
3—Always use a wooden mallet...never one of metal...in tapping.
4—When removing bung and rod from keg, tap the bung lightly on each side, alternately, until loose. Never use the rod as a lever, as this may bend it and cause it to become useless.
5—Don't have more barrels on tap than requirements call for.

Federal Regulations require revenue stamp to be defaced when tapping barrel by driving rod through stamp

Suggestions for keeping and serving beer. (*Courtesy the F. & M. Schaefer Brewing Company, New York, reprinted by permission of A. O. Smith Corporation*)

3. Bottled or canned beer may not be described as draft beer if it has been pasteurized, but the use of such terms as *draft brewed, draft beer flavor,* and *old-time on-tap* taste is permitted as long as the label or advertisement conspicuously states that the beer has been pasteurized.

DISPENSING DRAFT BEER

The three cardinal points of beer service are cleanliness, temperature, and pressure.

cleanliness

Beer is one of the most delicate and perishable food products a restaurant handles. It is highly susceptible to extraneous odors, to bacteria in the air, and to strong light. It should be stored by itself in a spotless room that is well ventilated and in which a constant temperature of 40 degrees Fahrenheit is maintained.

The dispensing equipment should be checked and thoroughly cleaned as often as possible, but at least once a week. If an establishment wishes to serve perfect beer, no detail is too small to be overlooked, no precaution too great, in maintaining and ensuring cleanliness of beer service.

temperature

One of the main causes for flat beer is the American tendency to serve it too cold. The ideal temperature is 45 degrees Fahrenheit for beer and 50 degrees Fahrenheit for ale, although it is customary to chill as low as 40 degrees for lager and 45 degrees for ale. Do not chill below 40 degrees; the nearer the beer is to 45 degrees, the better it tastes.

Imported beers should be served at 48 to 50 degrees Fahrenheit and English ale or Irish stout at 55 degrees.

Beer that is too cold is flat and cloudy. If it is too warm, the gas breaks away from the liquid and there is too much gas. Beer in this condition is called wild beer. Do not take any chances. Maintain a constant and uniform temperature. Use a thermometer and store the barrels as close to the dispensing unit or units as possible.

pressure

To maintain an even flow of beer from the tap, the pressure must be carefully watched and controlled. Since some of the natural pressure of the carbon dioxide gas is bound to be lost between the time the barrel is opened and the time the last glass of beer is drawn, additional pressure must be supplied. Some people prefer air and others carbon dioxide. Carbon dioxide, while more expensive, ensures a more even supply of gas from the first to the last glass and eliminates the possibility of foul air being drawn into the system, as may happen when air pressure is used. Just as the gasoline gauge on the dashboard

Final operation in a brewery—filling the aluminum kegs. (*Courtesy the F. & M. Schaefer Brewing Company, New York*)

As bottles of beer move along conveyor belts, inspectors make sure each bottle is properly filled. (*Courtesy Jos. Schlitz Brewing Company*)

of an automobile permits the driver to check his supply at a glance, so the gas pressure gauge should be at the bar where the operator may check and control the pressure.

HANDLING PACKAGED BEER

Bottled beer should be stored in a dark, cool place. Beer exposed to the direct rays of the sun in a shop window for display cannot be used, as beer is extremely sensitive to light and will, after only a few moments, take on a strange odor and flavor commonly called skunky. It may also become cloudy.

Beer in cans is not affected by light, but it should be kept in a cool place. In the home beer should be stored in the lowest, coolest part of the refrigerator. Storing bottled or canned beer in the door shelf of a refrigerator is risky because the constant jostling and the drafts of warm air from the kitchen could hasten the beer's deterioration.

Most cans today have the convenient aluminum snap-top openings. When *opening* opening a flat-topped can without this, make a small puncture to allow air to enter, then push the opener down as far as it will go on the opposite side of the lid.

When serving bottled or canned beer, allow the glass to remain on the table in an upright position. Pour the beer so that the stream flows straight into the center of the glass. Do not tilt the glass and pour down its side because you will not release enough carbon dioxide. Pour the beer in a natural manner and not too fast, which may cause overfoaming.

IMPORTANT SERVING NOTE. Glasses or containers to be used for serving beer or ale must never be washed with soap or soapy water. The soap leaves a fatty film on the inner surface of the glass that will break down the bubbles of carbon dioxide, thus destroying the desired collar of foam. Nonsoapy detergents may be employed, but always make sure that the glass is rinsed well before it is used.

UNITED STATES BEERS

The United States is the world's largest producer of malt beverages, producing all types of beers and ales. Most of the twenty-two gallons per capita consumed in this country is the nationally produced, light-colored, light-bodied beer. Large breweries, with nationwide distribution, brew toward a taste level that is pleasing to all areas of the country. The biggest breweries in the United States are Anheuser-Busch, Schlitz, Miller, Pabst, Coors, Falstaff, Olympia, and Schaefer. Most have breweries in many different cities.

Of the more than seven hundred breweries in the United States that sprang up after Prohibition, there are now only about seventy left. For small, local breweries costs are high and volume is low. They do, however, produce fine beers and fill a special need, brewing to local tastes. The beers are not mass produced, and the brewmaster can take time with each step, giving the brew extra aging. Since the beers are drunk near the breweries, they are fresher than those that are shipped great distances.

There are many fine producers dotted throughout the United States. Here is a partial list of cities with local breweries; there are, of course, many other local favorites.

Baltimore, Md.	National
Boston, Mass.	Dawson's, Croft's
Brooklyn, N.Y.	Rheingold
Chicago, Ill.	Peter Hand
Cincinnati, Ohio	Wiedermann's, Schoenling
Detroit, Mich.	Stroh's
Harrisburg, Pa.	Horlacher, Rolling Rock
Louisville, Ky.	Falls City, Drummond Brothers
Philadelphia, Pa.	Schmidt's, Ortlieb's, Prior
Rochester, N.Y.	Genesee
St. Louis, Mo.	Stag
San Antonio, Tex.	Pearl, Lone Star
San Francisco, Calif.	Anchor Steam Beer
Waltham, Mass.	Carling

BEERS OF OTHER LANDS

The beers of Europe that are most popular in America are the light brews, best exemplified by the famous Bohemian Pilsner Urquell of Pilsen, Czechoslovakia. Most of the German, Danish, and Dutch beers are similar to the Pilsner. They are very pale-colored, light, hop-tasting beers. From Munich, Germany, also come some much-favored darker-colored, richer, and slightly maltier-tasting beers.

England and Ireland have long supplied the American market with their famous ales and stouts. These brews are much darker, richer, and more bitter than those of the Continent.

In the Americas, Canada and Mexico have been the principal suppliers because of their proximity to the United States. Canada's very fine ales, in particular, enjoy an appreciative public, as do the very light, tart Mexican beers that are exported to the United States.

Many imported beers are aged a great deal longer than the average American beer and are fuller bodied, with more character. Some have a higher alcohol content than those produced in the United States. Beer devotees feel that the fuller beers are for sipping, while the lighter ones are for quaffing.

There are many famous beers and ales produced in the world. Each has its own individual character. A partial list of imported beers includes:

Argentina	Schneider, Río Segundo
Austria	Puntigan
Brazil	Brahma
Canada	Molson Ale, Labatt's Ale
Czechoslovakia	Pilsner Urquell
Denmark	Carlsberg, Tuborg
England	Bass Ale, Whitbread Ale, Mackeson's Stout
France	Kronenbourg
Germany	Dortmunder Union, Beck's, Würzburger, Löwenbräu
Holland	Amstel, Heineken
Ireland	Harp, Guinness Stout
Israel	Abir
Italy	Peroni
Japan	Asahi, Kirin
Mexico	Dos Equis, Carta Blanca
Norway	Frydenlunds, Ringness
Philippines	San Miguel
Sweden	Pripps
Uruguay	Salus

Many of the beers mentioned above are available both light and dark.

HOW AND WHEN TO SERVE BEER

Beer is one of the healthiest beverages one can consume. The alcohol and carbohydrates, with their food value, furnish energy. The proteins help assimilate food. The carbon dioxide gas, which gives the beer its head, or collar, helps create the cooling or refreshing effect that makes beer so popular in the summertime. The bitter hops stimulate the appetite.

Beer may be served at almost any hour and is appropriate during any season of the year. It blends with almost all foods, except heavy cream-sauce dishes and whipped-cream desserts. The characteristic sharp tang of beer adapts it to highly flavored or spicy dishes and to such foods as hamburger, steak, corned beef and cabbage, Irish stew, sausage, cold cuts, all pork dishes, fried dishes, curries, and broiled lobster, to mention only a few. All the sharper cheeses go well with either beer or ale.

The uses of beer in cooking are legion. Since many colonial recipes call for beer as an ingredient, it seems that the early Americans often depended on beer to give their dishes tang and character. A Yard of Flannel is a warm drink, popular with ale lovers, and is said to be an especially good cold remedy (see page 409).

SAKÉ

The word *saké* means "the essence of the spirit of rice." Saké, made from rice, is a specialized form of beer. Saké is produced in Japan, and a small amount is made in Hawaii. It is not a spirit; it is not a wine. Because of its high alcohol content, and because it looks like wine, many people call it Japanese rice wine.° Unlike beer, as we know it, saké is almost colorless and quite still. It has none of the carbon dioxide in solution that we find in creamy beers.

The preparation of saké is unique to brewing. Specially selected rice is polished, soaked in water for about twelve hours, and then steamed in a *koshiki*, a rice-steaming tub. Next, some of the steamed rice is treated with a culture of a special yeast spore, *Aspergillus oryzae*, which produces an enzyme that converts starch into sugar. This step takes about thirty-five hours and produces a culture called *koji* that is rich in the enzyme that converts starch into sugar. The *koji* is added to a thin paste of freshly steamed rice and water and another yeast is added. Development of the new yeast culture begins and continues slowly for two to three weeks, until the mash becomes a fully ripened *moto*. Finally, the *moto*, more *koji*, and water are slowly added to freshly steamed rice in progressive stages. A combined process consisting of two conversions, starch to sugar and sugar to alcohol and carbon dioxide, now occurs in a single vat. Within three weeks, with constant supervision of these reactions, the fermentation is completed. The liquor, now saké, is drawn off, filtered, allowed to settle, heated, and then run into casks to mature for a short period. Finally the saké is drawn out of the storage tanks and bottled or casked.

Saké is quite strong for a brewed beverage, usually having 14 to 16 percent alcohol by volume. It has a slightly sweet first taste and a dry aftertaste.

Drinking saké is accompanied by poetic ceremony. An old Japanese saying states, "Saké should be served warm . . . and by a warm-hearted woman." Traditionally, saké is served warm because heating releases its heady bouquet.

To warm saké, place the opened bottle in a pot of boiling water. Remove it when the saké is about 100 to 105 degrees Fahrenheit. To serve saké in the Japanese manner, decant the warm saké into small ceramic bottles, called *tokkuri*. Bring the saké to the table in the *tokkuri* and then pour it into tiny porcelain bowls, called *sakazuki*, which hold a little more than an ounce. The saké should be sipped. Often these *sakazuki* have a little tube on the outside, so that as you sip you draw in air and produce a whistling sound. Some saké producers enclose the tiny bowls, called singing saké cups, with bottles of saké.

It is not necessary to warm saké before drinking to enjoy its flavor and bouquet. It may be drunk at room temperature in standard glasses. Saké with bitter lemon, with Tom Collins mix, in place of vermouth in Martinis, or on the rocks is quite enjoyable.

° The B.A.T.F., in the Standards of Identity for Wine, lists saké in Class 6, wine from other agricultural products.

18
DISTILLED SPIRITS
IN GENERAL

I t is poetic to call the secret of distillation a gift of the gods, but it is more reasonable to suppose that it was discovered by some long-forgotten alchemist.

The essence of the principle of distillation is this: alcohol vaporizes—becomes a gas—at a lower temperature than water. The boiling point of water at sea level is 212 degrees Fahrenheit, when it vaporizes and becomes steam, while that of ethyl alcohol is 173 degrees Fahrenheit. Therefore, if heat is applied to a liquid that contains alcohol, and the temperature is kept below 212 degrees Fahrenheit, the alcohol may be separated from the original liquid. If, at the same time, an apparatus is used whereby the alcohol vapors are gathered and not allowed to escape into the air, it is possible to recondense them into liquid form. The result is an alcohol of high purity. This sounds simple and so it is, if one wishes to produce alcohol, but if one is trying to produce a potable alcoholic beverage, the problem is more difficult and, if the product is to be a fine one, more delicate.

Apparently the science of distillation was known to the ancient Egyptians and Chaldeans. Long before the Christian era the Chinese obtained a spirit from rice beer, and arak has been distilled from sugarcane and rice in the East Indies since 800 B.C. Later Aristotle (384–322 B.C.), the great Greek philosopher, stated in his *Meteorology* that "seawater can be made potable by distillation; wine and other liquids can be submitted to the same process." There are many such references to distilled spirits in ancient writings. Even Captain Cook, on his voyage of discovery to the South Pacific, found the natives of the islands familiar with the distillation process.

For practical purposes, however, the modern history of distillation may be said to have originated with the Arabs or Saracens. They gave us the words *alcohol* and *alembic;* the latter word means "a still" and is used in all but

history

English-speaking countries. The first mention of distillation is attributed to an Arabian alchemist of the tenth century, one Albukassen; later in the thirteenth century a Majorcan chemist and philosopher, Raymond Lully, described the process. Even before his time the Celts of Eire and Scotia, unaware of the efforts of the Arabs, were producing a potable spirit that they called *uisgebeatha* or *uisgebaugh* ("water of life").

Distilled liquids are called ardent spirits. The word *ardent* comes from the Latin *ardere*, which means "to burn" and hence to distill. Although modern science has progressed amazingly, and methods have grown more and more efficient, the apparatus used for distilling most spirits is still much the same, save for a few refinements, as the one used by the original distillers many centuries ago. Reduced to its two essential parts, it consists of a still and a worm condenser. The still is a copper pot with a broad, rounded bottom and a long, tapered neck. The worm condenser is a spiral copper tube that is connected to the still by a copper pipe. The worm passes through a jacket containing cold water to assist in a more rapid condensation of the vapors. Such an apparatus is known in the trade as a pot still. Pot stills produce spirits in individual batches and are used to a large extent in the distillation of brandies, Scotch and Irish whiskies, liqueurs, and some rums.

In 1826 Robert Stein, of a famous Scotch whisky-distilling family, invented the continuous still. This was later perfected by Aeneas Coffey, whose patent replaced Stein's and whose name has come down to us in connection with this type of still, which is known as a Coffey, or patent, still.

spirits   So far in this book we have discussed wines, which are the result of the natural processes of fermentation of the sugar contained in the grape juice, and beers, which are the result of the fermentation of grain. Now we are about to study what happens when the essence of the previously discussed wines or beers is distilled out to create alcoholic beverages. There are many of these, and while we shall consider each type in separate chapters, it is important to classify and define them.

BRANDY is a potable spirit, often aged in wood, obtained by distilling wine or a fermented mash of fruit. Examples are Cognac, Armagnac, Spanish brandy, Greek brandy, American brandy, Kirsch or Kirschwasser (cherry brandy), Calvados or applejack (apple brandy), Slivovitz, Mirabelle, Quetsch (plum brandies), and other fruit brandies.

WHISKY is a spirit, suitably aged in wood, usually oak, obtained from the distillation of a fermented mash of grain. Examples are Scotch whisky, Irish whiskey, Canadian whisky, rye whisky, and Bourbon whisky.

RUM is a potable spirit, suitably aged in wood, obtained from the distillation of a fermented mash of sugarcane juice or molasses. Examples are Jamaican rum, Demeraran rum, Barbados rum, Martinique rhum, Cuban ron, Puerto Rican ron, Haitian rhum, Philippine ron, Batavia arak, and others.

GIN is a flavored beverage, obtained by redistilling a high-proof spirit in the presence of juniper berries and other flavoring agents. Examples are English London Dry and Old Tom gins, Genever (Schiedam or Hollands) gin, American gins, and fruit-flavored gins. Gin may also be made by adding essential oils of juniper and other flavorings to spirits.

VODKA, made in America, is neutral spirits so distilled, or so treated after distillation with charcoal or other material, as to be without distinctive character, aroma, taste, or color. If any flavoring material is added to the distillate, the vodka is usually characterized with the name of the flavoring material used. Vodka made elsewhere may have some color, flavor, or aroma.

LIQUEURS AND CORDIALS are flavored beverages whose flavor is obtained either by infusion or by distillation of the flavoring agent, to which is then added simple syrup for sweetening. They may be artificially colored, if so stated on the label. All cordials or liqueurs are sweet. For tariff and taxation purposes, the regulations specify that a cordial or liqueur must have in excess of $2\frac{1}{2}$ percent sugar by volume. Examples are apricot liqueur, Bénédictine, blackberry liqueur, Chartreuse, Cointreau, crème de cacao, crème de cassis, crème de menthe, Grand Marnier, sloe gin, strawberry liqueur, and Triple Sec.

Other spirits are obtained by distilling various fermented starchy or sugar-containing products. They include Tequila, Aquavit, Okolehao, and bitters.

Potable spirits, obtained from a given basic material, have different trade names. But the factors that make them different from one another are the matters, aside from alcohol, that are necessarily distilled out with the alcohol: the flavoring elements; the small amounts of alcohols other than ethyl; and the solids and minerals, which differ in fruits, grains, and sugarcane.

If in distillation the separation could be carried out where only the alcohol is removed, the resultant spirit would be pure, or absolute, alcohol of 200 proof. Commercial distillation results in a "constantly boiling mixture" that never goes above 192 proof, or 96 percent. To achieve 200 proof, or 100 percent, alcohol, a dehydration procedure would have to be carried out in the laboratory. Such a spirit would be the same, whether obtained from fruit, grain, or molasses, and would have no character whatsoever. We are not concerned here with such a pure spirit—in fact, for all practical purposes a spirit of 190 proof is sufficiently neutral for blending, and such spirits are used by the trade daily. The trade term for them is *neutral spirits* or *cologne spirits*.

Newly distilled spirits, whether obtained from fruit, grain, molasses, or other raw materials, are colorless, have little character, and are quite similar. They have a sharp, biting aroma and taste. When they have been matured for a certain length of time in wood, however, congeners, or "impurities," which are extracted from the wood, change the spirits' aroma, taste, and character.

The various congeners in spirits consist of acids, esters, aldehydes, furfural, traces of fusel oils, extracts of mineral salts, and solids in minute quantities.

Fusel oils are a complex mixture of higher alcohols, mainly propyl, butyl, amyl, hexyl, heptyl, and the dialcohols, trialcohols, and their reaction products.

Acids found in spirits vary, but they include propionic, butyric, tartaric, lactic, succinic, and others.

Esters, produced by the chemical combination of the acids and the alcohols, are the volatile substances that give the aroma to the spirit.

Aldehydes are produced by the combination of the alcohols and air and are a contributing factor in giving a distinctive character to the spirit.

Furfural is an aldehyde. It is mostly obtained during distillation and partly extracted from the oak casks in which spirits are matured.

When the freshly distilled spirit flows from the still it is colorless and has a sharp, pungent, alcoholic aroma and sharp taste. If distilled out at 180 proof it would be difficult for any but experienced distillers to differentiate among distillates of grain, fruit (grape), or cane. When the spirit is distilled out at a lower proof, it contains more congeners and naturally has more character. Such a spirit, upon maturing in wood, undergoes certain changes in its composition that develop its flavor and character.

Once the spirit is placed in glass and sealed against air, no further change takes place. But as long as it is in wood there is constant change, brought about by the oxidizing effect of the oxygen in the air on the alcohol. The oxidation and wood aging cause the esters and acids to increase materially, the aldehydes to increase slowly, the fusel oils to remain practically the same, and a certain amount of loss of alcohol to take place. Furthermore, the spirit absorbs some tannin and other coloring material from the wood container and becomes less harsh and, in a sense, sweeter than it was originally.

proof   Before making distilled spirits became a science, the primitive distillers had a very simple method for determining the potable strength of the distillate. Equal quantities of spirit and gunpowder were mixed and a flame applied. If the gunpowder failed to burn, the spirit was too weak; if it burned too brightly, it was too strong. But if the mixture burned evenly, with a blue flame, it was said to have been proved.

Today we know that this potable mean was approximately 50 percent alcohol by volume, and we have adopted the term *proof* to describe the strength of alcoholic beverages. In the United States a 100-proof spirit is a spirit containing 50 percent alcohol by volume at a temperature of 60 degrees Fahrenheit. This is an arbitrary measurement. One proof gallon is equal to one measured wine gallon at 100 proof. Each degree of proof is equal to $\frac{1}{2}$ percent alcohol. Therefore, a spirit of 90 proof contains 45 percent alcohol, and one gallon at 90 proof would equal 0.9 proof gallons. A spirit of 150 proof contains 75 percent alcohol, and one gallon at 150 proof would equal 1.5 proof gallons.

The trade term for a spirit of more than 100 proof is an *overproof* spirit.

A tax gallon is the gallonage on which duties and revenue taxes are paid. When the duties and taxes are determined, the tax gallons are equivalent to proof gallons at 100 proof or higher. If the spirits are less than 100 proof, the tax gallons are the actual wine gallons as measured quantitatively. See Appendix O for British "Sikes" and metric "Gay-Lussac" tables.

What is rectifying? Theoretically it means to purify or improve, but practically it means anything that changes the character of a spirit. A rectification tax of $0.30 per tax gallon applies to most rectified spirits. Rectifying must be performed in a distilled spirits plant.

rectified spirits

What constitutes taxable rectification?

1. Blending two different spirits.
2. Blending two different whiskies, that is, whiskies distilled in different distilleries or in different seasons of the year.
3. Blending whisky with neutral spirits.
4. Redistilling whisky that has been stored in a barrel.
5. Adding coloring, flavoring, or anything except water to distilled spirits.
6. Redistilling neutral spirits for potable purposes.

Automated barrel-filling at Schenley's Bernheim Distillery in Louisville, Kentucky. (*Courtesy Schenley Industries, Inc., New York*)

7. Distilling neutral spirits over a flavoring agent.

8. Compounding spirits, essential oils, or other flavors and sugar to make cordials, liqueurs, and gin.

The following do *not* constitute taxable rectification and consequently are not subject to the rectification tax:

1. Blending whiskies that are four or more years old.

2. Blending rums that are two or more years old.

3. Making gin by original distillation or redistillation of spirits with juniper and other flavors.

4. Reducing the proof with water only.

THERAPEUTIC VALUE OF SPIRITS

The question of drinking, unhappily, has been invested with so much mumbo jumbo, loudly proclaimed by badly informed zealots of reform, that the quieter, more restrained voices of the scientific investigators have been drowned out. There is room in all this discussion for a balanced judgment that can recognize the beneficial qualities of alcoholic beverages and at the same time be aware of their faults.

Alcohol is a compound of several elements—carbon, hydrogen, and oxygen—and in itself it not only is not harmful to man but is a necessary constituent of his bloodstream. The normal alcohol content of the average person's blood is 0.003 percent; the lethal limit is around 0.7 percent.

Alcohol is the only food taken into the system that is unaffected by the digestive system. The stomach and intestines pass it into the bloodstream, unchanged, and it is diffused so rapidly that within a few minutes after being swallowed it has reached every part of the body. In the bloodstream it is carried to the liver, where most of it is filtered out, then to the heart, to the lungs, back to the heart, then through the aorta into the arteries, and throughout the body, finally coming to the brain and the higher nerve centers. This is where it has its most pronounced effect.

The popular idea is that alcohol is a stimulant. Pathologically that is not true. There is a false sense of stimulation because of the loss of control of the inhibitory nerve centers that control heartbeat, thus increasing the heartbeat and causing a sensation of warmth. Actually, the effect is relaxing rather than stimulating.

In regard to this sensation of warmth, alcohol dilates the peripheral blood vessels, increasing the flow of blood to the skin. It is actually only the surface of the body that is warmed, and in reality more heat is given off by the body than is supplied by the alcohol. As a matter of fact, alcohol is an excellent way of reducing body heat rapidly. This is why so much rum is drunk in the tropics; it is more cooling than ice water.

For the cardiac patient, the dilation of the blood vessels brings blood to the oxygen-starved heart muscles and to the rest of the body, helping the patient overcome shortness of breath at the same time. Alcohol provides energy and acts as a sedative to the brain, relaxing the patient.

All investigations made on the toxic effects of alcohol have been based on large doses of alcohol. These effects are materially reduced as dilution is increased, and when alcohol is a small part of other liquids, such as wine or beer, its intoxicating quality is reduced further.

A book that has done much to correct the misconceptions about the properties of alcohol is Morris E. Chafetz's *Liquor: The Servant of Man*, which states the following points:

Alcohol is actually manufactured in the human body, but is less toxic than most of the other natural secretions, such as thyroid, pituitary, adrenal, pancreas and bile.

Alcohol, if taken in anything remotely approaching customary amounts, is harmless to the body and in many cases beneficial.

Alcohol is one of the most valuable medicines in the world, both as a sedative and as a food, is useful for these and other reasons in many disease conditions, and is almost always indicated in old age.

Alcohol, to indulge in an understatement, has had a conspicuous position in the history of the race. It fathered religion and science and agriculture, provided more human confidence, and promoted good will toward men. It is the most efficient and practical relaxer of the driving force in the brain; it offers an immediate method of personal enjoyment; it is the greatest medium known for the purpose of permitting man to forget, at least for a little while, the shortness of life and the ludicrously helpless and infinitesimal part he plays in the functions of the universe.

Temperate alcohol use does not physically damage the nervous system or any of the healthy, important organs of the body, such as the heart, liver, kidneys, stomach, or brain.

points to remember about alcohol

Alcohol produces energy without making the body work because it is taken into the bloodstream in its original state. Alcohol itself does not produce fat. Other foods, which would normally produce the energy needed by the body, are stored, as an energy reserve, in the form of fat by those who drink regularly in substantial amounts.

The part of the body most quickly and directly affected by alcohol is the brain, and the effect is relaxing, not stimulating.

Once absorbed, excess alcohol cannot be "worked off" except by oxidation and excretion. The normal rate of elimination is about ten cubic centimeters° per hour, and this remains constant whether you lie in bed, walk around in the open, or sit in a Turkish bath.

° This is one-third of an ounce of absolute alcohol.

The best insulation against the effects of overindulgence is food to line the walls of the stomach. The best food is the fat of milk. In the order of their protective value, the foods you can take are cream, whole milk, butter, meat fats, olive oil, and meat.

The heart of a hangover is the accumulation of residual lactic acid in the muscles. Lactic acid normally occurs in the body as a waste product of energy production. Excess alcohol produces excess lactic acid in the body, which can be eliminated only by the blood and the kidneys. This process cannot be hastened, and the only cure is rest and time.

There is no evidence that alcohol in itself causes any disease. The principal danger of too much alcohol is social. One who is drunk, whether from imbibing one or ten drinks, has a narcotized brain—one that is not awake. In a moment of crisis, when a quick decision is necessary, the part of the brain that reasons may be awake, while the part that commands the muscles may be asleep, or vice versa. The result in either case is trouble.

Alcohol is prescribed in many ailments but is contraindicated in some for which the layman believes it most valuable. These are shock, snake bite, and fatigue. In the first two the blood pressure is lowered, and the additional lowering of blood pressure by alcohol is unnecessary. Fatigue means that you already have too much lactic acid in the system, and alcohol adds to it.

The conclusion one reaches is that alcoholic beverages in themselves are not damaging or harmful to man physically. When taken temperately, they are beneficial.

We do not advocate that anyone drink for the "kick." Drinking should be done for pleasure, relaxation, and the release to which the beverage contributes; it should be a part of the good life.

19
BRANDIES

Brandy is a potable spirit, suitably aged in wood, that is obtained from the distillation of wine or a fermented mash of fruit. An alcoholic beverage answering this description may be produced in any part of the world.

1. BRANDIES OF FRANCE

history

The art of distillation, although known to the ancients, was not applied to wine commercially until the sixteenth century, when the brandy trade began. Supposedly, a brisk trade in wine existed between the port of La Rochelle, on the Charente River in France, and Holland. All of this trade was carried on by sea, and the perils of war placed a premium on shipping.

Casks of wine take up quite a lot of space, particularly on small sailing vessels. The story is told of one very bright Dutch shipmaster who hit upon the idea of concentrating the wine—eliminating the water—and transporting the spirit, or the "soul," of the wine to Holland, where the water could be put back. In his thrifty mind he figured that he could save an enormous amount on the freight charges.

When this enterprising man arrived in Holland, however, with his "concentrated wine," his Dutch friends tasted it and liked it as it was. It would be a waste of water, they decided, to try to make it wine again. And thus the brandy trade had its inception. The Dutch called the new product *brandewijn* ("burned wine"), presumably because fire, or heat, is used in the process of distillation. In time this term was Anglicized to the present-day word—*brandy*.

COGNAC

When we say brandy, we usually mean the delightful "soul" of wine. There is one brandy that the world has accepted and recognized as superior to all others: Cognac. It is important to understand that all Cognac is brandy, but all brandies are not Cognac. Cognac is a brandy distilled from wines made of grapes grown within the legal limits of the Charente and Charente-Maritime departments of France.

The ancient city of Cognac, on the Charente River, is in the heart of the district that produces the brandies that have carried its fame throughout the world. In fact, they have done the job so well that *Cognac* is probably the best-known French word in the world.

The quality that makes Cognac superior to all other brandies is not only the special process of distillation that has been used in this district for centuries, but also the combination of ideal soil, climate, and other conditions. While it might be possible for another section to reproduce one or two of these essentials, the combination of all the factors cannot be achieved elsewhere.

The Cognac district, the Charentais, has seven subdivisions, which, in the order of quality, are:

SUBDIVISION	ACRES UNDER CULTIVATION
Grande Champagne	27,930
Petite Champagne	31,510
Borderies	8,750
Fins Bois	74,260
Bons Bois	43,840
Bois Ordinaires } Bois à Terroir }	8,780

The entire Cognac region was delimited by law in 1909; the seven subdivisions, in 1936. The Grande Champagne is a small district that is the kernel of the region. In it lies the town of Cognac, around which everything centers: the territory, the commerce, and the fame of the product. Almost completely surrounding it is the Petite Champagne. To the north, and situated at about the point where the encirclement of the Grande Champagne is incomplete, is the smallest district, the Borderies. Completely surrounding these first three districts are the Fins Bois. Around all these are the Bons Bois, and advancing from the Bons Bois to the Atlantic Ocean in the west are the Bois Ordinaires and the Bois à Terroir, sometimes considered one area.

If the Bordeaux system of classifying growths were to be followed, one might say that the two Champagnes would make up the great *crus;* the Borderies, the bourgeois *crus;* and the last four Bois, the ordinary *crus.*

In Cognac the small farmer may have his own still. Big shippers very often own a vineyard or two but they cannot possibly own the amount of vineyard land they would need to take care of the worldwide demand for their brands. It is the custom in Cognac, therefore, for all shippers to buy the brandy from the farmer. Each farmer has his little vineyard, gathers his grapes, makes his wine, and distills it as soon as it falls bright or has it distilled for him by one of the regional distillers. Distillation of brandy in France, and especially in Cognac, is supervised by government inspectors. There are padlocks and seals on every still. At vintage time the inspectors visit each farm, measure the wine, and tell the farmer how much brandy he can distill.

The subsoil in Cognac is chalky, and the more chalk, the more suitable are the wines produced for making Cognac. The two Champagne heartland regions have the highest amounts of chalk. Outside the Champagne area the chalky layer becomes shallower, while the earthy top layer becomes deeper. The Bois are so named because they used to be covered with woods, whose life cycle added to the soil layer. The Atlantic Ocean and the Gironde River modify the variations in temperature and help maintain humidity levels favorable to the production of Cognac.

REGION OF COGNAC

VENDÉE

La Rochelle

DEUX-SÈVRES

VIENNE

CHARENTE MARITIME

Charente R.

Aigre

Cognac
Jarnac

Royan

Angoulême

Segonzac

BAY OF BISCAY

Jonzac

CHARENTE

DORDOGNE

GIRONDE

☐ Grande Champagne

Petite Champagne

Bons Bois

Borderies

Bois Ordinaires

Fins Bois

Bois à Terroir

In 1936 French law decreed that wines that produce Cognac should be made from Folle Blanche, Saint-Émilion, and Colombard grapes, with up to 10 percent permitted to be made from other white grapes. Since then, Saint-Émilion, also known as Ugni Blanc, has emerged as the predominant variety because of its high yield of wines that are low in alcohol, about 8 percent, and high in acid. It is this type of wine, thin and unpleasant to drink, that produces the best Cognac. Cognac, by law, may be produced only from white grapes.

production   The grapes are picked, pressed, and allowed to ferment; skins, pips, and all are necessary to give the full character to the brandy.

At the distillery the wine is received in *demi-muids*, large wooden casks of 157-gallon capacity. As the wine producers make wine for both consumption and distillation, there is always the temptation to mix the lees and other deposits from the drinkable wine with the wine to be distilled. The new wine, therefore, passing from the receiving room to the stills, goes through settling basins where gravity draws out the excess impurities. The wine now enters the still. The stills are the old-fashioned pot stills, or alembics; there are no modern patent stills in Cognac.

Distillation begins in a simple boiler, heated directly by a coal or wood fire. On top of the boiler is a metal hood to collect the vapors produced from an initial batch of wine put into the boiler. These vapors travel through a thin, curved tube, which leads them to a preheating chamber, known as the *chauffe-vin*. Remaining in a coiled tube, the hot vapors preheat the wine, placed in the *chauffe-vin*, which is to be distilled. From the *chauffe-vin* this warmed wine now enters the boiler. The vapors, having given up some of their heat in the *chauffe-vin*, give up the rest of their heat in a condensing coil, which is surrounded by cold water. The vapors have now become a liquid, and it trickles out into a receiving pan. All of the metal used in a still of this type is pure copper.

The conversion of the wine into *eau-de-vie de Charente* is accomplished in two operations, the *première chauffe* and the *bonne chauffe*, which are ingeniously connected. In the *première chauffe* the first vapors that are distilled from the boiling wine are the heads, and they are collected separately, to be added back to a subsequent *première chauffe*. The middle distillate, or *brouilli*, is collected for use in the second distillation, known as the *bonne chauffe*. The alcohol content of the *brouilli* is 24 to 32 percent. What remains in the boiler, and what comes off with little alcohol, is called the tails. This, like the heads, is put back into the next *première chauffe* with a new lot of wine.

When enough *brouillis* have been collected, the *bonne chauffe* distillation begins. As before, the first vapors to come off, the heads, are collected separately and added back to the *bonne chauffe*. The middle-range vapors, or heart, will become Cognac. These vapors are condensed at an average of 70 percent alcohol. The remaining distillate, now called seconds, varies in alcoholic

Cognac still room showing the traditional alembics—copper pot stills—used for generations. (*Courtesy Cognac Producers of France, New York*)

strength from 50 percent to no alcohol at all. This is put back in the *bonne chauffe* with additional *brouilli* for further distillation.

Hand regulation of all steps is the key to traditional Cognac production. Most important are uniform procedures, evenness of heating, and precise control of the separation of distillates and the quantities produced. The alembics work continuously, twenty-four hours a day, seven days a week, during the distilling season, which starts in November and lasts from three to eight months, depending on the quantity of the vintage.

With so many different people carrying out this process of distillation, naturally there are many variations, so each shipper examines and tastes the young, new brandy. Sometimes the farmers decide to keep a puncheon or so of brandy, but usually they sell it as soon as it has been distilled. At that time, as with other spirits, it is colorless and has a sharp, but fruity, coppery bouquet and taste. The coppery character, *goût de cuivre*, passes after the brandy has been in wood for a year.

Cognac is aged in casks made of Limousin oak obtained from the forest near Limoges. After the first year the brandy is transferred from new casks to old ones to prevent the brandy from absorbing too much tannin from the wood. The cooperage must be very good to stand up for forty to fifty years. The casks are laid away in light-tight cellars or warehouses.

In the cask the Cognac changes by action of the wood and by contact with the oxygen in the air that enters through the pores of the wood, between the staves, and by the bung. In the same way that the air enters, the brandy evaporates.

There is a continual yearly loss in volume that amounts to 20 percent of the world's annual consumption. As the alcohol evaporates more rapidly than the water and other constituents of the brandy in the humid atmosphere around Cognac, there is a corresponding diminution of strength. It is rapid during the first few years and becomes more gradual after that, the average being about 2 percent a year. This loss of proof is considered essential to the proper development of Cognac. During this time the brandy gradually changes from a colorless state, taking on a beautiful amber tone, and the taste and perfume are changed, so that what finally results is a finished Cognac, a delicate mellow essence with a natural bouquet of grapes.

Today the demand is for a standard of quality that remains the same year in and year out. This requires large stocks being held by the brandy merchant as well as judicious and exact blending.

This *coupage*, or blending, is done many months before bottling. The various brandies are put into tremendous oak vats and are brought down to shipping strength—40 to 43 percent alcohol as required—by the addition of distilled water or diluted brandy. Coloring matter (caramel) is added to ensure uniform color in every bottle. Inside these vats wooden propellerlike paddles rotate from time to time, mixing the brandies. After several months the blend, thoroughly "married," is put in bottles, cased, and is ready for market.

The French government has passed laws to protect the public as to what is and is not Cognac. Every consignment travels with a certificate, called an *Acquit Régional Jaune d'Or*, which guarantees that the product comes from Cognac; it has nothing to do with age.

labeling   The various qualities of Cognacs are often indicated by stars: one, two, or three, in ascending quality. Wine people are superstitious. One of their firmest beliefs is that comet years produce fine wines. The legend is that in the comet year of 1811, when a superb brandy was produced, one of the shippers decided to designate the brandy of that year with a star. An equally excellent brandy was produced in the following year and this he designated by two stars. By this time he had acquired the habit, but fortunately he stopped when he reached five stars. The firm of Hennessy claims to have originated the system. Each house blends its brandies for uniformity of quality, which is maintained year in and year out. The standards represented by the stars vary with the different houses, but since 1946 French law has decreed that a three-star Cognac, the youngest blend on the market, must have spent at least one and a half years in wood. Most Cognacs average two to four years. In order to enter the United States, Cognac must be at least two years old. No age statements are permitted on the labels of Cognacs brought into the United States, so beware of so-called vintage Cognacs, which you may come across on your foreign travels.

Better-quality brandies are sometimes identified by letters to indicate quality. The letters, oddly enough, represent not French words but English, because of the traditional importance of the English market. They represent the following:

C means Cognac	*P* means Pale
E means Extra or Especial	*S* means Superior
F means Fine	*V* means Very
O means Old	*X* means Extra

These words used to appear on the label at the discretion of the producer. Since 1955 certain combinations of letters have had age significance. For instance the letters *VO* or *VSOP* not only mean Very Old or Very Superior Old Pale, respectively, but they also mean, as does the word *Réserve*, that the Cognac has been aged in wood at least four and a half years. In reality, VSOP Cognacs are usually aged seven to ten years.

Since Cognac by and large is a business of brands, many houses have abandoned the stars and letters and identify their various qualities either by proprietary names or by the district of origin.

Some other words producers use to describe their best Cognacs are now also regulated by French law. Extra, Napoléon, and Vieille Réserve require that the Cognac has been in cask for a minimum of $5\frac{1}{2}$ years. The romantic nonsense about the 80- and 104-year-old so-called Napoléon brandies is nothing but a ploy for the unknowing buyer.

Cognac improves in wood for roughly fifty to fifty-five years. The cost of aging the brandy for this length of time is very high, as the losses through evaporation and the risk of aging too long are considerable and make the ultimate selling prices excessive. Once the Cognac is bottled, it neither varies nor improves. A Cognac bottled in 1900 will taste exactly the same today as it did the day it was placed in the glass. Yet the question naturally arises: What is the best age for Cognac? It is at its best between the ages of twenty-five and forty.

From the consumer's point of view there are several other questions that are frequently asked.

What is Fine Champagne? This means that the brandies have been made from grapes grown in either the Grande or Petite Champagne, with at least 50 percent of the grapes coming from the Grande Champagne region. Consequently, a Fine Champagne Cognac should be very good.

What is *Fine de la Maison?* In France every restaurant includes among its list of brandies a *Fine de la Maison*. This is its bar brandy and can be anything the proprietor wishes to buy. More than likely it is not Cognac, but it is usually a sound enough French brandy. It does not mean that it is Fine Champagne Cognac. When you order a *Fine* (pronounced *feen*), all you can expect is brandy of some sort.

As for the oversize snifters, they are not best for the appreciation of Cognac. The large body and relatively small opening are good, but the size requires that too much be put in each glass. The glass should never be larger than one is capable of holding and warming in one hand. By the same token avoid the one-ounce pony or cordial glass. Heating the glass over a flame drives off much of the bouquet prematurely.

The question of bottles is also important. An old bottle means nothing. Distilled spirits do not change in corked bottles. Much better is an old brandy from the wood in a gleaming, newly labeled container. Large magnum bottles are bad. It is true that a bottle of Cognac need not be consumed at one sitting, as a bottle of wine should. However it stands to reason that the larger the bottle, the longer it remains partly full, and the combination of evaporation and oxidation in contact with air in time results in a flat and lifeless drink.

A good test of a fine Cognac is to empty a glass after it has been thoroughly wetted on the inside by the brandy. The glass should retain its delicious aroma for hours, even days.

ARMAGNAC

Second only to Cognac is the Armagnac brandy produced predominantly in the Department of Gers, southeast of Bordeaux in the heart of Gascony. The center of the trade is the city of Condom. There are three subregions: Bas-Armagnac, Haut-Armagnac, and the Ténarèze between them. Armagnac by itself on a label means that the liquid is a blend of brandies from two or three subregions. Brandies exclusively from any subregion are so named on the label, but few appear in the United States.

Only white grapes are permitted in making the wines for distillation into Armagnac. The predominant grape is the Saint-Émilion (Ugni Blanc), which, as in Cognac, is replacing the Folle Blanche in importance. Other varieties permitted are the Colombard, Meslier, Jurançon, and a few others. The hybrid Baco 22A has been planted in the sandier areas of the Bas-Armagnac. Armagnac has less chalk in the soil than Cognac.

A major difference in the systems of distilling Armagnac and Cognac is that in Armagnac the original and redistillation operations are continuous, whereas in Cognac they are two separate batch operations. Another difference lies in the fact that the Armagnac aging casks are made of black oak from the Monlezun Forest, instead of the Limousin oak used in Cognac.

Armagnac is regulated and labeled similarly to Cognac, with the same age requirements for three-star, VSOP, and so on. Age statements may appear on the label. Armagnac is often seen at ten years old.

Some people prefer Armagnac to Cognac for its drier, more pungent smell and surprising smoothness on the palate.

MARC

Brandies distilled from the grape pomace of the wine press are called *eaux-de-vie de Marc* (pronounced *mar*) and are obtained in various parts of France, but notably in Burgundy. They have a strawlike, woody taste and rustic character appreciated by some devotees.

OTHER FRENCH BRANDIES

Substantial quantities of good brandy, not necessarily made from pomace, are distilled in various parts of France, outside the delimited Cognac and Armagnac regions. They are, generally speaking, good, clean, pleasant brandies that do not pretend to have the character or quality of Cognac. Their production is less restricted, and they are less costly.

2. BRANDIES OF OTHER LANDS

AMERICAN BRANDY

Almost all of the beverage brandy distilled in the United States is obtained in California from wines of that state, where production is fifteen million gallons annually. In addition there is now an average annual production of thirty-three million gallons of high-proof brandy, which is used in processing fortified wines and as a base for cordials.

Beverage brandy is produced mainly from Thompson Seedless and Flame Tokay grapes, which possess characteristics especially suitable for brandy. The pot still, such as predominates in Cognac, is found in 20 percent of the brandy distilleries, but the patent, or continuous, still is preferred in California because it yields an extremely clean distillate and at the same time retains the highly desired congeners of the wine when distillation is performed at appropriate proof strength. It is also more efficient and produces a more uniform product.

White oak barrels of fifty-gallon capacity are used for storage and aging, during which time the wood imparts the characteristic oak flavor and a light golden color to the brandy.

Ample stocks of sound, mature American brandy—forty-five million tax gallons—have now been accumulated, despite the fact that the industry was compelled to start from scratch in 1933, and official government records show that consumption of California beverage brandy multiplied more than elevenfold between 1934 and 1974.

California brandy, like Armagnac, is different from Cognac brandy and stands on its own merits.

GERMAN BRANDY

From Germany comes a soft grape brandy with characteristic mellow taste and fine aroma and bouquet. It is blended from especially selected distillates of wines from Germany, as well as from other countries, and is matured in oak. It has a great deal of finesse.

GREEK BRANDY

A great deal of brandy is distilled in Greece and much of it is exported. Greek brandy is becoming more popular. It usually has a clean flavor, with a touch of sweetness from the caramel used to give it color. The most popular Greek brandy in the United States, Metaxa, is technically a liqueur since it has been sweetened just enough to give it wider appeal.

Cyprus is an independent country today, but it cannot separate itself from its Greek heritage. Cypriot brandies are good and very similar to those of Greece.

ISRAELI BRANDY

Good, sound, clean grape and other fruit brandies have been distilled in the Holy Land for many years, but it is only since the State of Israel came into being that any serious efforts have been made to export them. Israeli brandy is always kosher.

ITALIAN BRANDY

Italy produces an excellent, clean grape brandy whose foreign market popularity increases every year. It is a good, all-purpose brandy that has a touch of sweetness. Grappa brandy, like Marc, is distilled from grape pomace. Grappa is usually unaged and sharp in taste, and it has its devoted following.

MEXICAN BRANDY

Brandy was not produced in Mexico in any quantity before 1950, but in the past twenty-five years it has become the national drink, surpassing rum and Tequila. Many brandies are made in the Spanish style, following the Spanish methods of *solera* blending and aging, after local wines have been distilled. Some brandies are produced in pot stills and may have Limousin oak aging, in the French style.

PERUVIAN BRANDY

The brandy of Peru is Pisco, which takes its name from the port in southern Peru whence it is shipped. This brandy is distilled from Muscat wines produced in the Ica Valley, near Pisco. Pisco is matured in clay jars and is consumed in Peru quite young.

Pisco Punch, which is really a sour, is the most popular cocktail in Peru and also in Chile. It is a delightfully pleasant drink.

Muscat brandies are also produced in both Chile and Argentina.

PORTUGUESE BRANDY

Brandy has been distilled in Portugal in commercial quantities ever since Porto wine, as we know it today, was developed. Therefore, brandy-distilling know-how was always there, but very little effort was ever made to develop an export market. During and for some years after World War II, however, large quantities of Portuguese brandy were imported into the United States.

SPANISH BRANDY

Very little Spanish brandy is distilled from sherry wine. Spanish brandies are distilled from wines of other wine regions of Spain, mostly from Valdepeñas. They are developed, aged, and marketed by many sherry shippers. Spanish brandy has a distinctive aroma and flavor and is different from Cognac or Armagnac. It is a sweeter brandy with an earthy character.

This list would not be complete without mentioning that brandy is made in Yugoslavia, South Africa, Australia, and all other wine-producing countries in both hemispheres.

3. FRUIT BRANDIES

The fermented mash of fruits other than grapes is the source of a wide variety of unique brandies. They form three broad categories: brandies made with apples and pears; brandies made with stone fruits, such as cherries, plums, and apricots; and brandies made from berries, such as raspberries, strawberries, blackberries, and elderberries. These brandies come from Switzerland, France, Germany, Hungary, Israel, Yugoslavia, and the United States. Some of these fruits and the brandies they produce are as follows:

FRUIT	BRANDY
Apple	Apple brandy
	Applejack or apple jack
	Calvados
Apricot	Apricot brandy
	Barack Palinka
Blackberry	Blackberry brandy
Cherry	Kirsch
	Kirschwasser
Elderberry	Elderberry brandy
Pear	Pear brandy
	Eau-de-vie de poire
Pineapple	Pineapple brandy
Plum	Slivovitz
	Mirabelle
	Quetsch
	Prunelle
	Pflümli
Raspberry	Framboise
Strawberry	Fraise

APPLE BRANDY

The two principal sources of apple brandy are the United States and France. In the United States it is commonly called applejack, while in France the most famous is called Calvados, from the Department of Calvados in Normandy, center of apple and cider production in France. In France Calvados is also made in other parts of Normandy and in Brittany and Maine.

The production of Calvados begins with the juice of only sound, ripe cider apples. The juice is allowed to ferment for at least a month until no sugar remains, and it is then distilled. The best Calvados, with the appellation

Calvados du Pays d'Auge, is distilled only in pot stills. Patent stills are used to make a brandy with the appellation Reglementée Calvados. An ordinary French apple brandy that has no specific appellation is called *eau-de-vie de cidre.*

The Calvados du Pays d'Auge is double distilled, similar to the way Cognac is made. The first, or low, wines are redistilled to obtain the high wines, or brandy. These spirits are drawn off at around 140 proof and then aged in oak barrels, where they pick up color as they mature. Calvados may be aged up to forty years, when it can acquire the finesse of Cognac. Aged Calvados has a very pronounced apple flavor, and its bouquet combines wood and fruit. It is bottled at 80 to 100 proof.

Applejack is made in a manner similar to Calvados. The legal U.S. minimum age for applejack is two years in wood, but most is aged longer. Applejack is bottled as a straight brandy at 100 proof, or it may be blended with neutral spirits and bottled at 80 proof as a blended applejack. *Applejack* and *apple brandy* are synonymous terms.

PEAR BRANDY

Pear brandy, or *eau-de-vie de poire,* is made in both France and Switzerland. It is distilled from the Williams pear, which is the Bartlett pear of the United States. Pear brandy is unaged and colorless, with a distinct aroma. The production is similar to other colorless fruit brandies.

OTHER FRUIT BRANDIES

After apple brandy the most widely produced fruit brandies are distilled from cherries and plums. All are produced in a similar fashion, except that only some are aged.

Those that are aged in wood and have a golden brown color are the plum brandies of central Europe (Hungary, Romania, Yugoslavia), known as Slivovitz; the apricot brandy of Hungary, called Barack Palinka; and some blackberry brandy, whose color is enhanced by the addition of some dark-colored juice to the matured spirit.

The brandies that are unaged are always colorless and are generally referred to as white alcohols. They include those distilled from a fermented mash of cherries, from varieties of plums, from raspberries, from strawberries, as well as from Williams pears.

The source of the finest Kirschwasser (cherry brandy) is the small black wild cherry from the valley of the Rhine. Because of geopolitics, however, the three best sources are in three different countries: Switzerland, where the Rhine starts on its way to the sea; Alsace, on the French side of the Rhine; and the Black Forest, on the opposite side of the Rhine in Germany. One can always find those who will claim that the Kirschwasser of one of these three sources is superior to the others, but they are all excellent.

Fruit brandies are made in the following manner. The fully ripened fruit is gathered and thoroughly mixed or mashed with wooden paddles in a wooden tub, where it is allowed to ferment—stones and all. After six weeks, when fermentation is complete, the entire contents of the tub are placed in a pot still and distilled twice. A small amount of oil from the stones is distilled over with the spirit. This oil imparts the characteristic bitter almond flavor usually found in good Kirschwasser or Slivovitz.

All of these white brandies are distilled off at a fairly low proof, usually around 100 proof or slightly less. In this way the maximum fruit aroma and flavor are retained. Since this is their most attractive and desired characteristic, they are bottled promptly, without any further reduction, so they will not lose any of their fragrance, or else they are stored in either glass-lined casks or earthenware containers. If aged in plain oak they would take on color, which is not desirable. Slivovitz, however, is preferred with color, so it is matured in wood.

So much fruit is required to obtain these essences that white alcohols are very expensive and luxurious.

HOW AND WHEN TO SERVE BRANDIES

Aside from their medicinal uses, which are well established, all brandies, those obtained from wine in particular, find their primary use as after-dinner drinks. They are most attractive when served neat, although brandy and soda is a pleasant drink after dinner or at any time when a refreshing and relaxing long drink is desired. Since brandy was considered a sort of wine concentrate, it has traditionally been drunk with water also, either mixed into the brandy or on the side. Brandy is also excellent in coffee.

Brandies have many uses in the kitchen. They may be flamed, which leaves a concentration of flavor after the alcohol burns off.

Kirsch, or one of the other white alcohols, is a delightful addition to any fresh fruit cup and as one of the flavorings in the delicious French dish Crêpes au Kirsch. The intensity of the white alcohols makes it possible to impart flavor with very small amounts. They are especially good as flavorings in desserts, puddings, cakes, and ice creams. Unlike other brandies, the white alcohols are most enjoyable when served ice cold.

All brandies, both aged and unaged, may be used in making mixed drinks of all kinds.

When a palate cleanser is called for around the middle of a formal dinner, a small glass of Calvados may be served. This is known as a *Trou Normand* and is said to aid digestion.

20
WHISKIES

After the process of distillation was discovered, it was inevitable that man should use the product closest at hand, easiest to obtain, and least expensive. As a result, where there is an abundance of grain, whisky is distilled.

The word *whisky* comes from the Celtic *uisgebeatha* or *uisgebaugh* (pronounced *whis-geh-BAW*), the Scottish and Irish words, respectively, for "water of life." Whether it was the Scots or the Irish who first used the word or first distilled whisky is a source of never ending argument between them.

the word whisky— its origin

The English found the Celtic word too difficult and too long so they shortened and Anglicized it to *whisky*. The Canadians and the Scottish use the same spelling, without the *e*; the Irish keep the *e*. The United States used to use the *e*; the B.A.T.F. now omits it in the Standards of Identity but permits its use in a traditional context.

SCOTCH WHISKY

In the beginning every Highland laird had his own still, and the spirits he obtained were rough and harsh, with a smoky pungency appreciated only by the Caledonians. The whiskies were distilled freely and their distillers paid no taxes. In 1814 distillation from all stills of less than five hundred gallons' capacity was prohibited in Scotland, and the law almost caused a revolution. The government finally convinced the irate Highlanders that they would be wiser to sell their whisky legally, and within a few years illicit distilling became a rare thing in Scotland. A similar situation prevailed in Ireland at the same time.

Four regions of Scotland produce malt whisky: the Highlands, the Lowlands, Campbeltown, and Islay (pronounced *I-lay*). Each produces a whisky with an individual character.

*making Scotch
malt whisky*

Scotch whisky is obtained primarily from barley, which is grown, prefera-bly, in Scotland, but in recent years barley from California, Canada, India, Africa, and other countries has been imported for distilling purposes.

There are five main stages in making Scotch: malting, mashing, fermenting, distilling, and maturing and blending.

On arrival at the distillery the barley goes into the barley-receiving room, where it is dressed, that is, sieved, or passed over screens so that small and inferior grain will be eliminated, after which the best grain is stored. When required for use, it is placed in tanks, called steeps, where it is soaked in water until thoroughly softened. It is then spread out on the floor of the malting house and sprinkled with warm water for about three weeks, during which time the grain begins to germinate, that is, to sprout.

When the sprouts are about three-quarters of an inch long, the water is turned off and the grain is known as green malt. It is already malt, for malt is germinated grain. During this germination process a chemical change occurs in the grain, as explained on page 289, that is important in its future function of producing whisky. The enzyme amylase, traditionally called diastase in the beverage industry, is produced and has the property of converting the starch into sugars—maltose and dextrin—which are fermentable, whereas the starch in its original state is not.

The green malt is transferred to a kiln, where it rests on a screen directly above a peat° fire. Like green wood, peat gives off a much more acrid and oilier smoke than soft coal. This swirls around the grain, which becomes so impregnated with the aroma of the smoke that it is carried over into the spirit later distilled from it.

The kilning, or drying, process is very important, as it is here that the malt acquires a good part of its character, and a variation occurs here in the various regions. The malt in the Lowlands is kilned less than that in the Highlands, whereas the Campbeltown and Islay grains are more heavily roasted.

The kilned malt is now screened to remove the culm, or dried sprouts, after which it goes to the mill room, where it is ground into meal, or grist.

The next step is mashing. The ground malt is thoroughly mixed with warm water in a mash tun, also referred to as a mash tub, where it soaks until the water has liquefied all of the starches and the diastase has converted them into sugar. When the water has absorbed all of the goodness from the grain, it is drawn off, cooled, and is known as wort.

The wort now passes into the fermenting vats, where a small quantity of carefully cultivated pure yeast is added and fermentation takes place. The yeast acts upon the sugars in the wort in the same manner as the natural yeasts act upon the sugars in grape juice, producing alcohol and carbon dioxide gas.

° Peat is coal in its primary stage and consists of partially carbonized vegetable material, usually found in bogs. Pressed and dried peat is used for fuel.

SCOTLAND

ORKNEY IS.

NORTH SEA

LEWIS

CAITHNESS

ROSS AND CROMARTY

SKYE

NAIRN

MORAY

BANFF

Inverness

Glenlivet

Aberdeen

INVERNESS

ABERDEEN

Spey R.

Balmoral

H I G H L A N D S

Perth

Dundee

FIRTH OF TAY

HIGHLAND LINE

FIRTH OF FORTH

Leith

Edinburgh

Glasgow

Greenock

Clyde R.

ISLAY

KINTYRE

ARRAN

L O W L A N D S

CAMPBELTOWN

ATLANTIC OCEAN

ENGLAND

L.M.

When fermentation is completed, the liquid is known as beer, or wash. To this point the process is identical with that of brewing ales and beers, except for the omission of hops.

The beer now goes into a pot still, which is known as the wash still. The result of the first distillation is a distillate of low alcoholic strength, which is known as low wines. The low wines pass into the spirit pot still where they are redistilled. The first and last part of the distillation (the heads and tails—called the feints) are gathered separately from the middle portion, which is the useful part of the distillation. At the beginning and at the end of the distillation operation too high a percentage of impurities is carried over with the spirit, which, if used, would impair the flavor of the spirit when matured. The feints, however, contain a substantial quantity of useful alcohol and are returned to the spirit still with the next charge of low wines, and the alcohol is distilled out. The impurities are disposed of with the residual slop from the spirit still operation, that is, the waste material that is thrown out.

The useful spirit, distilled off at between 140 and 142 proof, is now known as whisky and flows into a spirit vat from where it is put into casks. These casks, generally made of American white oak, vary in size from the 34-gallon quarter cask to the 132-gallon butt. The different sizes are used for convenience. They may be new or old, and very often they are casks in which sherry has been shipped. More often than not, the casks have been previously used for maturing whisky.

At the time of barreling the whisky is reduced in proof to 124 to 126.8 by the addition of water. According to Dr. P. Schidrowitz, whose notes are quoted by Peter Valaer in his excellent paper on Scotch whisky, "It is held that the best water is that which has its origin as a spring served with water which has passed through a red granite formation, and which, after rising from its source, passes through peaty country. Such waters are generally very soft and possess certain qualities which are apparently due to the peaty soil or heather-clad moor through or over which the water passes on its way to the distillery."

blended Scotch whisky   Until 1853 Scotch whiskies were always straight malt whiskies, but at that time the firm of Andrew Usher & Company, and later other companies, began the practice of blending malt whiskies with grain whiskies. These grain whiskies, produced primarily from corn with a small amount of barley malt, came from distilleries in lower Scotland and were distilled in the patent still. Grain whisky in Scotland is *whisky* and not neutral spirits, as some people believe. The Scotch grain whiskies are distilled out at slightly over 180 proof. They are reduced to 124 proof when barreled in seasoned sherry or Bourbon casks for aging. (See pages 334–36 for a description of how grain whisky is made.)

Before this time the taste for Scotch had been confined to Scotland, but after blending became a general practice, Scotch whisky became popular in

Line-up of modern wash and low-wine spirit copper pot stills, Tormore Distillery at Advie, Grantown-on-Spey, Morayshire, Scottish Highlands. (*Courtesy Long John Distilleries, Ltd., Glasgow*)

England and throughout the rest of the world. Blending grain whiskies with malt whiskies produced a drink that people generally liked.

The blending is done after the whiskies are three to four years old. A master blender examines them and indicates the exact proportions of Highland, Lowland, Campbeltown, and Islay malts of various ages and of grain whisky that are to be married. This is accomplished by placing the whiskies in a large vat where they are thoroughly mixed both by rotating paddles and by compressed air blown up from the bottom. The whisky is then returned to the sherry or Bourbon casks for a further period of maturing (marrying) before bottling or shipping in bulk.

The usual Scotch blend contains 20 to 50 percent malt whisky, the balance being grain whisky. The original object of using grain whiskies, which are always distilled in patent stills, was to reduce the cost, but in doing so a lighter whisky was produced that appealed much more to the other peoples of the world than had the fuller, smokier Scotch whiskies previously made.

The essential difference between blends is the proportions used of the four types of malts. Of these the Highland malts are considered the finest and are always the most costly. They are fairly light in body and flavor and do not have too much smoke. The finest Highland section is Banffshire, and within it the Glen Livet and Speyside regions are considered the best. Next in importance is Moray. Lowland malts are also light in body, but not as smoky in flavor. Almost all of the grain whisky distilleries are in the Lowlands. Campbeltown malts are very full in body and quite smoky. The Islay malts are also very full, smoky, and pungent.

In the last analysis, the reasons for blending are to obtain a smoother, more balanced product than any of the blend's single components and to ensure uniform continuity of a given brand. In this way the consumer can expect the same character, flavor, taste, and quality year in and year out. A Scotch whisky blend can very easily be the result of a marriage of as many as thirty or forty malt whiskies, together with five or more grain whiskies.

The ages of the individual whiskies at the time of blending may vary widely, since no single whisky is employed before it has reached its proper maturity. The number of years required for this is governed by the character of the whisky itself and the climatic conditions under which it is matured. The fuller-bodied malts of Islay and Campbeltown take much longer, sometimes ten to twelve years, while the Highland and Lowland malts may be ready in six to eight years, and the grain whiskies may require only four years. The greater the climatic dampness, the slower the aging process.

The secret of fine Scotch whisky, therefore, lies in the art of the blender. On his unique ability depend the polish, smoothness, and uniformity of the whisky. There are 130 distilleries in Scotland (95 Highland malt, 11 Lowland malt, 8 Islay malt, 2 Campbeltown malt, and 14 grain whisky distilleries) producing whiskies that make up into over 4,000 brands or blends. As we have already indicated, there are many reasons why Scotch whisky from one area differs from Scotches of other areas. Local conditions, such as water, peat, and climate, and traditional distilling practices of individual distilleries are all contributing factors. But to understand fully the Scotch picture, it is important to remember that there are many distilleries, each one turning out a whisky that has its own individual characteristics. By combining the full-flavored malt whiskies with gentler grain whiskies, the blenders obtain the individuality of character and quality that distinguishes their brands. Blends may also be tailored to producers' interpretations of consumer preferences, even to having different blends produced for various countries under the same label. The United States is Scotland's best customer, consuming nearly half of all the Scotch whisky sold each year. Consequently the Scotch whisky blender tries to supply what appeals most to his very important American customer.

light Scotch whisky   There has been an unquestioned trend in the United States toward lightness of flavor and body in most of the beverages Americans consume. An indication of this is the doubling in ten years (1965 to 1975) of the share of the market in the United States held by "white goods" (gin, vodka, rum, and Tequila).

Those brands of Scotch whisky that have been blended for lightness by judicious selection of light-bodied, lighter-flavored malts are among the largest-selling brands in the United States. The American public has come to associate paleness or lack of color with lightness and dryness. This is nonsense, of course, since the depth of color in a Scotch whisky as shipped is governed by the amount of caramel (burned sugar) that is used in all blends to ensure color uniformity.

all-malt whisky

Even though more than 99 percent of the Scotch whisky consumed outside Scotland is blended whisky as described previously, there are also marketed in small quantities straight, unblended Highland malt whiskies, as well as blends of only malt whiskies, in which no grain whisky has been used. Such whiskies are much fuller bodied and usually are of very fine quality.

liqueur Scotch

A liqueur Scotch whisky is one that, through proper aging and blending, has acquired a mellow softness both in the bouquet and on the palate. The word *liqueur,* when used with Scotch whisky, applies to older, finer whiskies, particularly the premium brands, and should not be confused with a sweetened cordial or liqueur. These whiskies are rare and expensive.

age in Scotch whisky

The high regard for age statements in the United States may frequently lead us astray. A Scotch whisky with a ten-year-old age statement on the label is not necessarily a better whisky than one with no age statement at all. Naturally aging is important in making a Scotch (or any other whisky) mellow and more palatable, but the quality of the whisky and the skill of the blender's hand must be there first. Some fully aged Scotch is laid away in casks, after it has been blended, for marrying for periods of up to one year. The law stipulates an aging period of at least three years for Scotch whisky, and none can enter the United States under four years of age. Practically all Scotch malts remain in their casks for a minimum of five years. Blends with higher percentages of malt whiskies are usually aged longer than those with more grain whiskies.

Scotland versus U.S. bottled

The duty and Internal Revenue tax on imported distilled spirits is levied on a wine- or tax-gallon basis instead of on a proof-gallon basis, as is the case for domestically produced spirits. This means that a case of imported 86-proof Scotch whisky containing 2.4 liquid gallons is subject to the same duty and tax as it would be if imported at 100 proof. If this same whisky is imported in bulk at 100 proof or higher, the duty and tax are calculated on the proof gallons, that is, the equivalent wine gallons at 100 proof. When it is reduced to 86 proof with distilled or deionized water, this represents a 14 percent duty and tax saving. If this lower tax cost is passed along to the consumer, it represents a substantial price advantage over the bottled-in-Scotland whisky. There are also savings in freight and handling. Even though there is a difference in costs, there is no difference in flavor of whisky bottled in Scotland or in the United States. Distilled or deionized water is used universally to bring whisky down to bottling proof.

Competition for the market being what it is, and as long as the excise tax remains at the high rate of $10.50 per proof gallon, more and more Scotch whisky and other spirits will be imported in bulk for bottling in the United States. In 1975 bulk imports accounted for 41 percent of all Scotch imports.

IRISH WHISKEY

There is a common belief that Irish whiskey is a potato whiskey. This is not true at all. No doubt the misconception stems from the fact that the Irish refer to illicitly distilled whiskey as *poteen,* a term derived from the pot still in which it has traditionally been distilled.

Whiskey in Ireland is distilled from a fermented mash of grains, namely, malted barley, unmalted barley, corn, rye, wheat, and oats.

The barley malt is dried in a kiln that has a solid floor. Even when peat was used as a fuel the smoke could not come in contact with the malt. Now peat has been replaced by smokeless anthracite, and the malt is not smoke cured, as is the case in Scotland.

Much Irish whiskey is distilled in the pot still. There are three distinct distilling operations. The wash is first distilled in a large wash still, yielding the low wines. These low wines are then distilled in a smaller pot still, producing strong and weak feints, which are collected separately. Thus far the process is similar to the distillation of Scotch malt whisky. The distillation of Irish whiskey differs from Scotch whisky, however, in that a third pot still is used to obtain the final whiskey from the distillation of the strongest feints. That is why Irish whiskey is said to be triple distilled.

Some houses distill grain whiskey in column, or patent, stills. These are blended with pot-still whiskies to produce lighter-bodied and lighter-flavored whiskies, mostly for export.

Irish whiskies must be aged in seasoned cooperage for at least four years, but usually they are aged seven to eight years before being shipped.

Irish is a particularly smooth whiskey, with medium body and a clean, unique flavor. It is consumed in the same manner as Scotch whisky and also is popularly used in Irish Coffee.

AMERICAN WHISKY

history   Early American settlers brought spirituous liquors with them, as they were considered essential in withstanding the hardships of an ocean voyage and a

Average proportions of grain used in producing Bourbon. In practice, proportions vary with the distiller's formula. LEFT TO RIGHT: Corn, 51 to 88 percent; rye, 2 to 37 percent; barley malt, approximately 10 percent. The bins in the rear contain the grains shown in the glass. (*Courtesy Bourbon Institute, New York*)

medicine in cases of illness in the new, savage land. For a long time spirits had to be imported from Europe.

The first commercially distilled spirit in what is the present-day United States was New England rum. Distilling whisky on a commercial scale began over a century later.

There is a record of distilling on Staten Island in New York in 1640, but it was not until the early eighteenth century that whisky distilling began to develop. The grains used along the eastern seaboard were rye and barley. As the settlements began extending westward, however, it became apparent that transporting newly grown grain back to the populous seaboard cities was difficult for the settlers, particularly those in western Pennsylvania. They found it was simpler to distill their grain, both rye and corn, into whisky. It not only kept longer, but it was easier to transport to the cities. Whisky and furs, indeed, became the best means of exchange, particularly during the Revolutionary War, when Continental currency was worth less than five cents on the dollar.

Whisky played a prominent part in our early history, in determining our right and ability to be a self-governed nation. Whisky had always been distilled in small, family-owned distilleries without legal interference from any government. In 1791, not long after George Washington became president, money being a crying need for the new nation, an excise tax was levied on whisky.

The independent Pennsylvania distillers resented the tax on their product, and the tax collectors in some cases were even tarred and feathered. There were riots and stormy scenes in these "western" communities, and President

Washington, in great haste, sent a force of militia to quell the insurrection. It was done without bloodshed and accomplished its object. While in itself the insurrection was of minor importance, it was of tremendous significance to the future of the federal government and is still known as the Whiskey Rebellion.

Many of the disgruntled Dutch, Scottish, and Irish farmer-distillers decided to move out of reach of the tax collector, which meant going farther west into Indian territory. They found the proper water for distilling in southern Indiana and Kentucky.

The first whisky distilled in Kentucky is generally attributed to the Reverend Elijah Craig at Georgetown, in Bourbon County. The grain he employed was corn (maize), as it was more plentiful than rye. His product became known as Bourbon County whisky, and the name Bourbon has remained as the designation of whiskies distilled from a corn mash.

The important whisky-distilling areas in the United States are not located where they are by pure chance but because of the most important factor in making whisky—the quality of the water. It comes from springs that pass up through layer on layer of limestone rock. The limestone mantle runs along western Pennsylvania and cuts across southern Indiana over into Kentucky. There is another isolated limestone region in Maryland around Baltimore.

With the advancement of science and the development of inexpensive water technology the distiller has been freed from the necessity of locating his

Flow diagram showing entire modern grain distillery operation from the arrival of the grain to the barreling of whisky and grain neutral spirits and the processing of the spent grain into various types of fodder. (*Courtesy Joseph E. Seagram & Sons, Inc., New York*)

DISTILLERY OPERATIONS / FLOW DIAGRAM

production at or near these limestone mantle outcroppings. Today he can and does distill whisky in many other parts of the United States.

The early distillers used very crude and primitive equipment. Fermentation was carried on in open mash tubs, the yeast being the wild varieties the air afforded. Since that day tremendous changes have taken place. *grain whisky production*

Briefly the steps in making whisky are as follows:

1. Upon arrival at the distillery the grain is carefully inspected and cleaned of all dust.

2. It is ground in the gristmill to a meal.

3. The meal is first cooked to release starch from its tough cellular coating, then malt is added to convert the starches.

4. Pure cultured yeast is propagated in increasingly large containers—a flask in the laboratory, a dona tub in the yeast room, the yeast tub in the distillery.

5. The cooled wort is yeasted with the propagated yeast and goes to the fermenting vats to become beer.

6. The beer goes into a patent, or double-column, still. The result is whisky, which is distilled out at below 160 proof. It is then reduced in proof to 100 to 125 by adding deionized (demineralized) water.

All new whisky (except corn whisky and light whisky) is placed in *new* charred white oak barrels to mature in a bonded warehouse, where it must remain under Treasury Department control until the Internal Revenue tax has been determined. The time limit had been eight years and was later extended to twenty years. A whisky or any other distilled spirit still in bond after twenty years is then subject to payment of the Internal Revenue tax, whether it can be sold or not.

proof changes through aging

Spirits are generally matured in porous containers so the air can seep in to oxidize and mellow the alcohol. The most common container is made of wood (generally oak). Wood is a porous substance, and when liquid is stored in a wooden barrel, even though it be tightly closed, some of it seeps through, that is, evaporates or escapes through the pores of the wood.

Aged spirits, such as brandy, rum, and Scotch whisky, are barreled for aging at proofs varying from 124 to 150 proof. These spirits lose some alcoholic strength as they mature because they are stored under humid conditions.

American whiskies, on the other hand, are barreled at 100 to 125 proof (50 to $62\frac{1}{2}$ percent alcohol), and as they mature their alcoholic strength increases because of the warm, dry conditions under which they are stored.

To illustrate this point, after four years of aging a fifty-gallon barrel of new whisky at 100 proof (twenty-five gallons of alcohol and twenty-five gallons of water) has lost ten gallons of liquid, but the alcoholic strength is 110 proof. This means that 55 percent of the forty gallons remaining is alcohol (twenty-two gallons) and the remaining eighteen gallons are water.

Newly distilled Bourbon (LEFT) and samples at one, two, four, six, and eight years of age. Note how Bourbon whisky picks up color year by year as it matures in new charred oak barrels. Evaporation also takes place, reducing the amount of whisky in a 50-gallon barrel by as much as $1\frac{1}{2}$ gallons per year. (*Photograph by Marty Cobin, courtesy Joseph E. Seagram & Sons, Inc., New York*)

NEW   1   2   4   6   8

No one knows exactly how the advantage of charring barrels was learned. *origin of* One legend is that as a result of a fire in a warehouse in Jamaica some barrels of *charring* rum were heavily charred. After some time it was learned that the rum in the *barrels* charred barrels had acquired both color and quality it had lacked before.

Another explanation is that in order to bend the barrel staves into the proper shape for the barrel, the early Kentuckians heated them before an open fire, and often they became charred. Discovering that the more charred the staves the more palatable the whisky, charring became an accepted practice. Kentuckians were also said to have burned out the inside of used barrels so that the whisky would not pick up off-flavors. It is likely that none of these stories is true, as it is probable that the virtues of charring the barrels in which whisky was to be stored were stumbled upon quite by accident. Staves average one inch in thickness, and one-eighth-inch depth of char is most common.

There are two yeasting processes used in America—the sweet-mash, or *sweet and* yeast-mash process, and the sour-mash, or yeasting-back process. The sour- *sour mash* mash process is used primarily in making Bourbon whisky.

A sweet mash is produced by adding all or almost all freshly developed yeast to the mash, that is, little or no spent beer from a previous fermentation is mixed with the fresh mash. It is allowed to ferment from thirty-six to fifty hours and the fermenter can be, and usually is, refilled almost immediately upon becoming empty.

A sour mash is produced by adding at least one-quarter of the volume of the fermenter of spent beer (working yeast) from a previous fermentation to the fresh mash and fresh yeast. The mash is allowed to ferment from seventy-two to ninety-six hours. Fermentation generally takes place in open fermenting vats at low temperatures. When emptied, the fermenters are sterilized, aerated, and allowed to "sweeten" for twenty-four hours before being used again.

Sour mash offers a favorable pH for yeast growth and inhibits bacterial contamination. Sweet mash is more difficult to control and must be done above 80 degrees Fahrenheit to end quickly and avoid contamination.

There are three main categories of whiskies produced in America: straights, blends, and light whiskies. Each one has several subcategories. Because these products are often blended together, a whisky may appear in more than one category.

A straight whisky, under federal regulations, is one that has been distilled *straight whisky* off at a proof not exceeding 160, aged in new, charred white oak barrels for at least two years, and reduced by the addition of water at the time of bottling to no lower than 80 proof, from a minimum of 51 percent of a grain. Nothing may be added other than the water. Straights include Bourbon, Tennessee, rye, corn, and wheat whiskies.

The higher the proof at which a spirit is distilled out, the lighter it will be in character, flavor, and body. This is because more and more of the congeners (flavor and body components) are eliminated as the proof of the spirit is increased.

Under U.S. regulations the theoretical critical point is reached at 190 proof (95 percent alcohol). Any spirit distilled out at 190 proof or higher is called a neutral spirit and should not possess any noticeable aroma, flavor, or character. Conversely, the lower the proof of distillation the greater the amount of congeners that will be distilled over and become a part of the distillate to give character, aroma, flavor, and body. Since straight whisky by regulation cannot be distilled out at a strength exceeding 160 proof, it possesses very definite aroma, flavor, and body characteristics when suitably aged in wood.

The predominant grain used in the mash formula determines the final designation under which the whisky is labeled and marketed. If 51 percent or more of the grain is corn, it is straight Bourbon; 51 percent or more rye grain makes it a straight rye; 51 percent wheat, straight wheat whisky; 51 percent barley malt or rye malt, straight malt whisky or straight rye malt whisky; 80 percent or more corn, aged in uncharred oak barrels or reused charred oak barrels, is designated straight corn whisky.

Tennessee whisky is a straight whisky that must be distilled in Tennessee from a fermented mash containing 51 percent or more of any grain, usually corn.

Barrels of Ancient Age Bourbon whisky aging in a modern temperature- and humidity-controlled warehouse at Frankfort, Kentucky. In the background the operator is ricking a barrel. (*Courtesy Schenley Industries, Inc., New York*)

Straight whiskies may be mixed, provided the mixture is made up of whiskies of the same distilling period and from the same distillery. Such whiskies do not lose their straight whisky designation.

Straight whiskies of different distilling periods and from different distilleries may also be mixed or blended, but they must be labeled blended Bourbon whisky, blended rye whisky, and so on. When straight whiskies that are homogeneous are mixed, the mixture carries the age of the youngest whisky it contains. Most straight whiskies on the market greatly exceed the minimum age requirement because each distiller attempts to age his product until he feels his whisky has reached the ripeness or maturity that is ideal for that particular whisky. Most authorities agree that the average Bourbon attains this stage in about six years, but this varies with the flavor intensity of the initial distillate.

A little more than half of the American-distilled whisky consumed in the United States is straight whisky or blends of straight whiskies, either of which may be bottled in bond.

The term *bottled in bond* is generally misunderstood, not only by the public but too often by people in the retail liquor trade itself. The term is *not* a guarantee of quality; it refers only to the Internal Revenue tax. Only straight whiskies are bottled in bond.

bottled in bond

The Bottled in Bond Act of 1894 permitted distillers to bottle whisky (or other distilled spirits) without paying the excise taxes, provided the whisky was at least four years old, distilled at one plant by the same proprietor, and bottled at 100 proof, under the supervision of the U.S. Treasury Department. After bottling, the whisky remains in the bonded warehouse until the distiller is ready to sell it, at which time the tax must be paid or determined, before withdrawing the whisky from bond.

Other distilled spirits may also be bottled in bond provided they meet the specifications of the Bottled in Bond Act of 1894: namely, that they have been distilled out below 160 proof, are straight, are four or more years old, and are bottled at 100 proof. Examples are rum, grape brandy, apple brandy, and gin.

If the distiller wishes to bottle his whisky before it is four years old, he must pay or determine the taxes and withdraw the whisky to his free bottling premises.

"The Bottled-in-Bond stamp," reads the Treasury Department's Decision No. 1299, "is no guarantee as to purity or quality of the spirits, and the government assumes no responsibility with respect to claims by dealers in this connection in advertising Bottled-in-Bond spirits." Since all straight whiskies are now matured in bonded warehouses for up to twenty years, consumer interest in the Bottled in Bond label has decreased.

blended whisky　　Nearly half of the American-produced whisky consumed in the United States is blended whisky. The blender devotes his art to mixing carefully selected, full-bodied, straight whiskies with grain spirits and/or light whiskies to produce a lighter, more harmoniously balanced whole and to duplicate, day in and day out, an identical, uniform product. The straight whiskies contribute aroma, flavor, and body, while the grain spirits and/or light whiskies give the final product lightness and smoothness without sacrificing character.

To be a blended whisky, at least 20 percent of the blend must be straight whisky. The balance may be grain neutral spirits, grain spirits, and/or light whiskies. Grain neutral spirits are spirits that are distilled out at over 190 proof and have no recognizable aroma or flavor. Grain spirits are neutral spirits that have been aged in reused oak barrels to give them a delicate flavor and soft mellowness. It is important that the barrel be compatible with the flavor intensity of the grain neutral spirits, since the woody character of a new barrel would overwhelm the light flavor of the grain neutral spirits. Light whiskies, the newest category, have become an important component for the blender.

Regulations also permit the use of certain blending materials in blended whiskies, up to $2\frac{1}{2}$ percent by volume. Those most often employed are sherry wine (a special heavy blending sherry made from the Pedro Ximenez grape) and prune or peach juice.

There is an unending discussion as to the merits and demerits of blended whisky in comparison to straight whisky. Both usually are fine, very drinkable products. The one you enjoy more—the one that pleases your palate—is the one you should choose. It is absurd to consider one inferior to the other; they are simply different. The straight whisky is full bodied and full flavored, while the blended whisky is comparatively light bodied and light in flavor.

Curiously, many people in the northeastern states refer to blended whisky as rye. It is not. While this is probably the result of the long tradition of using a great deal of rye in making whisky in that area, true rye whisky contains at least 51 percent of that grain and has a pronounced rye flavor. If someone unknowingly gets a true rye whisky, the strong flavor and full body may shock his palate.

light whisky　　Light whisky is whisky that has been distilled in the United States at more than 160 proof and less than 190 proof and stored in used or uncharred new oak containers. This whisky is permitted to be entered for storage at proofs higher than 125. The B.A.T.F. adopted this standard of identity on January 26, 1968, and it became effective on July 1, 1972.

The primary purpose for this category was to permit the production of light distillates that could be aged in seasoned oak casks—that is, reused cooperage—which are more compatible in developing the lower flavor intensities found in this type of whisky.

One of the newest and most modern distilleries in the nation, at Lawrenceburg, Indiana, showing the towering distilling columns and the complex control panel by which precise temperatures and distilling proofs can be maintained scientifically. (*Courtesy Schenley Distillers, Inc., New York*)

In general, the techniques used in the production of straight whisky and grain neutral spirits are followed in making light whisky. The proportions and types of cereal grains used in the formula are left entirely to the discretion of the distiller, but most distillers use corn (up to 90 percent) as the major portion of their formula. The main emphasis in this process is on distillation techniques. The higher proof requirements permit the use of more sophisticated distillation systems, such as those used in distilling grain spirits. The distiller also has a wide range of proofs in which to work. At 161 proof the whisky is still flavorful; at 189 proof it is extremely light in flavor and character. At almost every level of proof in between, a changing relative amount of flavor components is left in the distillate to affect the body, flavor, and character of the whisky. The distiller can distill his light whisky out at any of these proofs and achieve different weights of flavor. He can mix different batches of different proofs for his final product.

Typical distillery tasting room at Lawrenceburg, Indiana, where tasters evaluate samples. (*Courtesy Schenley Distillers, Inc., New York*)

The age of light whisky as it is withdrawn for bottling affects its final character. As with America's straight whiskies and imported whiskies, a major factor in the character of the light whisky brands is their maturity or approach to perfection when bottled. As stocks of light whiskies continue to mature, age labels may play an increasingly important role in the market. Federal regulations provide that when the whiskies are less than four years old, a back label must identify them by volume and age; otherwise the back label is optional.

Light whisky is available in three ways:

1. As light whisky, in the bottle as distilled and reduced in proof, and including mixtures of these distillates.

2. As blended light whisky, a mixture of less than 20 percent straight whisky at 100 proof with light whisky.

3. In the traditional blended whisky, with the light whisky portion unidentified in a mixture with 20 percent or more straight whisky at 100 proof.

For more precise information about these whiskies, refer to the Standards of Identity for distilled spirits in Appendix P.

CANADIAN WHISKY

According to U.S. federal regulations, "Canadian whisky is a distinctive product of Canada, manufactured in Canada in compliance with laws of the Dominion of Canada . . . containing no distilled spirits less than three years old . . . such whisky is blended Canadian whisky. Canadian whisky shall not be designated as straight."

According to Canadian law, Canadian whisky must be produced from cereal grain only. While the Canadian Excise Tax Bureau exercises the customary controls to ensure proper collection of the tax, the government sets no other limitation as to grain formulas, distilling proofs, or special type of aging cooperage. It believes the distillers are better judges than the government of what the public, both at home and abroad, wants in a Canadian whisky.

Many people believe Canadian whisky is a rye whisky. Corn, rye, wheat, and barley malt are the grains generally used. The proportions of each in the grain formulas are the trade secret of each individual distiller.

The methods of production are similar but the procedures of maturing differ somewhat from U.S. standards and practices. For example, any loss from evaporation may be made up by adding new whisky to replace the amount lost.

Canadian whisky may be bottled in bond when it is three years old, and it can be bottled at 90 proof. However, practically all Canadian whisky is six years old or older when it is marketed. If it is less than four years old, its age must be listed on the label.

The distillers have developed a whisky with a delicate flavor and light body. They obtain these characteristics with mash formulas designed to produce lightness and delicacy and by distilling out at varying strengths, ranging from 140 to 180 proof.

JAPANESE WHISKY

The Japanese wine and spirits industry is an old one, going back into antiquity. However, until relatively recent times (about 1870) it was in large part devoted to such traditional beverages as saké, Umeshu (a Japanese plum wine made by infusion), and Umechu (a Japanese medicinal wine). With the advent of Westernizing influences in Japan, distillation was also introduced. Since then products such as Japanese whisky, liqueurs, brandies, and Sochu (a neutral spirit made from grain or sweet potatoes) have become part of the Japanese culture.

Although historically much of the technique of distillation was learned from the West, especially Scotland and France, the Japanese adapted the methods to their own economy. For example, their whisky is primarily a blended whisky made up of varying percentages of fuller-bodied whiskies produced in pot stills and lighter-bodied whiskies produced by continuous distillation using column stills, many of which were adapted from French designs. While the original Japanese whiskies were an attempt to duplicate Scotch whisky, the grains employed in these whiskies were different from those used in Scotland. Japan now produces a whisky different from any currently made in the United States and from any of the other imported whiskies entering the United States.

Many of the fuller-bodied whiskies are made from malted barley, some small portion of which is cured over peat. Most of the whisky used in blended Japanese whisky is made from millet, corn, Indian corn, some small quantities of rice, and other grains in varying proportions in their mash bill (formula). Wheat and rye are seldom used. The milling and fermentation procedure is similar to that of the Western methods. The saccharification method differs, however, in that most of the lighter whisky uses the Japanese *koji* enzyme, an enzyme similar to that used in making saké (see page 302) to convert the starch to sugar.

The proofs of the whiskies, when removed from the stills, vary from about 130 proof for the fuller-bodied whiskies to about 180 proof for the lighter-bodied whiskies. The whiskies are aged separately in used charred oak barrels before blending. Blending, the subsequent marrying period, and further aging last from months to years, depending on the quality of the whisky. The laws of Japan define various classes of whisky primarily for Japanese tax purposes and regulate the aging and handling of whisky.

OTHER WHISKIES

Whisky types are also produced in Holland, Germany, Denmark, and Australia. In Australia the Scotch method—first producing malt whisky and then a blend of malts and grains—is followed. Although made on the Scotch pattern, Australian whisky has a distinctive character.

TASTE OF WHISKIES

The principal taste distinction of Scotch whisky is its smoky peat flavor, whereas Irish whiskey has a similar barley-malt whisky character without the smoky flavor. Both are somewhat lighter in body than American straight whiskies because high proof, very light-bodied grain whiskies are used for blending. Also, because Scotch and Irish whiskies are matured in old, previously used cooperage they require a longer aging period. This is usually seven to eight years, and up to twelve for the heavier distillates, which require more time to smooth out.

Rye and Bourbon whiskies have the distinctive tastes and characters of the rye and corn grains used. Because of the different methods of mashing and the lower proofs at which they are distilled out, which give them a higher congeneric content, they are both sweeter and fuller bodied than Scotch or Irish. Furthermore, aging in new charred oak cooperage makes it possible for the American whiskies to reach maturity sooner.

HOW AND WHEN TO SERVE WHISKIES

Aside from their most common use as a straight drink or on the rocks, whiskies may be used in innumerable cocktails, punches, and other mixed drinks. They are also very popular in long drinks, such as highballs and coolers (see Chapter 26).

21
VODKAS

When this book first appeared in 1940, only half a page was devoted to vodka. In the short space of four decades this most neutral of spirits has risen from its "also ran" listing among the "other spirits" to a degree of popularity that has made it the largest-selling individual type of spirits in the United States, replacing Bourbon and blended whisky. It was not until 1950 that vodka was separately reported in trade statistics. In 1955 it represented only 3.4 percent of the total distilled spirits market, and by 1976 it had risen to 20.4 percent.

history   The word *vodka* is a diminutive of the Russian word for "water," *voda,* and it was the Russians who originated this particular "water of life." In Russia, Finland, Czechoslovakia, Poland, and elsewhere in northern and eastern Europe, spirits have long been distilled to a very high proof, resulting in a minimum of flavor.

According to many historians vodka was first produced in Russia in the fourteenth century. The vast Smirnoff distilleries in Moscow, dating from 1818, passed out of the family's control with the 1917 revolution. The formula was brought to America in the 1930s via Paris, and Smirnoff was the first and only American-made vodka for many years. It alone can be given credit for generating a new fashion of drinking in the United States.

how vodka   Vodka has always been distilled from the most plentiful and least expensive
is made   materials available to the distiller, wherever he might be. Vodka is made from potatoes and various grains, principally corn, with some wheat added. The best export vodkas, and all those produced in the United States, are made from grain.

Vodka, like whisky, is an alcoholic distillate from a fermented mash. Whisky, however, is distilled at low proof to retain flavor. Vodka is distilled at high proof and then processed still further, if required, to extract all congeners.

346

In a sense vodka is like gin, but with one big difference. Both are made from neutral spirits; neither has to be aged. But in making American gin, as will be described in Chapter 22, the neutral spirits are delicately flavored with juniper and aromatics. In making vodka nothing is added to the neutral spirits; instead all character is absent, leaving the spirits colorless and without distinctive odor or taste.

Vodka is made neutral by either of two processes. In the first, neutral spirits flow continuously through tanks containing no less than one and a half pounds of vegetable charcoal for each gallon of spirits, so that the spirits are in intimate contact with the charcoal for a minimum of eight hours. At least 10 percent of the charcoal is replaced after each forty hours of operation. In the second method spirits are agitated for a minimum of eight hours in contact with no less than six pounds of new vegetable charcoal for every one hundred gallons of spirits. Vodka can also be made by purifying or refining the spirits by any other method that the government finds will result in a product without distinctive character, aroma, or taste. American vodka is bottled at proofs ranging from 80 to 100, the majority of sales being at the lower figure. (See Appendix P for the U.S. Standards of Identity for vodka.)

Inspecting activated charcoal used for filtering vodka. (*Courtesy Ste. Pierre Smirnoff Fls., Hartford, Connecticut*)

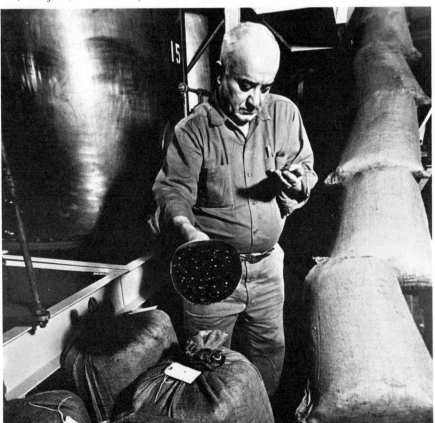

IMPORTED VODKAS

The most significant and prestigious imported vodkas are those from the original Russian, Finnish, and Polish sources. With vodka's increasing popularity, however, an increased flow has come from England, France, Holland, Czechoslovakia, and China, and there is a kosher vodka from Israel.

FLAVORED VODKAS

Flavored varieties of vodka are popular, particularly in Poland and Russia, where infusions and mixtures with herbs, grasses, leaves, spices, and seeds are involved. Some of these vodkas are colored and, as vodka-based liqueurs, are sweetened and fruit flavored. The most common of the flavored vodkas, which range from 70 proof up, are:

ZUBROWKA. Flavored with a type of grass found only in the forests of eastern Poland. These grasslands are the breeding grounds for a particular species of bison indigenous to Poland, and the zubrowka ("bison grass vodka") has a slightly yellowish tinge and an aromatic bouquet. Exceptionally soft and smooth, it is normally served ice cold and drunk straight.

STÁRKA ("old"). Vodka aged for about ten years in special oak casks previously used for fine-quality wines. This maturing imparts an amber color and flavor to Stárka, which is a vodka for brandy lovers.

YUBILEYNEYA OSOBAYA ("jubilee vodka"). Contains brandy, honey, and other ingredients.

PERTSOVKA. A dark brown Russian pepper vodka with a pleasant aroma and burning taste. It is prepared from an infusion of capsicum, cayenne, and cubeb. History records that Czar Peter the Great seasoned his vodka with pepper, and numerous Russians apparently continue to enjoy its sharp bite.

OKHOTNICHYA ("hunter's vodka"). A spirit flavored with many herbs; has a scent that suggests heather honey.

Russian vodka makers produce about thirty other vodkas with a wide range of flavors, some of which are available in the United States.

Fruit-flavored vodka is made in the United States. There are orange, lemon, cherry, and other fruit flavors. American flavored vodka is a product of rectification and pays the $0.30-per-gallon rectification tax.

HOW AND WHEN TO SERVE VODKA

In the middle of the twentieth century general consumption of vodka was confined almost entirely to Russia, Poland, and the Baltic states. Vodka has been produced in the United States since 1933, but until 1948 it was an exotic specialty consumed by a few people of eastern European origin. It was drunk straight, ice cold, in a small, one-ounce glass, at one gulp, and almost always with a sharp-tasting appetizer. Drinking vodka in this way, however, did not have much appeal for Americans, and it would have remained little known except for an accident of chance—an accident that had nothing to do with vodka.

After World War II a Hollywood restaurant owner found himself with a large and unsalable stock of ginger beer. Realizing that he had to find a new use for it or take a heavy loss, he tried mixing it with any number of products without success, until he used vodka. He added half a lime, served it in a copper mug, and named it the Moscow Mule. The Mule caught on, and other distillers made vodka and created new drinks. From Hollywood the vodka fashion swept across the country.

Because it has no flavor of its own, vodka was quickly recognized as the most versatile of all mixers. It combines exceedingly well with fruit juices and flavors of all types. This fact, perhaps more than any other, accounts for the remarkable growth of vodka's popularity. The Screwdriver (vodka and orange juice) was one of the earliest drinks specially created. The most significant vodka drink, which has become part of the American scene, is the Bloody Mary (vodka and tomato juice). Vodka and Tonic is also enormously popular, and vodka is substituted freely for gin in the Martini and other drinks.

America has also begun to enjoy vodka straight—chilled in the refrigerator or freezer—particularly with spicy appetizers, smoked salmon, and caviar. Vodka is often served on the rocks.

22
GINS

Gin is one of the few liquors in whose production man plays a more important part than nature. In the wines and spirits studied so far, we have seen that natural forces age and develop the liquor. But here man has manufactured the whole product. Gin did not happen by chance; it was created quite intentionally for a specific purpose. Credit for this belongs to Franciscus de la Boe (1614–1672), also known as Doctor Sylvius, a seventeenth-century physician and professor of medicine at Holland's famed University of Leyden.

Doctor Sylvius was not thinking of a beverage spirit, much less a Dry Martini. His objective was medicinal in the purest sense. Knowing the diuretic properties of the oil of the juniper berry (*Juniperus communis*), he felt that by redistilling a pure alcohol with the juniper berry he could obtain its therapeutic oil in a form that would provide an inexpensive medicine. And he succeeded. Within a few years all Holland found itself suffering from ills that could be cured only by Dr. Sylvius's medicine. He named it Genièvre, the French name for the juniper berry. The Dutch called it Genever, which they still do, and today it is also known in the Netherlands as Hollands and Schiedam (a gin-distilling center near Rotterdam). The English shortened and Anglicized it to gin.

The popularity of gin in England came about as the result of a demand for distilled spirits that were palatable and also inexpensive. During the reign of Queen Anne (1702–1714) the only way distillers knew how to satisfy this demand was to take the lees of wine or beer and distill out the alcohol. Such seventeenth-century spirits did not possess a very pleasant flavor, and something had to be done about it. The solution was found in gin.

English soldiers returning from the seventeenth-century wars on the Continent brought back a taste for "Dutch Courage," as they dubbed the beverage. In no time at all gin became the national drink of England, as it has

350

remained ever since. (Contrary to the general belief, the popularity of Scotch whisky among the English is quite recent, only a little more than a century old.)

Queen Anne helped matters along by raising the duties and taxes on French wines and brandies and at the same time lowering the excise tax on English distilled spirits. Naturally the production of this new, inexpensive beverage flourished. In fact, gin was so cheap for a time in England that one innkeeper put up a sign that read:

> Drunk for a penny,
> Dead drunk for twopence,
> Clean straw for nothing!

This gives a mild idea of the kind of gin that was made, although it is unlikely it was much worse than the kind many people drank in America during the bathtub gin era of the twenties.

During the course of the years tremendous improvements have been made in production methods. Today making gin is a highly refined science, with very precise quality controls to ensure continuous uniformity. This does not mean that all gins are identical. Each distiller has his own closely guarded secret formula and method of making gin.

There are only two basic styles or types of gin: Dutch—Hollands, Genever, or Schiedam gin—and Dry—English or American gin.

Dutch gins are very full flavored and full bodied and possess a complex, malty aroma and taste.

English and American gins are quite light in flavor and body by comparison. They are more aromatic and flavorful.

HOLLANDS GIN

In the Netherlands gin is generally made in the following manner:

1. A grain formula of approximately equal parts of barley malt, corn, and rye is mashed, cooked, and fermented into a beer.

2. The resulting beer is distilled in a pot still and the distillate may be redistilled once or twice. The final spirits, known as malt wine, are distilled off higher than the first distillates, but still at a very low proof, between 100 and 110.

3. The malt wine is then redistilled, together with juniper berries, in another pot still. The first gin is distilled off at between 94 and 98 proof. (Other botanicals are included with the juniper berries, but not in the quantity or variety employed in England and the United States.)

Some of the botanicals used to impart distinctive flavor to gin. (*Courtesy Joseph E. Seagram & Sons, Inc., New York*)

Because of the low proof at which it is distilled, Hollands, Genever, or Schiedam is a very full-bodied gin with a clean but pronounced malty aroma and flavor. Dutch gin cannot be mixed with other ingredients to make cocktails because its own definite taste will predominate and overshadow whatever other wine or spirit it is mixed with.

DRY GIN—ENGLISH

Originally the term *London Dry Gin* signified gin produced in or near London, where most English gin has always been distilled, but today the term has been adopted by American gin distillers as well as gin producers in other countries. Therefore it has lost its geographical significance. The term *dry* does not have much meaning either, since all English, American, and Dutch gins are equally dry.

English and American gins are very different in character from Dutch gins. This is the result of the different production methods used.

In England making gin begins with a grain formula made up of 75 percent corn, 15 percent barley malt, and 10 percent other grains. This is mashed, cooked, and fermented, much the same as the mash is handled for the production of whisky. After fermentation is completed, the wort, or beer, is distilled and rectified in a column still to obtain a rather pure spirit of from 180 to 188 proof. This is reduced to 120 proof by the addition of distilled water. The reduced spirit is placed in a gin still, which is usually a pot still, and redistilled in the presence of the flavoring agents, primarily juniper berries. However, other flavoring materials, known as botanicals, are used in rather small quantities to add flavor nuances to the gin. Among those generally used are dried lemon and orange peel, cardamom and coriander seeds, bitter almonds, angelica and orris root, as well as anise, caraway, fennel, licorice, and so on. The precise formula is always a secret. There is also a variation in the method of distilling. Some producers mix the botanicals with the spirit and distill the entire mash, while others place the botanicals on wire mesh trays that are suspended above the spirit in the still, so that the alcohol vapors, upon rising, will pass through and around the botanicals, thus becoming impregnated with the aromatic flavoring oils they contain.

The resulting spirit comes off the gin still at 150 to 170 proof and is recovered as gin. Character can be influenced by adjusting the cutoff in the run, since the aromatics are extracted in varying amounts during the process. Only the heart of the run is used, and it is reduced in proof to bottling strength—80 to 97 proof—and is ready to be marketed. If it is not to be bottled at once, it is stored in glass-lined or stainless steel tanks, since gin is generally not aged.

There is a difference in character between English and American gin, primarily because of the slightly lower proof of the spirits employed by English distillers. These spirits retain some character.

other English gins

While virtually the whole trade in gin in the British Isles is concerned with London Dry, there are some other varieties. The most important of these is Plymouth Gin. It is a heavier, more strongly flavored gin than the London Dry type.

A few English gin distillers still produce in small amounts a sweetened gin labeled Old Tom Gin. It is rarely sold today.

DRY GIN—AMERICAN

American gin is either distilled or compounded. Distilled gin can be made by adding the flavor ingredients as part of a continuous process, during which the alcohol is first distilled from the mash, or by redistilling distilled spirits.

In some cases the botanicals are suspended above the liquid so that the flavor is removed by the alcohol vapor. In other cases, when redistillation occurs, the ingredients may be put directly into the alcohol to be redistilled.

Compound gin is made by combining distilled spirits with essential oils or extracts of the botanicals. The main characteristic flavor must be from juniper berries, although many other ingredients are used, each according to the formula of the maker.

Grain alcohol passes into the still to be evaporated by the heat from a steam coil. In some instances botanicals are mixed with the spirits in the gin still and heated. The vapor, rich with the essence of the botanicals, passes to a condenser, through a tail box for control, and into the storage tank.

Gin produced by original distillation or redistillation may be designated distilled. Compound gin needs no special designation. In every case the type of spirits used must be mentioned on the label.

To make a quality gin the producer must start with neutral spirits that are clean and free of any foreign flavor. The juniper berries and other botanicals must also be of the best grades. Because botanicals vary in flavor content each season, the distilier must continually adjust the proportions to maintain his brand's consistency.

As stated earlier, virtually all gins on the market use the word *dry* as descriptive of the brand. The label may read Dry Gin, Extra Dry Gin, Very Dry Gin, London Dry Gin, or English Dry Gin, but all express the same meaning—lacking in sweetness.

Dry gin is also produced in Germany, Italy, Israel, Norway, the Balkans, and Africa.

FRUIT-FLAVORED GINS

In all gin-producing countries there are people who enjoy a gin with a special flavor: orange, lemon, pineapple, mint, and so forth. These are gins to which the specific flavoring has been added and the name of the flavor put on the label. In the United States these are considered the product of rectification and pay the $0.30-per-gallon rectification tax.

For a product to be a gin the one requirement sine qua non is that its principal flavoring agent be juniper berries. There is one exception, however: sloe gin. Sloe gin is a gin in name only since it is a cordial; it will be discussed in Chapter 25.

AGING GIN

U.S. regulations do not permit any age claims to be made for gin. In fact, gin does not require aging to be smooth, palatable, and drinkable. It is ready for consumption when it comes off the gin still and has been reduced to potable strength. Some producers in the United States do age their gin in wood for short periods of time, which gives the gin a light golden color. This product is often called Golden Gin, but the producers cannot advertise or make any age claims on the label.

There is a general misconception about Dutch gins being aged. In the Netherlands aging is not recognized by law, although it would still not be illegal to practice it. Whether labeled Hollands, Genever, or Schiedam, the gin is not aged. As it comes from the still it is stored for bottling, either in large, glazed earthenware vats or more often in glass-lined tanks. Any slight yellowish or golden color to be found in Dutch gin is the product of a slight amount of caramel coloring that has been added.

HOW AND WHEN TO SERVE GIN

Hollands gin should be drunk straight; in the East Indies, however, it is drunk with bitters. Take a regular whisky glass and add two dashes of bitters, roll the glass around until the inside of the glass is covered with the bitters, then throw out the rest. Fill with Hollands gin. It is a quick drink and a good aperitif.

The most popular dry gin cocktail by far is the Dry Martini, but it is only one of hundreds of gin cocktails, such as the Alexander, Negroni, Gibson, and Gimlet. Dry gin is also widely used in long drinks, such as the Gin and Tonic, Tom Collins, Gin Rickey, and Gin and Bitter Lemon, all especially refreshing in warm weather (see Chapter 26).

23
RUMS

Rum,° the name of that multifaceted alcoholic beverage, conjures up pictures of Sir Henry Morgan, the Spanish explorers in the New World, and the smugglers, or rum runners, of Prohibition. Its career has been romantic, colorful, and replete with legends, some of which are doubtless apocryphal.

Rum comes from a grass whose botanical name is *Saccharum officinarum,* *history* but it is more commonly known as sugarcane. The earliest mention we have of sugarcane dates back to 327 B.C., when Alexander the Great returned from his expedition to India. Whether sugarcane originated in the northeastern valleys of India or in the islands of the South Pacific we may never know, but it was finally brought to Europe by the Arabs after A.D. 636. Still, crystallized sugar was a costly rarity until Columbus took cane cuttings from the Canary Islands to the West Indies. It prospered so well there that sugar made from cane became inexpensive and could be enjoyed by everyone.

Almost at once, distillation of rum sprang up as a by-product of the sugar factory. Today it is made in all parts of the world, wherever sugarcane grows.

Rum is any alcoholic distillate or a mixture of distillates from the fermented juice of sugarcane, sugarcane syrup, sugarcane molasses, or other sugarcane by-products distilled at less than 190 proof (whether or not such proof is further reduced before bottling to not less than 80 proof). The distillate must possess the taste, aroma, and characteristics generally attributed to rum.

The early Spanish settlers of the West Indies noted that the residual molasses of their primitive sugar factories fermented easily, so it was natural that they experimented with distilling. The result was a pleasant-tasting alcoholic beverage. The freebooters of the period took the product back to Europe, where it found ready acceptance.

° *Ron* (Spanish); *rhum* (French).

357

How rum got its name is a matter of conjecture. Its origin is lost among the legends of sixteenth-century swashbuckling pirates. Purists believe it is a shortened form of the Latin *saccharum*, which means "sugar." Another idea is that the wild lads of the Spanish Main first called the product *rumbullion* or *rumbustion*.

Still others credit the name to the English Navy. In 1745 Admiral Vernon discovered that his men were suffering from scurvy. Not knowing what to do about it, he cut the daily ration of beer from their diet and replaced it with the strange, new West Indian beverage, which conquered the scurvy problem and won him the lasting regard of his men, who referred to him affectionately as Old Rummy and in his honor called the new drink rum. (In eighteenth-century England the word *rum* was a slang expression used to describe people, things, or events that were very good, the very best. Thus, when the British sailors named the beverage rum it was the highest accolade they could bestow upon it.)

For over three hundred years rum has been made in the West Indies, but it is also produced in other sugarcane-growing sections of the world. It was made in New England, which imported molasses from the West Indies for this purpose. Many New England shipping families engaged in an infamous cycle of trade in the production of New England rum.

Rum, distilled in New England, was carried to Africa, perhaps with stops at Madeira, the Azores, or the Canaries, where some of it was sold. The remainder was exchanged for African blacks, who were brought back to the West Indies to become slaves, in exchange for molasses that was brought back to New England to be distilled into rum so that the cycle could begin all over again..

production   The production of rum begins with harvesting the cane. The freshly cut cane is brought to the sugar mills, where it is passed through enormous, very heavy crushing rollers that express the juice. The juice is boiled to concentrate the sugar and evaporate the water. Then it is clarified. The result is a heavy, thick syrup.

The syrup is pumped into high-speed centrifugal machines, whirling at over twenty-two hundred revolutions per minute, where the sugar in the syrup is crystallized and separated from the other solids. After the sugar is removed, what remains is molasses. Sometimes this still retains up to 5 percent sugar. The only economical way to recover, or not to lose, the residue of sugar is to ferment this molasses and distill it into rum.

classifications   There are four main classifications of rum: the first is the very dry, light-bodied rums, generally produced in the Spanish-speaking countries, of which Puerto Rican rum is today's outstanding example; the second is the medium-bodied rums; the third is the rich, full-bodied, pungent rums usually produced in the English-speaking islands and countries, the best example of which is

Cutting sugarcane in Puerto Rico, the first step of many in making rum. (*Courtesy Bar Management, New York*)

Jamaican rum; and the fourth is the light-bodied but pungently aromatic East Indian Batavia arak rum from Java.

The rums of the various islands of the West Indies, as well as those from elsewhere, all have their own individual character. So we have Jamaican rum, Puerto Rican rum, and so forth. The B.A.T.F. declares that the word *type* cannot be used in identifying a rum, as is done in the case of many wines; rather a rum must carry the name of the locality from which it comes. Therefore there cannot be a Jamaica-type rum made in some other place.

Light-bodied rums generally found in international trade today are those of Puerto Rico, the Virgin Islands, the Dominican Republic, Mexico, and Venezuela. Medium-bodied rums, which are more in the style of the light rums, include those from Haiti, Barbados, Trinidad, and Guyana (Demeraran). The full-bodied, pungent rums come primarily from Jamaica and Martinique. This does not mean that Puerto Rico produces only light-bodied and Jamaica only full-bodied rums. Both countries can produce both types, but they are better known for their own traditional type.

Bacardi distillery at Palo Seco, San Juan—the world's largest rum plant. (*Courtesy Bacardi & Company, Ltd., Miami, Florida*)

PUERTO RICAN RUM

The molasses is placed in large vats holding thousands of gallons. Water is added, together with a substantial proportion of mash from a previous distillation. Special yeast strains are added to a small amount of molasses in a test tube. Fermentation begins, and the mixture is transferred to successively larger containers until it reaches the fermenting tanks. Fermentation lasts two to four days.

After fermentation is completed, the fermented mash, containing about 7 percent alcohol, is pumped into a column still, where the spirit is distilled off at 160 proof or higher. Distilling at a high proof produces a spirit low in congeners, light in body, and fairly neutral in flavor.

Only the middle rum (middle part of the distillation), the *madilla*, also called *aguardiente* in the trade, is used for rum. It is aged in seasoned oak barrels, some charred and some uncharred, when color is not desired.

When the rum has matured—after a minimum of one year under Puerto Rican law to more than six years for some special aged rums—it is passed through a filtering and leaching vat. At this point the younger rums are clear with a very light taste and lightness of body. These clear, more neutral rums are designated as White or Silver.

Deeper-colored and more flavored rums, designated as Amber or Gold, are aged a minimum of three years and have caramel added to give a deeper, more uniform color. In the case of rum, caramel does not affect the flavor because rum is a sugar-based product. Most of these rums are marketed at 80 proof.

The characteristic taste of the White and Gold Label rums is dry, with a very slight molasses flavor, the Gold Label being slightly mellower and having a more pronounced taste.

The older "liqueur" rums are usually shipped under brand names. While these rums are generally quite dry, they have a fine, mellow, rummy bouquet and flavor. Because of their dryness they can be likened to a fine old brandy. Puerto Rican producers now offer full-bodied rums in addition to the light. These may be labeled either Red Label or Heavy Dark, for Planter's Punch.

VIRGIN ISLANDS RUM

The Virgin Islands have always been known for three things: rum (the kind you drink), bay rum (the kind you put on your hair), and as pirate hangouts during the days of the Spanish Main.

Purchased by the United States in 1917, the Virgin Islands were subject to our Prohibition laws and had to confine their efforts to bay rum until 1933. The islands were in bad financial straits, and our Department of Insular Affairs decided to assist the islands by reestablishing the Virgin Islands rum industry. Eventually the first shipments of the new rum arrived amid the greatest fanfare of free publicity any liquor ever had. Virgin Islands rum is of the light-bodied type. The best rums are from the island of Saint Croix.

OTHER LIGHT-BODIED RUMS

While Puerto Rico, the Virgin Islands, and Cuba are the principal areas that produce light-bodied rums, this type is also distilled in the Dominican Republic, Venezuela, Mexico, Brazil, Argentina, Peru, Paraguay, and more recently in Jamaica and Guyana. Light-bodied rum is also made in Hawaii, the Philippines, and the continental United States.

MEDIUM RUMS

Among others in this group are rums from Haiti and Martinique that are made from sugarcane juice rather than from the traditional molasses. They are made in pot stills and develop a fine mellow bouquet.

DEMERARAN RUM

Demeraran rum is distilled from sugarcane molasses grown along the Demerara River in Guyana (formerly British Guiana), South America. The chief difference between Demeraran rum and fuller-bodied rum is the result of the variations in character of the sugarcane and the soil and the fact that Demeraran rum is distilled in column stills. Demeraran rum is much darker and not nearly as pungent as Jamaican rum.

Demeraran rum is obtainable in this market at 80, 86, and 151 proofs. The overproof rum is used in northern lumber camps, by the Grand Banks fishermen, and in Alaska. After exposure to intense cold, these outdoorsmen need a very strong bracer to thaw them out. The rum is generally consumed in the form of grog, that is, mixed half and half with very hot water, as well as in many fancy rum drinks.

When the Zombie became a popular drink, the 151-proof Demeraran rum found a new outlet.

JAMAICAN RUM

The typical Jamaican rum is a full-bodied rum, and its manufacture differs considerably from that of light-bodied rum.

To the molasses in the fermentation vats are added the skimmings from previous distillations—the dunder, known also as burned ale. The natural yeast spores in the air promptly settle on the surface of the liquid mass, multiply rapidly, and cause fermentation to begin.

Some call this wild fermentation and others spontaneous fermentation. The correct term is *natural* fermentation. In addition to the dunder, usually a certain amount of the residue from a previous fermentation is added. This natural free method of fermentation is slower, taking anywhere from five to twenty days, depending on the abundance of free yeast spores and climatic or temperature conditions at the time.

This also permits a larger amount of congeners to develop, which in turn are carried over in the distillation.

The fermented liquor is pumped into a pot still, where it is distilled, producing a low wine. This is then redistilled in another pot still. Only the middle rum, taken off after the heads and before the tails begin to come over, is used.

The new rum is taken off between 140 and 160 proof, sometimes lower. The result is a very full-bodied, very pungent rummy spirit.

The new rum, like all distillates, is colorless, but with time in oak puncheons (casks) it takes on a golden hue. The depth of color of Jamaican rum, however, is governed by the amount of caramel added. Jamaican rums are always blended, and being full bodied and rich in congeners they require more aging than lighter-bodied rums, anywhere from five to seven years and more. Some "liqueur" rums of Jamaica are aged fifteen years before bottling.

Dark mahogany-colored rums have become very popular because they give greater color to the drinks made with them. These darker rums are generally labeled "for Planter's Punch," as this is the drink in which they are used most often. The intense color is produced by adding caramel.

Jamaica's best market is Great Britain, where much of the rum is shipped for aging and blending. The damp climate is excellent for maturing rum. (Jamaican rums are usually shipped to Britain at their original high proof. They are reduced to potable strength at the time of bottling by adding only water.) Such rums, when they are stored and blended in bonded warehouses at the London docks, are known in the trade as London Dock rums.

Jamaican rums are usually marketed at 86 to 97 proof and occasionally at 151 proof. Traditional Jamaican rum is the most pungent of all alcoholic beverages. It has a unique, buttery molasses aroma and flavor. Recently some producers have installed column stills and are making light rums.

BATAVIA ARAK

Arak is a rum produced from molasses that comes from the sugar factories near Batavia, on the island of Java, Indonesia. Because of the special treatment given the molasses and the special quality of the river water used in fermentation, a dry, highly aromatic rum results. The quality of arak owes much, too, to the wild, uncultured yeast *Saccharomyces vordermanni* and to the little cakes of specially cooked and dried red Javanese rice that are placed in the fermenting tubs of molasses.

The arak is aged for three or four years in Java, after which it is shipped to Holland, where it is aged for another four to six years, blended, and then bottled.

Arak is a brandylike rum of great pungency and rumminess and is used as is any other rum. In Sweden, however, its greatest use is for making Swedish Punsch.

NEW ENGLAND RUM

New England rum is now obsolete and was eliminated from the U.S. Standards of Identity in 1968. It was straight rum, distilled at less than 160 proof, with considerable body and pungency.

HOW AND WHEN TO SERVE RUM

In rum-producing countries rum is drunk straight, rather than in mixtures, and this is the best way to appreciate the qualities of a fine rum. In the United

States the most popular ways of drinking rum are with cola, in Daiquiris (see page 392 for recipe), on the rocks, with water and other mixers, such as 7-Up, tonic, and orange juice, and as a substitute for gin in Martinis.

There has been a great change in the market in the last few years, and exotic drinks made with rum, while still consumed, particularly in Polynesian restaurants, have been overtaken by the more usual drinks, which are simpler to prepare.

Rums are used extensively in the kitchen for making sauces, for desserts, and in ice creams and candies.

Finally, rum, when it has been denatured to make it unsuitable for beverage purposes, and thus not subject to high consumption taxes, is one of the most widely used flavors in the tobacco industry.

24
OTHER SPIRITS

In all countries where spirits are produced, man has always used the most available and least costly basic material. Thus we find brandies where grapes and fruits are grown, whiskies where corn and barley are grown, and rum where sugarcane is grown.

This chapter will discuss some of the more interesting and popular spirits produced from, and occasionally flavored by, local products.

ANISE/LICORICE-FLAVORED SPIRITS

No alcoholic beverage has been less understood than absinthe, poetically described as "the water of the Star Wormwood—the Green Muse." It was supposed to be wicked, to drive the drinker insane, and to have killed many. In France its sale was prohibited before World War I because of the belief that it would cause a decrease in the birthrate. Possibly it could have done all these terrible things, as it was one of the most potent of all alcoholic beverages. It was not, however, because of the wormwood that it was so dangerous, but rather because of its alcoholic strength. Absinthe was generally shipped at a proof of 136 (68 percent alcohol). The sale of absinthe is prohibited in Switzerland, where it was invented, as well as in France, the United States, and most other countries.

Just what was this absinthe of which we heard so much and of which we know so little? The "elixir" absinthe was composed of aromatic plants, *Artemisia mayoris* and *vulgaris,* balm-mint, hyssop, fennel, star-anise, and a high-proof spirit. It was invented toward the end of the eighteenth century by a physician and pharmacist, Dr. Ordinaire, a French exile living in Couvet, Switzerland. In 1797 Henri-Louis Pernod acquired the recipe, and since that time the Pernod name has been so closely associated with absinthe that they have become synonymous.

The classic absinthe drink was the Absinthe Drip, which required a special two-piece drip glass. A jigger of absinthe was poured into the glass, then a cube of sugar placed over the drip hole of the upper section, which was then packed with cracked ice. Cold water was added to fill the dripper. When all of the water had dripped through, the drink was ready. Some people preferred a slightly sweeter drink, which was made by using one ounce of absinthe and one ounce of anisette. This drink was an excellent restorative in cases of seasickness, airsickness, and nausea. One was enough.

Since absinthe is prohibited in the United States and other countries, the Pernod firm produces, in France, an anise-flavored spirit of 90 proof that is reminiscent in flavor and character of absinthe. It has a light yellow-green color and a sharp, pronounced aroma, in which the dominant note is licorice. When it is mixed with water (as it always should be), it changes color, becoming streaked, then milky, and finally a cloudy opalescent color. It is intriguing to look at and to drink.

The highly concentrated natural essential oils that give the flavor to these products are more soluble in alcohol than in water. Therefore when water is added the oils precipitate, making the mixture cloudy. If a great deal of water is added, they become clear again. Since anise has a strong flavor, up to five parts water are added to these spirits for general consumption.

There are other anise products produced throughout the world. They vary one from another, but none is absinthe, since the formulas do not contain wormwood. They are popular drinks of the countries bordering the Mediterranean. The product is known in each country by its local name—thus in Spain it is Ojen; in France it is Pastis, the best-known brand of which is Ricard; in Italy it is Anesone; in Greece it is Ouzo and Mastikha; and in Turkey it is Raki. They are rarely ever drunk neat but usually mixed with water, similarly to Pernod, producing a long opalescent cooler. They are served both as aperitifs and as refreshers.

AQUAVIT (AKVAVIT)

It is an old Scandinavian custom at formal gatherings to drink as many toasts as there are buttons on the men's dress vests. The number of buttons may vary, but the spirit, surely, does not. It is Aquavit, the beverage of Scandinavia.

The method of producing Aquavit is similar in Denmark (where it is called Akvavit), Norway, Sweden, and Iceland, although there are some variations, mainly in the proportions of flavorings.

Aquavit may be made from a fermented mash of either barley malt and grain or potatoes; it is flavored with caraway seeds. Aquavit is first distilled as a neutral spirit at 190 proof, reduced with water to 120 proof, and then redistilled with the flavorings. Caraway is the principal flavoring, but others, such as lemon and orange peel, cardamom, and anise, are used. This is quite similar to the production of gin, except that the main flavor in Aquavit is caraway rather than juniper berries.

Aquavit generally is unaged, except for a specific Norwegian brand that is traditionally sent on an ocean voyage across the Equator and back before bottling.

Many people describe Aquavit by saying that it is Kümmel (see page 375) before the sweetening syrup is added; it tastes like Kümmel, except that it is much drier. Its alcoholic strength is 86 to 90 proof, whereas Kümmel's is 70 to 80 proof.

Aquavit is always served ice cold. It is usually taken with food—appetizers, canapés, or sandwiches—and usually with a beer chaser. The usual portion of Aquavit is one ounce, and it is not sipped but is taken at one swallow. It is customarily drunk to this Scandinavian toast:

> *Skaal! Min skaal—din skaal,*
> *Alla vackra flickornas skaal!*

> Health! My health—your health,
> All the pretty girls' health!

BITTERS

Bitters consist of bitter and aromatic essences and flavors incorporated into an alcohol base. The flavors come from fruits, plants, seeds, flowers, leaves, bark, roots, and stems. Most bitters are made from closely guarded formulas, proprietary secrets handed down from generation to generation. These products are the result of infusion and distillation processes and their one common characteristic is bitterness.

Bitters are classified into two categories: fit for use as beverages and not fit for use as beverages. Those fit for beverages are subject to the Internal Revenue tax of $10.50 per tax gallon plus $0.50 per tax gallon duty if imported. Bitters not fit for beverage use made in the United States have a $1.00 per tax gallon Internal Revenue tax. If bitters are imported and are not fit for beverages, there is no Internal Revenue tax and the applicable duty is $0.94 per tax gallon.

Bitters not fit for beverages contain components of such nature or in such amounts that only small quantities of the bitters can be used as flavoring agents in cocktails and general cuisine. The best known of this type is Angostura Bitters, which is made in Trinidad. Other such bitters are Peychaud's from New Orleans, Underberg from Germany, and various orange bitters.

Bitters fit for beverages include stomachics or aids to digestion such as Fernet Branca and Unicum from Italy. Campari is a beverage bitter from Italy, where its consumption is so pervasive that premixed and bottled Campari and soda is sold everywhere.

OKOLEHAO

Hawaii has made several contributions to our way of life, but the most exotic offering is Okolehao, or Oke, as it is known on the islands.

According to the producer of Okolehao, it is distilled solely from fermented mash of the roots of the sacred ti plant of Hawaii (*Cordyline australis*).

Okolehao was first made by an Australian, William Stevenson, about 1790. He cooked the ti roots, which are rich in levulose (fructose), and allowed the mash to ferment in the bottom of a canoe. He then distilled the fermented mash in a still constructed from a ship's cooking pot, with an inverted calabash for a lid and a water-cooled gun barrel for a coil.

Today, of course, Okolehao is distilled in a modern distillery employing column stills and all the most advanced scientific mashing and distilling control techniques.

Okolehao is not aged. After distillation it is filtered through charcoal. Both a Crystal Clear and a Golden Oke are produced. It has an unusual and subtle flavor. Okolehao is marketed at 80 proof. It is drunk straight, on the rocks, in tall drinks, and in highballs, and it is employed in the preparation of a number of intriguingly named cocktails, such as Mahalo, which means "thank you" in Hawaiian, Ti A'A Sour, Scratch Me Lani, Okole-Wow, No-Mo-Pain, Aloha, and Coke and Oke.

PIMM'S CUP

Pimm's Cup is a drink that dates back more than a century. The story is that a bartender in a Pimm's restaurant in the London financial district invented the original gin sling many years ago, and the patrons liked it so much they used to ask that it be prepared for them in quantity so they could take it up to the country when they went on holiday. From the numerous requests of this nature, it was natural that the drink be prepared commercially. As it is bottled, Pimm's is rather bittersweet and heavy, but when mixed with soda and garnished with a slice of lemon and a piece of cucumber rind, it makes a very satisfying, cooling thirst quencher.

TEQUILA AND PULQUE

Tequila is a descendant of the first alcoholic beverage produced in North America, the origins of which are interwoven with Aztec history. Before the Spaniards brought the art of distillation to Mexico in the early 1500s, the Aztecs were drinking a winelike liquid called pulque. Pulque is a product of the mezcal plant, which belongs to the genus *agave* (which the Spanish referred to as *maguey*).

Guillermo Freytag holds the 100 millionth *agave* "pineapple" to be harvested at the Cuervo plantation, near Tequila, in the state of Jalisco, Mexico. (*Courtesy Liquor Publications, Inc.*)

The mezcal plant takes ten to twelve years to reach proper maturity, at which time the sap flows to the base. When the plant reaches maturity, the outer leaves are removed and the base, resembling a pineapple but larger and heavier, weighing 75 to 150 pounds, is cut from the plant, leaving only a stump.

These "pineapples," or hearts of the plant, are heavy with sweet sap called *aguamiel* ("honey water"), which is allowed to ferment slowly for about ten days to form *madre pulque* ("mother pulque"). A small amount is added to fresh *aguamiel*, which ferments rapidly and is ready for consumption in a day or two. Pulque is not readily available very far from its source because it is always consumed freshly made.

Pulque has a rather heavy flavor resembling sour milk, but it is much appreciated by the Mexicans because of its cooling, wholesome, and nutritional properties.

When pulque is distilled it makes an interesting *maguey* brandy, known as *vino mezcal*. The best *vino mezcal* is Tequila, which comes from the upland valleys surrounding the town of Tequila, near Guadalajara, in the state of Jalisco, Mexico.

The best species of mezcal plant, grown near Tequila, is the *Agave tequileana* Weber, commonly called the blue *agave*. There are hundreds of varieties of the proliferous mezcal *agave* plant, and their differences are marked enough that one makes a good Tequila and another does not. The blue *agave* is cultivated for Tequila production. Many people believe that the mezcal plant is a type of cactus, but technically it belongs to the amaryllis family (*Amarillydaceae*).

When the matured *agave* "pineapples" arrive at the distillery they are split open and placed in an oven, where they are steamed for nine to twenty-four hours at 200 degrees Fahrenheit. This causes a considerable amount of the *aguamiel* to run off freely, while the balance of the starch is converted to sugar. The "pineapples" are then shredded and the remaining juice is expressed by mechanical means. The juices are placed in large vats to ferment.

To start fermentation and to ensure uniform character, a small amount of must from a previous fermentation is added to each new batch. Fermentation takes about two and a half days. The fermented product is distilled in copper pot stills, and the finished Tequila, after double distillation, is drawn off at 104 to 106 proof.

The Tequila shipped to this country as White is unaged and is bottled when it leaves the still and is reduced to 80 to 86 proof. Some Tequila is shipped to the United States in bulk and is bottled here. A few producers ship a Gold Tequila, which is purported to be aged in oak vats for two to four or more years. The Gold Tequila has no official government recognition and is aged and colored before bottling at the discretion of the producer. An *añejo* ("aged") Tequila, which has been aged for at least one year, is recognized officially.

The Mexican government has recently decreed that only the superior *vino mezcal* from a carefully delineated section of Jalisco may be called Tequila, just as the French, for example, earlier declared that only brandies from the province of Charente could be called Cognac.

Tequila has a distinctive flavor, quite different from other spirits. Its flavor is assertive and reveals its herbaceous origins. Tequila has a natural affinity to lime juice and salt. The traditional method of drinking Tequila in Mexico is a ceremony in itself. The imbiber takes a wedge of lime or lemon, puts a pinch of salt on his thumbnail or on the back of his hand, and pours a chilled jigger of Tequila. He then bites the lime, licks the salt, and gulps down the Tequila.

Another way Mexicans enjoy Tequila is with Sangrita, a spicy tomato and citrus juice mixture that is held in one hand while the Tequila is held in the other. They are sipped alternately.

The Margarita, a Tequila cocktail developed in Los Angeles, was the springboard to Tequila consumption in this country. Since 1969, when Tequila imports were 770,000 gallons, or 0.2 percent of the total distilled spirits market, consumption has jumped to 7 million gallons in 1976, or 1.6 percent of the market. This is a remarkable increase of 900 percent.

25
LIQUEURS AND
CORDIALS

A closely sheltered room, a thin, ascetic individual wearing a black robe with flowing sleeves bending over strange vessels and retorts, stirring up a fire in search of gold and the everlasting life! This is a picture of the early distiller, the alchemist who was thought to be in communion with the devil. The medieval distiller was the magician of his day; he was trying to find the chemical secret of obtaining gold from baser metals—at which he failed—and an elixir that would prolong life beyond the normal span. If this medieval magician did not learn how to prolong life, at least he learned the secret of making it more interesting, for his experiments produced the first liqueurs.

Originally liqueurs were used as medicinal remedies, love potions, aphrodisiacs, and general cure-alls. It is unnecessary to explain the medicinal and therapeutic value of certain seeds, herbs, and roots that were used at that time, as most of them are found in a modern pharmacopoeia; caraway seed, coriander, angelica root, oil of orange, oil of lemon, and various herbs rich in iodine are but a few.

In his *Wines and Spirits* the late André L. Simon said: "In the making of wine . . . the art of man intervenes only to make the best use possible of Nature's own gift . . . but in the making of liqueurs, man has a much wider field wherein to exercise his ingenuity; he is at liberty to give to his liqueurs practically any shade or color he thinks best to attract the attention, raise the curiosity, and charm the eye; he also has at his command all the fruits of the earth from which to extract an almost unlimited variety of aromas and flavors, wherewith to please the most fastidious taste and flatter the most jaded palate."

By the same token it is theoretically possible to make any liqueur with equal success in any part of the world, but the theory works only up to a point. Certain countries have produced such excellent liqueurs that their products are recognized throughout the world as standards of quality. Foremost in this respect are France and Holland, although certain specialties of great repute are produced in other countries, such as Italy's Strega, Liquore Galliano, and

Dalmatian Maraschino; Germany's Gilka Kümmel and Danziger Goldwasser; Sweden's Swedish Punsch; Denmark's Peter Heering; and Spain's Anis del Mono.

Liqueurs and cordials have been known by many names and described at one time or another as balms, crèmes, elixirs, oils, and so on. The terms *liqueur* and *cordial* are synonymous, with the former said to apply more to European products and the latter to American products. Liqueurs are alcoholic beverages prepared by mixing or redistilling various spirits (brandy, whisky, rum, gin, or other spirits) with certain flavoring materials. These materials can be fruits, flowers, herbs, seeds, barks, roots, peels, berries, juices, or other natural flavoring substances or extracts derived from them.

Liqueurs and cordials differ from all other spirits because they must contain at least $2\frac{1}{2}$ percent sugar by weight. The sugar may be beet, maple, cane, honey, corn, or a combination of these. There are no hard rules. The United States has very white, stable sugar. Between the $2\frac{1}{2}$ percent minimum and a 10 percent sugar content the product is still not very sweet, and it may include the word *dry* on the label. Most liqueurs and cordials contain up to 35 percent of a sweetening agent.

PRODUCTION OF LIQUEURS AND CORDIALS

There are two basic ways of extracting flavors when making liqueurs. They are, simply, the cold method and the hot method. The method chosen depends on the flavor to be made and the source of that flavor. Generally, fruit flavors are extracted by the cold method, and other plant products, such as seeds, peels, and flowers, have their flavors extracted by the hot method. Each method encompasses several processes, and each fruit or plant product is handled differently.

infusion or maceration

The cold method is used when the flavoring material is sensitive to heat and would be damaged by it. Cold extractions can take up to a year, but attempts to make the process go faster by using heat would destroy the flavor. One cold method can be either infusion or maceration and is very much like making tea. If crushed fruits are steeped in water, the process is called infusion. If the fruits are steeped in alcohol, such as 120- to 130-proof brandy, it is maceration. The water or brandy eventually absorbs almost all of the aroma, flavor, and color of the fruit or berry.

In some cases, when the stones (seeds) of the fruit are present, some of the oil from the stones is also extracted, which accounts for the slight bitter almond undertone sometimes found in such liqueurs as apricot, peach, and cherry.

When ready, the liquid is drawn off, allowed to rest for several days in a storage tank that will not impart any flavor (such as stainless steel), and then filtered.

The mass of remaining fruit still contains both useful alcohol and some essential flavorings. In order to recover them, the mass is placed in a still and the last drop of flavor is extracted by distillation. The resultant distillate may then be added to the original maceration in order to give it more character.

The finished maceration is then sweetened to the desired richness by adding sugar and/or other sweetening material in syrup form. The finished product is sometimes aged before bottling.

percolation

Another method of cold extraction is percolation, or brewing, which is somewhat like making coffee. The flavoring agent, in the form of leaves or herbs, is placed in the upper part of an apparatus, the principle of which is the same as that of a coffee percolator. Brandy or another spirit is in the lower part and is pumped up over the flavoring and allowed to percolate through it, extracting and carrying down the aroma and flavor. The pumping and percolation are repeated continuously for weeks or months until most of the flavor constituents have been obtained. The spirit-soaked flavoring agent is then distilled to obtain whatever flavor remains. This distillate may be mixed with the percolate, and the whole is filtered, sweetened with sugar syrup, and often bottled at once, although some plant liqueurs of this group are aged for a time.

distillation

The hot extraction method is used mostly for seeds and flowers, such as anise, caraway, orange peel, mint, roses, and violets. These materials can withstand some heat and benefit from a quicker extraction of flavor than the slower cold methods.

The distillation method is normally carried out in small to medium-size copper pot stills, in many cases similar to a gin still.

The normal procedure is to steep the flavoring agent—plant, seed, root, or herb—in alcohol for several hours, after which it is placed in the still with additional spirits and distilled. The heads and tails are either discarded or redistilled.

A variation of the distillation process is used on delicate flowers and herbs, such as mint, roses, and violets, whose flavors disappear soon after picking. These are distilled quickly and gently in an aqueous solution rather than in a spirit. A vacuum is created so that distillation can take place at a lower temperature, preserving more of the floral aroma.

The resultant distillate, always colorless, is sweetened with simple syrup and colored with natural vegetable coloring matter or approved food dyes. Thus the producer can give his Curaçao or crème de menthe whatever hue he wishes. We have seen crème de menthe colorless, as well as various shades of green, gold, red, and blue.

fruit and plant liqueurs

The liqueur family is divided into two main branches: the natural-colored, or fruit, liqueurs and the plant liqueurs, which are colorless. The principal fruit liqueurs marketed are apricot, blackberry, cherry, crème de cassis, maraschino, peach, and sloe gin. Leading examples of plant liqueurs are anisette, crème de cacao, crème de menthe, and Kümmel.

Some liqueurs fall into a borderline category because they are made from the peels or stones of a particular fruit, not from the fruit itself. Examples of these are Curaçao and Triple Sec, made from orange peels, and crème de noyaux, an almond-flavored liqueur made from pits of fruits such as peaches or cherries.

Whereas fruit liqueurs derive their color and flavor naturally from one informing fruit, plant liqueurs very often require more than one flavoring agent to balance or bring out the desired flavor. For example, vanilla is often part of the formula in crème de cacao. Plant liqueurs, such as Bénédictine, Chartreuse, or Drambuie, result from blending flavors obtained from many plants, seeds, roots, and herbs, as many as fifty different ones in some cases. Because these herb and spice liqueurs were originally made by monks, they are sometimes known as monastery types.

GENERIC LIQUEURS AND CORDIALS SHIPPED BY MANY HOUSES

Many producers all over the world make and market a wide variety of liqueurs under generic or universally used names. In the following list are those shipped by most general liqueur producers, together with a description of their principal flavor and usual proof. Since many producers use different flavoring formulas, there are variations in brands of the same type of liqueur.

ADVOCAAT. Sometimes called Egg Brandy, made in Holland from eggs, sugar, and brandy. It is creamy and thick, with an eggnog flavor. 30 proof.

AMARETTO. Almond flavor comes from apricot stones. 48 to 56 proof.

ANESONE. Anise/licorice-flavored liqueur made in Italy and the United States. 90 proof.

ANIS. Spanish spelling of anisette, when made in Spain and Latin America. 78 to 96 proof.

ANISETTE. Flavor is obtained principally from aniseed. 50 to 60 proof.

APRICOT LIQUEUR. Principal flavor is from apricots. Often shipped under a trade name such as Abricotine or Apry. 60 to 70 proof.

BLACKBERRY LIQUEUR. Obtained generally from blackberries, but occasionally has a small amount of red wine added to it. 60 proof.

CHERRY LIQUEUR. Flavor is obtained generally from small wild black cherries. 48 to 60 proof.

COFFEE LIQUEUR. Based on coffee beans. Many sold under proprietary names. 53 to 60 proof.

CRÈME DE BANANES. Artificial banana flavor. 50 to 60 proof.

CRÈME DE CACAO. Flavor is obtained from cacao and vanilla beans, produced either white or brown. The word *Chouao* often found on crème de cacao labels indicates that the beans come from the Chouao region of Venezuela—considered to produce the finest cacao beans in the world. 54 to 60 proof.

CRÈME DE CASSIS. Flavor is obtained primarily from black currants. 32 to 40 proof.

CRÈME DE MENTHE. Flavor is obtained from several varieties of mint but principally peppermint. Both white and green are usually shipped. The only difference is that the green has harmless certified coloring added. 60 proof.

CRÈME DE NOYAUX. Flavor is obtained primarily from fruit stones, resulting in a bitter almond flavor. 50 to 60 proof.

CRÈME DE ROSE. Flavor is obtained primarily from the essential oil of rose petals and vanilla. 60 proof.

CRÈME DE VANILLE. Flavor is obtained primarily from the finest Mexican vanilla beans. 60 proof.

CRÈME DE VIOLETTE. Flavor is obtained from essential oil of violets and green oranges from the island of Curaçao. Produced in orange, white, and blue colors. 54 to 80 proof.

CURAÇAO. Flavor is obtained primarily from the dried peel of the famous green oranges from the island of Curaçao, produced in orange, white, and blue colors. 54 to 80 proof.

GINGER. Flavor is obtained from ginger root. 70 proof.

KÜMMEL. Flavor is obtained principally from caraway seeds. If the Kümmel has crystallized sugar in it, it is sold as Kümmel Crystallizé. 70 to 82 proof.

MANDARINE. Flavor is obtained primarily from dried peel of mandarines (tangerines). 80 proof.

MARASCHINO. Flavor is obtained from the special Dalmatian Marasca cherry. 60 to 78 proof.

PEACH LIQUEUR. Flavor is obtained from fresh and dried peaches. 60 to 72 proof.

PEPPERMINT SCHNAPPS. Mint liqueur, lighter bodied and less sweet than crème de menthe. 40 to 60 proof.

PRUNELLE. Flavor is obtained from European blackthorn plum. 60 to 80 proof.

ROCK AND RYE. A liqueur with a rye whisky base, but including grain neutral spirits, rock candy syrup, and sometimes fruits—lemons, oranges, and cherries. 60 to 70 proof.

SAMBUCA. Licorice flavor, obtained from the elderbush, whose Latin name is *sambucus.* 70 to 84 proof.

SLOE GIN. Flavor is obtained from the sloe berry. 42 proof.

STRAWBERRY. Flavor is obtained from strawberries. 44 to 60 proof.

TRIPLE SEC. A white Curaçao (orange flavor). 60 to 80 proof.

WISHNIAK. A wild cherry liqueur from Russia, Poland, and Czechoslovakia. 48 to 60 proof.

While generic liqueurs may be made by any producer, there are many that have trademarked names and that may be made only by a single producer. For example, anyone may make crème de menthe, but only Cusenier may make Freezomint. Similarly, any producer may make apricot liqueur, but only Garnier may make Abricotine and only Marie Brizard may make Apry.

fruit-flavored brandies

At this point the misuse of the word *brandy* as applied to liqueurs should be explained. In most countries the word *brandy* is used very loosely in connection with liqueurs, and it is quite common to find these products labeled apricot brandy, cherry brandy, peach brandy, and so forth. Under these circumstances, apricot brandy and apricot liqueur would be the same thing.

In the United States brandy must be a distillate obtained solely from the fermented juice, mash, or wine of fruit. Therefore, a liqueur made from fruit cannot be labeled or marketed as a brandy. True fruit brandies are marketed under specific designations such as Kirschwasser or Slivovitz. (See Chapter 19.)

This regulation caused some confusion for the public who believed apricot brandy and apricot liqueur were the same product (as they are in other countries). For this reason the U.S. government established a category of fruit-flavored brandies, which are the equivalent of the fruit brandies or fruit liqueurs seen abroad. These products must be made solely with a brandy base, be 70 proof (minimum), and contain more than $2\frac{1}{2}$ percent sugar by weight. To the best of our knowledge, all fruit-flavored brandies marketed in the United States are produced in this country; none is imported.

Most producers make some or all of the following: apricot-flavored brandy, blackberry-flavored brandy, cherry-flavored brandy, coffee-flavored brandy, ginger-flavored brandy, and peach-flavored brandy.

spirit liqueurs

So-called spirit liqueurs, such as gin liqueur, Scotch liqueur, and rum liqueur, are spirits that have a minimum of $2\frac{1}{2}$ percent sweetening. These used to be in vogue but are now dying out.

FAMOUS PROPRIETARY BRANDS

These are, in most cases, world-famous specialty liqueurs that are produced under closely guarded secret formulas and marketed under registered trademark brands. Every producer believes the formula he uses is unique and is his secret, and he goes to great lengths to guard it. These liqueurs are made in each case by only one house. Most of them have centuries of tradition behind them and have become household names.

Battery of copper pot stills employed to distill the various herbs, flowers, and plants used to flavor Bénédictine liqueurs at Fécamp, France. (*Courtesy Julius Wile Sons & Co., Inc., New York*)

Stained glass window at Bénédictine Distillerie, Fécamp, France, showing Dom Bernardo Vincelli directing his brother Bénédictines in his medieval laboratory. (*Courtesy Julius Wile Sons & Co., Inc., New York*)

BÉNÉDICTINE.   To the best of our knowledge, the oldest liqueur is the world-famous D.O.M Bénédictine, which is still produced on the spot where its secret formula was developed in 1510.

If you should visit this corner of France, you would see the duplicate of the original Bénédictine Abbey of Fécamp, where Dom Bernardo Vincelli first gave his brother monks his new elixir to comfort them when they were fatigued or ill. D.O.M, which appears on every label, stands for the Latin words *Deo Optimo Maximo,* "To God, Most Good, Most Great."

Today Bénédictine has no connection with any religious order but is produced by a family-owned corporation founded by Alexandre Le Grand in 1863.

The formula for Bénédictine is one of the most closely guarded secrets in the world. Only three people ever know the complete details. It is a tribute to their ability to keep the secret inviolate that every attempt to imitate this liqueur—and attempts have been made in every part of the world—has failed. At the distillery at Fécamp they point to their *Salon de Contrefaçons* ("Hall of Counterfeits"), where the walls are lined with cabinets filled with examples of hundreds of attempted imitations. This is one liqueur of which can truly be said, "There is only one."

Bénédictine is a plant liqueur made from twenty-seven different herbs, plants, and peels on a fine Cognac brandy base. It is made in a number of operations; not all of the flavors are distilled out at the same time. They are obtained separately and are then skillfully blended. Bénédictine is aged for four years before being bottled.

In the 1930s the heads of the firm were convinced that a substantial amount of Bénédictine was drunk in the form of Bénédictine and brandy by people who preferred a drier liqueur. They therefore decided to prepare their own uniform B & B liqueur, D.O.M, which creates a drier Bénédictine. They are each 86 proof.

In 1977 a third liqueur was introduced, Café Bénédictine, a blend of Bénédictine D.O.M and French coffee liqueur. It is 60 proof.

CHARTREUSE. The most famous liqueur still made by a religious order is Chartreuse. It is made from a secret formula given to Les Pères Chartreux (the Carthusian Fathers) of the convent of the Grande Chartreuse at Grenoble, France, in 1605 by the Maréchal d'Estrées. The original formula was slightly modified and perfected in 1737 by one of the monks, Brother Gérome Maubec, whom a writer of the period described as a "very clever apothecary."

In 1903, because of a law against religious orders passed in France, the Carthusian Fathers were expelled from their monastery of the Grande Chartreuse. The clever fathers, who still had their secret formula, repaired to another monastery of their order in Tarragona, Spain, where they continued to produce their famous liqueur. The Spanish bottles bore two labels: the original

LEFT: A monk working amid the Chartreuse distilling and blending tanks at Voiron. RIGHT: A monk removing residue from a Chartreuse pot still. (*Courtesy Chartreuse, Voiron, France*)

label used before the expulsion from France and a second that carried the legend Liqueur Fabriquée à Tarragone par Les Pères Chartreux.

During the order's absence from France, the French government tried to duplicate the formula without success. By 1927, when the production company was bankrupt and the shares were selling for almost nothing, some local businessmen from Voiron bought the shares, thus gaining legal control of the company. They mailed these shares, as a gift, to the Carthusian Fathers in Tarragona. With the distillery back in their possession, the monks began their secret return to France. Although the Carthusians were in France illegally, the French government chose not to prosecute, and the monks were producing Chartreuse by 1929. When the distillery was destroyed by a mud slide after eleven days of heavy rains in 1935, the French government even sent army engineers to help rebuild (and relocate) the distillery. The new distillery was established in the town of Voiron, but rather than place it on its original site on a mountainside, it was located near the railroad station where the monks already had warehouses to store the Chartreuse before shipping.

After World War II the French government lifted the expulsion order, making the monks legal residents once again of their own country.

Two types of Chartreuse—yellow (80 and 86 proof) and green (110 proof)—have been faithfully made according to the original formula. Both yellow and green Chartreuse are plant liqueurs with a spicy, aromatic flavor, made on a brandy base, the green being much drier and somewhat more aromatic than the yellow.

CHÉRI-SUISSE is a chocolate-cherry liqueur from Switzerland. 60 proof.

CHOCOLAT SUISSE is a chocolate-flavored Swiss liqueur with miniature squares of chocolate floating in the bottle. 60 proof.

COINTREAU is a brand name for one of the finest Triple Secs. While the Cointreau family formerly made many flavors of liqueurs, the name Cointreau has come to be synonymous with orange liqueur, and the other flavors are now produced under the Regnier label. 80 proof.

CORDIAL MÉDOC is a cocktail of liqueurs—a blend of fine brandy, orange Curaçao, and crème de cacao—produced in Bordeaux, France. 80 proof.

DANZIGER GOLDWASSER. The flavor is obtained primarily from orange peel, anise, and various other spicy herbs and plants. It contains tiny flecks of genuine gold leaf that are harmless when consumed. 80 proof.

DRAMBUIE liqueur was originally made from a private recipe of Prince Charles Edward Stuart (Bonnie Prince Charlie). When the prince arrived from France in 1745, one of his attendants brought with him the recipe of his master's favorite liqueur. After the battle of Culloden Moor, where the Scottish rebels were defeated, the prince was hunted and a price was put on his head. One of his Highland friends, Mackinnon of Strathaird, protected the prince and helped him escape back to France. In gratitude the prince presented Mackinnon with his secret recipe. Since then the Mackinnon family has been making this liqueur. It is made with old Highland malt Scotch whisky and heather honey. 80 proof.

FIOR D'ALPE ISOLABELLA is a spicy Italian liqueur bottled with an herb sprig inside the bottle and made with an excess of sugar that crystallizes on the sprig. The recipe for this liqueur is centuries old and involves the numerous herbs found in the Alps, such as juniper, mint, thyme, arnica, wild marjoram, and hyssop. 92 proof.

FORBIDDEN FRUIT is a liqueur made and sold in America and exported to Europe. It is made from a type of grapefruit, called the shaddock, steeped in fine brandy. 64 proof.

GILKA BERLINER KÜMMEL, made in Germany, has for almost a century been accepted as the standard of quality. The old firm of Bols in Holland, however, claims that their Bolskümmel was the original Kümmel, distilled by Erven Lucas Bols in 1575. This is said to have so impressed a Russian czar that he took the recipe back to Russia and eventually made Russia the principal producer and consumer of Kümmel. Kümmel is flavored principally with caraway seed and cumin seed. 86 proof.

GRAND MARNIER is one of the finest orange Curaçao liqueurs. It is made on a Cognac base and is produced in Cognac, France. 80 proof.

IRISH MIST is a spicy Irish whiskey and heather honey liqueur from Tulloch Mhor. During an exodus of warriors after certain battles in 1692, the recipe was lost. It was eventually located in Austria and returned to Ireland. 80 proof.

IZARRA is produced in two forms—green (100 proof) and yellow (86 proof). Its brandy base is flavored from plants grown in the French Pyrénées.

KAHLÚA is the extremely popular coffee-flavored liqueur from Mexico. 53 proof.

LIQUORE GALLIANO was created in the late 1800s and was named after the Italian Major Giuseppe Galliano. It is made from herbs and flowers and is a golden, spicy, aromatic liqueur. 80 proof.

PASHA is a coffee liqueur from Turkey. 53 proof.

PETER HEERING, formerly known as Cherry Heering, is made in Copenhagen, Denmark, and is recognized as one of the finest cherry liqueurs in the world. 49 proof.

SABRA is a popular liqueur of Israel, made from a blend of Jaffa oranges and chocolate. 60 proof.

SOUTHERN COMFORT is an American specialty. It was known originally as Cuff and Buttons around 1875, when this phrase meant "white tie and tails." According to the legend it was Louis Herron, a bartender in St. Louis, Missouri, who gave it the very apt name of Southern Comfort.

The liqueur is prepared in the same manner as Louis Herron made it. To Bourbon whisky is added a moderate quantity of peach liqueur and freshly pitted and peeled peaches. The fruit and the liqueur help mellow the robust body of the whisky, even though it is bottled at 100 proof.

STREGA is a famous spicy plant liqueur from Italy. 80 proof.

TIA MARIA from Jamaica is claimed to be the original coffee-flavored liqueur. It is made on a rum base with local Blue Mountain coffee. 63 proof.

VANDERMINT is a chocolate-mint liqueur from Holland. 60 proof.

VIEILLE CURE is an aromatic plant liqueur blended with Cognac and Armagnac and produced in Bordeaux. It is made both green and yellow. Each is 86 proof.

As has been noted, Peter Heering's cherry liqueur is considered the best cherry liqueur and Cointreau and Grand Marnier are considered the best orange-flavored liqueurs. There are a few generic liqueurs that have achieved proprietary status because of their quality and perfection. For example, the anisette considered to be finest is Marie Brizard's, and Get's Pippermint crème de menthe is most highly regarded.

HOW AND WHEN TO SERVE LIQUEURS AND CORDIALS

Liqueurs, being sweet and potent and containing certain beneficial, essential oils, are natural digestives. For this reason they are most popular as after-dinner drinks, their primary use today. During Prohibition, however, liqueurs came into wide use as cocktail ingredients because their rich sweetness was helpful in covering up the harsh bite of the spirits bootleggers supplied. Many cocktails invented during that period call for liqueurs as an important ingredient. In fact, many people have found that a dash of a liqueur in a cocktail gives it added smoothness, texture, and palatability.

In France certain liqueurs are used in various ways aside from their customary use as after-dinner drinks. Most of the crème de menthe used in France, for instance, is drunk in the form of highballs. Crème de cassis, made from black currants, is drunk mixed with French vermouth and soda or with white wine. A popular way of serving liqueurs is as frappés, which are made by filling a small glass with finely shaved ice and then pouring the liqueur into it. Liqueurs are compatible with sweet cream, other liqueurs, liquors, and mixers.

In addition to all these uses, liqueurs and syrups are used in cooking, in baking, to flavor ices and ice creams, in making sauces for puddings, in fruit dishes, and in desserts in general.

liqueurs in the kitchen

SPECIFIC GRAVITY OF LIQUEURS AND CORDIALS

In France a Pousse-Café is a brandy or cordial served to "push down the coffee." In the United States the Pousse-Café is a colorful combination of "floated" liqueurs. For those who want to prepare this delightful creation, we offer the following table of colors and specific gravities (densities) of some of the more popular liqueurs and cordials. Not all liqueur manufacturers use identical formulas and consequently the densities vary slightly among different shippers, but this should serve as a fairly good guide. To pour each layer of the Pousse-Café so that one colored liqueur will settle on another without disturbing the earlier ones in the glass, pour each liqueur over an inverted spoon. The heaviest liqueur goes on the bottom, and each lighter product floats on the denser one. Pousse-Cafés can be prepared ahead of time for use at a party or to end a special dinner. They will keep for at least an hour in the refrigerator before the layers start to blend.

LIQUEUR OR CORDIAL	COLOR	SPECIFIC GRAVITY
Kirsch	Clear	0.940
Sloe gin	Red	1.040
B & B liqueur	Amber	1.045
Kümmel	Clear	1.055
Rock and Rye	Amber	1.065
Triple Sec	Clear	1.075
Peach-flavored brandy	Peach	1.085
Blackberry liqueur	Dark red	1.110
Blue Curaçao	Blue	1.120
Apricot liqueur	Apricot	1.125
Crème de cacao	Brown	1.150
	Clear	1.150
Crème de menthe	Green	1.160
	Clear	1.160
Crème de cassis	Deep purple	1.170
Crème de bananes	Yellow	1.180

N.B.: The higher the specific gravity, the heavier the liqueur.

Because of the rapidly expanding interest in liqueurs and cordials, many new brands and combinations of flavors are constantly entering the market. From 1970 to 1976 consumption of liqueurs and cordials has increased about 60 percent.

26
COCKTAILS
AND OTHER
MIXED DRINKS

The cocktail is a purely American institution, and there are almost as many versions of the origin of its name as there are legends about the beds George Washington is said to have slept in. Actually, the first cocktail was made by the first person who mixed his wine with a bit of honey or an herb or two to give it zest.

history

One story is that Betsy Flanagan, a spirited Irish lass who had a tavern near Yorktown, New York, was responsible for naming the cocktail. In 1779 Betsy's Tavern was a meeting place for the American and French officers of Washington's army. Here they came to relax and to fortify themselves for the rigors of the campaign with a concoction called a bracer. The officers used to tease Betsy about the fine chickens owned by a Tory neighbor, until one day she threatened to make them eat their words.

No true patriot would buy anything from a Tory, but Betsy arranged for the patrons of her tavern to have a Tory chicken feast, and when it was over they repaired to the bar to continue the celebration with bracers. To their amusement, they found each bottle of bracer decorated with a cock's tail from the Tory farmer's roost. A toast was called for, and one of the Frenchmen exclaimed: *"Vive le cock tail."* Thenceforth Betsy's concoctions were known as cocktails, a name that has prevailed to this day.

mixing guidelines

A cocktail is a fairly short drink made by mixing liquor and/or wine with fruit juices, eggs, and/or bitters, by either stirring or shaking in a bar glass. A mixed drink is liquor with a mixer, usually served in a tall glass over ice.

Cocktails made from liquor and wine are always stirred, except in a few private clubs, where traditionally they are shaken. Cocktails that include sugar or eggs are always shaken. Mixing in an electric blender gives the same effect as shaking.

The object of a cocktail is to mix two or more ingredients so that the result is a pleasant, palatable drink. No single ingredient should overshadow the rest. An unbalanced mixture produces an unsatisfying drink. Because cocktails are always mixed with ice, their strength varies with the length of time they remain in contact with the ice, which dilutes the liquor as it melts.

If you want to be sure that your cocktails are always the same, use a measure for the ingredients and always use exactly the same quantities. While experienced bartenders usually measure by eye, their drinks vary. This does not necessarily mean that they produce a good cocktail and then a bad one, but simply that at a large bar, where there are several bartenders, no two will make identical cocktails unless they all use a measuring jigger. Here are some important measurements:

A jigger is 1½ liquid ounces
A pony is 1 liquid ounce
A dash is ⅙ teaspoon, or about 10 drops
A teaspoon is ⅙ ounce
A wineglass is 4 ounces

Sometimes recipes are given in parts, as cocktail glasses vary greatly in size. Melting ice adds from ½ to ¾ ounce liquid to a cocktail if it is shaken for ten seconds, and proportionately more if shaken longer.

basic rules   There are a few fundamentals that if followed with care will contribute to making pleasant, palatable mixed drinks.

1. Accuracy in the formula ensures uniformity. Follow recipes carefully.
2. Measure ingredients. Use a measuring jigger.
3. Mixed drinks are only as good as the ingredients used. Always use the best, whether it be liquor, fruit juice, or mixer.
4. Always use fresh, clean ice. Never rinse or reuse ice even for making a new batch of the same cocktail. Use ice cubes for long drinks and cocktails that are stirred. Use cracked ice for cocktails that are shaken. Shaved ice is too fine in a hand-shaken cocktail; it will melt and dilute before chilling the drink properly. When making drinks in a blender, however, shaved ice is the most practical to use.
5. To remove the snowy look on ice cubes, sprinkle them with lukewarm water.
6. Use only perfect, fresh fruit. Do not slice oranges or lemons too thinly; they will curl and appear to droop. Cover the sliced fruit with a damp napkin to keep it fresh and prevent it from drying out. When preparing orange or lemon peel for garnish, remove the white pithy underlining, as it is bitter. A twist is a small strip of peel that is twisted over the glass to release its aromatic oils. It is then dropped into the drink.

7. Lemons and oranges give more juice if you first soak them in warm water.

8. Use only the best mixer, be it soda water,° tonic (or quinine water), ginger ale, or whatever. A mediocre or poor mixer will spoil the finest liquor.

9. For aromatic bitters† or other ingredients where the recipe usually specifies only a dash, use a special dasher stopper. This will ensure the proper dash, which is ⅙ teaspoon.

10. Whenever granulated sugar is called for, use superfine sugar, as it will dissolve more easily than the standard granulated sugar.

11. Use white of egg only for foaming cocktails.

12. When mixing the ingredients for a cocktail, always add the liquor last. For a mixed drink, put the liquor in first.

13. Stir briskly cocktails that should be stirred. These are generally mixtures of liquor and wine. Stir long enough to mix—approximately seven stirs.

14. Shake firmly (do not rock) cocktails that are shaken. These are usually cocktails that contain sugar, fruit juices, cordials, or cream.

15. To muddle ingredients, use a wooden muddler or the back of a spoon to crush solid pieces so they may be mixed with the liquid.

16. Glassware should sparkle.

17. Always strain cocktails before serving them.

18. Do not leave ice in the "dividend" remaining in the cocktail shaker. It will dilute the remains and produce a watery second round.

19. Serving a cocktail in a prechilled glass will keep it cold longer than serving it in a warm glass. If you wish to frost the rim of the cocktail glass, moisten the rim lightly and dip it in powdered sugar.

syrups

Sometimes recipes call for a syrup, three of which are described below. These may be either made or purchased.

SUGAR SYRUP may be prepared in advance and stored in the refrigerator. To make sugar syrup, dissolve 2 cups sugar in 1 cup water in a saucepan. Simmer for 5 to 10 minutes. Pour into a bottle or jar, cool, and cover. Larger amounts may be prepared for punches. Use wherever recipes call for sugar syrup or simple syrup.

GRENADINE is sweet and has a deep red color and the flavor of pomegranates. In fact, the French word for pomegranate is *grenadier*. Grenadine is available without alcohol or with very little alcohol, about 5 proof. It is an ingredient in certain mixed drinks, but it may also be used as a general sweetening agent.

FALERNUM is a pleasant flavoring syrup, with a small amount of alcohol (6

° Wherever soda water is mentioned, it is used as a generic term that includes sparkling water, charged water, mineral water, seltzer, and club soda.

† Wherever aromatic bitters are mentioned, use Angostura brand.

percent), made up of simple syrup, lime, almond, ginger, and other spices. It is milky colored.

Falernum was invented over two hundred years ago in Barbados, British West Indies, and was named after the ancient Falernian wine of Roman times. Aside from this, Falernum has no connection with wine or Italy, for it is made in the West Indies and the United States. Its principal use is as a flavoring and sweetening ingredient in rum drinks.

ORGEAT is a sweet, white, nonalcoholic, almond-flavored syrup.

types of mixed drinks   Mixed drinks have a very special nomenclature. The following list should be helpful in identifying the type of mixed drink, the glass in which it is served, and the ingredients of which it is made.

TYPES OF MIXED DRINKS

DRINK	GLASS°	INGREDIENTS	ICE
Aperitif	Wine or cocktail	Straight and mixed	Chill
	Old-fashioned		Cubes
Cobbler	Stemmed goblet	Whisky, sherry, or port; sugar; fruit	Cracked or shaved
Cocktail	Cocktail	According to recipe	Cracked—in shaker only
	Old-fashioned		Cubes
Collins	Collins	Liquor, lemon juice, sugar, soda water, fruit	Cracked
Cooler	Collins	Liquor, lemon juice, ginger ale or soda water, grenadine or powdered sugar, bitters, fruit if desired	Cracked
Crusta	Wine	Liquor, orange slice, lemon juice, maraschino, aromatic bitters (sugar rim of glass)	Cracked—in shaker only
Cup	Stem glass or cup (serve in pitcher or bowl)	Liquor, Curaçao, cucumber rind, brandy, fruit, mint	Cubes or block

° Glassware is described in Chapter 28.

DRINK	GLASS	INGREDIENTS	ICE
Daisy	Highball or metal stein	Liquor, grenadine, lemon juice, soda water, fruit	Shaved
Eggnog	Cup or old-fashioned	Liquor, egg, milk, sugar, nutmeg	Cracked—in shaker only
Fix	Highball	Liquor, lemon juice, sugar, water, fruit	Shaved
Fizz	Highball	Liquor, lemon juice, sugar, soda water	Cubes
Flip	Cocktail	Liquor, sugar, egg, nutmeg	Cracked—in shaker only
Frappé	Cocktail or saucer	Liqueur	Shaved
Highball	Highball	Liquor, ginger ale or soda water	Cubes
Hot Buttered Rum	Mug	Rum, sugar, hard butter, cinnamon, cloves, nutmeg	Boiling water
Julep	Tankard or Collins	Liquor, sugar, mint	Shaved
Puff	Collins	Brandy, fresh milk, tonic	Cubes
Punch	Cup, Collins, or tankard (serve in bowl)	According to recipe	Cubes or block
Rickey	Highball	Liquor, lime, soda water	Cubes
Sangaree	Highball	Liquor, sweetening, nutmeg	Cracked
Sling	Collins	Liquor, fruit juice, liqueurs, soda water, fruit	Cubes
Smash	Old-fashioned	Liquor, lump sugar, mint	Cubes
Sour	Sour	Liquor, lemon juice, sugar, fruit	Cracked—in shaker only
	Old-fashioned		Cubes

DRINK	GLASS	INGREDIENTS	ICE
Swizzle	Highball	Liquor, sweetening, soda water	Cubes
Toddy	Toddy (hot) Old-fashioned (cold)	Liquor, lemon, sugar, cloves, cinnamon	Boiling water Cubes

Martini   There is no standard recipe on which all professionals agree. Tastes change with time. The best example of this is the manner in which the fashion has changed for the Martini.

The Martini has always been the most popular cocktail. It is a dry, sharp, appetite-whetting drink, and it is simple to make, requiring less fuss and bother than many other mixtures. Consequently it is made more often in the home. Those who make this cocktail at home develop a taste for it and naturally order it when they go to a bar.

There is some question as to the origin of the Martini and how it got its name. The earliest recipe we have been able to find is for the Martinez Cocktail, which appeared in Professor Jerry Thomas's *Bon Vivant's Companion or How to Mix Drinks*, originally published in 1862. His recipe is a far cry from today's.

Through the years the cocktail became progressively drier. By the time it was referred to as a Martini it had become a mixture of equal parts gin and dry vermouth. Before World War I the accepted standard was two parts gin to one part dry vermouth, stirred briskly with large pieces of ice and strained into a cocktail glass. For twenty years after Repeal the standard recipe was four parts gin to one part dry vermouth. The ratio gradually crept up to fifteen to one, and eventually to the foolishness of chilled gin being called a Martini because it was served in a cocktail glass. When one of the basic ingredients of a recipe is totally eliminated, it is time to give the recipe a new name.

To give you a clearer picture of the development of the Dry Martini recipe, note the changes that have taken place over the past century.

MARTINEZ COCKTAIL
(*Professor Jerry Thomas's original recipe*)

1 dash bitters
2 dashes maraschino liqueur
1 pony Old Tom gin
1 wineglass vermouth
2 small lumps of ice

Shake up thoroughly and strain into a large cocktail glass. Put a quarter of a slice of lemon in the glass and serve. If the guest prefers it very sweet, add two dashes of gum syrup.

MARTINI COCKTAIL
(*Mauve Decade recipe*)

1 part gin
1 part dry vermouth

DRY MARTINI COCKTAIL
(*pre-Prohibition*)

2 parts gin
1 part dry vermouth
1 dash orange bitters

VERY DRY MARTINI COCKTAIL
(*pre–World War II*)

4 parts gin
1 part dry vermouth
1 dash orange bitters or
twist of lemon

MARTINI
(*post–World War II*)

15 parts gin
1 part dry vermouth
garnishes

NAKED MARTINI

gin on the rocks
garnishes

There appears to be a reversal taking place in Martini fashion. Some devotees who enjoy a not-so-dry Martini have reverted to the pre–World War II recipe of a four-to-one Martini. These ingredients are stirred in a mixing glass with ice, and in most bars a piece of lemon peel is twisted over the cocktail after it is strained into the glass to give the added zip of the oil from the peel. A Martini can also be served on the rocks and should be garnished with a small olive. If garnished with one or more pearl onions, the drink becomes a Gibson.

Some variations that have captured popular fancy are:

VODKA MARTINI

7 parts vodka
1 part dry vermouth

SAKÉ MARTINI (SAKINI)

3 parts gin
1 part saké
olive

COCKTAILS

The following are standard recipes for the most popular cocktails and long drinks. In addition to these, new cocktails are continuously being developed. Some are successful and endure, while others last only a short time.

ALEXANDER

½ ounce crème de cacao
½ ounce gin
½ ounce heavy cream

Shake well with cracked ice and strain into cocktail glass.

VARIATION: For a Brandy Alexander, substitute brandy for the gin.

AMERICANO

1½ ounces Campari
1½ ounces sweet vermouth

Pour over cracked ice in old-fashioned glass and stir. Add twist of lemon.

BACARDI

juice of ½ large or 1 small lime
½ teaspoon sugar
1 dash grenadine
1½ ounces Bacardi White Label rum

Shake lime juice, sugar, and grenadine with cracked ice until cold. Put in rum and shake until shaker frosts. Strain into cocktail glass.

BANSHEE

1 ounce cream
½ ounce simple syrup
¾ ounce white crème de cacao
¾ ounce crème de bananes°

Blend with shaved ice and strain into cocktail glass.

BETWEEN THE SHEETS

juice of ¼ lemon
½ ounce brandy
½ ounce Triple Sec or Cointreau
½ ounce light rum

Shake well with cracked ice and strain into cocktail glass.

° 1½ ounces chocolate banana liqueur may be substituted for the crème de cacao and crème de bananes.

BLACK RUSSIAN

1 ounce vodka
½ ounce Kahlúa

Pour over ice cubes in old-fashioned glass and stir.

VARIATION: For a White Russian, add ½ ounce cream.

BRANDY CRUSTA

Moisten the edge of a cocktail glass with lemon juice and dip in sugar. Cut the rind of half a lemon into a spiral and place in glass. To a bar glass add:

1 teaspoon lemon juice
1 teaspoon maraschino
¾ ounce Triple Sec
1½ ounces brandy
1 dash aromatic bitters

Shake well with cracked ice and strain into cocktail glass. Add slice of orange.

BRAVE BULL

1½ ounces Tequila
1 ounce Kahlúa

Pour over ice cubes in old-fashioned glass and stir. Add twist of lemon.

BRONX

In a mixing glass muddle several pieces of sliced orange that have a bit of the rind on them to give flavor. To this add:

½ ounce sweet vermouth
½ ounce dry vermouth
1 ounce gin

Shake well with cracked ice and strain into cocktail glass.

CHAMPAGNE COCKTAIL

Place 1 cube of sugar saturated with 1 dash of aromatic bitters in cocktail glass. Add cube of ice. Fill glass with chilled Champagne and add twist of lemon.

CLOVER CLUB

$\frac{3}{4}$ ounce lemon juice
white of 1 egg
$1\frac{1}{2}$ ounces gin
1 teaspoon grenadine

Shake well with cracked ice and strain into cocktail glass.

Daiquiri   This is the most popular cocktail made with light rum. The origin of the recipe is unknown, but the drink got its name shortly after the Spanish-American War of 1898, when a group of American engineers was invited to Santiago, Cuba, to help develop the Daiquiri iron mines. The job was hard, the climate was hot, and at the end of a long day's work the men needed a refreshing relaxer. It was made from the ingredients most readily available—rum, limes, ice, and sugar to balance the acidity of the lime juice. On weekends the engineers' headquarters in Santiago was the bar of the Venus Hotel, where the bartender would make this cocktail for them. On one such occasion, early in 1900, Jennings S. Cox, the chief engineer, suggested that the cocktail be named the Daiquiri after the mines, and so it has remained ever since.

Perhaps the biggest Daiquiri ever made was mixed right at the mines in honor of Charles M. Schwab, president of Bethlehem Steel Company, on one of his inspection trips. According to accounts, the hosts used half an oak barrel into which they emptied two big pails of ice, the juice of a hundred limes, a pound of sugar, and ten bottles of Bacardi Carta Blanca rum. This was stirred briskly with a wooden paddle and ladled out to Schwab and his entourage when they emerged from the mine pits.

If it is properly made, a Daiquiri is a most delightful and refreshing cocktail. It must never be made with lemon juice; only freshly squeezed lime juice will make a proper Daiquiri. You can also use the frozen Daiquiri mix, which contains lime juice. For the Daiquiri as it was prepared in the Floradida Bar in Havana, Cuba, add $\frac{1}{4}$ ounce maraschino.

DAIQUIRI

juice of $\frac{1}{2}$ lime, freshly squeezed
1 teaspoon sugar
$1\frac{1}{2}$ ounces light rum

Shake the lime juice and sugar with cracked ice until it gets cold. Add rum and shake until the shaker frosts. Strain into cocktail glass.

IMPORTANT: A Daiquiri should be drunk immediately because the rum, lime, and sugar tend to separate if the drink is allowed to stand.

FROZEN DAIQUIRI

For a Frozen Daiquiri, use the basic Daiquiri ingredients, with shaved ice instead of cracked ice, and mix in a blender.

DUBONNET COCKTAIL

½ ounce gin
1 ounce red Dubonnet

Stir well with cracked ice and strain into cocktail glass.

FRAPPÉ

Pour 1½ ounces of any liqueur into a cocktail or saucer glass filled with finely shaved ice. Serve with a straw.

GIMLET

½ ounce Rose's Lime Juice (unsweetened)
1½ ounces gin

Stir with an ice cube and strain into cocktail glass or serve over ice cubes in old-fashioned glass. Garnish with a slice of lime.

VARIATION: For a Vodka Gimlet, substitute vodka for the gin.

GODFATHER

1½ ounces Scotch whisky
1½ ounces amaretto

Pour over ice cubes in old-fashioned glass and stir.

GODMOTHER

1½ ounces vodka
1½ ounces amaretto

Pour over ice cubes in old-fashioned glass and stir. Some cream may be added.

GOLDEN CADILLAC

2 ounces light cream
¾ ounce Galliano liqueur
¾ ounce white crème de cacao

Shake well with cracked ice and strain into cocktail glass.

GRASSHOPPER

¾ ounce light cream
¾ ounce green crème de menthe
¾ ounce white crème de cacao

Shake well with cracked ice until very cold. Strain into cocktail glass.

HALF & HALF

2 ounces sweet vermouth
2 ounces dry vermouth

Pour over ice cubes in old-fashioned glass and stir. Add twist of lemon.

JACK ROSE

juice of ½ lime
1 teaspoon grenadine
1½ ounces applejack

Shake well with cracked ice and strain into cocktail glass.

MAI TAI

½ teaspoon sugar
½ ounce lime juice
1 ounce light rum
1 ounce dark rum
½ ounce Curaçao
½ ounce Orgeat
1 ounce grenadine

Shake well with cracked ice and strain into cocktail glass or serve over ice cubes in old-fashioned glass. Decorate with fresh pineapple and cocktail cherry.

MANHATTAN	or	DRY MANHATTAN
1½ ounces rye or blended whisky		1½ ounces whisky
¾ ounce sweet vermouth		¾ ounce dry vermouth
1 dash aromatic bitters		1 dash aromatic bitters

Stir well with cracked ice and strain into cocktail glass. Decorate with cocktail cherry or twist of lemon.

MARGARITA

juice of ½ lime or lemon
1½ ounces Tequila
½ ounce Triple Sec

Shake well with cracked ice and strain into cocktail glass rimmed with salt.

NEGRONI

1 ounce Campari
1 ounce sweet vermouth
1 ounce gin

Shake well with cracked ice and strain into cocktail glass.

VARIATION: For a tall drink pour over ice cubes in highball glass and fill with soda water.

OLD FASHIONED

Place in an old-fashioned glass:
1 cube sugar muddled with ½ jigger water
1½ ounces whisky
3 dashes aromatic bitters

Add ice cubes and stir. Garnish with slice of orange and cocktail cherry. Add twist of lemon and serve with cocktail pick.

ORANGE BLOSSOM

1 ounce orange juice
1 teaspoon sugar
1½ ounces gin

Shake well with cracked ice and strain into cocktail glass.

PINK LADY

1 egg white
juice of ½ lemon
1½ ounces gin
1½ ounces applejack
½ ounce grenadine

Shake well with cracked ice and strain into cocktail glass.

PINK SQUIRREL

1 ounce light cream
1 ounce crème de noyaux (almond) or cherry liqueur
½ ounce white crème de cacao

Shake well with cracked ice and strain into cocktail glass.

PRESIDENTE

1½ ounces light rum
¾ ounce dry vermouth
2 dashes Curaçao
1 dash grenadine

Shake well with cracked ice and strain into cocktail glass.

ROB ROY	or	DRY ROB ROY
¾ ounce Scotch whisky		¾ ounce Scotch whisky
¾ ounce sweet vermouth		¾ ounce dry vermouth
2 dashes aromatic bitters		2 dashes aromatic bitters

Shake well with cracked ice and strain into cocktail glass.

RUSTY NAIL

½ ounce Drambuie
1½ ounces Scotch whisky

Pour over ice cubes in old-fashioned glass and stir.

SALTY DOG

3 ounces grapefruit juice
1½ ounces gin
dash salt

Pour over ice cubes in old-fashioned glass and stir.

SAZERAC

1 cube sugar
1 teaspoon water
2 dashes Pernod or Ricard
1 dash aromatic bitters
1 dash Peychaud Bitters
2 ounces Bourbon whisky

Coat the inside of a chilled glass with the Pernod or Ricard. Discard any excess. Muddle the cube of sugar with the teaspoon of water and the 2 dashes of bitters. Add ice cubes. Pour in Bourbon and top with twist of lemon. If Peychaud Bitters are not available, use an extra dash of aromatic bitters.

SCARLETT O'HARA

2 ounces orange juice
1 ounce grenadine
$\frac{3}{4}$ ounce Southern Comfort

Pour over ice cubes in old-fashioned glass and stir.

SCOTCH MIST

Pour $1\frac{1}{2}$ ounces Scotch whisky into old-fashioned glass filled with shaved ice. Add twist of lemon.

VARIATION: For a Whisky Mist, substitute any whisky for the Scotch.

SHERRY FLIP

1 egg
1 teaspoon powdered sugar
$1\frac{1}{2}$ ounces sweet sherry

Shake well and pour over ice cubes in old-fashioned glass. Sprinkle a little nutmeg on top.

VARIATIONS: Brandy, port, rum, or whisky may be substituted for the sherry.

SIDE CAR

$\frac{1}{2}$ ounce lemon juice
$\frac{1}{2}$ ounce Triple Sec
$\frac{1}{2}$ ounce brandy

Shake well with cracked ice and strain into cocktail glass.

STINGER

$\frac{3}{4}$ ounce brandy
$\frac{3}{4}$ ounce white crème de menthe

Shake well with cracked ice and strain into cocktail glass. Add twist of lemon.

TEQUILA SUNRISE

4 ounces orange juice
1½ ounces Tequila
½ to ¾ ounce grenadine

Pour orange juice and Tequila over ice cubes in old-fashioned glass and stir. Add grenadine and let it settle to the bottom. Stir very gently and watch the "sunrise."

WHISKY SMASH

1 cube sugar
1 ounce water
mint sprigs
1½ ounces whisky

Muddle sugar with water and a few sprigs of mint in old-fashioned glass. Add ice cubes. Pour in whisky and stir. Decorate with four or five sprigs of mint. Serve with soda water on the side.

WHISKY SOUR

¾ ounce lemon or lime juice
1 teaspoon powdered sugar
1½ ounces Bourbon or blended whisky

Shake well with cracked ice and strain into sour glass. When served over ice cubes, use old-fashioned glass. Add cocktail cherry and slice of orange.

VARIATIONS: Scotch, gin, brandy, rum, Tequila, or vodka may be substituted for the whisky. For an Apricot Sour, substitute apricot-flavored brandy for the whisky.

LONG DRINKS

APRICOT COOLER

juice of ½ lemon or 1 lime
1½ ounces apricot-flavored brandy
2 dashes grenadine
soda water

Shake lemon or lime juice, apricot-flavored brandy, and grenadine well and pour over cracked ice in highball glass. Fill with soda water.

BLOODY MARY

3 ounces tomato juice
juice of ½ lemon
1½ ounces vodka
2 dashes Worcestershire sauce
dash of salt and pepper

Shake well (shaking produces a superb drink) and pour over ice cubes in highball glass. This recipe makes an excellent Bloody Mary, particularly when Sacramento or another thick tomato juice is used. Some people use more Worcestershire sauce, some add a dash of Tabasco sauce, and some substitute gin for the vodka.

BULL SHOT

1½ ounces vodka
4 ounces beef bouillon
dash of salt and pepper

Pour over ice cubes in highball glass and stir.

COFFEE ROYALE

5 ounces very hot black coffee
1 sugar cube
1½ ounces brandy

Pour coffee into a cup. Place spoon across cup and pour some brandy into spoon with sugar cube. Pour balance of brandy into the coffee. Place before guest and ignite brandy in spoon. Stir when flame subsides and add twist of lemon.

CUBA LIBRE

1½ ounces light or dark rum
6 ounces cola

Pour over ice cubes in highball glass and stir. Some people squeeze and insert a wedge of a fresh lime.

FRENCH 75

juice of 1 lemon
1 teaspoon sugar
1½ ounces brandy
Champagne

Shake lemon juice, sugar, and brandy well and pour over ice cubes in highball glass. Fill with chilled Champagne.

GIN AND BITTER LEMON

1½ ounces gin
6 ounces bitter lemon

Pour over ice cubes in highball glass and stir. Add twist of lemon.

VARIATION: For a Vodka and Bitter Lemon, substitute vodka for the gin.

GIN DAISY

juice of ½ lemon
½ teaspoon powdered sugar
1 teaspoon grenadine
1½ ounces gin
soda water

Shake lemon juice, sugar, grenadine, and gin well and pour over shaved ice in highball glass or metal stein. Add soda water as desired. Garnish with fruit.

VARIATIONS: Brandy, rum, vodka, or whisky may be substituted for the gin.

GIN FIX

juice of ¼ lemon
1 tablespoon powdered sugar
1 ounce water
1½ ounces gin

Shake well and pour into highball glass filled with shaved ice. Garnish with lemon slice and other fruit.

VARIATIONS: Brandy, rum, or whisky may be substituted for the gin.

GIN FIZZ

juice of ½ lemon
1 teaspoon sugar
1½ ounces gin
soda water

Shake lemon juice, sugar, and gin well and pour over ice cubes in highball glass. Fill with soda water and add twist of lemon.

VARIATION: For a Silver Fizz, make as above but shake with 1 egg white.

GIN RICKEY

juice and rind of ½ lime
2 ounces gin
soda water

Pour lime juice and gin over ice cubes in highball glass and stir. Fill with soda water and drop lime rind into drink.

VARIATION: For a Sloe Gin Rickey, substitute sloe gin liqueur for the gin.

GIN AND TONIC

1½ ounces gin
6 ounces tonic

Pour over ice cubes in highball glass and stir. Squeeze lime wedge and drop into drink.

VARIATION: For a Vodka and Tonic, substitute vodka for the gin.

HARVEY WALLBANGER

1 ounce vodka
6 ounces orange juice
½ ounce Galliano liqueur

Pour vodka and orange juice over ice cubes in highball glass and stir. Float liqueur on top.

HIGHLAND COOLER

juice of ½ lemon
1 teaspoon powdered sugar
1½ ounces Scotch whisky
2 dashes aromatic bitters
ginger ale

Shake lemon juice, powdered sugar, whisky, and bitters well and pour over ice cubes in Collins glass. Fill with ginger ale.

VARIATIONS: Gin, rum, or vodka may be substituted for the Scotch whisky.

HOT BUTTERED RUM

This is the classic warmer-upper of colonial days, and it is still popular today. It is guaranteed to take away cold stiffness if you have been skating, skiing, or out in the cold too long. We do not recommend it if you are going back out into the freezing cold weather.

1 teaspoon sugar
1½ ounces dark rum
5 ounces boiling water
1 pat hard butter
nutmeg or cloves
1 cinnamon stick

Rinse an 8-ounce mug or cup with hot water. Put in the sugar, rum, and boiling water. Float the pat of butter on the surface and sprinkle with nutmeg. Use the cinnamon stick as a stirrer. Inhale the wonderful aroma and drink while the mixture is good and hot.

IRISH COFFEE

This drink was made famous by the Buena Vista Café at San Francisco's Fisherman's Wharf shortly after World War II. It has since become popular all over the world.

1 teaspoon sugar
1½ ounces Irish whiskey
5 ounces very hot, strong black coffee
whipped cream

Rinse an 8-ounce stemmed goblet with very hot water. Place the sugar in the glass and pour in the Irish whiskey and coffee. Stir to dissolve sugar and top with whipped cream.

KIR

4 ounces chilled dry white Burgundy wine
¼ ounce crème de cassis (or to taste)

Pour over ice cubes in wineglass or highball glass and stir.

MIMOSA

2 ounces orange juice
6½ ounces (a split) Champagne
1 teaspoon Grand Marnier (optional)

Pour over ice cubes in highball glass and stir.

MINT JULEP

In a Collins glass or pewter tankard, dissolve 1 teaspoon sugar in just enough water to cover it. Fill with shaved ice. Pour in Bourbon whisky to within a half-inch of the top. Stir until glass is thoroughly frosted. Decorate generously with fresh mint.

If you want a more pronounced mint flavor, crush a sprig of mint together with the sugar and water and leave it in the glass. Then pack with ice, add the Bourbon, stir, and decorate.

MOSCOW MULE

$1\frac{1}{2}$ ounces vodka
juice of $\frac{1}{2}$ lime
ginger beer

Pour vodka and lime juice over ice cubes in an 8-ounce copper mug and stir. Fill with ginger beer. Garnish with wedge of lime.

PIÑA COLADA

$1\frac{1}{2}$ ounces cream of coconut
3 tablespoons crushed pineapple
3 ounces light rum

Blend with shaved ice and strain into Collins glass. Serve with a straw.

PLANTER'S PUNCH

1 ounce lime juice
1 teaspoon sugar
2 ounces Jamaican rum

Dissolve the sugar in the lime juice in a bar glass. Put in the rum and cracked ice and shake well. Strain into a highball glass that is half filled with finely cracked ice. Decorate with maraschino cherry, sliver of fresh pineapple, half a slice of orange, and sprig of mint. Serve with a straw.

PORT WINE SANGAREE

$2\frac{1}{4}$ ounces port wine
$\frac{1}{2}$ ounce simple syrup

Pour over ice cubes in highball glass and stir. Grate nutmeg on top.

RUM SWIZZLE

juice of 1 lime
1 teaspoon powdered sugar
$1\frac{1}{2}$ ounces light rum
2 dashes bitters
soda water

Shake lime juice, sugar, rum, and bitters well and pour over ice cubes in highball glass. Fill with soda water. Serve with swizzle stick.

VARIATIONS: Brandy, gin, or whisky may be substituted for the rum.

RUM TODDY

1 cube sugar
$1\frac{1}{2}$ ounces dark rum
boiling water
1 cinnamon stick
lemon slice
cloves

Place sugar cube and rum in toddy glass and fill with boiling water. Insert one small piece of cinnamon and one slice of lemon garnished with cloves. Stir. Serve with a spoon and a small pitcher of hot water on the side.

SCREWDRIVER

$1\frac{1}{2}$ ounces vodka
5 ounces orange juice

Pour over ice cubes in highball glass and stir.

SHERRY COBBLER

2 ounces sweet sherry
$\frac{3}{4}$ ounce simple syrup

Pour over shaved ice in stemmed goblet and stir. Decorate with fresh fruits, cubed or sliced, cocktail cherry, and sprig of mint. Serve with a straw.

VARIATIONS: Whisky or port may be substituted for the sherry.

SINGAPORE SLING

1 ounce lime juice
1 ounce cherry liqueur
2 ounces gin
soda water

Shake lime juice, cherry liqueur, and gin well and pour over ice cubes in Collins glass. Fill with soda water. Decorate with orange slice and sprig of mint. Then add through the middle with a dropper:

4 drops Bénédictine
4 drops brandy   (or 8 drops B & B)

This recipe is the original from the Raffles Hotel in Singapore.

SLOE GIN FIZZ

$\frac{3}{4}$ ounce lemon juice
1 teaspoon powdered sugar
$1\frac{1}{2}$ ounces sloe gin liqueur
soda water

Shake lemon juice, sugar, and sloe gin liqueur well and pour over ice cubes in highball glass. Fill with soda water.

TOM COLLINS

$\frac{3}{4}$ ounce lemon juice
1 teaspoon powdered sugar
$1\frac{1}{2}$ ounces gin
soda water

Shake lemon juice, sugar, and gin well and pour over ice cubes in Collins glass. Fill with soda water.

VARIATION: For a Vodka Collins, substitute vodka for the gin.

TOM AND JERRY

1 egg, separated
1 teaspoon powdered sugar
1 ounce brandy
1 ounce dark rum
hot milk or boiling water

In an 8-ounce cup mix the yolk of the egg with the sugar. Pour in brandy and rum. Stir thoroughly. Put in the beaten white of egg and, while stirring, pour in hot milk or boiling water to fill the cup. Sprinkle nutmeg on top.

VERMOUTH CASSIS

$1\frac{1}{2}$ ounces dry vermouth
$\frac{1}{4}$ ounce crème de cassis
soda water

Pour vermouth and crème de cassis over ice cubes in highball glass and stir. Fill with soda water.

WARD EIGHT

1 ounce lemon juice
1½ ounces whisky
1 teaspoon grenadine
soda water

Shake lemon juice, whisky, and grenadine well and pour over ice cubes in highball glass. Fill with soda water.

ZOMBIE°

¾ ounce lime juice
¾ ounce pineapple juice
1 teaspoon Falernum or simple syrup
1 ounce light rum
2 ounces medium rum
1 ounce Jamaican rum
½ ounce 151-proof Demeraran rum
½ ounce apricot liqueur

Shake well and pour into 14-ounce Zombie glass half-filled with shaved ice. Garnish with slice of orange and several sprigs of mint. Serve with a straw.

PUNCHES AND WINE CUPS

BRANDY MILK PUNCH

1 pint brandy
1 quart milk
4 teaspoons sugar

Stir together in a punch bowl. Add a small block of ice and dust top liberally with nutmeg. Serves twelve.

CHAMPAGNE CUP

1 tablespoon powdered sugar
4 ounces brandy
2 ounces Curaçao
1 ounce maraschino
1 ounce Grand Marnier
1 bottle Champagne

° The original recipe is supposedly still a closely guarded secret of Don the Beachcomber.

Stir together in a pitcher or bowl. Add a small block of ice and decorate with slices of orange and pineapple, one piece of cucumber rind, and sprigs of mint. Serve in a stem glass or punch cup.

VARIATIONS: Claret, Rhine wine, or Sauternes may be substituted for the Champagne.

FISH HOUSE PUNCH

¾ pound loaf sugar
1 to 2 quarts water
1 quart lemon juice
2 quarts Jamaican rum
1 quart Cognac
4 ounces peach liqueur

Dissolve loaf sugar in the water in punch bowl. When entirely dissolved, add lemon juice, then all the other ingredients. Put a large piece of solid ice in the punch bowl and allow the mixture to steep for about two hours, stirring occasionally. In winter, when ice melts slowly, more water may be used; in summer, less. The melting ice dilutes the mixture sufficiently. This will make 1½ gallons, depending on dilution.

This is the original Fish House Punch, made by the Fish House Club, now called the State in Schuylkill, founded in 1732. We are indebted to Anna Wetherill Reed, in whose *Philadelphia Cook Book of Town and Country* this recipe appears.

MAYWINE PUNCH

½ package Waldmeister°
13 bottles German or Alsatian wine
1 bottle Champagne
2 ounces Bénédictine
2 ounces Cognac
¼ pound sugar
1 quart soda water

Soak Waldmeister six hours in 1 bottle of wine. Strain and mix with 12 remaining bottles. Add Champagne, Bénédictine, and Cognac. Dissolve sugar in soda water and add. Decorate with strawberries and fresh Waldmeister. When sufficiently cold, serve in wineglasses from a punch bowl. To keep the punch cold, place a pitcher full of shaved ice in the center of the bowl. This will serve approximately 100 cups of 3½ ounces each.

° Waldmeister is sweet-scented woodruff, a European woodland herb.

MULLED RED WINE

2 cups water
1 cup sugar
4 cinnamon sticks
4 cloves
2 lemons
1 bottle claret or Burgundy

Boil the water with the sugar, cinnamon, and cloves for five minutes. Then add the lemons sliced very thin, cover, and let stand for ten minutes. Add the wine and heat gradually, but do not allow to boil. Serve very hot in a pitcher or brown jug. A spoon placed in each glass will prevent it from cracking.

SANGRIA

Throughout the Spanish-speaking world one of the traditional ways of enjoying wine is in the form of a wine cup, the Sangria. The recipe given is more time-consuming than using bottled Sangria, but the fresh fruit flavor more than compensates.

$\frac{1}{4}$ cup sugar (or to taste)
1 cup water
1 orange, thinly sliced
1 lime, thinly sliced
1 bottle red or white wine
6 ounces soda water

Dissolve sugar in water in large pitcher. Add fruit and wine, plus 12 or more ice cubes. Stir until cold. Add sparkling water. Serve, putting some of the fruit in each glass.

WASSAIL BOWL

2 cups water
1 teaspoon freshly ground nutmeg
2 teaspoons ground ginger
2-inch stick of cinnamon
6 whole cloves
6 allspice berries
4 coriander seeds
4 cardamom seeds
2 bottles cream sherry or Madeira
2 quarts ale
4 cups sugar
12 eggs, separated
1 cup Cognac or brandy
12 roasted slices of apples or 12 tiny roasted apples

Combine water and spices in a saucepan and simmer for 10 minutes. Add sherry and ale and stir in sugar. Heat, but do not boil. Beat 12 egg yolks until they are pale and thick; fold in 12 stiffly beaten egg whites. Strain half the ale and sherry mixture over the eggs. Turn into a warmed punch bowl. Bring the remaining ale and sherry to a boil and strain it into the punch bowl. Add Cognac and roasted apples or apple slices.

A YARD OF FLANNEL

1 quart ale
2 egg whites
4 egg yolks
4 tablespoons brown sugar
$\frac{1}{2}$ tablespoon nutmeg

Stir brown sugar and nutmeg into beaten egg yolks. Fold in beaten egg whites. Boil ale and gradually stir in egg-sugar-nutmeg mixture. Then pour it rapidly back and forth between two pans until the drink is smooth and finely frothed. Serve hot.

PREPARED COCKTAILS

Certain mixed drinks whose ingredients include wine and spirits can very easily be prepared in large quantities and stored and distributed in bottles and cans. These prepared cocktails are practical for those who do not have facilities in the home for mixing them fresh. They have the advantage of being uniform, and they can be put in the refrigerator until needed.

The most popular varieties are Martinis, Manhattans, Sours, and Daiquiris. But prepared cocktails also include Tequila Sours, Margaritas, Vodka Martinis, Scotch Mists, high-proof Martinis, Black Russians, Gin Collinses and Sours, Gimlets, Screwdrivers, Side Cars, Stingers . . . and many, many others.

The liquor industry had to overcome many obstacles in making prepared cocktails that would keep a long time. The aim was to make drinks that were uniform in quality, that would taste the same a week after the bottle was opened, and in which the sugar would not change flavor or crystallize. With the development of nondairy creamers that need no refrigeration, a new field of prepared drinks has opened up for the liquor industry. Prepared eggnogs, Brandy Alexanders, and Grasshoppers are examples of drinks that formerly had to be made with fresh cream but can now be purchased as finished beverages. In addition to these drinks, new products that taste like milkshakes but need no refrigeration are available in such soda-fountain flavors as chocolate, vanilla, and various fruits. They are sweet and creamy, with an alcoholic strength equivalent to that of fortified wine.

COCKTAIL MIXES

Cocktail mixes are expertly prepared cocktails with all the necessary ingredients except the liquor. To create a Manhattan, for example, add whisky to the appropriate mix.

There are two types of cocktail mixes now on the market: liquid and dry powder. The liquid mix, to which you just add liquor to make the appropriate drink, has been in existence for decades, although the range of cocktails has increased tremendously. The dry mix is a powder to which water and liquor are added to dissolve the powder and create the drink. Recently freeze-dried fruit has been added to dry mixes, making for fresher flavor.

In addition to being convenient, mixes allow the home bartender to be creative. He can add Scotch to the Manhattan mix and get a Rob Roy. The Daiquiri mix is a starting point for a Planter's Punch, Pink Lady, Clover Club, Ward Eight, or Gin Fizz. In addition, of course, the host can choose which brands of liquor he wants to use.

27
PREPARING
WINE LISTS
AND MENUS

In the Mauve Decade and the years before World War I, the art of wining and dining reached its height in this country, epitomized, perhaps, by the Waldorf-Astoria Hotel with its great Oscar as host to fashionable America. Prohibition brought a period of gastronomical and vinicultural depression. But since Repeal, and with the increase of travel, the country has recultivated the fine arts of good living, dining, wining, and stimulating conversation.

A new Waldorf-Astoria replaces the original, but no one can replace Oscar Tschirky, who was the Waldorf's banquet manager par excellence. The banquet manager serves an important function in a hotel. It is his job to know his menus and to know which dishes the chef prepares best for a small party and which for a large party. He must know his wines and how to sell them. He must be the epitome of tact, for it is his job to advise the host or hostess who consults him, suggest the wine or food the host should order, supervise the details of the gathering, and have insight into the tastes of the person he is advising. All in all, it is an important position requiring tact, intelligence, and ability.

The following menu is an example of an informal banquet dinner. A dry white wine can be served through the meal—a Burgundy such as Meursault, a Graves, or an Alsatian Riesling.

Crabmeat Cocktail
Essence of Mushrooms
Celery   Olives   Salted Nuts
Filet of Sea Bass, Bonne Femme
Roast Capon
Green Beans au Beurre
Pommes Anna
Asparagus, Sauce Vinaigrette
Fresh Strawberries
Parfait Glacé à la Vanille
Petits Fours
Coffee

411

For a more formal banquet the following menu with its full complement of wines was served by the Waldorf-Astoria in the 1930s.

APERITIF	Les Canapés Russes
	Amuse-Bouche Gabriel
SHERRY	Le Fumet de Gombo
	Paillettes Dorées
	Céleri Amandes Salées Olives
POUILLY-FUISSÉ 1928	Les Crabes de Californie
	en Turban
CHÂTEAU LÉOVILLE-POYFERRÉ 1928	L'Entrecôte Grillée Vendôme
	Bouquetière de Légumes
	Pommes Colorette
	Salade de Floride
ERNEST IRROY CHAMPAGNE 1928	Feuillantine Nesselrode
	Son Sabayon
COGNAC	Moka
LIQUEURS	

(Courtesy the late Oscar Tschirky, The Waldorf-Astoria Hotel)

The great interest in wining and dining has been evidenced by the formation, in serveral metropolitan centers, of branches of the Wine and Food Society, an organization founded in London by the late André L. Simon, who devoted himself to increasing the enjoyment of the better things of life. The Wine and Food Society holds periodic tastings of wines, spirits, and foods and occasional dinners. The object of the society is to acquaint its members with the most interesting wines or foods that the community affords. Its accomplishment is educational in the truest sense.

Several similar groups exist, and each in its own way also contributes to the general interest in better eating and drinking. The most important of these are the Confrérie des Chevaliers du Tastevin ("The Brotherhood of Gentlemen of the Tasting Cup"), devoted to a greater appreciation of the wines and food of Burgundy; Commanderie de Bordeaux, whose main interest is the wines and food of Bordeaux; and Confrérie de la Chaîne des Rôtisseurs ("The Fraternity of the Turners of the Roasting Spit"), who give their allegiance to good food, especially roasts and the wines that complement them best.

OPPOSITE: Induction dinner of the Confrérie des Chevaliers du Tastevin, January 24, 1977, at the Waldorf-Astoria Hotel in New York.

ESCRITEAU

"In Vino Veritas"

Comité Gastronomique
Chairman
Grand Officier Gordon Bass
Officier Commandeur Jules J. Bond
Officier Commandeur Dorothy McClure Buckner
Officier Commandeur Alfred Rosenthal
Commandeur George R. Suhr

Comité Oenologique
Chairman
Grand Historiographe Richard de Rochemont
Grand Sénéchal
H. Gregory Thomas
Grand Officier Thomas H. Ahrens
Grand Officier Henry N. Sachs
Grand Officier William Zeckendorf, Jr.
Officier Commandeur William E. Hutton
Commandeur Leonard S. Sheriff
Commandeur Maurice E. Blin

Pour la Réception
Les Coquillages de l'Atlantique
Le Saumon Fumé
Les Saucissons de France
La Gougère Bourguignonne

Tattinger Comtes de Champagne, 1966
Blanc de Blanci, Brut

Chablis Premier Cru, 1973
(Joseph Drouhin)
et
Cassis Cartron,
Pour le Kir

Pour l'Intronisation
Clos de Vougeot, 1971
J. Faiveley

Le Dîner

Première Assiette
L'Essence Neptune

Xérès La Ina
(Pedro Domecq)

Deuxième Assiette
Les Ris de Veau des Vignerons

Corton-Charlemagne, 1971
(Louis Jadot)

Troisième Assiette
Les Pigeonneaux Grand-mère
Les Petits Pois Mange-Touts

Richebourg, 1973
(Domaine de la Romanée-Conti)

Le Coup du Milieu
Le Granité de Mirabelle

Mirabelle Maisenez

Chaud-Froid
Le Filet de Charolais en Gelée
Les Fruits du Désert

Charmes Chambertin, 1962
(Prosper Maufoux)

Issue de Table
Le Plateau de Fromages

Pol Roger Brut, 1969

Le Predelvoro
Les Délices de Dijon

Le Café des Chevaliers
Friandises

Cognac Baron Otard
Chartreuse Verte
Kirsch de Zoug
Menthe Blanche (Marie Brizard)

Directeur de Banquets
RUDY MAZZONELLI

Chef Directeur de Cuisine
ARNO SCHMIDT

Maître d'Hôtel
GUNTHER NOETH

"Jamais en Vain
Toujours en Vin"

THE WINE LIST

The wine list is as important a silent salesman for wine as the menu is for food, and it should always be presented to a guest along with the menu.

It is not possible to prepare a wine list that would be equally useful in every establishment, as the wine list, like the menu, must reflect the character of a restaurant and therefore is prepared with a view to the taste of its patrons. While there is a similarity in certain price groups, each hotel or restaurant has to bear in mind its own clientele in preparing its wine list. A great hotel or fashionable restaurant will have an elaborate wine list, while a smaller establishment, whose atmosphere is simpler, will plan its list accordingly. It is not profitable to list a great number and variety of wines when experience shows that there is no demand for them.

The wine list should be simple and should list wines, spirits, beers, and mineral waters. It is no longer necessary to include a chart indicating the wine that should be served with a specific dish.

If there is enough space, it will add interest and invite a guest to peruse the entire wine list if short paragraphs describing each type of wine are included, such as a short account of Champagne or Bordeaux wines. Short descriptions of each wine, if there is room for them, assist a guest in selecting his wine.

In making up a wine list, check all spellings carefully, copying them from the labels on the bottles. Correct vintages should also be listed. Avoid repetition within classes of wine. For instance, one regional Sauternes is enough. There is no point in having three.

One of the best and most balanced wine lists in the United States is that of the New York Hilton at Rockefeller Center. Listing two hundred wines, it is very extensive yet practical for the Hilton. It embodies all of the recommended points, and at one time or another the hotel's guests have ordered all of the wines listed.

There are no arbitrary rules for the order in which wines should appear on a wine list or as to whether cocktails and mixed drinks should appear on a left-hand or right-hand page when a large single-fold list is used.

Our preference is for the following order:

Champagnes	Rhône wines
U.S. Champagnes	Alsatian wines
Sparkling wines (French, Italian, etc.)	Rhine and Moselle wines
Aperitif wines	Italian wines
White Bordeaux	U.S. wines
Red Bordeaux (clarets)	Wines from other countries
White Burgundies	Sherries
Red Burgundies	Portos
	Madeiras

THE WINES

The New York Hilton at Rockefeller Center believes the enjoyment of fine wine and fine food to be integral parts of the art of gracious living. Many months of careful searching, tastings, and retastings by a distinguished committee have gone into the final selection of the wines presented here. Our primary objective was to choose wines we hope will please you. The range of wines includes all the principal producing regions of the world. Our prices are reasonable and our staff has been specially trained to suggest and serve the wines properly. We can assure you that every wine is not only good, but that many are extraordinary . . . and some are unobtainable elsewhere. All of these wines and spirits have been produced by dedicated men with the fond hope that you will enjoy them. Please do!

WHICH WINE
WITH WHICH FOOD

Our simplest rule of thumb is to drink the robust wines with the hearty foods, the gentle wines with the delicate foods, the more expensive wines with the richer, more elegant dishes, and the inexpensive everyday wines with the less extravagant meals.

WE RECOMMEND:

Hors d'oeuvres	Champagne, Rosé Wine
Soups	Sherry
Fish	White Wine
Dark Meats	Red Wine
Light Meats	Rosé Wine or White Wine
Cheese	Red Wine
Dessert	Champagne

The cover of the wine list of the New York Hilton at Rockefeller Center in New York, one of the most complete and well-balanced wine lists in the United States. (*Courtesy the New York Hilton*)

Cognacs and brandies	Rums
Whiskies (blended, Bourbon, and Canadian)	Miscellaneous spirits
Whiskies (Scotch and Irish)	Liqueurs
Vodkas	Beers
Gins	

We list Champagne first because it is generally the most costly; it is good psychology for the guest to come upon the most glamorous wine when he first opens the list. The balance of the listings seem to us to be in a logical order.

Obviously this list does not include all the possibilities; on the other hand, not every establishment need have every category. Where only one or two wines of a given class are stocked, two or more may be listed under one heading, such as Porto and Madeira wines.

Wine lists need not be complicated or very long, but they should be appropriate to the type of restaurant in which they are used. A good selection of five or ten wines is better than a poor selection of fifty. Wine lists should be up to date, and above all they should be available and used. A menu that has changes and deletions is not acceptable in a good restaurant. Therefore it follows that a wine list is not acceptable if it lists items that are out of stock or has many changes.

The wine list should be as clear and clean and presentable as the menu from which the diner selects his food. Enough information should be given on the list so the customer knows what he is ordering without having to ask questions. The type of wine, the size of the bottle, the name of the wine, its vintage if there is any, and the name of the shipper are all important. Identifying each wine by a number may eliminate embarrassment in pronunciation.

In addition to the wine list many establishments with cocktail lounges find it profitable to print a small secondary list including the most popular bar drinks, such as cocktails, mixed drinks, and spirits. This is generally called the drink list. It should be printed on a card, which may be folded, and it may include a small selection of wines, particularly Champagnes.

Establishments doing a large banquet and function business often have a third list, called the banquet wine list, which includes a selection of the more popular mixed drinks, Champagnes, table wines, aperitif wines, spirits, and beers—in short, whatever experience shows is most frequently ordered at large functions. It is important for this list to contain a notation regarding corkage, which is customarily charged when guests bring their own beverages. In most cities this is $8 to $15 a bottle for Champagne and spirits and $5 to $10 for table wines.

OPPOSITE: A partial list of the wines now offered at the Waldorf-Astoria Hotel in New York. (*Courtesy the Waldorf-Astoria Hotel, New York*)

FRENCH CHAMPAGNE

Bin No.		Vintage	Half Bottle	Bottle
8179	LANSON BLACK LABEL, Brut	N.V.		$22.00
8169	TAITTINGER BRUT LA FRANCAISE	N.V.	$14.00	$26.00
8160	LAURENT PERRIER, Extra Dry	N.V.		$24.00
8178	CANARD-DUCHENE, Brut	N.V.		$25.00
8164	MOET et CHANDON WHITE STAR	N.V.		$24.00
8166	PIPER HEIDSIECK, Extra Dry	N.V.	$14.00	$26.00
8158	MUMM'S, Extra Dry	N.V.	$13.00	$24.00
8151	BOLLINGER, Brut	1970		$40.00
8157	MUMM'S CORDON ROUGE, Brut	1969/70	$17.00	$30.00
8165	PIPER HEIDSIECK, Brut	1969/70	$18.00	$35.00
8161	LAURENT PERRIER GRAND SIECLE	1966/69		$55.00
8163	MOET et CHANDON "CUVEE DOM PERIGNON"	1969		$55.00
8170	TAITTINGER COMTES de CHAMPAGNE Blanc de Blancs, Brut	1969		$56.00

FRENCH PINK CHAMPAGNE

Bin No.		Vintage	Half Bottle	Bottle
8167	PIPER HEIDSIECK, Pink	1969		$35.00
8171	TAITTINGER COMTES de CHAMPAGNE, Brut Rose	1969		$56.00

AMERICAN CHAMPAGNE

Bin No.		Vintage	Half Bottle	Bottle
8111	WALDORF-ASTORIA, Brut	N.V.	$6.00	$11.00
8134	TAYLOR'S BRUT, New York State	N.V.		$14.00
8109	PAUL MASSON BRUT, California	N.V.		$14.00
8132	GREAT WESTERN EXTRA DRY, New York State	N.V.	$7.50	$14.00
8106	KORBEL EXTRA DRY, California	N.V.		$15.00

SPARKLING WINE

IMPORTED

Bin No.		Vintage	Half Bottle	Bottle
8154	BOUVET BRUT	N.V.		$15.00
8193	ASTI SPUMANTE, Martini & Rossi	N.V.		$16.50
8176	CHAUVENET RED CAP	N.V.	$9.00	$16.50

AMERICAN

Bin No.		Vintage	Half Bottle	Bottle
8116	GREAT WESTERN SPARKLING BURGUNDY, New York State	N.V.		$14.00

HOTEL ST. REGIS WINE POLICY

Shortly after Repeal, the Hotel St. Regis recognized the potential of wine sales at moderate prices and published a leaflet entitled "Hotel St. Regis Wine Policy," from which we quote:

Convinced that poor wine lists and high prices were seriously retarding the use of wine and thus impeding the progress of gracious and temperate living, the Management of the Hotel St. Regis published in 1935 an extensive and carefully selected list of wines at prices which were recognized as phenomenally low.

This list attracted wide attention and was generally proclaimed the finest in the country—as it was designed to be.

In offering well-chosen wines at moderate cost we believed we were performing a public service and at the same time exhibiting intelligent self-interest. We expected, in short, to make up the difference between a small profit per bottle and a large profit per bottle by greatly increasing the volume of our sales.

Experience has justified this expectation. The public has cordially supported our wine policy.

FOUR SEASONS WINE POLICY

One of the first restaurants in New York to respond to the increased demand for a broad spectrum of wines at fair prices was the Four Seasons. It now has at least three hundred wines available, all chosen as very good examples of their class. The list includes a large selection of American wines, as well as those from France, Italy, Spain, Germany, and other countries.

The price of the wine to the dinner guest is determined carefully, with lower-priced wines marked up to three times the restaurant's cost and higher-priced wines marked up two and a half times the cost. This brings the price to about double that in a retail store, which is fair to the consumer and which includes a reasonable amount for the restaurant for service.

Another popular practice is selling wine by the glass. This makes it possible for someone to have a glass of white wine when others are having cocktails and makes it easier, during dinner, if one guest wants something other than the bottle of wine that the others in a party have ordered. The Four Seasons carries this policy one step further by offering Champagne by the glass, making this festive beverage more available.

Other New York restaurants that are notable for their extensive selections of wines at fair prices are Windows on the World and, especially for an excellent list of over sixty American white wines, the Oyster Bar in Grand Central Station.

Enlightened restaurateurs have learned that a smaller profit per bottle generates greater volume and encourages diners to explore different wines with different dishes.

HOW TO USE THE WINE LIST

Although the wine list is a silent salesman, it cannot perform its selling job unless it receives some assistance from the restaurant's selling staff.

First, the waiter who takes the food order should present the wine list together with the menu. At banquets two or three banquet wine lists should be on every table.

Second, if the guest or host of a party fails to order a beverage when ordering his meal, he should be asked, "Do you care to order cocktails or wine now?"

Third, to sell you must tell; to tell you must know. It is the duty of the management to have and to impart to the service staff complete information about the wines in stock. This can be done at the regular meetings all well-organized restaurants hold periodically to instruct the staff on house policies and service, deportment, and so forth. This is important, as we have never known anyone who could sell a product successfully without knowing anything about it.

As most waiters depend on tips for a considerable portion of their income, it should not be difficult to point out to them that they will make more money (through larger tips) when they sell a bottle of wine or some other alcoholic beverage to a guest.

The restaurant has everything to gain and nothing to lose by its wine sales. Wine sales are plus sales because they are often made at a time when the guest would normally not drink any other alcoholic beverage, and they are sold at no additional overhead to the restaurant.

While there are no set rules about what drinks should be served with specific dishes, there are some traditional customs that are observed because they are practical.

We do not agree with the theory that cocktails should not be served before a dinner at which wine is to be served. If a cocktail whets the appetite, then one should drink it. However, too many drinks on an empty stomach take away the desire for food instead of stimulating it, because the alcohol supplies food value and the system may be satisfied before the meal is begun.

A home dinner today may consist of an appetizer, a main dish with its accompanying vegetables, salad, dessert, and coffee. With such a dinner one wine is sufficient. This may be either white or red, depending on the main course and on one's personal preference. When entertaining informally this menu may be expanded to include a soup, but the one wine is still correct.

For more formal entertaining, where several wines are in order, the long-accepted order of service should be followed: dry sparkling wines; light, dry wines; full-bodied wines; and rich, sweet wines. Other suggestions for appropriate wine service are:

Do not serve a dry claret or Burgundy after a rich Sauternes—the red wines, being dry, would taste harsh on the sweetened palate.

When two vintages of the same type of wine are being served, the younger should precede the softer, mellower, older wine. The only exception is Champagne. In this case the older comes first, as it will seem to lack life and vigor if it follows a fresh, young wine.

When serving fine wines, it is advisable to avoid vinegar sauces.

When serving dry red or white wine, avoid dishes with sweet sauces. They will make the wine taste harsh.

Rich, well-seasoned food needs a full-bodied wine. Such food will interfere with the full enjoyment of a delicate wine, while a powerful, big wine will completely dominate any delicate, light dish. There should be harmony between them.

In printing menus for formal dinners or banquets, two forms are commonly used for listing the wines. One is to print the wines and spirits on the left side of the menu, listing each opposite the course with which it is to be served. The other is to list the wine or spirit (brandy or liqueurs) as part of the menu, putting each wine immediately below the course with which it is served. In listing wines on a formal dinner menu, full information as to name and vintage should be given. For example, 1959 Château Mouton-Rothschild or 1976 Gewürztraminer, Willm, would be proper listings.

OPPOSITE: Menu for the inauguration dinner of the New York chapter of Les Dames d'Escoffier, March 27, 1977, at the Carlyle Hotel in New York.

Le Premier Dîner
Les Dames d'Escoffier, New York

The Carlyle
March 27, 1977
Guest of Honor
Honorary Grande Dame Julia Child

Le Comité de la Bonne Bouche
Elayne Kleeman, Hôtesse
Cécile L. Cuming
Linda Downs
Grace Kent
Anna Muffoletto
Sylvia Schur
Jeanne Voltz
Robert Frédy – Directeur des Restaurants
Henri Thongs – Directeur de Cuisine

Chablis Les Preuses Grand Cru
Domaine de la Maladière 1974

Champagne Dom Ruinart Blanc de Blancs 1969

Château Figeac 1966

Muscat Ottonel Dr Konstantin Frank

Cognac and Liqueurs

La Réception
Les Huîtres de la Saison

La Matière
Mousse de Foie de Canard
*
Coquille Saint Jacques à la Nage

*

Selle d'Agneau Forestière
*
Asperges Sauce Moutarde

L'Apotéose
Soufflé Glacé à la Chartreuse
*
Mignardises
*
Café

28
BEVERAGE
SERVICE

1. GLASSWARE

The first wineglass is said to have been made from a bubble of seafoam cut in half by Aphrodite as she came forth from the sea—a pretty myth and one that has a point: the wineglass should be crystal clear.

Undoubtedly, the first cup man used was his hand. As he became more civilized and acquired tools with which to fashion implements, he made himself a drinking vessel. The earliest one was fashioned from a dried gourd. Later on he experimented with wood, shells, and metals, and finally, when he learned how to work with glass, he made the first of our present-day containers. The origin of glass is credited both to the early Assyrians and to the Egyptians. The examples of early glass drinking cups that survive today are misshapen and not very transparent, but even so they were useful and a great improvement on other containers of potables.

As time went on and the art of glassblowing was improved, much beauty and perfection of line were blown into wine bottles and goblets. Later the art of glass cutting further enhanced the elegance and beauty of the container.

The most famous glassmakers were the Venetians and Bohemians. They had a secret for coloring their glass that no one else possessed, and up to the end of the last century colored glasses for wine were still the fashion. There was a definite reason for color in wineglasses. More often than not the wine was not perfectly clear. It had sediment in it and was dull and uninteresting to look at. Today wines are perfectly brilliant when shipped, and advances in technology and sanitation ensure their clarity—therefore colored wineglasses are no longer necessary.

The enjoyment of beverages, and wine in particular, calls for using three senses: sight, smell, and taste. Before we smell or taste a wine, we see it. There is pleasure in the bright red of a claret, the deep ruby of a Burgundy, and the mellow, golden hue of a Sauternes, to say nothing of the dancing brightness of Champagne. The sight of wine shimmering in a transparent, delicately stemmed glass increases the pleasure of anticipation. A colored glass deprives us of this pleasure.

GLASSWARE FOR THE HOME

The glassware needed for a well-appointed house and that required for a hotel are two different requirements. For the home it is unnecessary to have many different shapes and sizes. Many beverages may be served in the same size glass.

A complete set of glassware for a household that entertains up to twelve guests at a dinner should include:

12 old-fashioned or on-the-rocks glasses (8 ounces)
12 cocktail glasses (4 or 4½ ounces)
12 highball glasses (10 ounces)
12 Champagne tulip glasses (8 ounces)
12 all-purpose wineglasses (9 ounces)
12 sherry or dessert wineglasses (6 ounces)
12 brandy snifters marked at 2 ounces

In their desire to be of service, the glassware people have done much to frighten the American public away from wine by advocating the use of a different glass for every type of wine. The number of types of glasses necessary and some difference of opinion as to what type of glass should be used with certain wines have prevented many people from serving wine at all.

the ideal wineglass

The ideal, all-purpose wineglass (one that is quite proper for red and white table wines and all sparkling wines) should:

1. Be beautiful to look at, with simple, graceful lines

2. Be generous—9 ounces—so you can pour enough wine (4 ounces) for a satisfying drink and still have room in the glass to swirl the wine around and get the full benefit of its aroma

Wineglasses. LEFT: Oversize 23-ounce capacity. RIGHT: All-purpose 9-ounce capacity. Both contain 4 ounces of wine. (*Photo by Andrew B. Wile*)

3. Have a mouth that is slightly smaller than the widest part of the bowl so that the wine's bouquet is concentrated for maximum enjoyment, but wide enough so that the upper edge does not strike the nose when the glass is tilted for drinking

HOTEL SERVICE

In a hotel or restaurant the problem of glass service is entirely different. Tradition and showmanship enter the picture and the requirements are stricter and more numerous.

A fine hotel or restaurant must have conventional glassware for both its bar service and its wine service.

The bar must have available the following assortment with sizes and quantities determined by the needs of the operation:

Shot glass (3/4 to 2 ounces, lined)
Delmonico (5 ounces)
Old-fashioned or on-the-rocks (8 to 12 ounces)
Highball (8 to 10 ounces)
Tom Collins (12 ounces)
Cocktail (4 to 4½ ounces, with a 3- or 3½-ounce line)
Whisky sour (3 to 6 ounces)
Champagne cocktail (5 ounces)
Port (3 to 4 ounces)
Sherry (3 to 4 ounces)
Liqueur (3 ounces, with a 1-ounce line)
Pony brandy (2 ounces, with a 1-ounce line)
Brandy snifter (6 to 12 ounces, with a 2-ounce line)
Beer (8 to 12 ounces)
Punch bowl
Wine cooler

A hotel dining room or restaurant must have available the following assortment of glassware:

Water goblet
Rhine wine, tall, stemmed,
   squat-bowled (6 ounces)
Graves, Sauternes, white
   Burgundy (6 ounces)

Tulip Champagne goblet (8 ounces)
Claret, red Burgundy, and red
   Rhône (9 ounces)
Sherry (4 ounces)
Port (4 ounces)

While in a private home the all-purpose wineglass may serve nicely, a hotel or restaurant that serves formal dinners or banquets must serve each wine in its traditional glass. A wine will not taste better in it, but, just as dinner clothes invest a formal gathering with a dignity that is lacking when informal dress is the rule, so the proper glassware for each wine lends dignity and elegance to the affair. Some restaurants go to the extreme in showmanship by using giant-size glasses containing up to twenty-four ounces. These glasses are often used as water goblets as well as for wine. Although oversized glasses are popular in many distinctive restaurants, some people consider them awkward and out of place in a formal setting.

Notwithstanding the foregoing, even in large luxury hotels the trend is to simplify, wherever possible, the service equipment, including glassware. Many new establishments have reduced wine glassware to just two sizes of the same shape: a six-ounce stemmed glass for serving rosé and white table wines and a similarly styled glass with a capacity of nine to twelve ounces for serving red wines and Champagne or sparkling wine.

placement of glasses

Depending on the amount of space on the table, glasses may be placed in a line or grouped into triangles or diamonds. If they are placed in a line, the first glass to be used goes to the far right. The rest of the glasses will go on a diagonal toward the left and center of the table.

To save space when several glasses are required, create a triangle or diamond by placing the first glass to the right of the knife. The second glass should be to the left of the first and slightly toward the center of the table, above the knife. The third should be centered above the first two, forming a triangle. If a fourth glass is used, it goes above the second glass, but slightly to the left, forming a diamond. This pattern can be followed for as many glasses as are necessary. The water goblet should always be at the extreme left.

If several wines are served, each glass is removed when the course with which it is served is finished. After-dinner liqueurs, when offered with coffee, may be served from a cart or buffet that holds suitable glasses.

2. HOW TO SERVE WINE

temperature

What beverages are served chilled? All white wines, all sparkling wines, all rosé wines, all beers, all cocktails, most mixed drinks, certain spirits that are consumed as aperitifs such as vodka and Aquavit, all aperitif wines, very dry sherry, very dry Madeira, and *eaux-de-vie* (clear, unaged fruit brandies).

The following generally are served at room temperature: all red wines, medium and rich sherries, Madeira, port, Marsala, and all spirits when taken neat, such as whisky, gin, rum, brandy, and liqueurs. Exceptions are vodka and Aquavit.

Exceptions make the rule, and even a liqueur, with all its sweetness, can be very pleasant in the summer if it is chilled. In fact, a liqueur such as crème de menthe is much more enjoyable if it is served over ice.

LEFT TO RIGHT: 1. Saucer, 5 ounces, which is ideal for serving ice cream or fruit cups but not Champagne or sparkling wine. Its flat shallowness exposes too great a surface of wine, allowing the bubbles to escape too rapidly. 2. All-purpose 9-ounce wineglass for red table wines and all sparkling wines. 3. Tulip Champagne glass, 8 ounces, developed by the Champagne producers of France. 4. and 5. Two Champagne flute glasses. 6. Sherry glass, 2 ounces, which is popular but inadequate. The normal portion of sherry is 2 ounces, which means this glass must be filled to the brim. 7. The ideal 4½-ounce glass for sherry, port, or Madeira. The 2-ounce portion can be served cleanly in this glass. 8. Wine carafe, 20 ounces. (*Photo by Al Levine*)

LEFT TO RIGHT: 1. Wineglass, 4 ounces, is inadequate and should not be used. 2. and 3. All-purpose wineglasses, 6½ and 8½ ounces, which are recommended. 4. Excellent 9-ounce glass for red wine and Champagne. 5. The Grossman all-purpose 8-ounce lead crystal glass without the 4-ounce fill line. 6. Baccarat 10-ounce thin lead crystal wineglass suitable for home use but too fragile for restaurant service. 7. Traditional 7-ounce Roemer wineglass for serving German wines. 8. and 9. Dramatic lead crystal glasses for serving white wine and red wine, respectively. (*Photo by Al Levine*)

LEFT TO RIGHT: 1. Shot glass. The etched line marks the ⅝-ounce fill. It is a dishonest glass, properly called a cheater in Canada. 2. Special shot glass approved by the Liquor License Board of Ontario that must be used by all Ontario licensees. The etched lines mark the 1-, 1¼-, and 1½-ounce fill. 3. Pony brandy or liqueur glass, 1 ounce. The normal 1-ounce portion cannot be served in this glass without spilling. 4. and 5. The 2-ounce brandy glass with an etched line marking the 1-ounce fill and the 3-ounce snifter are much more practical for both brandy and liqueurs. 6. The large, dramatic, 20-ounce crystal snifter is sometimes used for Cognac and other fine brandies. 7. Traditional 10-ounce Pilsner beer glass. 8. Elegant 16-ounce footed beer shell. 9. Absinthe drip glass. 10. Porcelain singing saké bottle and whistling saké cup from Japan. (*Photo by Al Levine*)

LEFT TO RIGHT: 1. Cocktail glass, 2½ ounces, is inadequate and should not be used. 2. Ideal 4½-ounce cocktail glass has an etched line showing the proper 3-ounce fill. 3. Cocktail glass, 6 ounces, filled to within ¼ inch of the brim holds 4½ ounces. 4. Waterford Irish crystal glass for serving Irish Coffee. 5. Sour glass, 6 ounces. 6. Highball glass, 8 ounces. 7. Collins glass, 12 ounces. 8. Delmonico glass, 5 ounces, better known today as a juice glass and rarely used in bars. 9. Old-fashioned or on-the-rocks glass, 6 ounces. 10. Footed old-fashioned glass, 7 ounces. (*Photo by Al Levine*)

How cold should wine be when it is served? It depends, in the last analysis, on the individual taste of the host in each case. The general rules are that sweeter wines should be served colder than dry and that no wine should be chilled below 42 degrees Fahrenheit (45 degrees is cold enough).

What does room temperature mean? In reality, not quite what it says. The room temperature criterion was established in Europe long before central heating was known. Even today rooms abroad are never heated as warmly as is customary in the United States, where 70 to 72 degrees Fahrenheit is usual. Room temperature for wine is 65 to 68 degrees Fahrenheit, which is the temperature at which red wines are most enjoyable. However, if you enjoy your red table wines either tepid (80 degrees) or very cold (45 degrees), by all means drink them that way, since it is your palate that must be pleased.

If the wine has been stored in a cellar where the temperature is lower, the wine may be brought to room temperature by standing the bottle for a few hours in the room where it is to be served. WARNING: Under no circumstances should the wine be warmed artificially, either by plunging the bottle in hot water or by placing it on or near a heater. This will harm the wine. It is better to drink a red wine too cold than to spoil it by heating it.

chilling the wine   There are two ways to chill wine for dining room service. One is to keep still white and sparkling wines in the refrigerator. A wine will be properly chilled after two to three hours. In some restaurants, and for luncheon service in almost any restaurant, this is the only kind of chilling used. The other way is to serve the wine in the conventional table cooler or ice bucket. Serving white wines at lunch ordinarily does not require the use of the cooler, which takes more time than either the staff or the guests have to spare at midday. Sparkling wines are nearly always served in coolers, however.

Dining rooms that use coolers usually have them available at the service bar together with stands or trays. Place a little shaved ice in the bottom of the cooler, then insert the bottle and add ice and water to fill the cooler. Water is added so the bottle can be reinserted in the cooler between servings. Also, water and ice together chill the bottle faster than ice alone. A wine will be properly chilled after twenty minutes in the cooler.

It is important to bring the wine to the table immediately after it is ordered. The cooler may be placed on the table if a stand is not available. When the bottle is removed from the cooler it should be wiped dry before the wine is poured.

An attentive waiter refills patrons' wineglasses promptly and spares the host the inconvenience of pouring the wine himself. But the cooler should be placed conveniently at the host's right so he may refill glasses in the waiter's absence. When the waiter empties the bottle, he should remove it and the cooler from the table. Turning the bottle upside down in the cooler is also practiced, although many guests (and wine stewards) feel that it is an impolite suggestion that it is time the host ordered another bottle of wine.

OPENING A BOTTLE OF WINE

After presenting the bottle, cut the capsule (the foil or plastic covering over the cork) to just below the bulge that is found on all wine bottles. Cut all the way around, pressing the knife firmly against the glass, and remove the capsule. Since the metal capsule is often corroded or moldy, the wine would taste tainted if it came in contact with the metal.

With a clean napkin wipe off the mold or *ullage* often found between the cork and the capsule, as it is impossible to pour wine from a bottle without some of the wine spilling or slipping over the lip.

Insert the point of the corkscrew (we recommend the single-lever type*) slightly off center, so that the worm will go down into the center of the cork. Turn the corkscrew until all of the worm has entered the cork, hook the lever onto the rim of the bottle, and raise the body of the corkscrew until the cork emerges. For very long corks you may need to ease out the final length of cork with a rocking motion. Do not jerk it out nervously, as that will shake up the wine.

If you use the T corkscrew, turn it into the cork, then grasp the bottle firmly with the left hand; hold the bottle so that the shoulder rests in the palm of your hand. Grasp the corkscrew with your right hand, hold the bottle between your knees, and pull slowly and evenly. Pull straight out. Do not rock or twist the cork while withdrawing it.

When the cork is out, smell it to see whether it is sound. Then wipe the mouth of the bottle both inside and out with the napkin. You are ready to serve.

---

* There are many types of corkscrews or cork pullers available, several of which are illustrated on page 432, but only a few are really practical. The object is to extract the cork from the bottle in one piece and as easily as possible so as not to disturb the wine. Ideally, the screw, or worm, should be 2 to $2\frac{1}{4}$ inches long. The metal should be rounded, and the point should be a continuation of the spiral. Avoid a corkscrew with a flattened, sharp cutting edge. Avoid any corkscrew that has the appearance of an auger. The single-lever type is the most practical cork puller for a waiter to use in a restaurant because it closes into a compact, flat instrument he can carry in his pocket. It is also practical for home use.

One of the best cork pullers we have found for older bottles is the wooden corkscrew with a counter screw. It functions easily and requires a minimum of effort to remove the cork, thus not disturbing any sediment. Steel and brass corkscrews that work on the same principle are also available.

The two-pronged cork extractor works by inserting the prongs on either side of the cork, between the cork and the neck of the bottle, and rocking them all the way down the side of the cork. The handle is then twisted and the cork comes out, held between the two prongs. This method does not pierce the cork.

Serving a bottle of wine.
1. Present the bottle to the guest. The towel, if used, should not cover the label.

2. Cut the capsule below the bulge in the neck of the bottle and remove upper portion of capsule.

3. An older bottle of wine may have some mold on top of the cork.

4. If this is the case, *before* the cork is pulled, clean the top of the cork and the rim of the bottle with a towel.

5. Insert worm of corkscrew slightly off center and twist.

6. Hook lever onto rim of bottle.

(Photos of Kevin Zraly, cellarmaster at Windows on the World, by Andrew B. Wile)

7. Lift up until cork emerges.

8. Sniff the cork to see whether it is sound.

Cork pullers. CLOCKWISE FROM LEFT: 1. Traditional T style. 2. Two-tined extractor. 3. Metal wing type. 4. Wooden cork puller with counterscrew. 5. Waiter's lever type with knife. (*Photo by Andrew B. Wile*)

OPENING A BOTTLE OF CHAMPAGNE OR SPARKLING WINE

If the bottle is presented in a cooler filled with fine ice or ice cubes and water, it should be stood upright. Holding a napkin in your hand, grasp the bottle by its neck and remove the bottle from the cooler. Wipe it dry and present it to the guest. It is incorrect to wrap the bottle in the napkin.

Locate and untwist the wire loop under the foil on the neck of the bottle. Loosen the wire cage, which will tear the foil or metal capsule covering the cork. Remove both together. (Some people prefer to remove the foil first.) Put your thumb over the cork immediately to prevent it from flying out. The pressure in a bottle of Champagne or sparkling wine is four to six atmospheres, or sixty to ninety pounds per square inch.

Holding the napkin in your hand, grasp the cork and tilt the bottle to a forty-five-degree angle away from your face. Twist the bottle and gently ease out the cork. After the cork is out, keep the bottle at an angle for about five seconds to let excess gas escape. If you return the bottle to its upright position too quickly, the gas will rush out and carry a good part of the wine with it.

Once the bottle is open, wipe the rim of the bottle with the napkin. Champagne and sparkling wines should be served in two motions. Pour wine until the froth almost reaches the brim of the glass. Stop. Wait a moment until this foaming froth subsides, then continue pouring to fill the glass one-third to one-half full. Be careful not to pour too rapidly or the wine will froth over.

SERVING WINE

In the Middle Ages a popular way of poisoning one's enemies was to ask them to dine and sometime during the festivities serve a goblet of poisoned wine. A guest had to be wary in those days.

Gradually the custom arose for the host to taste the wine before his guests to allay their fears. Today, too, the host samples the wine before his guests are served, but this practice now has a far more reasonable basis. It is the means of assuring the host that his wine is in perfect condition. At a dinner for twelve or more, the host and the sommelier or captain sample the wines beforehand. Wines are not presented for approval.

When serving at home, when there are no servants, the host should serve himself and then his guests. First he should fill his own glass about one-fourth full and satisfy himself on the quality of the wine. Then, around the table, counterclockwise, he should pour wine for everyone in turn. After everyone has been served, he should serve himself. The wineglass should not be more than one-third to one-half full.

When the wine is poured, the bottle should be held so that the label is always uppermost and can readily be seen. The bottle should be brought to the glass on the table—the glass should not be lifted to the bottle. When the glass is one-half full, the bottle should be twisted to distribute the last drop on the bottle's rim, preventing it from dripping. The wine should be served from the right side of the guest, as the glass is set at the right of the plate.

It is not necessary to drape either red or white wine in such a manner as to hide the label unless one is ashamed of the wine he is serving. However, a bottle that is in an ice bucket should be carefully wiped dry each time it is withdrawn to prevent drops of ice water from trickling down. It is a good idea to hold a napkin in your hand and place your hand under the bottle while pouring.

The open wine bottle may be kept at the right of the host. When there are servants, the bottle is usually placed on the sideboard until it is needed. Wines that are chilled should be kept at the right of the host in a cooler or, if there are servants, in a cooler on the sideboard. At every course the wine should be served before the food.

serving red wines

Red wine is a perfect companion to dark-meated fowl and all kinds of red meat however prepared and is excellent with cheese. As previously noted, it is generally served at room temperature. If brought directly from the wine cellar, it should be served at that temperature—*never warmed.* Some lighter-bodied red wines may be preferred when slightly chilled, particularly in summer.

Red wine often throws a sediment as it grows older. This is natural and shows that the wine is maturing in the bottle. For this reason, red wine should be handled carefully and gently. In fact, the Burgundy basket was created in

Serving a bottle of Champagne.
1. Bottle should be placed in cooler packed with ice and with a towel handy.

2. Present the bottle, wiping it off with the towel.

3. Locate and untwist the wire loop on cage.

4. Loosen and remove the wire cage.

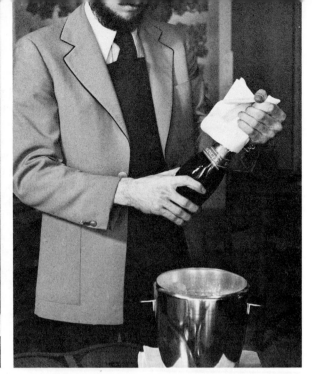

5. Holding a towel, grasp the neck of the bottle and tilt it to a forty-five-degree angle.

6. Twist the bottle and ease the cork out.

(Photos of Kevin Zraly, cellarmaster at Windows on the World, by Andrew B. Wile)

7. Wipe the rim of the bottle.

8. Pour Champagne gently so as not to drive out too much gas.

Burgundy for the sole purpose of removing the bottle from the cellar bin in the horizontal position in which it lies, so that the sediment in the bottle is not disturbed. If the bottle in the basket is carried under the arm and stirred up, the object of the basket is wasted. Its sole purpose is to leave the wine undisturbed. Baskets should not be used for wines that do not have any sediment.

When red wine is presented to a restaurant guest for his approval before opening, care should be taken not to disturb any sediment present. When using a Burgundy basket the bottle should be left in the basket while presenting, opening, and serving the wine.

Very old red wines should be decanted to draw off the clear wine and leave any sediment there might be in the bottle. It is not necessary to decant white wines, as any light tartrates that might precipitate are odorless and tasteless. Avoid using a filter in decanting wine, since it takes out some of the taste and body.

In decanting, the decanter must be perfectly clean and dry. Remove the capsule on the wine bottle completely, draw the cork, then place a candle or a strong light behind the bottle neck for visibility while pouring gently and steadily. At the moment you see any sediment coming over, stop pouring.

Aeration is the second good reason for decanting. However, if a decanter is not available, a clean empty wine bottle will do. Decanting is particularly advisable if the wine is young or from an off year. Contact with the air expands the bouquet and enhances the enjoyment of the wine by permitting any undesirable volatile aromas to dissipate.

serving white and rosé wines in restaurants   As previously stated, white and rosé wines should be served chilled. Traditionally, they are served with white meats—fowl, fish, and seafood—but tradition does not rule out the possibility that white wine may be drunk with red meat or red wine with fowl. When a guest orders a particular type and brand of wine, he should be served the wine he orders with no comment by the waiter.

When a guest asks for white or rosé wine, the waiter—or sommelier (wine steward)—should obtain the bottle from storage, set it in an ice cooler filled with ice and water, cover it with a clean, folded napkin, and bring this service into the dining room. The ice bucket, placed on a stand, is set to the right of

Burgundy basket.
(*Photo by Al Levine*)

the person who ordered the wine. The waiter or sommelier then takes the bottle out of the bucket and presents it to the guest with the label uppermost. The host thus has an opportunity to verify that his order has been filled correctly.

This bottle presentation is an important part of wine service and should not be overlooked. If the waiter has misunderstood the guest and brought the wrong wine—to which the guest will later object—the waiter can easily exchange this bottle for one the guest prefers. Had the waiter ignored this presentation ritual and opened the bottle without showing it to the guest for his approval, the bottle would have to be returned to storage and may become a loss. Furthermore, this bottle-presentation ceremony shows courtesy to the guest, regardless of his knowledge about wines, and adds to the atmosphere of the dining room.

Once the bottle is opened and the mouth cleaned, the waiter should pour about one ounce into the glass of the host (or whoever ordered the wine) so he or she can approve the wine. A towel should be held in the left hand when serving wine and used to wipe the bottle, particularly when it is taken out of the ice bucket. The bottle should not be wrapped in a towel since the guests may wish to see the label of the wine they are drinking.

When the host has approved the wine, it should be poured for the woman first, if a couple is being served. If a group is being served, then the person sitting to the host's right is served first. The waiter then proceeds around the table counterclockwise, filling the host's glass last. For white wine, the glasses should not be filled more than one-half full. This gives the guests an opportunity to savor the wine's aroma before sipping it.

When everyone has been served, the white wine bottle should be replaced in the ice bucket to the host's right. Waiters should always see that every guest's glass is replenished. It often produces the sale of an extra bottle of wine.

Wine should be brought to the table before it is time to serve it. If more than one wine is to be served, all wines should be either on a side table or chilled in coolers where the host and guests can see them.

serving appetizer and dessert wines

Appetizer and dessert wines are served in the manner of cocktails and other mixed drinks. It should be remembered that with wines—and cocktails and spirits too—no glass should ever be filled to the brim. It is impossible to carry it on a tray without spilling, and the result is sloppy service.

An increasingly popular way of serving sherry and other appetizer wines is over ice cubes in an old-fashioned glass.

In hotel service, when serving sherry or any product ordered by brand name, it is our opinion that the bottle should be brought to the table. It is not always practical, but wherever it is possible it makes a better impression on the guest if the waiter does this. Then there is no question that the customer is getting what he ordered.

29
BAR OPERATION

Bar profits depend on the economical and practical operation of the bar. In most instances a bar represents a substantial investment in plant, furniture, and decoration. This investment must be protected by maintaining a standard of service and quality of beverages on a par with the decor and the investment.

types of bars   There are two basic types of bars: the front, or stand-up, bar, where drinks are made in front of the patrons; and the service bar never seen by the patrons, from which drinks are dispensed. A service bar is sometimes called a back bar. The space behind a front bar is also sometimes called a back bar, although we prefer to call it the back-of-the-bar space.

The working arrangement of a bar is of the utmost importance. This matter is too often overlooked when the installation plans are made, and nine times out of ten the people who work behind the bar are not consulted. The space between the front and the back of the bar should be wide enough so that two bartenders can pass each other without jostling. The front section should not be too low, but so arranged that the bartender can reach ice, mixing glass, and bottles with ease.

front bar   In laying out a bar, try to keep the working stations well off the floor. Plumbing repairs will have to be made, and if there is plenty of working space the repairs will be completed in less time and at much less expense. More importantly, people will have to work in the fairly cramped space between the front and the back of the bar. In practically every new large bar layout we have observed over the years the bartender's comfort has been forgotten. The fact that a man must be on his feet for eight hours or longer is not taken into account. Wooden or plastic racks or cushioned rubber on the floor makes the difference between a smiling, efficient bartender and one who is tired and grouchy after a couple of hours of standing on a cold cement floor.

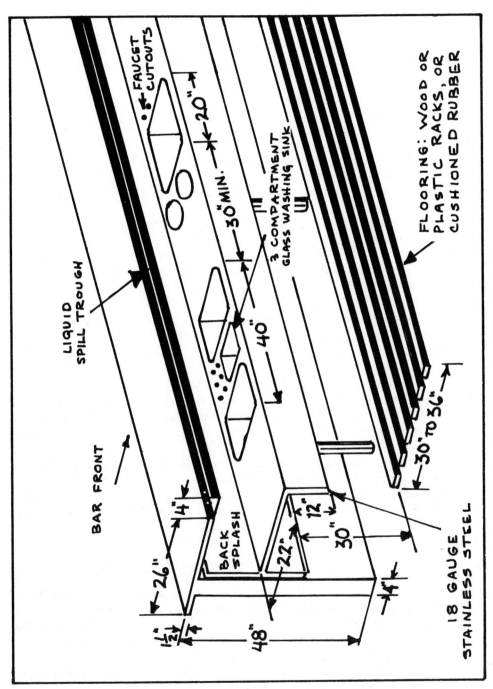

Layout for working stations behind the front bar. (*Drawing by William Lembeck*)

Floor racks can be built using clear pine laths three inches wide by one inch thick by three feet long; allow a one-inch separation between laths and hold the rack together by crosspieces of the same laths. This produces racks with a two-inch clearance off the floor. If the racks are longer than three feet, they become too heavy to lift for cleaning the floor.

If the bar is oval or some other shape whereby the customers standing on one side can see the working stations on the other, a cover should be hung in front of the stations to conceal the pipes and other equipment. Under the same circumstances, special thought must be given to the floor covering.

The working space between the front and the back of the bar should be at least thirty inches, and thirty-six inches is ideal. Doors of refrigerators set into the back-of-the-bar space should not be so wide that they block traffic when opened.

The back-of-the-bar space should also have storage cabinets and shelves to hold bottles.

Do not have a lighting system that consists of electric bulbs under glass shelves on which bottles are placed. The heat generated by the lights will be detrimental to the liquid contents.

service bar For service bars out of public sight, there need be no back work space. This space will be occupied by large refrigerators, while the bottles that ordinarily would be on the back of the bar are placed on overhead shelves above the counter.

The working space between the service bar and the back wall line must be at least ten feet, particularly if the bar services banquets. This provides the extra space needed for stacking cases of wines, liquors, and waters when they are to be served in quantities exceeding the capacity of the regular storage space.

A service bar should have one entrance and one exit. Some establishments prefer a turnstile at the entrance. If there is none, the rule must be enforced that once a waiter reaches the bar there can be no turning around and going out the way he came in. The waiter should exit past the service-bar manager.

THE BARTENDER'S JOB

the bartender Beverage dispensing should be done quietly and with dignity, creating an atmosphere of refinement and good taste. The job of the bartender is no different from that of any other retail salesman except that, because of the character of the goods he is selling, extra care should be taken to please customers and look after their welfare.

The bartender's day really starts the night before, for without sufficient rest he cannot do his best work on the job.

The bartender is often in close contact with the guest, and it is therefore imperative that he practice scrupulous personal hygiene.

Uniform coats or vests, as appropriate for the operation, should be provided by the employer, but it is the responsibility of the bartender to provide a white shirt, black tie, and dark trousers, or a white blouse and dark skirt for women. The full uniform must always be kept clean and pressed. Colored shirts should never be worn unless they are part of a uniform. Jewelry should be limited. Aprons are not considered in good form today, unless they are part of a specific uniform.

Care of the feet is important for the bartender. He cannot show the customer a happy face if his feet are tired and aching. It is a good idea to have two pairs of comfortable shoes and change once or twice during the day. Shoes with built-in arches are available and help prevent fatigue. Rubber heels also relieve the strain.

When not busy, the bartender should not slouch or stand around with his hands in his pockets. The bartender should refrain from smoking while on duty. Customers as a rule do not like smoking behind the bar, and smoking while handling food or drink is extremely unsanitary. The same is true of drinking—do *not* drink while on duty. Many times the bartender is asked to take a drink with a customer, but he should pass it up.

the bar

The first duty of the day, of course, is to report for work on time, whether the bartender is to open the bar or to relieve someone else. The bar should be inspected to see that it is spotlessly clean, that the floor, walls, windows, and furniture for table service are in perfect condition, that the room temperature is right, and that there are no offensive odors.

At the bar the woodwork should be polished, the back of the bar dusted, and bottles and glasses neatly arranged. The mirrors should be clean and shining. Liquor bottles should be wiped off with a damp cloth each morning. The work area sinks and drain board and the storage cabinets under the bar should be clean and ready for use.

Supplies of wines and liquors should be carefully checked so that the stock is up to par for the day. Any orders should be sent to the storeroom and followed up to make sure all supplies are on hand before the first customer arrives. Ice boxes should be filled with ice. Bottles of liquor should be in the speed racks or in their proper places on the shelves. Then the working equipment and the draft beer system should be checked.

There should be a supply of clean towels, which are properly kept behind the bar, not stuck into the belt or over the shoulder of the bartender.

garnishes

Next, the fruit and other garnishes should be prepared. These include oranges, lemons, limes, pineapples, olives, cherries, cocktail onions, and any special items that are ordered frequently or that are unique to the operation.

This should be done just before opening time so that the garnishes will be as fresh as possible. If the bar opens an hour or two before lunch, it is well to prepare only the fruits for which there will be a call during the luncheon hour. During the afternoon lull there is time to prepare such additional fruits as might be necessary for the cocktail hour and the evening.

Oranges should be of uniform size—about 216 to the crate is a good size—and either California or Florida fruit may be used. Floridas have more juice, but Californias have a better color, which is better for slices. Cut orange slices in half from top to bottom, about one-fourth inch thick, and discard the end pieces. Slices should be kept together as much as possible until used, to preserve their freshness. The main supply should be covered with a moist napkin and kept, if possible, in a refrigerator.

Lemon slices should also be about a quarter-inch thick. Begin by cutting the lemon in half in the middle as for juicing. Then slice each half, throwing the ends away.

Limes should be cut in wedges large enough to grasp and squeeze the juice into the drink. A forty-eight-to-fifty-four-count lime (forty-eight to fifty-four to

Elegant, intimate small bar at the Regency Hotel, New York. (*Courtesy Bar Management*)

the crate) should yield eight wedges. Begin by cutting each lime in half as for juicing. Place the flat side on the cutting board and cut into four equal wedges. Keep the finest fruits for slicing and peeling, reserving the less perfect fruit for squeezing.

Where twists of lemon or orange peel are called for, start at one end of the whole fruit and cut a strip about three-quarters of an inch wide, skin deep, the length of the fruit to the other end. If a long spiral piece of lemon or orange peel is called for, start at one end and cut a strip about three-quarters of an inch wide spirally, as when peeling an apple, until the other end is reached.

Fresh pineapple should be used for punches and special drinks. The best method of preparing this fruit is to cut it into strips about three inches long.

Olives and cherries should be placed in handy containers so they may be reached easily. Only small pitted green olives, especially prepared for cock-tails, should be used, never stuffed olives. Maraschino cherries especially prepared for cocktail use, pitted but with the stems left on, are the best. No broken fruit should be used.

Never use anything but tongs or picks when serving ice or fruit. It is unsanitary and undignified to use the fingers.

the juices

Juices needed for most situations are lemon, orange, pineapple, tomato, and sometimes grapefruit. Freshly squeezed orange and lemon juices yield superior cocktails, but because of cost and/or convenience, frozen orange concentrate and liquid or powdered lemon juice are widely used.

Lemon juice mixes can be purchased presweetened with sugar or artificial sweetener. The artificially sweetened ones often leave a bitter aftertaste, so it is best to sample them in a cocktail before purchasing them in any significant quantity.

Tomato, pineapple, and grapefruit juices are usually purchased canned. It is best to transfer the liquid to a pitcher or bottle if it is to be kept opened for any length of time without being used.

the drink

The appearance of a drink should have great eye appeal, since eye appeal is a factor in your guests' enjoyment as well as in merchandising. The profes-sional touch is given when a drink is well garnished with fruit. The glass should be filled to within one-eighth to one-fourth inch of the brim. Filling the glass to the brim or allowing it to overflow is sloppy.

Finally, the dishes on the bar should be filled with whatever appetizers the rules of the house call for—pretzels, cheese crackers, cheese, peanuts, and so forth. One of the functions of these salty foods is to stimulate the guests to further beverage consumption and they should be placed within reach without guests' having to ask for them.

SOME RULES FOR THE BARTENDER

1. Your manners will be reflected in your sales. After you have served a drink, step back from your customer or move away. Never appear to listen to a conversation and never take part in it unless you are directly addressed.

2. Cultivate a good memory for the faces and tastes of your regular customers and greet them pleasantly when they come in.

3. Handle complaints courteously. At the bar the customer is always right. If he complains about his drink, fix it or mix another. A bar quickly gets a reputation for fine drinks and courteous service—and it can lose it just as quickly.

4. Never hurry a customer or show that you are impatient. Don't show by your manner that you think a customer is drinking too much—or too little. If he is intoxicated he should be refused service courteously. It may be against the law to serve him and you could lose your license to sell alcoholic beverages if you do so.

5. If you must answer a telephone at the bar, do so quietly. If the call is for a patron, *never* say that he is there. Instead, say that you will inquire and leave it up to the patron to decide whether or not he wishes to answer the telephone.

6. Be cooperative and friendly with the other employees.

7. Be sure you know how to mix standard cocktails without referring to a book. A helpful trick in starting is to take a glass cutter and make a few tiny marks on the outside of the bar glass, showing where the main ingredients for Martinis and Manhattans come to for one, two, three, and four drinks. It is simpler to gauge ingredients if you put them in before adding the ice. Practice until you can fill four glasses to just the right height and not have a drop left over in your bar glass.

8. When a drink is ordered, first place the required glass on top of the bar. If more than one drink is ordered, place the glasses in a straight row with the rims touching. Then place your mixing glass on the bar and pour the ingredients into it where the customer can see. Allow for ice melting during the shaking process.

9. In pouring more than one drink, run your mixing glass back and forth over the row of glasses, filling them all first quarter full, then half full, then full. Never fill one glass first and then another.

10. As soon as you have mixed a drink, put the bottles back in their proper places, no matter how rushed you are. Discard the ice, rinse your bar glass, shaker, and strainer, and you are ready for the next one. Good, efficient work habits will save time in the long run.

11. As a rule, follow standard recipes, but you should also study regular patrons' likes and dislikes and make their drinks the way they prefer.

12. Many houses now require the use of the shot glass or jigger, as modern bar controls make it necessary to account for every drink. An inexperienced bartender often has a little left over in the shaker, which goes down the sink. This waste is trifling on one drink, but if it is repeated often during a day, the loss is substantial. Therefore, measure to be sure.

13. When preparing standard cocktails such as the Martini and Manhattan, use cracked ice or ice cubes. Finely shaved ice melts too rapidly and dilutes the cocktail too much.

14. Cocktails that are shaken should be shaken briskly and not too long, since the ice melts and weakens the drink.

15. In the past it was proper to wipe all glasses twice, once to dry and again to give them a polish. In view of present-day sanitation codes, however, it is best that all glasses air dry on racks to avoid unsanitary handling by wiping.

1. Put all bottles in their proper places and lock the liquor cabinet if required.   *closing procedures*

2. Clean all bar tools and utensils.

3. Wash all dirty glasses and ashtrays.

4. Wipe down the bar and clean your station thoroughly, including the outside of ice bins, beer boxes, and so forth.

5. Drain and wipe off the sinks and drain boards.

6. Write up your liquor order for the next day's operation.

7. Count out and turn in your receipts for the night.

8. Turn out lights and lock up after making sure that all tables have been cleaned off and wiped down by the person responsible.

IMPLEMENTS FOR THE BAR

Aside from the necessary glassware, which is discussed in Chapter 28, the person behind the bar needs a number of tools of the trade, some of which are stationary, some movable. The stationary equipment is the province of the architects who design the bar.

The principal implements needed in a bar are:

Bar spoons—assorted sizes	Cutting board
Beer can openers	Electric blender
Beer scraper	Electric drink mixer
Bottle openers	Electric juice extractor
Cocktail picks	Fruit knives
Cocktail shakers	Fruit tongs
Corkscrews—automatic and waiter's type	Ice crusher
	Ice pick

Ice scoops
Ice tongs
Lemon and lime squeezers
Mixing glasses—large and small
Muddlers—wooden
Nutmeg shakers or graters
Pitchers

Salt shakers
Speed pourers
Strainers
Sugar bowls
Swizzle sticks
Towels

SUGGESTIONS FOR MANAGERS

1. When you find a good bartender, make every effort to keep him.

2. It pays to listen to the bartender's suggestions.

3. If you have no confidence in your bartender, don't keep him on the job.

4. A good bartender is worth a good salary in the added business he brings you.

5. Show the bartender you are interested in him.

6. Set policy and guidelines, but avoid overly rigid rules, since exceptions are often necessary to please a customer.

7. Many organizations find they do better by training their own bartenders. After several weeks of group training, the best is gradually given more responsibility in accordance with his abilities.

THE HOME BAR

In some homes the closet or pantry where the supply of beverages is stored has to perform the added function of a bar, while in others a corner of the recreation room has a bar with all the necessary accouterments. Whichever one has, these are the implements or gadgets needed to make it a practical working bar and a corner of the house that host and guests will enjoy using.

USEFUL EQUIPMENT FOR A HOME BAR

Cocktail shaker
Mixing glass
Muddler
Jigger or measuring cup
Long mixing spoons (iced
  tea spoons will do)
Cocktail, highball, and
  all-purpose wineglasses
  (which can be used in a
  pinch for cordials and
  brandies)

Flat bar strainer
Corkscrew, bottle opener, and
  beer can opener
Sharp stainless steel knife
Lemon and lime squeezer
Ice bucket
Electric blender

It is difficult to say what supplies are indispensable, since this must be governed by the individual taste and by the assortment of drinks the host wishes to offer his guests.

The following list is offered in the nature of a guide. (In Chapter 30 recommendations are made for a number of basic and expanded wine cellars.)

USEFUL SUPPLIES FOR A HOME BAR

Lemons	Sweet vermouth
Limes	Medium sherry
Oranges	Tawny port
Maraschino cherries	Vodka
Small cocktail olives	Dry gin
Small cocktail onions	Tequila
Fresh mint	Puerto Rican rum
Sugar, both granulated	Jamaican rum
(superfine) and powdered	Bourbon whisky
Club soda	Blended whisky
Mineral water	Scotch whisky
Ginger ale	Applejack
Quinine water	Bénédictine
Bitter lemon	Cognac
Cola	Crème de cacao
Grenadine	Crème de menthe
Orange bitters	Kahlúa
Aromatic bitters	Triple Sec
Dry vermouth	

DOS AND DON'TS IN MIXING

Do not make up more cocktails than are needed to fill the exact number of glasses. "Dividends," the remains in the shaker, are usually tasteless and watery from melting ice.

Cocktails taste better when freshly made. If allowed to stand, some of the ingredients will separate. This is particularly the case with mixed drinks that contain fruit juices and sugar.

Cocktails made of liquor and wine may be prepared in quantity in advance of a party, but those that include fruit juices are better if mixed just before drinking.

If the recipe calls for lime juice, use fresh green limes for best results. The only exception to this rule is the frozen Daiquiri mix. In many tests we have found it the equal of fresh lime juice and we recommend it highly. Do not substitute lemon juice for lime juice in a drink. This is particularly important with rum drinks, such as the Daiquiri, Planter's Punch, or Swizzle. Lemon juice will not give the sharp acid tang necessary for best results with rum.

30
PURCHASING

Confidence is the foundation on which the wine and spirits trade has been built. The wholesale distributor has confidence in the producer or shipper, the retailer has confidence in the wholesaler, and the consumer has confidence in the retailer. The basis for this confidence is a combination of quality, price, and service.

QUALITY VERSUS PRICE

Quality is foremost in importance, for if this is lacking the other factors will not interest the purchaser. A product may be of good, sound quality and yet be inexpensive, while a similar product of better quality may be more costly. In both cases the purchaser gets his money's worth. It is value the purchaser looks for when he buys a product. Value is quality in relation to price.

Determining the quality of a product presents some difficulties unless samples are available. It is important for the buyer to know the product he purchases by actually tasting it. Comparative qualities can be determined only by comparative tastings. It is important that the salesman, whether wholesale or retail, be sold on a product himself before he can sell it to someone else.

For instance, if two whiskies are under consideration and the price of one is 25 percent higher than the other, the buyer must be satisfied that it is at least 25 percent better in quality, or the values will not be equal. When quality and price are equal, intangibles enter the picture. For example, if similar products of similar value at a similar price are offered for sale by different houses, the firm that gives the best service will usually get the order.

While the foregoing applies to trade buyers, it is equally important that the consumer or nonlicensee purchaser should also sample before making a quantity purchase of a given type of beverage. In most states, however, sampling in a retail store is not permitted. It is wise, in this case, to follow the wine merchant's suggestions on several brands and purchase a bottle of each. After tasting them, the purchaser can determine which he prefers and can rate its value in relation to its price.

DISTRIBUTOR'S SALES REPRESENTATIVE

The sales representative of the distributor or wholesaler is important to the retail trade buyer because he brings information about market changes. He can also provide merchandising ideas and render many little services that make the buyer's life easier than it might otherwise be.

The sales representative who approaches his work eager to render every reasonable service and assistance to his customer will find that the relationship will be a pleasant one of mutual confidence with profit to both. The greatest help a sales representative can give his customer is accurate, honest information about the products he is offering.

The B.A.T.F. and state A.B.C. board regulations are specific about what services a wholesaler is forbidden by law to render a retail establishment. There are many such prohibitions, but they are all designed with one broad principle in mind—to prevent offering inducements to the retailer to use a specific brand to the detriment of competing brands.

The salesman, in offering his brands, should use all the information he has about their quality and usefulness, but he should not disparage his competitor or his brands. This is bad salesmanship. It is always wise to remember that brands that have been selling successfully for generations have stayed on the market because the public has found them satisfactory. The salesman who bases his selling talk on the premise that the public does not know what it is buying is in for a sad awakening.

INVENTORY AND THE ECONOMICS OF TURNOVER

To operate successfully, a business establishment should have a variety and quantity of stock sufficient to meet all its normal needs. The amounts that must be kept in stock are governed by how near the source of supply is. If it is in the same city, and an order can be filled within the day, there is no point in carrying a very large stock. On the other hand, the farther away the source of supply, the greater must be the reserve stock to protect the business from losses because of lack of stock.

During periods when freight, insurance, and costs are likely to rise, it is good business to increase the stock of items affected by those conditions, as such purchasing is not a risky speculation.

A seven- to ten-time inventory turnover is considered normal business practice. That is, if the stock required to handle normal business is worth $20,000, the annual purchases should total $140,000; the stock turns over seven times during the year. A slower turnover means that either the establishment is overstocked or something should be done to stimulate more business.

A careful analysis of sales and keeping a perpetual inventory will soon indicate which types and brands of merchandise move most steadily and which are dead stock. With the exception of rare, fine-quality, high-priced brands on which a rapid turnover is not expected (but which may be compensated for by a larger profit), slow-moving brands or items should be removed from stock.

A profit is obtained on a given brand of merchandise only when it is sold. Bottles standing on the shelf or lying in a cellar bin cost money. They represent an investment, and unless the merchandise moves, it is costing at least 6 percent or more per annum on the purchase price, plus overhead.

Purchasing, therefore, is closely related to merchandising. Buying must always be done in proportion to the establishment's ability to sell. Where savings can be effected by quantity purchases and by cash discounts, it is elementary to avail oneself of the lower price; but if it takes six months to a year to sell a lot so purchased, the saving should be greater than the cost of carrying, as a portion of working capital has been tied up in dead stock that has been paid for but is not earning any income.

The proper stock for a store, restaurant, or distributor's cellar or warehouse depends entirely on the market it serves. In the East, for example, the public prefers blended and Scotch whiskies, while throughout the Middle West, South, and Southwest the public prefers Bourbons.

It is good merchandising to have as complete and varied an assortment on hand as is commensurate with good business practice, as this will make customers feel that they can obtain anything they need. It is impossible, of course, for either a retail or a wholesale outlet to carry every brand. A fairly complete assortment of types is possible, however, without too great an investment.

CONSUMER PURCHASING

Quality should always be the first consideration—with the consumer as well as with the wholesaler and retailer—although its relation to price and value should not be overlooked.

The most satisfactory system for the consumer who has not had an opportunity to taste many products is to find a supplier in whom he has confidence and ask his advice. In time each individual discovers, by actual tasting, which products and brands he prefers.

While in the long run the contents of a bottle are more important than the label, it must not be forgotten that the brand is important. Any brand that has been marketed successfully for generations—and sometimes for centuries—has maintained its popularity because its quality is satisfactory. People do not continue to accept famous brands only because of their reputation and advertising; they continue to buy because of the consistent quality maintained by the manufacturers of these brands. The moment quality is lowered, the public turns away.

In purchasing spirits, there is little advantage in stocking more than the necessary requirements, as spirits do not gain in value or in quality after they have been bottled. Very rare old brandies, whiskies, or rums of which there are limited supplies may, however, gain in value.

It is a different story where wines are concerned. Light beverage wines and Champagnes do change, improve, and, in the case of very fine wines, increase in value with time (when properly stored and cared for) and therefore often are worth purchasing with a view to future use.

In general we recommend allowing red wines several days' rest after receipt before serving. In other words, do not buy a bottle of wine this afternoon to serve with tonight's dinner. If the wine has any deposit it will be stirred up, giving the wine an unattractive, dull appearance. Some of the sturdier wines do not need all this care, but it is safer to err on the side of too much care than to risk handling wines carelessly.

When preparing to entertain, whether at a cocktail party, reception, or dinner, it is advisable to figure out in advance the quantities of beverages needed. Every host wishes to make sure his guests have as much as they wish. It is difficult to predict thirst accurately, but in general it is safe to approximate two drinks per person if the party lasts two hours, and three if it lasts three or four hours. Allow an extra half-drink per person, and there should be no shortage.

Guests' preferences should govern the beverages served. There must be enough soda water on hand for highballs, lemons and limes for cocktails, and so forth. Spirits and fortified wines do not spoil, so a few extra bottles may be purchased as a precaution against a shortage.

The following chart may help you calculate the number of bottles needed to entertain any number of guests.

PRODUCT	BOTTLE CONTENT	AVERAGE PORTION	NO. OF PORTIONS
Table wine	24.0 oz. (75 cl.)	4 oz. (12.5 cl.)	6
Champagne and sparkling wine	26.0 oz. (75 cl.)	4 oz. (12.5 cl.)	6
Sherry, Porto, and Madeira	24.0 oz. (75 cl.)	3 oz. (9 cl.)	8
Vermouth and aperitif wine	30.5 oz. (1 liter)	3 oz. (10 cl.)	10
Cognac and brandy	25.6 oz. (75 cl.)	1 oz. (3 cl.)	25
Whisky, vodka, and gin	25.6 oz. (75 cl.)	1½ oz. (4.5 cl.)	17
Rum and Tequila	25.6 oz. (75 cl.)	1½ oz. (4.5 cl.)	17
Liqueurs	23 to 25.6 oz. (75 cl.)	1½ oz. (4.5 cl.)	17
Mixers: soda water or ginger ale	32.0 oz. (1 liter)	4 oz. (12.5 cl.)	8
Beer on draft (in kegs)	15.5 gal.	8 oz.	250

In estimating the wine needed for a dinner party, the following should serve as a guide:

If one wine is served, two glasses (4 ounces each) per person
If two wines are served, one glass (4 ounces each) per person
If three wines are served, one glass (4 ounces each) per person

Have a reserve of one-half glass per person in case the guests wish more. When sherry, Madeira, or Champagne is served as an aperitif before the meal, allow one and one-half glasses per person.

WHAT THE CELLAR SHOULD CONTAIN

When one is limited by space or inclination to an inexpensive cellar, it is better to have a small, compact assortment of wines and spirits that provides a sufficient quantity of a given product rather than a wide assortment of single bottles.

The cellars suggested on the following pages can only serve as guides; personal taste should govern the selection. The only reason for cellaring these products is to buy early when prices are lower and to have the beverages available for serving.

THE STARTING CELLAR

3 bottles California red table wine (Zinfandel, Gamay Beaujolais, proprietary red)
3 bottles California or eastern white table wine (Chenin Blanc, Dutchess, proprietary white)
3 bottles French red table wine (Beaujolais, Bourgogne Rouge, claret)
3 bottles French white table wine (Graves, Sauternes, Mâcon Blanc)
3 bottles Italian red table wine (Bardolino, Chianti, Lambrusco)
2 bottles German white table wine (Rhine, Moselle)
2 bottles rosé wine (Anjou, eastern rosé)
2 bottles Champagne or sparkling wine (French, California)

A basic collection of wines and spirits that do not have to be laid away and may be purchased as needed is:

1 bottle medium-dry sherry
1 bottle dry vermouth
1 bottle sweet vermouth
2 bottles whisky—blended, Bourbon, or Canadian
2 bottles Scotch whisky

1 bottle gin
1 bottle vodka
1 bottle rum
2 half-bottles liqueurs (amaretto, B & B)

If one has twice as much to invest, a wider assortment is possible. Quantities can also be increased. For example, one can include several different wines of the regions mentioned above. Additions to the list can include:

Madeira
Porto
Cognac
A wider assortment of liqueurs (Drambuie, Grand Marnier, crème de menthe)

THE EXPANDED CELLAR

For one who enjoys a variety to please all tastes, this assortment should fill the bill:

6 bottles Champagne and sparkling wine (Brut French, California, *vin mousseux*)
6 bottles red California wine (Cabernet Sauvignon, Zinfandel, Petite Sirah)
6 bottles white California wine (Chardonnay, Johannisberg Riesling, Sauvignon Blanc)
3 bottles eastern white wine (Aurora, Seyval Blanc, Delaware)
12 bottles red and white regional Bordeaux wine (Médoc, Saint-Émilion, Graves, Sauternes)
6 bottles château-bottled Bordeaux wine, second and third growths (Cos d'Estournel, Gruaud-Larose, etc.)
3 bottles château-bottled Bordeaux wine, first growths (Latour, Margaux, Mouton-Rothschild, etc.)
6 bottles red Burgundy wine (Gevrey-Chambertin, Chambolle-Musigny, Pommard)
6 bottles white Burgundy wine (Pouilly-Fuissé, Puligny-Montrachet, Meursault)
6 bottles Rhine and Moselle wine (Liebfraumilch, Bernkasteler Riesling)
6 bottles rosé wine (Tavel, Portuguese, proprietary rosé)
6 bottles red and white Italian wine (Barolo, Valpolicella, Soave)
3 bottles red Spanish wine (Rioja)

A complementary liquor cabinet would include the following:

3 bottles Canadian whisky	1 bottle Cointreau or Grand Marnier
4 bottles Scotch whisky	1 bottle aromatic bitters
3 bottles vodka	2 bottles Cognac
2 bottles gin	1 bottle Madeira
1 bottle Tequila	2 bottles Porto
2 bottles rum	3 bottles sherry—dry, medium, sweet
1 bottle Calvados or applejack	2 bottles dry vermouth
1 bottle Bénédictine or B & B	2 bottles sweet vermouth

THE COLLECTOR'S CELLAR

The wine and spirits collector can stock his cellar with the assortment of wines mentioned in the starting and expanded cellars, but in greater quantities and with emphasis on the ones indicated in parentheses below, or vary it as his experience dictates. It is a good idea to try wines from the same grape or region from different producers.

18 bottles red California wine (Cabernet Sauvignon, Zinfandel, Pinot Noir, etc., from different regions)

18 bottles white California wine (Chardonnay, Johannisberg Riesling, Gewürztraminer), etc., from different regions)

6 bottles eastern varietal white wine (Johannisberg Riesling, Chardonnay, Seyval Blanc)

12 bottles red and white regional Bordeaux wine (Médoc, Saint-Émilion, Graves, Sauternes)

12 bottles Bordeaux wine, second and third growths (Lascombes, Léoville-Lascases, Kirwan, Palmer, etc.)

12 bottles Bordeaux wine, first growths (Lafite-Rothschild, Mouton-Rothschild, Margaux, Haut Brion, Latour)

6 bottles château-bottled Graves wine (Olivier, Bouscaut, Carbonnieux, etc.)

6 bottles Sauternes wine (d'Yquem, Suduiraut, Coutet, etc.)

12 bottles Mâcon and Beaujolais wine (Mâcon Viré, Brouilly, Moulin à Vent, etc.)

6 bottles red Côte de Nuits wine (Chambertin, Clos de Vougeot, Richebourg, etc.)

6 bottles red Côte de Beaune wine (Volnay, Beaune, Corton, etc.)

12 bottles white Burgundy wine (Meursault, Montrachet, Corton Charlemagne, Chablis, etc.)

6 bottles white Loire wine (Muscadet, Pouilly-Fumé)

12 bottles rosé wine (Anjou, Côtes de Provence, Tavel, California Cabernet Rosé, etc.)

6 bottles Alsatian wine (Riesling, Gewürztraminer, etc.)

6 bottles Moselle wine (Bernkasteler Doctor, Wehlener Sonnenuhr, Graacher Himmelreich, etc.)

12 bottles Rhine wine (Schloss Johannisberg, Oestricher Lenchen, Niersteiner Orbel, Forster Jesuitengarten, etc.)

6 bottles red Spanish wine (Rioja Reserva)

6 bottles Italian white wine (Verdicchio, Pinot Grigio, etc.)

6 bottles Chianti Classico or Valpolicella Amarone wine

12 bottles Barolo, Gattinara, and Sassella wine

A complementary fortified wines and spirits cabinet would contain the following:

6 bottles sherry—dry, medium, and sweet

3 bottles Vintage Porto

6 bottles Tawny and Ruby Porto

2 bottles Sercial and Malmsey Madeira

4 bottles aperitif wines (Dubonnet, St. Raphaël, Lillet, or Campari)

2 bottles dry vermouth

2 bottles sweet vermouth

2 bottles cherry or other fruit wine

2 bottles Cognac

2 bottles Puerto Rican rum

2 bottles Jamaican rum

2 bottles Calvados or applejack

4 bottles Scotch whisky (all malt, aged, etc.)

6 bottles American whisky (Bourbon, blended, Tennessee, etc.)

3 bottles Canadian whisky

1 bottle Irish whiskey

3 bottles gin (English, American, Dutch)

1 bottle Aquavit

3 bottles vodka

2 bottles Tequila

12 bottles assorted liqueurs (apricot, Bénédictine, Chartreuse, Cointreau, Grand Marnier, crème de menthe, Kahlúa, etc.)

2 bottles Kirsch, Framboise, or Poire

1 bottle aromatic bitters (Angostura)

1 bottle orange bitters

beer ⎫
ale ⎬ Quantities vary with personal requirements
stout ⎭ and coolness of storage conditions

The foregoing are only suggestions we offer as a beginning, but the collector's cellar can be varied and expanded as much as his taste, wishes, and pocketbook allow. It can include many finer wines, some in magnums, both table wines and Champagne, and increased quantities of less costly wines, as well as a supply of older spirits. The selection can be modified considerably, to include Armagnac, some of the rare Rhines and Moselles, and some of the other very interesting Italian wines, Hungarian Tokays, and so forth.

The sweeter-tasting white table wines such as Sauternes, Spätlese, Auslese, and even richer Beerenauslese and Trockenbeerenauslese German wines of the Moselle and Rhine districts can be quite long lived. We have enjoyed and found such wines magnificent after forty years in the bottle. This does not mean that all such rich white table wines will always last so long. They, like all white wines, tend to maderization with time, but when they are good, they can be extraordinarily good.

There is one recommendation we wish to make with regard to building up a private cellar. Do not purchase wines or spirits merely for the sake of collecting and storing them. Store them only for the purpose of aging. Wines, beers, and spirits are produced for only one purpose, and that is to be drunk, thereby giving pleasure, enjoyment, and satisfaction to appreciative consumers. Buy them, buy them generously, so that you may enjoy them generously with your guests. We make the admonition because on more than one occasion we have had the sad experience of having to appraise cellars filled with wines that bore magnificent names and vintages but had been hidden away and perhaps forgotten until, when we examined them, they were finished and worthless, no longer capable of being drunk and giving enjoyment.

As a final observation, we suggest purchasing only young vintages of white table wines, rosé wines, and Beaujolais. They are at their best, most attractive, and most enjoyable while they possess the fresh fruity charm of youth. This also means you should drink them young. You may find them disappointing if you keep them four or five years.

31
STORAGE AND
CELLAR TREATMENT

The care of wines, beers, and spirits is an important but fairly simple task. In a commercial establishment these beverages represent an investment on which a profit is expected, and they should be treated both with care and with regard for their perishable qualities. Just as a restaurant operator takes care to store dairy products, meats, and vegetables in a properly refrigerated room, so beverages must be carefully stored. While this applies more to beers and wines than it does to spirits, even the latter need to be safeguarded, preferably under lock and key, for otherwise the profits in them tend to "evaporate" mysteriously.

Assuming proper security, attention must be paid to the actual physical environment that surrounds the bottles. The most important factors are temperature, humidity, light, and vibrations. These should be considered when choosing a place for storing wines, beers, and spirits.

WINE STORAGE

The cardinal requirement of a cellar or storage space where wines are to be kept for some time is an even temperature. There is no single ideal temperature, but instead a range of acceptable storage temperatures that vary with the length of time the wines will be stored. For long-term storage (fifteen to thirty years) 55 to 60 degrees Fahrenheit would be the best range. For moderately long storage (five to fifteen years), anywhere from 55 to 65 degrees Fahrenheit would be satisfactory if the temperature is kept fairly constant and any changes are simply gradual seasonal changes. Violent swings in temperature should be avoided. For short-range laying away of wines (up to five years), the temperature can go as high as 70 degrees Fahrenheit, and any fluctuations must still be gradual. It is not advisable to store wine for any length of time in a room where the temperature goes above 70 degrees Fahrenheit. The storage area should be away from a heating plant or hot-water unit.

temperature

457

Whether the cellar is below ground or in the closet of an apartment, it should be ventilated to keep it free of odors and to maintain uniform conditions throughout the area.

Air conditioning makes ideal cellar conditions possible in any part of a building, provided the space is large enough. Air conditioning not only maintains the proper temperature, but it can provide needed ventilation to filter the air and maintain humidity control, both of which are important. One mistake that many people make is to install an air-conditioning unit in a small room or closet. This can lead to poor humidity control and excessive air currents and temperature fluctuations, which are bad for wine. Also, the coils of the unit may freeze, which will make the air conditioner unreliable. If you are thinking of installing an air conditioner, call in an expert who will select the proper-size unit or who may even suggest using a refrigeration system that can be adapted to smaller spaces.

White wines, either still or sparkling, may be stored in the refrigerator so that they will be properly chilled and immediately available. Nothing will happen to them if they are left in the refrigerator for a few months.

Large hotels and restaurants that sell a considerable amount of wine daily find it economical to have special refrigerators in which the white and sparkling wines for daily use are kept at serving temperature. This ensures prompt service to guests. Such refrigerators are also useful for chilling large numbers of bottles for banquet service.

humidity   Proper humidity is the most nebulous of all the physical conditions that affect wines. If the air is too damp, molds are encouraged to grow and labels, foils, and corks may deteriorate.

Air at different temperatures can hold different amounts of water vapor. The biggest problem occurs when the outside air is significantly warmer (20 to 30 degrees Fahrenheit) than the air inside the cellar. The cooler air holds less water vapor than the warmer air. If the cool cellar is ventilated (to avoid stale odors), the outside air mixes with the cooler cellar air. Condensation can occur when the outside air is cooled to the temperature existing in the cellar. To avoid the mustiness caused by the condensation, the cellar should not only be ventilated but it should also be dehumidified, keeping the air at a practical relative humidity of approximately 50 percent.

light   Sunlight is an indispensable friend of the vine but an implacable enemy of the wine it yields. Wines are injured by light, which is why most wine bottles are made of colored glass. Actually, all bright light is bad, and a wine cellar or storage location should be as dark as possible. No wine, of course, will be damaged by an hour or a day or even a week of any light except bright sunlight.

The proprietors of the Four Seasons restaurant in New York, Tom Margittai (left) and Paul Kovi (right), inside the wine cellar. (*Photo by S. Karin Epstein*)

Wine cellar and tasting room of Theodore Hutton's famous La Doña Luz Restaurant at Taos, New Mexico. (*Courtesy La Doña Luz Restaurant*)

vibrations   Constant vibrations can damage wine. For this reason do not put wine bottles directly on the floor, but rather keep them on shelves or in racks that are free of vibrations. If possible, locate the wine cellar away from machinery or the rumble of traffic.

manner of storing   Bottles of still and sparkling wines should always be stored on their sides so the wine is in contact with the inner surface of the cork. This keeps the cork expanded and prevents it from drying out. If the bottles are stored upright and the cork dries out, air could seep through and spoil the wine. In the case of Champagne and sparkling wines, a dried-out cork permits the gas to escape, resulting in flat wine.

Fortified wines and any spirits that are closed with corks should be stored in an upright position, since the alcohol, which is at a higher strength than that of table wine, has an adverse effect on the cork, resulting in seepage. The one exception is Vintage Porto, which is closed with an extralong cork for long-term horizontal storage.

Wines and spirits closed with plastic or metal stoppers or screw caps may be stored in any position. Upright is preferable, however, as there is a slight chance that a bottle with a loose cap may leak.

White and sparkling wines should be stored in the coolest part of the cellar in the lower bins or shelves, while red wines may be stored in the bins above them, with the topmost bins for fortified wines and spirits.

The arrangement should be determined by your own practical needs, with items most frequently in demand within easy reach.

Cased goods should be stored in an orderly fashion, stacked off the floor to permit ventilation and to prevent mold from forming. This can be accomplished by laying down two parallel two-by-four runners below the stacks.

corking   Eventually corks deteriorate. It is generally felt that a good cork will last about twenty-five years and should be changed after that. The best way to tell whether a cork needs to be changed is to examine the bottle for signs of *ullage* resulting from slight leaking.

Recorking is best left to a professional. Extracting a damaged cork is critical, and several tools are needed; the standard waiter's corkscrew can rarely be used. If there are several bottles of the same wine, all are usually recorked at the same time; one of the bottles is used to top off the others and reduce the amount of air space.

Sweet wines tend to "weep" more than clarets or red Burgundies, and the presence of some sticky liquid on the neck of a bottle of Sauternes or great German wine is usually not cause for alarm. Those corks need be replaced only if there is a substantial loss in the bottle.

Recently, the "21" Club in New York had its large, valuable cellar checked by a professional. Old bottles from the last century were recorked. They were also relabeled with the date and the name of the person who performed the recorking. These wines are part of "21's" carefully maintained wine museum.

All the adjuncts to beverage service, such as mineral water, ginger ale, and tonic water, may be stored in the wine cellar. Wine baskets and wine coolers may be stored here too, but the wine cellar should never become the repository for broken furniture and odds and ends. *adjuncts to beverage service*

The wine cellar should be separated from the rest of the cellar so it can be locked. In large establishments a time lock may be used or it will be difficult to maintain correct inventory balances.

PACKAGE STORES

Generally speaking, the same principles of cellar storage apply to stores as to hotels and restaurants.

In each case the cellar should be arranged so that the patrons of the establishment may be shown through the cellar. This is good sales promotion, since it arouses greater interest in the beverages, and viewing bottles and cases in a well-maintained storage area is far more enticing than a mere printed list.

A retail store cellar should be as attractive as the main part of the store. (*Courtesy Corti Brothers, San Francisco*)

LEFT: Wines stored in prefabricated triangular modules in apartment closet designed by Greg Lentz. (*Courtesy Harold J. Baron*) ABOVE: A wine vault unit that can be installed in a home. (*Courtesy Wine Vault, Inc.*)

HOME CELLAR

The home cellar can vary from simple racks to elaborately controlled environments. But whether it is a cupboard, a closet, or an actual cellar, it should serve the purposes of the owner.

For an apartment, select a closet that is not near any heating apparatus. Shelves can be built in of strong, three-fourths-inch-thick boards. Leave plenty of space above the top shelves on which to stand fortified wines and spirits. These bottles average thirteen to fourteen inches in height when the cork is half out. Then build the other shelves from twelve to fourteen inches apart, making them fourteen inches deep, for the wines to be stored on their sides.

When a cellar is in a house, a room away from the heating plant or hot-water unit should be selected. Bins made of wood planking or of metal should be installed along the walls, fourteen inches deep. If the room is large and is to store large quantities of wine, it is advisable to build additional rows of bins in the center of the room. If these are made of wood, we recommend crisscross bins. If made of metal, the bins should be square. Honeycomb units made of metal, wood, or plastic are available in different shapes and capacities and are useful if you have a large number of individual bottles. The disadvantage of individual binning is that it is difficult to tell what is in each cubicle without pulling out the bottle. One way to avoid this is to use press-on labels, available at most stationery stores, which can be placed on the capsule of the bottle or on the bottom, depending on which way the bottle is placed in the rack. This label should tell the name of the wine, or its bin number, and will eliminate excessive handling of bottles.

The cellar should have an adequate light source and contain a table and a cellar book in which a record is kept of all purchases of wines and spirits. A cellar book might also contain menus of dinner parties and guest lists, with notes on the wines that were served and their condition. In time this will become a record of some of your most pleasant memories.

For more controlled cellar conditions, although at greater expense, some self-contained storage units are available. Two brands that have given satisfactory service for a long time are the Wine Vault and the Cramer Wine Steward. Both have refrigeration units to maintain constant temperature and humidity.

Whether an elaborate system or simple shelves, remember to keep a strong lock on the cellar door.

32
MERCHANDISING

The principles of successful promotion and selling are fundamental. When the public clamors for a particular brand it is usually not only a good product but one that has been intelligently and aggressively merchandised. In the wine and spirits trade the brands most in demand are those that are most widely advertised and intensively merchandised.

The first important consideration is the salesman. Everyone engaged in the wine and spirits trade, whether producer, distributor, retailer, or owner of a restaurant, is necessarily a salesman. The whole object of producing, distributing, or selling these products is to make a profit from them. No one can sell anything about which he knows nothing. The more the salesman knows about the product he is selling, the more successfully he will sell it.

Therefore, it is basic that the members of the sales staff, from the president through the newest salesman down to the telephone operator, who very often takes orders and answers questions, should know as much as possible about the wines, beers, or spirits (and their uses and service) that are being sold.

RESTAURANT MERCHANDISING

We are convinced that if the food is good and the prices of the beverages are reasonable, the public will buy wine or other beverages when dining out, because in the proper atmosphere wine is enjoyed with well-cooked, well-presented meals.

We have never been able to understand why American restaurants work so hard at selling ice water. This is a beverage service that produces no revenue or profit, and yet this "service" is costly to the management. On the other hand, the nearest the restaurant comes to "selling" profitable beverages is "Do you wish a drink before dinner?" or "Do you want your coffee now or later?"

Another sales deterrent is overpricing. In far too many cases, wine sales in a restaurant are discouraged by outrageous prices. Wine is the only item

464

restaurants list that is sold in its original package. It is an item whose price the patron can compare with a known retail price. While he is willing to pay for service and surroundings, he is not prepared—nor should he be expected—to pay an excessively high premium. Most people resent any pricing that appears to take advantage of them. The average patron will enjoy good wines with his dinner if the price is not prohibitive. Marking up premium-quality wine 100 percent over the wholesale price yields the restaurant a small profit and is acceptable to the patron. We also suggest the cost-plus system as a suitable alternative.

The following table compares the most-used markup systems, showing them with various percentage markups for each. For a given wholesale cost of a bottle of wine (column A), the table shows the retail store price (column B), figuring the usual 50 percent markup taken by the retail wine merchant. Columns C and D show restaurant selling prices based on straight markups of 100 and 200 percent respectively.

Columns E and F, with 100 and 150 percent markups applied, also add $1 per bottle for fixed overhead expenses, which include wine service and glass-ware. With the cost-plus system, higher-priced wine, such as Champagne, can be offered at a more reasonable price and therefore increase sales and total profits. In fact, columns E and F are approximately double retail prices, with the more expensive bottles actually less than twice retail, which is an extremely reasonable price for a wine in a restaurant. Many restaurateurs use the straight markup system for their lower-priced wines and shift to the cost-plus system for the higher-priced wines.

BOTTLE COSTS AND MARKUPS

		RESTAURANT PRICE			
WHOLESALE COST	RETAIL STORE PRICE	STRAIGHT MARKUP		COST PLUS	
		100%	200%	100% PLUS $1.00	150% PLUS $1.00
A	B	C	D	E	F
$1.00	$ 1.50	$ 2.00	$ 3.00	$ 3.00	$ 3.50
1.50	2.25	3.00	4.50	4.00	4.75
2.00	3.00	4.00	6.00	5.00	6.00
2.50	3.75	5.00	7.50	6.00	7.25
3.00	4.50	6.00	9.00	7.00	8.50
4.00	6.00	8.00	12.00	9.00	11.00
5.00	7.50	10.00	15.00	11.00	13.50
6.00	9.00	12.00	18.00	13.00	16.00
7.00	10.50	14.00	21.00	15.00	18.50
8.00	12.00	16.00	24.00	17.00	21.00

If restaurants have wines and are not selling them, the investment in time, space, and money is not paying off. The sale of a bottle of wine with a meal can yield the restaurateur more solid net profit than the food itself.

How is the restaurant owner going to sell beverages? This is a serious problem, for obviously it is difficult to get the sales staff to learn about something in which they are not interested. How can the interest of the sales staff be aroused so that every member will want to know more about wines and spirits? The answer is money.

As an example, compare two dinner checks. The first check, for dinner without wine, amounts to $15.00, and the tip is $2.25. The second check includes cocktails and a half-bottle of wine and amounts to $25.00 Now the tip is $3.75.

Of course, before waiters can sell wines they must be familiar with what they are selling. Here are a few points they should learn:

1. Waiters should know exactly what wines and spirits the restaurant has to offer.

2. They must know which of these are red and which are white, as well as which are dry or sweet.

3. They must know which of the wines are table wines, such as claret, Sauternes, Burgundy, Rhine, and Moselle; which are sparkling wines; and which are fortified wines, such as sherry, port, and Madeira.

4. They must know which wines should be chilled and which should be served at room temperature.

5. They should know what wines to suggest for the various dishes on the menu.

6. When they do sell a bottle of wine, they should know the correct manner of presenting, opening, and serving the wine—described in Chapter 28. Too frequently wine is casually, sloppily, or incorrectly served. While a great deal of absurd ritual has grown up about serving wines and spirits, it is necessary that a hotel, restaurant, or club know the correct procedure in presenting, opening, and serving wine. There is always a little glamor about ordering wine. Play it up—it flatters the customer.

These are the bare essentials that a good staff should know in order to sell wines; any additional information given them will help. No one can expect a staff to learn everything overnight. The best way to equip them is to have a weekly class where these things are explained repeatedly until the staff is thoroughly versed. When waiters are trained, they in turn will be better able to serve guests.

Now for a few practical selling ideas:

1. A good, well-rounded wine list that is suited to the needs of the establishment's clientele is a must. A list is often placed on each table. Avoid repetition in listings. By this we mean that one Sauternes may be quite adequate.

2. Describe each wine as to taste in two or three words—especially the white wines, which vary greatly between sweet and dry.

3. Mention wines on the food menu. An appropriate wine suggestion printed next to the plat du jour will sell wine.

4. Certain dishes have an affinity for specific beverages. For example, one way to boost Porto sales is to offer a combination of cheese and Porto for one price. Beer goes well with dishes that have sauerkraut in them; offer them together.

5. Arrange a table at the entrance to the dining room with a few wines attractively displayed. This in itself suggests gracious dining, and it starts the guest thinking about wine before he is seated.

6. Table tents and menu riders will sell cocktails, wines, beer, and cordials.

7. We are greatly in favor of measuring all ingredients when making cocktails. That way they will always be uniform. This encourages repeat business.

8. Specialize in two or three cocktails made better than other restaurants make them.

9. Feature seasonal drinks. Tie in holidays with beverage merchandising.

10. Finally, and most important, while the foregoing ideas will help, the actual sale must still be made by the person taking the food order. The wine must be suggested. The wine list or wine card should be presented when the guest finishes ordering the food, if not before, and while he is psychologically in the ordering mood. It should be presented naturally, without fanfare, but as a matter of course, with a suggestion such as "Would you like to enjoy a pleasant bottle of Riesling with the fish you have ordered?" In other words, *suggest* a wine. You will be surprised by the number of sales.

From experience we know that the best advertisement for wine is the wine itself. We have long maintained that if the wine trade could distribute samples, as the food and cigarette industries do, our country would be much more of a wine-drinking nation.

The closest approach to this is the half-bottle, which can be sold inexpensively, making it possible for the person who has never tasted a certain wine to do so without risking too great a sum. In tests conducted by leading wine distributors, when half-bottles were featured the sale of the large bottles of the same wines increased because the half-bottles performed their sample function perfectly.

Another way to promote wine sales that has been used successfully is to offer small six- to eight-ounce decanters. These perform the same function as the half-bottle but are not as successful as selling tools, however, because the customer cannot see the actual bottle or label.

Splits and half-bottles have also been merchandised with equal success in retail stores and have produced repeat sales of regular-size bottles.

Wine sales are best when *all* waiters or waitresses suggest and serve wine to customers. For added showmanship some leading hotels and restaurants like to designate one person to specialize in the sale and service of wine, paying him a commission on the wine he sells. Usually, for practical purposes, this person is

A suitable display for either a liquor store or a restaurant. (*Courtesy* Liquor Store *Magazine*)

simply called the wine waiter, and his uniform need differ only in color from that of the other waiters. Any experienced waiter can acquire a knowledge of wine types and uses with a little extra training and inducement from the management. In turn, he can then aid the management in training other waiters in wine use. Since he is a wine salesman, it is important that the wine waiter have a pleasant personality and the ability to sell without high-pressure tactics.

There is another, more traditional, type of wine waiter, known as the sommelier, preferred by hotels or restaurants that want the maximum attention given to wine. The sommelier is more of a true wine expert, by custom, and he often wears a leather cellar apron and a silver chain, with a tasting cup and a medallion or giant key attached. These accessories are available from some restaurant supply firms.

It should be emphasized that neither the wine waiter nor the sommelier is necessary to a successful wine-selling program if the regular waiters or waitresses are properly trained. When a wine specialist is used, however, he can still work hand in hand with the regular waiter, and both benefit from the wine sale: one from his wine commission, one from his increased tip. In such an operation the regular waiter finds out quickly in taking the food order whether the customer likes the idea of wine with dinner. He then summons the wine waiter or sommelier to the table. The latter presents the wine list, suggests a specific type and brand, brings the wine promptly, and serves it. The wine price is added to the regular food check.

An important factor in any merchandising policy is maintaining a uniform and constant source of supply. The standard quality merchandise should be available to customers at all times. Bargains and close-outs do not build permanent trade. The customer who is pleased by a wine or spirit wants the same quality when he comes back a second time. If he is shifted from one brand or one quality to another, he will lose confidence in the establishment. This is a basic point that applies equally to restaurants and to retail establishments, and it should be stressed by the distributor's salesman.

STORE MERCHANDISING AND ADVERTISING

To sell you must tell. This may be accomplished by various methods:

1. In personal conversation with a customer
2. By a newspaper or magazine advertisement
3. By broadcasting the message over radio and television
4. By a letter
5. By catalogs and price lists
6. By displaying the merchandise both in the store and in the windows

ABOVE: Morrell & Company in New York City has a counter constructed of wooden liquor cases and displays oversize bottles atop its liqueur and brandy shelves. BELOW: A "supermarket" liquor store with a good selection of wines divided by regions. Note the displays at the end of each aisle of full and open cartons. (*Courtesy* Liquor Store *Magazine*)

The ideal method, of course, is personal discussion, during which the salesman may use arguments and counterarguments, answer questions, and render service in the most complete fashion. This method is necessarily limited to the number of people who enter the establishment because of a specific need for merchandise.

When a customer does come into an establishment, however, half of the selling problem has been solved because the customer has come to buy. The other half of the problem is to have the salesman serve the customer's needs if they are specific or to offer helpful suggestions if he is not certain what he wishes to purchase. In direct personal selling, even if the customer knows exactly what he wants, the alert merchant can find out by adroit questioning or conversation how the beverage will be used and base his selling on this information.

For example, if the merchandise is intended for a party, the merchant can advise the customer as to the quantities required for the number of guests expected. If it is for daily use, the merchant will be able to tell whether the customer should buy in half-bottle, bottle, or gallon sizes, depending on the customer's needs.

Merchants can inform customers, for example, that white wine, if promptly recorked after opening, may be kept in the refrigerator and will not spoil for a week or ten days, while red wine, if tightly recorked after opening, especially if decanted into a smaller bottle, will keep almost as long stored in a dark cabinet. Champagne and sparkling wines should be consumed when they are opened, as they cannot be recorked and will lose most of their effervescence in a few hours. Loss of gas can be retarded if the sparkling wine is kept very cold at all times. Offering this kind of useful information inspires customer confidence.

As desirable as personal contact with prospective customers is, it is limited, and therefore other media are useful and, when properly employed, profitable. Advertising reaches a far greater audience. Every advertisement should convey the personality of the store and reflect its reputation.

What sort of trade does the establishment wish to attract? Are low prices, or special offerings, or a complete range from low-priced to finest-quality products to be featured? Even if all three types of merchandise are stocked, start with one and feature it above the others.

Once store advertising policy is decided, select the medium best suited to reach the widest audience: local magazines, club magazines, fraternal publications, newspapers, local radio stations, or direct mail. First, of course, determine what audience these vehicles reach and what audience contains the largest proportion of potential customers. Check this against the cost of the medium you have chosen to determine the most profitable method.

It is advisable to find some merchandising device—a slogan, an illustration, a crest, or the store name—that will always associate the advertisement with the store at first glance.

In the advertisement feature your merchandise or simply the enjoyment the purchaser will derive from it. Perhaps the selling point is a very convenient location, or a fine telephone and delivery service; or perhaps the store specializes in certain types of beverages or sizes of packages. If so, feature these points.

This is known as institutional advertising—that is, selling primarily the store name, its policies, and its services to the public rather than employing the special offering form of advertisement where the primary attraction is price or availability of extraordinary items.

All advertising has a cumulative effect, and therefore repetition will, in time, produce the wanted sales.

newspapers   An important consideration in newspaper advertising is deciding on the right spot for the advertisement. There are society and women's pages, sports pages, food pages, and general news sections. Specify in what part of the paper your ad is to appear. The food page and pages 2, 3, and 4 are generally premium spots and may cost more than the general run of the paper. Some dealers prefer to specify these positions and pay the extra rate, as a small advertisement so placed will often be more productive than a larger one in another spot. Try this by test. The advertisement should be timed with the buying habits of the public.

To get double value for your advertising dollar, post a blow-up of an ad in the store after it has appeared in the newspaper. (*Courtesy* Liquor Store *Magazine*)

The National Association of Broadcasters accepts wine and beer adver- *radio and*
tisements for radio and television, but not spirits advertising. There are a *television*
number of different methods of using air time. Most popular are thirty- and
sixty-second radio spots and ten- and thirty-second television spots.

Direct solicitation by means of a convincingly worded letter has many *direct mail*
advantages, although it is one of the costlier methods of advertising. Its
principal advantage is that the list of names to which a letter is addressed is
made up of either customers who have actually purchased wines or spirits in
the store or those believed to be consumers of alcoholic beverages. The
productiveness of this form of advertising will only be as good as the list itself.
In view of this fact, and considering the cost of mailing, the list must be
updated constantly.

The primary object of a catalog or price list is to inform the customer of the *catalogs and*
products stocked and the prices at which they are sold. Price lists fall into two *price lists*
classes—a general catalog listing every item in inventory and condensed
offerings of specific products or groups of products.

The general price list or catalog should be revised periodically. In addition
to the prices and the list of products, it should contain information that is useful
to the customer, such as cocktail recipes, punch recipes, and uses of wines and
spirits. The more useful this information is to the customer, the longer he will
keep the catalog and the more often he will refer to it and be reminded of the
name of the store and its products.

The special offering should state clearly that it is for a limited time only. Its *special*
object is to stimulate quick sales, and therefore it should be concise, direct, and *offerings*
dramatic.

These points may be accomplished in several ways. If a lower price than
normal is offered, show the regular price and indicate the savings involved.

If it is a new product, describe it briefly.

If it is a seasonal or holiday offering, an illustration or a short paragraph
about the seasonal use of the product may be effective.

The main point is that to be effective, the special-offering price list must
encourage people to buy at once, to take advantage of a special opportunity.

Every window display should be designed to be an "interrupting factor" to *window*
the eye of the passerby. What accomplishes this? Certainly not a display of *displays*
standard merchandise with standard prices arranged in rows. Arrange a
window so that attention is focused on some one thing. That may be an item of
merchandise or it may be some related subject, a well-set table, for instance,
that indicates how a beverage can be used, such as:

To show customers one way to set up a wine tasting, this window arrangement displays the program from a Wine & Food Society tasting and bottles of all the wines served. (*Photo by David Amster, courtesy Manhattan Château Wine and Liquor Corp.*)

1. A brilliant scarlet riding coat, a pair of boots, a riding crop, and bottles of Bourbon whisky; or a punch bowl, Jamaican rum, and the other ingredients for several different punches.

2. A casserole, an artificial chicken, and a bottle of claret; or a chafing dish, pancakes, and bottles of brandy and Triple Sec.

3. A top hat, a pair of white gloves, a cane, and a bottle of Champagne and a couple of tulip glasses.

4. A bottle of Rock and Rye, a pair of rubbers, and an umbrella.

5. Bottles of wines that would be interesting to compare, along with wineglasses and a tasting list, can suggest ideas for wine tastings.

All of the objects used can be obtained from local merchants, who will usually be glad to lend them, providing a credit is placed in the window.

In states where standard merchandise prices are fixed, there is no advantage in displaying bottles with prices that are identical to competitors'; therefore, it is better merchandising to display fewer bottles but arrange the display attractively, either with a quantity of a given item, a picture background, or a seasonal motif with the merchandise of the season featured.

warning! Were a person to be placed in a window under the direct rays of the sun, he would get sunburned and possibly sunstruck. Wine is also affected by too much

ABOVE: Grouping moderately priced wines by area simplifies a customer's choice and shows the range of wines available from a specific region. BELOW: A promotional wine-of-the-month display encourages people to try a variety of wines throughout the year. (*Courtesy* Liquor Store *Magazine*)

(A Chateau Margaux Label of the 1860's)

1967	Chateau Margaux	Margaux		19.50
1969	Chateau Margaux	Margaux		22.50
1969	Chateau Margaux	Margaux (Tenths)		12.00
1971	Chateau Margaux	Margaux	256.50	23.75
1967	Chateau Maucaillou	Moulis		6.50
1969	Chateau Maucaillou	Moulis		4.50
1970	Chateau Maucaillou	Moulis		5.95
1961	Chateau Meyney	St. Estephe	186.30	17.25
1967	Chateau La Mission-Haut-Brion	Graves	129.60	12.00
1970	Chateau La Mission-Haut-Brion	Graves	161.46	14.95
1971	Chateau La Mission-Haut-Brion	Graves		14.49

(A Chateau La Mission-Haut-Brion Label of the 1860's)

1971	Chateau Monbousquet	St. Emilion	61.56	5.70
1971	Chateau Monbousquet	St. Emilion (Magnums)	61.56	11.40
1971	Chateau Moulin de Cadet	St. Emilion, Avery	61.56	5.70
1966	Chateau Mouton Baron Philippe	Pauillac		11.95
1967	Chateau Mouton Baron Philippe	Pauillac	120.60	12.00
1970	Chateau Mouton Baron Philippe	Pauillac	85.32	7.90
1970	Chateau Mouton Baron Philippe	Pauillac (Magnums)	96.93	17.95

35

Pages from two attractive retail wine catalogs. (RIGHT: *Courtesy Draper & Esquin, San Francisco.* BELOW: *Courtesy Sherry-Lehmann, Inc., New York)*

RED BORDEAUX	SALE	
continued	Bottle	Case

CHATEAU MOUTON ROTHSCHILD 1973 (Pauillac)   11.95   136.25

<u>We have an intriguing story to tell.</u> We all know that it has been a practice of Baron Philippe de Rothschild to persuade the world's greatest artists to creat a label for each of his vintage years. We have seen the works of Chagall in 1970, Miro in 1969, Braque in 1965. The only one missing was Pablo Picasso. World opinion developed quickly that Baron Philippe was never able to persuade Picasso. The truth is that Picasso did create a label for the good Baron but asked that it not be used until after his death.

<u>Picasso died in 1973</u> – the very year Chateau Mouton Rothschild was officially declared a <u>First Growth</u> – the first change in the 1855 classification in over a century. To commemorate the event, and the memory of Picasso, Baron Rothschild declared his art the official label for the 1973 vintage, a very good year at Mouton Rothschild.

<u>The wine has just arrived.</u> It promises to be a collector's item – not only for the extraordinary beauty of the label that Picasso created for this Mouton Rothschild 1973. It is not an easy wine to come by and the <u>price has mounted dramatically in Bordeaux.</u> We offer our first shipment at the opening price of only <u>$11.95 the bottle</u>, <u>$136.25 the case.</u> Also available in <u>magnums</u> at $139.25 the case of six.

light. Wherever possible, use dummy bottles for window displays; if they are unobtainable, keep the awnings down so that the direct rays of the sun do not strike the wines. They become blind, or dull looking, and lose their brilliance. The flavor of the wine is affected in the same manner—the wine becomes flat in taste. Sparkling wine may become overheated and the bottle may burst.

Liqueurs that are artificially colored may change or lose their color if exposed too long to the sun. The afternoon sun is worse than that of the morning, because the actinic rays are stronger after midday. This is partly the reason for using colored glass in wine bottles. The dark green, brown, or black glass protects the wine against the light. (The original reason for dark-colored glass in wine bottles, however, was to hide the cloudy condition of the wines themselves.)

interior displays

Several effective merchandising principles should be considered. One well-recognized and highly productive principle is the related sale, that is, grouping items in relation to each other. For example, cocktail ingredients, the wine for a meal, and the cordial or brandy to finish it can make an attractive island display set in a central spot in the store to attract attention.

Grouping a dozen half-bottles of wine of different types encourages a customer to buy a few bottles in order to find out which wine he or she likes best.

The intimate sale display, where merchandise is arranged helter skelter in a basket so customers will not hesitate to pick up and examine a bottle, helps them to overcome the hesitancy they feel about disturbing a neatly arranged stack.

chilled wines

A selection of more popular white and rosé table wines and Champagne and sparkling wines should be kept in refrigerated storage. This is an accommodation for the customer who wants a bottle for lunch or dinner and does not have the facilities for chilling one on short notice. If the shop is located near a pier for cruise ships, having chilled Champagne on hand for bon voyage parties is a must.

shelf display

Merchandise with which the customer is not familiar and which has a slow sale should be placed in the most prominent part of the store—in the front— while the standard merchandise can be placed in the center or rear so as to draw the customer back into the store to see the island displays as well as the shelf merchandise.

Put signs on floor stackings, on middle-of-the-floor and island displays, and in the windows. Signs should tell more than just the price and should have a professional look. Keep them clean and neat.

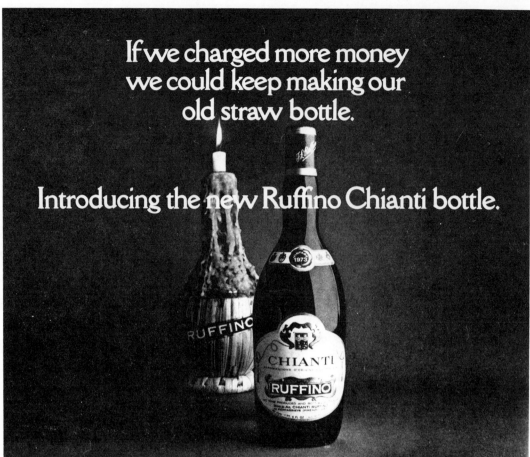

If we charged more money we could keep making our old straw bottle.

Introducing the new Ruffino Chianti bottle.

The old straw Ruffino bottle is being replaced by a distinctive new bottle, and you may be wondering why.

Blame it on the impossible high cost of making the straw package, or inflation, or a lot of things. It doesn't matter where the blame lies. The simple fact is if we don't replace the straw Ruffino Chianti bottle, we would have to charge an inflationary price for our Chianti.

Instead we're making a change for the better: we are replacing the straw-wrapped bottles with a new line of bottles in popular sizes, (24 oz. illustrated above).

Best of all, this new bottle enables us to keep the 24 oz. and 12 oz. prices the same as before. And that's going to make your sales go up.

Ruffino. We became America's best selling premium Chianti by making a great bottle of wine. It's the same great wine in a new wine bottle.

Ruffino. It's Chianti's first name.

Imported by Schieffelin & Co., New York

Good importer advertising helps educate the public. Here Ruffino explains why their popular straw-covered bottle was discontinued. (*Courtesy Schieffelin & Co., New York*)

Well-designed stores put the customer at ease. ABOVE: Fluorescent lighting and natural wood panels create a bright, modern decor in this store. Wines from each country are located under shipping-case signs. Designer: Display Fixtures, Inc., Minneapolis, Minnesota, photograph by H. M. Schawang. BELOW: This Northfield, Illinois, store is classical and traditional. Each alcove holds wines from a different country, and expensive wines are locked in a "rare-wine" cellar. Designer: Florio, Inc., Franklin Park, Illinois. (*Photos courtesy* Liquor Store *Magazine*)

seasonal promotions

There is a holiday or a seasonal merchandising motif in nearly every month of the year, and these should be tied up with advertising and window displays.

The gift-giving holidays should be featured with the logical type of merchandise for the season or holiday. Other holidays indicate weekend parties and entertaining. Stress these facts.

New Year's is a Champagne holiday.

In the spring rums and gins should be featured with the lighter wines.

In May begin promoting Champagne for June weddings and summer garden parties.

In June prestigious brands should be displayed for Father's Day.

In the summer feature beverages that may be used in preparing cooling drinks; also promote light white table wines.

In the fall, with approaching cold weather, whiskies, brandies, and fuller-bodied wines should be promoted.

For the football season feature whiskies and brandies.

Throughout the winter the richer products will be more popular.

At Christmastime, the peak selling season in the trade for the entire year, be sure to bring out the finest-quality merchandise and the fancy packaged liqueurs. This is the best season for these products; anyone giving wines and spirits as a gift wants to feel he is making a gift of something that is not only fine but that will give pleasure and enjoyment to the recipient.

sales

Special offerings of slow-moving merchandise help inventory turn over.

Keep duplicates of sales slips and, at the end of each month or at the end of six months, find out how many customers bought two bottles of an item and how many were pint buyers. From these sales slips you can determine the buying habits of customers. If you find that a good portion of them are multiple buyers, try the device, which has proved very successful in certain large stores, of offering a small discount over the one-bottle price in lots of three bottles. Customers who are constant group-bottle buyers may be interested in buying a case of the same item if they can save something by doing so.

how to sell oneself to one's customers

There is only one road to the goal of a flourishing neighborhood business, and that is confidence. The soundest ways to establish confidence are knowledge of the products, courtesy to customers, quality and value in the merchandise stocked, and the service given. Added to this is personality, a great intangible. Some people have this faculty of approach, the ready smile, the confident air—and it is helpful for the store owners to develop a pleasant manner.

Before customers can be convinced that the merchant's advice is sound, that he is honest in his suggestions, he must know something about the products and how they should be used. Some customers want advice, others feel they know more about it than the merchant does. Let them have their own way about it or they will go elsewhere.

IF YOU CAN TASTE FOOD, YOU CAN TASTE WINE.

Contrary to popular belief, you don't have to come from Oxford or talk funny in order to taste wine.

Anyone, man or woman, with a nose, a mouth and a tongue can become proficient in the art of wine tasting. All it takes is a desire to learn, some practice and the discipline to stick to the guidelines which we are now going to set forth for you free of charge.

There is something in it for us, however, in that if more people developed their palates, more Inglenook Wine would probably be sold, because the taste of our wine is complex enough to challenge the best of wine tasters.

8 PALATES ARE BETTER THAN 1.

If you're just getting into wine tasting, do it among friends.

For one thing, it's cheaper because the cost of the wines can be defrayed. And this is one case where too many cooks don't spoil the broth, for it helps

to have several opinions on a wine that is particularly difficult to judge. So select 6 or 8 friends who are as interested in learning how to taste wine as you are and get them together. But tell them to check their cigarettes at the door. Wine tasting is a difficult enough business under ideal conditions, and the last thing you need is a smoke screen between you and the wine.

TO SPIT OR TO SWALLOW.

A good wine list should include a selection of related wines. They should have something in common, such as vintage, region, varietal, or brand. This gives the palate a better chance to compare one wine with another and it gives the tasting a theme. Eight to ten wines is about right for a good tasting. Any more than this and your taste buds start to get confused. Always cover the labels when tasting and spit, don't swallow. Remember, this is a wine tasting, not a drinking bout, and if you swallow the wine your impressions of the last few wines will be anything but clear. A wine case half-full of sawdust can serve as an excellent make-shift spitoon.

NEVER TRUST YOUR MEMORY.

Even the best of wine tasters will forget a wine's name if he forgets to take notes. So always have paper and pen handy. Note the date of the tasting, name of the wine, vintage year, bottler, price, and a description of the wine's appearance, bouquet, and taste.

Try to keep your descriptions brief and to the point. Describe the wine as clearly as possible so that later, when you refer to your notes, you will be able to recall the wine.

ACIDITY: Natural sourness which bites the tongue.
AROMA: The perfume of the grape.
BOUQUET: The smell of the wine itself.
BODY: The feeling of weight in the mouth.
CHARACTER: Complexity in a wine.
CLEAN: Absence of foreign matter.
DEEP: A bouquet of full, rich and lasting quality.
DRY: Complete absence of sweetness.
EARTHY: A mineral or organic taste of the soil.
FRUITY: A ripe but not necessarily grapy smell.
FULL-BODIED: Thick in the tactile sense.
MELLOW: Soft, ripe and well-matured.
WOODY: A smell derived from aging in oak casks.

Armed with this information and willing to put in several hours a week, you should be able to tuck away 25 to 30 wines a year in your memory. Considering the fact that there are over 5,000 wines in the world, this should keep you busy until around the year 2169.

WINE IS LIKE MUSIC.

There are only two kinds of wine: wine you gulp and wine you taste. Trying to learn wine tasting with a "gulp" wine is like trying to learn music theory on a kazoo.

In our opinion, the better tasting wines should be the following:

A. Estate bottled. This means that every grape used in the wine's production was grown, picked and crushed under the direct supervision of the vintner. It takes this kind of care to produce a truly great wine.

B. Napa Valley. The Napa Valley of California is, in our opinion, the finest wine producing area outside of France, and it consistently produces wines worthy of tasting.

C. Vintage dated. Sunshine and rainfall have a tremendous effect on a wine's taste, and only when a wine is marked with its year of production will you begin to make an association between its taste and the weather.

One wine which fulfills all of these requirements is Inglenook Estate Bottled Wine.

We mention this because any ad that explains wine tasting would have been incomplete without it.

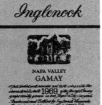

INGLENOOK

In Europe, there are many great wines.
In America, there is Inglenook.

In a four-part advertising series, Inglenook concentrated on education. This ad gives the basics of wine tasting. (*Courtesy Inglenook Vineyards*)

*community
relations*

Watch the daily announcements in the newspaper and keep alert to the happenings in your neighborhood. In the society page announcements there are valuable leads for large sales: not only for events such as coming-out parties, engagements, weddings, and births, but for organization outings, conventions, and so forth.

*sales
representatives*

The foregoing discussion of merchandising is as applicable to the producer's or distributor's representatives as it is to the retail trade. The services that these experts, calling on an account, can render will have a great deal to do with the volume of business the account will produce. The services include helping prepare wine and price lists, giving the customer new display or advertising ideas, suggestions for and placement of point-of-sale material, and new or varied factual information about the products the representative has sold to the customer. The salesman who brings a customer ideas he can use profitably is the one who will get the bulk of the business.

TRADE TASTINGS

One of the best methods of introducing or promoting wines is through wine tastings. Importers and producers of domestic products often hold tastings for their wholesalers and retailers. Retailers, in some states, may also hold tastings for their customers.

A range of wines from one shipper or producer might be shown—either to potential buyers at the various levels, the company's own sales force in order to familiarize them with the line, or, perhaps, to local journalists. These tastings can be of particular advantage to retailers, who can then advise their customers with greater confidence.

Each tasting must be tailored to the specific purpose of the occasion. Points to be considered are which wines or spirits are to be shown, to whom they are to be shown, and how they will be presented. Tastings may be held with everyone standing or seated and may or may not have a commentator.

33
BEVERAGE
CONTROL

1. ACCOUNTING FOR HOTELS, RESTAURANTS, AND BARS

A watchful eye makes any business prosper. If you could buy, receive, and sell without depending on anyone else, you would need few beverage controls; but this is never possible. You must have help from others, and you can maintain a watchful eye over your business by establishing an orderly control over each phase.

Beverage control encompasses all the records and checks on the movement of beverages from their purchase, receipt, and storage to their use or sale. It is important, since the information obtained reflects the health—the profit or loss—of your business.

We believe strongly in a practical beverage control system keyed to your specific needs. You should employ the necessary inventory and sales records to keep you informed at all times of the state of your business but avoid excessive, costly control systems that go beyond your needs.

WINE STEWARDS AND BEVERAGE MANAGERS

A wine steward need not have spent a lifetime in the business and sport a set of symbolic cellar keys hung about his neck. Today the wine steward, in addition to being thoroughly experienced in his own specialty, is an accredited executive with responsibility for accounting records and statistical information in his department and for supervising personnel.

Today even the title itself has been changed and the position is better known as beverage manager, and the person who has charge of the wine cellar is known as the wine steward. The function of the beverage manager is to maintain constant supervision over all divisions of the department. He usually has a wine steward, an assistant, and a supervisor for the bartenders to help him. The beverage manager's responsibility should extend over the wine cellar, service bars, and public bars up to the point of service. He should have charge of employing and discharging employees in this department.

483

WINE CELLARS

Wine cellars need not be cellars at all but may be located many floors above street level as long as they are air conditioned to maintain the proper temperature for storing cases of wines. The layout of a cellar must, of course, be based on the physical condition of the building, but there are a number of points regarding its construction that can be applied generally.

security   Square foot for square foot, the bottled-goods storeroom is the most valuable space in the house, except perhaps for the office safe. In one operation, for example, the average value of merchandise in the food storage rooms and refrigerators was $8.34 per square foot, while in the cellar it was $66.67. Therefore, all possible safeguards are mandatory.

There should be only one entrance to the bottled-goods storage room, and the refrigerators and bins should be inside this area. The door should be strongly locked. Some clubs even have old safe doors, complete with combination and/or time locks, to protect this important space. Time locks are useful, as they print the time and the code of the key used to unlock the door on a tape inside a locked box. This tape can be inspected for the length of time the door was open, the number of times it was opened, and any unusual occurrences.

Traffic in this space should be kept to a minimum, and nothing from any other department should be stored therein.

A layout that permits physical contact with all or a majority of the bars, through either small pass-through windows or a dumbwaiter if the cellar is on a lower level, is ideal. Such interior contact prevents bottles from "disappearing" from the halls, keeps cases and empties out of the guest areas, and speeds up filling requisitions. All of these supplemental entrances should also be well locked.

If the cellarman orders the wine, a telephone should be available, and if there are more than two bars, some system of communication between them is necessary.

tools   The cellar should be equipped with these tools:

> Wire and metal tape cutter
> Carton cutter (for cardboard)
> Case hammer (not a regular hammer)
> Dustpan and broom
> Mop and bucket
> Self-supporting rolling ladder
> Marking pencils
> Thumbtacks
> Bottle breaker and trash cans
> Desk or work table and chair

BEVERAGE DEPARTMENT PROCEDURES

In a large hotel or restaurant the beverage department is in charge of every aspect of acquiring and controlling stock. The beverage manager must oversee purchasing, receiving, and sometimes returning goods, security, case and bottle storage, bin cards and bottle tags, perpetual inventory, and issuing stock.

purchasing

When the wine cellar needs an item, whether it be a new one or a reorder, a requisition must be written for it. Any form is acceptable, as long as each set of two sheets is numbered in sequence. The requisition is made in duplicate; the original goes to the beverage manager's office and the cellar retains the copy.

When the request reaches the beverage manager's office, it is transferred to a purchase order form, which is made out in triplicate. This form should provide plenty of room for writing in the names of the items. Some wines have long names, and when the vintage and shipper's name are added, as should always be done, ample space is needed. The form may also state conditions of the purchase. The original copy of the order is sent to the purveyor; the duplicate, to which is attached the cellar requisition, goes to the accounting office; and the third copy is sent back to the food and beverage receiving clerk as a receiving copy.

receiving

When the goods arrive, the food and beverage receiving clerk receives them and completes a receiving clerk's daily report (RCDR), listing the items fully and accurately. He also checks the copy of the original order against the invoice to verify correct prices, extensions, totals, and the merchandise being delivered. The invoices and the RCDR are now sent to the beverage manager's office and are compared again with the original purchase order for price and quantity. After scrutinizing the invoices, the beverage manager should approve each bill, if correct, and return it to the accounting department for payment.

A copy of the RCDR, with all pertinent details on it, is kept by the beverage manager. These details include the date, quantity, vendor, price, discount, tax, additional charges, order number, net cost per case and per bottle, and selling price per bottle. This record gives a complete history of the beverage department's purchases. While the accounting department may duplicate some of the records maintained by the beverage manager's office, the RCDR has the advantage of containing all the information on one form. By referring to it while ordering new stock, the beverage manager can easily find out how many cases of a certain product were purchased previously and at what price.

returned goods

The receiving clerk is also responsible for returning goods to a purveyor. On a credit memo form (which should be prepared in duplicate, with the sets

```
┌─────────────────────────────────────────────────────────────────────────┐
│                    THE CULINARY INSTITUTE OF AMERICA                       │
│                      North Road, Hyde Park, N. Y. 12538                    │
│                        REQUEST FOR CREDIT MEMO                             │
│   To: _____      № 1701            │
│   Address: _____                  │
│   City, State: _____ Zip Code: _____    DATE _____  │
│                                                                           │
│       GENTLEMEN: Please send us Credit Memo for the following:            │
└─────────────────────────────────────────────────────────────────────────┘
```

INVOICE NO.	ITEM	QUANTITY	UNIT of SALE	UNIT PRICE	EXTENSION
					TOTAL

REASON:

By _____

Title _____

numbered consecutively) he enters the name of the dealer, the date, and the items being returned. Both copies must be signed by the trucker making the pickup. The original is sent to the dealer with the merchandise. The duplicate is listed on the day's RCDR and is attached to it with the day's invoices. The RCDR is then handed to the beverage manager, who holds it pending receipt of credit advice from the dealer. Inventory records can be adjusted from the duplicate copy.

Occasionally, "dry breakers" (bottles broken in shipment from which the wine has evaporated without leaving stains on the outside of the case), "leakers" (bottles from which part of the wine has drained because of a poor cork), and "dummies" (unfilled bottles) may be encountered. Usually the purveyor replaces or issues credit for these, providing the still-sealed necks are presented. It is unethical to try to get credit for bottles broken in your own cellar.

case storage   As soon as the wines or spirits are received, a small case card (about $2\frac{1}{2}$ by 3 inches) with the code number printed in large letters should be tacked or taped onto the upper left-hand corner of the case, which carries the name of

Case card.

```
┌─────────────────┐
│   M24-4         │
│  #  1   OF      │
│   4   CASES     │
└─────────────────┘
```

the product. It may also be helpful to indicate the number of cases in the shipment and assign a specific number to that particular case, as shown. The cases should be stacked so that these cards are on the aisle ends and the bottles placed either on their sides or bottom up, so the corks will be kept moist. All cases should be stacked on 2-by-4-inch slats. If stored next to a wall, they should be placed at least 2 inches from the wall to permit air circulation.

Shelves are also needed for the standing storage of liquors and the horizontal storage of wines. Liquors may also be stored horizontally, if that is more convenient.

bottle storage

Each bin should be marked by a bin card. It should list, in addition to the code number, the name, year, and producer or importer. The minimum number of bottles to which the stock may be reduced before reordering should also be listed. This is determined by experience.

bin cards

Costs and selling prices are not indicated on the bin card, as they are better kept in a price book. Requisitions can be priced much faster when the cellarman is seated at a desk than when he must go up and down the aisles with a clipboard. Moreover, costs and selling prices should be checked at least once every six months by the accounting office to make sure they are current. The cellarman, of course, makes changes in either figure in his price book when new shipments with different costs arrive.

The price book is maintained by someone who does not work in the storeroom. The information contained in it is garnered from invoices for merchandise received and requisitions for merchandise issued. It shows all receipts, issues, and the amount of stock on hand for all items at any time. These amounts are checked periodically against the actual stock on the shelves in order to uncover any discrepancies. The maximum and minimum guidelines act as signals that stock is running low and indicate what amounts to reorder.

Writing issues and receipts on bin cards is time consuming and serves little practical value. Information about usage can be obtained from delivery dates

M 24-4
GEVREY- CHAMBERTIN '49
RESERVE DU PATRON
SICHEL - REORDER 9

Bin card.

and a physical count or by referring to a perpetual inventory sheet. The monthly inventory should be taken on pretyped sheets or in a book from which the previous month's figures have been transferred. This forces the cellarman to count each bottle each month and prevents him from skipping a bin or a bank of bins.

The supplemental bin card is thumbtacked alongside the bin card and indicates where extra cases of that wine are stored, both for inventory purposes and in the event someone other than the cellarman fills a requisition. It is altered or removed as that wine is transferred to the bin.

Supplemental bin card.

> M 24 - 4
> 2 ARE ON TOP
> OF ROW 5

bottle tags   When the wines are binned, we suggest that three price tags be placed on the bottle—one over the end of the cork and two near or on the label. These tags can be self-sticking labels or labels prepared from an automatic price labeler, like those used by grocery and department stores. They should show the code number and the price of the wine.

Bottle tags.

> M 24-4
> $10.50
> - - - -
> M 24-4
> $10.50
> - - - -
> M 24-4
> $10.50

The tag on the cork is an aid in taking inventory and in locating the bottle—particularly when it is placed in service storage bins that may be too small to permit the use of bin cards. When the bottle is used, the two tags near the label are removed. One is placed on the guest check and the other on the daily requisition sheet kept by the bar checker or the person responsible for

Perpetual inventory card.

in-service storage. If an empty bottle is returned to the cellar with a tag still on it, it indicates that one of these two operations probably has been overlooked.

Bottles should also be tagged with hotel identification. This is important, particularly for full-bottle sales at banquets, since all bottles carrying this identification are proved property of the house. In instances where corkage is charged, this procedure is of the utmost importance, since it eliminates the possibility of an argument and a disgruntled guest.

perpetual inventory

The perpetual inventory, while not generally used in food storerooms because of the large number and variety of items carried, is essential in keeping a day-to-day running inventory of what is inside the beverage storeroom. A perpetual inventory, which should be recorded on a perpetual inventory card, should be done by someone outside the storeroom. Because it indicates what the maximum and minimum quantities of stock on hand are to be, the perpetual inventory is valuable to the cellarman when he orders; it is also useful if he needs to check for pilferage.

issuing stock

One of the best methods of issuing stock from the storeroom to the bar is using a requisition and a bottle-for-bottle exchange system.

The bartender fills out a full-bottle sales slip any time a bottle is sold and taken from the bar. This slip is used in place of the empty bottle for requisitioning and maintaining the par bar, which will be described shortly. The night barman, or whoever checks the bar inventory, makes out the requisition in triplicate based on the number of empty bottles and full-bottle sales slips from that day's sales.

WILLIAM ALLEN & CO., N. Y. STOCK FORM 7169

FULL BOTTLE SALES SLIP

DATE	TABLE-ROOM NO.	CHECK NO.	SERVER NO.

QUANTITY	SIZE	DESCRIPTION	STOCK NO.	VALUE	ISSUED

N⁰ 1490   SERVER_____

Wm. Allen & Co., N. Y. Stock Form 7042

BAR REQUISITION   No. 25055

Bar_____   Date_____

List No.	Size	Description	Quantity	COST		SALE VALUE	
				Unit	Total	Unit	Total

Requisitioned by: Issued by: Received by:

_____   _____   _____

One copy of the requisition is kept at the bar for record purposes. The original and the other copy are sent, along with the empty bottles, to the storeroom. The storeroom clerk issues a new bottle only upon receipt of the requisition and an empty bottle or full-bottle sales slip for each item listed. This is known as a bottle-for-bottle exchange. When the empty bottles have been received and checked, they are destroyed, usually by breaking them. This ensures that the bottles will not be reused for illicit purposes.

The storeroom clerk signs the original and the copy of the requisition, verifying that the order has been filled. This copy is then sent to the beverage manager for daily cost records and adjustment to the perpetual inventory.

The original requisition is taken back to the bar with the filled order and signed by the bartender on duty to acknowledge receipt, after he has checked it against the order and his copy of the requisition. It is then turned in to the accounting office, with that day's receipts, for their records.

This requisitioning procedure ensures good control by assigning responsibility to specific individuals throughout the ordering and receiving process.

Another essential element in control that supports the bottle-for-bottle exchange is maintaining what is known as a par bar.

The par bar is a list used to maintain a safe level of bar stock. Par stock levels are one and a half times the greatest amount used of any bottle on the busiest day. The par levels may, from time to time, have to be modified, and a current list should always be kept on hand; but they virtually guarantee that there is adequate stock at the bar at all times.

A par bar can also be used to make periodic comparisons between the par stock list and the number of bottles—full, empty, or partial—at the bar. There should be no discrepancies. The bottle-for-bottle exchange system, as explained previously, makes this possible. If there is a difference, something has gone awry, and it is the beverage manager's responsibility to correct the problem.

DRINK PRODUCTION CONTROLS

One of the most important aspects of good bar management is uniformity of drinks. This uniformity ensures that drinks taste the same each time they are ordered and that the proper cost of drinks is maintained. Drink production controls have three components: standard recipes, standard serving-glass sizes, and standard measures.

Standard recipes that provide for the same ingredients and amounts to be used are essential if cocktails are to taste and cost the same each time they are made.

When the same drink is served in different-size glasses, it leads to the appearance of a slipshod operation and may cause guests to be dissatisfied with their drinks. Use standard sizes and shapes of glasses for specific drinks.

measuring   Standard measures are necessary so that recipe quantities and costs are adhered to. Many different methods, such as shot glasses, measured pourers, and automatic bars, can be used to measure spirits accurately. Shot glasses or jiggers are the most common. One of the best types to use is the lined glass, which has a thin line printed at some height around the glass to indicate a specific amount. Measured pourers that can be attached to the bottle can be purchased. When the bottle is turned for pouring, a specific amount flows into the pourer and then into the glass. Automatic bars have become popular recently and are gaining more and more acceptance in the trade. Some automatic bars are based on gravity: the bottles are placed upside down in a rack and a premeasured shot is poured when a lever is pushed or pulled. Others use a pump to get the spirits to a dispensing head. At the push of a button, spirits that are kept in a separate storeroom are pumped, through lines, to a spigot head at the bar.

All of these measuring methods have their individual advantages and disadvantages, which must be weighed according to the specific operation before you decide which to use. All are preferable to free pouring, however, which is practical only if the bartender can pour accurately. Free pouring is even frowned upon by some guests who wish to see that they are getting the proper amount. Others, who don't like to see measuring and like free pouring, can be reassured by using lined shot glasses and pouring slightly above the line. The main problem with free pouring, from the standpoint of good bar management, is that it leaves a large gap in the control system and can be exploited by an unscrupulous bartender.

SALES CONTROLS

Sales controls enable the beverage manager to know whether revenue and costs are in line with what has been planned and budgeted.

There are many areas of sales controls, all of which depend, either largely or in part, on the use of cash registers and checks.

cash register   The most practical business control agent ever devised was invented by a tavern owner in Dayton, Ohio, and was patented on November 4, 1879. It was called Ritty's Incorruptible Cashier, later improved and sold as James Ritty's New Cash Register and Indicator. Today James Ritty's invention, somewhat improved to be sure, is known throughout the world as the National Cash Register. While there are quite a number of cash register manufacturers in the world, National is the leading producer, supplying the majority of all cash registers used anywhere.

Today's cash registers are mechanical and electronic marvels. In our opinion, no matter how large or small the business operation, the cash register and check are your most important beverage control tools. The register issues

OPTION #1 — HISTORY

STATE CUSTOMER	NUMBER	DESCRIPTION	PER CASE	RETAIL BOTTLE PRICE	RETAIL CASE PRICE	SALES	RECEIPTS	ON HAND	INVENTORY VALUE RETAIL BOTTLE PRICE	ACTUAL $ SALES THIS PERIOD	MONTH TO-DATE	1ST MO PREVIOUS	2ND MO PREVIOUS	3RD MO PREVIOUS	YEAR TO-DATE	REMARKS
1 027:1	0210	10TH CUTTY SARK	24	3.58	81.62	1		44	157.52	3.58	5	24	27	21	77	
1 027:1	0211	5TH CUTTY SARK	12	6.68	76.08	1		26	173.68	6.68	2	9	30	12	53	
1 027:1	0212	QT. CUTTY SARK	12	8.29	94.51			23	190.67		1	4	20	2	27	
1 027:1	0213	10TH DEW WHT LBL	24	3.58	81.62	4	24	28	100.24	14.32	7	20	13	8	48	
1 027:1	0214	5TH DEW WHT LBL	12	6.79	77.21			19	129.01		2	11	17	14	44	
1 027:1	0215	QT. DEW WHT LBL	12	8.39	95.65	1		8	67.12	8.39	1	3	2		6	
1 027:1	0216	10TH GLEN ROSSI	24	2.49	56.77	4	--	19	47.31	9.96	6	17	15	10	48	
1 027:1	0217	5TH GLEN ROSSI	12	4.99	56.89	2	12	12	59.88	9.98	3	9	10	4	26	
1 027:1	0218	QT. GLEN ROSSI	12	5.99	68.29	2		7	41.93	11.98	4	4	5	2	15	
1 027:1	0219	10TH VL MACNISH	24	3.49	79.57			5	17.45		1	1			2	
1 027:1	0220	5TH VL MACNISH	12	6.66	75.92	1		4	26.64	6.66	1	1	2	1	5	
GROUP TOTAL						16	36	195	1011.45	71.55	32	103	142	74	351	
1 027:1	0230	10 GRANTS 8 YRS	24	3.65	83.22	1		23	83.95	3.65	1	3		1	5	
1 027:1	0231	5TH GRANTS 8 YRS	12	6.96	79.34	2	6	9	62.64	13.92	3	2	4	1	10	
027:1	0232	12 GRANTS & H SST	24	3.49	79.57			25	87.25	10.47			12			

OPTION #2 — COST

STATE CUSTOMER	DESCRIPTION	PER CASE	RETAIL BOTTLE PRICE	BOTTLE COST	SALES	RECEIPTS	ON HAND	INVENTORY VALUE RETAIL BOTTLE PRICE	INVENTORY VALUE @ BOTTLE COST	ACTUAL $ SALES THIS PERIOD	GROSS PROFIT THIS PERIOD	MONTH TO-DATE	1ST MO PREVIOUS	2ND MO PREVIOUS	YEAR TO-DATE	REMARKS
1 027:2 0405	PT. SCHNLY RESRV	24	3.00	2.40	5	24	79	237.00	189.60	15.00	3.00	8	34	95	137	
1 027:2 0406	5TH SCHNLY RESRV	12	4.79	3.83	14		49	234.71	187.67	67.06	13.44	16	25	43	84	
1 027:2 0407	QT. SCHNLY RESRV	12	5.90	4.72	2		28	165.20	132.16	11.80	2.36	2	9	20	31	
1 027:2 0408	PT. SEGRM 7 CRWN	24	3.00	2.40	62	48	77	231.00	184.80	186.00	37.20	96	131	212	439	
1 027:2 0409	5TH SEGRM 7 CRWN	12	4.79	3.83	21		15	71.85	57.45	100.59	20.16	38	81	112	231	
GROUP TOTAL					104	72	248	939.76	751.68	380.45	76.16	160	280	482	922	
1 027:2 0410	PT. SEAGRAM VO	24	3.99	3.19	36		92	367.08	293.48	143.64	28.80	59	84	142	285	
1 027:2 0411	5TH SEAGRAM VO	12	6.40	5.12	15	12	70	448.00	358.40	96.00	19.20	27	46	175	248	
027:2 0412	QT. SEAGRAM VO	12	7.95	6.36			52	413.40	330.72					16		

Typical National Cash Register inventory control reports—daily, weekly, or monthly.
(*Courtesy National Cash Register Company, Dayton, Ohio*)

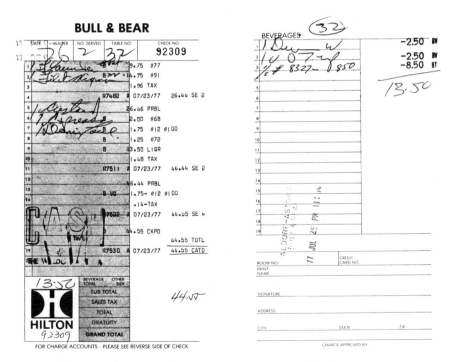

A check from the Bull & Bear Restaurant at the Waldorf-Astoria Hotel in New York.
Notice that the wine and liquor charges are entered and totaled on the back of the
check. These charges are then entered on the front of the check when the total bill is
rung up on the cash register. (*Courtesy Waldorf-Astoria Hotel, New York*)

an itemized, mechanically added receipt, prints separate and total charges on a waiter's check, and accumulates and stores totals of the several kinds of information you desire for daily verification. Many of the newer registers help reduce losses from human error. Those that are programmed with the prices of every food and drink item can avoid waiters' mistakes in prices, as well as addition mistakes, undercharges, illegible figures, and overlooked items.

Registers can be equipped with eight or more separate category keys and can total separately the transactions of each category. They can even separate the sales made by each cash drawer, when there are several.

Just how you use the cash register is up to you and your individual needs, whether your business is a small tavern, a restaurant, a retail store, or a large hotel whose entire data-processing system from bar checks, room bills, large banquets, and payrolls is handled by a whole assortment of registers, including an electronic computer that collates and analyzes the data from all of the small registers.

Only one control form is used behind the bar. This is to account for losses through accidents. When drinks are spilled, either by employees or by customers, a regular check must be made for it and the word *accident* written across its face and signed by the bar captain. If for any reason a drink is not acceptable and is returned, the same procedure is followed. In both instances the cause for the loss or the return of the drink should be stated. Most of these losses can be prevented, and the beverage manager's office should scrutinize such records daily and initiate remedial action within the department if necessary.

Another control is to compare actual consumption with revenue taken in for the amount supposedly consumed. This control can be done three ways.

The inventory, or ounce, method compares ounces used (determined by physical inventory) with ounces sold (determined by counting drinks written on sales checks). There should be only slight differences.

A mechanical counting system incorporated into an automatic pouring head is another method. As the mechanical device pours the premeasured shot, it also records how many shots or ounces have been poured. Revenues taken in must tally with these recorded amounts. Some systems are so advanced that either the machine will not dispense the drink until a check is placed in the cash register and rung up as the drink is poured, or the register will deliver a chit with the name of the drink and the price that must be presented to the bartender before he may dispense the drink.

In the third control method potential revenues and cost percentages are projected for each bottle sold at the bar. These potentials are compared with the actual revenue received, and there should be very little difference, if any.

banquet sales   A separate division of the beverage department that is of great importance to a hotel is the banquet bar. Ordering and stocking this bar follow the

TO: Mr. Monetti, Chef, Headwaiter, Steward, Linen Room, Florist, Food Checker, Wine
       Room, Beverage Department, Banquet Auditor, Supt. of Service, Room Service

FROM: Mr. Herb Rose

Thursday, June 23, 1977   Democratic National Committee Salute to
East Foyer, Silver Corridor   the President
Grand Ballroom   Reception/Dinner Dance
Time: (See below)   Attendance: About 700 guests

EXTRA ITEMS AND ARRANGEMENTS

Time:	Invitations	7:00 p.m.
	Grand Ballroom Doors Open	8:00 p.m.
	Service Begins	8:15 p.m.
	Program Begins	10:00 p.m.
	Conclusion	11:00 p.m.

Control: By invitation. Tickets are to be collected as soon as the guests are seated. COMMITTEE TABLES - Four (4) six-foot committee tables in the Silver Corridor.
Special Note: As soon as tickets are collected, number stands are to be removed from the table.

Checkroom: Flat rate added to the account. *NO TIPPING* sign displayed.

Restrooms: Flat rate added to the account. *NO TIPPING* sign displayed.

Beverages: Three (3) bars and seven (7) bartenders. To serve assorted highballs at bottle prices, cocktails and mixed drinks at individual prices.
With Fish Course: We will serve Dr. Konstantine Frank New York State Pinot Chardonnay. Two (2) bottles per table.
With Main Course: We will serve Ingelnook California Pinot Noir. Two (2) bottles per table.
All other beverages during dinner entirely à la carte. Cashier required.
On the bar during the reception, have Clement Colombet, red and white.

Special Note to Steward: Silver wine buckets to be used as much as possible. Please have all available wine buckets in the Ballroom Kitchen.

Room Set-Up: *Reception, East Foyer:* Two bars, one on the south wall, one on the north wall. South bar with two bartenders; north bar, triple bar with three bartenders. Remainder set Vanderbilt style with cocktail tables for four (4) and five (5) guests.

Silver Corridor: To be set reception style with cocktail tables of four and five guests. Bar at north end of corridor in front of Basildon Room doors.

Decorations: *Linen:* White
Candles: Three (3) 16-inch white tapers on each table.
Flowers: Own arrangements.

Some of the banquet list requirements furnished to beverage manager and wine cellar
in advance of a function. (*Courtesy Waldorf-Astoria Hotel, New York*)

procedure previously outlined for bars in general, except that a banquet bar requires a larger stock, both of wine and of liquor items, because the bulk of the business is done in full-bottle sales. This fact also necessitates keeping a complete record of all full bottles of liquor sold so that the proper internal financial adjustment can be made. Since the bar has been debited for all beverages at selling prices per drink, the bottle sales show a decrease from this debit total. For example:

The bar is charged with 16 drinks at $1.20 each	$19.20
And sells a bottle at	15.00
Full-bottle sales adjustment due the bar is	$ 4.20

From the record of bottles sold at each party, data are obtained for the beverage manager's future use. Here is a splendid chance to procure a detailed record of these parties and form a comparison for the following year. A list of the wines sold should also be added to the records. One of the most convenient ways to keep such data is on five-by-eight cards. The name of the person or organization giving the party is essential. The day and date are important for future comparison, as is the type of function, for if the next party should be a dance instead of a dinner, the beverage requirements would be entirely different. The number of persons attending and the original number guaranteed would be useful, too. Use the term *bar cash* to indicate à la carte sale of beverages and *bar signed* to denote the inclusive items that the party may have ordered in advance. On the face of the card in the left-hand column enter the number of bottles sold, followed by the type of beverage:

> 54 B Scotch
> 10 B Rye
> 9 B Champagne

To know the brands used, refer to the bar captain's figures.

The item most commonly served at banquets is a cocktail for each guest, either in the reception room or when the guests are seated at the tables. A choice of cocktails is invariably offered. In large establishments where there can be anywhere from five to a dozen parties going on at the same time, this basic choice should be limited. If we consider the possibility not only of this choice of drinks, but of sherry with the soup, dry white wine with the fish, red wine with the roast, and sweet wine with dessert, then we can understand how complicated the service can become and how necessary it is to give this phase careful advance attention. The detailed information concerning the beverage service of each banquet is, of course, collected at the banquet department, where it originates. It should be typed on a list six days before the date of the function, with copies to everyone in the beverage department and to others connected with any of the functions. This includes the wine cellar, each bar, and the beverage manager's office.

2. ACCOUNTING FOR RETAIL STORES

Accounting for stock and sales in a retail liquor store depends to a great extent on the size of the store and the statutory requirements of the state in which it is located. There usually are prescribed forms, too numerous to cite here, in state-controlled stores. It is our intent to outline the internal control any liquor store needs to ensure intelligent operation, without stressing any type of record keeping.

Individual practices may vary, but in general the previously described routine used by hotels and restaurants for requisitioning, purchasing, receiving, stocking, and recording broken merchandise is applicable to a retail store.

In a large number of retail stores it is the custom to have a unit control ticket pasted on the bottle before it is placed in stock. The price is entered from the duplicate purchase order, and the ticket also states the type of merchandise, the size of the bottle, the bin, and the purchase order number for identification. When the bottle is sold, half the ticket is torn off and either attached to the sales slip or collected for further classification.

unit control ticket

A retail store should maintain a perpetual inventory record for each individual brand and size of product. For example, if you have quarts, fifths, pints, and half-pints of a Pennsylvania rye whisky, you should have an inventory sheet for each size.

perpetual inventory

This record sheet should provide columns for entering dates, purchase order numbers, and sales ticket numbers; columns for the units purchased and units sold; and a column for units in stock at the close of each day. At the bottom of the sheet there should be space for the unit cost price, if the proprietor wishes to enter it; the selling price per unit and per case, and the maximum and minimum stock to be carried. This last, of course, is not constant but varies according to the time of the year.

The perpetual inventory record works as follows:

1. Enter in an "in" column merchandise received as shown by the vendor's invoice and the receiving department ticket. Also enter sales returns from the duplicate tickets.

2. Enter in an "out" column total unit daily sales, arrived at by classifying the duplicate sales ticket and/or the unit control tickets; also enter merchandise returned to vendors as shown on the duplicate return ticket. Sales prices should be carefully compared with schedules on inventory sheets, as these provide an opportunity to audit daily sales. Breakages should be entered individually and so labeled.

3. Stock on hand, as reflected in the perpetual inventory at the end of a

day, is arrived at by adding to the previous day's inventory the merchandise put into stock and by deducting the sales, returns to vendors, and breakages. Some new cash registers do this automatically.

Physical inventory of the merchandise should be taken at regular intervals and the results checked against the perpetual inventory.

returned goods   Merchandise to be returned to vendors should be taken out of stock and the unit tickets removed and attached to the returned goods memorandum, which is made out in triplicate. One copy of this memorandum is to be sent to the accounting department. The merchandise, with the original and the remaining copy of the return ticket, should be sent to the shipping department, from where it is either delivered by the store itself or picked up by the vendor, at which time a receipt is obtained and sent to the accounting department. On the return slip should be indicated the originating department, the date, the vendor, the quantity and description of merchandise, and the reason for the return. Returns should always be made promptly.

The manager or owner of the store is held responsible for all merchandise returned by customers. The regular returned goods slip may be used for this purpose and on it should be entered the goods returned, the reason for the return, and the amount of the refund involved. The merchandise should then be entered back into stock, unless it is faulty.

sales   In states permitting sales on credit, stores should use a standard accounts-receivable system, with a separate account being maintained for each customer. In some states credit cards may now be used as well.

At the end of each day an analysis of sales shows the types of merchandise sold. These quantities must agree with the unit control tickets and the perpetual inventory.

vendor's invoices   Invoices should be compared with the bills of lading from the receiving department, and the condition of the wines and spirits should be checked. After the person who made the purchase checks the price, discount if any, quantity, and type of merchandise, the invoices are approved for payment, attached to the bills of lading, and entered in the regular purchase register.

customer orders   When a customer orders wine to be sent C.O.D., the wines are packed immediately and the order is written up on a C.O.D. order form, which has instructions that the amount due should be collected before the wines are left at their destination. This transaction is completed quickly.

If a customer telephones for some wines for which he will send payment before they are delivered, a memo is kept of the order, but nothing is written up and the wines are not necessarily held aside. After the customer's check arrives, the wines are packed and the order is written up on a paid-send order form. The wines are then delivered to the customer.

INTERSTATE BUSINESS FORMS

LICENSE No. L-1331

PLEASE PRINT—USE PRESSURE

S 12191

NO. OF BOTTLES

NO. OF PACKAGES

TO

ADDRESS

CITY

APARTMENT

DATE

52158

COD

Telephone

TEMPLETON 8-7500

SHERRY LEHMANN, INC.

WINE & SPIRITS MERCHANTS

679 MADISON AVE. at 61st ST., NEW YORK 10021 •

THE WINE AND SPIRIT CENTER OF NEW YORK

QUANTITY	SIZE	BIN	DESCRIPTION	PRICE	AMOUNT
		A			
		B			
		C			
		D			
		E			
		F			
		G			
		H			
		J			
		K			
		L			
		M			

COLLECT

NOTE: Payment in advance, or C.O.D. . . . Section 100, New York State Alcoholic Beverage Control Law Provides . . .
"No retail licensee shall sell any alcoholic beverages on credit."

SHERRY-LEHMANN, INC.
WINE & SPIRITS MERCHANTS
679 Madison Ave. At 61 St., New York, N.Y. 10021 · Templeton 8-7500

Name..............................

Address..........................

FOR DELIVERY TO YOUR OWN ADDRESS

Quantity	NO.	DESCRIPTION	UNIT	AMOUNT
			TAX	
			TOTAL	

☐ Check Enclosed (Add 8% Sales Tax Within City Limits)
☐ Send C.O.D. (Add applicable % in remainder of N.Y. State)

DELIVERY INFORMATION

WITHIN U.P.S. ZONE: No charge for delivery within west U.P.S. zone on orders of $25 or more. This includes the five boroughs — Long Island, Westchester, and most of Rockland County. Below $25, kindly add $3.00 for each delivery.

BEYOND U.P.S. ZONE: (but within New York State) No charge for delivery on orders of $200 or more. Below $200, kindly add $10 for each delivery — the minimum charge that trucking companies impose for upstate deliveries. During mid-winter some upstate areas may not be serviced by truck. If there are any questions as to trucking facilities, kindly inquire.

ORDERS TO BE SENT TO OTHERS

Quantity	DESCRIPTION	SEND TO	AMOUNT
		Name	
		Address	
		City	
		Name	
		Address	
		City	
		Name	
		Address	
		City	
		Name	
		Address	
		City	
		Name	
		Address	
		City	

☐ Send Card to each with my name
☐ Cards Enclosed

TAX →
TOTAL →

Convenient Order Form — Tear Out and Mail

Prompt Delivery Service Throughout United Parcel Zone

LEFT: An in-store C.O.D. order form. RIGHT: A customer mail-order form. (*Courtesy Sherry-Lehmann, Inc., New York*)

34
REGULATORY
BODIES AND LAWS

A great many volumes could be written on the regulation of the alcoholic beverage trade in the United States and the rest of the world. For the purposes of this book, a brief history of the laws and regulations concerning alcoholic beverages will illustrate American attitudes toward these products and how our present-day laws have developed.

history   Liquor restrictions in our country go back to colonial days. At that time the legislative regulations regarding liquor were mainly for revenue and, later, to encourage sobriety among the Indians, the slaves, and finally the working classes.

In 1630, only ten years after the Pilgrims landed, some agitation against the use of strong liquor began. The first organized attempt to curtail the consumption of hard liquor, however, came in 1733 when Governor Oglethorpe of Georgia prohibited the importation of hard liquors into that colony.

Probably the strongest impetus given to the organized temperance movement was caused by the publication, in 1785, of "The Effects of Ardent Spirits upon the Human Mind and Body" by Dr. Benjamin Rush of Philadelphia. The publication of this essay converted many medical as well as nonmedical persons to the temperance ideal.

Both for revenue and as a deterrent, a tax was levied on the selling of distilled liquors in 1790. This led to the Whiskey Rebellion in 1794 in Pennsylvania, an uprising that was put down by federal troops.

In 1816 the first prohibitory law, forbidding the selling of liquor on Sundays, was passed in Indiana. By the end of 1833 there were more than five thousand organized temperance groups, with a membership totaling more than one million people. In 1838 Massachusetts limited the amount of liquor that one person could buy at a time. Many people in this country felt that drinking was a problem and that it should be controlled or stopped.

In 1846 Maine passed the first statewide prohibition law. As the opposition to hard liquor increased, people began to drink more malt and vinous beverages, and brewing operations developed into a major industry.

The groundswell against alcohol consumption reached such proportions that on January 16, 1920, the National Prohibition Amendment (the Eighteenth Amendment to the Constitution) became law. Although the amendment was adopted nationwide, the public was not ready for such drastic controls and violations flourished. It has been estimated that the cost to the government alone approached $1 billion per year, including loss in federal, state, county, and municipal revenues. It is also estimated that the American people spent a total of $36 billion for bootleg and smuggled liquor during Prohibition. Clearly some other form of control was necessary.

On December 5, 1933, the Twenty-first Amendment repealed the Eighteenth Amendment, and the way was cleared for new controls. A system of federal regulations concerning trade practices and requiring permits was set up. This concern for regulations to avoid any possible return to prohibition marked the start of a new period for liquor control.

FEDERAL CONTROLS

Under authority of the 1933 National Industrial Recovery Act (N.I.R.A.), the president approved codes of fair competition for the industry, which continued in force until 1935, when the Federal Alcohol Control Administration, which had been previously established to administer the codes, was abolished and the N.I.R.A. was invalidated by the Supreme Court.

The Federal Alcohol Administration (F.A.A.) was created and 1935, 1936, and 1937 saw a new legislative trend. Much fair trade legislation was passed, both by the federal government and by individual states.

In 1940 the F.A.A. was abolished, and its functions were transferred to the Alcohol Tax Unit (A.T.U.) of the Treasury Department. In 1952, when the functions of the A.T.U. were increased by adding responsibilities for tobacco administration, the name was enlarged to the Alcohol and Tobacco Tax Division of the U.S. Treasury Department (A.T.T.D.). In 1968, with increased responsibilities for firearms control, the name was further enlarged to the Alcohol, Tobacco, and Firearms Division of the U.S. Treasury Department (A.T.F.D.). In 1972 the name was changed to the Bureau of Alcohol, Tobacco, and Firearms (B.A.T.F.), still a division of the Treasury Department.

The B.A.T.F. enforces the codes and laws established by the legislative and executive branches of the U.S. government.

There are three broad areas where the B.A.T.F. exercises control over the alcoholic beverage industry: public protection, trade practices, and revenue collection.

The public is protected by the prevention of adulteration and/or misbranding of products and from the misuse of advertising.

labeling   Control of labeling° is a prime function of the B.A.T.F. All alcoholic beverage labels must conform to certain regulations and must have B.A.T.F. approval before they may be used. Labels *must* include such information as the identity of the product; the manufacturer, bottler, or importer; the liquid contents; and the alcohol content—except for wine containing 14 percent or less alcohol by volume. In this special case the percentage of alcohol may be stated, or the label may simply mention the type designation (table wine or light wine). Distilled spirits must indicate the percentage of neutral spirits used and the source of those neutral spirits (except for cordials, liqueurs, and specialties).

Certain statements are also specifically prohibited, such as those that disparage a competitor's product; those that are false, misleading, indecent, or obscene; or those that use the name of a person or organization to imply that the product has been endorsed by such a person or organization. There may also not be any consumer deception regarding the age, manufacturing processes, analyses, guarantees, or other irrelevant matters.

These labeling regulations require a certificate of label approval or a specific exemption from this requirement if the product is sold only within the state where it is produced. Once a product is sold interstate, it must comply with federal codes.

Imported products are also controlled by the B.A.T.F. in close cooperation with the customs branch of the Treasury Department. All stipulations listed previously apply, and the country of origin must be clearly marked.

The certificate of label approval must conform, to the last period and comma, with the actual labels on the bottles. If an imported or domestic product does not conform, except for certain allowed variables, the product may be withheld from the market by Internal Revenue and customs officials.

advertising   Advertisements of any alcoholic beverages must contain much of the mandatory label information, such as the class and type of the product, the percentage of alcohol as it appears on the label, and the source of any neutral spirits in distilled products when it appears on the label. The lettering of this information must be clear and legible, and the name and address of the advertiser must be present.

As with the labeling regulations, there may be no false or misleading assertions, disparagement of a competitor's product, or any other statements that would be prohibited on a label. There may be no medicinal or therapeutic claims that might be misleading. Also, a label is not allowed to imply that a

° For a basic federal document on labeling information and requirements, write to the U.S. Government Printing Office for Document 27CFR-4.

product is from a country other than that where it was produced. Confusion of brands is forbidden, and two or more products may not be advertised together if the advertisement implies that what is said about one product also applies to the other. The American flag or other government symbol may not be used to mislead the consumer into thinking that the product has been produced for or supervised by the government.

The B.A.T.F. exercises a further protective control over the many branches of the industry by regulating just what services a distiller, brewer, rectifier, blender, producer, importer, or wholesaler may or may not render a retailer. A retailer may not be induced to purchase certain alcoholic beverages to the exclusion of competing beverages by bribery, bonuses, premiums, or direct or indirect compensation. *trade practices*

Also prohibited are consignment sales, conditional sales with the privilege of return, or sales involving the acquisition of other alcoholic beverages. The bona fide return of merchandise to a vendor for usual commercial reasons arising after the merchandise is sold is permitted.

Distilled spirits in the possession of a retail dealer must be in bottles or similar containers that bear Internal Revenue tax stamps. This applies to whisky, gin, rum, brandy, vodka, alcohol, cordials containing distilled spirits, and other similar liquors. A portion of the strip stamp must be kept affixed to each opened bottle. Liquors not stamped in compliance with these requirements are subject to seizure and forfeiture. The penalty for having unstamped liquors is a fine of not more than $10,000 and imprisonment for not more than five years, or both. *tax stamps and revenue controls*

New strip stamps are available from the office of the regional directors of the B.A.T.F. Replacement of the stamp may be necessary when:

1. The strip stamp is missing from an unopened bottle of distilled spirits.

2. The strip stamp is mutilated to the extent that the genuineness of the stamp is in question.

3. The contents of the container are available without breaking the stamp.

A retail liquor dealer must for a period of two years keep all records that relate to purchases of, and payment for, distilled spirits, wines, and fermented malt beverages. Invoices and bills must be kept in book form showing the quantity, from whom received, and the date received.

For specific tax information, see Appendix R.

STATE CONTROL

In addition to the federal government's control of the industry, the individual states exercise a secondary control. Laws vary from state to state but cannot conflict with federal laws, and each state must meet all federal regulations. State regulations may be stricter than federal regulations, however. For example, federal law allows a wine from any state to be labeled with the name of that state if 75 percent of the wine in the bottle is from there. California law, however, requires that 100 percent of the wine be from California.

State control of the sale of alcoholic beverages falls into three types:

OPEN-LICENSE STATES, where private business makes both on-premise (restaurants, bars, and some retail outlets where consumption is permitted) and off-premise (retail or package stores) sales of alcoholic beverages to all types of consumers.

The operations vary in these states because of different taxes imposed on wines, spirits, and beers and because of different license fees imposed on wholesalers and retailers. Furthermore, each state and, as a rule, each municipality, may have different hours for opening and closing, and different provisions with respect to the number of licenses permitted.

CONTROL (MONOPOLY) STATES that control the sale of all alcoholic beverages distributed in their territories.

CONTROL (MONOPOLY) STATES that control the sale of distilled spirits and certain kinds of wines.

In the open-license states trade is conducted as in other competitive businesses. Open states collect revenues from excise taxes and sales tax. In the control states, however, whether those that control the sale of all alcoholic beverages or those that control only a part of the trade and permit the open sale of other beverages, it must be borne in mind that the states themselves are in the liquor business and their function, public statements to the contrary, is to make money. As a result, these states stock only those brands they believe will have the most sales, thereby limiting consumer choice.

CONTROLS OF OTHER COUNTRIES

Throughout this book we have discussed the laws governing wine production in other countries. We have seen how the *Appellation d'Origine Contrôlée* laws of France, the *Denominazione di Origine Controllata* of Italy, and German wine laws control every phase of wine production. These stringent regulations from the largest exporting nations also serve to protect the consumer and should not be overlooked.

35
SUMMARY

Since Repeal the wine and spirits trade has established the fact that the American public drinks its alcoholic beverages in moderation. Consumption of spirits has gradually increased to a moderate 2 gallons per capita, while that of wine and beer has increased progressively to over $1\frac{3}{4}$ gallons and 22 gallons respectively. This does not mean that individuals are drinking a great deal more, but rather that a greater number of people are enjoying the pleasant relaxation that wines, beers, and spirits offer. It reflects as well the lowering of the legal age for drinking and the states, counties, and cities that have shifted from "dry" to "wet" areas.

We are convinced that our consumption of spirits will remain fairly steady and that beer drinking will not decrease, and we see every indication that wine consumption will increase steadily until we become one of the wine-drinking countries of the world. The popularity of white wine as an aperitif is a step in this direction.

There has been an increased interest in the art of good living. A dinner complemented with wine gives the diner greater enjoyment and makes the food more appetizing. Both the diner and the restaurant (or host if it is a home dinner) will be pleased, and everyone benefits.

There is little likelihood of prohibition returning to the United States. Yet the trade itself, as a matter of protection, must advocate temperance. Temperance education is becoming a function of our public school systems, and we are seeing some cooperative action between the beverage trade and the educational boards to teach children the real meaning of moderation and the value as well as the dangers of alcoholic beverages of all types.

The trade has made little attempt to place before the medical community the value of wines and spirits in the treatment of patients. In other countries alcoholic beverages have a place in this field and in time many doctors in the United States may prescribe them in similar ways.

The increased knowledge and technology of viniculture are spreading throughout the world, and with them the interest of the general public has grown. Wine publications and articles on alcoholic beverages in leading popular magazines contain specific information demanded by the consumer. Another happy occurrence is the space devoted to both the use and the service of these beverages in the food sections of our important daily newspapers. Editors are satisfying their readers' demands for information and are also tacitly showing that wine is, indeed, considered a food.

The more accurate information people have about alcoholic beverages, the better off they are. Much educational work has been done but there is much more still to be done. The future should usher in an era of freedom, but *not* one of unlimited license and abuse.

Of one thing we are convinced: the American public demands the best. It is the best-informed buying public in the world. The person who attempts to fool the public with poor quality or shoddy imitations is fooling only himself. Any brand can be sold, provided it has the quality claimed for it. No company can stay in the wine and spirits trade unless people are convinced that the firm's products are good.

The more the wine and spirits merchant learns about the product he is presenting, the prouder he will be to find himself engaged in a profession whose honorable and ancient traditions have evolved through the centuries.

Our aim has been to compress into this book available information on alcoholic beverages required for the producer, seller, and consumer. The crowning knowledge about the beverages we have described can come only firsthand by actual tasting.

We lift our glass to wish you profit in the reading, pleasure in the tasting, and your very good health!

APPENDICES

APPENDIX A
QUICK GUIDE TO WINES AND SPIRITS

Any wine can accompany any food, and you should choose a wine according to personal preference. Certain combinations of wine and food have developed, however, because they are generally pleasing. These are listed here for general guidance but should not be taken as hard and fast rules. The best guide is your own experience. Remember also that many chilled wines, either still or sparkling, may be enjoyed by themselves, as hospitality wines, or as aperitifs.

NAME	PHONETIC SPELLING	SOURCE	TYPE	COLOR	TASTE	SERV. TEMP.	SERVE WITH
Adabag	ah-DAH-bah	Turkey	Table wine	Red	Dry	*	Ch, G, & RM
Adom Atic	ah-DOHM ah-TEEK	Israel	Table wine	Red	Dry	*	Ch, G, & RM
Advocaat	AHD-voh-kaht	Holland	Prepared eggnog	Yellow	Sweet	* or ***	AD
Afames	ah-FAHM-ees	Cyprus	Table wine	Red	Dry	*	Ch, G, & RM
Affentaler	AH-fen-tah-lehr	Baden, Ger.	Table wine	Red	Dry	*	RM
Aigle	AY-gul	Switzerland	Table wine	White	Med. dry	***	F, P, & LM
Ale		Various	Malt beverage	Straw to dark amber	Bittersweet	***	Hosp
Aleatico	ah-leh-AH-tee-koh	California & Italy	Dessert wine	Red	Sweet	*	AD
Alella	ah-LAY-yah	Spain	Table wine	Red or white	Dry	* or ***	Varies with color
Aloxe-Corton	ah-lohs-kor-toh(n)	Côte de Beaune, Fr.	Table wine	Red	Dry	*	Ch, G, & RM
Amarone della Valpolicella	ah-mah-roh-neh deh-lah vahl-poh-lee-CHAY-lah	Veneto, I	Table wine	Red	Dry	*	Ch, G, & RM
Amer Picon	ah-mehr pee-koh(n)	France	Aperitif	Dark	Bitter	***	BD
Amontillado	ah-mohn-tee-YAH-doh	Jerez, Sp.	Sherry	Amber	Dry	**	Hosp
Angelica	ahn-JEL-ee-kah	California	Fortified wine	Gold	Sweet	*	Hosp
Angostura Bitters	ahn-gus-TOO-rah	Trinidad	Aromatic bitters	Reddish brown	Bitter	*	C & Pun
Anisette	ah-nee-zet	Various	Liqueur	White	Aniseed	*	AD
Anjou	ah(n)-zhoo	Loire, Fr.	Table wine	White or pink	Med. sweet	***	F, P, & LM
Anninger Perle	on-ing-ehr PEHR-luh	Austria	Table wine	White	Dry	***	F, P, & LM
Applejack		U.S.	Apple brandy	Amber	Dry, fruity	*	AD
Apricot liqueur		Various	Liqueur	Amber	Sweet, fruity	*	AD
Aquavit	AHK-wa-veet	Denmark	Spirit	White	Caraway	***	BD
Armagnac	ar-mah-nyahk	Gers, Fr.	Brandy	Amber	Dry	*	AD
Assmannshausen	AHS-mahnz-howz-en	Rheingau, Ger.	Table wine	Red	Dry	*	RM
Asti Spumante	ahs-tee spoo-MAHN-teh	Piedmont, It.	Sparkling wine	White	Sweet	***	Desserts
Aurora	oh-RORE-uh	New York State	Table wine	White	Dry	***	F, P, & LM
Avdat	AHV-daht	Israel	Table wine	Red or white	Dry	* or ***	Varies with color
Baco Noir	bah-koh nwahr	New York State	Table wine	Red	Dry	*	P & RM
Badacsonyi Rizling	BAHD-ah-choh-nee reez-ling	Hungary	Table wine	White	Dry	***	F, P, & LM
Badacsonyi Szürkebarát	BAHD-ah-choh-nee tsoor-keh-BAH-raht	Hungary	Table wine	White	Med. dry	***	F, P, & LM
Banyuls	bah-nyuls	Banyuls, Fr.	Fortified wine	White	Sweet	*	AD
Barack Palinka	BAR-ahks PAH-leen-kah	Hungary	Apricot brandy	Orange	Dry	*	AD

Service temperature: *—Room temperature / **—Slightly chilled / ***—Cold
Serve with: AD—After dinner / BD—Before dinner / C—Cocktails / Ch—Cheese / F—Fish / Fr—Fruits / G—Game /
    H—Highballs / Hosp—Hospitality / LM—Light meats / P—Poultry / Pun—Punches / RM—Red meats / S—Straight
1855 classification: 1st—First growth / 2nd—Second growth, etc.; *wines of Burgundy:* GC—*Grand Cru* / PC—*Premier Cru*

NAME	PHONETIC SPELLING	SOURCE	TYPE	COLOR	TASTE	SERV. TEMP.	SERVE WITH
Barbaresco	bar-bah-REHZ-koh	Piedmont, It.	Table wine	Red	Dry	*	Ch, G, & RM
Barbera	bar-BEH-rah	Piedmont, It., & California	Table wine	Red	Dry	*	Ch, G, & RM
Bardolino	bar-doh-LEEN-oh	Veneto, It.	Table wine	Red	Dry	*	Ch, G, & RM
Barolo	bah-ROH-loh	Piedmont, It.	Table wine	Red	Dry	*	Ch, G, & RM
Barsac	bar-sahk	Barsac, Fr.	Table wine	White	Sweet	***	Fr & desserts
Bâtard-Montrachet (GC)	bah-tar-moh(n)-rah-shay	Côte de Beaune, Fr.	Table wine	White	Dry	***	F, P, & LM
Batavia arak	bah-TAY-vee ah AHR-ahk	Java, Indonesia	Spirit	Straw	Dry, aromatic	***	C, Pun, & H
Beaujolais	boh-zhoe-lay	Beaujolais, Fr.	Table wine	Red	Dry	* or **	All foods
Beaune	bone	Côte de Beaune, Fr.	Table wine	Red	Dry	*	Ch, G, & RM
Beaune-Grèves (PC)	bone-grehv	Côte de Beaune, Fr.	Table wine	Red	Dry	*	Ch, G, & RM
Beaune-Les Fèves (PC)	bone-lay-fehv	Côte de Beaune, Fr.	Table wine	Red	Dry	*	Ch, G, & RM
Beer, lager	LAH-gur	Various	Malt beverage	Pale gold	Dry	***	Hosp
Bénédictine	bay-nay-deek-teen	Fécamp, Fr.	Liqueur	Gold	Spicy, sweet	*	AD
Bernkasteler Doctor	behrn-kahs-tel-ehr DAWK-tohr	Moselle, Ger.	Table wine	White	Med. dry	***	F, P, & LM
Bienvenue-Bâtard-Montrachet (GC)	bya(n)-veh-noo-bah-tahr-moh(n)-rah-shay	Côte de Beaune, Fr.	Table wine	White	Dry	***	F, P, & LM
Binger Scharlachberg	bing-ehr SHAHR-lahk-behrk	Rheinhessen, Ger.	Table wine	White	Dry	***	F, P, & LM
Bitters		Various	Spirit	Reddish brown	Bitter	***	C, H, & Pun
Blackberry liqueur		Various	Liqueur	Dark red	Sweet, fruity	*	AD
Blanc de Blancs	blah(n) duh blah(n)	Champagne, Fr.	Sparkling wine	White	Dry	***	All foods & Hosp
Bonnes Mares, Les (GC)	lay bun mahr	Côte de Nuits, Fr.	Table wine	Red	Dry	*	Ch, G, & RM
Bordeaux Blanc	bor-doh blah(n)	Bordeaux, Fr.	Table wine	White	Dry, semisweet	***	F, P, & LM
Bordeaux Rouge	bor-doh roozh	Bordeaux, Fr.	Table wine	Red	Dry	*	Ch, G, & RM
Bourbon whisky		U.S.	Spirit	Brown	Dry		S, C, H, & Pun
Bourgogne Blanc	boor-gun-yeh blah(n)	Burgundy, Fr.	Table wine	White	Dry	***	F, P, & LM
Bourgogne Rouge	boor-gun-yeh roozh	Burgundy, Fr.	Table wine	Red	Dry	*	Ch, G, & RM
Brachetto	brah-KET-oh	Piedmont, It.	Table wine	Red	Dry	*	Ch, G, & RM
Brandy	BRAN-dee	Various	Fruit spirit	Amber	Dry, fruit	*	BD, C, & H
Brauneberger Juffer	brown-uh-behrk-ehr YOO-fehr	Moselle, Ger.	Table wine	White	Dry	***	F, P, & LM
Brouilly	brwee-yee	Beaujolais, Fr.	Table wine	Red	Dry	*	Ch, G, & RM
Bual (Boal)	boo whal	Madeira	Fortified wine	Gold	Sweet	*	Hosp
Bucelas	boo-SEL-ush	Portugal	Table wine	White	Med. sweet	***	LM & Fr
Buzbag	BOOZ-bah	Turkey	Table wine	Red	Dry	*	Ch, G, & RM
Cabernet Sauvignon	kah-behr-nay soh-vee-nyoh(n)	Various	Table wine	Red	Dry	*	Ch, G, & RM
Calvados	kahl-vah-dohs	Normandy, Fr.	Apple brandy	Brown	Dry, fruit	*	AD
Campari	kahm-PAR-ee	Italy	Aperitif	Red	Bitter	***	BD
Canadian whisky		Canada	Spirit	Brown	Dry, rich	* or ***	C, H, Pun, & S
Capri	KAH-pree	Capri, It.	Table wine	White	Dry	***	F, P, & LM
Carcavelos	kar-sah-VEL-ush	Portugal	Fortified wine	White	Sweet	***	AD
Carema	kah-RAY-mah	Piedmont, It.	Table wine	Red	Dry	*	Ch, G, & RM

Service temperature: *—Room temperature / **—Slightly chilled / ***—Cold
Serve with: AD—After dinner / BD—Before dinner / C—Cocktails / Ch—Cheese / F—Fish / Fr—Fruits / G—Game /
       H—Highballs / Hosp—Hospitality / LM—Light meats / P—Poultry / Pun—Punches / RM—Red meats / S—Straight
1855 classification: 1st—First growth / 2nd—Second growth, etc.; wines of Burgundy: GC—Grand Cru / PC—Premier Cru

NAME	PHONETIC SPELLING	SOURCE	TYPE	COLOR	TASTE	SERV. TEMP	SERVE WITH
Carruades de Château Lafite-Rothschild	kah-rwahd duh shah-toh lah-feet-roh-sheeld	Médoc, Fr.	Table wine	Red	Dry	*	Ch, G, & RM
Catawba	kuh-TAW-bah	New York State & Ohio	Table or sparkling wine	White	Sweet	***	Fr & Hosp
Chablis	shah-blee	Chablis, Fr.	Table wine	White	Dry	***	Oysters, P, & LM
Chablis Blanchots (GC)	shah-blee blah(n)-shoh	Chablis, Fr.	Table wine	White	Dry	***	Oysters, P, & LM
Chablis Bougros (GC)	shah-blee boo-groh	Chablis, Fr.	Table wine	White	Dry	***	Oysters, P, & LM
Chablis Grenouilles (GC)	shah-blee grah-nwee	Chablis, Fr.	Table wine	White	Dry	***	Oysters, P, & LM
Chablis Les Clos (GC)	shah-blee lay kloh	Chablis, Fr.	Table wine	White	Dry	***	Oysters, P, & LM
Chablis Les Preuses (GC)	shah-blee lay pruhz	Chablis, Fr.	Table wine	White	Dry	***	Oysters, P, & LM
Chablis Valmur (GC)	shah-blee vahl-moor	Chablis, Fr.	Table wine	White	Dry	***	Oysters, P, & LM
Chablis Vaudésir (GC)	shah-blee voh-day-zeer	Chablis, Fr.	Table wine	White	Dry	***	Oysters, P, & LM
Chambertin, Le (GC)	luh shah(m)-behr-ta(n)	Côte de Nuits, Fr.	Table wine	Red	Dry	*	Ch, G, & RM
Chambertin-Clos de Bèze (GC)	shah(m)-behr-ta(n)-klohd-behz	Côte de Nuits, Fr.	Table wine	Red	Dry	*	Ch, G, & RM
Chambolle-Musigny	shah(m)-bohl-moo-see-nyee	Côte de Nuits, Fr.	Table wine	Red	Dry	*	Ch, G, & RM
Chambolle-Musigny-Les Amoureuses (PC)	shah(m)-bohl-moo-see-nyee layz ah-muh-ruhz	Côte de Nuits, Fr.	Table wine	Red	Dry	*	Ch, G, & RM
Champagne	shah(m)-pah-nye	Champagne, Fr.	Sparkling wine	White or light red	Dry to sweet	***	All foods & Hosp
Chapelle-Chambertin (GC)	shah-pehl-shah(m)-behr-ta(n)	Côte de Nuits, Fr.	Table wine	Red	Dry	*	Ch, G, & RM
Charbono	shar-BOH-noh	California	Table wine	Red	Dry	*	Ch, G, & RM
Charmes-Chambertin (GC)	shahrm-shah(m)-behr-ta(n)	Côte de Nuits, Fr.	Table wine	Red	Dry	*	Ch, G, & RM
Chartreuse	shahr-truhz	Voiron, Fr.	Liqueur	Yellow or green	Spicy, sweet	*	AD
Chassagne-Montrachet	shah-sah-nyuh-moh(n)-rah-shay	Côte de Beaune, Fr.	Table wine	White or red	Dry	* or ***	Varies with color
Château Ausone	shah-toh oh-sohn	Saint-Émilion, Fr.	Table wine	Red	Dry	*	Ch, G, & RM
Château Batailley (5th)	shah-toh bah-tie-yay	Médoc, Fr.	Table wine	Red	Dry	*	Ch, G, & RM
Château Beauséjour	shah-toh boh-say-zhewr	Saint-Émilion, Fr.	Table wine	Red	Dry	*	Ch, G, & RM
Château Belair	shah-toh bel-ehr	Saint-Émilion, Fr.	Table wine	Red	Dry	*	Ch, G, & RM
Château Belgrave (5th)	shah-toh bel-grahv	Médoc, Fr.	Table wine	Red	Dry	*	Ch, G, & RM
Château Bellevue	shah-toh bel-vuh	Saint-Émilion, Fr.	Table wine	Red	Dry	*	Ch, G, & RM
Château Beychevelle (4th)	shah-toh baysh-vehl	Médoc, Fr.	Table wine	Red	Dry	*	Ch, G, & RM
Château Bouscaut	shah-toh boo-skoh	Graves, Fr.	Table wine	Red or white	Dry	* or ***	Varies with color
Château Boyd-Cantenac (3rd)	shah-toh-bwahd-kah(n)-teh-nahk	Médoc, Fr.	Table wine	Red	Dry	*	Ch, G, & RM
Château Branaire-Ducru (4th)	shah-toh brah-nehr-doo-croo	Médoc, Fr.	Table wine	Red	Dry	*	Ch, G, & RM

NAME	PHONETIC SPELLING	SOURCE	TYPE	COLOR	TASTE	SERV. TEMP.	SERVE WITH
Château Brane-Cantenac (2nd)	shah-toh brahn kah(n)-teh-nahk	Médoc, Fr.	Table wine	Red	Dry	*	Ch, G, & RM
Château Broustet (2nd)	shah-toh broo-stay	Barsac, Fr.	Table wine	White	Sweet	***	Desserts
Château Caillou (2nd)	shah-toh kah-yoo	Barsac, Fr.	Table wine	White	Sweet	***	Desserts
Château Calon-Ségur (3rd)	shah-toh kah-loh(n) say-goor	Médoc, Fr.	Table wine	Red	Dry	*	Ch, G, & RM
Château Camensac (5th)	shah-toh kah-men-sahk	Médoc, Fr.	Table wine	Red	Dry	*	Ch, G, & RM
Château Canon	shah-toh kah-noh(n)	Saint-Émilion, Fr.	Table wine	Red	Dry	*	Ch, G, & RM
Château Cantemerle (5th)	shah-toh kha(n)-teh-mehrl	Médoc, Fr.	Table wine	Red	Dry	*	Ch, G, & RM
Château Cantenac-Brown (3rd)	shah-toh kha(n)-teh-nahk-brown	Médoc, Fr.	Table wine	Red	Dry	*	Ch, G, & RM
Château Carbonnieux	shah-toh car-boh-nyuh	Graves, Fr.	Table wine	Red or white	Dry	* or ***	Varies with color
Château Certan-Giraud	shah-toh sehr-ta(n)-zhee-roh	Pomerol, Fr.	Table wine	Red	Dry	*	Ch, G, & RM
Château Châlon	shah-toh-shah-loh(n)	Jura, Fr.	Table wine	White	Dry	***	BD
Château Cheval-Blanc	shah-toh sheh-vahl-blah(n)	Saint-Émilion, Fr.	Table wine	Red	Dry	*	Ch, G, & RM
Château Clerc-Milon-Mondon (5th)	shah-toh klehr-mee-loh(n)-moh(n)-doh(n)	Médoc, Fr.	Table wine	Red	Dry	*	Ch, G, & RM
Château Climens (1st)	shah-toh klee-mah(n)	Barsac, Fr.	Table wine	White	Sweet	***	Desserts
(Château) Clos Fourtet	shah-toh kloh foor-tay	Saint-Emilion, Fr.	Table wine	Red	Dry	*	Ch, G, & RM
(Château) Clos Haut-Peyraguey (1st)	shah-toh kloh oh-pay-rah-gay	Sauternes, Fr.	Table wine	White	Sweet	***	Desserts
Château Cos d'Estournel (2nd)	shah-toh koh deh-toor-nel	Médoc, Fr.	Table wine	Red	Dry	*	Ch, G, & RM
Château Cos-Labory (5th)	shah-toh koh-lah-boh-ree	Médoc, Fr.	Table wine	Red	Dry	*	Ch, G, & RM
Château Couhins	shah-toh k̲ wah(n)	Graves, Fr.	Table wine	White	Dry	***	F, P, & LM
Château Coutet (1st)	shah-toh koo-tay	Barsac, Fr.	Table wine	White	Sweet	***	Desserts
Château Croizet-Bages (5th)	shah-toh krwah-zeh-bahzh	Médoc, Fr.	Table wine	Red	Dry	*	Ch, G, & RM
Château d'Arche (2nd)	shah-toh dahrsh	Sauternes, Fr.	Table wine	White	Sweet	***	Desserts
Château Dauzac (5th)	shah-toh doh-zahk	Médoc, Fr.	Table wine	Red	Dry	*	Ch, G, & RM
Château de Malle (2nd)	shah-toh duh mahl	Sauternes, Fr.	Table wine	White	Sweet	***	Desserts
Château d'Issan (3rd)	shah-toh dee-sah(n)	Médoc, Fr.	Table wine	Red	Dry	*	Ch, G, & RM
Château de Rayne-Vigneau (1st)	shah-toh duh rayn-vee-nyoh	Sauternes, Fr.	Table wine	White	Sweet	***	Desserts
Château Doisy-Daene (2nd)	shah-toh dwah-zee-dane	Barsac, Fr.	Table wine	White	Sweet	***	Desserts
Château Doisy-Védrines (2nd)	shah-toh dwah-zee-vay-dreen	Barsac, Fr.	Table wine	White	Sweet	***	Desserts
Château Ducru-Beaucaillou (2nd)	shah-toh doo-croo-boh-kah-yoo	Médoc, Fr.	Table wine	Red	Dry	*	Ch, G, & RM

Service temperature: *—Room temperature / **—Slightly chilled / ***—Cold
Serve with: AD—After dinner / BD—Before dinner / C—Cocktails / Ch—Cheese / F—Fish / Fr—Fruits / G—Game / H—Highballs / Hosp—Hospitality / LM—Light meats / P—Poultry / Pun—Punches / RM—Red meats / S—Straight
1855 classification: 1st—First growth / 2nd—Second growth, etc.; *wines of Burgundy:* GC—*Grand Cru* / PC—*Premier Cru*

NAME	PHONETIC SPELLING	SOURCE	TYPE	COLOR	TASTE	SERV. TEMP.	SERVE WITH
Château Duhart-Milon-Rothschild (4th)	shah-toh doo-ar-mee-loh(n)-roh-sheeld	Médoc, Fr.	Table wine	Red	Dry	*	Ch, G, & RM
Château Durfort-Vivens (2nd)	shah-toh duhr-for-vee-vah(n)	Médoc, Fr.	Table wine	Red	Dry	*	Ch, G, & RM
Château du Tertre (5th)	shah-toh doo tehrtr	Médoc, Fr.	Table wine	Red	Dry	*	Ch, G, & RM
Château d'Yquem (1st)	shah-toh dee-kem	Sauternes, Fr.	Table wine	White	Sweet	***	Desserts
Château Ferrière (3rd)	shah-toh fehr-yehr	Médoc, Fr.	Table wine	Red	Dry	*	Ch, G, & RM
Château Fieuzal	shah-toh fyuh-zahl	Graves, Fr.	Table wine	Red	Dry	*	Ch, G, & RM
Château Figeac	shah-toh fee-zhahk	Saint-Émilion, Fr.	Table wine	Red	Dry	*	Ch, G, & RM
Château Filhot (2nd)	shah-toh fee-loh	Sauternes, Fr.	Table wine	White	Sweet	***	Desserts
Château Gazin	shah-toh gah-za(n)	Pomerol, Fr.	Table wine	Red	Dry	*	Ch, G, & RM
Château Giscours (3rd)	shah-toh zhis-koor	Médoc, Fr.	Table wine	Red	Dry	*	Ch, G, & RM
Château Grand-Puy-Ducasse (5th)	shah-toh grah(n)-pwee-doo-kahs	Médoc, Fr.	Table wine	Red	Dry	*	Ch, G, & RM
Château Grand-Puy-Lacoste (5th)	shah-toh grah(n)-pwee-lah-kohst	Médoc, Fr.	Table wine	Red	Dry	*	Ch, G, & RM
Château Grillet	shah-toh gree-yay	Côtes du Rhône, Fr.	Table wine	White	Dry	***	F, P, & LM
Château Gruaud-Larose (2nd)	shah-toh groo-oh-lah-rohz	Médoc, Fr.	Table wine	Red	Dry	*	Ch, G, & RM
Château Guiraud (1st)	shah-toh zhwee-roh	Sauternes, Fr.	Table wine	White	Sweet	***	Desserts
Château Haut-Bages-Libéral (5th)	shah-toh oh-bahzh-lee-beh-rahl	Médoc, Fr.	Table wine	Red	Dry	*	Ch, G, & RM
Château Haut-Bailly	shah-toh oh-bay-yee	Graves, Fr.	Table wine	Red	Dry	*	Ch, G, & RM
Château Haut-Batailley (5th)	shah-toh oh-bah-tie-yay	Médoc, Fr.	Table wine	Red	Dry	*	Ch, G, & RM
Château Haut-Brion (1st)	shah-toh oh-bree-oh(n)	Graves, Fr.	Table wine	Red	Dry	*	Ch, G, & RM
Château Haut-Brion Blanc	shah-toh oh-bree-oh(n) blah(n)	Graves, Fr.	Table wine	White	Dry	***	F, P, & LM
Château Kirwan (3rd)	shah-toh kir-wah(n)	Médoc, Fr.	Table wine	Red	Dry	*	Ch, G, & RM
Château La Conseillante	shah-toh lah koh(n)-say-ah(n)t	Pomerol, Fr.	Table wine	Red	Dry	*	Ch, G, & RM
Château Lafaurie-Peyraguey (1st)	shah-toh lah-foh-ree-pay-rah-gay	Sauternes, Fr.	Table wine	White	Sweet	***	Desserts
Château Lafite-Rothschild (1st)	shah-toh lah-feet-roh-sheeld	Médoc, Fr.	Table wine	Red	Dry	*	Ch, G, & RM
Château La Fleur-Pétrus	shah-toh lah fluhr-pay-troos	Pomerol, Fr.	Table wine	Red	Dry	*	Ch, G, & RM
Château Lafon-Rochet (4th)	shah-toh lah-foh(n)-roh-shay	Médoc, Fr.	Table wine	Red	Dry	*	Ch, G, & RM
Château La Gaffelière	shah-toh lah gah-fel-yehr	Saint-Émilion, Fr.	Table wine	Red	Dry	*	Ch, G, & RM
Château La Garde	shah-toh lah gahrd	Graves, Fr.	Table wine	Red	Dry	*	Ch, G, & RM
Château Lagrange (3rd)	shah-toh lah-grah(n)zh	Médoc, Fr.	Table wine	Red	Dry	*	Ch, G, & RM
Château La Lagune (3rd)	shah-toh lah lah-goon	Médoc, Fr.	Table wine	Red	Dry	*	Ch, G, & RM
Château La Mission Haut Brion	shah-toh lah mee-syoh(n) oh bree-oh(n)	Graves, Fr.	Table wine	Red	Dry	*	Ch, G, & RM
Château Lamothe (2nd)	shah-toh lah-moht	Sauternes, Fr.	Table wine	White	Sweet	***	Desserts

NAME	PHONETIC SPELLING	SOURCE	TYPE	COLOR	TASTE	SERV. TEMP.	SERVE WITH
Château Langoa-Barton (3rd)	shah-toh lah(n)-goh ah-bahr-toh(n)	Médoc, Fr.	Table wine	Red	Dry	*	Ch, G, & RM
Château Laroze	shah-toh lah-rohz	Saint-Emilion, Fr.	Table wine	Red	Dry	*	Ch, G, & RM
Château Larrivet Haut Brion	shah-toh lah-ree-veh oh-bree-oh(n)	Graves, Fr.	Table wine	White	Dry	***	F, P, & LM
Château Lascombes (2nd)	shah-toh lahs-coh(m)b	Médoc, Fr.	Table wine	Red	Dry	*	Ch, G, & RM
Château Latour (1st)	shah-toh lah-toor	Médoc, Fr.	Table wine	Red	Dry	*	Ch, G, & RM
Château La Tour-Blanche (1st)	shah-toh lah toor-blah(n)sh	Sauternes, Fr.	Table wine	White	Sweet	***	Desserts
Château La Tour-Carnet (4th)	shah-toh lah toor-car-nay	Médoc, Fr.	Table wine	Red	Dry	*	Ch, G, & RM
Château La Tour Haut Brion	shah-toh lah toor oh bree-oh(n)	Graves, Fr.	Table wine	Red	Dry	*	Ch, G, & RM
Château La Tour-Martillac	shah-toh lah toor-mahr-tee-yahk	Graves, Fr.	Table wine	Red or white	Dry	* or ***	Varies with color
Château Latour-Pomerol	shah-toh lah-toor-pohm-rohl	Pomerol, Fr.	Table wine	Red	Dry	*	Ch, G, & RM
Château Laville Haut Brion	shah-toh lah-vee yoh bree-oh(n)	Graves, Fr.	Table wine	White	Dry	***	F, P, & LM
Château Léoville-Barton (2nd)	shah-toh lay-oh-veel-bar-toh(n)	Médoc, Fr.	Table wine	Red	Dry	*	Ch, G, & RM
Château Léoville-Lascases (2nd)	shah-toh lay-oh-veel-lahs-kahz	Médoc, Fr.	Table wine	Red	Dry	*	Ch, G, & RM
Château Léoville-Poyferré (2nd)	shah-toh lay-oh-veel-pwah-feh-ray	Médoc, Fr.	Table wine	Red	Dry	*	Ch, G, & RM
Château L'Évangile	shah-toh lay-vah(n)-zheel	Pomerol, Fr.	Table wine	Red	Dry	*	Ch, G, & RM
Château Lynch-Bages (5th)	shah-toh leensh-bahzh	Médoc, Fr.	Table wine	Red	Dry	*	Ch, G, & RM
Château Lynch-Moussas (5th)	shah-toh leensh-moo-sah	Médoc, Fr.	Table wine	Red	Dry	*	Ch, G, & RM
Château Magdelaine	shah-toh mahg-duh-lehn	Saint-Émilion, Fr.	Table wine	Red	Dry	*	Ch, G, & RM
Château Malartic-Lagravière	shah-toh mah-lahr-teek-lah-grahv-yehr	Graves, Fr.	Table wine	Red or white	Dry	***	Varies with color
Château Malescot-Saint-Exupéry (3rd)	shah-toh mah-lehs-koh-sa(n)-tex-oo-peh-ree	Médoc, Fr.	Table wine	Red	Dry	*	Ch, G, & RM
Château Margaux (1st)	shah-toh mahr-goh	Médoc, Fr.	Table wine	Red	Dry	*	Ch, G, & RM
Château Marquis d'Alesme-Becker (3rd)	shah-toh mahr-kee dah-lehm-beh-ker	Médoc, Fr.	Table wine	Red	Dry	*	Ch, G, & RM
Château Marquis de Terme (4th)	shah-toh mahr-kee duh tehrm	Médoc, Fr.	Table wine	Red	Dry	*	Ch, G, & RM
Château Montrose (2nd)	shah-toh moh(n)-rohz	Médoc, Fr.	Table wine	Red	Dry	*	Ch, G, & RM
Château Mouton-Baron-Philippe (5th)	shah-toh moo-taw(n)-bah-roh(n)-fee-leep	Médoc, Fr.	Table wine	Red	Dry	*	Ch, G, & RM
Château Mouton-Rothschild (1st)	shah-toh moo-taw(n)-roh-sheeld	Médoc, Fr.	Table wine	Red	Dry	*	Ch, G, & RM

Service temperature: *—Room temperature / **—Slightly chilled / ***—Cold
Serve with: AD—After dinner / BD—Before dinner / C—Cocktails / Ch—Cheese / F—Fish / Fr—Fruits / G—Game /
H—Highballs / Hosp—Hospitality / LM—Light meats / P—Poultry / Pun—Punches / RM—Red meats / S—Straight
1855 classification: 1st—First growth / 2nd—Second growth, etc.; *wines of Burgundy:* GC—*Grand Cru* / PC—*Premier Cru*

NAME	PHONETIC SPELLING	SOURCE	TYPE	COLOR	TASTE	SERV. TEMP.	SERVE WITH
Château Myrat (2nd)	shah-toh mee-rah	Barsac, Fr.	Table wine	White	Sweet	***	Desserts
Château Nairac (2nd)	shah-toh nay-rahk	Barsac, Fr.	Table wine	White	Sweet	***	Desserts
Château Nenin	shah-toh nuh-neen	Pomerol, Fr.	Table wine	Red	Dry	*	Ch, G, & RM
Châteauneuf-du-Pape	shah-toh-nuf-doo-pop	Rhône, Fr.	Table wine	Red	Dry	*	Ch, G, & RM
Château Olivier	shah-toh oh-lee-vyay	Graves, Fr.	Table wine	Red or white	Dry	* or ***	Varies with color
Château Palmer (3rd)	shah-toh pahl-mehr	Médoc, Fr.	Table wine	Red	Dry	*	Ch, G, & RM
Château Pape-Clément	shah-toh pop-klay-mah(n)	Graves, Fr.	Table wine	Red	Dry	*	Ch, G, & RM
Château Pavie	shah-toh pah-vee	Saint-Émilion, Fr.	Table wine	Red	Dry	*	Ch, G, & RM
Château Pédesclaux (5th)	shah-toh pay-dehs-kloh	Médoc, Fr.	Table wine	Red	Dry	*	Ch, G, & RM
Château Petit-Village	shah-toh puh-tee-vee-lahzh	Pomerol, Fr.	Table wine	Red	Dry	*	Ch, G, & RM
Château Pétrus	shah-toh peh-troos	Pomerol, Fr.	Table wine	Red	Dry	*	Ch, G, & RM
Château Pichon-Longueville (Baron) (2nd)	shah-toh pee-shoh(n)-loh(n)g-veel (bah-roh(n))	Médoc, Fr.	Table wine	Red	Dry	*	Ch, G, & RM
Château Pichon-Longueville-Comtesse (2nd)	shah-toh pee-shoh(n)-loh(n)g-veel-coh(m)-tehs	Médoc, Fr.	Table wine	Red	Dry	*	Ch, G, & RM
Château Pontet-Canet (5th)	shah-toh poh(n)-teh-kah-neh	Médoc, Fr.	Table wine	Red	Dry	*	Ch, G, & RM
Château Pouget (4th)	shah-toh poo-zhay	Médoc, Fr.	Table wine	Red	Dry	*	Ch, G, & RM
Château Prieuré-Lichine (4th)	shah-toh pree-uh-ray-lee-sheen	Médoc, Fr.	Table wine	Red	Dry	*	Ch, G, & RM
Château Rabaud-Promis (1st)	shah-toh rah-boh-proh-mee	Sauternes, Fr.	Table wine	White	Sweet	***	Desserts
Château Rausan-Ségla (2nd)	shah-toh roh-zah(n)-say-glah	Médoc, Fr.	Table wine	Red	Dry	*	Ch, G, & RM
Château Rauzan-Gassies (2nd)	shah-toh roh-zah(n)-gah-see	Médoc, Fr.	Table wine	Red	Dry	*	Ch, G, & RM
Château Rieussec (1st)	shah-toh ree-uh-sehk	Sauternes, Fr.	Table wine	White	Sweet	***	Desserts
Château Ripeau	shah-toh ree-poh	Saint-Émilion, Fr.	Table wine	Red	Dry	*	Ch, G, & RM
Château Romer (2nd)	shah-toh roh-mehr	Sauternes, Fr.	Table wine	White	Sweet	***	Desserts
Château Saint-Pierre (4th)	shah-toh sa(n)-pyehr	Médoc, Fr.	Table wine	Red	Dry	*	Ch, G, & RM
Château Sigalas-Rabaud (1st)	shah-toh see-gah-lah-rah-boh	Sauternes, Fr.	Table wine	White	Sweet	***	Desserts
Château Smith-Haut-Lafitte	shah-toh smith-oh-lah-feet	Graves, Fr.	Table wine	Red	Dry	*	Ch, G, & RM
Château Suau	shah-toh soo-oh	Barsac, Fr.	Table wine	White	Sweet	***	Desserts
Château Suduiraut (1st)	shah-toh soo-dwee-roh	Sauternes, Fr.	Table wine	White	Sweet	***	Desserts
Château Talbot (4th)	shah-toh tahl-boh	Médoc, Fr.	Table wine	Red	Dry	*	Ch, G, & RM
Château Trimoulet	shah-toh tree-moo-lay	Saint-Émilion, Fr.	Table wine	Red	Dry	*	Ch, G, & RM
Château Troplong-Mondot	shah-toh troh-loh(ng)-moh(n)-doh	Saint-Émilion, Fr.	Table wine	Red	Dry	*	Ch, G, & RM
Château Trotanoy	shah-toh trwah-tah-nwah	Pomerol, Fr.	Table wine	Red	Dry	*	Ch, G, & RM
Château Trottevieille	shah-toh troht-vyay	Saint-Émilion, Fr.	Table wine	Red	Dry	*	Ch, G, & RM
(Château) Vieux Château Certan	(shah-toh) vyuh shah-toh sehr-ta(n)	Pomerol, Fr.	Table wine	Red	Dry	*	Ch, G, & RM

NAME	PHONETIC SPELLING	SOURCE	TYPE	COLOR	TASTE	SERV. TEMP.	SERVE WITH
Chefoo	chay-foo	China	Dessert wine	Red or white	Sweet	***	Desserts
Chelois	shel-wah	New York State	Table wine	Red	Med. dry	**	P & RM
Chenin Blanc	sheh-neen blah(n)	California & France	Table wine	White	Med. dry	**	F, P, & LM
Cherry liqueur		Various	Liqueur	Red	Sweet, cherry	*	AD
Chevalier-Montrachet (GC)	sheh-vahl-yay moh(n)-rah-shay	Côte de Beaune, Fr.	Table wine	White	Dry	***	F, P, & LM
Chianti	kee-AHN-tee	Tuscany, It.	Table wine	Red	Dry	*	All foods
Chiaretto del Garda	kee-ah-RET-oh del gar-dah	Veneto, It.	Table wine	Pink	Med. dry	***	All foods
Cider		Spain & England	Sparkling or still wine	Straw	Sweet, fruity	***	Hosp
Clos de la Roche (GC)	kloh duh lah rohsh	Côte de Nuits, Fr.	Table wine	Red	Dry	*	Ch, G, & RM
Clos des Lambrays (PC)	kloh day lah(m)-bray	Côte de Nuits, Fr.	Table wine	Red	Dry	*	Ch, G, & RM
Clos des Mouches (PC)	kloh day moosh	Côte de Beaune, Fr.	Table wine	Red	Dry	*	Ch, G, & RM
Clos de Tart (GC)	kloh-duh tahr	Côte de Nuits, Fr.	Table wine	Red	Dry	*	Ch, G, & RM
Clos de Vougeot (GC)	kloh duh voo-zhoh	Côte de Nuits, Fr.	Table wine	Red	Dry	*	Ch, G, & RM
Clos Saint-Denis (GC)	kloh sa(n)-duh-nee	Côte de Nuits, Fr.	Table wine	Red	Dry	*	Ch, G, & RM
Clos Sainte-Odile	kloh sa(n)-toh-deel	Alsace, Fr.	Table wine	White	Med. dry	***	All foods
Clos Saint-Jacques (PC)	kloh sa(n)-zhahk	Côte de Nuits, Fr.	Table wine	Red	Dry	*	Ch, G, & RM
Cognac	koh-nyahk	Cognac, Fr.	Brandy	Brown	Dry	*	AD
Cointreau	kwa(n)-troh	Angers, Fr.	Liqueur	White	Sweet, orange	*	AD
Colares	koh-LAHR-esh	Portugal	Table wine	Red	Dry	*	Ch, G, & RM
Combettes, Les (PC)	lay co(m)-bet	Côte de Beaune, Fr.	Table wine	White	Dry	***	F, P, & LM
Commandaria	koh-mahn-dah-REE-ah	Cyprus	Dessert wine	White	Sweet	*	AD
Cortaillod	kohr-tie-oh	Switzerland	Table wine	Red	Dry	*	Ch & RM
Cortese	kohr-TAY-zee	Piedmont, It.	Table wine	White	Dry	***	F, P, & LM
Corton, Le (GC)	luh kohr-toh(n)	Côte de Beaune, Fr.	Table wine	Red	Dry	*	Ch, G, & RM
Corton-Charlemagne (GC)	kor-toh(n)-shahr-leh-mah-nyuh	Côte de Beaune, Fr.	Table wine	White	Dry	***	F, P, & LM
Corton-Clos du Roi (GC)	kor-toh(n)-kloh doo rwah	Côte de Beaune, Fr.	Table wine	Red	Dry	*	Ch, G, & RM
Corton-Pougets (GC)	kor-toh(n)-poo-zheh	Côte de Beaune, Fr.	Table wine	Red	Dry	*	Ch, G, & RM
Corvo	kohr-voh	Sicily, It.	Table wine	Red or white	Dry	* or ***	Varies with color
Côteaux de la Loire	koh-toh duh lah lwahr	Loire, Fr.	Table wine	White	Med. sweet	***	All foods
Côte Rôtie	koht roh-tee	Rhône, Fr.	Table wine	Red	Dry	*	Ch, G, & RM
Cotnari Grasa	koht-NAR-ee GRAH-sah	Romania	Dessert wine	Gold	Sweet	***	Desserts, AD
Crème de bananes	krehm deh bah-nahn	Various	Liqueur	Gold	Sweet, banana	*	AD
Crème de cacao	krehn duh kah-kah oh	Various	Liqueur	Brown or white	Sweet, chocolate	*	AD

Service temperature: *—Room temperature / **—Slightly chilled / ***—Cold
Serve with: AD—After dinner / BD—Before dinner / C—Cocktails / Ch—Cheese / F—Fish / Fr—Fruits / G—Game /
     H—Highballs / Hosp—Hospitality / LM—Light meats / P—Poultry / Pun—Punches / RM—Red meats / S—Straight
1855 classification: 1st—First growth / 2nd—Second growth, etc.; *wines of Burgundy:* GC—*Grand Cru* / PC—*Premier Cru*

NAME	PHONETIC SPELLING	SOURCE	TYPE	COLOR	TASTE	SERV. TEMP.	SERVE WITH
Crème de cassis	krehm duh kah-sees	Various	Liqueur	Red	Sweet, currant	***	H & C, aperitifs
Crème de menthe	krehm duh mah(n)t	Various	Liqueur	White or green	Sweet, mint	***	AD
Crème de noyaux	krehm duh noy-oh	Various	Liqueur	Cream	Sweet, nut	*	AD
Crème de violettes	krehm duh vee-oh-let	Various	Liqueur	Violet	Sweet, violet	*	AD
Crème Yvette	krehm ee-vet	Connecticut	Liqueur	Blue or violet	Sweet, violet	*	AD
Criots-Bâtard-Montrachet (GC)	kree-ut-bah-tahr-moh(n)-rah-shay	Côte de Beaune, Fr.	Table wine	White	Dry	***	F, P, & LM
Csopaki Furmint	CHO-pah-kee foor-mint	Hungary	Table wine	White	Dry	***	F, P, & LM
Curaçao	kuh-rah-soh	Various	Liqueur	Orange	Sweet, orange	*	AD
Cynar	CHEE-nar	Italy	Aperitif	Brown	Bitter	***	BD
Danziger Goldwasser	dahnt-zeeg-ehr GOHLD-vahs-ehr	Danzig, Ger.	Liqueur	White	Sweet	*	AD
Dão	dow	Portugal	Table wine	Red or white	Dry	* or ***	Varies with color
Debröi Hárslevelü	DEH-broy harsh-leh-vel-yoo	Hungary	Table wine	White	Med. sweet	***	All foods
Deidesheimer Leinhöhle	die-dehs-hie-mehr LINE-hoyl-eh	Rheinpfalz, Ger.	Table wine	White	Med. dry	***	F, P, & LM
Demeraran rum	dem-eh-RAH-rahn	Guyana	Spirit	Dark brown	Med. sweet	***	C, H, Pun, & S
Demestica	deh-MES-tee-kah	Greece	Table wine	Red or white	Dry	* or ***	Varies with color
Dézaley	day-zah-lay	Switzerland	Table wine	White	Dry	***	F, P, & LM
Dolcetto	dohl-CHET-oh	Piedmont, It.	Table or sparkling wine	Red	Dry or sweet	* or ***	All foods
Dôle de Sion	dohl duh see oh(n)	Switzerland	Table wine	Red	Dry	*	Ch, G, & RM
Domaine de Chevalier	duh-men duh sheh-vahl-yay	Graves, Fr.	Table wine	Red or white	Dry	* or ***	Varies with color
Drambuie	dram-BOO EE	Scotland	Liqueur	Gold	Sweet, spicy	*	AD
Dubonnet	doo-boh-nay	France & U.S.	Aperitif	Red or white	Sweet	***	BD
Dürkheimer Michelsberg	doork-hie-mehr MEEK-els-behrk	Rheinpfalz, Ger.	Table wine	White	Med. dry	***	F, P, & LM
Dürkheimer Spielberg	doork-hie-mehr SHPEEL-behrk	Rheinpfalz, Ger.	Table wine	White	Med. dry	***	F, P, & LM
Eau de Vie de Marc	ode-vee duh mahr	France	Brandy	Brown	Dry	*	AD
Eau de Vie de Poire	ode-vee duh pwahr	Various	Pear brandy	White	Dry, pear	***	AD
Echézeaux, Les (GC)	lays ay-sheh-zoh	Côte de Nuits, Fr.	Table wine	Red	Dry	*	Ch, G, & RM
Egri Bikavér	eg-ree BEE-kah-vehr	Hungary	Table wine	Red	Dry	*	Ch, G, & RM
Eiswein	ICE-vine	Rhine & Moselle, Ger.	Table wine	White	Sweet	***	Desserts
Enkircher Steffensberg	eng-keer(kh)-ehr SHTEF-ens-behrk	Moselle, Ger.	Table wine	White	Med. dry	***	F, P, & LM
Erbacher Marcobrunn	EHR-bahk-ehr MAHR-koh-bruhn	Rheingau, Ger.	Table wine	White	Med. dry	***	F, P, & LM
Erdener Treppchen	ehrd-eh-nehr TREPF-shen	Moselle, Ger.	Table wine	White	Med. dry	***	F, P, & LM
Escherndorfer Lump	eh-shehrn-dorf-ehr LOOMP	Franconia, Ger.	Table wine	White	Med. dry	***	F, P, & LM
Est! Est!! Est!!!	ehst-ehst-EHST	Latium, It.	Table wine	White	Dry	***	F, P, & LM
Falerno	fah-LEHR-noh	Campania, It.	Table wine	Red or white	Dry	* or ***	Varies with color

NAME	PHONETIC SPELLING	SOURCE	TYPE	COLOR	TASTE	SERV. TEMP.	SERVE WITH
Fendent de Sion	fah(n)-dah(n) duh see oh(n)	Switzerland	Table wine	White	Dry	***	F, P, & LM
Fernet Branca	fehr-net BRAHN-kah	Italy & U.S.	Bitters	Reddish brown	Bitter	*	C & H
Fino	FEE-noh	Jerez, Sp.	Sherry	Straw	Dry	**	Bd
Fior d'Alpe	fyor DAHL-pay	Italy	Liqueur	Gold	Sweet	*	AD
Fleurie	fluh-ree	Beaujolais, Fr.	Table wine	Red	Dry	*	All foods
Folle Blanche	fohl blah(n)sh	California	Table wine	White	Dry	***	F, P, & LM
Forster Kirchenstück	forsh-ter KEER(KH)-en-shtuk	Rheinpfalz, Ger.	Table wine	White	Med. dry	***	F, P, & LM
Forster Ungeheuer	forsh-ter OONG eh-hoy-er	Rheinpfalz, Ger.	Table wine	White	Med. dry	***	F, P, & LM
Fraise	frehz	Various	Strawberry brandy	White	Dry	***	AD
Framboise	frah(m)-bwahz	Various	Raspberry brandy	White	Dry, raspberry	***	AD
Frascati	frahs-KAH-tee	Latium, It.	Table wine	White	Med. sweet	***	F, P, & LM
Frecciarossa	freh-chah-ROH-sah	Lombardy, It.	Table wine	Red or white	Dry	* or ***	Varies with color
Freisa	FRAY-sah	Piedmont, It.	Table wine	Red	Dry	*	Ch, G, & RM
French vermouth		Midi, Fr.	Aromatized wine	White	Dry	***	BD & C
Galliano	gahl-YAH-noh	Milan, It.	Liqueur	Gold	Sweet	*	AD
Gamay	gah-may	France & California	Table wine	Red	Dry	**	Ch, G, & RM
Gattinara	gah-tee-NAH-rah	Piedmont, It.	Table wine	Red	Dry	*	Ch, G, & RM
Geisenheimer Mäuerchen	gie-zen-hie-mehr MOY-er-shen	Rheingau, Ger.	Table wine	White	Med. dry	***	F, P, & LM
Geisenheimer Rothenberg	gie-zen-hie-mehr RAHTH-en-behrk	Rheingau, Ger.	Table wine	White	Med. dry	***	F, P, & LM
Genever (gin)		Holland	Spirit	White	Dry	**	BD, S, & H
Gevrey-Chambertin	zhev-ray-shah(m)-behr-ta(n)	Côte de Nuits, Fr.	Table wine	Red	Dry	*	Ch, G, & RM
Gewürztraminer	geh-VURTZ-trah-meen-er	Alsace, Fr., & California	Table wine	White	Med. dry	***	All foods
Gin, dry	jin	Various	Spirit	White	Dry	***	C, H, & S
Girò	zhee-roh	Sardinia, It.	Dessert wine	Red	Sweet	*	AD
Graacher Himmelreich	grah-kehr HIM-el-rie(kh)	Moselle, Ger.	Table wine	White	Med. dry	***	F, P, & LM
Gragnano	grah-NYAH-noh	Campania, It.	Table wine	Red	Dry	*	Ch, G, & RM
Grand Marnier	grah(n) mahr-nyay	Cognac, Fr.	Liqueur	Orange	Sweet, orange	*	AD
Grands Echézeaux, Les (GC)	lay grah(n) zay-sheh-zoh	Côte de Nuits, Fr.	Table wine	Red	Dry	*	Ch, G, & RM
Graves	grahv	Bordeaux, Fr.	Table wine	Red or white	Dry	* or ***	Varies with color
Greco di Gerace	greh-koh dee jeh-RAH-chay	Calabria, It.	Table wine	White	Med. dry	***	F, P, & LM
Grenadine	GREHN-ah-deen	Various	Syrup	Red	Sweet	***	C & Pun
Grignolino	gree-nyoh-LEE-noh	Piedmont, It.	Table wine	Red	Dry	*	Ch, G, & RM
Grinzinger	GRINT-zing-ehr	Austria	Table wine	White	Dry	***	F, P, & LM
Griotte-Chambertin (GC)	gree-ut-shah(m)-behr-ta(n)	Côte de Nuits, Fr.	Table wine	Red	Dry	*	Ch, G, & RM
Grumello	groo-MEL-oh	Lombardy, It.	Table wine	Red	Dry	*	Ch, G, & RM
Gumpoldskirchner	GOOM-pohls-keer(kh)-nehr	Austria	Table wine	White	Dry	***	F, P, & LM

Service temperature: *—Room temperature / **—Slightly chilled / ***—Cold
Serve with: AD—After dinner / BD—Before dinner / C—Cocktails / Ch—Cheese / F—Fish / Fr—Fruits / G—Game /
     H—Highballs / Hosp—Hospitality / LM—Light meats / P—Poultry / Pun—Punches / RM—Red meats / S—Straight
1855 classification: 1st—First growth / 2nd—Second growth, etc.; *wines of Burgundy:* GC—*Grand Cru* / PC—*Premier Cru*

NAME	PHONETIC SPELLING	SOURCE	TYPE	COLOR	TASTE	SERV. TEMP.	SERVE WITH
Haitian rum	hay-shun	Haiti	Spirit	Straw	Dry	***	C, Pun, H, & S
Hallgartener Schönhell	hahl-gar-ten-ehr SHOYN-hel	Rheingau, Ger.	Table wine	White	Med. dry	***	F, P, & LM
Hattenheimer Engelmannsberg	haht-ten-hie-mehr AYNG-el-mahns-behrk	Rheingau, Ger.	Table wine	White	Med. dry	***	F, P, & LM
Hattenheimer Nussbrunnen	haht-ten-hie-mehr NOOS-broon-en	Rheingau, Ger.	Table wine	White	Med. dry	***	F, P, & LM
Hermitage	ehr-mee-tahzh	Rhône, Fr.	Table wine	Red or white	Dry	* or ***	Varies with color
Hochheimer Domdechaney	hok-hie-mehr DOHM-deh-shah-nay	Rheingau, Ger.	Table wine	White	Med. dry	***	F, P, & LM
Hochheimer Kirchenstück	hok-hie-mehr KEER(KH)-en-shtuk	Rheingau, Ger.	Table wine	White	Med. dry	***	F, P, & LM
Hohenwarther	HOH-hen-vahr-tehr	Austria	Table wine	White	Dry	***	F, P, & LM
Hollands (gin)		Holland	Spirit	White	Dry	*	BD, S, & H
Hospices de Beaune	ohs-pees duh bone	Côte de Beaune, Fr.	Table wine	Red or white	Dry	* or ***	Varies with color
Inferno	een-FEHR-noh	Lombardy, It.	Table wine	Red	Dry	*	Ch, G, & RM
Iphofener Julius-Echter-Berg	ip-hah-fehn-er YOOL-yuhs-eh(kh)t-ehr-behrk	Franconia, Ger.	Table wine	White	Dry	***	F, P, & LM
Irish whiskey		Ireland	Spirit	Brown	Dry, rich	* or ***	C, H, AD, & S
Ischia	EESK-yah	Campania, It.	Table wine	White	Dry	***	F, P, & LM
Italian vermouth		Italy	Aromatized wine	Red	Bittersweet	***	C & BD
Jamaican rum	jah-MAY-kun	Jamaica, B.W.I.	Spirit	Dark brown	Med. sweet	***	C, H, Pun, & S
Johannisberger Erntebringer	yoh-hahn-is-behrk-ehr EHRN-teh-bring-ehr	Rheingau, Ger.	Table wine	White	Med. dry	***	F, P, & LM
Johannisberg Riesling	yoh-hahn-is-behrk REES-ling	California	Table wine	White	Med. dry	***	F, P, & LM
Juliénas	yoo-lee-eh-nahs	Beaujolais, Fr.	Table wine	Red	Dry	*	All foods
Kadmon	KAHD-mahn	Israel	Dessert wine	Amber	Sweet	*	AD
Kahlúa	kah-LOO-ah	Mexico	Liqueur	Brown	Sweet, coffee	*	AD
Kalebag	kah-LAY-bah	Turkey	Table wine	Red	Dry	*	Ch, G, & RM
Kéknyelü	KAYK-nee-el-yoo	Hungary	Table wine	White	Dry	***	F, P, & LM
Kirsch	keersh	Various	Cherry brandy	White	Dry, cherry	***	AD
Kirschwasser	KEERSH-vahs-ehr	Various	Cherry brandy	White	Dry, cherry	***	AD
Klosterneuburger	klos-tir-NOY-boorg-ehr	Austria	Table wine	White	Dry	***	F, P, & LM
Knipperlé	k nip-ehr-lay	Alsace, Fr.	Table wine	White	Dry	***	All foods
Kokineli	koh-kee-NAY-lee	Cyprus	Table wine	Red	Dry, non-resinated	*	Ch, G, & RM
Kokineli	koh-kee-NAY-lee	Greece	Table wine	Red	Dry, resinated	**	F, P, & LM
Kremser	KREHM-zer	Austria	Table wine	White	Dry	***	F, P, & LM
Kröver Nacktarsch	kroy-vehr NAHK-tarsh	Moselle, Ger.	Table wine	White	Med. dry	***	F, P, & LM
Kümmel	KUHM-mel	Various	Liqueur	White	Sweet, caraway	*	AD
Lacrima Christi	lah-creem-ah KREES-tee	Campania, It.	Table wine	White	Med. dry	***	All foods
Lambrusco	lahm-BROOS-coh	Emilia, It.	Sparkling wine	Red	Med. sweet	***	All foods
Latricières-Chambertin (GC)	lah-tree-syehr-shah(m)-behr-ta(n)	Côte de Nuits, Fr.	Table wine	Red	Dry	*	Ch, G, & RM
Leányka Edes	LAY-ahn-kyah a-dehsh	Hungary	Table wine	White	Med. sweet	***	F, P, & LM
Leányka Szaras	LAY-ahn-kyah ZHAH-rahzh	Hungary	Table wine	White	Dry	***	F, P, & LM
Liebfraumilch	LEEB-frow-mil(kh)	Rhine, Ger.	Table wine	White	Med. dry	***	F, P, & LM
Lillet	lee-lay	France	Aperitif	White	Bitter	***	BD

NAME	PHONETIC SPELLING	SOURCE	TYPE	COLOR	TASTE	SERV. TEMP.	SERVE WITH
Mâcon	mah-coh(n)	Burgundy, Fr.	Table wine	White	Dry	***	F, P, & LM
Madeira	mah-DEHR-ah	Madeira	Fortified wine	Dark brown	Dry or sweet	*	Hosp
Málaga	MAH-lah-gah	Málaga, Sp.	Fortified wine	Dark brown	Sweet	*	Hosp
Malmsey	MALM-zee	Madeira	Fortified wine	Dark brown	Sweet	*	Hosp
Malvasia delle Lipari	mahl-vay-see ah deh-leh lee-PAH-ree	Sicily, It.	Fortified wine	Gold	Sweet	*	Hosp
Manzanilla	mahnt-sah-NEE-yah	Sanlúcar, Sp.	Sherry	Straw	Dry	**	Hosp
Maraschino	mah-rahs-KEE-no	Various	Liqueur	White	Sweet, cherry	*	AD
Marsala	mahr-SAH-lah	Sicily, It.	Dessert wine	Brown	Sweet	*	Hosp
Mastikha	MAHS-tee-kah	Greece	Liqueur	Cloudy white	Sweet	***	BD & H
Mavrodaphne	mahv-roh-DAHF-nee	Greece	Dessert wine	Red	Sweet	*	AD
Maximim Grünhauser Herrenberg	mahx-ee-meen GRUHN-hoyz-ehr HEHR-ehn-behrk	Moselle, Ger.	Table wine	White	Med. dry	***	F, P, & LM
May wine		Germany & U.S.	Table wine	White	Med. sweet	***	All foods
Mazis-Chambertin (GC)	mah-zee-shah(m)-behr-ta(n)	Côte de Nuits, Fr.	Table wine	Red	Dry	*	Ch, G, & RM
Médoc	may-dohk	Médoc, Fr.	Table wine	Red	Dry	*	Ch, G, & RM
Mercurey	mehr-kyu-ray	Chalonnais, Fr.	Table wine	Red	Dry	*	Ch, G, & RM
Meursault	muhr-soh	Côte de Beaune, Fr.	Table wine	White	Dry	***	F, P, & LM
Meursault-Charmes (PC)	muhr-soh-shahrm	Côte de Beaune, Fr.	Table wine	White	Dry	***	F, P, & LM
Meursault-Genevrières (PC)	muhr-soh-zhah(n)-eh-vryehr	Côte de Beaune, Fr.	Table wine	White	Dry	***	F, P, & LM
Meursault-Perrières (PC)	muhr-soh-pehr-yehr	Côte de Beaune, Fr.	Table wine	White	Dry	***	F, P, & LM
Mirabelle	mee-rah-bel	Alsace, Fr.	Plum brandy	White	Dry, plum	***	AD
Montilla	mohn-TEE-yah	Cordoba, Sp.	Aperitif wine	Straw	Dry	***	Hosp & BD
Montrachet, Le (GC)	luh moh(n)-rah-shay	Côte de Beaune, Fr.	Table wine	White	Dry	***	F, P, & LM
Moore's Diamond		New York State	Table wine	White	Dry	***	F, P, & LM
Moscatel de Setúbal	mohs-kah-tel duh seh-TOO-bahl	Portugal	Fortified wine	Gold	Sweet	***	AD
Moscatel de Sitges	mohs-kah-tel duh SEET-yes	Catalonia, Sp.	Fortified wine	Gold	Sweet	*	Hosp
Moscato di Salento	mohs-KAH-toh dee sah-LEN-toh	Apulia, It.	Fortified wine	Gold	Sweet	*	Hosp
Moscato Fior d'Arancio	mohs-KAH-toh fyor dah-RAHN-choh	Sicily, It.	Fortified wine	Gold	Sweet	*	Hosp
Moselblümchen	MOH-zel-bloom-shehn	Moselle, Ger.	Table wine	White	Med. dry	***	F, P, & LM
Moulin-à-Vent	moo-la(n)-ah-vah(n)	Beaujolais, Fr.	Table wine	Red	Dry	*	Ch, G, & RM
Muscadet	moos-kah-day	Loire, Fr.	Table wine	White	Dry	***	F, P, & LM
Muscatel	mus-kah-tel	California	Fortified wine	Gold	Sweet	*	AD
Musigny, Les (GC)	lay moo-see-nyee	Côte de Nuits, Fr.	Table wine	Red	Dry	*	Ch, G, & RM
Muskotaly	MOOSH-koh-tah-lee	Hungary	Table wine	White	Dry	***	F, P, & LM
Nackenheimer Rothenberg	nok-en-hie-mehr ROTH-ehn-behrk	Rheinhessen, Ger.	Table wine	White	Med. dry	***	F, P, & LM

Service temperature: *—Room temperature / **—Slightly chilled / ***—Cold
Serve with: AD—After dinner / BD—Before dinner / C—Cocktails / Ch—Cheese / F—Fish / Fr—Fruits / G—Game / H—Highballs / Hosp—Hospitality / LM—Light meats / P—Poultry / Pun—Punches / RM—Red meats / S—Straight
1855 classification: 1st—First growth / 2nd—Second growth, etc.; wines of Burgundy: GC—Grand Cru / PC—Premier Cru

NAME	PHONETIC SPELLING	SOURCE	TYPE	COLOR	TASTE	SERV. TEMP.	SERVE WITH
Nebbiolo	nehb-yoh-loh	Piedmont, It.	Table wine	Red	Dry	*	Ch, G, & RM
Neuchâtel	nuh-shah-tel	Switzerland	Table wine	White	Dry	***	F, P, & LM
Niersteiner Auflangen	neer-shtine-ehr OWF-lahng-en	Rheinhessen, Ger.	Table wine	White	Med. dry	***	F, P, & LM
Niersteiner Heiligenbaum	neer-shtine-ehr HIE-lee-gen-bowm	Rheinhessen, Ger.	Table wine	White	Med. dry	***	F, P, & LM
Niersteiner Hipping	neer-shtine-ehr HIP-ing	Rheinhessen, Ger.	Table wine	White	Med. dry	***	F, P, & LM
Niersteiner Oelberg	neer-shtine-ehr OHL-behrk	Rheinhessen, Ger.	Table wine	White	Med. dry	***	F, P, & LM
Niersteiner Rehbach	neer-shtine-ehr RAY-bahkh	Rheinhessen, Ger.	Table wine	White	Med. dry	***	F, P, & LM
Nuits-Saint-Georges	nwee-sa(n)-zhorzh	Côte de Nuits, Fr.	Table wine	Red	Dry	*	Ch, G, & RM
Nussberger	NOOS-behrk-ehr	Austria	Table wine	White	Dry	***	F, P, & LM
Oeil de Perdrix	oy duh pehr-dree	Burgundy, Fr., Switzerland, & U.S.	Sparkling or still wine	Pale pink	Med. dry	***	All foods
Oloroso	oh-loh-ROH-soh	Jerez, Sp.	Sherry	Gold	Sweet	*	Hosp
Opol	oh-POHL	Yugoslavia	Table wine	Light red	Dry	***	All foods
Oppenheimer Daubhaus	ah-pen-hie-mehr DOWB-howss	Rheinhessen, Ger.	Table wine	White	Med. dry	***	F, P, & LM
Oppenheimer Herrenberg	ah-pen-hie-mehr HEHR-en-behrk	Rheinhessen, Ger.	Table wine	White	Med. dry	***	F, P, & LM
Oppenheimer Kreuz	ah-pen-hie-mehr KROYTS	Rheinhessen, Ger.	Table wine	White	Med. dry	***	F, P, & LM
Oppenheimer Sackträger	ah-pen-hie-mehr ZAHK-tray-gehr	Rheinhessen, Ger.	Table wine	White	Med. dry	***	F, P, & LM
Orgeat	or-zhah	France	Syrup	Gray	Sweet, almond		C & Pun
Orvieto	orv-YEHT-oh	Umbria, It.	Table wine	White	Dry or semisweet	***	F, P, & LM
Othello	oh-THEL-loh	Cyprus	Table wine	Red	Dry	*	Ch, G, & RM
Ouzo	OO-zoh	Greece	Liqueur	Cloudy white	Sweet, licorice	***	H & C
Partom	PAR-tohm	Israel	Dessert wine	Red	Sweet	*	Desserts, AD
Pastis de Marseilles	pahs-tees duh mahr-say	Marseilles, Fr.	Liqueur	Cloudy white	Sweet, licorice	***	H & BD
Pavillon Blanc du Château Margaux	pah-vee-yoh(n) blah(n) doo shah-toh mahr-goh	Médoc, Fr.	Table wine	White	Dry	***	F, P, & LM
Peach liqueur		Various	Liqueur	Brown	Sweet, fruity	*	AD
Perlan	pehr-lah(n)	Switzerland	Table wine	White	Dry	***	F, P, & LM
Pernand-Vergelesses	pehr-nah(n)-vehrzh-uh-les	Côte de Beaune, Fr.	Table wine	Red	Dry	*	Ch, G, & RM
Pernod	pehr-noh	France	Liqueur	Green gold	Sweet, licorice	***	BD & H
Perry		England	Sparkling or still pear wine	Straw	Sweet	***	Desserts
Peter Heering		Denmark	Liqueur	Red	Sweet, cherry	*	AD
Pfaffstätter	FAHF-shtay-tehr	Austria	Table wine	White	Dry	***	F, P, & LM
Piesporter Goldtröpfchen	pees-port-ehr GOHLD-trehpf-shen	Moselle, Ger.	Table wine	White	Med. dry	***	F, P, & LM
Pineau des Charentes	pee-noh day shah-rah(n)t	Cognac, Fr.	Fortified wine	White	Sweet	***	BD
Pinot Blanc	pee-noh blah(n)	France & California	Table wine	White	Dry	***	F, P, & LM

NAME	PHONETIC SPELLING	SOURCE	TYPE	COLOR	TASTE	SERV. TEMP.	SERVE WITH
Pinot Chardonnay	pee-noh shahr-doh-nay	France & California	Table wine	White	Dry	***	F, P, & LM
Pinot Noir	pee-noh nwahr	Various	Table wine	Red	Dry	*	Ch, G, & RM
Pisco	PEES-koh	Pisco, Peru	Brandy	Gold	Dry	*	AD & Pun
Pommard	poh-mahr	Côte de Beaune, Fr.	Table wine	Red	Dry	*	Ch, G, & RM
Pommard-Clos-de-la-Commareine (PC)	poh-mahr-kloh-duh-lah-kuhm-ah-rehn	Côte de Beaune, Fr.	Table wine	Red	Dry	*	Ch, G, & RM
Pommard-Garollières (PC)	poh-mahr-gah-rohl-yehr	Côte de Beaune, Fr.	Table wine	Red	Dry	*	Ch, G, & RM
Pommard-Les-Epenots (PC)	poh-mahr-lay-zay-puh-noh	Côte de Beaune, Fr.	Table wine	Red	Dry	*	Ch, G, & RM
Pommard-Platière (PC)	poh-mahr-plah-tyehr	Côte de Beaune, Fr.	Table wine	Red	Dry	*	Ch, G, & RM
Pommard-Rugiens (PC)	poh-mahr-roo-zhyens	Côte de Beaune, Fr.	Table wine	Red	Dry	*	Ch, G, & RM
Port		U.S.	Fortified wine	Red	Sweet	*	Hosp
Porter		England & Ireland	Malt beverage	Dark brown	Bitter	**	Hosp
Porto		Portugal	Fortified wine	Red	Sweet	*	Hosp
Pouilly-Fuissé	pwee-yee-fwee-say	Mâconnais, Fr.	Table wine	White	Dry	***	F, P, & LM
Pouilly-Fumé	pwee-yee-foo-may	Loire, Fr.	Table wine	White	Med. sweet	***	F, P, & LM
Pousse-Café	poos-kah-fay	France	Liqueur	Various	Sweet	*	AD
Prunelle	proo-nel	France	Liqueur	Brown	Sweet, plum	*	AD
Puerto Rican rum		Puerto Rico	Spirit	White	Dry	***	C, H, Pun, & S
Puligny-Montrachet	poo-lee-nyee-moh(n)-rah-shay	Côte de Beaune, Fr.	Table wine	White	Dry	***	F, P, & LM
Quetsch	kwehtch	Alsace, Fr.	Plum brandy	White	Dry	***	AD
Quinquina	ka(n)-ka(n)-nah	France	Aperitif	Red or white	Bittersweet	***	BD
Raki	RAHK-ee	Turkey	Liqueur	White	Sweet, licorice	***	AD
Randersackerer Pfülben	rahn-dehr-zahk-ehr-ehr FOOL-ben	Franconia, Ger.	Table wine	White	Dry	***	F, P, & LM
Randersackerer Teufelskeller	rahn-dehr-zahk-ehr-ehr TOY-fels-kel-ehr	Franconia, Ger.	Table wine	White	Dry	***	F, P, & LM
Rauenthaler Baiken	row-en-tahl-ehr BY-ken	Rheingau, Ger.	Table wine	White	Med. dry	***	F, P, & LM
Rauenthaler Gehrn	row-en-tahl-ehr GAYRN	Rheingau, Ger.	Table wine	White	Med. dry	***	F, P, & LM
Rauenthaler Langenstück	row-en-tahl-ehr LAHNG-en-shtuk	Rheingau, Ger.	Table wine	White	Med. dry	***	F, P & LM
Rauenthaler Wülfen	row-en-tahl-ehr VIL-fen	Rheingau, Ger.	Table wine	White	Med. dry	***	F, P, & LM
Recioto Nobile	reh-chee-OH-toh NOH-bee-lay	Veneto, It.	Sparkling wine	Red	Sweet	***	All foods
Retsina	reht-SEE-nah	Greece	Table wine	White	Dry, resinated	***	All foods
Rhoditys	roh-DEE-tis	Greece	Table wine	Light red	Dry	***	All foods
Ricard	ree-kahr	France	Liqueur	Brown	Semisweet	***	BD
Richebourg, Le (GC)	luh reesh-boor	Côte de Nuits, Fr.	Table wine	Red	Dry	*	Ch, G, & RM
Riesling	REES-ling	Various	Table wine	White	Dry or sweet	***	Varies with sweetness

Service temperature: *—Room temperature / **—Slightly chilled / ***—Cold
Serve with: AD—After dinner / BD—Before dinner / C—Cocktails / Ch—Cheese / F—Fish / Fr—Fruits / G—Game /
     H—Highballs / Hosp—Hospitality / LM—Light meats / P—Poultry / Pun—Punches / RM—Red meats / S—Straight
1855 classification: 1st—First growth / 2nd—Second growth, etc.; *wines of Burgundy:* GC—*Grand Cru* / PC—*Premier Cru*

NAME	PHONETIC SPELLING	SOURCE	TYPE	COLOR	TASTE	SERV. TEMP.	SERVE WITH
Rioja	ree-OH-hah	Spain	Table wine	Red or white	Dry	* or ***	Varies with color
Rizling Szemelt	REEZ-ling tseh-mehlt	Hungary	Table wine	White	Dry	***	F, P, & LM
Romanée, La (GC)	lah roh-mah-nay	Côte de Nuits, Fr.	Table wine	Red	Dry	*	Ch, G, & RM
Romanée-Conti (GC)	roh-mah-nay-kah(n)-tee	Côte de Nuits, Fr.	Table wine	Red	Dry	*	Ch, G, & RM
Romanée-Saint-Vivant (GC)	roh-mah-nay-sa(n)-vee-vah(n)	Côte de Nuits, Fr.	Table wine	Red	Dry	*	Ch, G, & RM
Ruby Porto		Portugal	Fortified wine	Red	Sweet	*	Hosp
Ruchottes-Chambertin (GC)	roo-shot-shah(m)-behr-ta(n)	Côte de Nuits, Fr.	Table wine	Red	Dry	*	Ch, G, & RM
Rüdesheimer Berg Rottland	roo-des-hie-mehr behrk ROHT-lahnt	Rheingau, Ger.	Table wine	White	Med. dry	***	F, P, & LM
Rüdesheimer Berg Schlossberg	roo-des-hie-mehr behrk SHLAWS-behrk	Rheingau, Ger.	Table wine	White	Med. dry	***	F, P, & LM
Rüdesheimer Klosterberg	roo-des-hie-mehr KLOHS-tehr-behrk	Rheingau, Ger.	Table wine	White	Med. dry	***	F, P, & LM
Rum		Various	Spirit	Various	Slightly sweet	***	C, H, Pun, & S
Ruppertsberger Hoheburg	roo-pehrts-behrk-ehr HOH-heh-boorg	Rheinpfalz, Ger.	Table wine	White	Med. dry	***	F, P, & LM
Ruppertsberger Linsenbusch	roo-pehrts-behrk-ehr LEEN-zen-bush	Rheinpfalz, Ger.	Table wine	White	Med. dry	***	F, P, & LM
Ruppertsberger Nussbien	roo-pehrts-behrk-ehr NOOS-been	Rheinpfalz, Ger.	Table wine	White	Med. dry	***	F, P, & LM
Ruppertsberger Spiess	roo-pehrts-behrk-ehr SHPEES	Rheinpfalz, Ger.	Table wine	White	Med. dry	***	F, P, & LM
Saint-Amour	sa(n)-tah-moor	Beaujolais, Fr.	Table wine	Red	Dry	*	Ch, G, & RM
Saint-Émilion	sa(n)-tay-meel-yohn	Saint-Émilion, Fr.	Table wine	Red	Dry	*	Ch, G, & RM
Saint-Estèphe	sa(n)-tehs-tef	Médoc, Fr.	Table wine	Red	Dry	*	Ch, G, & RM
Saint-Julien	sa(n)-zhul-yen	Médoc, Fr.	Table wine	Red	Dry	*	Ch, G, & RM
Saint-Raphaël	sa(n)-rah-fah-el	France	Aperitif	Red	Bitter	***	BD
Saké	SAH-kee	Japan	Rice beer	White	Dry	100°F	All foods
Sancerre	sa(n)-sehr	Loire, Fr.	Table wine	White	Dry	***	F, P, & LM
Santenay	sa(n)-teh-nay	Côte de Beaune, Fr.	Table wine	Red	Dry	*	Ch, G, & RM
Sassella	sah-SAY-lah	Lombardy, It.	Table wine	Red	Dry	*	Ch, G, & RM
Saumur	soh-moor	Anjou, Fr.	Still or sparkling wine	White	Med. sweet	***	F, P, & LM
Sauterne	soh-tehrn	U.S.	Table wine	White	Dry	***	All foods
Sauternes	soh-tehrn	Sauternes, Fr.	Table wine	White	Sweet	***	Desserts
Sauvignon Blanc	soh-vee-nyoh(n) blah(n)	California & France	Table wine	White	Dry or sweet	***	F, P, & LM
Schaumwein	SHOHM-vine	Germany	Sparkling wine	White	Dry or sweet	***	All foods
Scheidam (gin)	SKEE-dahm	Holland	Spirit	White	Dry	***	S & H
Schloss-Böckelheimer-Mühlberg	shlawss-BUHK-el-hie-mehr-mewl-behrk	Nahe, Ger.	Table wine	White	Dry	***	F, P, & LM
Schloss Johannisberg	shlawss yoh-hahn-is-behrk	Rheingau, Ger.	Table wine	White	Med. dry	***	F, P, & LM
Schloss Vollrads	shlawss FAWL-rahds	Rheingau, Ger.	Table wine	White	Med. dry	***	F, P, & LM
Scotch whisky		Scotland	Spirit	Brown	Dry, smoky	* or ***	C, H, & S
Scuppernong		Southeastern U.S.	Table wine	White	Sweet	***	All foods
Sekt	sehkt	Germany	Sparkling wine	White	Dry or sweet	***	All foods

NAME	PHONETIC SPELLING	SOURCE	TYPE	COLOR	TASTE	SERV. TEMP.	SERVE WITH
Sémillon	seh-mee-yoh(n)	California	Table wine	White	Dry or sweet	***	All foods
Sercial	SIR-shahl	Madeira	Fortified wine	Gold	Med. dry	**	Hosp
Sharir	shah-REER	Israel	Dessert wine	Gold	Med. dry	*	Hosp
Sherry		Jerez, Sp., & various	Fortified wine	Amber	Dry to sweet	* or **	Hosp
Sidra	SEE-drah	Northern Spain	Sparkling cider	Gold	Sweet, apple	***	Hosp
Slivovitz	SHLIV-oh-wits	Various	Plum brandy	Brown	Dry, plum	*	AD
Sloe gin		England & U.S.	Liqueur	Red	Sweet, astringent	* or ***	AD & C
Soave	suah-veh	Veneto, It.	Table wine	White	Dry	***	F, P, & LM
Somlói Furmint	SHOHM-loy ye foor-mint	Somlói, Hungary	Table wine	White	Dry	***	F, P, & LM
Spanish brandy		Spain	Brandy	Brown	Med. dry	*	AD
Sparkling Burgundy		Burgundy, Fr., & U.S.	Sparkling wine	Red or white	Med. sweet	***	All foods
Steinberger	SHTINE-behrk-ehr	Rheingau, Ger.	Table wine	White	Med. dry	***	F, P, & LM
Stout		England & Ireland	Malt beverage	Dark brown	Bitter	**	Hosp
Strega	STRAY-gah	Benevento, It.	Liqueur	Gold	Sweet	*	AD
Suze	sooz	France	Aperitif	Brown	Bittersweet	***	BD
Swedish Punsch		Sweden	Liqueur	Yellow	Sweet, rummy	***	AD
Sweet Catawba		Ohio & New York State	Table wine	White	Sweet	***	Desserts
Sylvaner	zil-vah-nehr	Alsace, Fr., & Germany	Table wine	White	Med. dry	***	All foods
Szilvanyi Zold	ZIL-vahn-yuh zuhld	Hungary	Table wine	White	Med. sweet	***	F, P, & LM
Tâche, La (GC)	lah tahsh	Côte de Nuits, Fr.	Table wine	Red	Dry	*	Ch, G, & RM
Tavel	tah-vel	Rhône, Fr.	Table wine	Pink	Dry	***	All foods
Tawny Porto		Portugal	Fortified wine	Red	Sweet	*	Hosp
Tequila	teh-KEE-lah	Jalisco, Mex.	Spirit	White	Dry	*	C & S
Tia Maria	tee-ah mah-REE-ah	Jamaica	Liqueur	Brown	Sweet, coffee	*	AD
Tokaji Aszú	TOHK-ah ye ah-zoo	Hungary	Dessert wine	Amber	Sweet	**	Hosp & AD
Tokaji Szamorodni	TOHK-ah ye SAH-mah-rohd-nee	Hungary	Dessert wine	White	Med. dry	***	Hosp
Topaz	TOH-paz	Israel	Dessert wine	Gold	Sweet	*	Desserts & AD
Trakya	TRAHK-yah	Turkey	Table wine	White	Dry	***	F, P, & LM
Triple Sec		Various	Liqueur	White	Sweet, orange	*	AD
Trittenheimer Altärchen	trit-en-hie-mehr AHLT-ehr-shen	Moselle, Ger.	Table wine	White	Med. dry	***	F, P, & LM
Trittenheimer Apotheke	trit-en-hie-mehr ah-poh-TAY-kuh	Moselle, Ger.	Table wine	White	Med. dry	***	F, P, & LM
Tsingtao	TSEENG-tow	China	Aperitif	Red or white	Dry	* or ***	BD
Ürziger Würzgarten	oor-tsee-gehr VURTZ-gahr-ten	Moselle, Ger.	Table wine	White	Med. dry	***	F, P, & LM
Valdepeñas	vahl-day-PAYN-yahs	La Mancha, Sp.	Table wine	Red	Dry	*	Ch, G, & RM
Valpolicella	vahl-poh-lee-CHAY-lah	Veneto, It.	Table wine	Red	Dry	*	Ch, G, & RM
Valtellina	vahl-tel-LEE-nah	Lombardy, It.	Table wine	Red	Dry	*	Ch, G, & RM
Van Der Hum	VAN der huhm	South Africa	Liqueur	Gold	Sweet	*	AD
Verdelho	vehr-DEL-yo	Madeira	Fortified wine	White	Sweet	*	AD & Hosp
Verdicchio	vehr-DEEK-yoh	Marches, It.	Table wine	White	Dry	***	Shellfish
Vernaccia	vehr-NAH-chah	Italy	Table wine	White	Sweet	***	Fr

Service temperature: *—Room temperature / **—Slightly chilled / ***—Cold
Serve with: AD—After dinner / BD—Before dinner / C—Cocktails / Ch—Cheese / F—Fish / Fr—Fruits / G—Game /
       H—Highballs / Hosp—Hospitality / LM—Light meats / P—Poultry / Pun—Punches / RM—Red meats / S—Straight
1855 classification: 1st—First growth / 2nd—Second growth, etc.; wines of Burgundy: GC—Grand Cru / PC—Premier Cru

NAME	PHONETIC SPELLING	SOURCE	TYPE	COLOR	TASTE	SERV. TEMP.	SERVE WITH
Villányi-Pècs	VIL-ahn-yee-pehch	Hungary	Table wine	Red	Dry	*	G & RM
Vinho Verde	VEE-nyoh vehr-deh	Portugal	Table wine	Red or white	Dry	* or ***	Varies with color
Vin (Vino) Santo	veen (VEE-noh) SAHN-toh	Italy	Table wine	White	Sweet	***	All foods
Vodka	VAHD-kah	Various	Spirit	White	Dry	***	C, H, & S
Volnay	vuhl-nay	Côte de Beaune, Fr.	Table wine	Red	Dry	*	Ch, G, & RM
Vöslau	FOYS-low	Austria	Table wine	Red	Dry	*	Ch, G, & RM
Vosne-Romanée	vohn-roh-mah-nay	Côte de Nuits, Fr.	Table wine	Red	Dry	*	Ch, G, & RM
Vouvray	voo-vreh	Loire, Fr.	Table wine	White	Med. sweet or sweet	***	Fr
Wachenheimer Schlossberg	vah(kh)-en-hie-mehr shlawss-behrk	Rheinpfalz, Ger.	Table wine	White	Med. dry	***	F, P, & LM
Waldracher Hubertusberg	vahlt-rah(kh)-ehr uh-BEHR-toos-behrk	Ruwer, Ger.	Table wine	White	Med. dry	***	F, P, & LM
Wehlener Nonnenberg	VAY-len-ehr NAWN-en-behrk	Moselle, Ger.	Table wine	White	Med. dry	***	F, P, & LM
Wehlener Sonnenuhr	VAY-len-ehr ZAWN-en-oor	Moselle, Ger.	Table wine	White	Med. dry	***	F, P, & LM
Whisky	WISS-kee	Various	Spirit	Brown	Dry, rich	* or ***	C, H, Pun, & S
White Porto		Portugal	Aperitif	Gold	Sweet	*	Hosp & BD
Wiltinger Schlangengraben	vilt-ing-ehr SHLAHNG-en-grah-ben	Moselle, Ger.	Table wine	White	Med. dry	***	F, P, & LM
Wisniowka	vish-nyoof-kah	Poland	Liqueur	Red	Sweet, cherry	**	AD
Würzburger Innere Leiste	vurtz-behrk-ehr IN-ehr-eh LICE-teh	Franconia, Ger.	Table wine	White	Dry	***	F, P, & LM
Würzburger Stein	vurtz-behrk-ehr SHTINE	Franconia, Ger.	Table wine	White	Dry	***	F, P, & LM
Zeller Schwarze Katz	tsel-ehr SHVAHRT-seh kahts	Moselle, Ger.	Table wine	White	Med. dry	***	F, P, & LM
Zeltinger Himmelreich	tselt-ing-ehr HIM-mel-rie(kh)	Moselle, Ger.	Table wine	White	Med. dry	***	F, P, & LM
Zeltinger Schlossberg	tselt-ing-ehr SHLAWSS-behrk	Moselle, Ger.	Table wine	White	Med. dry	***	F, P, & LM
Zeltinger Sonnenuhr	tselt-ing-ehr ZAWN-en-oor	Moselle, Ger.	Table wine	White	Med. dry	***	F, P, & LM
Zinfandel	TZIN-fan-del	California	Table wine	Red	Dry	*	Ch, G, & RM
Zubrowka	zoo-BROHV-kah	Russia & Poland	Flavored spirit	Straw	Dry	***	C, H, & S

APPENDIX B
VINTAGE INFORMATION —
FRANCE, ITALY, GERMANY, PORTUGAL,
AND THE UNITED STATES

Every vintage chart is a compilation of many opinions that tends to even out the extremes. There are often exceptional bottles in average years and average bottles in excellent years. The vintage chart must always be considered the indicator of the general quality.

FRENCH AND GERMAN VINTAGE CHART

	'59	'60	'61	'62	'63	'64	'65	'66	'67	'68	'69	'70	'71	'72	'73	'74	'75	'76
Red Bordeaux	9C	6D	10C	7C	2D	8C	X	9B	7C	X	7C	9B	8B	5B	6B	6A	9A	7A
Dry White Bordeaux	X	X	X	X	X	9	X	8	X	X	5	9	9	7	7	7	8	7
Sweet White Bordeaux	9	X	10	9	X	X	X	7	7	X	7	8	9	6	6	6	9	6
Red Côte d'Or Burgundy	9D	X	10C	8D	X	9C	X	9C	5C	X	10B	7C	10B	7B	7B	7B	5C	10A
Red Beaujolais Burgundy	X	X	X	X	X	X	X	X	X	X	X	8D	9D	7C	7C	6C	5B	10B
White Burgundy	X	X	X	7D	X	8D	X	10D	7D	X	10C	9C	10C	7C	7C	7C	9B	7B
Loire	X	X	X	X	X	X	X	X	X	X	X	10	9	6	9	8	9	8
Rhône	8	8	9	8	X	8	7	9	9	6	9	10	8	8	7	6	6	9
Rhine	10	X	8	X	X	9	X	9	7	X	9	9	10	7	7	6	9	10
Moselle	9	X	7	X	X	10	X	8	X	X	8	7	9	6	7	6	9	10

Number ratings:

1 to 10 relate to potential quality when fully mature. A mature wine of modest rating should be preferred to an immature wine whatever its potential quality (10 is finest grade).

Letter code for red Bordeaux and Burgundy:

A = Not at present ready for drinking
B = Can be drunk now but development still to come
C = Fully ready for drinking
D = Approach with caution; could be good, but could be past best

The format of this vintage chart is based on charts developed by Austin, Nichols & Co.

NOTES ON RED BORDEAUX VINTAGES

1945 Very small yield, but quality superb. Excellent to drink now, but will continue to develop.

1946 Generally very light wines.

1947 A great vintage. Big, fine wines that are long lived. Some are starting to decline.

1948 A good vintage that was overshadowed by those of '47 and '49.

1949 An important vintage although the quantity was somewhat below average. Very fine wines.

1950 Abundant vintage. Quality good. Now old.

1951 Small yield, but wines were better than average. Now old.

1952 Wines somewhat hard and slow in developing, long lived. In general a great year.

1953 Big vintage produced under optimum conditions. Wines much softer and earlier developing than the '52s. They are still excellent.

1954 Small crop. Some useful wines but on the whole thin and short lived.

1955 Smaller vintage than '54, but the wines have body. Many good wines and some great wines were produced.

1956 A very small vintage because of severe frosts. Very light, thin wines.

1957 Quantity small. Quality fairly good. Quite hard wines that are now starting to soften.

1958 Quantity small. Light, pleasant, drinkable wines. Now old.

1959 Good harvest. Quality excellent. On the whole big, balanced wines that have developed quickly and are now fully mature.

1960 Better than average quantity. Wines somewhat light and not long lived.

1961 Very small vintage because of rains at time of flowering. Excellent quality. Wines show concentration and are well balanced. These will be very long lived.

1962 Better than average quantity. Well-made wines, pleasant, soft. At their peak now.

1963 Quality generally poor. A few pleasant light wines were produced.

1964 Rains at harvest time produced wines of variable quality. In Saint-Émilion and Pomerol and in those parts of the Médoc that harvested early some very good wines were made.

1965 A rainy summer produced thin wines.

1966 An excellent year. Big, full-bodied, well-balanced wines. Will be long lived.

1967 A larger harvest than in '66. The wines are lighter than those of '66, maturing earlier, but have charm and elegance.

1968 Generally a very poor year.

1969 Light wines that are generally pleasant.

1970 Very good quantity. Quality excellent. Big wines with character. Will be long lived.

1971 Quantity small but quality excellent. Big, concentrated wines, in many cases comparable to '70s.

1972 Light wines. Many lack fruit and charm. Some pleasant wines. Not long lived.

1973 Very abundant quantity. Variable quality. Some good light wines but will not be long lived.

1974 Good quantity. Quality average. Sound wines that will mature quickly.

1975 Small quantity, less than half that of '74. Quality appears to be very good. Wines have high alcohol and tannin and should be long lived.

1976 Large quantity. Wines are rich and dark with a great deal of fruit. Lack tannin and consequently will mature early.

NOTES ON WHITE BORDEAUX VINTAGES

1959 Sauternes excellent—sweet, rich, and luscious. Dry wines were very good.

1960 Dry wines were very good. Sweet wines poor.

1961 Some excellent sweet wines produced. These should be long lived. Dry whites were very good to excellent. High in alcohol.

1962 Very good for sweet wines, many excellent. Good to very good for dry wines, which are now too old.

1963 Fair for dry wines, poor for sweet.

1964 Some good dry wines were produced. Very poor sweet wines.

1965 Very poor year for Sauternes. Dry wines were fair to good.

1966 Some very good sweet wines were produced. The dry wines were good to very good.

1967 Very good Sauternes—sweet, rich, and luscious. Some very good dry wines were produced.

1968 Generally poor year for sweet and dry wines.

1969 Good dry wines. Sweet wines are variable, but generally good.

1970 An excellent year. Sauternes are rich and elegant, will live long. Graves are well balanced and elegant.

1971 Excellent vintage for Sauternes—elegant, outstanding, long-lived wines. Dry wines also excellent—good depth and character.

1972 Quality is variable. Dry wines generally better than the sweet.

1973 Very large quantity. Dry wines better than the sweet.

1974 Abundant quantity. Quality only fair.

1975 Excellent, luscious sweet wines. Dry wines also excellent and high in alcohol.

1976 September rain washed away the noble rot, and few quality sweet wines were produced. Some good dry wines, high in acidity, were made from grapes harvested before the rain.

NOTES ON RED AND WHITE BURGUNDY VINTAGES

1945 Small quantity. A great year. Slow maturing.

1946 Quick-maturing wines.

1947 Wines made with sufficient care were of excellent quality.

1948 A very good vintage.

1949 Excellent vintage.

1950 Above average quantity. Light red wines. White wines good.

1951 Poor quality.

1952 Good, sturdy wines of fine color and bouquet.

1953 Very fine, balanced wines of finesse, body, and flavor.

1954 Very large quantity. Quality variable. Some good wines produced.

1955 Good, well-rounded wines.

1956 Very poor quality. Light wines.

1957 Fair quantity. Good wines of fine color and good body.

1958 Reds fair—some wines have good, fruity flavor. Whites were good.

1959 A great vintage in all respects. One of the best of the century. White wines tend to be overrich.

1960 Fair.

1961 Excellent quality for both red and white wines. Grand Cru reds still excellent for present consumption.

1962 Quality almost up to 1961 wines.

1963 Large quantity. Quality variable.

1964 Large quantity. Well-made wines. Early maturing.

1965 Poor quality.

1966 Abundant quantity. Quality was good. Big, full wines. Some fast-maturing wines produced; others will live a long time.

1967 Generally light and fast-maturing wines.

1968   Generally light wines. Whites better than reds.

1969   Low quantity. A great year. Deeply colored, big, full wines. Reds matured faster than expected.

1970   Good quantity. Good quality. Fast-maturing wines.

1971   Small quantity. Full-bodied, concentrated wines. Good color, long lived. Perhaps comparable to the '69s.

1972   Good quantity. Wines somewhat hard, but generally good quality. Will be long lived.

1973   Very large quantity. Variable quality. Many light wines produced. Fast maturing.

1974   A long period of heavy rains lowered the quality.

1975   Quantity small. With good grape selection some good reds were made. Whites tend to be better than the reds, with Chablis producing excellent, full wines.

1976   Average quantity. Very hot summer required early harvest. Red wines are dark in color, have good alcohol, and are well balanced. They have exceptional potential and should be long lived. Some whites may lack acidity but are very full and round.

NOTES ON CHAMPAGNE VINTAGES*

1961   Good quantity. Top quality, light and delicate wines.

1962   Good quantity. Excellent quality. Wines are full bodied.

1963   Not a vintage year.

1964   Good quantity. Excellent quality, very full-bodied wines.

1965   Not a vintage year.

1966   Very good quality, well-balanced wines.

1967   Good quality when grapes carefully selected by the producer.

1968   Not a vintage year.

1969   Small quantity. Good quality, full-bodied wines.

1970   Large quantity. Good quality, light, fragrant wines.

1971   Very small quantity. Very good quality, full-bodied wines.

1972   Not a vintage year.

1973   Not a vintage year.

1974   Not a vintage year.

1975   Large quantity. Good quality, very full wines.

1976   Large quantity. Good quality, very full wines. Unusual to have two such years in a row.

*Some houses may produce a vintage Champagne in years when the majority of houses do not. The decision is up to each producer. When vintage wines are not produced, the wines of that year are used to replenish blending stocks, so that each house may maintain its unique style and continuity.

NOTES ON RHÔNE VINTAGES

1945
1949
1952   } All long-lived, full-bodied wines.
1955
1957

1959   Selectivity needed in choosing wines.

1960   A very good year.

1961   Good wines produced.

1962   Quantity small. Quality fair.

1963   Quantity very small. Quality poor.

1964   Quality average.

1965   One of the few regions to produce good wines during this year.

1966   An excellent year. Long-lived wines.

1967   Well-balanced, long-lived wines.

1968   Some pleasant, drinkable wines were produced.

1969 Quantity small. Variable quality. Excellent in the north, good in the south.

1970 Large quantity. Excellent quality. Long-lived wines with great potential.

1971 Small quantity. Very good quality. Full body and high alcohol. Need some time.

1972 Big, full-bodied wines. Need time to soften.

1973 Enormous quantity. Most areas suffered from overproduction. Most wines pleasant and light. Some good wines produced.

1974 In general, good-quality wines.

1975 Limited quantity and variable quality in the northern Rhône. Good quantity as well as good quality in the south.

1976 Quantity good. Very good quality because of very warm growing conditions. Wines should be long lived with high alcohol and very full body.

NOTES ON ALSATIAN VINTAGES*

1959 One of the finest Alsatian vintages. Well-balanced wines full of fragrance. Elegant and rich.

1960 Quite good.

1961 Very good vintage. Excellent wines.

1962 Not quite as fine as those of '61.

1963 Average quality. Short-lived wines.

1964 Good quality.

1965 Poor quality.

1966 Excellent quality.

1967 Excellent vintage.

1968 Poor quality.

1969 Good quality. Full-bodied wines.

1970 Very large quantity. Quality good.

1971 Excellent quality. Wines high in alcohol.

1972 Quality fair.

1973 Quantity very large. Quality good.

1974 Quality good.

1975 Quantity about average. Quality good. Well-balanced wines.

1976 Average quantity, with above average amount of Beerenauslesen produced. Excellent quality with delicate bouquet and superior elegance.

*Wines older than those of 1969 are no longer at their prime. The chart indicates the quality of the vintage at that time.

ITALIAN VINTAGE CHART*

	'61	'62	'63	'64	'65	'66	'67	'68	'69	'70	'71	'72	'73	'74	'75
Barbaresco (Piedmont)	9B	8B	2D	10B	6B	2D	8A	6C	7A	8B	10A	2D	6C	9A	6A
Barbera (Piedmont)	8B	7B	4D	9B	5B	2D	7A	6C	7A	7B	9A	2D	5C	8A	5A
Bardolino (Veneto)	6D	9D	2D	8D	6D	7D	7D	7D	9C	7D	8D	5D	7C	7C	8B
Barolo (Piedmont)	10B	8C	3D	10B	8B	4D	8A	6C	7A	8A	10A	2D	6C	9A	6A
Brunello di Montalcino	6D	7C	4D	10A	6C	8B	8A	6B	7B	10A	9A	4D	6B	7B	9A
Cabernet Trentino	6D	4D	6D	10A	2D	6D	6D	4D	10B	10B	8B	4C	4C	4C	6A
Castel del Monte (Apulia)	6D	4D	4D	4D	10D	8D	6D	10C	8D	6D	6D	6D	8A	8A	8A
Chianti (Tuscany)	4D	8C	2D	6C	4C	4C	6B	8B	8B	8A	8A	4D	4C	8B	8A
Chianti Classico Riserva	5D	9C	2D	9C	6C	6C	9B	9B	9B	9A	10A	5D	5C	9B	9A
Corvo Rosso (Sicily)	—	—	—	—	—	—	—	—	—	—	9B	8B	8B	8B	8B
Frecciarossa (Lombardy)	10C	10C	6D	10C	6C	6C	10B	8C	10B	10B	8B	8B	8B	8B	8A
Gattinara (Piedmont)	8B	6B	2D	10B	6B	4D	6A	8C	8A	8A	4C	2D	4C	10A	6A
Ghemme (Piedmont)	6D	8B	2D	8C	4D	3D	6B	6D	6A	8A	8A	6C	8C	10A	6A
Inferno (Lombardy)	8D	4D	4D	10C	2D	4D	6C	4C	8B	8B	8A	4B	6A	6A	7A
Sassella (Lombardy)	8D	4D	4D	10B	2D	4D	6C	4C	8B	8B	8A	4A	6A	4A	6A
Sforsato (Lombardy)	8D	4D	4D	10B	2D	4D	6C	4C	8B	8B	8A	4A	6A	4A	6A
Torgiano (Umbria)	6D	8D	6D	6C	6C	9C	8C	9B	8C	8B	9B	8B	8B	7B	7B
Valpolicella (Veneto)	8D	8D	4D	8D	4D	7D	8D	7D	8C	8C	9C	6C	7C	7C	8A
Valpolicella Recioto Amarone (Veneto)	7C	8B	6C	10B	5D	7C	8B	7C	9B	7B	8A	6B	7A	9A	9A
Vino Nobile di Montepulciano	6D	8C	2D	8C	2D	6C	10B	8B	8B	10A	6A	4D	8C	6B	10A

*All Italian white wines should be consumed while young.

Number ratings:
1-2 = Less than average
3-4 = Average
5-6 = Good
7-8 = Very good
9-10 = Exceptional

Letter ratings:
A = Best if aged further
B = Can improve with more aging
C = Ready for drinking
D = Probably past its prime

NOTES ON GERMAN VINTAGES

(1921 was considered one of the greatest vintages ever.)

1953   A great vintage. The fine Auslesen, Beerenauslesen, and Trockenbeerenauslesen are long lived.

1954   Generally fair wines were produced.

1955   Small quantity. Variable quality. Some good wines were made.

1956   In general poor quality.

1957   Quantity below average. Many good wines were made.

1958   Fairly large vintage. Wines were generally good.

1959   A fine vintage in all respects. Wines very rich.

1960   One of the largest vintages. Quality fair to good.

1961   Quantity fair. Wines on the whole were excellent.

1962   Quantity below normal. Quality generally good, especially in the finer vineyards.

1963   Average quality. Wines were for early consumption.

1964   Excellent vintage. Full-bodied wines were produced. Spätlesen and Auslesen still good.

1965   Large quantity. Average quality.

1966   Very good quality. Spätlesen and Auslesen show some elegance.

1967   Produced extraordinary Auslesen, Beerenauslesen, and Trockenbeerenauslesen with abundant fruit. Wines made from grapes picked earlier are good in quality.

1968   Some useful, good-quality wines were produced.

1969   Good quality. Good fruit and acidity.

1970   Very good quantity. Good, light, attractive wines.

1971   A great vintage. *Edelfäule* produced wines of great concentration and depth. Spätlesen and higher will be very long lived.

1972   Generally light, attractive wines. Rhine wines better than Moselles.

1973   Extremely large quantity. Fruity and well-balanced wines best consumed young.

1974   Small quantity. Agreeable but undistinguished.

1975   Average quantity. Great vintage. Extremely high proportion of top-category wines. Almost no Tafelwein was produced.

1976   Small quantity. Long, hot summer produced predominantly Spätlesen and higher-quality wines, but some lack acid.

NOTES ON PORTO VINTAGES

Vintage Porto is made only in fine years, and even then not every producer makes a Vintage Porto. The number of producers who declare a vintage has ranged from two (in 1931) to thirty (in 1927). The average number of producers who declare a vintage is fourteen.

1945   Classic vintage; wines are rich with good color and body.

1947   Good year; wines are fruity and delicate.

1948   Wines are full and powerful with depth.

1950   Lighter wines, faster to mature.

1955   Good year; wines are long lasting and full.

1958   Lighter wines, more delicate.

1960   Good quality, not too dark, can be drunk now.

1963   Big, fat wines, good fruity bouquet, dark color. Drink in 1980s.

1966   Fresh and fruity, not as big as '63s. Drink from 1980 on.

1967   Borderline vintage, few declared; on the light side.

1970   Superb year, good color and body. Drink in the 1990s.

1975   Exceptional year; wines are very dark and intense.

CALIFORNIA VINTAGE CHART

(Cabernet Sauvignon, Zinfandel, Pinot Noir, and Chardonnay)

	'51	'52	'53	'54	'55	'56	'57	'58	'59	'60	'61	'62	'63
Cabernet Sauvignon	10	8	8	8	8+	8	8+	9+	9+	9+	7+	7	6+
Zinfandel	10	8	8	8	8+	8	8+	9+	8	9	7+	7	6+
Pinot Noir	7	7	7	7	7+	7	7	9	7	7	7+	7	6+
Chardonnay*	—	—	—	—	—	—	—	—	—	—	—	—	—

	'64	'65	'66	'67	'68	'69	'70	'71	'72	'73	'74	'75
Cabernet Sauvignon	8+	8+	8+	8	9+	8+	10	9	6+	9+	10	9
Zinfandel	8+	8+	8+	8	9+	8+	10	8	6+	9+	10	9
Pinot Noir	8+	7	8	7+	9+	8+	7+	8	6+	9	9+	8+
Chardonnay*	—	—	—	—	—	—	9+	8	7	10	10	8

6 = Fair
7 = Average
8 = Good
9 = Very Good
10 = Exceptional

*Other California white wines are best when consumed within five years of bottling.

APPENDIX C
THE CLASSIFIED GROWTHS OF BORDEAUX
OFFICIAL CLASSIFICATION OF 1855

The Official Classification of 1855 listed the red wines of the Médoc and the sweet white wines of the Sauternes in order of quality. The one exception was the inclusion of Château Haut-Brion, from Graves, among the first growths of Médoc. The following list, which uses the current spelling of the names of some of the châteaux, also lists some châteaux that were not originally part of the 1855 classification but which came into existence when a château that had been originally listed was divided up. These wines are shown bracketed, signifying that they were once a single château.

Château Mouton-Rothschild, which is now listed as a first growth, was listed as a second growth from 1855 to 1973, although it always brought prices commensurate with those of the first growths.

MEDOC WINES

FIRST GROWTHS
Château Lafite-Rothschild
Château Margaux
Château Latour
Château Haut-Brion
Château Mouton-Rothschild

SECOND GROWTHS
Château Rausan-Ségla
Château Rauzan-Gassies
{ Château Léoville-Lascases
{ Château Léoville-Poyferré
{ Château Léoville-Barton
Château Durfort-Vivens
Château Gruaud-Larose
Château Lascombes
Château Brane-Cantenac
{ Château Pichon-Longueville, Baron de Pichon
{ Château Pichon-Longueville, Comtesse de
    Lalande
Château Ducru-Beaucaillou
Château Cos d'Estournel
Château Montrose

THIRD GROWTHS
Château Kirwan
Château d'Issan
Château Lagrange
Château Langoa-Barton
Château Giscours
Château Malescot-Saint-Exupéry
{ Château Boyd-Cantenac
{ Château Cantenac-Brown
Château Palmer
Château La Lagune

Château Desmirail
Château Calon-Ségur
Château Ferrière
Château Marquis d'Alesme-Becker

FOURTH GROWTHS
Château Saint-Pierre
Château Talbot
Château Branaire-Ducru
Château Duhart-Milon-Rothschild
Château Pouget
Château La Tour-Carnet
Château Lafon-Rochet
Château Beychevelle
Château Prieuré-Lichine
Château Marquis de Terme

FIFTH GROWTHS
Château Pontet-Canet
{ Château Batailley
{ Château Haut-Batailley
{ Château Grand-Puy-Lacoste
{ Château Grand-Puy-Ducasse
Château Lynch-Bages
Château Lynch-Moussas
Château Dauzac
Château Mouton-Baron-Philippe
Château du Tertre
Château Haut-Bages-Libéral
Château Pédesclaux
Château Belgrave
Château Camensac
Château Cos-Labory
Château Clerc-Milon-Mondon
Château Croizet-Bages
Château Cantemerle

SAUTERNES (INCLUDING BARSAC)

FIRST SUPERIOR GROWTH
Château d'Yquem

FIRST GROWTHS
Château La Tour-Blanche
{ Château Lafaurie-Peyraguey
{ Clos Haut-Peyraguey
Château de Rayne-Vigneau
Château Suduiraut
Château Coutet
Château Climens
Château Guiraud
Château Rieussec
{ Château Rabaud-Promis
{ Château Sigalas-Rabaud

SECOND GROWTHS
Château Myrat
{ Château Doisy-Daene
{ Château Doisy-Dubroca
{ Château Doisy-Védrines
Château d'Arche
Château Filhot
{ Château Broustet
{ Château Nairac
Château Caillou
Château Suau
Château de Malle
{ Château Romer (R. Farges, prop.)
{ Château Romer (A. du Hayot, prop.)
{ Château Lamothe
{ Château Lamothe-Bergey

OFFICIAL CLASSIFICATIONS OF OTHER BORDEAUX

The wines of Graves and Saint-Émilion were not classified until 1953 and 1955, respectively. The 1955 list still holds for Saint-Émilion, but the Graves list was redone and finalized in 1959. All of these wines are listed in alphabetical order, with the exception of Châteaux Ausone and Cheval-Blanc, which are listed ahead of the other Premiers Grands Crus Classés of Saint-Émilion. In the list of the classified wines of the Graves, Château Haut-Brion appears in Crus Classés—Red, even though it remains listed as a first growth of the 1855 classification.

The wines of Pomerol have never been officially classified. Château Pétrus, however, is considered to be an outstanding growth, equal to the first growths of the Médoc. The rest of the listed Pomerol wines are those generally considered to be the best wines after Château Pétrus.

GRAVES
1959 Official Classification

CRUS CLASSÉS—RED
Château Bouscaut
Château Carbonnieux
Domaine de Chevalier
Château Fieuzal
Château Haut-Bailly
Château Haut-Brion
Château La Mission Haut Brion
Château La Tour Haut Brion
Château La Tour-Martillac
Château Malartic-Lagravière
Château Olivier

Château Pape-Clément
Château Smith-Haut-Lafitte

CRUS CLASSÉS—WHITE
Château Bouscaut
Château Carbonnieux
Domaine de Chevalier
Château Couhins
Château La Tour-Martillac
Château Laville Haut Brion
Château Malartic-Lagravière
Château Olivier

SAINT-ÉMILION
1955 Official Classification

PREMIERS GRANDS CRUS CLASSÉS
Château Ausone
Château Cheval-Blanc

Château Beauséjour (Lagrosse, prop.)
Château Beauséjour (Fagouet, prop.)
Château Belair

Château Canon
Château Figeac
Château La Gaffelière
Château Magdelaine
Château Pavie
Château Trottevieille
Clos Fourtet

GRANDS CRUS CLASSÉS

Château L'Angélus
Château L'Arrosée
Château Balestard-La Tonnelle
Château Bellevue
Château Bergat
Château Cadet-Bon
Château Cadet-Piola
Château Canon-La Gaffelière
Château Cap-de-Mourlin
Château Chapelle-Madeleine
Château Chauvin
Château Corbin (Giraud, prop.)
Château Corbin (Michotte, prop.)
Château Coutet
Château Croque-Michotte
Château Curé-Bon
Château Fonplégade
Château Fonroque
Château Franc-Mayne
Château Grand-Barrail-Lamarzelle-Figeac
Château Grand-Corbin-Despagne
Château Grand-Corbin-Pécresse
Château Grand-Mayne
Château Grand-Pontet
Château Grandes-Murailles
Château Guadet-Saint-Julien
Château Jean-Faure
Château La Carte
Château La Clotte
Château La Cluzière
Château La Couspaude

Château La Dominique
Château Larcis-Ducasse
Château Lamarzelle
Château Larmande
Château Laroze
Château Lassere
Château La Tour-du-Pin-Figeac (Bélivier, prop.)
Château La Tour-du-Pin-Figeac (Moueix, prop.)
Château La Tour-Figeac
Château Le Châtelet
Château Le Couvent
Château Le Prieuré
Château Mauvezin
Château Moulin-du-Cadet
Château Pavie-Décesse
Château Pavie-Macquin
Château Pavillon-Cadet
Château Petit-Faurie-de-Souchard
Château Petit-Faurie-de-Soutard
Château Ripeau
Château Sansonnet
Château Saint-Georges-Côte-Pavie
Château Soutard
Château Tertre-Daugay
Château Trimoulet
Château Trois-Moulins
Château Troplong-Mondot
Château Villemaurine
Château Yon-Figeac
Clos des Jacobins
Clos La Madeleine
Clos Saint-Martin

POMEROL

CRU EXCEPTIONNEL

Château Pétrus

PREMIERS CRUS

Château Beauregard
Château Certan-Giraud
Château Certan-de-May
Château Gazin
Château La Conseillante
Château La Croix-de-Gay
Château Lafleur
Château La Fleur-Pétrus
Château Lagrange

Château La Pointe
Château Latour-Pomerol
Château L'Église-Clinet
Château L'Évangile
Château Nenin
Château Petit-Village
Château Rouget
Château Trotanoy
(Château) Vieux Château Certan

Source: *Bordeaux et Ses Vins* by Ch. Cocks et Éd. Féret, 12th edition, 1968, 1974.

APPENDIX D
PRINCIPAL VINEYARDS OF
THE CÔTE D'OR, BURGUNDY

The ranking of wines of Burgundy has developed by tradition. Over the years, the best wines were judged to be Grands Crus, followed by Premiers Crus. These opinions have generally held to this day.

In this compilation of Grands and Premiers Crus, which is arranged by communes from north to south, Grand Cru vineyards appear in boldface type. Where the spelling of a vineyard has changed slightly from the original, the current spelling is used.

CÔTE DE NUITS

COMMUNE	*VINEYARD (CLIMAT)*	
FIXIN (mostly red)	Les Arvelets Aux Cheusots Le Clos-du-Chapitre	Les Hervelets Les Meix-Bas La Perrière
GEVREY- *CHAMBERTIN* (only red)	**Chambertin** **Chambertin-Clos de Bèze** **Chapelle-Chambertin** **Charmes-Chambertin** (**Mazoyères-Chambertin**)	**Griotte-Chambertin** **Latricières-Chambertin** **Mazis-Chambertin** **Ruchottes-Chambertin**
	Au Closeau Aux Combottes Bel-Air Cazetiers Champeaux Champitonnois Champonnets Cherbaudes Clos-du-Chapitre Clos-Prieur Le Clos Saint-Jacques Combe-aux-Moines	Les Corbeaux Craipillot Ergots Estournelles Le Fonteny Les Gemreaux Les Goulots Issarts Lavaut La Perrière Poissenot Les Véroilles
MOREY-SAINT- *DENIS* (mostly red)	**Bonnes Mares** (partly in Chambolle-Musigny) **Clos de la Roche**	**Clos de Tart** **Clos Saint-Denis**
	Aux Charmes Les Bouchots Calouères Chabiots Les Chaffots Les Charrières Les Chénevery Le Clos-Baulet Clos-Bussière Clos-des-Lambrays Le Clos-des-Ormes Le Clos-Sorbès Côte Rôtie	Les Façonnières Les Fremières Les Froichots Les Genevrières Les Gruenchers Maison-Brûlée Les Mauchamps Meix-Rentiers Les Millandes La Riotte Les Ruchots Les Sorbès

COMMUNE	VINEYARD (CLIMAT)

CHAMBOLLE-MUSIGNY
(mostly red)

Bonnes Mares
Musigny
Musigny Blanc (white)

Les Amoureuses	Les Fousselottes
Aux Beaux-Bruns	Les Fuées
Aux Combottes	Les Gras
Les Baudes	Les Groseilles
Les Bonnes Mares	Les Gruenchers
Les Borniques	Les Hauts-Doix
Les Charmes	Les Lavrottes
Les Chatelots	Les Noirots
Les Combottes	Les Plantes
Derrière-la-Grange	Les Sentiers

VOUGEOT
(mostly red)

Clos de Vougeot

Le Clos-Blanc (white)	Les Cras
Clos-de-la-Perrière	Les Petits-Vougeots

VOSNE-ROMANÉE
(only red)

Richebourg   **Romanée-Saint-Vivant**
Romanée   **La Tâche**
Romanée-Conti

Aux Brûlées	La Grande Rue
Aux Malconsorts	Les Petits-Monts
Les Beaumonts	Les Reignots
Les Chaumes	Les Suchots
Le Clos des Réas	

FLAGEY-ECHÉZEAUX
(only red)

Echézeaux
Grands Echézeaux

NUITS-SAINT-GEORGES
(mostly red)

Les Argillats	Clos-des-Forêts
Aux Argillats	Clos-des-Grandes-Vignes
Aux Boudots	Le Clos Saint-Marc
Aux Bousselots	Les Corvées-Paget
Aux Chaignots	Les Didiers
Aux Champs-Perdrix	En la Chaîne-Carteau
Aux Cras	Les Hauts-Pruliers
Aux Crots	La Perrière
Aux Damodes	Perrière-Noblet
Aux Murgers	Les Porets
Aux Perdrix	Les Poulettes
Aux Thorey	Le Procès
Aux Vignes-Rondes	Les Pruliers
Les Cailles	La Richemone
Les Chaboeufs	La Roncière
Clos-Arlots	Rue-de-Chaux
Clos-de-la-Maréchale	Les Saint-Georges
Clos-des-Argillières	Les Vallerots
Clos-des-Corvées	Les Vaucrains

CÔTE DE BEAUNE

COMMUNE	VINEYARD (CLIMAT)

ALOXE-CORTON
(mostly red)

Corton or **Corton** plus vineyard name: Bressandes, Clos du Roi, Languettes, Perrières, Pougets, Renardes, La Vigne-au-Saint, etc.

Corton-Charlemagne (white)

Les Chaillots	Les Maréchaudes
En Pauland	Les Meix
Les Fournières	Les Valozières
Les Guérets	Les Vercots

LADOIX-SERRIGNY
(mostly red)

Basses-Mourettes	La Maréchaude
La Coutière	Les Petites Lolières
Les Grandes-Lolières	La Toppe-au-Vert

PERNAND-VERGELESSES
(mostly red)

Les Basses-Vergelesses	En Caradeux
Creux-de-la-Net	Les Fichots

SAVIGNY-LES-BEAUNE
(mostly red)

Aux Clous	La Dominode
Aux Fourneaux	Les Hauts-Jarrons
Aux Grands-Liards	Les Hauts-Marconnets
Aux Gravains	Les Jarrons
Aux Guettes	Les Lavières
Aux Guettes	Les Marconnets
Aux Petits-Liards	Les Narbantons
Aux Serpentières	Petits-Godeaux
Aux Vergelesses	Les Peuillets
Basses-Vergelesses	Redrescuts
Bataillière	Les Rouvrettes
Les Charnières	Les Talmettes

BEAUNE
(mostly red)

Les Aigrots	Les Épenottes
A l' Écu	Les Fèves
Aux Coucherias	Les Grèves
Aux Cras	Les Marconnets
Les Avaux	La Mignotte
Le Bas-des-Teurons	Montée-Rouge
Les Blanches-Fleurs	Les Montrevenots
Les Boucherottes	Les Perrières
Les Bressandes	Pertuisots
Les Cent-Vignes	Les Reversées
Champs-Pimont	Les Seurey
Les Chouacheux	Les Sisies
Le Clos-de-la-Mousse	Sur-les-Grèves
Le Clos-des-Mouches	Les Teurons
Clos-du-Roi	Tiélandry or Clos-Landry
En Genêt	Les Toussaints
En l'Orme	Les Vignes-Franches

COMMUNE	VINEYARD (CLIMAT)	
POMMARD (only red)	Les Argillières Les Arvelets Les Bertins Les Boucherottes La Chanière Les Chanlins-Bas Les Chapponières Clos-Blanc Clos-de-la-Commareine Clos-du-Verger Le Clos-Micot Les Combes-Dessus Les Croix-Noires Derrière-Saint-Jean	Les Épenots Ès-Charmots Les Fremiers Les Garollières Les Petits-Épenots Les Pézerolles La Platière Les Poutures La Refène Les Rugiens Les Rugiens-Bas Les Rugiens-Hauts Les Sausilles
VOLNAY (only red)	Les Angles Les Aussy La Barre or Clos-de-la-Barre Bousse-d'Or Les Brouillards Caillerets-Dessus Carelle-Dessous Carelle-sous-la-Chapelle Chanlin Le Clos-des-Chênes Les Clos-des-Ducs En Caillerets En Champains En Chevret	En l'Ormeau En Verseuil Fremiers Les Lurets Les Mitans Les Petures (red) Les Pitures-Dessus Pointe-d'Angles Robardelle Ronceret Les Santenots (red) Taille-Pieds Village-de-Volnay
MONTHÉLIE (mostly red)	Le Cas-Rougeot Les Champs-Fulliot Le Château-Gaillard Le Clos-Gauthey Duresse	Le Meix-Bataille Les Riottes Sur Lavelle La Taupine Les Vignes-Rondes
AUXEY-DURESSES (predominantly red)	Les Bas-des-Duresses Les Bretterins La Chapelle La Chapelle Clos-du-Val	Les Duresses Les Écusseaux Les Grands-Champs Reugne
MEURSAULT (mostly white)	Aux Perrières Les Bouchères Les Caillerets Les Charmes-Dessous Les Charmes-Dessus Les Cras Les Genevrières-Dessous Les Genevrières-Dessus La Goutte d'Or La Jennelotte	Les Perrières-Dessous Les Perrières-Dessus Les Petures La Pièce-sous-le-Bois Le Poruzot Le Poruzot-Dessus Les Santenots-Blancs Les Santenots-du-Milieu Sous-le-dos-d'Ane

COMMUNE	VINEYARD (CLIMAT)	
PULIGNY-MONTRACHET (mostly white)	**Bâtard-Montrachet** (partly in Chassagne-Montrachet) **Bienvenues-Bâtard-Montrachet**	**Chevalier-Montrachet** **Montrachet** (partly in Chassagne-Montrachet)
	Le Cailleret Les Chalumeaux Le Champ-Canet Clavoillons Les Combettes Les Folatières	La Garenne Hameau-de-Blagny Les Pucelles Les Referts Sous-le-Puits
CHASSAGNE-MONTRACHET (majority red)	**Bâtard-Montrachet** (partly in Puligny-Montrachet) **Criots-Bâtard-Montrachet**	**Montrachet** (partly in Puligny-Montrachet)
	Abbaye-de-Morgeot La Boudriotte Les Brussoles Les Champs-Gain Les Chenevottes Clos-Saint-Jean En Cailleret	Grandes-Ruchottes Les Macherelles La Maltroie Morgeot La Romanée Les Vergers
SAINT-AUBIN (predominantly red)	Champlot La Chatenière Les Combes En Remilly	Les Frionnes Les Murgers-des-Dents-de-Chien Sur Gamay Sur-le-Sentier-du-Clou
SANTENAY (mostly red)	Beauregard Beaurepaire Clos-de-Tavannes La Comme	Les Gravières La Maladière Le Passe-Temps

Source: Pierre Poupon and Pierre Forgeot, *The Wines of Burgundy*, 5th ed. (Paris: Presses Universitaires de France, 1974).

HOSPICES DE BEAUNE

Founded in 1443 by Nicolas Rolin and his wife, Guigone de Salins, the Hospices de Beaune is a charity hospital whose entire financial support has always come from the sale of the wines produced on the vineyard parcels deeded to it by charitable Burgundian vineyard owners. Originally the sales were private, but since 1858 the wines have been sold at a public auction held each year on the third Sunday of November.

Hospices de Beaune wines are auctioned in lots under the name of the donor, for example, Beaune-Cuvée Nicolas Rolin, Beaune-Cuvée Guigone de Salins, Corton-Cuvée Docteur Peste, Corton-Cuvée Charlotte Dumay. The buyers purchase the wine in cask with the right to label it "Hospices de Beaune Cuvée Docteur Peste" or whatever the *cuvée* may be.

The Hospices de Beaune *cuvées* are:

RED WINES

AUXEY-DURESSES "Boillot"
BEAUNE "Hugues et Louis Bétault"
BEAUNE "Brunet"
BEAUNE "Clos des Avaux"
BEAUNE "Dames Hospitalières"
BEAUNE "Maurice Drouhin"
BEAUNE "Guigone de Salins"
BEAUNE "Nicolas Rolin"
BEAUNE "Rousseau-Deslandes"
CORTON "Charlotte Dumay"
CORTON "Docteur Peste"
CORTON-VERGENNES "Paul Chanson"
MONTHÉLIE "J. Lebelin"
PERNAND-VERGELESSES
    "Rameau-Lamarosse"
POMMARD "Billardet"
POMMARD "Dames de la Charité"
SAVIGNY-LES-BEAUNE "Forneret"
SAVIGNY-LES-BEAUNE "Fouquerand"
SAVIGNY-LES-BEAUNE "Arthur Girard"
VOLNAY "Blondeau"
VOLNAY "Général Muteau"
VOLNAY-SANTENOTS "Gauvain"
VOLNAY-SANTENOTS "Jehan de Massol"

WHITE WINES

CORTON-CHARLEMAGNE "François de Salins"
MEURSAULT "Jehan Humblot"
MEURSAULT "Loppin"
MEURSAULT-CHARMES "de Bahèzre de
    Lanlay"
MEURSAULT-CHARMES "A. Grivault"
MEURSAULT-GENEVRIERE "P. le Bon"
MEURSAULT-GENEVRIÈRES "Baudot"
MEURSAULT-GOUREAU

Source: *Le Bien Public*, November 1976.

APPENDIX E
D.O.C. WINES AND
PRINCIPAL GRAPE VARIETIES OF ITALY
D.O.C. WINES OF ITALY
(by region from north to south)

VALLE D'AOSTA

Donnaz
Enfer d'Arvier

PIEDMONT

Asti Spumante
Barbaresco
Barbera d'Alba
Barbera d'Asti
Barbera del Monferrato
Barolo
Boca
Brachetto d'Acqui
Caluso Passito
Caluso Passito Liquoroso
Carema
Colli Tortonesi (Barbera, Cortese)
Dolcetto d'Acqui
Dolcetto d'Alba
Dolcetto d'Asti
Dolcetto delle Langhe Monregalesi
Dolcetto di Diano d'Alba
Dolcetto di Dogliani
Dolcetto di Ovada
Erbaluce di Caluso
Fara
Freisa d'Asti
Freisa di Chieri
Gattinara
Gavi or Cortese di Gavi
Ghemme
Grignolino d'Asti
Grignolino del Monferrato Casalese
Malvasia di Casorzo d'Asti
Malvasia di Castelnuovo Don Bosco
Moscato d'Asti
Moscato Naturale d'Asti
Nebbiolo d'Alba
Rubino di Cantavenna
Sizzano

LOMBARDY

Botticino
Cellatica
Franciacorta Pinot
Franciacorta Rosso
Lugana
Oltrepò Pavese (Barbacarlo, Barbera, Bonarda, Buttafuoco, Cortese, Moscato, Pinot red, rosé, and white, Riesling, Sangue di Giuda)
Riviera del Garda (Rosso and Chiaretto)
Tocai di San Martino della Battaglia
Valtellina
Valtellina Superiore (Inferno, Grumello, Sassella, Valgella)

TRENTINO–ALTO ADIGE

Alto Adige (Cabernet, Lagrein, Malvasia, Merlot, Moscato Giallo, Moscato Rosa, Pinot Bianco, Pinot Grigio, Pinot Nero, Riesling Italico, Riesling Renano, Sauvignon, Schiave, Sylvaner, Traminer Aromatico)
Caldaro or Lago di Caldaro
Casteller
Colli di Bolzano
Meranese or Meranese di Collina
Santa Maddalena
Terlano
Teroldego Rotaliano
Valdadige
Valle Isarco (Muller Turgau, Pinot Grigio, Sylvaner, Traminer, Veltliner)
Vini del Trentino (Cabernet, Lagrein, Marzemino, Merlot, Moscato, Pinot, Pinot Nero, Riesling, Traminer Aromatico di Termeno, Vin Santo)

VENETO

Bardolino
Bianco di Custoza
Breganze (Bianco, Rosso, Cabernet, Pinot Bianco, Pinot Nero, Vespaiolo)
Cabernet di Pramaggiore
Colli Berici (Cabernet, Garganega, Merlot, Pinot Bianco, Sauvignon, Tocai Bianco, Tocai Rosso)
Colli Euganei (Bianco, Moscato, Rosso, Spumante)
Gambellara (Recioto, Vin Santo)
Merlot di Pramaggiore
Prosecco di Conegliano-Valdobbiadene
Recioto della Valpolicella Amarone
Recioto Soave
Soave
Tocai di Lison
Valpolicella
Vini del Piave (Cabernet, Merlot, Tocai, Verduzzo)

FRIULI-VENEZIA-GIULIA

Aquileia
Colli Goriziano or Collio (Cabernet Franc, Cabernet Sauvignon, Malvasia, Merlot, Pinot Bianco, Pinot Grigio, Pinot Nero, Riesling Italico, Tocai, Traminer)
Colli Orientale del Friuli (Cabernet Franc, Cabernet Sauvignon, Merlot, Picolit, Pinot Bianco, Pinot Grigio, Pinot Nero, Ribolla, Riesling Renano, Refosco Nostrano, Tocai, Verduzzo)
Grave del Friuli (Cabernet Franc, Cabernet Sauvignon, Merlot, Pinot Bianco, Pinot Grigio, Refosco Nostrano or Penduncolo Rosso, Tocai, Verduzzo)
Isonzo
Latisana

LIGURIA

Cinqueterre
Cinqueterre Sciacchetrà
Rossese di Dolceacqua or Dolceacqua

EMILIA-ROMAGNA

Albana di Romagna
Colli Bolognese Monte San Pietro
Gutturnio dei Colli Piacentini
Lambrusco di Sorbara
Lambrusco Grasparossa di Castelvetro
Lambrusco Reggiano
Lambrusco Salamino di San Croce
Monterosso Val d'Arda
Sangiovese di Romagna
Trebbianino Val Trebbia
Trebbiano di Romagna

TUSCANY

Bianco della Valdinievole
Bianco di Pitigliano
Bianco Vergine Val di Chiana
Brunello di Montalcino
Carmignano
Chianti
Elba Bianco and Rosso
Montecarlo Bianco
Parrina
Rosso delle Colline Lucchesi
Vernaccia di San Gimignano
Vino Nobile di Montepulciano

MARCHES

Bianchello del Metauro
Bianco dei Colli Maceratesi
Falerio dei Colli Ascolani
Rosso Conero
Rosso Piceno
Sangiovese dei Colli Pesaresi
Verdicchio dei Castelli di Jesi
Verdicchio di Matelica
Vernaccia di Serrapetrona

UMBRIA

Colli dei Trasimeno
Orvieto
Torgiano

LATIUM

Aleatico di Gradoli
Bianco Capena
Cerveteri
Cesanese del Piglio or Piglio
Cesanese di Affile or Affile
Cesanese di Olevano Romano or Olevano Romano
Colli Albani
Colli Lanuvini
Cori

Est! Est!! Est!!! di Montefiascone
Frascati
Marino
Merlot di Aprilia
Montecompatri Colonna
Sangiovese di Aprilia
Trebbiano di Aprilia
Velletri
Zagarolo

ABRUZZI AND MOLISE

Montepulciano d'Abruzzi
Trebbiano d'Abruzzi

CAMPANIA

Greco di Tufo
Ischia Bianco
Ischia Bianco Superiore

Ischia Rosso
Solopaca
Taurasi

APULIA

Aleatico di Puglia
Castel del Monte
Locorotondo
Martina or Martina Franca
Matino

Moscato di Trani
Ostuni
Primitivo di Manduria
Rosso di Cerignola
San Severo

BASILICATA

Aglianico del Vulture

CALABRIA

Cirò
Donnici

Pollino
Savuto

SICILY

Bianco Alcamo or Alcamo
Cerasuolo di Vittoria
Etna
Malvasia delle Lipari
Marsala

Moscato di Noto
Moscato di Pantelleria Naturale
Moscato di Siracusa
Moscato Passito di Pantelleria

SARDINIA

Cannonau di Sardegna
Girò di Cagliari
Malvasia di Bosa
Malvasia di Cagliari
Monica di Cagliari
Monica di Sardegna

Moscato di Cagliari
Moscato di Sorso-Sennori
Nasco di Cagliari
Nuragus di Cagliari
Vermentino di Gallura
Vernaccia di Oristano

Source: Italian Trade Commission, 1977, New York.

PRINCIPAL GRAPE VARIETIES OF ITALY

red grapes

GRAPE	REGIONS WHERE GROWN*	WINES
Aglianico	Basilicata	Aglianico del Vulture
	Campania	Taurasi
Aleatico	Latium	Aleatico di Gradoli
(Muscato Nero)	Apulia	Aleatico di Puglia
Barbera	Piedmont	Barbera d'Alba
		Barbera d'Asti
		Barbera del Montferrato
	Lombardy	Botticino
		Cellatica
		Franciacorta
		Oltrepò Pavese
		Riviera del Garda
	Emilia-Romagna	Gutturnio dei Colli Piacentini
Bombino Nero	Apulia	Castel del Monte
Bonarda	Piedmont	Boca
		Fara
		Ghemme
		Sizzano
Brunello di Montalcino	Tuscany	Brunello di Montalcino
Cabernet Sauvignon	Veneto	Breganze Cabernet
	Trentino–Alto Adige	Trentino Cabernet
	Friuli-Venezia-Giulia	Grave del Friuli Cabernet
		Colli Orientale del Friuli Cabernet
Canaiolo Nero	Tuscany	Chianti
		Vino Nobile di Montepulciano
Corvina	Veneto	Bardolino
Veronese		Valpolicella
Dolcetto	Piedmont	Dolcetto d'Acqui
		Dolcetto di Ovada
Freisa	Piedmont	Freisa d'Asti
Girò	Sardinia	Girò di Cagliari
Grignolino	Piedmont	Grignolino d'Asti
Gropello	Lombardy	Gropello Amarone
		Riviera del Garda
Lagrein	Trentino–Alto Adige	Trentino Lagrein
Lambrusco	Emilia-Romagna	Lambrusco Reggiano
(several varieties)		Lambrusco di Sorbara, etc.
Merlot	Friuli-Venezia-Giulia	Colli Orientale del Friuli Merlot
		Grave del Friuli Merlot
	Trentino–Alto Adige	Trentino Merlot
	Veneto	Breganze Rosso
Montepulciano	Abruzzo	Montepulciano d'Abruzzo
	Marches	Rosso Conero
		Rosso Piceno
	Apulia	San Severo

*These are the regions where the grapes are most important. Many of these grapes are grown elsewhere in Italy in smaller amounts.

GRAPE	REGIONS WHERE GROWN	WINES
Nebbiolo (called Spanna around Gattinara)	Piedmont	Barbaresco Barolo Boca Carema Fara Gattinara Ghemme Sizzano
(here called Chiavennesca)	Lombardy	Grumello Inferno Sassella Valgella
Perricone	Sicily	Corvo Rosso
Pinot Nero	Friuli-Venezia-Giulia	Colli Orientale del Friuli Pinot Nero Collio Pinot Nero
	Lombardy	Oltrepò Pavese Pinot
	Trentino–Alto Adige	Trentino Pinot Nero
	Veneto	Breganze Pinot Nero
Rondinella	Veneto	Bardolino Valpolicella
Sangiovese (several varieties)	Emilia-Romagna	Sangiovese di Romagna
	Latium	Sangiovese di Aprilia
	Marches	Sangiovese dei Colli Pesaresi
	Tuscany	Chianti Elba Rosso
	Umbria	Torgiano Rosso
	Veneto	Riviera del Garda
Schiava (several varieties)	Lombardy	Botticino Cellatica
	Trentino–Alto Adige	Caldaro Santa Maddalena
Vespolina	Piedmont	Boca Fara Ghemme Sizzano

white grapes

GRAPE	REGIONS WHERE GROWN	WINES
Albana	Emilia-Romagna	Albana di Romagna
Ansonica (Inzolia)	Sicily	Corvo
		Marsala
	Tuscany	Parrina Bianco
Biancolella	Campania	Ischia Bianco
Bombino Bianco	Abruzzo	Trebbiano d'Abruzzo
	Apulia	San Severo Bianco
Catarratto	Sicily	Alcamo
		Corvo
		Etna Bianco
		Marsala
Cortese	Lombardy	Oltrepò Pavese Cortese
Erbaluce	Piedmont	Caluso Passito
		Caluso Passito Liquoroso
Garganega	Veneto	Gambellara
		Soave
Greco	Calabria	Cirò Bianco
	Campania	Greco di Tufo
	Latium	Frascati
Grillo	Sicily	Marsala
Malvasia (several varieties)	Latium	Colli Albani
		Est! Est!! Est!!!
		Frascati
		Marino
	Tuscany	Chianti
		Vin Santo
	Umbria	Orvieto
	Marches	Verdicchio
	Sardinia	Malvasia di Bosa
Moscato Bianco	Piedmont	Asti Spumante
	Sardinia	Moscato di Cagliari
Müller-Thurgau	Trentino–Alto Adige	Trentino Riesling
Picolit	Friuli-Venezia-Giulia	Colli Orientale del Friuli-Picolit
Pinot Bianco	Friuli-Venezia-Giulia	Collio Pinot Bianco
		Colli Orientale del Friuli Pinot Bianco
		Grave del Friuli Pinot Bianco
	Trentino–Alto Adige	Trentino Pinot
	Veneto	Breganze Pinot Bianco
Pinot Grigio	Friuli-Venezia-Giulia	Collio Pinot Grigio
		Colli Orientale del Friuli Pinot Grigio
		Grave del Friuli Pinot Grigio
	Trentino–Alto Adige	Trentino Pinot
	Veneto	Breganze Pinot Grigio
Prosecco	Veneto	Prosecco di Conegliano-Valdobbiadene

GRAPE	REGIONS WHERE GROWN	WINES
Riesling Italico Riesling Renano	Friuli-Venezia-Giulia Lombardy Trentino–Alto Adige	Colli Orientale del Friuli Riesling Oltrepò Pavese Riesling Trentino Riesling
Tocai Friulano	Friuli-Venezia-Giulia Lombardy Veneto	Colli Orientale del Friuli Tocai Collio Tocai Tocai di San Martino della Battaglia Tocai di Lison Breganze Bianco Piave Tocai
Traminer Aromatico (Gewürztraminer)	Friuli-Venezia-Giulia Trentino–Alto Adige	Collio Traminer Trentino Traminer
Trebbiano (several varieties)	Emilia-Romagna Latium Lombardy Tuscany Umbria Veneto	Trebbiano di Romagna Est! Est!! Est!!! Frascati Lugana Chianti Elba Bianco Montecarlo Vin Santo Orvieto Torgiano Bianco Lugana Soave
Uva di Troia	Apulia	Castel del Monte
Verdicchio (several varieties)	Marches	Verdicchio dei Castelli di Jesi Verdicchio di Matelica
Verduzzo Friulano	Friuli-Venezia-Giulia Veneto	Colli Orientale del Friuli Verduzzo Grave del Friuli Verduzzo Piave Verduzzo
Vernaccia (several varieties)	Sardinia Tuscany	Vernaccia di Oristano Vernaccia di San Gimignano
Vespaiolo	Veneto	Breganze Vespaiolo
Zibibbo (Moscato di Alessandria)	Sicily	Marsala Moscato di Pantelleria Moscato Passito di Pantelleria

Source: Pier Giovanni Garoglio, *Enciclopedia Vitivinicola Mondiale* (Milan: Unione Italiana Vini, 1973).

APPENDIX F
PRINCIPAL GERMAN WINE REGIONS AND GRAPE VARIETIES

AHR
6 percent of Germany's harvest

1 subregion (*Bereich*): Walporzheim/Ahrtal
1 collective vineyard (*Grosslage*): Klosterberg
43 single vineyards (*Einzellagen*) around 11 villages (*Gemeinden*)
485 hectares under cultivation
Main grapes: Spätburgunder (red), 27 percent; Portugieser (red), 26 percent; Riesling, 22 percent; Müller-Thurgau, 19 percent
No principal wines distributed in the United States

MOSEL-SAAR-RUWER
4.2 percent of Germany's harvest

4 subregions (*Bereichen*): Zell, Bernkastel, Saar-Ruwer, Obermosel
19 collective vineyards (*Grosslagen*): Weinhex, Goldbäumchen, Rosenhang, Grafschaft, Schwarze Katz, vom Heissen Stein, Schwarzlay, Münzlay, Badstube, Beerenlay, Kurfürstlay, Michelsberg, St. Michael, Probstberg, Römerlay, Schwarzberg, Königsberg, Gipfel
524 single vineyards (*Einzellagen*) around 161 villages (*Gemeinden*)
11,500 hectares under cultivation
Main grapes: Riesling, 66 percent; Müller-Thurgau, 19 percent; Elbling, 10 percent
Principal wines distributed in the United States: Zeller Schwarze Katz (*Grosslage*), Erdener Treppchen, Zeltinger Himmelreich, Zeltinger Sonnenuhr, Wehlener Sonnenuhr, Graacher Domprobst, Graacher Himmelreich, Bernkasteler Badstube (*Grosslage*), Bernkasteler Doctor und Graben, Bernkasteler Kurfürstlay (*Grosslage*), Piesporter Michelsberg (*Grosslage*), Piesporter Goldtröpfchen, Maximin Grünhauser Herrenberg, Scharzhofberger, Trittenheimer Apotheke, Ockfener Bockstein, Ürziger Würzgarten, Ayler Kupp, Eitelsbacher Kronenberg, Kröver Nacktarsch (*Grosslage*), Brauneberger Juffer

MITTELRHEIN
1 percent of Germany's harvest

3 subregions (*Bereichen*): Rheinburgengau, Siebengebirge, Bacharach
11 collective vineyards (*Grosslagen*): Burg Hammerstein, Lahntal, Marksburg, Gedeonseck, Burg Rheinfels, Loreleyfelsen, Schloss Schönburg, Herrenberg, Petersberg, Schloss Stahleck, Schloss Reichenstein
120 single vineyards (*Einzellagen*) around 55 villages (*Gemeinden*)
1,000 hectares under cultivation
Main grapes: Riesling, 80 percent; Müller-Thurgau, 12 percent
No principal wines distributed in the United States

RHEINGAU
4 percent of Germany's harvest

1 subregion (*Bereich*): Johannisberg
10 collective vineyards (*Grosslagen*): Burgweg, Steil, Erntebringer, Honigsberg, Gottesthal, Deutelsberg, Mehrhölzchen, Heiligenstock, Steinmächer, Daubhaus
117 single vineyards (*Einzellagen*) around 28 villages (*Gemeinden*)
2,900 hectares under cultivation
Main grapes: Riesling, 76 percent; Müller-Thurgau, 11 percent; Sylvaner, 5 percent
Principal wines distributed in the United States: Rüdesheimer Bischofsberg, Rüdesheimer Berg Rottland,

Rüdesheimer Rosengarten, Geisenheimer Rothenberg, Johannisberger Erntebringer (*Grosslage*), Johannisberger Klaus, Schloss Johannisberg, Schloss Vollrads, Oestricher Lenchen, Hattenheimer Nussbrunnen, Steinberger, Erbacher Marcobrunn, Eltviller Rheinberg, Eltviller Sonnenberg, Rauenthaler Baiken, Hochheimer Domdechaney, Hochheimer Kirchenstück

NAHE
5 percent of Germany's harvest

2 subregions (*Bereichen*): Kreuznach, Schloss Böckelheim
7 collective vineyards (*Grosslagen*): Schlosskapelle, Sonnenborn, Pfarrgarten, Kronenberg, Rosengarten, Burgweg, Paradiesgarten
340 single vineyards (*Einzellagen*) around 79 villages (*Gemeinden*)
4,380 hectares under cultivation
Main grapes: Müller-Thurgau, 31 percent; Sylvaner, 28 percent; Riesling, 24 percent
Principal wines distributed in the United States: Schloss Böckelheimer Kupfergrube, Schloss Böckelheimer Mühlberg

RHEINHESSEN
25 percent of Germany's harvest

3 subregions (*Bereichen*): Bingen, Nierstein, Wonnegau
24 collective vineyards (*Grosslagen*): Sankt Rochuskapelle, Abtey, Rheingrafenstein, Adelberg, Kurfürstenstück, Kaiserpfalz, Sankt Alban, Domherr, Gutes Domtal, Spiegelberg, Rehbach, Auflangen, Güldenmorgen, Krötenbrunnen, Vogelsgärten, Petersberg, Rheinblick, Sybillenstein, Bergkloster, Pilgerpfad, Gotteshilfe, Burg Rodenstein, Domblick, Liebfrauenmorgen
430 single vineyards (*Einzellagen*) around 140 villages (*Gemeinden*)
21,800 hectares under cultivation
Main grapes: Müller-Thurgau, 36 percent; Sylvaner, 28 percent; Scheurebe, 6 percent; Riesling, 5 percent; Portugieser (red), 5 percent
Principal wines distributed in the United States: Niersteiner Gutes Domtal (*Grosslage*), Niersteiner Spiegelberg (*Grosslage*), Niersteiner Rehbach (*Grosslage*), Niersteiner Pettenthal, Niersteiner Hipping, Niersteiner Auflangen (*Grosslage*), Niersteiner Orbel, Oppenheimer Krötenbrunnen (*Grosslage*)

RHEINPFALZ
30 percent of Germany's harvest

2 subregions (*Bereichen*): Mittelhaardt Deutsche Weinstrasse, südliche Weinstrasse
26 collective vineyards (*Grosslagen*): Schnepfenflug vom Zellertal, Grafenstück, Höllenpfad, Schwarzerde, Rosenbühl, Kobnert, Feuerberg, Saumagen, Honigsäckel, Hochmess, Schenkenböhl, Schnepfenflug an der Weinstrasse, Mariengarten, Hofstück, Meerspinne, Rebstöckel, Pfaffengrund, Mandelhöhe, Schloss Ludwigshöhe, Ordensgut, Trappenberg, Bischofskreuz, Königsgarten, Herrlich, Kloster Liebfrauenberg, Guttenberg
Approximately 330 single vineyards (*Einzellagen*) around 160 villages (*Gemeinden*)
20,800 hectares under cultivation
Main grapes: Müller-Thurgau, 24 percent; Sylvaner, 23 percent; Riesling, 14 percent; Portugieser (red), 12 percent
Principal wines distributed in the United States: Forster Mariengarten (*Grosslage*), Forster Jesuitengarten, Deidesheimer Herrgottsacker, Deidesheimer Hohenmorgen, Deidesheimer Paradiesgarten, Ruppertsberger Hoheburg, Ungsteiner Herrenberg, Bad Dürkheim Feuerberg (*Grosslage*), Wachenheimer Gerümpel

HESSISCHE BERGSTRASSE
0.3 percent of Germany's harvest

2 subregions (*Bereichen*): Umstadt, Starkenburg
3 collective vineyards (*Grosslagen*): Rott, Wolfsmagen, Schlossberg
19 single vineyards (*Einzellagen*) around 9 villages (*Gemeinden*)
350 hectares under cultivation
Main grapes: Riesling, 53 percent; Müller-Thurgau, 20 percent; Sylvaner, 12 percent
No principal wines distributed in the United States

FRANKEN
4 percent of Germany's harvest

4 subregions (*Bereichen*): Mainviereck, Maindreieck, Steigerwald, Bayerischer Bodensee

17 collective vineyards (*Grosslagen*): Reuschberg, Heiligenthal, Burg, Rosstal, Ravensburg, Ewig Leben, Olspiel, Teufelstor, Hofrat, Honigberg, Kirchberg, Schild, Herrenberg, Schlossberg, Burgweg, Schlosstück, Kapellenberg

Approximately 130 single vineyards (*Einzellagen*) around 115 villages (*Gemeinden*)

3,400 hectares under cultivation

Main grapes: Müller-Thurgau, 45 percent; Sylvaner, 35 percent

Principal wines distributed in the United States: Escherndorfer Lump, Sommerhausen Ölspiel (*Grosslage*)

WÜRTTEMBERG
8 percent of Germany's harvest

3 subregions (*Bereichen*): Kocher-Jagst-Tauber, Württembergisch Unterland, Remstal-Stuttgart

16 collective vineyards (*Grosslagen*): Tauberberg, Kocherberg, Staufenberg, Lindelberg, Salzberg, Schozachtal, Wunnenstein, Kirchenweinberg, Heuchelberg, Stromberg, Schalkstein, Weinsteige, Kopf, Wartbühl, Sonnenbühl, Hohenneuffen

Approximately 200 single vineyards (*Einzellagen*) around 230 villages (*Gemeinden*)

8,500 hectares under cultivation

Main grapes: Trollinger (red), 25 percent; Riesling, 23 percent; Müller-Thurgau, 10 percent; Schwarzriesling, 9 percent

Principal wines distributed in the United States: Stettener Heuchelberg, Cannstatter Zuckerle (red wine)

BADEN
12.5 percent of Germany's harvest

7 subregions (*Bereichen*): Badisches Frankenland, Badische Bergstrasse Kraichgau, Bodensee, Ortenau, Breisgau, Kaiserstuhl-Tuniberg, Markgräflerland

16 collective vineyards (*Grosslagen*): Tauberklinge, Hohenberg, Mannaberg, Stiftsberg, Rittersberg, Sonnenufer, Fürsteneck, Schloss Rodeck, Burg Zähringen, Burg Lichteneck, Schutterlindenberg, Attilafelsen, Vulkanfelsen, Vogtei Rötteln, Burg Neuenfels, Lorettoberg

Approximately 340 single vineyards (*Einzellagen*) around 300 villages (*Gemeinden*)

13,100 hectares under cultivation

Main grapes: Müller-Thurgau, 33 percent; Blauer Spätburgunder (red), 22 percent; Ruländer, 14 percent; Gutedel, 11 percent; Riesling, 7 percent; Sylvaner, 5 percent

Principal wines distributed in the United States: Affentaler Spätburgunder, Kenzinger Hummelberg, Attilafelsen Niederrimsinger (*Grosslage*), Freiburger Lorettoberg Gutedel (*Grosslage*)

Source: *German Wine Atlas and Vineyard Register* (New York: Hastings House, 1977).

MOST WIDELY GROWN GRAPE VARIETIES
(in hectares)

GRAPE	Ahr	Mittelrhein	Mosel-Saar-Ruwer	Nahe	Rhein-hessen	Rhein-pfalz	Rhein-gau	Hessische Berg-strasse	Baden	Württem-berg	Franken	Total
							REGION					
Bacchus	•	1	129	41	187	97	—	—	—	—	5	460
Burgunder (white)	1	1	1	48	71	278	•	—	366	4	5	775
Elbling	1	—	1,116	•	•	•	•	•	73	2	5	1,243
Gewürztraminer	•	2	1	14	111	138	16	•	155	10	•	447
Gutedel (white)	—	—	—	—	—	—	—	—	1,184	3	2	1,198
Kerner	2	13	81	34	226	584	10	—	16	257	29	1,274
Morio-Muskat	—	1	5	54	1,062	1,426	•	—	3	—	9	2,560
Müller-Thurgau	87	89	2,095	1,316	7,813	4,784	288	55	4,174	585	1,329	22,641
Riesling (white)	115	706	7,775	1,051	1,182	2,833	2,219	142	860	1,746	105	18,740
Ruländer	1	3	7	103	443	591	25	21	1,741	105	18	3,067
Scheurebe	•	3	11	176	1,208	625	9	1	15	2	42	2,092
Sylvaner	•	33	12	1,338	6,756	5,077	152	40	614	708	1,149	15,879
Traminer	•	1	1	6	37	192	•	•	85	—	38	360
Others	14	5	216	72	385	367	46	11	249	20	75	2,297
White varieties, total	221	862	11,457	4,326	20,388	17,448	2,795	270	9,535	3,442	2,948	73,791
Burgunder (black)	120	8	•	9	74	83	53	—	2,312	293	16	2,968
Limberger	•	•	•	•	•	•	•	•	17	382	•	399
Müllerrebe	•	•	•	•	•	•	•	•	62	787	—	878
Portugieser	137	5	1	36	1,089	2,512	4	2	63	610	18	4,478
Trollinger	—	•	•	•	•	•	—	—	15	1,866	—	1,884
Others	5	1	1	7	42	98	9	•	104	310	1	582
Red varieties, total	262	14	2	52	1,217	2,697	66	2	2,573	4,248	43	11,175
Wine grapes, total	483	876	11,459	4,378	21,605	20,145	2,862	272	12,108	7,690	2,991	84,966

• = less than 0.5 hectares

Source: Statistisches Bundesamt, Wiesbaden, 1973; courtesy German Wine Academy, Kloster Eberbach.

APPENDIX G
COMMERCIALLY IMPORTANT BONDED WINERIES AND BONDED WINE CELLARS OF THE UNITED STATES

ARKANSAS

Center Ridge Winery
Springfield, AR

De Salvo's Winery
Center Ridge, AR

Freyaldenhoven's Winery
Morrilton, AR

Mount Bethel Winery
Altus, AR

Post Winery, Inc.
Altus, AR

Wiederkehr Wine Cellars, Inc.
Altus, AR

CALIFORNIA

Alexander Valley Vineyards
Healdsburg, CA

Alex's Winery
(California Cellarmaster)
Lodi, CA

Almadén Vineyards
San Francisco, CA

Bandiera Wines
Cloverdale, CA

B & R Vineyards, Inc./Rapazzini Winery
Gilroy, CA

Barengo Vineyards, Inc.
Campbell, CA

Bargetto's Santa Cruz Winery
Soquel, CA

Bear Mountain Winery
DiGiorgio, CA

Beaulieu Vineyard
Rutherford, CA

Bella Napoli Winery
Manteca, CA

Beringer Vineyards/Los Hermanos Vineyards
(Division of Wine World, Inc.)
St. Helena, CA

Bernardo Winery
Escondido, CA

Bertero Winery
(also known as Italian California Wine Co.)
Gilroy, CA

Bisceglia Bros. Wine Co.
(Canandaigua Wine Company, Inc.)
Madera, CA

J.F.J. Bronco Winery
Ceres, CA

Brookside Enterprises, Inc.
(subsidiary of Beatrice Foods, Inc.)
Guasti, CA

David Bruce Winery, Inc.
Los Gatos, CA

Buena Vista Winery and Vineyards
(The Haraszthy Cellars)
Sonoma, CA

Burgess Cellars
St. Helena, CA

Butte Creek Vineyards, Inc.
Chico, CA

Davis Bynum Winery
Healdsburg, CA

Cadenasso Winery
Fairfield, CA

Cadlolo Winery
Escalon, CA

California Growers Winery, Inc.
San Francisco, CA

California Mission Wines
McFarland, CA

California Wine Association
(subsidiary of A. Perelli-Minetti & Sons)
Burlingame, CA

Callaway Vineyard and Winery
Temecula, CA

Cambiaso Winery & Vineyards
Healdsburg, CA

Carneros Creek Winery
Napa, CA

Caymus Vineyards
Rutherford, CA

Chalone Vineyard
(Gavilan Vineyards, Inc.)
Soledad, CA

Chappellet Winery
St. Helena, CA

Château Chevalier Winery
St. Helena, CA

Château Montelena Winery
Calistoga, CA

Château St. Jean, Inc.
Kenwood, CA

Château Vintners
San Leandro, CA

Louis Cherpin Winery
Fontana, CA

Clos du Val Wine Co., Ltd.
Napa, CA

Concannon Vineyard
Livermore, CA

Anselmo Conrotto Winery
Gilroy, CA

Cresta Blanca Winery
Ukiah, CA

Cucamonga Top Winery
Etiwanda, CA

Cucamonga Vineyard Company
Cucamonga, CA

Cuvaison, Inc.
Calistoga, CA

D'Agostini Winery
Plymouth, CA

Dehlinger Winery
Sebastopol, CA

Delano Growers Cooperative Winery
(Delwine)
Delano, CA

Delicato Vineyards
Manteca, CA

Del Rey Cooperative Winery Association
Fresno, CA

J.E. Digardi Winery
Martinez, CA

Dry Creek Vineyard, Inc.
Healdsburg, CA

East-Side Winery
Lodi, CA

Edmeades Vineyards
Philo, CA

Enz Vineyards
Hollister, CA

Ferrara Winery
Escondido, CA

Fetzer Vineyards
Redwood Valley, CA

Ficklin Vineyards
Madera, CA

Filice Winery, Inc.
Acampo, CA

J. Filippi Vintage Co.
Mira Loma, CA

The Firestone Vineyard
Los Olivos, CA

L. Foppiano Wine Co.
Healdsburg, CA

Fortino Winery
Gilroy, CA

Franciscan Vineyards
Rutherford, CA

Franzia Brothers Winery
(Franzia Brothers Champagne Cellars)
Ripon, CA

James Frasinetti and Sons
Sacramento, CA

Chris A. Fredson Winery
Geyserville, CA

Freemark Abbey Winery
St. Helena, CA

Frei Brothers
Santa Rosa, CA

Galleano Winery, Inc.
Mira Loma, CA

E. & J. Gallo Winery
Modesto, CA

Gemello Winery Corp.
Mountain View, CA

Geyser Peak Winery
San Rafael, CA

A. Ghianda Winery
Oroville, CA

Gibson Wine Co.
Sanger, CA

Peter and Harry Giretti
Gilroy, CA

Giumarra Vineyards Corp.
Bakersfield, CA

Golden State Winery
Fresno, CA

Gold Mine Winery
Madera, CA

Grand Cru Vineyards
Glen Ellen, CA

Emilio Guglielmo Winery
Morgan Hill, CA

Guild Wineries and Distilleries
Lodi, CA

Gundlach-Bundschu Winery
Vineberg, CA

Hacienda Wine Cellars
Sonoma, CA

Hanzell Vineyards
Sonoma, CA

Hecker Pass Winery
Gilroy, CA

Heitz Wine Cellars
St. Helena, CA

Kenwood Vineyards
Kenwood, CA

Kirigin Cellars
(formerly Bonesio Winery)
Gilroy, CA

F. Korbel & Bros.
Guerneville, CA

Hanns Kornell Champagne Cellars
St. Helena, CA

Charles Kreck Winery
Healdsburg, CA

Charles Krug Winery
(C. Mondavi & Sons)
St. Helena, CA

Thomas Kruse Winery
Gilroy, CA

Lambert Bridge
Healdsburg, CA

Landis Vineyard
Fresno, CA

Landmark Vineyards
Windsor, CA

Liberty Winery, Inc.
Acampo, CA

Llords & Elwood Winery
Beverly Hills, CA

Lodi Vintners, Ltd.
Acampo, CA

Louis M. Martini
St. Helena, CA

Martini & Prati Wines, Inc.
Santa Rosa, CA

Paul Masson Vineyards
Saratoga, CA

J. Mathews Napa Valley Winery
Newport Beach, CA

Mayacamas Vineyards
Napa, CA

Giuseppe Mazzoni
Cloverdale, CA

Mirassou Vineyards
San Jose, CA

Robert Mondavi Winery
Oakville, CA

Monterey Peninsula Winery
Monterey, CA

The Monterey Vineyard
Gonzales, CA

Montevina
Plymouth, CA

Mont La Salle Vineyards
Napa, CA

Mount Eden Vineyards
Saratoga, CA

Mount Palomar Winery
Temecula, CA

Mt. Veeder Winery and Vineyards
Napa, CA

Napa Valley Cooperative Winery
St. Helena, CA

Nichelini Vineyards
St. Helena, CA

Noble Vineyards, Inc.
Kerman, CA

A. Nonini Winery
Fresno, CA

Oakville Vineyards
Oakville, CA

Opici Winery, Inc.
Alta Loma, CA

Papagni Vineyards
Madera, CA

Parducci Winery, Ltd.
(d.b.a. Parducci Wine Cellars)
Ukiah, CA

Pastori Winery
Cloverdale, CA

Pedrizzetti Winery
Morgan Hill, CA

J. Pedroncelli Winery
Geyserville, CA

A. Perelli-Minetti & Sons
Delano, CA

Pesenti Winery
Templeton, CA

Joseph Phelps Vineyards
St. Helena, CA

L. Pocai & Sons
Calistoga, CA

Pope Valley Winery
Pope Valley, CA

A. Rafanelli Winery
Healdsburg, CA

Rancho de Philo
Alta Loma, CA

Raymond Vineyard & Cellar
St. Helena, CA

A. Rege Wine Co.
San Francisco, CA

Richert & Sons Winery
Morgan Hill, CA

Ridge Vineyards, Inc.
Cupertino, CA

Rio Vista Winery
Selma, CA

Rotta Winery
Templeton, CA

Rubidoux Winery
Riverside, CA

Russian River Vineyards
Forestville, CA

Rutherford Hill Winery
St. Helena, CA

San Antonio Winery, Inc.
Los Angeles, CA

San Benito Vineyards, Inc.
Hollister, CA

San Martin Vineyards Co., Inc.
San Martin, CA

San Pasqual Winery
San Diego, CA

Santa Barbara Winery
Santa Barbara, CA

V. Sattui Winery
St. Helena, CA

Sausal Winery
Healdsburg, CA

Peter Scagliotti
(d.b.a Live Oaks Winery)
Gilroy, CA

Schenley Distillers, Inc.
Fresno, CA

Schramsberg Vineyards Co.
Calistoga, CA

Sebastini Vineyards
Sonoma, CA

Seghesio Winery, Inc.
Cloverdale, CA

Selma Winery, Inc.
Selma, CA

Sierra Wine Corporation
Fresno, CA

Silver Oak Cellars
Oakville, CA

Simi Winery
Healdsburg, CA

Soda Rock Winery
Healdsburg, CA

Sommelier Winery
Mountain View, CA

Sonoma County Cellars
Healdsburg, CA

Sonoma County Cooperative Winery
Windsor, CA

Sonoma Vineyards
Windsor, CA

Sotoyome Winery
Healdsburg, CA

Souverain Cellars
(d.b.a. Souverain of Rutherford and
  Souverain of Alexander Valley)
Geyserville, CA

Spottswoode Cellars
St. Helena, CA

Spring Mountain Vineyards
St. Helena, CA

Stag's Leap Wine Cellars
Napa, CA

Sterling Vineyards
Calistoga, CA

Stockton Distillery Corp.
Lodi, CA

Stonegate, Inc.
(d.b.a. Stonegate Winery)
Calistoga, CA

Stony Hill Vineyard
St. Helena, CA

Stony Ridge Winery
(formerly Ruby Hill Vineyard Co.)
Pleasanton, CA

Sutter Home Winery, Inc.
St. Helena, CA

Joseph Swan Vineyards
Forestville, CA

Thomas Vineyards
Cucamonga, CA

Torgeon-Lohr Winery
San Jose, CA

Trefethen Vineyards
Napa, CA

Trentadue Winery
Geyserville, CA

United Vintners, Inc.
San Francisco, CA

Valley of the Moon Winery
Glen Ellen, CA

Veedercrest-Ringsbridge Cellars
Emeryville, CA

Vie-Del Company
Plant No. 1: Fresno, CA
Plant No. 2: Kingsburg, CA

Villa Armando Winery
Pleasanton, CA

Villa Mt. Eden Winery
Oakville, CA

Weibel, Inc.
(d.b.a. Weibel Champagne Vineyards)
Mission San Jose, CA

Wente Brothers
Livermore, CA

Woodbridge Vineyard Assn.
Lodi, CA

Wooden Valley Winery
Suisun, CA

York Mountain Winery
Templeton, CA

Yverdon Vineyards
St. Helena, CA

FLORIDA

Bartels Winery, Inc.
Pensacola, FL

Fruit Wines of Florida, Inc.
Tampa, FL

Todhunter International, Inc.
West Palm Beach, FL

GEORGIA

Monarch Wine Co. of Georgia
Atlanta, GA

ILLINOIS

Gem City Vineland Co., Inc.
Nauvoo, IL

Mogen David Wine Corp.
Chicago, IL

Thompson Winery
Monee, IL

INDIANA

Banholzer Winecellars Ltd.
New Carlisle, IN

Oliver Wine Co., Inc.
Bloomington, IN

Villa Medeo Vineyards Winery
Madison, IN

IOWA

Ackerman Winery, Inc.
South Amana, IA

Colony Village Winery
Williamsburg, IA

Colony Wines, Inc.
Amana, IA

Council Bluffs Grape Growers Assn., Inc.
Council Bluffs, IA

Old Wine Cellar Winery
Amana, IA

Colcord Winery, Inc.
Paris, KY

Kentucky River Products, Inc.
Frankfort, KY

MARYLAND

Boordy Vineyard
Riderwood, MD

Provenza Vineyards
Brookeville, MD

Mountbray Wine Cellars Ltd.
Westminster, MD

MICHIGAN

Boskydel Vineyard
Lake Leelanau, MI

Lakeside Vineyard, Inc.
Harbert, MI

Bronte Champagne & Wines Co., Inc.
Detroit, MI

Milan Wineries
Detroit, MI

Château Grand Travers, Inc.
Travers City, MI

St. Julian & La Salle Wine Co., Inc.
Paw Paw, MI

Fenn Valley Vineyards
Fennville, MI

Tabor Hill Vineyard and Winecellar, Inc.
Buchanan, MI

Frontenac Vineyards, Inc.
Paw Paw, MI

Warner Vineyards, Inc.
Paw Paw, MI

MISSOURI

Ambrose & Co.
Kansas City, MO

Mount Pleasant Vineyards
Augusta, MO

Ashby Vineyards, Inc.
(d.b.a. Rosati Winery)
St. James, MO

St. James Winery
St. James, MO

Stoltz Vineyards Winery, Inc.
Rolla, MO

Bardenheier's Wine Cellars
St. Louis, MO

Stone Hill Wine Co., Inc.
Hermann, MO

Garco Wine Co.
St. Louis, MO

Weston Wine Cellars
Weston, MO

Green Valley Vineyards
Portland, MO

NEW HAMPSHIRE

White Mountain Vineyards
Laconia, NH

NEW JERSEY

Balic Winery
Mays Landing, NJ

Monte Carlo Wine Industries, Ltd.
New Brunswick, NJ

B & B Vineyards, Inc.
Stockton, NJ

Renault Winery, Inc.
Egg Harbor City, NJ

Gross' Highland Winery
Absecon, NJ

Tomasello Winery
Hammonton, NJ

Jacob Lee Winery
Bordentown, NJ

Tribuno Wines, Inc.
Lodi, NJ

NEW MEXICO

Gros Winery
Albuquerque, NM

NEW YORK

The Barry Wine Co., Inc.
Conesus, NY

Benmarl Wine Co.
Marlboro, NY

Brotherhood Corp., Inc.
Washingtonville, NY

Canandaigua Wine Co., Inc.
Canandaigua, NY

Delmonico's
Brooklyn, NY

Ebi's Champagne, Inc.
Williamson, NY

Dr. Konstantin D. Frank & Sons
(Vinifera Wine Cellars)
Hammondsport, NY

Fredonia Products Co., Inc.
Dunkirk, NY

Gold Seal Vineyards, Inc.
Hammondsport, NY

Hammondsport Wine Co., Inc.
(Canandaigua Wine Co., Inc.)
Hammondsport, NY

Hudson Valley Wine Co., Inc.
Highland, NY

Italian & French Wine Co. of Buffalo, Inc.
Buffalo, NY

Frederick S. Johnson Vineyards
Westfield, NY

Long Island Vineyards, Inc.
Cutchogue, NY

Marlboro Industries, Ltd.
Marlboro, NY

Monarch Wine Co., Inc.
Brooklyn, NY

Pleasant Valley Wine Co.
Hammondsport, NY

Robin Fils & Cie, Ltd.
Batavia, NY

Royal Wine Corporation
Bronx, NY

Schapiro's Wine Co., Ltd.
New York, NY

Seneca Foods Corp.
(Boordy Vineyards Division)
Penn Yan, NY

Solano Winery, Inc.
Brooklyn, NY

Distillerie Stock U.S.A., Ltd.
Woodside, NY

Walter S. Taylor Bully Hill Wine Co.
Hammondsport, NY

The Taylor Wine Co., Inc.
Hammondsport, NY

Transamerica Wine Corp.
New York, NY

Widmer's Wine Cellars, Inc.
Naples, NY

NORTH CAROLINA

Wine Cellars, Inc.
Edenton, NC

OHIO

American Vineyards Co., Inc.
Cleveland, OH

Leslie J. Bretz
Middle Bass, OH

Catawba Island Wine Co.
(d.b.a. Mon Ami Champagne Co.)
Catawba Island, Port Clinton, OH

Cedar Hill Wine Co.
Cleveland Heights, OH

Chalet Debonne Vineyards
Madison, OH

Cohodas Vineyards, Inc.
Geneva, OH

Dover Vineyards, Inc.
Westlake, OH

Edward L. Feick
Sandusky, OH

The Hammer Company
Cleveland, OH

Heineman Winery
Put-in-Bay, OH

Edward W. Johlin
Oregon, OH

Klingshirn Winery
Avon Lake, OH

Le Boudin Vineyard & Winery
Cardington, OH

Mantey Vineyards, Inc.
Sandusky, OH

Markko Vineyard
Conneaut, OH

Meier's Wine Cellars, Inc.
Cincinnati, OH

Moyer Vineyards
Manchester, OH

Pompei Winery, Inc.
Cleveland, OH

Rini Wine Company
Cleveland, OH

Steuk Wine Company
Sandusky, OH

Warren J. Sublette Winery Co.
Cincinnati, OH

Tarula Farms
Clarksville, OH

Valley Vineyards Farm, Inc.
Morrow, OH

Willoughby Winery
Willoughby, OH

OKLAHOMA

Pete Schwarz Winery
Okarche, OK

OREGON

Bjelland Vineyards
Roseburg, OR

Henry Endres Winery
Oregon City, OR

The Eyrie Vineyards
Dundee, OR

Hillcrest Vineyard
Roseburg, OR

Honeywood Fruit Winery
Salem, OR

Knudsen-Erath Winery
Dundee, OR

Nehalem Bay Wine Co.
Nehalem, OR

Oak Knoll Winery, Inc.
Hillsboro, OR

Pioneer Homestead Winery, Inc.
Sandy, OR

Tualatin Vineyards, Inc.
Forest Grove, OR

PENNSYLVANIA

Bucks Country Vineyards, Inc.
New Hope, PA

Château Piatt Winery, Inc.
Allentown, PA

Conestoga Vineyards, Inc.
Birchrunville, PA

Kasser Distillers Prod. Corp.
Philadelphia, PA

Mazza Vineyards, Inc.
North East, PA

James Moroney, Inc.
Philadelphia, PA

A & R Nissley, Inc.
(d.b.a. Conoy Winery)
Bainbridge, PA

Penn-Shore Vineyards, Inc.
North East, PA

Presque Isle Wine Cellars
North East, PA

RHODE ISLAND

Sakonnet Vineyards
Little Compton, RI

SOUTH CAROLINA

Oakview Plantations, Inc., Vintners
Woodruff, SC

Tenner Brothers, Inc.
(Canandaigua Wine Co., Inc.)
Patrick, SC

TENNESSEE

Southwestern Wine & Liquor, Inc.
Memphis, TN

TEXAS

Guadalupe Valley Winery
New Braunfels, TX

Rio Grande Valley Citrus Winery
Progreso, TX

Llano Estacado Winery
(Staked Plains)
Lubbock, TX

Val Verde Winery
Del Rio, TX

VERMONT

Vermont Wineries, Inc.
Danby, VT

VIRGINIA

K. C. Arey & Co., Inc.
Danville, VA

Meredyth Vineyard
Middleburg, VA

Dixie Wine Company
Richmond, VA

Richard's Wine Cellars, Inc.
(Canandaigua Wine Co., Inc.)
Petersburg, VA

La Abra Farm & Winery
Lovingston, VA

WASHINGTON

Alhambra Wine Company
Selah, WA

Ste. Michelle Vintners
(d.b.a. National Wine Co. and the
    Pommerelle Co.)
Woodinville, WA

Associated Vintners, Inc.
Redmond, WA

Preston Wine Cellars
Pasco, WA

Manfred J. Vierthaler Winery
Sumner, WA

WISCONSIN

Fruit of the Woods Wine Cellar, Inc.
Three Lakes, WI

Von Stiehl Wine, Inc.
Algoma, WI

Stone Mill Winery, Inc.
Cedarburg, WI

The Wollersheim Winery, Inc.
Prairie Du Sac, WI

Source: *Wines & Vines*, Directory of the Wine Industry in North America, San Francisco, 1977.

APPENDIX H
EXPLANATION OF
ALCOHOLIC FERMENTATION

The juice from the freshly crushed grape berry contains sugars, acids, and other cell-sap-soluble components of the easily disrupted cells. Juice-insoluble substances and the contents of cells not easily broken, which may be important to the composition and quality of the wine, are dissolved in the wine by the alcohol and by other effects produced by fermentation. The metabolic activities of the fermenting wine yeast produce a theoretical conversion of 51 percent of the weight of sugar fermented to ethanol and the rest to carbon dioxide. Actual yields are slightly lower because the yeast produces a series of compounds other than alcohol. Some of the sugar is used to synthesize new yeast cells. The energy necessary for this synthesis and waste heat energy are produced by the yeast during the sequence of fermentation reactions terminating in ethanol, a by-product of the activity of anaerobic yeast. The ethanol, acetaldehyde, higher alcohols (fusel oils), and other products of alcoholic fermentation are important attributes of wine. The variable proportions of them contribute to type, flavor, and quality differences among wines. Some yeast cells die and "leak" or break up (autolyze) to contribute their soluble constituents to the solution. Therefore, the composition of the wine may be affected by the grape, by the direct and indirect reactions of alcoholic fermentation on grape must, by yeast-cell breakdown products, by activity of other microorganisms, and by reactions during processing.

The biochemistry of fermentation not only beautifully illuminates and clarifies the ancient art of making wine, but also explains and makes possible a calculated control of many of the "mysteries" which baffled the artisan winemaker. Aesthetics, however, is still a part of (and should not be displaced from) wine production and wine appreciation, but mystique should not remain if knowledge can be substituted.

* * *

The word *yeast* is believed to have reached English from the Anglo-Saxon *gist* via Greek *zestos* ("boiled") and Sanskrit *yasyati* ("it seethes"). To ferment is to seethe, or "boil" without a great deal of heat. The term *fermentation* today is used loosely to include all processes in which chemical changes are brought about in organic substances by the action of microorganisms (or less commonly by other cells or free enzymes). Important commercial examples include the production of antibiotics by submerged aerobic mold and actinomycete fermentations. With some exceptions, such as vinegar production, the "natural" food fermentations observed by housewives and farmers of long ago were usually capable of changing foods in sealed or deep containers—that is, were anaerobic. This includes sauerkraut, pickle, and olive fermentations by lactic-acid bacteria, as well as the alcoholic fermentation by yeasts. This "boiling" without heat was a great mystery to the ancients and was one of the first subjects studied in the emerging life sciences. The knowledge resulting from the study of wine fermentations and the so-called diseases of wine was a major contributor to the development and early progress of the modern sciences of microbiology and biochemistry.

Only a little over a hundred years ago it was discovered that alcoholic fermentation could occur naturally only in the presence of small living "ferments," the yeasts. Pasteur, from his studies in the 1860s, defined fermentation as life without air (anaerobic life), in contrast to the respiration of animals and higher plants which require air (are aerobic). In 1897 Edward Buchner reported that yeasts could be broken up and the cell-free juice would still produce alcohol from sugar. Thus the idea arose that there were "organized" ferments (cells of microorganisms) which could be broken down to "unorganized" ferments. These we know now as the enzymes, proteinaceous molecules which catalyze each of the metabolic reactions of the cell. Originally it was assumed that one enzyme of the yeast produced alcohol from sugar, but further study revealed that separate enzymes carry on steps in the process. The process of sugar catabolism to ethyl alcohol by yeasts and to lactic acid by the muscles of animals was eventually found to be essentially the same process except for the very last steps. This pathway of carbohydrate utilization by living organisms is usually called the Embden-Meyerhof pathway, after two of the many scientists who have contributed to our present understanding of this biochemical process.

The process of fermentation of one molecule of a simple sugar to alcohol was shown to result in two molecules of ethyl alcohol (more simply called ethanol) and two molecules of carbon dioxide. This was formulated by Gay-Lussac in 1810 into the equation which bears his name. This equation on the overall process can be written in a slightly modernized version as:

$$1 \text{ glucose } (C_6H_{12}O_6) \rightarrow 2 \text{ ethanol } (CH_3CH_2OH) +$$
$$2CO_2 + \text{ about 56 kilocalories of energy}$$

Thus 180 grams of glucose (the molecular weight in grams computed from the atomic weights of carbon 12, hydrogen 1, and oxygen 16) should produce a total of 92 grams of ethanol and 88 grams of carbon dioxide when completely fermented. This represents the maximum theoretical ethanol yield, which is 51.1 percent of the weight of the sugar (hexose) fermented. Although actual yields in winemaking approach this level, they are slightly lower owing to the diversion of some of the sugar's atoms to other products, incorporation of sugar derivatives into the yeast cells, losses by volatilization, and so on.

The Embden-Meyerhof pathway of conversion of sugars to ethanol does not require oxygen, and in fact the mixture of air into the fermenting solution decreases the yield of ethanol. Under truly aerobic conditions no alcohol is produced even though yeast growth is excellent, and if ethanol is already present the yeast cells, in the presence of air, can eventually metabolize it completely to carbon dioxide and water. The normal condition for alcoholic fermentation, then, is the absence of air or oxygen. This is relatively simple to accomplish, since any oxygen dissolved in the solution to be fermented is rapidly consumed by the yeast cells during initial (aerobic) multiplication. Access of further oxygen during fermentation in the typical deep liquid layer is not usually a serious problem, particularly since carbon dioxide is produced in large volume, and as it escapes it sweeps away the air.

The 56 kilocalories of energy indicated in the Gay-Lussac equation as a product of fermentation of one gram molecular weight of glucose represents the total energy change during the reaction. If glucose is "burned" either actually or by complete metabolic combustion to carbon dioxide and water, the total heat energy released is 673 kilocalories. The yeast cell ferments sugar *not* to get alcohol and carbon dioxide; it has no use for them and thus they accumulate or escape. It does need energy, and this is the "profit" the yeast gains from fermenting the sugar. The energy is needed to do the chemical work of synthesizing the substances of more yeast cells; without it no reproduction of the yeast can occur. It is obvious that if 673 kilocalories are produced when yeast converts 180 grams of glucose to carbon dioxide and water by complete oxidation, and only 56 kilocalories are produced by alcoholic fermentation, more than twelve times the amount of energy is potentially available for producing new yeast cells aerobically than anaerobically. To put it another way, yeasts must metabolize more than twelve times as much sugar to produce the same amount of cellular growth when growing anaerobically as they would if oxygen were available to them. This is fortunate for us, because it means that during alcoholic fermentation the yeasts must "process" a great deal of sugar to alcohol with relatively little cell multiplication and therefore relatively little consumption of the sugar and other nutrients to build cells. If our object is to produce a large number of yeast cells, whether for use in inoculation of musts for wine fermentation or as pressed yeast cakes for the baker, the pumping of oxygen (air) through the solution containing the yeast will produce up to twelvefold more cells per unit of sugar consumed and lower or eliminate the production of ethanol. The fact that the addition of oxygen to fermenting yeasts inhibits the conversion of glucose to ethanol, and gives more cells per unit of glucose consumed, was observed by Pasteur and is termed the Pasteur effect.

The total amount of energy released during conversion of glucose to ethanol by yeasts (about 56 kilocalories/mole) is not available to the yeast for metabolic work. About 40 percent of this amount, or 22 kilocalories, is captured in a usable form by the yeast. The rest is lost to the yeast and appears as heat. Thus the temperature of the fermenting solution is increased significantly. The usable energy is captured and transferred to other uses by the yeast cell in the form of a complex chemical, adenosine triphosphate, usually abbreviated ATP. A phosphate ion from the fermenting solution is combined by enzymes of the yeast with adenosine diphosphate, ADP, to give ATP. This illustrates one important reason why yeasts require the presence of phosphate for growth. The formation of ATP requires energy, and the energy is obtained by the yeast from specific steps in the conversion of sugar to ethanol. Once "built into" ATP, this energy can be temporarily stored, transferred, and used by the yeast for a multitude of metabolic reactions requiring energy. In fact, ATP is the primary energy-exchanging substance for all activities of living organisms including the muscular work you are doing right now as you breathe.

Converting sugar to alcohol requires at least a dozen enzymes, each of which catalyzes one step in the process sequence of the Embden-Meyerhof pathway. The enzymes acting first are those necessary to get the particular sugar being fermented phosphorylated and isomerized into the form of fructose-1,6-diphosphate. This hexose phosphate is necessary for starting the remainder of the breakdown reactions, and two molecules of ATP are consumed in its formation from the fermentable simple sugars. The next reaction splits the 6-carbon unit, fructose-1,6-diphosphate, into two 3-carbon triose phosphates. These are dihydroxyacetone phosphate and glyceraldehyde-3-phosphate, which can be converted one into the other by the action of an isomerase (enzyme). A series of reaction steps, each with its own enzyme, then occurs, and eventually two molecules of pyruvic acid result. During these reactions hydrogen is transferred to a coenzyme carrier and two new molecules of ATP are formed for each 3-carbon unit, or a total of four, giving a net gain of two ATP per sugar molecule fermented. Each new gram molecule of ATP represents about 11 kilocalories of useful energy gained by the yeast and therefore accounts for the 22 kilocalories of energy yeasts gain in converting one mole of glucose to two moles of ethanol.

The pyruvic acid (CH_3—CO—COOH) is converted to acetaldehyde (CH_3CHO) by loss of one molecule of carbon dioxide (or two per original hexose sugar.) This escaping carbon dioxide is one of the major products of fermentation. The acetaldehyde is ordinarily reduced by the addition to it of the hydrogen transferred to the coenzyme carrier at the earlier step mentioned. This final reaction—

$$CH_3CHO + H_2 \rightarrow CH_3CH_2OH$$

—is catalyzed by the enzyme alcohol dehydrogenase. It is a reversible reaction, and acetaldehyde can be produced from ethanol. All the reactions in this sequence are reversible if the proper conditions, enzymes, and energy are supplied, except that of the decarboxylation (carbon dioxide loss) of pyruvic acid. The reversal of the sequence would produce sugars from smaller molecules and has several features in common with the way in which the grapevine makes its sugar.

This reaction system may seem a bit complicated, but it has been substantiated by chemists and is one of the fundamentals of modern biochemistry. It clearly explains the origin of the major products of alcoholic fermentation. It also explains the presence of at least small amounts of many of the intermediate compounds in the sequence, such as acetaldehyde and pyruvic acid. Acetaldehyde reacts with sulfur dioxide, or rather the bisulfite ion in solution, to form an addition product which cannot be reduced to ethanol by the coenzyme hydrogen carrier system. The hydrogen is diverted under this condition to reduce the triose dihydroxyacetone to glycerol. Some glycerol (also called glycerine, CH_2OH—$CHOH$—CH_2OH) is produced to the extent of about 0.2 to 1.5 percent in every wine fermentation, but considerably more may be produced under certain conditions, including the presence of high amounts of bisulfite. Glycerol production for explosives (nitroglycerine) by fermentation was an important development in the First World War. Glycerol is a slightly sweet substance and *may* contribute to the viscosity and apparent "body" of some wines.

Glycerol is a constituent of fats, and as such some of it is incorporated into the yeast cell. Pyruvic acid is partly converted to alanine, one of the amino acids of yeast proteins. Reactions such as these divert some of the atoms from the original sugar molecule into yeast-cell constituents and decrease the yield of ethanol. Other reactions, such as the enzymatic reduction of a small amount of pyruvic acid to lactic acid or the conversion of some acetaldehyde to acetic acid, not only divert some of the carbon source to products other than alcohol, but also explain the presence of small amounts of these compounds which may contribute to a wine's flavor.

Yeasts are able to grow aerobically and can convert ethanol to acetaldehyde and then, via a series of reactions known as the Krebs cycle, after its discoverer, to carbon dioxide and water. Various degrees of temporary, partial, or incomplete aerobic metabolism can occur or be produced in wine fermentation. In the production of *flor* sherry, for example, the level of acetaldehyde and certain other flavor-producing substances is much increased by aerobic growth of yeast in or on the surface of previously fermented wine. In any typical wine fermentation, some oxygen gains access to the wine even though relatively anaerobic conditions must exist to produce wine. Again, as a result, more or less of the carbon source is diverted from ethanol production to other products. Among these products are citric acid, succinic acid, fumaric acid, malic acid, and α-ketoglutaric acid. Not all compounds that are found in wine got there from the action of yeasts, however, for the Krebs cycle occurs in grapes, too, and produces the greater part of the total acids found in wine.

These many possible and actual diversions of the carbon of sugar during wine fermentation explain the fact that whereas 51.1 percent of the weight of glucose theoretically should appear as ethanol, only about 48 percent actually does so. Since the yeast does produce 90 to 95 percent of the theoretical amount of ethanol, it might be assumed that the small amounts of other products are unimportant. This is far from the truth, because many of the constituents minor in amount in wine are major in importance to flavor and aroma. Many of the important esters and other odorous constituents are present in very small amounts and in complex mixtures which are difficult to analyze; yet they determine the quality and distinctiveness of wines and most other food products. In wines many of these important trace compounds arise from the grapes themselves, but many are produced or are modified as the yeasts play their role in the process of winemaking.

Higher alcohols, sometimes called fusel oils, occur in fermented beverages. By higher alcohols is meant those like ethanol, but with more than two carbon atoms. Particularly the 5-carbon or amyl alcohols, 4-carbon butanols, and 3-carbon propyl alcohols or propanols may occur in wine in various isomers and proportions. These compounds arise in large part during alcoholic fermentation, and their relative concentration in wines and spirits is a factor in the flavor and quality of the product, although they ordinarily total rather less than 0.1 percent of the wine. It was believed, based upon the work of Ehrlich, that these compounds arose by the action of the yeast enzymes upon the amino acids in wine musts. An example is the conversion of leucine into isoamyl alcohol:

$$(CH_3)_2—CH—CH_2—CH(NH_2)—COOH + H_2O$$
$$\rightarrow (CH_3)_2—CH—CH_2—CH_2OH + NH_3 + CO_2$$

This is an oversimplification because, among other things, more higher alcohols are produced under some conditions than can be accounted for by complete conversion of all the respective amino acids present in the medium. Rather, it is now known, the carbon skeletons which the yeast produces to make its amino acids can also be diverted to produce these alcohols. This is another example of the complex and intimate interplay among the numerous chemical reactions which characterize the metabolism of living cells, and alcoholic fermentation in particular.

As we have seen, the grape berry contains sugars, acids, pigments, tannins, and odorous compounds; and some of these ingredients, particularly sugars and amino-acid derivatives, are used and transformed by yeasts during fermentation. Fermentation, particularly the alcohol produced, affects the solvent powers of the fluid and influences the composition of the wine. The pigments, many of the odorous compounds, and part of the tannin compounds are localized within the cells of the skin of the grape berry. Another large portion of the total tannin of the berry is found in the seeds. Some of these compounds are not released at all and some do not go completely into the solution merely as a result of the crushing of the grapes. Time for diffusion from the cells and the extractive effect of alcohol are both provided during fermentation, if the solid parts of the berry remain in the must during this period. The turbulence in the fermentation vessel and perhaps the enzymic actions of the yeast also affect the transfer of less soluble grape-cell components to the solution. Thus, although the grape produces the tannin, anthocyanin pigment, and aroma compounds, and the yeast may not produce any synthesis or chemical change of these compounds, their content in the wine can be strongly influenced by events during the fermentation process.

Source: Maynard Amerine and V.L. Singleton, *Wine: An Introduction.* Copyright © 1965, 1977 by The Regents of the University of California; reprinted by permission of the University of California Press.

APPENDIX 1
MUST WEIGHT AND
SUGAR CONTENT MEASUREMENTS

The specific gravity of a liquid is the relative density of the liquid compared with water, the specific gravity of which is designated as 1.000.

The German *Öchsle* reading is a hydrometer determination of the specific gravity of the grape must. The hydrometer is calibrated to indicate the specific gravity directly, with the number 1 to the left of the decimal point understood. In the table below the average minimum *Öchsle* values for must that can produce Kabinett, Spätlese, Auslese, Beerenauslese, and Trockenbeerenauslese wines are indicated by the letters within parentheses. Slightly lower values are allowed in the Moselle region.

The Brix or Balling hydrometer readings are calibrated to indicate directly the sugar content of the unfermented must. Thus a Balling reading of 22 indicates 22 percent sugar by weight in the unfermented grape must.

The Dujardin hydrometer, when inserted in the unfermented must, indicates the potential alcoholic percentage by volume of the finished wine, assuming that all of the sugar is converted to alcohol. Since high must weight wines usually have residual sugar, their alcohol content would be lower than indicated in the table, as not all of the sugar is converted to alcohol by the yeast.

Specific gravity	German Öchsle reading	Percent sugar by weight	Brix or Balling hydrometer reading	Approximate Dujardin hydrometer reading
1.035	35	9	9.0	4.0
1.039	39	10	10.0	4.5
1.043	43	11	11.0	5.0
1.047	47	12	12.0	5.5
1.052	52	13	13.0	6.3
1.056	56	14	14.0	7.1
1.059	59	15	15.0	7.5
1.064	64	16	16.0	8.2
1.068	68	17	17.0	9.0
1.072	72(K)	18	18.0	9.5
1.077	77	19	19.0	10.3
1.081	81	20	20.0	11.0
1.086	86(S)	21	21.0	11.6
1.090	90	22	22.0	12.2
1.095	95(A)	23	23.0	13.0
1.099	99	24	24.0	13.9
1.104	104	25	25.0	14.4
1.109	109	26	26.0	15.2
1.113	113	27	27.0	16.0
1.118	118	28	28.0	16.7
1.123	123(BA)	29	29.0	17.5
1.127	127	30	30.0	18.2
1.150	150(TBA)	35	35.0	21.0

APPENDIX J
CALORIC VALUES OF ALCOHOLIC BEVERAGES

Wines	Calories per ounce (approx.)
Red table wine	18
Dry white table wine	20
Champagne (brut)	21
Champagne (extra dry)	29
Catawba (sweet)	30
Madeira	32
Port (U.S.)	43
Porto (imported)	39
Sherry (U.S.)	36
Sherry (dry, imported)	32
Vermouth (dry, French)	27
Vermouth (sweet, Italian)	44

Malt beverages	Calories per 8 ounces
Beer	100
Ale	150

Spirits	Calories per ounce (approx.)
Vodka, gin, whiskies, etc.	65-85

Liqueurs	Calories per ounce (approx.)
Bénédictine, Chartreuse, Drambuie, and other proprietary and generic liqueurs	100-120

Bitters	Calories per teaspoon
Aromatic bitters	10

APPENDIX K

TEMPERATURE CONVERSIONS

Degrees Fahrenheit (°F) to Degrees Celsius (°C)*

°F	°C	°F	°C	°F	°C
+ 0	− 17.78	+ 60	+ 15.56	+ 120	+ 48.87
1	17.22	61	16.11	121	49.44
2	16.67	62	16.67	122	50.00
3	16.11	63	17.22	123	50.56
4	15.56	64	17.78	124	51.11
+ 5	− 15.00	+ 65	+ 18.33	+ 125	+ 51.67
6	14.44	66	18.89	126	52.22
7	13.89	67	19.44	127	52.78
8	13.33	68	20.00	128	53.33
9	12.78	69	20.56	129	53.89
+ 10	− 12.22	+ 70	+ 21.11	+ 130	+ 54.44
11	11.67	71	21.67	131	55.00
12	11.11	72	22.22	132	55.56
13	10.56	73	22.78	133	56.11
14	10.00	74	23.33	134	56.67
+ 15	− 9.44	+ 75	+ 23.89	+ 135	+ 57.22
16	8.89	76	24.44	136	57.78
17	8.33	77	25.00	137	58.33
18	7.78	78	25.56	138	58.89
19	7.22	79	26.11	139	59.44
+ 20	− 6.67	+ 80	+ 26.67	+ 140	+ 60.00
21	6.11	81	27.22	141	60.56
22	5.56	82	27.78	142	61.11
23	5.00	83	28.33	143	61.67
24	4.44	84	28.89	144	62.22
+ 25	− 3.89	+ 85	+ 29.44	+ 145	+ 62.78
26	3.33	86	30.00	146	63.33
27	2.78	87	30.56	147	63.89
28	2.22	88	31.11	148	64.44
29	1.67	89	31.67	149	65.00
+ 30	− 1.11	+ 90	+ 32.22	+ 150	+ 65.56
31	0.56	91	32.78	155	68.33
32	0.00	92	33.33	160	71.11
33	+ 0.56	93	33.89	165	73.89
34	1.11	94	34.44	170	76.67
+ 35	+ 1.67	+ 95	+ 35.00	+ 175	+ 79.44
36	2.22	96	35.56	180	82.22
37	2.78	97	36.11	185	85.00
38	3.33	98	36.67	190	87.78
39	3.89	99	37.22	195	90.56
+ 40	+ 4.44	+ 100	+ 37.78	+ 200	+ 93.33
41	5.00	101	38.33	205	96.11
42	5.56	102	38.89	210	98.89
43	6.11	103	39.44	215	101.67
44	6.67	104	40.00	220	104.44
+ 45	+ 7.22	+ 105	+ 40.56	+ 225	+ 107.22
46	7.78	106	41.11	230	110.00
47	8.33	107	41.67	235	112.78
48	8.89	108	42.22	240	115.56
49	9.44	109	42.78	245	118.33
+ 50	+ 10.00	+ 110	+ 43.33	+ 250	+ 121.11
51	10.56	111	43.89	255	123.89
52	11.11	112	44.44	260	126.67
53	11.67	113	45.00	265	129.44
54	12.22	114	45.56	270	132.22
+ 55	+ 12.78	+ 115	+ 46.11	+ 275	+ 135.00
56	13.33	116	46.67	280	137.78
57	13.89	117	47.22	285	140.56
58	14.44	118	47.78	290	143.33
59	15.00	119	48.33	295	146.11

Water freezes $\begin{bmatrix} 32°F \\ 0°C \end{bmatrix}$

Ethyl alcohol boils $\begin{bmatrix} 173°F \\ 78.5°C \end{bmatrix}$

Water boils $\begin{bmatrix} 212°F \\ 100°C \end{bmatrix}$

The formula used to derive the table is:
$$°C = 5/9 \, [°F − 32]$$

*Degrees Celsius was formerly called degrees Centigrade. The change was made to honor Anders Celsius (1701-1744) in accordance with the scientific custom of naming units of measurement after famous scientists who have contributed to that field.

APPENDIX L
METRIC CONVERSIONS
FOR WEIGHTS AND MEASURES IN
THE UNITED STATES AND ENGLAND

WEIGHTS AND MEASURES IN THE UNITED STATES AND
GREAT BRITAIN AND METRIC SYSTEMS

For most purposes the modern units used for measures and weights in the United States are the same as those used in Great Britain. The major exception is in the measurement of capacity. In the following tables, therefore, there are three systems for liquid capacity—U.S., British, and metric—instead of the two major systems—U.S.-British combined and metric.

The S.I. system (*Système Internationale*), a refinement of the long-used metric system, will in time become the universal system of measurement. Britain is already committed to a complete transfer to this system, and the United States has approved transfer on a voluntary, industry-by-industry, basis.

*United States
Great Britain*

Metric or S.I.

LENGTH

12 inches	= 1 foot	10 millimeters	= 1 centimeter
3 feet	= 1 yard	10 centimeters	= 1 decimeter
1,760 yards	= 1 mile	10 decimeters	= 1 meter
5,280 feet	= 1 mile	10 meters	= 1 dekameter
6,080 feet	= 1 nautical mile	10 dekameters	= 1 hectometer
		10 hectometers	= 1 kilometer

AREA

144 square inches	= 1 square foot	100 square centimeters	= 1 square decimeter
9 square feet	= 1 square yard	100 square decimeters	= 1 square meter (centare)
4,840 square yards	= 1 acre	100 square meters	= 1 square dekameter (are)
43,560 square feet	= 1 acre	10,000 square meters	= 1 hectare
640 acres	= 1 square mile	100 hectares	= 1 square kilometer

VOLUME AND DRY CAPACITY

1,728 cubic inches	= 1 cubic foot	1,000 cubic centimeters	= 1 cubic decimeter
27 cubic feet	= 1 cubic yard	1,000 cubic decimeters	= 1 cubic meter
1 dry pint	= 33.6 cubic inches	1,000 cubic meters	= 1 cubic dekameter
1 dry quart (2 pints)	= 67.201 cubic inches	1,000 cubic dekameters	= 1 cubic hectometer
1 peck (8 quarts)	= 537.6 cubic inches	1,000 cubic hectometers	= 1 cubic kilometer
1 bushel (4 pecks)	= 2,150.42 cubic inches		

United States
Great Britain
(avoirdupois weight)

Metric or S.I.

WEIGHT

437.5 grains	= 1 ounce		1,000 milligrams	= 1 gram
16 ounces	= 1 pound		1,000 grams	= 1 kilogram
100 pounds	= 1 cental		100 kilograms	= 1 quintal
2,000 pounds	= 1 short ton		1,000 kilograms	= 1 metric ton
2,240 pounds	= 1 long ton			

(Also in Great Britain)

14 pounds	= 1 stone
2 stones	= 1 quarter
4 quarters	= 1 hundredweight
20 hundredweights	= 1 long ton

LIQUID CAPACITY

United States

16 fluid ounces	= 1 pint
2 pints	= 1 quart
4 quarts	= 1 gallon
5 fifths	= 1 gallon
1 fluid ounce	= 1.8 cubic inches
1 pint	= 28.88 cubic inches
1 quart	= 57.75 cubic inches
1 gallon	= 231 cubic inches

Great Britain

20 fluid ounces	= 1 imperial pint
2 imperial pints	= 1 imperial quart
4 imperial quarts	= 1 imperial gallon*
1 fluid ounce	= 1.735 cubic inches
1 imperial pint	= 34.68 cubic inches
1 imperial quart	= 69.35 cubic inches
1 imperial gallon	= 277.4 cubic inches
*1.2 American gallons	= 1 imperial gallon

Metric or S.I.

10 milliliters	= 1 centiliter
100 centiliters	= 1 liter
100 liters	= 1 hectoliter
10 hectoliters	= 1 kiloliter
1 milliliter	= 1 cubic centimeter
1 liter	= 1,000 cubic centimeters
1 hectoliter	= 100,000 cubic centimeters

CONVERSION TABLES FOR U.S. AND METRIC EQUIVALENTS

	To Change	To	Multiply by
LENGTH	centimeters	inches	0.394
	inches	centimeters	2.540
	meters	feet	3.281
	feet	meters	0.305
	kilometers	miles	0.621
	miles	kilometers	1.609
AREA	square centimeters	square inches	0.155
	square inches	square centimeters	6.451
	square meters	square feet	10.764
	square feet	square meters	0.093
	hectares	acres	2.471
	acres	hectares	0.405
	square kilometers	square miles	0.386
	square miles	square kilometers	2.590
VOLUME	cubic centimeters	cubic inches	0.061
	cubic inches	cubic centimeters	16.387
	cubic meters	cubic feet	35.315
	cubic feet	cubic meters	0.0283
LIQUID CAPACITY	centiliters	fluid ounces	0.338
	fluid ounces	centiliters	2.957
	liters	gallons	0.264
	gallons	liters	3.785
	hectoliters	gallons	26.418
	gallons	hectoliters	0.0378
WEIGHT	grams	ounces	0.035
	ounces	grams	28.35
	kilograms	pounds	2.205
	pounds	kilograms	0.454
	metric ton	long ton	0.984
	long ton	metric ton	1.016
	metric ton	short ton	0.907
	short ton	metric ton	1.102

APPENDIX M
BEVERAGE CONTAINER CAPACITIES

BOTTLE SIZES

Pre-metric terminology	Metric terminology	Metric capacity	Fluid-ounce capacity
		WINES	
Miniature	Miniature	100 ml*	3.4
Split	Small	187 ml	6.3
Tenth	Medium	375 ml	12.7
Fifth	Regular	750 ml	25.4
Quart	Large	1.0 liters†	33.8
Magnum	Magnum	1.5 liters	50.7
Jeroboam	Extra Large	3.0 liters	101.4
Rehoboam§	—	4.5 liters	156
Methuselah§	—	6.0 liters	179-208
		SPIRITS	
Miniature	Miniature	50 ml*	1.7
Half-Pint	Small	200 ml	6.8
Pint	Medium	500 ml	16.9
Fifth	Regular	750 ml	25.4
Quart	Large	1.0 liter†	33.8
Half-Gallon	Extra Large	1.75 liters	59.2

Note: Liqueurs and cordials previously were exempt from standards of fill requirements and the number of available bottle sizes eventually reached an extreme of thirty-nine. Liqueur and cordial bottles must now conform to metric sizes, and as with other spirits the permitted number is six.

*ml means milliliters, or 1/1000 liter.

†1 liter equals 1,000 milliliters.

§These sizes are not presently accepted by the B.A.T.F.

TRADITIONAL WINE AND SPIRIT CASK STANDARDS WITH LITER EQUIVALENTS

	Approx. gallons	Approx. liters
Barrique of Bordeaux (24 cases)	59	225
Tonneau of Bordeaux (4 *barriques*)	238	900
*Pièce** of Burgundy (24-25 cases)	60	228
Queue of Burgundy (2 *pièces*)	120	456
*Pièce** of Champagne	54	200
Fuder of the Moselle	264	1,000
Stück of the Rhine	317	1,200
Halbstück (Fass) of the Rhine	158	600
Pipe of Porto or Tarragona	138	522
Pipe of Madeira	110	418
Butt of sherry	132	500
Hogshead of sherry (one-half butt)	66	250
Hogshead of Cognac	72	272
Puncheon of rum (varies in value)	112	422

*The term *pièce* is also used in the Loire and Rhône and denotes varying capacities, all approximately 60 gallons.

HISTORICAL BEVERAGE CAPACITIES IN GREAT BRITAIN

2 mouthfuls	=	1 jigger (handful!)
2 jiggers	=	1 jack (jackpot)
2 jacks	=	1 jill (gill)
2 jills	=	1 cup (half-pint)
2 cups	=	1 pint (jug)
2 pints	=	1 quart
2 quarts	=	1 pottle
2 pottles	=	1 wine gallon
2 gallons	=	1 peck (flagon)
4 pecks	=	1 bushel
2 bushels	=	1 cask
2 casks	=	1 barrel
2 barrels	=	1 hogshead
2 hogsheads	=	1 pipe (butt)
2 pipes	=	1 tun

The units listed in this table, whose order is essentially derived from a doubling process, varied greatly throughout English history. One of the measurements that varied most was the barrel. Originally there were two types of barrels, the ale barrel and the beer barrel. The ale barrel contained 32 corn gallons (1 corn gallon = 268 cubic inches). It then was changed to hold 32 ale gallons (1 ale gallon = 282 cubic inches). The original beer barrel contained 36 wine gallons (1 wine gallon = 231 cubic inches). Thus the later ale barrel contained 32 x 282 = 9,024 cubic inches, as against the beer barrel's 36 x 231 = 8,316 cubic inches. One had to know what type of barrel one was dealing with to avoid being confused or cheated.

The conversion of all capacities to metric measurements eventually should eliminate the inconsistencies of the past.

Source: H. Arthur Klein, *The World of Measurements* (New York: Simon & Schuster, 1974).

APPENDIX N
VINEYARD AND WINERY YIELDS
AND CONVERSIONS

The weight of grapes grown in a unit area of a vineyard is known as *grape yield*. The units used to measure this yield in some of the major wine regions of the world are:

UNITED STATES		FRANCE		ITALY		GERMANY
$1 \dfrac{\text{short ton}}{\text{acre}}$	=	$2.25 \dfrac{tonne}{\text{hectare}}$	=	$22.5 \dfrac{quintale}{\text{hectare}}$	=	$22.5 \dfrac{Doppelzentneren}{Hektar}$

Weight conversion factors:

$$1 \text{ short ton } = 0.9 \text{ metric } tonne = 9 \; quintale = 9 \; Doppelzentneren$$

The volume of table wine that is produced from a specific quantity of grapes varies from winery to winery and from region to region. The range is from 150 to 200 gallons of table wine produced from a short ton of grapes crushed. An average yield is 170 gallons per ton. With this average figure as a base, some conversions into other units are:

	UNITED STATES	FRANCE	ITALY	GERMANY
WINE YIELD	$170 \dfrac{\text{gallons}}{\text{ton}}$	$7 \dfrac{\text{hectoliters}}{tonne}$	$70 \dfrac{\text{liters}}{quintale}$	$70 \dfrac{\text{liters}}{Doppelzentner}$
CASE* YIELD	$70 \dfrac{\text{cases}}{\text{ton}}$	$78 \dfrac{\text{cases}}{tonne}$	$7.8 \dfrac{\text{cases}}{quintale}$	$7.8 \dfrac{\text{cases}}{Doppelzentner}$

Another important vineyard term is *harvest yield*. This can range from 1 ton per acre to 16 tons per acre. To determine the wine yield in gallons per acre, multiply:

$$\text{Harvest yield} \quad \times \quad 170 \frac{\text{gallons}}{\text{ton}} \quad = \quad \frac{\text{gallons}}{\text{acre}}.$$

To convert gallons per acre into hectoliters per hectare, multiply by 10.69. To convert cases per acre into cases per hectare, multiply by 2.47.

*A case is 12 bottles at 75 centiliters.

Source: William Lembeck.

575

APPENDIX O

COMPARISON OF U.S. PROOF, BRITISH "SIKES," AND METRIC "GAY-LUSSAC" TABLES OF ALCOHOLIC STRENGTHS—at 60° F

U.S. PROOF	BRITISH SIKES U.P.*	GAY-LUSSAC Alcohol by volume	U.S. PROOF	BRITISH SIKES U.P.*	GAY-LUSSAC Alcohol by volume	U.S. PROOF	BRITISH SIKES U.P.*	GAY-LUSSAC Alcohol by volume	U.S. PROOF	BRITISH SIKES O.P.*	GAY-LUSSAC Alcohol by volume
0	100	0	52	54.5	26.0	104	8.9	52.0	149	30.5	74.5
1	99.1	0.5	53	53.6	26.5	105	8.1	52.5	150	31.3	75.0
2	98.2	1.0	54	52.7	27.0	106	7.2	53.0	151	32.2	75.5
3	97.4	1.5	55	51.8	27.5	107	6.3	53.5	152	33.1	76.0
4	96.5	2.0	56	51.0	28.0	108	5.4	54.0	153	34.0	76.5
5	95.6	2.5	57	50.1	28.5	109	4.6	54.5	154	34.9	77.0
6	94.7	3.0	58	49.2	29.0	110	3.7	55.0	155	35.7	77.5
7	93.9	3.5	59	48.3	29.5	111	2.8	55.5	156	36.6	78.0
8	93.0	4.0	60	47.5	30.0	112	1.9	56.0	157	37.5	78.5
9	92.1	4.5	61	46.6	30.5	113	1.1	56.5	158	38.4	79.0
10	91.2	5.0	62	45.7	31.0	114	0.2	57.0	159	39.2	79.5
11	90.4	5.5	63	44.8	31.5				160	40.1	80.0
12	89.5	6.0	64	44.0	32.0	114.3	0.0 Proof	57.1	161	41.0	80.5
13	88.6	6.5	65	43.1	32.5				162	41.9	81.0
14	87.7	7.0	66	42.2	33.0	*U.S. PROOF	BRITISH SIKES O.P.*	GAY-LUSSAC Alcohol by volume*	163	42.7	81.5
15	86.9	7.5	67	41.3	33.5				164	43.6	82.0
16	86.0	8.0	68	40.5	34.0				165	44.5	82.5
17	85.1	8.5	69	39.6	34.5				166	45.4	83.0
18	84.2	9.0	70	38.7	35.0	115	0.7	57.5	167	46.2	83.5
19	83.4	9.5	71	37.8	35.5	116	1.6	58.0	168	47.1	84.0
20	82.5	10.0	72	37.0	36.0	117	2.3	58.5	169	48.0	84.5
21	81.6	10.5	73	36.1	36.5	118	3.3	59.0	170	48.9	85.0
22	80.7	11.0	74	35.2	37.0	119	4.2	59.5	171	49.7	85.5
23	79.9	11.5	75	34.3	37.5	120	5.1	60.0	172	50.6	86.0
24	79.0	12.0	76	33.5	38.0	121	6.0	60.5	173	51.5	86.5
25	78.1	12.5	77	32.6	38.5	122	6.8	61.0	174	52.4	87.0
26	77.2	13.0	78	31.7	39.0	123	7.7	61.5	175	53.2	87.5
27	76.4	13.5	79	30.8	39.5	124	8.6	62.0	176	54.1	88.0
28	75.5	14.0	80	29.9	40.0	125	9.5	62.5	177	55.0	88.5
29	74.6	14.5	81	29.1	40.5	126	10.3	63.0	178	55.9	89.0
30	73.7	15.0	82	28.2	41.0	127	11.2	63.5	179	56.7	89.5
31	72.9	15.5	83	27.3	41.5	128	12.1	64.0	180	57.6	90.0
32	72.0	16.0	84	26.4	42.0	129	13.0	64.5	181	58.5	90.5
33	71.1	16.5	85	25.6	42.5	130	13.8	65.0	182	59.4	91.0
34	70.2	17.0	86	24.7	43.0	131	14.7	65.5	183	60.2	91.5
35	69.4	17.5	87	23.8	43.5	132	15.6	66.0	184	61.1	92.0
36	68.5	18.0	88	22.9	44.0	133	16.5	66.5	185	62.0	92.5
37	67.6	18.5	89	22.1	44.5	134	17.3	67.0	186	62.9	93.0
38	66.7	19.0	90	21.2	45.0	135	18.2	67.5	187	63.7	93.5
39	65.8	19.5	91	20.3	45.5	136	19.1	68.0	188	64.6	94.0
40	65.0	20.0	92	19.4	46.0	137	20.0	68.5	189	65.5	94.5
41	64.1	20.5	93	18.6	46.5	138	20.8	69.0	190	66.4	95.0
42	63.2	21.0	94	17.7	47.0	139	21.7	69.5	191	67.3	95.5
43	62.3	21.5	95	16.8	47.5	140	22.6	70.0	192	68.1	96.0
44	61.5	22.0	96	15.9	48.0	141	23.5	70.5	193	69.0	96.5
45	60.6	22.5	97	15.1	48.5	142	24.3	71.0	194	69.9	97.0
46	59.7	23.0	98	14.2	49.0	143	25.2	71.5	195	70.8	97.5
47	58.8	23.5	99	13.3	49.5	144	26.1	72.0	196	71.6	98.0
48	58.0	24.0	100	12.4	50.0	145	27.0	72.5	197	72.5	98.5
49	57.1	24.5	101	11.6	50.5	146	27.8	73.0	198	73.4	99.0
50	56.2	25.0	102	10.7	51.0	147	28.7	73.5	199	74.3	99.5
51	55.3	25.5	103	9.8	51.5	148	29.6	74.0	200	75.1	100.0

*U.P. = Underproof; O.P. = Overproof.

APPENDIX P
U.S. STANDARDS OF IDENTITY
FOR DISTILLED SPIRITS

Subpart C—Standards of Identity for Distilled Spirits

§ 5.21 Application of standards.

The standards of identity for the several classes and types of distilled spirits set forth in this part shall be applicable only to distilled spirits for beverage or other nonindustrial purposes.

§ 5.22 The standards of identity.

Standards of identity for the several classes and types of distilled spirits set forth in this section shall be as follows . . . :

(a) *Class 1; neutral spirits or alcohol.* "Neutral spirits" or "alcohol" are distilled spirits produced from any material at or above 190° proof, and, if bottled, bottled at not less than 80° proof.

(1) "Vodka" is neutral spirits so distilled, or so treated after distillation with charcoal or other materials, as to be without distinctive character, aroma, taste, or color.

(2) "Grain spirits" are neutral spirits distilled from a fermented mash of grain and stored in oak containers.

CAUTION: Section 5.22(a) (2) becomes effective July 1, 1972.

(b) *Class 2; whisky.* "Whisky" is an alcoholic distillate from a fermented mash of grain produced at less than 190° proof in such manner that the distillate possesses the taste, aroma, and characteristics generally attributed to whisky, stored in oak containers (except that corn whisky need not be so stored), and bottled at not less than 80° proof, and also includes mixtures of such distillates for which no specific standards of identity are prescribed.

(1)(i) "Bourbon whisky," "rye whisky," "wheat whisky," "malt whisky," or "rye malt whisky" is whisky produced at not exceeding 160° proof from a fermented mash of not less than 51 percent corn, rye, wheat, malted barley, or malted rye grain, respectively, and stored at not more than 125° proof in charred new oak containers; and also includes mixtures of such whiskies of the same type.

(ii) "Corn whisky" is whisky produced at not exceeding 160° proof from a fermented mash of not less than 80 percent corn grain, and if stored in oak containers stored at not more than 125° proof in used or uncharred new oak containers and not subjected in any manner to treatment with charred wood; and also includes mixtures of such whisky.

(iii) Whiskies conforming to the standards prescribed in subdivisions (i) and (ii) of this subparagraph, which have been stored in the type of oak containers prescribed, for a period of 2 years or more shall be further designated as "straight"; for example, "straight bourbon whisky," "straight corn whisky," and whisky conforming to the standards prescribed in subdivision (i) of this subparagraph, except that it was produced from a fermented mash of less than 51 percent of any one type of grain, and stored for a period of 2 years or more in charred new oak containers shall be designated merely as "straight whisky." No other whiskies may be designated "straight." "Straight whisky" includes mixtures of straight whiskies which are homogeneous under section 5025(e) (5), Internal Revenue Code (26 U.S.C. 5025 (e) (5)), and implementing regulations in 26 CFR Part 201, and also mixtures of straight whiskies of the same type produced by the same proprietor at the same distillery all of which are not less than 4 years old.

(2) "Whisky distilled from bourbon (rye, wheat, malt, or rye malt) mash" is whisky produced in the United States at not exceeding 160° proof from a fermented mash of not less than 51 percent corn, rye, wheat, malted barley, or malted rye grain, respectively, and stored in used oak containers; and also includes mixtures of such whiskies of the same type. Whisky conforming to the standard of identity for corn whisky must be designated corn whisky.

(3) "Light whisky" is whisky produced in the United States at more than 160° proof, on or after January 26, 1968, and stored in used or uncharred new oak containers; and also includes mixtures of such whiskies. If "light whisky" is mixed with less than 20 percent of straight whisky on a proof gallon basis, the mixture shall be designated "blended light whisky" (light whisky—a blend).

CAUTION: Section 5.22(b) (3) becomes effective July 1, 1972.

577

(4) "Blended whisky" (whisky—a blend) is a mixture which contains at least 20 percent of straight whisky on a proof gallon basis and, separately or in combination, whisky or neutral spirits. A blended whisky containing not less than 51 percent on a proof gallon basis of one of the types of straight whisky shall be further designated by that specific type of straight whisky; for example, "blended rye whisky" (rye whisky—a blend).

(5) "A blend of straight whiskies" (blended straight whiskies) is a mixture of straight whiskies. A blend of straight whiskies consisting entirely of one of the types of straight whisky, and not conforming to the standard for "straight whisky," shall be further designated by that specific type of straight whisky; for example, "a blend of straight rye whiskies" (blended straight rye whiskies).

(6) "Spirit whisky" is a mixture of neutral spirits and not less than 5 percent on a proof gallon basis of whisky, or straight whisky, or straight whisky and whisky, if the straight whisky component is less than 20 percent on a proof gallon basis.

(7) "Scotch whisky" is whisky which is a distinctive product of Scotland, manufactured in Scotland in compliance with the laws of the United Kingdom regulating the manufacture of Scotch whisky for consumption in the United Kingdom: *Provided*, That if such product is a mixture of whiskies, such mixture is "blended Scotch whisky" (Scotch whisky—a blend).

(8) "Irish whisky" is whisky which is a distinctive product of Ireland, manufactured either in the Republic of Ireland or in Northern Ireland, in compliance with their laws regulating the manufacture of Irish whisky for home consumption: *Provided*, That if such product is a mixture of whiskies, such mixture is "blended Irish whisky" (Irish whisky—a blend).

(9) "Canadian whisky" is whisky which is a distinctive product of Canada, manufactured in Canada in compliance with the laws of Canada regulating the manufacture of Canadian whisky for consumption in Canada: *Provided*, That if such product is a mixture of whiskies, such mixture is "blended Canadian whisky" (Canadian whisky—a blend).

(c) *Class 3; gin.* "Gin" is a product obtained by original distillation from mash, or by redistillation of distilled spirits, or by mixing neutral spirits, with or over juniper berries and other aromatics, or with or over extracts derived from infusions, percolations, or maceration of such materials, and includes mixtures of gin and neutral psirits. It shall derive its main characteristic flavor from juniper berries and be bottled at not less than 80° proof. Gin produced exclusively by original distillation or by redistillation may be further designated as "distilled." "Dry gin" (London dry gin), "Geneva gin" (Hollands gin), and "Old Tom gin" (Tom gin) are types of gin known under such designations.

(d) *Class 4; brandy.* "Brandy" is an alcoholic distillate from the fermented juice, mash, or wine of fruit, or from the residue thereof, produced at less than 190° proof in such manner that the distillate possesses the taste, aroma, and characteristics generally attributed to the product, and bottled at not less than 80° proof. Brandy, or mixtures thereof, not conforming to any of the standards in subparagraphs (1) through (8) of this paragraph shall be designated as "brandy," and such designation shall be immediately followed by a truthful and adequate statement of composition.

(1) "Fruit brandy" is brandy distilled solely from the fermented juice or mash of whole, sound, ripe fruit, or from the standard grape, citrus, or other fruit wine, with or without the addition of not more than 20 percent by weight of the pomace of such juice or wine, or 30 percent by volume of the lees of such wine, or both (calculated prior to the addition of water to facilitate fermentation or distillation). Fruit brandy shall include mixtures of such brandy with not more than 30 percent (calculated on a proof gallon basis) of lees brandy. Fruit brandy, derived from grapes, shall be designated as "grape brandy" or "brandy," except that in the case of brandy other than neutral brandy, pomace brandy, marc brandy, or grappa brandy) distilled from the fermented juice, mash, or wine of grapes, or the residue thereof, which has been stored in oak containers for less than 2 years, the statement of class and type shall be immediately preceded, in the same size and kind of type, by the word "immature." Fruit brandy, other than grape brandy, derived from one variety of fruit, shall be designated by the word "brandy" qualified by the name of such fruit (for example, "peach brandy"), except that apple brandy may be designated "applejack." Fruit brandy derived from more than one variety of fruit shall be designated as "fruit brandy" qualified by a truthful and adequate statement of composition.

(2) "Cognac," or "cognac (grape) brandy," is grape brandy distilled in the Cognac region of France, which is entitled to be so designated by the laws and regulations of the French Government.

* * *

(e) *Class 5; blended applejack.* "Blended applejack" (applejack—a blend) is a mixture which contains at least 20 percent of apple brandy (applejack) on a proof gallon basis, stored in oak containers for not less than 2 years, and not more than 80 percent of neutral spirits on a proof gallon basis if such mixture at the time of bottling is not less than 80° proof.

(f) *Class 6; rum.* "Rum" is an alcoholic distillate from the fermented juice of sugarcane, sugarcane syrup, sugarcane molasses, or other sugarcane by-products, produced at less than 190° proof in such manner that the distillate possesses the taste, aroma, and characteristics generally attributed to rum, and bottled at not less than 80° proof; and also includes mixtures solely of such distillates.

(g) *Class 7; Tequila.* "Tequila" is an alcoholic distillate from a fermented mash derived principally from the Agave Tequilana Weber ("blue" variety), with or without additional fermentable substances, distilled in such manner that the distillate possesses the taste, aroma, and characteristics generally attributed to Tequila and bottled at not less than 80° proof, and also includes mixtures solely of such distillates. Distinctive product of Mexico.

(h) *Class 8; cordials and liqueurs.* Cordials and liqueurs are products obtained by mixing or redistilling distilled spirits with or over fruits, flowers, plants, or pure juices therefrom, or other natural flavoring materials, or with extracts derived from infusions, percolation, or maceration of such materials, and containing sugar, dextrose, or levulose, or a combination thereof, in an amount not less than 2½ percent by weight of the finished product.

(1) "Sloe gin" is a cordial or liqueur with the main characteristic flavor derived from sloe berries.

(2) "Rye liqueur," "bourbon liqueur" (rye, bourbon cordial) are liqueurs, bottled at not less than 60° proof, in which not less than 51 percent, on a proof gallon basis, of the distilled spirits used are, respectively, rye or bourbon whisky, straight rye or straight bourbon whisky, or whisky distilled from a rye or bourbon mash, and which possess a predominant characteristic rye or bourbon flavor derived from such whisky. Wine, if used, must be within the 2½ percent limitation provided in § 5.23 for coloring, flavoring, and blending materials.

(3) "Rock and rye," "rock and bourbon," "rock and brandy," "rock and rum" are liqueurs, bottled at not less than 48° proof, in which, in the case of rock and rye and rock and bourbon, not less than 51 percent, on a proof gallon basis, of the distilled spirits used are, respectively, rye or bourbon whisky, straight rye or straight bourbon whisky, or whisky distilled from a rye or bourbon mash, and, in the case of rock and brandy and rock and rum, the distilled spirits used are all grape brandy or rum, respectively; containing rock candy or sugar syrup, with or without the addition of fruit, fruit juices, or other natural flavoring materials, and possessing, respectively, a predominant characteristic rye, bourbon, brandy, or rum flavor derived from the distilled spirits used. Wine, if used, must be within the 2½ percent limitation provided in § 5.23 for harmless coloring, flavoring, and blending materials.

(4) The designation of a cordial or liqueur may include the word "dry" if the sugar, dextrose, or levulose, or a combination thereof, are less than 10 percent by weight of the finished product.

(5) Cordials and liqueurs shall not be designated as "distilled" or "compound."

(i) *Class 9; flavored brandy, flavored gin, flavored rum, flavored vodka, and flavored whisky.* "Flavored brandy," "flavored gin," "flavored rum," "flavored vodka," and "flavored whisky" are brandy, gin, rum, vodka, and whisky, respectively, to which have been added natural flavoring materials, with or without the addition of sugar, and bottled at not less than 70° proof. The name of the predominant flavor shall appear as a part of the designation. If the finished product contains more than 2½ percent by volume of wine, the kinds and percentages by volume of wine must be stated as a part of the designation, except that a flavored brandy may contain an additional 12½ percent by volume of wine, without label disclosure, if the additional wine is derived from the particular fruit corresponding to the labeled flavor of the product.

(j) *Class 10; imitations.* Imitations shall bear, as a part of the designation thereof, the word "imitation" and shall include the following:

(1) Any class or type of distilled spirits to which has been added coloring or flavoring material of such nature as to cause the resultant product to simulate any other class or type of distilled spirits;

(2) Any class or type of distilled spirits (other than distilled spirits required under § 5.35 to bear a distinctive or fanciful name and a truthful and adequate statement of composition) to which have been added flavors considered to be artificial or imitation. In determining whether a flavor is artificial or imitation, recognition will be given to what is considered to be "good commercial practice" in the flavor manufacturing industry;

(3) Any class or type of distilled spirits (except cordials, liqueurs, and specialties marketed under labels which do not indicate or imply that a particular class or type of distilled spirits was used in the manufacture thereof) to which has been added any whisky essence, brandy essence, rum essence, or similar essence or extract which simulates or enhances, or is used by the trade or in the particular product to simulate or enhance, the characteristics of any class or type of distilled spirits;

(4) Any type of whisky to which beading oil has been added;

(5) Any rum or Tequila, to which neutral spirits or distilled spirits other than rum or Tequila, respectively, have been added;

(6) Any brandy made from distilling material to which has been added any amount of sugar other than the kind and amount of sugar expressly authorized in the production of standard wine; and

(7) Any brandy to which neutral spirits or distilled spirits other than brandy have been added, except that this provision shall not apply to any product conforming to the standard of identity for blended apple-jack.

(k) *Class 11; geographical designations.* (1) Geographical names for distinctive types of distilled spirits (other than names found by the Director under subparagraph (2) of this paragraph to have become generic) shall not be applied to distilled spirits produced in any other place than the particular region indicated by the name, unless (i) in direct conjunction with the name there appears to the word "type" or the word "American" or some other adjective indicating the true place of production, in lettering substantially as conspicuous as such name, and (ii) the distilled spirits to which the name is applied conform to the distilled spirits of that particular region. The following are examples of distinctive types of distilled spirits with geographical names that have not become generic: Eau de Vie de Dantzig (Danziger Goldwasser), Ojen, Swedish punch. Geographical names for distinctive types of distilled spirits shall be used to designate only distilled spirits conforming to the standard of identity, if any, for such type specified in this section, or if no such standard is so specified, then in accordance with the trade understanding of that distinctive type.

(2) Only such geographical names for distilled spirits as the Director finds have by usage and common knowledge lost their geographical significance to such extent that they have become generic shall be deemed to have become generic. Examples are London dry gin, Geneva (Hollands) gin.

(3) Geographical names that are not names for distinctive types of distilled spirits, and that have not become generic, shall not be applied to distilled spirits produced in any other place than the particular place or region indicated in the name. Examples are Cognac, Armagnac, Greek brandy, Pisco brandy, Jamaica rum, Puerto Rico rum, Demerara rum.

(4) The words "Scotch," "Scots," "Highland," or "Highlands," and similar words connoting, indicating, or commonly associated with Scotland, shall not be used to designate any product not wholly produced in Scotland.

(1) *Class 12; products without geographical designations but distinctive of a particular place.* (1) The whiskies of the types specified in paragraph (b), (1), (4), (5), and (6) of this section are distinctive products of the United States and, if produced in a foreign country, shall be designated by the applicable designation prescribed in such paragraphs, together with the words "American type" or the words "produced (distilled, blended) in ___," the blank to be filled in with the name of the foreign country: *Provided*, That the word "bourbon" shall not be used to describe any whisky or whisky-based distilled spirits not produced in the United States. If whisky of any of these types is composed in part of whisky or whiskies produced in a foreign country there shall be stated, on the brand label, the percentage of such whisky and the country of origin thereof.

(2) The name for other distilled spirits which are distinctive products of a particular place or country, an example is Habanero, shall not be given to the product of any other place or country unless the designation for such product includes the word "type" or an adjective such as "American," or the like, clearly indicating the true place of production. The provision for place of production shall not apply to designations which by usage and common knowledge have lost their geographical significance to such an extent that the Director finds they have become generic. Examples are Slivovitz, Zubrovka, Aquavit, Arrack, and Kirschwasser.

§ 5.23 Alteration of class and type.

(a) *Additions.* (1) The addition of any coloring, flavoring, or blending materials to any class and type of distilled spirits, except as otherwise provided in this section, alters the class and type thereof and the product shall be appropriately redesignated.

(2) There may be added to any class or type of distilled spirits, without changing the class or type thereof, (i) such harmless coloring, flavoring, or blending materials as are an essential component part of the particular class or type of distilled spirits to which added, and (ii) harmless coloring, flavoring, or blending materials such as caramel, straight malt or straight rye malt whiskies, fruit juices, sugar, or wine, which are not an essential component part of the particular distilled spirits to which added, but which are customarily employed therein in accordance with established trade usage, if such coloring, flavoring, or blending materials do not total more than 2½ percent by volume of the finished product.

(3) "Harmless coloring, flavoring, and blending materials" shall not include (i) any materials which would render the product to which it is added an imitation, or (ii) any material whatsoever in the case of neutral spirits or straight whisky, or (iii) any material, other than caramel and sugar, in the case of Cognac brandy.

(b) *Extractions.* The removal from any distilled spirits of any constituents to such an extent that the product does not possess the taste, aroma, and characteristics generally attributed to that class or type of distilled spirits alters that class and type thereof, and the product shall be appropriately redesignated. In addition, in the case of straight whisky the removal of more than 15 percent of the fixed acids, or volatile acids, or esters, or soluble solids, or higher alcohols, or more than 25 percent of the soluble color, shall be deemed to alter the class or type thereof.

(c) *Exceptions.* This section shall not be construed as in any manner modifying the standards of identity for cordials and liqueurs, flavored brandy, flavored gin, flavored rum, flavored vodka, and flavored whisky or as authorizing any product which is defined in § 5.22(j), Class 10, as an imitation to be otherwise designated.

Source: "Regulations under the Federal Alcohol Administration Act, Title 27, Code of Federal Regulations, Part 5, Subpart C."

APPENDIX Q
PRODUCTION AND CONSUMPTION OF WINES, BEERS, AND SPIRITS

PRODUCTION OF WINE IN VARIOUS COUNTRIES*

Position in 1974	Country	1973 (1,000 hectoliters)	1974 (1,000 hectoliters)	1973 (millions of U.S. gallons)	1974 (millions of U.S. gallons)
1	Italy	76,716	76,867	2,027	2,031
2	France	82,425	75,482	2,178	1,994
3	Spain	39,995	36,374	1,057	961
4	U.S.S.R.	22,593	27,638	597	730
5	Argentina	22,566	27,183	596	718
6	United States	16,300	15,220	431	402
7	Portugal	11,086	13,803	293	365
8	Romania	8,865	7,982	234	211
9	Algeria	6,500†	7,400†	172†	195†
10	West Germany	10,697	6,895	283	182
11	Yugoslavia	7,701	5,876	203	155
12	Greece	5,079	5,698	134	151
13	Republic of South Africa	5,490	4,990	145	132
14	Chile	5,690	4,665	150	123
15	Hungary	6,231	4,442	165	117
16	Bulgaria	3,892	3,246	103	85.8
17	Australia	2,730	2,947	72.1	77.9
18	Brazil	1,300†	2,000†	34†	53†
19	Austria	2,404	1,665	63.5	44.0
20	Mexico	1,415	1,568	37.4	41.4
21	Poland	1,500†	1,500†	40†	40†
22	Morocco	1,264	1,297	33.4	34.3
23	Tunisia	840†	1,238	22†	32.7
24	Uruguay	918†	918†	24†	24†
25	Czechoslovakia	1,456	854	38.5	22.6
26	Switzerland	1,203	694	31.8	18.3
27	Canada	516	550†	13.6	15†
28	Turkey	530†	540†	14†	14†
29	Cyprus	308	500†	8.1	13†
30	Israel	402	403	10.6	10.6
31	New Zealand	336	330†	8.9	9†
32	Japan	218	235	5.8	6.2
33	East Germany	200†	200†	5†	5†
34	Albania	158†	169†	4†	4.5†
35	Azores	85	150†	2.2	4†
36	Luxembourg	186	138	4.9	3.6
37	Cuba	100†	100†	2.5†	2.5†
38	Madeira	99	100†	2.6	2.5†

*In some cases much of the total wine production is distilled into brandy.
†Estimated.

Source: *Produktschap Voor Gedistilleede Dranken*, 1976.

Position in 1974	Country	1973 (1,000 hectoliters)	1974 (1,000 hectoliters)	1973 (millions of U.S. gallons)	1974 (millions of U.S. gallons)
39	Peru	80†	71†	2†	2†
40	Egypt	60†	62†	1.5†	1.5†
41	Lebanon	40†	40†	1†	1†
42	Libya	30†	30†	0.8†	0.8†
43	Venezuela	25†	25†	0.7†	0.7†
44	Macao	20	20†	0.53	0.5†
45	Malta	19†	19†	0.5†	0.5†
46	Madagascar	18†	19†	0.5†	0.5†
47	Jordan	15†	15†	0.4†	0.4†
48	Paraguay	7	8†	0.18	0.2†
49	Belgium	8	7	0.21	0.18
50	Syria	7†	7†	0.2†	0.2†
51	Bolivia	6†	6†	0.15†	0.15†
52	Iran	4†	4†	0.1†	0.1†
53	Panama	3	3†	0.08	0.1†
54	Colombia	1†	1†	0.03†	0.03†
55	Netherlands	—	—	—	—
	World Production	350,400	342,000	9,257	9,035

†Estimated.

Source: *Produktschap voor Gedistilleede Dranken*, 1976.

CONSUMPTION OF WINE PER CAPITA
IN VARIOUS COUNTRIES

POSITION	COUNTRY	YEAR	LITERS	U.S. GALLONS
1	Portugal	1975	± 120	31.7
2	Italy	1975	107.5	28.4
3	France	1975	103.7	27.4
4	Argentina	1975	85.7	22.64
5	Spain	1975	76	20.07
6	Switzerland	1975	43.9	11.60
7	Luxembourg	1975	41.3	10.91
8	Chile	1975	± 40	10.57
9	Greece	1975	38	10.04
10	Hungary	1975	37	9.77
11	Austria	1975	35.1	9.27
12	Romania	1975	33	8.72
13	Yugoslavia	1974	28.6	7.56
14	Uruguay	1974	25.1	6.63
15	West Germany	1975	23.2	6.13
16	Bulgaria	1974	19.98	5.28
17	Belgium	1975	17.2	4.54
18	U.S.S.R.	1975	± 16	4.23
19	Czechoslovakia	1975	± 15	3.96
20	New Zealand	1975	11.8	3.12
21	Denmark	1975	11.48	3.03
22	Australia	1974/75	11.2	2.96
23	Republic of South Africa	1975	10.41	2.75
24	Netherlands	1975	10.25	2.71
25	Finland	1975	8.86	2.34
26	Sweden	1975	8.25	2.18
27	Poland	1975	7.4	1.95
28	Canada	1974/75	6.68	1.77
29	East Germany	1975	± 6.6	1.74
30	United States	1975	6.53	1.73
31	Cyprus	1975	6.2	1.64
32	England	1975	5.21	1.38
33	Israel	1975	3.75	0.99
34	Republic of Ireland	1975	± 3.5	0.93
35	Norway	1975	3.34	0.83
36	Tunisia	1975	± 3.3	0.82
37	Iceland	1975	3.04	0.80
38	Brazil	1975	± 2	0.52
39	Morocco	1975	± 2	0.52
40	Lebanon	1974	± 2	0.52
41	Paraguay	1974	1.9	0.51
42	Cuba	1972	1.6	0.42
43	Peru	1975	± 1	0.26
44	Venezuela	1975	0.75	0.19
45	Turkey	1975	0.55	0.15
46	Algeria	1975	± 0.5	0.13
47	Japan	1975	0.45	0.12
48	Mexico	1975	0.23	0.06

Source: *Produktschap voor Gedistilleede Dranken*, 1976.

CONSUMPTION OF BEER PER CAPITA
IN VARIOUS COUNTRIES

POSITION	COUNTRY	YEAR	LITERS	U.S. GALLONS
1	West Germany	1975	147.80	39.05
2	Czechoslovakia	1975	142.2	37.57
3	Australia	1974/75	142.1	37.54
4	Belgium	1975	± 140	36.98
5	New Zealand	1975	133.2	35.19
6	Luxembourg	1975	129.0	34.08
7	East Germany	1975	117.6	31.07
8	England	1975	117.6	31.06
9	Denmark	1975	117.19	30.96
10	Austria	1975	103.8	27.42
11	Canada	1974/75	85.9	22.69
12	Ireland	1975	84.37	22.29
13	United States	1975	81.7	21.58
14	Netherlands	1975	78.92	20.85
15	Switzerland	1975	71.8	18.97
16	Hungary	1975	62.9	16.62
17	Sweden	1975	60.2	15.9
18	Finland	1975	54.7	14.45
19	Bulgaria	1974	± 52	13.74
20	Venezuela	1975	± 50	13.21
21	Spain	1975	47.0	12.42
22	Norway	1975	45.44	12.00
23	France	1975	45.22	11.95
24	Yugoslavia	1974	44.3	11.7
25	Poland	1975	36.8	9.72
26	Japan	1975	35.4	9.35
27	Uruguay	1974	33.7	8.9
28	Mexico	1975	33.0	8.72
29	Portugal	1975	32.7	8.64
30	Colombia	1975	32.6	8.62
31	Romania	1975	30	7.93
32	Peru	1975	± 28	7.4
33	Cuba	1972	25.6	6.72
34	Surinam	1972	21.7	5.73
35	U.S.S.R.	1975	21.5	5.68
36	Republic of South Africa	1975	19.5	5.15
37	Cyprus	1975	18.2	4.81
38	Greece	1975	± 17	4.49
39	Argentina	1975	16.8	4.44
40	Iceland	1975	± 16	4.23
41	Brazil	1975	± 15	3.96
42	Italy	1975	12.7	3.36
43	Israel	1975	10.35	2.73
44	Chile	1975	8.0	2.11
45	Tunisia	1975	± 6	1.59
46	Paraguay	1974	6.2	1.64
47	Algeria	1975	± 4.5	1.19
48	Lebanon	1974	± 4.1	1.08
49	Turkey	1975	3.85	1.02
50	Morocco	1975	1.5	0.4

Source: *Produktschap voor Gedistilleede Dranken*, 1976.

CONSUMPTION OF DISTILLED SPIRITS
PER CAPITA IN
VARIOUS COUNTRIES

POSITION	COUNTRY	YEAR	LITERS PURE ALCOHOL (200 PROOF)	U.S. GALLONS (80 PROOF)
1	Poland	1975	4.6	3.04
2	Japan	1975	3.95	2.61
3	Canada	1974/75	3.61	2.38
4	Luxembourg	1975	3.5	2.31
5	East Germany	1975	± 3.4	2.25
6	Netherlands	1975	3.39	2.24
7	U.S.S.R.	1975	± 3.3	2.18
8	United States	1975	3.13	2.07
9	West Germany	1975	3.04	2.01
10	Yugoslavia	1974	± 3	1.99
11	Hungary	1975	± 3	1.99
12	Czechoslovakia	1975	2.98	1.97
13	Sweden	1975	2.97	1.96
14	Finland	1975	2.8	1.85
15	France	1975	± 2.6	1.72
16	Spain	1975	2.6	1.72
17	Surinam	1972	± 2.5	1.65
18	Iceland	1975	2.4	1.59
19	Romania	1970	2.4	1.59
20	Republic of Ireland	1975	2.03	1.34
21	Italy	1975	± 2	1.32
22	Bulgaria	1974	± 2	1.32
23	Belgium	1975	1.99	1.31
24	Switzerland	1975	1.94	1.28
25	Norway	1975	1.84	1.22
26	Cyprus	1975	1.8	1.19
27	Denmark	1975	1.79	1.12
28	New Zealand	1975	± 1.7	1.12
29	Austria	1975	1.65	1.09
30	England	1975	1.46	0.96
31	Peru	1975	± 1.4	0.92
32	Republic of South Africa	1975	1.38	0.91
33	Australia	1974/75	± 1.3	0.86
34	Cuba	1972	1.0	0.66
35	Portugal	1975	± 0.9	0.59
36	Israel	1975	0.9	0.59
37	Mexico	1975	± 0.7	0.46
38	Turkey	1975	± 0.5	0.33

Source: *Produktschap voor Gedistilleede Dranken*, 1976.

TOTAL ALCOHOL CONSUMPTION
(WINES, BEERS, AND SPIRITS)
IN VARIOUS COUNTRIES
(in order of per capita consumption)

POSITION	COUNTRY	YEAR	LITERS OF PURE ALCOHOL (200 PROOF)	U.S. GALLONS (AT 80 PROOF)
1	France	1975	17.0	11.23
2	Portugal	1975	16.9	11.16
3	Spain	1975	14.1	9.31
4	Italy	1975	13.4	8.85
5	West Germany	1975	12.5	8.26
6	Luxembourg	1975	12.3	8.12
7	Argentina	1975	11.1	7.33
8	Austria	1975	11.1	7.33
9	Switzerland	1975	10.5	6.94
10	Belgium	1975	10.1	6.67
11	New Zealand	1975	9.8	6.47
12	Australia	1974/75	9.7	6.41
13	Hungary	1975	9.5	6.27
14	Czechoslovakia	1975	9.1	6.01
15	Canada	1974/75	9.0	5.9
16	Denmark	1975	8.9	5.88
17	Netherlands	1975	8.8	5.81
18	Yugoslavia	1974	8.6	5.68
19	England	1975	8.1	5.35
20	Romania	1975	7.9	5.22
21	East Germany	1975	7.7	5.09
22	Poland	1975	7.3	4.82
23	United States	1975	7.0	4.62
24	Bulgaria	1975	6.7	4.43
25	Republic of Ireland	1975	6.7	4.43
26	U.S.S.R.	1975	6.3	4.16
27	Finland	1975	6.3	4.16
28	Sweden	1975	6.2	4.1
29	Japan	1975	5.4	3.57
30	Greece	1975	5.4	3.57
31	Chile	1975	5.2	3.43
32	Uruguay	1974	4.7	3.10
33	Norway	1975	4.3	2.84
34	Iceland	1975	3.7	2.44
35	Republic of South Africa	1975	3.6	2.38
36	Surinam	1972	3.6	2.38
37	Cyprus	1975	3.5	2.31
38	Peru	1975	2.9	1.92
39	Venezuela	1975	2.6	1.72
40	Cuba	1972	2.4	1.59
41	Mexico	1975	2.2	1.45
42	Israel	1975	1.9	1.26
43	Brazil	1975	1.0	0.66
44	Turkey	1975	0.8	0.53
45	Tunisia	1975	0.7	0.46
46	Paraguay	1974	0.5	0.33
47	Lebanon	1973	0.4	0.26
48	Morocco	1975	0.3	0.2
49	Algeria	1975	0.3	0.2

Source: *Produktschap voor Gedistilleede Dranken, 1976.*

APPENDIX R
CUSTOMS DUTIES
AND INTERNAL REVENUE TAXES

HISTORY OF FEDERAL EXCISE (INTERNAL REVENUE) TAXES ON ALL ALCOHOLIC BEVERAGES

WINES
(rates are per wine gallon)

Date effective	0-14% alcohol	14-21% alcohol	21-24%* alcohol	Sparkling wine	Carbonated wine
Sept. 9, 1916	$0.04	$0.10	$0.25	$1.92	$0.96
Feb. 25, 1919	0.16	0.40	1.00	7.68	3.84
Jan. 12, 1934	0.10	0.20	0.40	0.80	0.40
June 26, 1936	0.05	0.10	0.20	0.40	0.20
July 1, 1938	0.10	0.15	0.20	0.40	0.10
July 1, 1940	0.06	0.18	0.30	0.48	0.24
October 1, 1941	0.08	0.30	0.65	1.12	0.56
November 1, 1942	0.10	0.40	1.00	1.60	0.80
April 1, 1944	0.15	0.60	2.00	2.40	1.60
November 1, 1951	0.17	0.67	2.25	2.72	1.92
January 1, 1955, to present	0.17	0.67	2.25	3.40	2.40

The Internal Revenue Code imposes a tax upon all wines, including imitation, standard, or artificial wine, and compounds sold as wine, produced in or imported into the United States. These taxes are determined at the time of removal for consumption or sale.

The tax imposed on wines does not apply to wine produced by the duly registered head of a family for family use and not for sale, or to wine removed from a bonded wine cellar for family use where the head of a family operates the bonded wine cellar as an individual owner. The quantity produced or removed during a year may not exceed 200 gallons per family.

*All wines containing more than 24 percent alcohol by volume are classified as distilled spirits and are taxed accordingly.

BEERS
(per barrel of 31 gallons)

Date effective	Tax	Date effective	Tax
Sept. 1862	$1.00	Oct. 4, 1917	$3.00
Mar. 3, 1863	0.60	Feb. 25, 1919	6.00
Apr. 1, 1864	1.00	Jan. 12, 1934	5.00
Jun. 14, 1898	2.00	Jul. 1, 1940	6.00
Jul. 1, 1901	1.60	Nov. 1, 1942	7.00
Jul. 1, 1902	1.00	Apr. 1, 1944	8.00
Oct. 23, 1914	1.50	Nov. 1, 1951, to present	9.00

587

DISTILLED SPIRITS

Date effective	Amount per tax gallon (proof gallon)
July 1, 1791	$0.09-0.25 according to proof
July 1, 1792	$0.07-0.18 according to proof
July 1, 1802	No tax
Jan. 1, 1814	No tax
Feb. 1, 1815	$0.20
Jan. 1, 1818	No tax
Sept. 1, 1862	$0.20
March 7, 1864	0.60
July 1, 1864	1.50
Jan. 1, 1865	2.00
July 20, 1868	0.50
Aug. 1, 1872	0.70
March 3, 1875	0.90
Aug. 27, 1894	1.10
Oct. 3, 1917—World War I	
Basic rate	2.20
Withdrawn for beverage use	3.20
Feb. 25, 1919—Prohibition	
Basic rate	2.20
Withdrawn for (from Nov. 23, 1921, if "diverted to") beverage use	6.40*
Jan. 1, 1927	1.65
Diverted to beverage use	6.40*
Jan. 1, 1928	
Basic rate	1.10
Diverted to beverage use (prior to repeal of Prohibition, Dec. 6, 1933)	6.40*
Jan. 12, 1934	2.00
July 1, 1938	
Distilled spirits generally	2.25
Brandy	2.00
July 1, 1940	
Distilled spirits generally	3.00
Brandy	2.75
Oct. 1, 1941	4.00
Nov. 1, 1942—World War II	6.00
April 1, 1944	9.00
Nov. 1, 1951, to present time	10.50

*During Prohibition.

CUSTOMS DUTIES AND INTERNAL REVENUE TAXES
ON IMPORTED ALCOHOLIC BEVERAGES

WINES	Customs duties (per wine gallon)		Internal Revenue taxes (per wine gallon)
Champagne and other sparkling wines	$1.17	($6.00)	$3.40
Artificially carbonated wines	1.17	($6.00)	2.40
Rice wine or saké	0.25	($1.25)	*
Still wines produced from grapes:			
Containing not over 14 percent alcohol by volume:			
In containers holding each			
Not over one gallon	0.37½	($1.25)	0.17
Over one gallon	0.62½	($1.25)	0.17
Containing over 14 percent alcohol by volume:			
Marsala or Marsala types in containers each holding not over one gallon	0.31½	($1.25)	0.67†
Sherry	1.00	($1.25)	0.67†
Other	1.00	($1.25)	0.67†
Vermouth, in containers holding each			
Not over one gallon	0.21	($1.25)	0.67†
Over one gallon	0.32	($1.25)	0.67†
Other fermented alcoholic beverages	0.25	($1.25)	§

Imitation wines are subject to the highest rate of duty for the product to be represented, but not less than $3.75 per proof gallon; the Internal Revenue tax is payable at the same rate as genuine wine according to the latter's classification, that is, Champagne, still wine, and so on. Still wines containing over 24 percent alcohol by volume are dutiable and taxable as distilled spirits.

BEER	Customs duties		Internal Revenue tax
Beer, ale, porter, and stout	$0.06	($0.50)	At the rate of $9.00 per 31 gallons computed upon the actual quantity in a container

*Internal Revenue tax same as for beer when product is made like beer; when alcohol has been added, it is taxed as still wine.

†Internal Revenue tax on still wines containing more than 21 percent and not exceeding 24 percent alcohol by volume, $2.25 per wine gallon.

§Internal Revenue tax same as for still wines according to alcohol content thereof.

DISTILLED SPIRITS	Customs duties (proof gallon)		Internal Revenue taxes** (proof gallon)
Aquavit	$0.42	($5.00)	$10.50
Arak	1.00	($5.00)	10.50
Bitters of all kinds containing spirits:			
Not fit for use as beverages	0.94	($5.00)	
Fit for use as beverages	0.50	($5.00)	10.50
Brandy:			
Pisco and Singani:			
In containers each holding not over 1 gallon:			
Valued not over $9 per gallon	0.62	($5.00)	10.50
Valued over $9 per gallon	1.25	($5.00)	10.50
In containers each holding over 1 gallon:			
Valued not over $9 per gallon	0.50	($5.00)	10.50
Valued over $9 per gallon	1.00	($5.00)	10.50
Other:			
In containers each holding not over 1 gallon:			
Valued not over $9 per gallon	0.62	($5.00)	10.50
Valued over $9 but not over $13 per gallon	1.25	($5.00)	10.50
Valued over $13 but not over $17 per gallon	3.00	($5.00)	10.50
Valued over $17 per gallon	5.00	($5.00)	10.50
In containers each holding over 1 gallon:			
Valued not over $9 per gallon	0.50	($5.00)	10.50
Valued over $9 per gallon	1.00	($5.00)	10.50
Valued over $9 but not over $17 per gallon	3.00	($5.00)	10.50
Valued over $17 per gallon	5.00	($5.00)	10.50
Cordials, liqueurs, Kirschwasser, and Ratafia	0.50	($5.00)	10.50
Ethyl alcohol for beverage purposes	1.12	($5.00)	10.50
Gin	0.50	($5.00)	10.50
Rum	1.75	($5.00)	10.50
Whisky:			
Irish and Scotch	0.51	($5.00)	10.50
Canadian and other	0.62	($5.00)	10.50
Tequila:			
In containers each holding not over 1 gallon	1.25	($5.00)	10.50
In containers each holding over 1 gallon	1.25	($5.00)	10.50
Other spirits and preparations in chief value of distilled spirits, fit for use in beverages or for beverage purposes:			
Spirits—vodka and other	1.25	($5.00)	10.50
Preparations in chief value of distilled spirits	1.25	($5.00)	10.50
Imitations of brandy and other spirituous beverages	2.50	($5.00)	10.50

**Customs duties and Internal Revenue tax rates are based upon proof gallon, or wine gallon when below proof.

Source: National Association of Alcoholic Beverage Importers, Inc., Statistical Report, Table 23, 1976.

The duties on imported alcoholic beverages are in *addition* to federal and state excise taxes that are also charged for alcoholic beverages. To determine the total tax on an imported beverage, add the federal tax for its category, then add the state tax, which varies from state to state, and finally add the import duty. There may also be local sales taxes.

Rates of duties shown in parentheses on the preceding chart are the full rates that were in effect on January 1, 1934, and are applicable to products of countries found by the president to be Communist controlled. These countries pay "penalty" rates. They include: Albania, Bulgaria, China (any part that may be under Communist control or domination), Cuba,* Czechoslovakia, Estonia, Germany (the Soviet zone and the Soviet sector of Berlin), Hungary, Indochina (any part of Cambodia, Laos, or Vietnam that may be under Communist control or domination), Korea (any part that may be under Communist control or domination), Kurile Islands, Latvia, Lithuania, Outer Mongolia, Southern Sakhalin, Tanna Tuva, Tibet, Union of Soviet Socialist Republics and the area in East Prussia under the provisional administration of the U.S.S.R.

Poland, Romania, and Yugoslavia, while part of the Communist sphere, have been accorded most-favored-nation status. Alcoholic beverages from these countries do not pay the higher "penalty" rate, but pay the same rates of duties as countries not mentioned in the above list.

*Proclamation 3447, February 3, 1962, prohibited importation into the United States of all goods of Cuban origin and all goods imported from or through Cuba. As of August 21, 1975, the embargo was lifted as to trade by U.S. companies through third countries. The embargo continues on direct United States-Cuban trade.

Source: *General Headnotes and Rules of Interpretation of the Tariff Schedules of the United States,* January, 1976.

APPENDIX S
GLOSSARY

The abbreviations Aus., Eng., Fr., Hun., It., Port., Sp., and Yug. represent the countries of origin Austria, England, France, Hungary, Italy, Portugal, Spain, and Yugoslavia respectively.

abboccato (It.). Semidry.

Abfüllung, Abf. (Ger.). Bottling.

Abstich (Ger.). Racking.

acerbe (Fr.). Green, acid.

acid, acidity. Compounds in wine that provide a tart freshness and contribute to the wine's ability to age.

acqua vita, aqua vitae (It., Latin). Water of life—spirits.

adega (Port.). Equivalent of *bodega*, wine warehouse.

aftertaste. The taste in the back of the throat after a wine has been swallowed. A lingering aftertaste is an indication of a complex wine.

agrafes (Fr.). Metal clips used in Champagne cellars to hold the temporary corks in place.

aguardiente (Sp.). Spirits, primarily brandy or whisky.

aigre (Fr.). An acid undertone.

albariza (Sp.). Chalky-white soil of best Jerez sherry vineyards in Spain.

alcohol (ethyl). Chemically C_2H_5OH, one of the results of fermenting liquids containing sugar.

aldehydes. By-products of alcoholic liquids resulting from the combination of alcohol, acid, and air.

alembic, *alambic, alambique* (Eng., Fr., Sp.). Still.

alt (Ger.). Old.

amabile (It.). Semisweet.

amaro (It.). Bitter or very dry.

amélioré (Fr.). Improved, usually by the addition of sugar to the must before fermentation.

amertume. (Fr.). Bitter.

amontillado (Sp.). Dry type of sherry.

amoroso (Sp.). Medium-dry type of sherry.

ampelography. Science of grapevine culture.

añada (Sp.). Wine of one vintage.

ansprechend (Ger.). Attractive, engaging.

aperitif. Appetizer wine or spirit.

Appellation d'Origine Contrôlée (Fr.). Term that appears on labels of fine French wines signifying origin and right to the name it bears, guaranteed by French law.

âpre (Fr.). Harsh, rough.

arenas (Sp.). Sandy soils of the Jerez sherry vineyards in Spain.

arome, aroma (Fr., Sp.). Odor or bouquet of a wine or spirit.

arroba (Sp.). Wine measure holding 16⅔ liters.

arrope (Sp.). Concentrated wine used to sweeten and give color to sherries. See also *vino de color*.

artig (Ger.). Smooth, rounded.

asciato (It.). Dry.

astringence. Puckering or drying sensation in the mouth after drinking certain tannic wines.

aszú (Hun.). Sweeter type of Tokay wine.

Auslese (Ger.). A wine made from selected grapes.

balance. The harmony of a wine in which none of the components is overly apparent.

Balthazar. Oversize Champagne bottle, holding 16 regular bottles, or 416 ounces.

Banvin, Ban de Vendange (Fr.). Ancient French custom of fixing the date when the gathering of the grapes might begin.

barrique, barrica (Fr., Sp.). Hogshead, cask.

barros (Sp.). Clayish soils of the Jerez sherry vineyards in Spain.

basto (Sp.). Coarse.

B.A.T.F. Bureau of Alcohol, Tobacco, and Firearms, U.S. Treasury Department.

Baumé. Measurement of the degree of sweetness in wines and spirits. Hydrometer and scales invented by the French chemist Antoine Baumé.

Beerenauslese (Ger.). A wine made from individually selected, perfectly ripe grapes.

beste (Ger.). Best.

bianco (It.). White.

binning. Storing wines in bins in a cellar for development.

blanc de blancs (Fr.). Wine made from the juice of white grapes only.

blanco (Sp.). White.

blending. Marrying two or more similar products to obtain a better and more uniform quality.

Blume (Ger.). Bouquet, aroma.

blumig (Ger.). Good bouquet.

Bocksbeutel (Ger.). Squat, flasklike bottle used for Frankenwein.

bocoy (Sp.). Large cask holding approximately 162 gallons.

bodega (Sp.). Ground-level wine warehouse.

body. The term employed to describe the consistency of beverages. For example, a thin wine has less body than a full one.

bond, in. A wine or spirit on which duty and Internal Revenue tax has not been paid must remain under government supervision as "bond" that same will be paid.

bonded warehouse. Warehouse under government supervision.

bon goût (Fr.). Good or pleasant taste.

592

bor (Hun.). Wine. *Fehérbor* is white wine; *Vörösbor* is red wine. Both are pluralized with the suffix *-ok*, as in *borok*.

bota (Sp.). Butt, sherry cask, holding 132 gallons.

bottle, *bouteille, botella* (Eng., Fr., Sp.). A wine bottle containing from 23 to 26 ounces.

Bottled in Bond. U.S.: Term signifying a straight whisky, at least four years old, bottled at 100 proof, under government supervision, before taxes have been paid on same. Canada: Term signifying a blended whisky, at least three years old, bottled at 100 proof, under government supervision, before taxes have been paid on same.

bouchonné (Fr.). Corky, as a wine that has taken on an unpleasant taste of cork.

bouquet. Aroma or fragrance of a wine or spirit.

Bowle (Ger.). Wine cup prepared with fresh fruit, wine, herbs, and liqueurs or brandy.

brandewijn, Branntwein (Dutch, Ger.). Brandy; literally, "burned wine."

breed. The character or degree of excellence a wine attains.

brouilli (Fr.). The middle distillate (about 24 to 32 percent alcohol), collected for the second distillation in Cognac.

brut (Fr.). Dry. Also, the driest type of Champagne.

bukettreich (Ger.). Rich, pronounced bouquet.

butt. Standard shipping cask for sherry, 132 gallons.

Cabinet-wein (Ger.). Term used before 1971 to denote the finest quality of certain Rhine wines, specially reserved and so marked.

cantina (It.). Cellar, winery, or bar.

cantina sociale (It.). Wine growers' cooperative.

capataz (Sp.). Foreman or *bodega* master in Jerez.

capiteux (Fr.). Spirity, heady.

capsule. Protector made of metal or plastic for wine and spirit bottle cork.

caque (Fr.). Basket in which grapes are carried from the vineyard to the press.

casco (Sp.). Cask or large barrel, usually made of oak, used for developing (aging) and/or shipping wines and spirits.

cask. Large container, usually made of oak, for wines or spirits.

casse (Fr.). Chemical disease of wines resulting from excess iron.

catalyst. Chemical agent that induces chemical changes in other substances by its presence but itself remains unchanged.

cave, celler, cellier (Fr.). Warehouse (usually underground) or cellar for storing wines and/or spirits.

cellar. Warehouse for storing wines.

centiliter. 1/100 part of a liter.

cep (cépage), cepa (Fr., Sp.). The vinestock.

chai (Fr.). Ground-level or aboveground warehouse, usually kept totally dark, for wines and/or spirits.

chambrer (Fr.). To bring red wine to room temperature (65-68 degrees Fahrenheit) gradually.

chaptalization. The practice of increasing the natural sugar content of the grape juice, before fermentation begins, by the addition of sugar or concentrated grape must when there is such a deficiency, especially in poor vintage years.

charnu (Fr.). Full bodied.

château-bottled. Wine bottled at the château, estate, or vineyard where grapes from which it was made are grown. Applies to Bordeaux wines primarily.

chiaretto (It.). Very light red.

clarete (Sp.). Light red or dark rose.

classified growths. Bordeaux wines listed according to merit in 1855, 1955, and 1959.

climat (Fr.). Vineyard.

cochylis. A disease of the vine.

collage (Fr.). Fining or clearing a wine.

commune (Fr.). Parish, a subdivision of a district.

Confréries (Fr.). Wine and gastronomic fraternities, mostly of ancient "guild" origin, such as Burgundy's *Confrérie des Chevaliers du Tastevin* (Brotherhood of Gentlemen of the Tasting Cup) and the *Confrérie de la Chaîne des Rôtisseurs* (Fraternity of the Turners of the Roasting Spit).

consejo regulator (Sp.). Organization for the control and promotion of the *Denominacion de Origen.*

consorzio (It.). Local growers' association with legal standing.

consumo (Port., Sp.). Ordinary wine for local consumption.

cordial. See liqueur.

corks. Stoppers for bottles made from the spongy bark of the cork oak. Portuguese cork is the finest for this purpose.

corky wine. A wine with an unpleasant odor imparted by a diseased cork. This can happen to even the finest wines.

corps (Fr.). Body, richness in alcohol and other substances.

corsé (Fr.). Full bodied.

cosecha (Sp.). Crop or vintage.

coulant (Fr.). Easy, pleasant.

couleur, color (Fr., Sp.). The color of a wine.

coupage (Fr.). Blending or mixing of wines.

coupé (Fr.). A blended wine.

courtier, corredor (Fr., Sp.). Wine broker.

crémant (Fr.). Crackling or slightly sparkling. Given appellation status by I.N.A.O.

criadera (Sp.). Nursery stage in the sherry maturing system.

criado y embotellado por (Sp.). Grown and bottled by.

cru (Fr.). Vineyard, growth.

cru classé (Fr.). See classified growths.

crust. The heavy deposit thrown off by red wines that have been long in bottles. Applies principally to Vintage Portos.

cuit, cotto (Fr., It.). A wine that has been heated or "cooked."

cup. Iced wine flavored with fresh fruits, brandy, liqueurs, and/or herbs.

cuvaison (Fr.). The period of first or violent fermentation during which the must remains in contact with the grape skins to obtain its color. Applies only to red wines.

cuvée (Fr.). The blend.

decanter. A glass bottle or container into which wines or spirits are poured from their original containers, for serving.

decanting. Transferring a wine or spirit from one bottle to another.

dégorgement (Fr.). Disgorging process used in production of Champagne to remove the sediment.

délicat (Fr.). Delicate, not harsh or coarse.

delimited area. A certain area whose regional name by law is given to the wine or spirit produced within the geographical limits of the region.

demi (Fr.). Half.

demijohn. A fat-bellied, wicker-encased bottle holding 4 to 10 gallons.

demi-muid (Fr.). Cask holding 157 gallons used in Cognac.

demi-queue (Fr.). A Burgundy cask measuring 228 liters, a half-*queue*.

demi-sec (Fr.). Semidry. Also, a fairly sweet type of Champagne.

Denominacion de Origen (Sp.). Guarantee of origin and authenticity of a wine.

density. See specific gravity.

deposit. Normal sediment precipitated by a wine as it matures in the bottle.

dépôt (Fr.). Natural sediment that all wines deposit; more visible in red wines.

dextrin. One of the sugars resulting from starch being exposed to the action of malt.

diastase. The enzyme, formed by malting barley, that causes the starch in grains to be converted into sugars.

dolce (It.). Sweet.

domaine (Fr.). Followed by a name, it denotes ownership. For example, Domaine de la Romanée-Conti.

Domäne (Ger.). Usually a state-owned and/or state-managed vineyard property.

dosage (Fr.). The amount of sugar used in preparing Champagne.

douil (Fr.). An open cask holding 7 to 8 hectoliters in which the grapes are carted from the vineyard to the pressing house in the Bordeaux wine region.

doux (Fr.). Sweet. Also, the sweetest type of Champagne.

dry. The opposite of sweet, literally, lacking in sugar.

duftig (Ger.). Fragrant, fine bouquet.

dulce (Sp.). Sweet.

dulce apagado (Sp.). See mistelle.

dunder. Sugarcane juice remains, used in making full-bodied rums.

dur (Fr.). Hard, harsh.

earthy. A flavor in wines reminiscent of earth or soil, highly prized in Burgundy where it is called *goût de terroir*.

eau de vie (Fr.). Spirits, generally brandy. Literally, "water of life."

eau de vie de marc (Fr.). A brandy distilled from the fermented pomace or husks of grapes after they have been pressed for wine.

echt (Ger.). Genuine.

edel (Ger.). Noble, extra fine.

Edelbeerenauslese (Ger.). Term used before 1971 to denote an especially fine Beerenauslese.

Edelfäule (Ger.). Noble mold that settles on overripe grapes. See also *pourriture noble*.

Edelsüsse (Ger.). Great natural, noble sweetness.

edes (Hun.). Sweet.

égrappage (Fr.). Process of destemming grapes before they are pressed.

égrappoir (Fr.). Apparatus used to perform the *égrappage*.

Ehrwein (Ger.). Very fine wine.

Eigene abfüllung (Ger.). Bottled by the producer.

Eiswein (Ger.). A wine produced from perfectly ripened grapes that have been partially frozen while still hanging on the vine. Eiswein used to be very rare, appearing perhaps once every twenty or twenty-five years. It is now made more often but only in very limited quantities. Eiswein is quite elegant and very rich and may be considered between an Auslese and an Edelbeerenauslese.

élégance (Fr.). A term used to denote a wine of a poor vintage with delicacy and lightness but that does not promise longevity.

éleveur (Fr.). See *négociant-éleveur*.

élixir (Fr.). Old term used in France for liqueur.

enology, oenology. The science or study of wines.

enzymes. The organic catalysts of yeasts and other substances, which cause various reactions, including alcoholic or vinous fermentation.

Erben (Ger.). Heirs of, or estate of.

erdig (Ger.). Earthy.

espumoso (Sp.). Sparkling.

Essenz, Eszencia (Hun.). Essence. The rarest and richest Tokay wine.

estate-bottled. Produced and bottled by the vineyard owner-producer, traditionally in Burgundy.

esters. The volatile compounds formed by the combination of organic acids with the alcohols. Esters give the bouquet of a wine or spirit.

estufa (Port.). Hothouses or heated cellars where Madeiras are baked when young.

ether. A sweet-smelling compound that contributes to the bouquet of a wine, formed by the dehydration of alcohol molecules.

ethyl alcohol. The principal alcohol found in all alcoholic beverages.

extra sec. Extra dry. Also, a type of dry Champagne, somewhat sweeter than *brut*.

fad (Ger.). Insipid.

faible (Fr.). Thin, weak.

Fass (Ger.). A cask of 600-liter capacity employed in all German wine regions except the Moselle, where the cask is called *Fuder*.

fein, feine, feinste (Ger.). Fine, very fine, finest.

feints. The first and last parts of a distillation, also called the heads and tails.

ferme (Fr.). Firm, full.

fermentation. The chemical process whereby sugars are broken down into ethyl alcohol, carbon dioxide, and other by-products.

fett (Ger.). Full, big; literally, fat.

fiasco (It.). Raffia-wrapped flask employed for bottling Chianti, Orvieto, and some other Italian wines. Plural *fiaschi*.

filter. To clarify liquids by passing them through a fine screen or permeable membrane.

finage (Fr.). All of the vineyards of a given subdistrict.

fine. To clarify wine by adding materials that combine with the particles floating in it and, after a short period, settle to the bottom, leaving the wine clear.

fine maison (Fr.). The house brandy served in a restaurant.

finesse (Fr.). Fineness, delicacy.

fino (Sp.). The driest type of sherry.

flagon. An ancient wine flask.

flask. A flat-sided bottle usually holding 12½ ounces but with a capacity of anywhere from 8 to 32 ounces.

flinty. See *pierre-à-fusil*.

flor (Sp.). See flower.

flower, flowering. Unique property of the yeast in the Jerez sherry region of Spain. Multiplying profusely, the yeast forms a film on the surface of the wine in the cask, especially in the case of the drier, more delicate fino types, giving sherry its nutty character. A similar flowering of the yeast also occurs in the casks of the *vin jaune* and *vin de paille* of Château-Châlon and Château-d'Arlay, in the Côtes de Jura region of France, and in South Africa.

flowery. A pleasing, fragrant perfume in some white wines.

fort (Fr.). Strong, with high alcohol.

fortified wines. Wines whose natural alcoholic strength is increased by the addition of brandy. Term not recognized by the B.A.T.F.

foudre (Fr.). A large storage cask for wines.

foxiness. The very pronounced grapey flavor found in wines produced from American grapes in the eastern United States.

franc (Fr.). Natural-tasting, clean.

frappé (Fr.). Iced. A liqueur served with finely cracked ice.

Freiherr (Ger.). Baron.

frisch (Ger.). Fresh, sprightly.

frizzante (It.). Semisparkling, crackling.

fruity, *fruité, fruchtig* (Eng., Fr., Ger.). Describes the frank taste of the grape found in good wines.

Fuder (Ger.). A Moselle wine cask holding 1,000 liters.

Fülle (Ger.). Richness, fullness.

fumet (Fr.). A pronounced bouquet.

fumeux (Fr.). Spirited, heady.

fungus. Mold that appears when wine is kept carelessly and when the most careful hygiene is not observed.

Fürst (Ger.). Prince.

fusel oil. The higher alcohols found in all spirits.

gallon. A liquid measure containing 128 fluid ounces.

Gay Lussac. French inventor of the alcoholometer and the standard metric measures of alcoholic strengths, in use today, that bear his name.

gefällig (Ger.). Pleasing, harmonious.

gefüllt (Ger.). Full, rich.

Gemarkung (Ger.). The boundary of a district in which wine is grown.

généreux (Fr.). Generous, warming.

Gewächs (Ger.). Growth or vineyard. Always followed by the name of the proprietor, to denote ownership.

gezuckert (Ger.). Sugared or improved.

glatt (Ger.). Smooth.

goût (Fr.). Taste.

goût américain (Fr.). Sweet Champagne to please the South American market.

goût anglais (Fr.). A very dry Champagne for the English market.

goût de bois (Fr.). Woody taste.

goût de bouchon (Fr.). Corky taste.

goût de paille (Fr.). Straw, musty taste.

goût de pique (Fr.). Vinegary taste.

goût de terroir (Fr.). Earthy taste.

goût d'event (Fr.). Flat, lifeless taste.

gradi, gradi alcool, grado alcoolico (It.). Followed by a number, percentage of alcohol by volume.

Graf (Ger.). Count.

grain spirits. Patent still spirits obtained from malted and unmalted grain.

grappa (It.). Brandy distilled from grape pressings in Italy and California. See also *marc*.

green. Very young, light, such as *vinho verde* ("green wine") of Portugal.

gros producteur (Fr.). A vine variety that produces large quantities of grapes but not fine-quality wines.

grossier (Fr.). Harsh, coarse.

growth. A vineyard (*cru* in French).

grün (Ger.). Young, green, immature.

gut (Ger.). Good.

habzó (Hun.). Sparkling.

Halb-fuder (Ger.). The standard Moselle wine cask containing 500 liters, a half-*Fuder*.

Halb-stück (Ger.). The standard Rhine wine cask containing 600 liters, a half-*Stück*.

harmonisch (Ger.). Harmonious, well-balanced.

hart (Ger.). Hard, acid, even vinegary.

heads. The spirits obtained at the beginning of distillation.

hecho (Sp.). Made. A completed wine ready for bottling and shipping.

hectare. 100 ares, equaling 2.47 acres.

hectoliter. 100 liters, equaling 26.418 gallons.

herb (Ger.). Bitter.

high wines. The useful spirits obtained in distillation after eliminating heads and tails.

Hochgewächs (Ger.). Superior vineyard or growth.

Hock. The English abbreviation for Hochheimer that today denotes any Rhine wine.

hogshead. Cask of varying measure. A hogshead of sherry contains 66 gallons.

honigartig (Ger.). Honeylike.

Hospices de Beaune (Fr.). A charitable hospital in Beaune, Burgundy, supported by an annual public sale of wine.

hübsch (Ger.). Nice, delicate.

hydrometer. An apparatus used to measure the density of alcoholic beverages and other liquids.

imbottigliato (It.). Bottled.

impériale (Fr.). An oversize Bordeaux bottle with a capacity of 8 bottles, or 6 liters; known as a Methuselah when used for Champagne.

I.N.A.O. (Fr.). *Institut National des Appellations d'Origine des Vins et Eaux-de-Vie.*

informing grape. The principal grape that gives a wine its varietal character.

isinglass. Substance made from fish gelatine; used as a fining material.

jarra (Sp.). Wooden or metal jar holding 11½ to 12½ liters, used in all sherry blending operations as the basic unit of measure.

Jeroboam or double magnum. Oversize Bordeaux or Champagne bottle, holding 4 regular bottles or 104 ounces.

jigger. The standard 1½-ounce measure used in cocktail and mixed drink recipes.

jung (Ger.). Young, immature.

Kabinett (Ger.). The driest wine of Qualitätswein mit Prädikat.

keg. A small, stout cask.

Keller (Ger.). Cellar.

Kellerabfüllung, kellerabzug (Ger.). Bottled at the cellar or estate.

kilogram, kg. 1,000 grams, or 2.2 pounds.

klein (Ger.). Small.

Körper (Ger.). Body.

kräftig (Ger.). Robust, rich in alcohol.

kräusen (Ger.). A method of carbonating beers.

lagar (Sp., Port.). The pressing and treading trough.

Lage (Ger.). Vineyard site.

lager. To store beer for aging and sedimentation. All American beers today are lagered.

lebendig (Ger.). Fresh, racy.

lees. The sediment that settles on the bottom of a cask of wine.

léger (Fr.). Light, lacking in body.

levante (Sp.). Hot, searing wind that blows over the sherry region, said to originate in the Sahara Desert.

lías (Sp.). Wine lees.

licoroso (Sp.). Rich, sweet, fortified.

Limousin (Fr.). The oak used for the casks in which Cognac is aged.

liqueur (Fr.). A sweetened, flavored distilled spirit.

liqueur de tirage (dosage) (Fr.). In Champagne, the sugar solution added at the time of bottling to ensure a proper secondary fermentation.

liqueur d'expédition (Fr.). In Champagne, the sugar solution added at the time of disgorging to give the varying degrees of sweetness.

liquoreux (Fr.). Rich, sweet.

lodges. The warehouses where Porto wines are stored in Vila Nova de Gaia, Portugal. Also, the warehouses where Madeira wines are stored in Funchal, Madeira.

low wines. In pot still distillation, the spirits obtained from the first operation.

maderisé (Fr.). A white wine that has become very dark and taken on a woody character because of oxidation and exposure to heat.

mager (Ger.). Thin, lacking in body, undistinguished.

magnum. A double-size bottle.

maigre (Fr.). Thin, weak.

malt. Grain, generally barley, that has been allowed to germinate for a short period so that the enzyme diastase may be formed.

malts. Scotch whisky made entirely from malted barley.

marc (Fr.). The grapes required to load a Champagne press for a pressing; also a distillate of skins, pips, or husks remaining after the grapes have been pressed.

mashing. The operation of mixing ground meal and malt with water to liquefy the starches so they may be converted into sugars by the diastase in the malt.

Master of Wine, M.W. Professional title in England acquired by members of the trade after many years of study and rigorous examinations.

metallic. See *pierre-à-fusil.*

Methuselah. Oversize Champagne bottle, holding 7 to 8 regular bottles or 179 to 208 ounces.

mildew. A disease that attacks the vines in rainy or damp seasons.

millésime (Fr.). Vintage year.

mise d'origine (Fr.). Bottled by the shipper.

mis en bouteille à la propriété (Fr.). Bottled by the shipper.

mis en bouteille au château (Fr.). Bottled at the château where the grapes are grown in Bordeaux.

mis en bouteille au domaine (Fr.). Bottled at the property where it is made in Burgundy; estate-bottled.

mistelle (Fr.). Grape must whose fermentation is halted by adding sufficient brandy to give it an alcohol content of 15 percent. The natural unfermented grape sugar remains as sweetening. *Mistelles* are used as sweetening wines, particularly in making vermouths and aperitif wines.

moelleux (Fr.). Soft, velvety.

Monimpex (Hun.). The Hungarian state export monopoly.

monopole (Fr.). A trademark name.

mou (Fr.). Flabby, lacking in character.

mousseux (Fr.). Sparkling.

mûr (Fr.). Balanced, fruity.

must, *moût, Moot, mosto* (Eng., Fr., Ger., Sp.). Grape juice before and during fermentation.

mustimeter. See saccharometer.

musty. Moldy, unpleasant.

muté (Fr.). *Mistelle* or a sweet wine whose fermentation has been inhibited by the addition of brandy.

Mycodermae aceti. The vinegar yeast.

Mycodermae vini. The yeast responsible for vinous fermentation.

Natur, Naturrein, Naturwein (Ger.). Completely natural wine to which no sugar has been added.

nature (Fr.). Term used in Champagne labeling interchangeably with *brut.* Also denotes still Champagne.

Nebuchadnezzar. Extraordinary Champagne bottle size holding 20 regular bottles or 520 ounces.

négociant-éleveur (Fr.). A merchant who buys wine from the grower, blends, bottles, and then markets it.

nero (It.). Very dark red.

nerveux (Fr.). Vigorous, with long-keeping qualities.

nervig (Ger.). Good, full-bodied.

neutral spirits. Spirits distilled out from any material at a proof of 190 or more, regardless of whether they are later reduced in proof.

Nicolauswein (Ger.). Denotes a wine produced from grapes gathered on December 6, St. Nicholas Day.

nip. Miniature bottle of spirits.

nose. The bouquet or aroma of a wine or spirit.

nu (Fr.). "Bare." Term denoting that the price quoted for a barrel of wine does not include the cost of the cask.

nube (Sp.). Cloudiness.

Öchsle (Ger.). The German scale for measuring the sugar content of the grape must before fermentation. The determination is made by the higher weight in grams of the must in relation to an equal volume of water, or its specific gravity. Twenty-five percent of this greater weight is known to be sugar. Thus, 100 liters of must with a reading of 100 *Öchsle* contains 25 kilograms of natural grape sugar.

octave, *octavilla* (Eng., Sp.). An eighth of a cask. In the sherry trade, 16½ gallons.

oeil de perdrix (Fr.). Partridge eye. Describes pale or still pink sparkling wine, usually from Burgundy, Switzerland, or California.

oenology. See enology.

oïdium. A fungus disease that attacks the vines.

ölig (Ger.). Having high consistency that gives wine the impression of being oily as it is poured..

oloroso (Sp.). The full-bodied, deeper-colored sherries. Although very dry in their *soleras,* they are usually shipped as sweet-tasting sherries by blending sweet wines with them.

organoleptic examination. The method of judging the quality of wines, beers, and spirits by the human organs of sight, smell, and taste.

Originalabfüllung, Originalabzug (Ger.). Term used before 1971 to denote original bottling. Equivalent to estate bottling.

overproof. A spirit whose alcoholic strength is more than 100 proof.

palma (Sp.). The special chalk marking used to identify a very fine fino sherry (𝑌).

palo cortado (Sp.). The special marking used to denote *dos rayas,* sherries that have developed fino characteristics (𝟋).

Passe Tout Grains (Fr.). A Burgundy wine made of a mixture of at least one-third Pinot Noir and the balance Gamay grapes.

passito (It.). A wine made from partially dried grapes.

Pasteur, Louis (1822-1895). Great French scientist whose studies on malt and vinous fermentations gave the first complete explanation of these phenomena.

pasteurization. A process discovered by Louis Pasteur of arresting, making inactive, or killing the ferments in wine, beer, milk, and other liquids through heating the liquid and holding it for a brief time at 131 to 158 degrees Fahrenheit.

patent still. The two-column or continuous still "patented" by Aeneas Coffey in 1832.

pelure d'oignon (Fr.). Onion skin. The brown tinge that certain red wines take on after aging.

perfume. The fragrance of a wine or spirit.

Perlwein (Ger.). Slightly sparkling wine.

pétillant (Fr.). Crackling or semisparkling.

petit (Fr.). Small, thin.

Pfarrgut (Ger.). Vineyard owned by a church whose product is given to the parson or preacher as part of his remuneration.

Phylloxera vastatrix. The American grape louse.

pièce (Fr.). A cask holding approximately 60 gallons, used in many French wine regions.

pierre-à-fusil (Fr.). Gun flint. A sharp, metallic tang sometimes noticed in bone-dry wines, especially those from Chablis.

pikant (Ger.). Attractive, intriguing.

pint. Liquid measure of 16 ounces.

pipe. The cask used in the Porto, Lisbon, and Tarragona wine trades containing 138 gallons and in the Madeira trade where a pipe holds 110 gallons.

piquant (Fr.). A pleasant point of acidity. Generally applied to dry white wines.

piqué (Fr.). A term used to describe a wine that has begun to turn and whose only use is for vinegar.

piquette (Fr.). A common, ordinary wine used in certain parts of France.

pisador (Sp.). One who treads the grapes at vintage time in the sherry region.

plastering. The system of adding *yeso* or gypsum to grapes when they are treaded and pressed in the *lagar* in Jerez, Spain.

plat (Fr.). Dull, flat, lifeless.

plein (Fr.). Full bodied.

pony. One-ounce brandy or liqueur glass.

portes-greffes (Fr.). The hardy *Phylloxera*-resistant American rootstocks on which the fine vines of Europe are grafted.

pot still. The old-fashioned, fat-bellied, tapered-neck still that requires two distinct operations to produce the spirit that is eventually bottled.

pourriture noble (Fr.). "Noble rot," the state of overripeness of the grapes of the Sauternes region of Bordeaux. It is in reality a yeast or mold known scientifically as *Botrytis cinerea*.

précoce (Fr.). Precocious, maturing rapidly.

pressoir, prensa (Fr., Sp.). Wine press.

proof. An arbitrary system of measuring the alcoholic strength of a liquid. In America, a spirit of 100 proof is one that contains exactly 50 percent alcohol by volume at 60 degrees Fahrenheit. Each degree of proof represents ½ percent alcohol.

puncheon. A large cask of varying capacities.

pupitres (Fr.). The special racks used in the Champagne cellars during *remuage* (shaking sediment onto the cork).

puttony (Hun.). The measure in which grapes are gathered in Tokay-Hegyalja. Plural *puttonos*.

Qualitätswein (Ger.). Superior table wine subject to certain controls, from any of eleven designated regions.

Qualitätswein mit Prädikat (Ger.). As above, but with more stringent controls and special attributes.

quart. Liquid measure of 32 ounces.

quarter bottle. Wine bottle containing 6 to 6½ ounces, one-fourth the size of a regular bottle.

quarter cask. In cases where the standard cask, pipe, or butt is too large for a merchant, casks containing one-fourth the original are used. Quarter casks vary in contents, depending on the wine region where they are used.

queue (Fr.). Burgundy casks holding 2 *pièces*, a total of 120 gallons or 456 liters.

quinquina (Fr.). Quinine. Most French aperitif wines use the word as a description because they are quinined wines.

quinta (Port.). Vineyard or winery estate in Portugal, similar to château in the Bordeaux wine region.

quintal, quintale (Fr., It.). 100 kilograms.

race (Fr.). Breed.

racking. The drawing of wine off its lees into a fresh, clean cask. Also, the transference of any alcoholic beverage from one cask or vat to another.

rancio (Sp.). A term used to describe a sweet fortified wine that has lost some color through age in the bottle. Such a wine acquires a special aroma.

rassig (Ger.). With race and breed.

rauh (Ger.). Raw, harsh.

raya (Sp.). The chalk mark used in the sherry region to identify wines that will become finos or amontillados (/).

récemment dégorgé (Fr.). Recently disgorged.

récolte (Fr.). Vintage.

rectifying. Anything that changes the natural state of a spirit, such as redistilling after it has been barreled or adding coloring matter, sweetening, or any other flavoring material. Adding water to reduce proof does not constitute rectifying.

redondo (Sp.). Round, well-balanced.

reduce. To lower alcoholic strength of a spirit by the addition of water.

red wine. Any wine that has the slightest part of red coloring, obtained from the pigment found on the inside of the grape skin.

refresh. To add young wine to an older one (in cask) to give the old wine new life. This term is also used in the same manner with respect to spirits, particularly brandies.

Rehoboam. Oversize Champagne bottle holding 6 regular bottles or 156 ounces.

reif (Ger.). Ripe, fine, sweet.

rein (Ger.). Pure.

reintönig (Ger.). Well-balanced, very good.

remuage (Fr.). The "shaking-down" operation employed in the production of Champagne, whereby the bottles are placed head downward and periodically shaken and turned slightly to cause the sediment to settle on the cork. In the United States the term used is *riddling*.

Rentamt (Ger.). Collection office.

reserva (Sp.). Mature quality.

riche (Fr.). Having a generous bouquet, flavor, and fullness of body.

rick. Framework or rack in a warehouse in which barrels of distilled spirits are stored for aging. Also, to place or rack barrels.

riddling. See *remuage*.

riserva (It.). Mature quality.

robe. The sheen of color left on the inside of a glass from a highly pigmented red wine.

rociar (Sp.). To refresh an old solera with young new wine.

rondeur (Fr.). Roundness.

rosè, *rosato, rosado* (Eng., It., Sp.). A pale red wine obtained by removing the grape skins as soon as the required amount of color has been attained.

rosso (It.). Red.

Rotwein (Ger.). Red table wine.

ruby. A port of a very deep red color, usually quite young, in contrast to one that has been aged for some time in wood and has become "tawny," pale in color, through repeated finings.

rund (Ger.). Round, harmonious.

saccharometer. Instrument used to measure the sugar content of must or of wines or liqueurs.

saftig (Ger.). Juicy, succulent.

Salmanazar. Oversize Champagne bottle holding 10 to 12 regular bottles or 270 to 312 ounces.

sancocho (Sp.). Syrup produced by simmering or cooking must to one-third its original volume. Used in the sherry blend to sweeten and color the wine.

sauber (Ger.). Clean, pure.

scantling. The stout wooden beams or supports on which the casks rest in the cellar.

schal (Ger.). Musty, tired.

Schaumwein (Ger.). Sparkling wine.

Schloss (Ger.). Castle.

schlossabzug (Ger.). Bottled at the castle's cellars, equivalent to estate-bottled.

schnapps. Generic Dutch and German term denoting spirituous liquors.

Schwefel (Ger.). Sulfur smell in the bouquet of the wine.

sec (Fr.). Dry. Also, a medium-sweet Champagne.

secco, seco (It., Sp.). Dry.

sediment. The natural deposit found in wines as they mature, formed by the crystallization and settling or precipitation of bitartrates, tannins, and pigments.

Sekt (Ger.). Sparkling wine.

self whiskies. Used in the Scotch whisky trade to denote a "straight" or unblended Scotch malt whisky.

sève (Fr.). Sappy, aromatic, vigorous.

Sikes (Sykes). Hydrometer and tables for measuring alcoholic strengths that are in use in England; invented by Bartholomew Sikes.

skunky. Describing the off aroma in beer that has been exposed to excessive light and heat.

slatko (Yug.). Sweet.

solear (Sp.). Sunning. The exposure of the grapes to the sun (*sol*) for 24 to 48 hours in the sherry region.

solera (Sp.). The system of tiered casks used to blend sherry.

sophistiquer (Fr.). To falsify a wine or to ameliorate a defective wine with anything that will cover up its defects.

souche (Fr.). *Cep* or vine rootstock.

sour mash. Yeasting process in which at least one-quarter of the working yeast from a previous fermentation *and* fresh yeast may be added to the mash to induce fermentation.

soutirer (Fr.). To rack clear wine from one cask into a fresh one.

soyeux (Fr.). Silky, smooth, soft roundness. Lacking in roughness.

Spätlese (Ger.). Late gathered. A wine made from late-picked bunches of grapes. Generally sweeter than wine made from grapes gathered earlier.

specific gravity. A measure of the density of a liquid or solid; the ratio of the weight of any volume of a liquid or solid to the weight of an equal volume of water.

spirits. The generic term for distilled beverages.

split. See quarter bottle.

spritzig (Ger.). Prickling, slightly effervescent.

spumante (It.). Sparkling.

stahlig (Ger.). Steely, austere.

still. The apparatus in which, by application of heat, the alcohol in a liquid may be separated and recovered. Pot still is the original form of still or alembic; Coffey still, patent still, and double-column still are three names applied to the continuous-operation still.

still wine. Table wine without any additional alcohol, carbon dioxide, or flavorings.

stirrup-cup. A cup for the parting drink. The name comes from an old custom of having a last drink with a guest after he had mounted his horse.

stolno vino (Yug.). Table wine.

Stück, Stückfasser (Ger.). The standard of cask measure, used in the Rhine, containing 1,200 liters.

suho (Yug.). Dry.

süss (Ger.). Sweet.

sweet mash. Yeasting process in which fresh yeast is added to the mash to induce fermentation.

Tafelwein (Ger.). Ordinary table wine from any of the five Tafelwein regions.

tannin, tannic. Organic compounds found mostly in red grapes, their woody stems, and new wood casks used for aging wines. They give the wine astringency and some bitterness when young, and they give the wine the ability to develop and age. Tannin is a large part of the sediment that eventually forms in sturdy red wines.

tawny. The quality of paleness that Portos acquire when matured in wood. This loss of red color comes from repeated finings. Such wines are Tawny Portos.

teinturier (Fr.). Grapes used primarily for the abundance of color they contribute to the must.

tendre (Fr.). A rather light and delicate wine, usually a young wine.

tête de cuvée (Fr.). Outstanding growth; generally used in Burgundy.

tierce, terzo, tercero (Fr., It., Sp.). A cask holding one-third of a butt or pipe.

tilts. Bars used for adjusting casks or scantlings to the desired position.

tinto (Sp.). Red.

tirage (Fr.). Drawing off wines or spirits into other containers, usually from casks into bottles.

tonelero (Sp.). Cooper.

tonneau (Fr.). Tun. Term used in the Bordeaux wine trade representing 4 *barriques* of 225 liters, or 900 liters. This is the unit of measure in which wines are sold in the bulk trade, the equivalent of 96 cases of finished wine.

Traube (Ger.). Bunch of grapes.

Traubenkelter (Ger.). Hydraulic grape press.

trocken (Ger.). Dry.

Trockenbeerenauslese (Ger.). Wine made from individually selected, dry, raisinlike grapes. Weather conditions must be perfect throughout the summer and the late vintage season for a Trockenbeerenauslese wine to be made. It is very rare and very sweet.

uisgebeatha, uisgebaugh (Celtic). Water of life, whisky.

ullage. The air space in a cask or bottle due to evaporation or leakage. May result in deterioration of contents.

underproof. Describes a spirit whose alcoholic strength is below proof. In the United States this is a spirit of less than 100 proof, as opposed to an overproof spirit having a strength of over 100 proof.

ungezuckert (Ger.). Unsugared, pure.

usé (Fr.). A wine that has passed its peak and is on the decline.

uva (Sp.). Grape.

vats. The containers in which alcoholic beverages are fermented or blended.

vatting. Mixing or blending in a vat.

velouté (Fr.). Rich, mellow, velvety, soft.

vendange (Fr.). Grape harvest.

vendange tardif (Fr.). Late-picked wine, implying more strength and/or sweetness.

vendangeur (Fr.). Grape harvester.

vendemmia, vendimia (It., Sp.). Vintage or harvest.

venencia (Sp.). The special cup used for drawing samples from the sherry butts in the *bodega.* It is a cylindrical silver cup attached to a long, flexible strip of whalebone.

viejo (Sp.). Old.

vif (Fr.). Lively, brisk.

vigne (Fr.). Vine.

vigneron (Fr.). Vine grower.

vignoble (Fr.). Vineyard.

vin (Fr.). Wine.

viña (Sp.). Vine. Also, vineyard in Argentina and Chile.

vin blanc (Fr.). White wine.

vin cuit (Fr.). A concentrated wine used to improve thin wines.

vin de garde (Fr.). A wine worth keeping, for laying down.

vin de goutte (Fr.). Wine made from the last pressing. It is generally of poor quality.

vin de messe (Fr.). Altar wine.

vin de paille (Fr.). White wine made from grapes that have been spread on straw (*paille*) mats to dry in the sun, before pressing.

vin de pays (Fr.). Small wines of each region, consumed locally.

vin doux (Fr.). A sweet wine.

vine. Climbing plant, one variety of which produces grapes.

viñedo (Sp.). Vineyard.

vineux (Fr.). Vinosity.

vin gris (Fr.). A pale pink wine made in Lorraine.

vinho (Port.). Wine.

vinho claro (Port.). Natural wine.

vinho estufado (Port.). Madeira wine after it has been baked in the *estufa.*

vinho generoso (Port.). Fortified wine.

vinho surdo (Port.). Fortified wine. According to Portuguese law, Porto wine must be a *vinho surdo.*

vinho verde (Port.). Light, young white or red wine produced in northern Portugal.

viniculture. The science of making wine.

vini tipici (It.). Typical or standard wines.

vin mousseux (Fr.). Sparkling wine.

vin nature (Fr.). Natural, unsweetened wine.

vino (It., Sp.). Wine.

vino corriente (Sp.). Ordinary wine for local consumption.

vino crudo (Sp.). Young or immature wine.

vino de añada (Sp.). Young wine of one vintage, ready for the *criadera* reserves.

vino de color (Sp.). Concentrated wine used in the sherry *bodega* to give color and sweetness to the final blend.

vino de crianza (Sp.). A suitable wine destined to become sherry.

vino de mesa (Sp.). Table wine.

vino frizzante (It.). A lightly sparkling type of wine in Italy.

vino liquoroso (It.). Very sweet wine.

vino maestro (Sp.). Master wine. A sweet, full wine used to lend character and body to weaker, thinner wine.

vin ordinaire (Fr.). Ordinary cheap wine for immediate consumption.

vinosity. The character of a wine, the balance of its bouquet, flavor, and body.

vino spumante (It.). Sparkling wine.

vinous. Pertaining to wine.

vin rosé (Fr.). Pink wine.

vin rouge (Fr.). Red wine.

Vin (Vino) Santo (It.). Sweet white wine produced from dried grapes in the Chianti region of Tuscany.

vin sec (Fr.). Dry wine.

vintage. Gathering the grape crop and making the wine. Also, the year when the wine is made, which often appears on wine labels.

vintage wine. In certain wine regions, particularly Champagne and Porto, the product of exceptional years only is dated. In other regions wines are dated each year.

virgin brandy. Unblended Cognac brandy.

viticulture. The science of growing grapes.

vitis (Latin). Vine.

vornehm (Ger.). Noble, aristocratic.

vörös (Hun.). Red.

Wachstum (Ger.). See *Gewächs*.

wash. In a distillery (usually whisky), the fermented liquor when it is ready to go to the still. In a Scotch distillery, the still that receives the wash is known as the wash still.

weepers. Bottles that show leakage through the cork.

Wein (Ger.). Wine.

Weinbau (Ger.). Viticulture.

Weingut (Ger.). Vineyard or estate.

Weinkeller (Ger.). Wine cellar.

Weisswein (Ger.). White wine.

wernig (Ger.). Vinous, vinosity.

wine. The fermented juice of fruit, usually grapes unless otherwise specified. Ideally, wine is the naturally fermented juice of freshly gathered ripe grapes that have been pressed at or near the place where gathered.

wine broker. An intermediary who acts for buyers and for a vineyard owner.

Winzergenossenschaft (Ger.). Wine growers' cooperative.

woody. The taste of a wine or spirit that has spent too much time in wood, sometimes called *goût de bois*.

wormwood. A perennial herb, *Artemisia absinthium*, aromatic, tonic, and bitter. Formerly used in the preparation of absinthe, certain liqueurs, and vermouths.

würzig (Ger.). Spicy, desirable, flowery.

yayin. A biblical Hebrew term for wine.

yeast. The plant organism whose fermentative qualities cause sugars to break down into alcohol and carbon dioxide gas.

yema (Sp.). The must resulting from the treading before the grapes are subjected to pressure. *Yema* is Spanish means "yolk of an egg" or the core of any product.

yeso (Sp.). Powdered gypsum (calcium sulfate) sprinkled on the grapes in the *lagar* at the time of treading and pressing to fix the tartaric acid during fermentation of the must into sherry wine.

zapatos de pisar (Sp.). Special nail-studded shoes worn by the men who tread the grapes in the *lagar* in the Jerez sherry region.

zymase. The enzyme in yeast cells that causes vinous fermentation and whose catalytic action converts sugars into alcohol and carbon dioxide gas.

APPENDIX T
BIBLIOGRAPHY

This bibliography has been arranged into several sections: reference books; general books on wines, beers, and spirits, including travel information and essays; technical books for those who want more information on the chemistry and physics of winemaking; and a how-to section that covers making wines, beers and liqueurs, mixing drinks, and cooking with wines and spirits.

REFERENCE BOOKS

Cocks, Ch., et Féret, Ed. *Bordeaux et ses Vins*, 12th ed. Bordeaux: Féret et Fils, 1969, 1974.

Garoglio, Pier Giovanni. *Enciclopedia Vitivinicola Mondiale*, 10 vols. Milan: Unione Italiana Vini, 1973.

Gavin-Jobson Associates. *Liquor Handbook*. New York: Jobson, 1977. Annual.

_____. *Wine Marketing Handbook*. New York: Jobson, 1977. Annual.

German Wine Atlas and Vineyard Register. Introduction by Edmund Penning-Rowsell. New York: Hastings House, 1977. Paper.

Jeffs, Julian. *Dictionary of World Wines, Liqueurs, and Other Drinks*. Toronto: Pagurian Press, 1973.

Lichine, Alexis. *New Encyclopedia of Wines and Spirits*. New York: Alfred A. Knopf, 1976.

Poupon, Pierre, et Forgeot, Pierre. *The Wines of Burgundy*, 5th rev. ed. Paris: Presses Universitaires de France, 1974. Paper.

Robards, Terry. *The New York Times Book of Wine*. New York: Quadrangle, 1976.

Schoonmaker, Frank. *Encyclopedia of Wine*, rev. ed. New York: Hastings House, 1975.

Société d'Action et de Gestion Publicitaire. *Les Grands Vins de Bordeaux*. Bordeaux: Delmas, 1972.

GENERAL BOOKS

Abrahamson, E. M., and Pezet, A. W. *Body, Mind and Sugar*, rev. ed. New York: Pyramid, 1971. Paper.

Adams, Leon D. *The Commonsense Book of Wine*. Boston: Houghton Mifflin, 1975.

_____. *The Wines of America*. San Francisco Book Co./Boston: Houghton Mifflin, 1973.

Allen H. Warner. *Romance of Wine*. New York: Dover, 1971. Paper.

Ambrosi, Hans. *Where the Great German Wines Grow*. Translated by Gavin Hamilton and Thom Pringle. New York: Hastings House, 1976.

Anderson, Will. *The Beer Book: An Illustrated Guide to American Breweriana*. Princeton: The Pyne Press, 1973; Des Moines: Wallace-Homestead, 1976. Paper.

Bach, Johann S. *Wine and Taxes*, facsimile ed. New York: Pierpont Morgan, 1970. Paper.

Balzer, Robert L. *Adventures in Wine: Legends, Histories, Recipes*, 3rd ed. Edited by Anna M. Peterson. Los Angeles: The Ward Ritchie Press, 1976. Paper.

Barnard, Alfred. *Whiskey Distilleries of the United Kingdom*. Fairfield, N.J.: A. M. Kelley, 1887.

Benson, Robert. *Great Winemakers of California*. Santa Barbara: Capra Press, 1977.

Bespaloff, Alexis. *Signet Book of Wine*. New York: New American Library, 1971. Paper.

_____, ed. *The Fireside Book of Wine: An Anthology for Wine Drinkers*. New York: Simon & Schuster, 1977.

Blumberg, Robert S., and Hannum, Hurst. *Fine Wines of California*. New York: Doubleday, 1973. Paper.

Bosdari, C. D. *Wines of the Cape*, 3rd rev. ed. New York: International Publications Service, 1966.

Brennan, John M., ed. *Buying Guide to California Wines: 1977 Edition*, 3rd rev. ed. San Diego: Wine Consultants of California, 1977.

Brillat-Savarin, Jean A. *Physiology of Taste*. Translated by M. F. Fisher. New York: Alfred A. Knopf, 1971.

Broadbent, Michael. *Wine Tasting*. New York: (Christie Wine Publications) International Publications Service, 1974.

Chroman, Nathan, and Boss, David. *Treasury of American Wines*. New York: Crown, 1973.

Churchill, Creighton. *The New World of Wines*. New York: Collier, 1974. Paper.

Dallas, Philip. *The Great Wines of Italy*. New York: Doubleday, 1974.

Gold, Alec. *Wine and Spirits of the World*. Coulsdon, Surrey: Virtue & Co., 1971.

Gordon, Alvin. *Of Vines and Missions*. Flagstaff, Ariz.: Northland Press, 1971.

Gorman, Marion, and de Alba, Felipe P. *The Tequila Book*. Chicago: Henry Regnery, 1976. Paper.

Gorman, Robert. *Gorman on California Premium Wines*. Berkeley, Calif.: Ten Speed Press, 1976. Paper.

Grossman, Harold J. *Practical Bar Management*. Rochelle Park, N.J.: Hayden, 1959.

Gunyon, R. E. *The Wines of Central and Southeastern Europe*. New York: International Publications Service, 1971.

Halász, Zoltán. *Hungarian Wine Through the Ages*. New York: International Publications Service, 1962.

Hallgarten, Peter. *Liqueurs*. New York: International Publications Service, Corner, 1973.

Hallgarten, S. F. *Alsace and Its Wine Gardens*. New York: International Publications Service, 1973.

Hamlyn, Paul. *How to Make Your Own Wine Cellar*. Sydney: Paul Hamlyn Pty. Ltd., 1973.

Hannum, Hurst, and Blumberg, Robert S. *Brandies and Liqueurs of the World*. New York: Doubleday, 1976.

Hasler, G. F. *Wine Service in the Restaurant*, rev. ed. London: Wine & Spirit Publications, Ltd., 1973.

Haszonics, J. J., and Barratt, S. *Wine Merchandising*. New York: Radio City, n.d.

Hazelton, Nika. *American Wines*. New York: Grosset & Dunlap, 1976. Paper.

Horwath, Ernest B., et al. *Hotel Accounting*, 3rd rev. ed. New York: Ronald Press, 1970.

James, Margery K. *Studies in the Medieval Wine Trade*. Edited by Elspeth M. Veale. New York: Oxford University Press, 1971.

Jeffs, Julian. *Wines of Europe*. New York: Taplinger, 1971.

Johnson, Hugh. *Wine*, rev. ed. New York: Simon & Schuster, 1975.

_____. *World Atlas of Wine*. New York: Simon & Schuster, 1976. Paper.

Kressman, Edouard. *Wonder of Wine*. New York: Hastings House, 1968.

Layton, T. A. *Cognac and Other Brandies*. New York: International Publications Service, 1973.

_____. *Winecraft: Encyclopedia of Wines and Spirits*. London: Wine & Spirit Publications, Ltd., 1963.

Leedom, William S. *The Vintage Wine Book*, rev. ed. New York: Vintage Books, 1975. Paper.

Lichine, Alexis. *Wines of France*, 5th rev. ed. New York: Alfred A. Knopf, 1969.

Lucia, Salvatore P. *A History of Wine as Therapy*. New York: Lippincott, 1963.

Massee, William E. *An Insider's Guide to Low-Priced Wines*. New York: Doubleday, 1974. Paper.

_____. *Massee's Guide to Wines of America*. New York: Saturday Review Press, 1974. Paper.

_____. *Massee's Wine Handbook*. New York: Doubleday, 1971.

Melville, John, and Morgan, Jefferson. *Guide to California Wines*, 5th rev. ed. New York: E. P. Dutton, 1976. Paper.

Misch, Robert J. *Quick Guide to Wine*, rev. ed. New York: Cornerstone Library, 1976.

_____. *Quick Guide to the Wines of All the Americas*. New York: Doubleday, 1977.

Morgan, Jefferson. *Adventures in the Wine Country*. San Francisco: Chronicle Books, 1971. Paper.

Pellegrini, Angelo M. *Wine and the Good Life*. New York: Alfred A. Knopf, 1965.

Penning-Rowsell, Edmund. *Wines of Bordeaux*, rev. ed. New York: Stein & Day, 1972.

Pohren, D. E. *Adventures in Taste: The Wines and Folk Food of Spain*. Manhattan, Kans.: Society of Spanish Studies, 1972.

Postgate, Raymond. *Alphabet of Wines*. Cedar Knolls, N.J.: Wehman Bros., 1952.

_____. *The Plain Man's Guide to Wine*. Revised by John Arlott. New York: Paul S. Eriksson, 1976.

_____. *Portuguese Wine*. New York: International Publications Service, 1969.

Pratt, James N., and De Caso, Jacques. *The Wine Bibber's Bible*, rev. ed. San Francisco: 101 Productions, 1975. Paper.

Price, Pamela V. *Aperitifs and Liqueurs*. New York: Stein & Day, 1976.

_____. *Wine-Lover's Handbook*. New York: Fireside (Simon & Schuster), 1970. Paper.

Ray, Cyril. *Cognac*. New York: Stein & Day, 1973.

_____. *Lafite*. New York: Stein & Day, 1969.

_____. *The Wines of Italy*, rev. ed. New York: Penguin, 1972. Paper.

Roncarati, Bruno. *Viva Vino: DOC Wines of Italy*. London: Wine & Spirit Publications, Ltd., 1976.

Sichel, Peter M. F., and Ley, Judy. *Which Wine? The Wine Drinker's Buying Guide*. New York: A & W, 1977. Paper.

Simon, André L. *All about Wines*, 8 vols. Brooklyn, N.Y.: Shalom, n.d. Paper.

_____. *History of the Wine Trade in England*, 3 vols. Williamstown, Mass.: Corner House, n.d.

_____. *Wine Primer*, 18th ed. Levittown, N.Y.: Transatlantic Arts, 1972.

_____. *Wines of the World*, rev. ed. New York: McGraw-Hill, 1972.

Stanislawsky, Dan. *Landscapes of Bacchus: The Vine in Portugal*. Austin: University of Texas Press, 1969.

Stokes, John W. *How to Manage a Restaurant or Institutional Food Service*, 2nd ed. Dubuque, Iowa: William C. Brown, 1976.

Storm, John. *An Invitation to Wines*, rev. ed. New York: Fireside, 1971. Paper.

Sunset Editors. *California Wine*. Menlo Park, Calif.: Lane, 1973. Paper.

_____. *California Wine Country*, rev. ed. Menlo Park, Calif.: Lane, 1975. Paper.

Thompson, Bob, and Johnson, Hugh. *The California Wine Book*. New York: William Morrow, 1976.

Todd, William J. *Handbook of Wine: How to Buy, Serve, Store and Drink It*. Brooklyn, N.Y.: Revisionist Press, 1974.

Waugh, Alec. *Wines and Spirits*. New York: Silver & Time-Life, 1968.

Waugh, Harry. *Diary of a Winetaster: Recent Tastings of the Wines of France and California*. New York: Quadrangle, 1972.

_____. *Winetaster's Choice*. New York: Quadrangle, 1974.

Weiner, Michael A. *The Taster's Guide to Beer: Brews and Breweries of the World*. New York: Macmillan, 1977.

Wildman, Frederick S., Jr. *A Wine Tour of France: A Convivial Guide to French Vintages and Vineyards*, rev. ed. New York: Vintage Books, 1976. Paper.

Younger, William. *Gods, Men and Wine*. Atlantic Highlands, N.J.: Humanities, 1966.

Yoxall, Harry W. *The Wines of Burgundy*, rev. ed. New York: Stein & Day, 1973.

TECHNICAL BOOKS

Amerine, M. A., and Joslyn, M. A. *Table Wines: The Technology of Their Production*, 2nd rev. ed. Berkeley: University of California Press, 1970.

Amerine, M. A., and Roessler, Edward B. *Wines: Their Sensory Evaluation*. San Francisco: W. H. Freeman, 1976.

Amerine, M. A., and Singleton, V. L. *Wine: An Introduction*, rev. ed. Berkeley: University of California Press, 1977.

Amerine, M. A.; Berg, H. W.; and Cruess, W. V. *Technology of Wine Making*. 3rd rev. ed. Westport, Conn.: AVI, 1972.

Austin, Cedric. *Science of Wine*. New York: Elsevier-North Holland, 1968.

Conant, James B., ed. *Pasteur's Study of Fermentation*. Cambridge, Mass.: Harvard University Press, 1952. Paper.

Massel, A. *Applied Wine Chemistry and Technology*. New York: Heineman, 1969.

Wagner, Philip M. *American Wines and Winemaking*, rev. ed. New York: Alfred A. Knopf, 1974.

_____. *Grapes into Wine: The Art of Winemaking in America*. New York: Alfred A. Knopf, 1976. Paper.

_____. *Wine-Grower's Guide*, rev. ed. New York: Alfred A. Knopf, 1965.

Weaver, Robert J. *Grape Growing*. New York: John Wiley & Sons, 1976.

Winkler, A. J., et al. *General Viticulture*. Berkeley: University of California Press, 1975.

MAKING WINES, BEERS, AND LIQUEURS

Adkins, Jan. *Craft of Making Wine*. New York: Walker, 1972.

Anderson, Stanley F., and Hull, Raymond. *The Advanced Wine Maker's Practical Guide*. New York: Hawthorn Books, 1976. Paper.

_____. *Art of Making Beer*. New York: Hawthorn Books, 1971. Paper.

_____. *Art of Making Wine*. New York: Hawthorn Books, 1971. Paper.

Austin, Cedric. *The Whys and Wherefores of Winemaking*. New York: British Book Centre, 1973. Paper.

Beadle, Leigh. *Brew It Yourself: A Complete Guide to the Making of Beer, Wine, Liqueurs and Soft Drinks*, 3rd rev. ed. New York: Farrar, Straus & Giroux, 1975.

Bravery, H. E. *Complete Book of Winemaking*. New York: Macmillan, 1973. Paper.

De Chambeau, André. *Creative Winemaking*. Edited by Robert A. Fowler. Rochester, N.Y.: WWWWW Info. Services, 1972.

Jagendorf, Moritz. *Folk Wines, Cordials and Brandies: How to Make Them, Along with the Pleasures of Their Lore*. New York: Vanguard Press, 1963.

Taylor, Walter S., and Vine, Richard P. *Home Winemaker's Handbook*. New York: Harper & Row, 1968.

Tritton, S. M. *Guide to Better Wine and Beer Making for Beginners*, 2nd rev. ed. New York: Dover, 1969. Paper.

MIXED DRINKS

Craddock, Harry. *The Savoy Cocktail Book*. 1930. Reprint, New York: Arno Press, 1976.

Duffy, Patrick Gavin. *Official Mixer's Manual*. Revised by James A. Beard. New York: Doubleday, 1956.

Embury, David A. *The Fine Art of Mixing Drinks*. New York: Doubleday, 1958.

Esquire Magazine Editors. *Esquire Drink Book*. New York: Bantam Books, 1967. Paper.

Haimo, Oscar. *Cocktail and Wine Digest: The Barman's Bible*, 37th rev. ed. New York: Oscar Haimo, 1977.

Ramos, Adam, and Ramos, Joseph. *Ramoses' Guide: 680 Mixed Wine Drinks.* Berkeley, Calif.: Apple Pie Press, 1975. Paper.

Trader Vic. *Trader Vic's Bartender's Guide,* rev. ed. New York: Doubleday, 1972.

COOKING WITH WINES AND SPIRITS

Ald, Roy. *Creative Wine Cookery.* New York Pyramid, 1972. Paper.

Amunategui, Francis. *Masterpieces of French Cuisine.* New York: Macmillan, 1971.

Barbour, Beverly. *Cooking with Spirits.* San Francisco: 101 Productions, 1976. Paper.

Beard, James A. *Fireside Cookbook.* New York: Simon & Schuster, 1969.

_____. *How to East and Drink Your Way Through a French or Italian Menu.* New York: Atheneum, 1971. Paper.

Chamberlain, Samuel. *Clementine in the Kitchen,* rev. ed. New York: Hastings House, 1963.

Chase, Emily. *Pleasures of Cooking with Wine.* Englewood Cliffs, N.J.: Prentice-Hall, 1960. Paper.

Child, Julia. *From Julia Child's Kitchen.* New York: Alfred A. Knopf, 1975.

Child, Julia, et al. *Mastering the Art of French Cooking,* vol. 1. New York: Alfred A. Knopf, 1961.

Child, Julia, and Beck, Simone. *Mastering the Art of French Cooking,* vol. 2. New York: Alfred A. Knopf, 1970.

Church, Ruth Ellen. *Entertaining with Wine.* New York: Rand McNally, 1976.

Claiborne, Craig. *Craig Claiborne's Kitchen Primer.* New York: Random House, 1972. Paper.

_____. *The New York Times Cookbook.* New York: Harper & Row, 1975.

Curnonsky. *Cuisine et Vins de France.* New York: Larousse, n.d.

Délu, Christian Roland. *French Provincial Cuisine.* New York: Barron's, 1976.

Dodd, Marguerite. *America's Cookbook,* rev. ed. New York: Scribners, 1974.

Galloping Gourmet. *The Graham Kerr Cookbook.* New York: Bantam, 1973. Paper.

Garvin, Fernande S. *Art of French Cooking.* New York: Bantam, 1969. Paper.

Hatch, Ted. *American Wine Cook Book.* New York: Dover, 1971. Paper.

Krieg, Saul. *Spirit of Grand Cuisine.* New York: Macmillan, 1969.

Logan, Anne M. *Wine and Wine Cooking.* New York: Arco, 1972. Paper.

Lucia, Salvatore P., and Chase, Emily. *Wine Diet Cook Book.* New York: Bantam Books, 1976. Paper.

Martin, Pol. *The Art of Cooking: The French Way.* New York: Doubleday Dolphin, 1975. Paper.

Montagne, Prosper. *Larousse Gastronomique: The Encyclopedia of Food, Wine, and Cooking.* Edited by Charlotte Turgeon and Nina Froud. New York: Crown, 1961.

Price, Pamela V. *Cooking with Wines, etc.* Cedar Knolls, N.J.: Wehman Bros., 1952.

Reynolds, Mary. *Good Cooking with Wine.* New York: Hamlyn-America, 1976.

Root, Waverly. *Food of France.* New York: Alfred A. Knopf, 1958.

Simon, André L. *Bibliotheca Bacchica Wine and Cooking Bibliography.* West Orange, N.J.: Albert Saifer, n.d.

Stockli, Albert. *Splendid Fare: The Albert Stockli Cookbook.* New York: Alfred A. Knopf, 1970.

Sunset Editors. *Cooking with Wine.* Menlo Park, Calif.: Lane, 1972. Paper.

Taylor, Greyton H. *The Treasury of Wine and Wine Cookery.* New York: Harper & Row, 1963.

Trader Vic. *Trader Vic's Rum Cookery and Drinkery.* New York: Doubleday, 1974.

Van Zuylen, Guirne. *Eating with Wine.* Levittown, N.Y.: Transatlantic Arts, 1972.

Waldo, Myra. *The Complete Book of Wine Cookery.* New York: Bantam Books, 1973. Paper.

Wine Advisory Board. *Easy Recipes of California Winemakers.* Blue Earth, Minn.: Piper Publishing, 1970.

_____. *Wine Cookbook of Dinner Menus.* Compiled by Emily Chase. Blue Earth, Minn.: Piper Publishing, 1971.

Wood, Morrison. *More Recipes with a Jug of Wine.* New York: Farrar, Straus & Giroux, 1956.

APPENDIX U
APHORISMS OF BRILLAT-SAVARIN*

The world would have been nothing if it were not for life; and all who live, eat.

Animals feed, man eats; only a man of culture knows how to dine.

Tell me what you eat and I will tell you what you are.

The pleasure of the table belongs to all ages, conditions, countries, and times; it accompanies all other joys and remains the last to console us for the loss of them.

Good living is an act of our judgment by which we show preference for those things that are agreeable to the taste over those that do not have this quality.

The discovery of a new dish is more beneficial to humanity than the discovery of a new star.

The dyspeptic and the drunkard do not know how to eat or drink.

The order of drinking is from the mildest to the fuller-bodied, and to the richest in bouquet.

Punctuality is the most important quality of the cook, and it should also be that of the guests.

To wait too long for a tardy guest denotes a lack of consideration for those who are present.

He who invites his friends and then neglects to give his personal attention to the food served to them does not deserve to have friends.

The hostess should always see to it that the coffee is excellent, and the host that the liqueurs are of first quality.

When we invite someone, we make ourselves responsible for his happiness while he is under our roof.

*Jean Anthelme Brillat-Savarin (1755-1826), a renowned French epicure, was a lawyer, political economist, mayor of the town of Belley, magistrate, musician, and literary man. His book *Physiologie du Goût* is a classic. The *Académie de Gastronomie Brillat-Savarin*, in Paris, is a culinary academy named in his honor.

INDEX